W9-CHN-752

CP-3	Work Sheet: Trial balance totals, $1,426,915; adjusted trial balance totals, $1,436,250

7-1	No key figure
7-2	No key figure
7-3	Adjusted cash balance, $47,556
7-4	(a) Adjusted cash balance, $31,142.30
7-5	(a) Adjusted cash balance, $21,142.30
7-6	(a) Adjusted cash balance, $21,146.50
7-7	(a) Adjusted cash balance, $21,007.29
7-8	(a) Cash shortage, $8,150
7-9	(a) Adjusted cash balance, $18,334
7-10	(b) Adjusted cash balance, $8,552
7-11	(b) Adjusted cash balance, $8,214.50
7-12	No key figure

8-1	(a) Estimated uncollectible accounts, $18,120
8-2	(a) Estimated uncollectible accounts, $12,960
8-3	(a) Estimated uncollectible accounts, $23,080
8-4	(b) Net accounts receivable, Jan. 31, $461,280
8-5	(a) Estimated uncollectible accounts, $6,740
8-6	(b) Estimated uncollectible accounts, $52,500
8-7	(a) (3) Debit uncollectible accounts expense, $726,000
8-8	(a) (2) Number of days' sales collected, Digital, 81 days
8-9	(a) (1) Accounts receivable turnover, Molson, 12 times
8-10	(a) Feb. 2, cash collected from note, $20,459
8-11	(a) Feb. 2, cash collected from note, $42,653
8-12	(c) Total current assets, $373,179
8-13	(c) Total current assets, $741,232
8-14	(c) Sales revenue, $176,000
8-15	(c) Sales revenue, $300,000

9-1	No key figure
9-2	(a) Inventory, May 31, $315
9-3	(a) Inventory, Sept. 30, $3,350
9-4	(b) (3) Inventory (FIFO), Jan. 15, $4,750
9-5	(a) (3) Ending inventory, LIFO, $18,550
9-6	(a) (2) Ending inventory, FIFO, $18,700
9-7	(b) (2) Write-down to market, $2,250
9-8	(a) (2) Ending inventory, LIFO, $93,240
9-9	(a) (2) Ending inventory, FIFO, $7,420
9-10	(a) Gross profit, 2001, $318,400
9-11	(b) (3) Gross profit, $273,720
9-12	(b) (2) Current ratio, 4.5 to 1

10-1	(c) Total cost, $96,870
10-2	Total cost, $237,326
10-3	Depreciation for 2001, (b) $61,500; (c) $64,800
10-4	Depreciation for 2000, (b) $10,000; (c) $20,000
10-5	Depreciation for 2002, (1) $18,000; (2) $32,000
10-6	Apr. 1, gain on sale, $275,000
10-7	(b) (1) Book value, $13,600
10-8	(b) (1) Book value, $25,500
10-9	No key figure
10-10	No key figure
10-11	No key figure
10-12	(c) Accumulated depletion, $3,069,000

CP-4	(a) Revised total assets, Alpine, $499,900, Nordic, $486,300; (b) Revised cumulative net income, Alpine, $195,000, Nordic, $219,000

11-1	No key figure
11-2	(a) Current liabilities, $375,403
11-3	(b) Interest expense for National Bank note, $4,704
11-4	(b) Interest Expense for Royal Bank note, $3,200
11-5	(a) Monthly interest expense, $425
11-6	(c) Total current liabilities, $337,186.50
11-7	(c) Unpaid balance, Jan. 1, 2000, $539,370
11-8	(a) Unpaid balance, Dec. 31, 2001, $8,331
11-9	No key figure
11-10	(b) Total payroll cost, $27,764
11-11	(b) (4) Total payroll cost, $250,058
11-12	(c) Total cost, $15,604

12-1	No key figure
12-2	No key figure
12-3	No key figure
12-4	No key figure
12-5	No key figure
12-6	(a) 2001, Percentage of completion, $1 million; instalment method, $2 million
12-7	(a) (1) Gross profit, $184,000
12-8	No key figure
12-9	No key figure

13-1	(b) Total assets, $187,400
13-2	(b) Total assets, $220,800
13-3	(b) Glen's capital balance, Dec. 31, $65,000
13-4	(a) Net income, $114,000; (c) total assets, $277,720

(continued on inside back cover)

ACCOUNTING

The Basis for Business Decisions

EIGHTH CANADIAN EDITION

Volume 1

ACCOUNTING

The Basis for Business Decisions

EIGHTH CANADIAN EDITION

Volume 1

ROBERT F. MEIGS

San Diego State University

MARY A. MEIGS

San Diego State University

MARK BETTNER

Bucknell University

RAY WHITTINGTON

San Diego State University

WAI P. LAM

University of Windsor

McGraw-Hill Ryerson

Toronto   Montréal   New York   Burr Ridge   Bangkok   Bogotá   Caracas
Lisbon   London   Madrid   Mexico City   Milan
New Delhi   Seoul   Singapore   Sydney   Taipei

McGraw-Hill
Ryerson Limited
A Subsidiary of The McGraw·Hill Companies

ACCOUNTING: THE BASIS FOR BUSINESS DECISIONS
Eighth Canadian Edition
Volume 1

Copyright © 1999, 1995, 1991, 1988, 1985, 1981, 1976, 1973, 1964 by McGraw-Hill Ryerson Limited, a Subsidiary of The McGraw-Hill Companies. Copyright © 1999, 1993, 1990, 1987, 1984, 1981, 1977, 1972, 1967, 1962 by McGraw-Hill, Inc. All rights reserved. No part of this publication may be reproduced or transmitted in any form or by any means, or stored in a data base or retrieval system, without the prior written permission of McGraw-Hill Ryerson Limited, or in the case of photocopying or other reprographic copying, a licence from CANCOPY (the Canadian Copyright Licensing Agency), 6 Adelaide Street East, Suite 900, Toronto, Ontario, M5C 1H6.

Any request for photocopying, recording, or taping of any part of this publication shall be directed in writing to CANCOPY.

ISBN: 0-07-560501-5

2 3 4 5 6 7 8 9 10   GTC   8 7 6 5 4 3 2 1 0

Printed and bound in Canada

Care has been taken to trace ownership of copyright material contained in this text. The publishers will gladly take any information that will enable them to rectify any reference or credit in subsequent editions.

Sponsoring Editor: Jennifer Dewey
Associate Editor: Janet Piper
Production Editor: Gail Marsden
Production Co-ordinator: Nicla Dattolico
Cover Designer: Dianna Little
Cover Illustration: Boris Lyubner/SIS©
Typesetter: Carlisle Communications, Ltd.
Printer: Transcontinental Printing

Canadian Cataloguing in Publication Data

Main entry under title:

Accounting: the basis for business decisions

8th Canadian ed.
Includes index.
ISBN 0-07-560501-5 (v. 1)   ISBN 0-07-560502-3 (v.2)

1. Accounting.   I. Meigs, Robert F.

HF5635.M49 1999   657'.044   C99-930219-1

CONTENTS

PREFACE

Welcome to the first financial accounting course. This course provides an introduction to the field of financial accounting and to the development and use of accounting information in the business world. It is intended for ***everyone,*** not just those students who may pursue careers in accounting. Today's students are tomorrow's business decision makers. And as we say in the title of this textbook, ***accounting is the basis for business decisions.***

There is more diversity today in the content of introductory financial accounting courses than at any time in the recent past. For example, the course may be structured to emphasize accounting techniques and procedures, accounting theory, or the interpretation and use of accounting information. There are many accounting textbooks available today, each with its own approach to the introductory course. Let us briefly explain ours.

OUR GOALS IN THIS EIGHTH CANADIAN EDITION

We have tried to improve this Eighth Canadian Edition in many ways. But three of our top priorities have been to:

1. Better develop the student's understanding of today's business environment.
2. Increase emphasis upon the ***interpretation*** and ***use*** of accounting information.
3. Retain a course structure that is familiar to faculty and meets the content requirements of most universities and colleges.

Providing Students with a Better "Business Background"

If students are to appreciate the nature of accounting, they first must understand the activities that accounting information describes. We find, however, that many introductory students lack this background. Often the introductory accounting course is also the students' first course in the business curriculum. In this edition, we give increased attention to explaining the nature of business activities before discussing the related accounting issues. Also, we add realism to the discussion and understanding of accounting issues by using real world events in the form of Case in Point boxes and in the assignment materials.

Our focus is upon the ***current and emerging*** business environment, not that of the past. We recognize the challenging reality that today's students will be ***just beginning*** their careers as we enter the twenty-first century.

Emphasizing the Interpretation and Use of Accounting Information

In today's business world, relatively few first-year accounting students will become professional preparers of accounting information. All, however, will become life-long ***users*** of this information. For this reason, we have reduced our emphasis on the techniques of preparing information, and increased our emphasis on its ***interpretation*** and ***use.***

This shift in perspective affects the text in several ways. For example, the assignment materials place greater emphasis on developing students' analytical, decision-making, and communication skills. Accordingly, these skills are required to solve the "Analytical and Decision Problems and Cases" in the final section of the assignment materials.

A more "user-oriented" approach also affects topical content and emphasis. Topics of crucial importance to decision makers are addressed, even if these topics traditionally have been deferred to later accounting courses. Examples include postretirement costs, income tax considerations, audits, and how different accounting methods affect key financial ratios.

The analysis and use of financial statement information, both by management and other users, are introduced in the early chapters and reinforced throughout the text. Thus, analytical ratios and other financial relationships are discussed throughout the text.

Some "traditional" accounting topics relate primarily to the preparation of accounting information and are of little significance to information users. Examples include the preparation of work sheets and alternative methods of recording accruals and deferrals. In our more user-oriented approach, such topics receive less emphasis.

Retaining a Familiar Course Structure

We regard our changes in this Eighth Canadian Edition as ***evolutionary,*** not revolutionary. Instructors who have used our past editions will find much that is familiar. They will also find that this edition supports—indeed encourages—evolutionary change from one semester to the next.

FOCUS AND ORGANIZATION OF THIS EIGHTH CANADIAN EDITION

This Eighth Canadian Edition, organized into two volumes, is focused on financial accounting. However, it also includes a brief introduction to managerial accounting.

Volume I covers the accounting cycle, merchandising operations and classified financial statements, accounting systems and internal control, assets, common liabilities, and accounting concepts, professional judgment, and ethical conduct.

Volume 2 covers partnerships, corporations, special types of liabilities, investments in corporate securities, income taxes, cash flows, analysis and interpretation of financial statements, and an introduction to managerial accounting.

ELEMENTS OF THE TEXTBOOK

This Eighth Canadian Edition is accompanied by a wide variety of in-the-text learning aids.

Chapter Introductions and Learning Objectives

Each chapter now starts with a "photo-opener." These photographs enable us to use non-technical images in describing each chapter's theme. Each chapter also includes a short set of ***learning objectives*** which are integrated with the text discussions and assignment materials.

Case in Point Boxes

A distinctive feature of our text is the use of short **Case in Point** boxes based upon real world events. This edition makes far greater use of this feature—it is part of our effort to more closely relate the study of accounting with today's business world. These Cases in Point are both informative and interesting. There are almost 100 of them in this edition.

Actual Annual Report and Financial Statements

The financial statements and other selected portions of the 1997 Annual Report of Loblaw Companies Limited are presented at the end of both *Volume 1* and *Volume 2*. The financial statements and other annual report information are referred to in these volumes to bring realism into classroom discussions. This represents another example of our efforts to more closely relate the study of accounting with today's business world.

Supplemental Topics and Appendixes

Several chapters are accompanied by ***Supplemental Topic*** sections. These topics are not "optional" or unimportant. Rather, they relate closely to the chapter content. Students **always** should read the *Supplemental Topic* sections. However, instructors may decide whether these topics are of sufficient general interest for inclusion in class discussions, homework assignments, and examinations.

In contrast to the *Supplemental Topics*, our four **Appendixes** provide self-contained coverage of specialized topics. We consider these topics optional; students are **not** expected to read the appendixes unless they are assigned by the instructor.

End-of-Chapter Reviews

Each chapter is followed by a variety of learning aids. These include a **Glossary of Key Terms, Self-Test Questions,** and in most chapters, a **Demonstration Problem.** Solutions to the Self-Test Questions and Demonstration Problems are also provided.

Assignment Materials

A substantial number of new questions, exercises, problems, and cases have been incorporated into this Eighth Canadian Edition. Many of these new assignment materials are based on real world situations, such as the financial statements of internationally well-known corporations. In fact, there is a separate section of real world problems and cases in Chapter 20.

One of the distinctive features of this edition is the nature and variety of its assignment material. Increased emphasis is placed upon the development of students' analytical, decision-making, communication, and interpersonal skills.

There are five basic categories of assignments (1) *Discussion Questions,* (2) *Exercises,* (3) *Problems,* (4) *Analytical and Decision Problems and Cases* and (5) *Comprehensive Problems.*

Discussion Questions are short and usually call for expository answers. In addition to developing communication skills, these questions enhance students' conceptual understanding of accounting.

Exercises are short assignments, usually focusing upon a single concept. They are designed to illustrate basic concepts quickly, allowing more class time for discussing assignments such as the *Analytical and Decision Problems and Cases*.

Problems are longer than the *Exercises* and address several concepts at one time. Many problems require students to explain, interpret, or make use of the information they produce.

Users of prior editions will notice that we now have a single series of problems, rather than the traditional *A* and *B* sets. This single series enables us to offer ***greater variety*** in our assignment material.

Analytical and Decision Problems and Cases are intended to develop students' analytical, decision-making, and communication skills. These assignments readily lend themselves to group analysis and to class discussions.

Comprehensive Problems tie together concepts presented over a span of chapters. The text includes ***six*** of these problems, ranging in length from 50-minute assignments to term projects. These problems are described in detail in the prefaces to both the *Solutions Manual* and the *Instructor's Guide.*

A ***checklist of key figures*** for all *Problems* and *Comprehensive Problems* appears on the front and back inside covers of the text. The purpose of these figures is to aid students in verifying their solutions and discovering their own errors. Also, a supplemental package of ***partially completed work sheets*** supporting all *Problems* and *Comprehensive Problems* is available through campus bookstores.

NEW FEATURES AND SUPPLEMENTARY MATERIALS

Traditionally, we have included in our *Preface* brief descriptions of new and extensively revised chapters and of the many supplemental materials which accompany this text. As these discussions are of greater interest to faculty than to students, we have moved them to the several pages immediately following the *Preface.*

A NOTE TO STUDENTS: SOME GUIDELINES ON CONDUCTING INTERVIEWS

Several of our *Analytical and Decision Problems and Cases* call for you—or a member of your study group—to interview people in the business community. Please appreciate that business people granting these interviews are donating their time for your benefit. For this reason, we ask that you observe a few basic guidelines:

- Please make an appointment for the interview, don't just walk in expecting to talk to someone. And be on time—recognize that time is a very valuable commodity in the business world.
- Dress appropriately and conduct yourself in a business-like manner.

- Learn the name of the person you will be interviewing, including the correct spelling and pronunciation, and his or her position within the organization.
- Plan and write down *in advance* all of the questions you plan to ask.
- Take notes during the interview. You should never attempt to quote the person's statements from memory.
- Realize that business people may not want certain information about their business "spread around town." Tell them *in advance* that the general content of the interview will be discussed within your study group and, perhaps, in your classroom. Respect any requests that specific comments be kept "off-the-record."

ACKNOWLEDGMENTS

It is with great pleasure that I acknowledge the contributions of the instructors and students who used the preceding edition. Their helpful comments were much appreciated.

My sincere thanks go to those reviewers who provided perceptive and constructive suggestions and to those who bestowed on me valuable advice. Their suggestions and advice have greatly improved the text and assignment materials. Now, let me thank each of the following individuals:

Cecile Ashman, Algonquin College
Elizabeth Grasby, Richard Ivey School of Business, University of Western Ontario
Elizabeth Hicks, Mount Saint Vincent University
Ross Johnston, University of Windsor
Loris Macor, PricewaterhouseCoopers
Bob Madden, St. Francis Xavier University
Jerry Mus, Assiniboine Community College
Penny Parker, Fanshawe College
Joe Pidutti, Durham College
Brenda Warner, University of Windsor
Betty Wong, Athabasca University

I appreciate the expert advice and assistance of the staff of McGraw-Hill Ryerson, especially Susan Calvert, Janet Piper, and Jennifer Dewey. Gail Marsden's professional and friendly approach to editing has made this project a more enjoyable experience. Also, I owe my thanks to Sandy Berlasty for her assistance in typing part of the manuscript.

Finally, let me express my gratitude to my family members—Jean, Gloria, Lambert, and Angela—for their support and understanding. I particularly want to thank Jean and Gloria for their excellent job in helping with various aspects of this project, especially in doing library research, and in typing, editing, and proofreading the manuscript of the text and solutions.

W.P. Lam

SOME ADDITIONAL INFORMATION

NEW OR EXTENSIVELY REVISED CHAPTERS

Many chapters in this Eighth Canadian Edition are either new or have been extensively revised. Among the changes which will be noticed most readily are:

The **first four** chapters utilize a new continuing example, are less procedural, and place more emphasis on the interpretation and use of accounting information. In **Chapter 1**, the coverage of the three forms of organizations has been revised and expanded. We now complete our coverage of the accounting cycle in **Chapter 3**, and our coverage of adjusting entries in that chapter has been expanded. **Chapter 4**, "Year-End!," provides a broader description of the many activities that make year-end the "busy season." Substantially less emphasis is given to the work sheet, which now appears in a *Supplemental Topic* section.

Chapter 5 continues to emphasize perpetual inventory systems, but the coverage of periodic systems has been expanded. Additional merchandising transactions have been moved from a supplemental topic to the main part of the chapter. Also "More About a Periodic Inventory System," is now an appendix, rather than a supplemental topic to this chapter.

Chapter 6, our accounting systems chapter, retains its focus on computer-based systems. However the chapter now is supplemented by Appendix B, illustrating the use of manual special journals, and by **THE NEXT DIMENSION**, which is our most challenging *Comprehensive Problem*. (NEXT makes an excellent group term project.)

Chapter 10, "Capital Assets: Plant and Equipment, Intangible Assets, and Natural Resources," emphasizes the depreciation methods that businesses use most—straight-line, declining balance, and units-of-production.

Chapter 12, "Accounting Concepts, Professional Judgment, and Ethical Conduct," is quite similar to that in our preceding edition. But we want to remind instructors that this chapter is at once a review of the first semester and an introduction to the second. It may well be worth repeating at the beginning of the second semester—particularly if students are returning from a long summer vacation.

Chapter 13, "Partnerships," has two significant changes. The first is the explanation of the distinction of the limited life of a partnership from the legal standpoint and the practical viewpoint, as many partnerships, such as accounting and law firms, continue to exist in spite of the changes of their partners. The second is the added discussion on the adequacy of partnership net income and the evaluation of partnership solvency.

Chapter 14, "Corporations: Organization and Shareholders' Equity," has been stream-lined. It also includes a new section on publicly owned and closely held corporations.

Chapter 15, "Reporting Special Events and Special Equity Transactions," has been updated by deleting the topic on prior period adjustments, as it is no longer a *CICA Handbook* recommendation.

Our coverage of bonds payable, in **Chapter 16**, differs substantially from past editions and from most accounting textbooks. For too long, coverage of long-term liabilities has focused upon the mechanics of amortizing bond discounts and premiums. But we find that bonds are almost never issued at a premium, and discounts generally are immaterial in dollar amount. Therefore, Chapter 16 now focuses upon topics of greater importance in today's business world, such as postretirement costs and the evaluation of credit risk. Bonds are addressed thoroughly in the chapter, but amortization of discount and premium is treated as a *Supplemental Topic*.

Chapter 19, "Measuring Cash Flows," is based on the most recent *CICA Handbook* recommendations, and consequently, this chapter is virtually new. The direct method for the preparation of the cash flow statement is covered in the main material of the chapter, while the indirect method is covered as a supplemental topic. The direct method is easier to understand and is preferred by the *CICA Handbook*.

Chapter 20, "Analysis and Interpretation of Financial Statements," has been revised and updated. The cash flow statement is now included and analyzed in this chapter. Also, the discussion on the measures of profitability has been revised and expanded.

One new feature to the assignment materials is a separate section of real world problems and cases, based on well-known corporations in North America.

Following this chapter is the new *Comprehensive Problem*. This problem requires the analysis and interpretation of the financial statements and other annual report information of Loblaw Companies Limited.

Chapter 21, "Introduction to Managerial Accounting; Accounting for Manufacturing Operations," is the final chapter of the text. While this chapter is essentially the same as it was in the previous edition, a new appendix on "The New Manufacturing Environment; Activity-Based Costing," has been added.

SUPPLEMENTARY MATERIALS

The text is accompanied by a large number of supplementary learning and teaching aids. These supplements are described below, with emphasis upon the features new to this eighth edition.

For the Student

1. *Study Guide.* The *Study Guide* enables students to measure their progress by providing immediate feedback. It includes a summary of the highlights of each chapter and an abundance of questions ranging from true/false to multiple choice to short problems and exercises. In fact, we have increased the number of short problems and exercises. The solutions are included at the end of each chapter with full explanations and worked-out solutions.

2. *Accounting Work Sheets.* Available in two volumes, (one for Chapters 1–12 and one for Chapters 13–21), students are provided with the appropriate type of working papers for each problem and comprehensive problem in the text.

3. ***Adders 'N Keyes,*** Fourth Edition, by Brenda Mallouk, *Adders 'N Keyes* is a sole proprietorship practice set that gives students exposure to a real life business setting.
4. ***Interactive Financial Accounting Lab*** by Ralph Smith, Rick Birney, and Alison Wiseman.
5. ***Student's Name CDs*** by Harvey Freedman. *Student's Name CDs* is an accounting practice set that requires students to analyze transactions using real life source documents.

U.S. Supplements For The Student

6. ***General Ledger Application Software***
7. ***Student SPATS for Accounting***
8. ***Tutorial Software—Windows***
9. ***Freewheel Practice Set***
10. ***Republic Practice Set***
11. ***Cogg Hill Practice Set***
12. ***Fast Mart Inc. Practice Set***

For the Instructor

The supplements listed here may accompany *Accounting: The Basis for Business Decisions.* Please contact your McGraw-Hill Ryerson representative for details concerning policies, prices, and availability as some restrictions may apply.

1. ***Solutions Manual.*** A comprehensive manual containing descriptions of each problem and case with the estimated time for completion and difficulty rating; suggested answers to the discussion questions; and solutions to the exercises, problems, cases, and comprehensive problems. All assignment material and solutions were developed by the authors of the text.
2. ***Instructor's Manual with PowerPoint Presentation.*** For each chapter, the *Instructor's Manual* contains a brief, topical outline, suggested assignment and topic coverage chart, teaching objectives, descriptions of new features, chapter outline, and teaching suggestions. In-class tests are a valuable new addition. These 3 to 4 question, 10 minute quizzes are a terrific new feature.

    A PowerPoint presentation and teaching transparencies are also included in the *Instructor's Manual.*
3. ***Computerized Test Bank.***

    The *Study Guide, Instructor's Manual with PowerPoint Presentation,* and *Computerized Test Bank* were adapted by the following:
    W.P. Doyle, Mt. Saint Vincent University
    E.A.G. Hicks, Mt. Saint Vincent University
    A.C. MacGillivary, Mt. Saint Vincent University
    J.R. Tilley, Mt. Saint Vincent University

U.S. Instructor Supplements

4. ***Instructor Spreadsheet Application Templates***

PART 1

An Introduction to Accounting

In today's business world, an understanding of accounting is not just useful—it's often a *survival skill*. Count on it.

CHAPTER 1

Accounting: The Language of Business

Accounting is the language of business. It's the way business people set goals, measure results, and evaluate performance. And it's difficult to participate if you don't speak the language.

1. Define accounting and explain why people other than professional accountants benefit from an understanding of accounting.
2. Explain the purpose of accounting, financial reporting, financial statements, public information, and generally accepted accounting principles.
3. Prepare a balance sheet and describe its content.
4. Describe the accounting principles involved in asset valuation.
5. Indicate the effects of business transactions upon the accounting equation and the balance sheet.
6. Describe the three forms of business organizations.
7. Use a balance sheet to evaluate the solvency of an organization.
8. Identify factors contributing to the reliability of financial statements.
9. Discuss the importance of professional judgment and ethical conduct in accounting practice.
10. Describe the relationship between professional accountants and top corporate executives.
*11. Describe various career opportunities in accounting.

WHAT IS ACCOUNTING?

LO 1: Define accounting and explain why people other than professional accountants benefit from an understanding of accounting.

Accounting is technically defined as the process of identifying, measuring, recording, interpreting, and communicating the results of economic activities. Thus, some people think of accounting as a highly specialized field that is practised only by professional accountants. However, accounting is simply the means by which we measure and describe the results of economic activities. Therefore, whether you are involved with an economic activity of managing a business, making an investment, preparing your tax return, or just paying your phone bill, you are working with accounting concepts and accounting information. So, nearly everyone deals with some aspects of accounting on an almost daily basis.

Accounting often is called the "language of business" because it is so widely used in describing all types of business activities. Every investor, manager, and business decision maker needs a clear understanding of accounting terms and concepts if he or she is to participate and communicate effectively in the business community.

But the use of accounting information is not limited to the business world. We live in an era of accountability. An individual may be required to account for his or her income and file an income tax return. Often an individual must supply personal accounting information in order to qualify for a loan or to obtain a credit card. The federal government, the provinces, the cities, and the school board all use accounting information as the basis for controlling their resources and measuring their accomplishments. Accounting is just as important to the successful operation of a government, a social program, or a church as it is to a business organization.

The study of accounting should not be limited to students majoring in accounting or finance. Everyone who engages in economic activity—**which means everyone**—will benefit from understanding the nature, significance, and limitations of accounting information.

---

*Supplemental Topic, "Careers in Accounting."

The Purpose of Accounting

LO 2: Explain the purpose of accounting, financial reporting, financial statements, public information, and generally accepted accounting principles.

The basic purpose of accounting is to provide decision makers with ***information useful in making economic decisions.*** As illustrated below, the input to the accounting process is economic activity; the output is useful information.

Accounting from a User's Perspective

Our primary goals in this text are to develop your ***understanding*** of accounting information and your ***ability to use it effectively.*** The diagram below not only illustrates the role of accounting in society, it also describes the content of this textbook.

Accounting "links" decision makers with economic activities—and with the results of their decisions

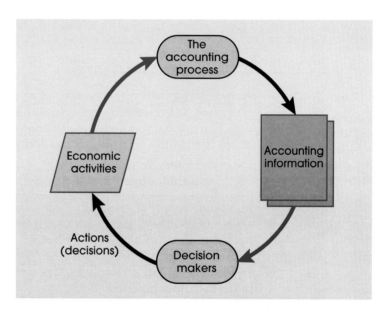

In order to use accounting information effectively, you must understand:

- The ***nature of the economic activities*** described in accounting reports.
- The ***assumptions*** and ***measurement techniques*** involved in the accounting process.
- How to ***relate the accounting information*** to the decision at hand.

We will address these topics throughout this book.

Types of Accounting Information

Just as there are many types of economic decisions, there are many types of accounting information. The terms ***financial accounting, management accounting,*** and ***tax accounting*** often are used in describing the types of accounting information most widely used in the business community.

Financial Accounting—"General-Purpose" Information   Financial accounting refers to information describing the financial resources, obligations, and activities of an economic entity (either an organization or an individual). Accountants use the term **financial position** to describe an entity's financial resources and obligations at one point in time, and the term *results of operations* to describe its financial activities during an accounting period such as a month or a year.

Financial accounting information (or simply financial information) is designed primarily to assist investors and creditors in deciding where to place their scarce investment resources.[1] Such decisions are important to society, as they determine which companies and industries will receive the financial resources necessary for growth, and which will not.

However, many other decision makers also make use of financial accounting information. A company's managers and employees constantly need such information in order to run and control daily business operations. For example, they need to know the amount of money in the company's bank accounts, the types and quantities of merchandise in the company's warehouse, and the amounts owed to specific creditors. Financial accounting information also is used in income tax returns. In fact, financial accounting information is used for so many different purposes that it often is called "general-purpose" accounting information.

Management Accounting   Management (or managerial) accounting involves the development and interpretation of accounting information intended *specifically to aid management* in running the business. Managers use this information in setting the company's overall goals, evaluating the performance of departments and individuals, deciding whether to introduce a new line of products—and in making virtually all types of managerial decisions.

Much "management accounting" information is financial in nature, but has been organized in a manner relating directly to the decision at hand. However, management accounting information often includes evaluations of "nonfinancial" factors, such as political and environmental considerations, product quality, customer satisfaction, and worker productivity.

Tax Accounting   The preparation of income tax returns is a specialized field within accounting. To a great extent, tax returns are based upon financial accounting information. However, the information often is adjusted or reorganized to conform with income tax reporting requirements.

The most challenging aspect of tax accounting is not the preparation of an income tax return, but *tax planning.* Tax planning means anticipating the "tax effects" of business transactions and structuring these transactions in a manner that will legally minimize the income tax burden.

Focus of This Book   In this book, we begin by introducing the basic concepts of financial accounting. These discussions will emphasize both the process of *financial reporting* to investors and creditors and the usefulness of financial information to an organization's management and employees. In the last chapter, we will introduce management accounting.

---

[1]CICA, *CICA Handbook* (Toronto), section 1000.11.

Major income tax concepts are discussed at various points throughout the text, and Chapter 18 is devoted entirely to this topic. Comprehensive coverage of income taxes, however, must be deferred to more advanced accounting courses.

Remember that the fields of financial, management, and tax accounting are *closely related.* Thus, we often address financial reporting requirements, management's information needs, and income tax considerations within a single chapter. Our emphasis throughout this book will be upon the accounting information developed in *profit-oriented business organizations.*

FINANCIAL REPORTING

All of the accounting information developed within an organization is available to management. However, much of the company's financial information also is distributed to people **outside** of the organization. These "outsiders" may include investors, creditors, financial analysts, labour unions, the general public—even the company's competitors (see the illustration on page 11). Each of these groups either supplies money to the business or has some other interest in the company's financial activities.

The process of supplying general-purpose financial information to people outside the organization is termed **financial reporting**. In Canada and most other industrialized countries, **publicly owned corporations** make much of their financial information "public"—that is, available to everyone.[2] These countries generally have laws to ensure that the *public information* provided by these companies is reliable and complete.

Small businesses generally do not provide financial information to the public. However, banks or other major creditors frequently insist upon receiving this information from the business as a condition for making a loan.

Financial Statements

The principal means of reporting general-purpose financial information to persons outside a business organization is a set of accounting reports called **financial statements**. The persons receiving these reports are termed the *users* of the financial statements.

A set of financial statements consists of four related accounting reports that summarize in a few pages the financial resources, obligations, profitability, and cash transactions of a business. A complete set of financial statements includes:

1. A **balance sheet,** showing at a specific date the *financial position* of the company, by indicating the resources that it owns, the debts that it owes, and the amount of the owner's *equity* (investment) in the business.

---

[2]A company is "publicly owned" whenever ownership "shares" in the company are offered for sale to the general public. Public information about a business can be obtained by writing to the company's corporate secretary.

2. An **income statement,** indicating the ***profitability*** of the business over the preceding year (or other time period).
3. A **statement of owner's equity**, explaining certain changes in the amount of the owner's equity in the business. (In businesses that are organized as corporations, the statement of owner's equity is replaced by a **statement of retained earnings**.)
4. A **cash flow statement**, summarizing the cash receipts and cash payments of the business over the same time period covered by the income statement.

In addition, a complete set of financial statements include several pages of ***notes,*** containing additional information that accountants believe is useful in the interpretation of the financial statements.

The basic purpose of financial statements is to assist users in evaluating the ***financial position, profitability,*** and ***future prospects*** of a business. In Canada, the annual and quarterly financial statements of all publicly owned corporations are public information.[3] (The annual financial statements of Loblaw Companies Limited, a publicly owned corporation, are illustrated at the end of this book.)

In deciding where to invest their limited resources, investors and creditors often compare the financial statements of many different companies. For such comparisons to be valid, the financial statements of these different companies must be reasonably ***comparable***—that is, they must present similar information in a similar format. To achieve this goal, financial statements are prepared in conformity with a set of "ground rules" called ***generally accepted accounting principles (GAAP).***

Financial Statements and Income Tax Returns   Revenue Canada requires corporations and individuals with taxable income to file annual income tax returns. ***Taxable income*** is a legal concept defined by income tax laws and regulations. In many instances, income tax laws are similar to generally accepted accounting principles; but in other cases, they are quite different. Therefore, an income tax return is a special accounting report, separate from the company's financial statements. A corporation's income tax return is sent only to tax authorities such as Revenue Canada, it is ***not*** public information.

The Functions of an Accounting System

Most business organizations have an **accounting system** for preparing financial statements, income tax returns, reports to managers, bills to customers, and other types of accounting information. An accounting ***system*** consists of the personnel, procedures, devices, forms, and records used by an entity in developing accounting information and in communicating this information to decision makers. Accounting systems often make use of computers and other electronic devices, as well as handwritten forms and

---

[3]In ***annual*** financial statements, the time period covered by the income statement, statement of owner's equity (or retained earnings), and cash flow statement is one year. In ***quarterly*** statements, the period covered in these statements is a quarter of a year (three months).

records. In fact, the accounting system of any large business organization includes all of these components.

In every accounting system, the economic activities of the organization are identified, measured, and then *recorded* in the accounting records. Next, the recorded data are *classified* within the system to accumulate subtotals for various types of economic activities. Finally, the information is *summarized* in accounting reports designed to meet the information needs of various decision makers, such as investors, managers, and governmental agencies.

The "Transactions Approach" to Recording Economic Activity   Accounting reports summarize information that has been recorded in the accounting system. In recording economic activities, accountants focus upon completed **transactions**—that is, events that (1) cause an *immediate change* in the financial resources or obligations of the business and (2) can be *measured objectively* in monetary terms. Examples of transactions include purchasing or selling goods or services, receiving cash, and making cash payments.

The primary strength of this "transactions approach" lies in the *reliability* of the information that is recorded. The recorded information is based upon past events, for which the financial effects upon the business can be measured with a reasonable degree of **objectivity**.[4]

In another respect, accountants' emphasis upon transactions *lessens* the usefulness of accounting reports. Some important events are not recorded in the accounting records, because they do not meet the definition of a "transaction." For example, the retirement or death of a key executive, a technological breakthrough by the company's research department, or the introduction of a new product by a competitor are not "transactions," and therefore are not recorded in the accounting records. These events may cause significant *future* changes in the financial resources and obligations of the business, but they do not cause *immediate* changes. In addition, the financial effects of these events cannot be measured with much objectivity.

The preceding events are examples of important "nonfinancial" information. Although these events are not recorded in the accounting records, they are recorded elsewhere in the company's information system. In addition, these events often are disclosed to decision makers outside of the business organization through press conferences, notes to the financial statements, or the news media.

Internal Control

The decisions made by management are based to a considerable extent upon information developed by the accounting system. Therefore, manage-

---

[4]Accountants use the term *objective* to mean neutral, free from bias, and verifiable in amount. The concept of *objectivity* is a generally accepted accounting principle and has a profound effect upon accounting practices and accounting information. This concept is discussed further on page 16 and at many points throughout the book.

ment needs assurance that the accounting information it receives is accurate and reliable. This assurance is provided by the company's ***internal control structure or system.***

A simple example of an internal control measure is the use of serial numbers on cheques issued. Accounting for an unbroken sequence of serial numbers provides assurance that every cheque issued has been recorded in the accounting records.

The **internal control structure** includes ***all*** measures used by an organization to guard against errors, waste, and fraud; to assure the reliability of accounting data; to promote compliance with management policies; and to evaluate the level of performance in all divisions of the company. In short, the internal control structure is intended to ensure that the entire organization ***operates according to plan.***

There is a strong ***interrelationship*** between accounting and internal control. We have stated that the internal control structure includes measures designed to promote the reliability of accounting information. At the same time, one goal of the accounting system is to provide management with information useful in establishing internal control throughout the organization. Thus, the topic of internal control goes hand in hand with the study of accounting.

Audits of Financial Statements

What assurance do outsiders have that the financial statements issued by management provide a complete and reliable picture of the company's financial position and operating results? In large part, this assurance is provided by an ***audit*** of the company's financial statements, performed by a firm of ***public accountants.*** These auditors are experts in the field of financial reporting and are ***independent*** of the company issuing the financial statements.

An **audit** is an ***investigation*** of a company's financial statements, designed to determine the "fairness" of these statements. Accountants and auditors use the term **"fair"** in describing financial statements that are reliable and complete, conform to generally accepted accounting principles, and are ***not misleading.***

As part of the audit, the auditors investigate the quality of the company's internal control structure, count or observe many of the company's assets, and gather evidence both from within the business and from outside sources. Based upon this careful investigation, the public accounting firm expresses its ***professional opinion*** as to the fairness of the financial statements. This opinion is contained in the **auditors' report** which accompanies the financial statements distributed to persons outside the business organization.

Auditors do not "guarantee the accuracy" of financial statements; they only express their ***expert opinion*** as to the fairness of the statements. However, public accounting firms stake their reputations on the thoroughness of their audits and the dependability of their audit reports. Over many years, audited financial statements have established an impressive track record of reliability.

Annual Reports

As part of the financial reporting process, large business organizations prepare **annual reports** for distribution to investors and to anyone requesting a copy. Included in these annual reports are audited financial statements for each of the last several years. These *comparative* financial statements enable users to identify *trends* in the company's performance and financial position. Annual reports also include the auditors' reports on the comparative statements and discussions by top management of the company's financial position, profitability, and future prospects. In addition, they contain much nonfinancial information about the company's objectives, products, and operations.

CASE IN POINT   McDonald's Corporation devoted much of a recent annual report to the company's concern for the environment. Included in the report were discussions of the company's programs for solid waste management, resource conservation, and recycling. (The annual report was printed on recycled paper.)

The flow chart on the following page summarizes the preparation and distribution of annual reports by publicly owned companies. Notice the many types of decision makers that make use of this information. Because annual reports are public information, even *competitors* have ready access to them—and so do you.

Financial Reporting: A Multimedia Process

Although financial statements are the *primary* means of financial reporting, they are not the *only* means. Information about a business is also made available to outside decision makers through news conferences, press releases, and filings of public information with governmental agencies. In addition, many financial analysts, investment advisory services, and business magazines continually evaluate the financial position, profitability, and future prospects of publicly owned companies. Many of these evaluations are available to the public at little or no cost.

CASE IN POINT   Financial analysts and financial reporters share their evaluations of the financial position, profitability, and future prospects of many publicly owned companies in such business publications as *The Financial Post**, *Canadian Business, Investor's Digest, Financial Post Survey of Industrials, The Investment Reporter,* and *Value Line Investment Survey.*

*Now part of the *National Post.*

THE PROCESS OF FINANCIAL REPORTING

(Audited Financial Statements and Annual Reports)

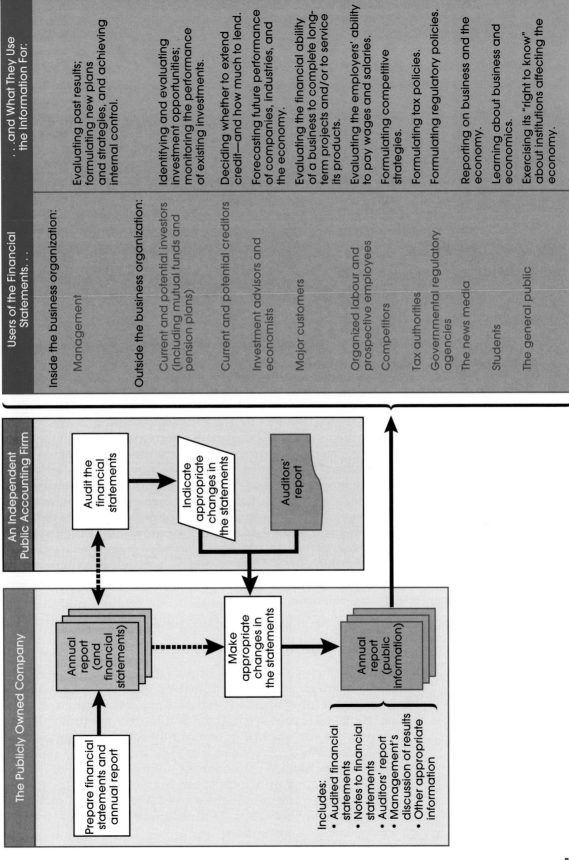

GENERALLY ACCEPTED ACCOUNTING PRINCIPLES (GAAP)

Generally accepted accounting principles (or **GAAP**) are the "ground rules" for financial reporting. These principles provide the general framework determining what information is included in financial statements, and how this information is to be presented. The phrase "generally accepted accounting principles" encompasses the basic objectives of financial reporting, as well as numerous broad concepts and many detailed rules. Thus, such terms as objectives, standards, concepts, assumptions, methods, and rules often are used in describing specific generally accepted accounting "principles."

We already have mentioned two concepts embodied in generally accepted accounting principles: ***comparability*** (among different companies) and ***reliability.*** In this chapter we will discuss six other generally accepted accounting principles: the business entity concept, the cost principle, the going-concern assumption, the objectivity principle, the stable-dollar assumption, and the concept of adequate disclosure. These and other accounting principles will be considered further at many points throughout this book.

Let us emphasize, however, that ***there is no comprehensive list of generally accepted accounting principles.*** In fact, new accounting principles emerge continuously as business organizations enter into new forms of business activity.

The Nature of Accounting Principles

Accounting principles are not like physical laws; they do not exist in nature awaiting discovery by us. Rather, they are developed by us, in light of what we consider to be the most important objectives of financial reporting. In many ways generally accepted accounting principles are similar to the rules established for an organized sport, such as football or hockey. For example, accounting principles, like sports rules:

- Originate from a combination of tradition, experience, and official decree.
- Require authoritative support and some means of enforcement.
- Are sometimes arbitrary.
- May change over time as shortcomings in the existing rules come to light.
- Must be clearly understood and observed by all participants in the process.

Unfortunately, accounting principles vary somewhat from country to country. The phrase "generally accepted accounting principles" refers to the accounting concepts in use in Canada. However, the principles in use in the United States, Great Britain, and a number of other countries are quite similar. Also, foreign companies that raise capital from Canadian investors usually issue financial statements in conformity with the generally accepted accounting principles in use in Canada.

Several international organizations currently are attempting to establish greater uniformity among the accounting principles in use around the world.

Organizations Influencing Accounting Practice

In Canada, the **Canadian Institute of Chartered Accountants (CICA)** is the most prominent and influential organization in developing generally accepted accounting principles and in improving the quality of financial reporting. The CICA, through its **Accounting Standards Board,**[5] has issued a significant number of recommendations on accounting standards. The recommendations are contained in the *CICA Handbook* and are considered as generally accepted accounting principles. Both the Canada Business Corporations Act and the provincial securities commissions have recognized the *CICA Handbook* accounting recommendations as generally accepted accounting principles. The CICA is a self-regulated body, not a government agency.

A number of other organizations outside Canada also have an influence on Canadian accounting practices—the Financial Accounting Standards Board (FASB), the American Institute of Certified Public Accountants (AICPA), and the Securities and Exchange Commissions (SEC) in the United States, and the International Accounting Standards Committees located in the United Kingdom.

The FASB is a self-regulated body that issues Statements of Financial Accounting Standards. These statements represent authoritative expression of generally accepted accounting principles in the United States.

"Authoritative Support" for Accounting Principles To qualify as "generally accepted," an accounting principle must have substantial authoritative support. Accounting recommendations set forth by the CICA's Accounting Standards Board automatically qualify as generally accepted accounting principles. However, many concepts and practices gain substantial authoritative support from ***unofficial*** sources, such as widespread use, or recognition in textbooks and other "unofficial" accounting literature. Thus, the phrase "generally accepted accounting principles" includes more concepts and practices than appear in the "official" literature.

FINANCIAL STATEMENTS: THE STARTING POINT IN THE STUDY OF ACCOUNTING

The preparation of financial statements is not the first step in the accounting process, but it is a logical point to begin the ***study*** of accounting. Financial statements convey to management and to interested outsiders a concise picture of the profitability and financial position of a business. These statements summarize, in a few pages, the thousands or even millions of transactions recorded during the year in the company's accounting system. Thus, financial statements are the ***end product*** of the accounting process. The student who acquires a clear understanding of the nature and content of

---

[5]The CICA's Accounting Standards Board is composed of a cross section of individuals with various backgrounds and occupations: eight members are appointed by the CICA, and one member is appointed by each of these five organizations—the Canadian Academic Accounting Association, Canadian Council of Financial Analysts, Certified General Accountants' Association of Canada, Financial Executives Institute Canada, and Society of Management Accountants of Canada. However, the Certified General Accountants' Association of Canada has declined to appoint its representative to serve on the Board. At least two-thirds of the voting board members will be members of the CICA.

these statements is in a better position to appreciate the objectives of the earlier steps of recording and classifying business transactions.

The three most widely used financial statements are the **balance sheet,** the **income statement,** and the **cash flow statement.** In this introductory chapter and in Chapter 2, we shall explore the nature of the balance sheet, or **statement of financial position,** as it is sometimes called. Once we have become familiar with the form and arrangement of the balance sheet and with the meanings of technical terms such as assets, liabilities, and owner's equity, it will be as easy to read and understand a report on the financial position of a business as it is for an architect to read a blueprint for a proposed building. (We shall discuss the income statement in Chapter 3, and the cash flow statement in a later chapter.)

The Balance Sheet

LO 3: Prepare a balance sheet and describe its content.

The purpose of a balance sheet is to show the **financial position** of a given business entity at a specific date. Every business prepares a balance sheet at the end of the year, and many companies prepare one at the end of each month. A balance sheet consists of a listing of the assets, the liabilities, and the owner's equity of a business. The **balance sheet date** is important, as the financial position of a business may change quickly. A balance sheet is most useful if it is relatively recent. The following balance sheet shows the financial position of Vagabond Travel Agency at December 31, 1999.

A balance sheet shows financial position at a specific date

VAGABOND TRAVEL AGENCY
Balance Sheet
December 31, 1999

Assets		Liabilities & Owner's Equity	
Cash	$ 22,500	**Liabilities:**	
Notes receivable	10,000	Notes payable	$ 41,000
Accounts receivable . .	60,500	Accounts payable . .	36,000
Supplies	2,000	Salaries payable	3,000
Land	100,000	Total liabilities	$ 80,000
Building	90,000	**Owner's equity:**	
Office equipment	15,000	Terry Crane, capital . .	220,000
Total	$300,000	Total	$300,000

Let us briefly describe several features of this balance sheet. First, the heading sets forth three things: (1) the name of the business entity, (2) the name of the financial statement, and (3) the balance sheet date. The body of the balance sheet also consists of three distinct sections: **assets, liabilities,** and **owner's equity.**

Notice that cash is listed first among the assets, followed by notes receivable, accounts receivable, supplies, and any other assets that will **soon be converted into cash or used up in business operations.** Following these relatively "liquid" assets are the more "permanent" assets, such as land, buildings, and equipment.

Liabilities are shown before owner's equity. Each major type of liability (such as notes payable, accounts payable, and salaries payable) is listed separately, followed by a figure for total liabilities.

Finally, notice that the amount of total assets ($300,000) is *equal* to the total amount of liabilities and owner's equity (also $300,000). This relationship *always exists*—in fact, the *equality of these totals* is one reason that this financial statement is called a *balance* sheet.

The Concept of the Business Entity   Generally accepted accounting principles require that a set of financial statements describe the affairs of a specific business entity. This concept is also called the *accounting entity concept* or *entity principle.*

A **business entity** is an economic unit that engages in identifiable business activities. For accounting purposes, the business entity is regarded as *separate from the personal affairs of its owner.* Therefore, the assets and liabilities are related to a specific business, not related to the owner personally. For example, Vagabond is a business organization operating as a travel agency. Its owner, Terry Crane, may have a personal bank account, a home, a car, and even another business, such as a cattle ranch. These items are not involved in the operation of the travel agency and should not appear in Vagabond's financial statements.

If the owner were to intermingle his or her personal affairs with the transactions of the business, the resulting financial statements would fail to describe clearly the financial position and operating results of the business organization.

Assets

Assets are economic resources that are owned by a business and are expected to benefit future operations. Assets may have definite physical form such as buildings, machinery, or an inventory of merchandise. On the other hand, some assets exist not in physical or tangible form, but in the form of valuable legal claims or rights; examples are accounts receivable (amounts due from customers), investments in government bonds, and patent rights.

One of the most basic and at the same time most controversial problems in accounting is determining the dollar values for the various assets of a business. At present, generally accepted accounting principles call for the valuation of most assets in a balance sheet at *cost,* rather than at current market values. The specific accounting principles supporting cost as the basis for asset valuation are discussed below.

LO 4: Describe the accounting principles involved in asset valuation.

The Cost Principle   Assets such as land, buildings and equipment are typical of the many economic resources that will be used in producing income for the business. The prevailing accounting view is that such assets should be recorded at their acquisition cost. When we say that an asset is shown in the balance sheet at its *historical cost,* we mean the original cost of the asset to the business entity; this amount may be very different from the asset's current market value.

For example, let us assume that a business buys a tract of land for use as a building site, paying $100,000 in cash. The amount to be entered in the accounting records as the value of the asset will be the cost of $100,000. If we assume a booming real estate market, a fair estimate of the market value of the land 10 years later might be $250,000. Although the market price or economic value of the land has risen greatly, the accounting value as shown in the accounting records and on the balance sheet would continue unchanged at the cost of $100,000. This policy of accounting for assets at their acquisition cost is often referred to as the **cost principle** of accounting.

In reading a balance sheet, it is important to bear in mind that the dollar amounts listed do not necessarily indicate the prices at which the assets could be sold, nor the prices at which they could be replaced. Perhaps the greatest limitation of a balance sheet is that this financial statement **_does not_** necessarily show how much the business currently is worth.

The Going-Concern Assumption It is appropriate to ask **_why_** accountants do not change the recorded values of assets to correspond with changing market prices for these properties. One reason is that the land and building being used to house the business were acquired for **_use_** and not for resale; in fact, these assets cannot be sold without disrupting the business. The balance sheet of a business is prepared on the assumption that the business is a continuing enterprise, a **going concern**. Consequently, the current market prices at which the land and buildings could be sold are of less importance than if these properties were intended for sale.

The Objectivity Principle Another reason for using cost rather than current market values in accounting for assets is the need for a definite, factual basis for valuation. The cost of land, buildings, and many other assets purchased for cash or equivalent consideration can be rather definitely determined. Accountants use the term **_objective_** to describe asset valuations that are factual and can be verified by independent experts. For example, if land is shown on the balance sheet at cost, any public accountant who performed an audit of the business would be able to find objective evidence that the land was actually valued at the cost incurred in acquiring it. Estimated market values, on the other hand, for assets such as buildings and specialized machinery are not factual and objective. Market values are constantly changing, and estimates of the prices at which assets could be sold are largely a matter of personal opinion.

At the date an asset is acquired, the cost and market value are usually the same. With the passage of time, however, the current market value of assets is likely to differ considerably from the cost recorded in the owner's accounting records.

The Stable-Dollar Assumption Severe inflation in several countries in recent years has raised serious doubts as to the adequacy of the conventional cost basis in accounting for assets. When inflation becomes very severe, historical cost values for assets simply lose their relevance as a basis for making business decisions. Much consideration has been given to the use of balance sheets that would show assets at current appraised values or at replacement costs rather than at historical cost.

Accountants in Canada, by adhering to the cost basis of accounting, are implying that the dollar is a stable unit of measurement, as is the litre or the kilometre. The cost principle and the **stable-dollar assumption** work very well in periods of stable prices, but are less satisfactory under conditions of rapid inflation. For example, if a company bought land 20 years ago for $100,000 and purchased a second similar tract of land today for $500,000, the total cost of land shown by the accounting records would be $600,000. This treatment ignores the fact that dollars spent 20 years ago had far greater purchasing power than today's dollar. Thus, the $600,000 total for cost of land is a mixture of two kinds of dollars with very different purchasing power.

After much research into this problem, the CICA's Accounting Standards Board required on a trial basis that large corporations annually disclose financial data adjusted for the effects of inflation. But after several years of experimentation, it was concluded that the costs of developing this information exceeded its usefulness. Thus, the disclosure requirement was eliminated. At the present time, the stable-dollar assumption continues in use in Canada—perhaps until challenged by more severe inflation sometime in the future.

Liabilities

Liabilities are debts. The person or organization to whom the debt is owed is called a **creditor**.

All businesses have liabilities; even the largest and most successful companies often purchase merchandise, supplies, and services "on account." The liabilities arising from such purchases are called ***accounts payable.*** Many businesses borrow money to finance expansion or the purchase of high-cost assets. When obtaining a loan, the borrower usually must sign a formal note payable. A ***note payable*** is a written promise to repay the amount owed by a particular date, and usually calls for the payment of interest as well.

Accounts payable, in contrast with notes payable, involve no written promises and generally do not call for interest payments. In essence, a note payable is a ***more formal*** arrangement.

When a company has both notes payable and accounts payable, the two types of liabilities are listed separately in the balance sheet. Other types of short-term liabilities, such as salaries payable, may either be listed separately or combined with the amount shown as accounts payable.

The order in which ***short-term*** liabilities are listed is not important, although either notes payable or accounts payable usually appears first.[6] The liabilities section of the balance sheet should include a subtotal indicating the total amount of liabilities, as illustrated on page 14.

Creditors' Claims Have Priority Over Those of Owners

Liabilities represent claims against the borrower's assets. As we shall see, the owners of a business ***also*** have claims to the company's assets. But in the eyes of the law, creditors' claims ***take priority*** over those of the owners. This means that creditors are entitled to be ***paid in full,*** even if such payment should exhaust the assets of the business and leave nothing for its owners.

---

[6]Short-term liabilities are those due within one year. Long-term liabilities are shown separately in the balance sheet, after the listing of all short-term liabilities.

Owner's Equity

Owner's equity represents the ***owner's claim*** to the assets of the business. Because creditors' claims have legal priority over those of the owner, owner's equity is a ***residual amount.*** If you are the owner of a business, you are entitled to "whatever's left" after the claims of creditors have been satisfied in full. Therefore, owner's equity is always equal to ***total assets minus total liabilities.*** For example, using the data from the illustrated balance sheet of Vagabond Travel Agency (page 14):

Vagabond has total assets of	*$300,000*
And total liabilities of	*80,000*
Therefore, the owner's equity **must be**	*$220,000*

Owner's equity does ***not*** represent a specific claim to cash or any other particular asset. Rather, it is the owner's "overall financial interest" in the entire company.

Increases in Owner's Equity   The owner's equity in a business comes from two sources:

1. ***Investment*** by the owner
2. ***Earnings*** from profitable operation of the business

Only the first of these two sources of owner's equity is considered in this chapter. The second source, an increase in owner's equity through earnings of the business, will be discussed in Chapter 3.

Decreases in Owner's Equity   Decreases in owner's equity also are caused in two ways:

1. ***Withdrawals of cash or other assets*** by the owner (in businesses organized as corporations, these withdrawals are termed ***dividends***)
2. ***Losses*** from unprofitable operation of the business

Accounting for withdrawals and net losses will be addressed in Chapter 3.

The Accounting Equation

A fundamental characteristic of every balance sheet is that the total figure for assets always equals the total of liabilities plus owner's equity. This agreement or balance of total assets with the total of liabilities and owner's equity is one reason for calling this financial statement a ***"balance" sheet.*** But ***why*** do total assets equal the total of liabilities and owner's equity? The answer can be given in one short paragraph:

The dollar totals on the two sides of the balance sheet are always equal because these two sides are ***merely two views of the same business resources.*** The listing of assets shows us what resources the business owns; the listing of liabilities and owner's equity tells us who supplied these resources to the business and how much each group supplied. Everything that a business owns has been supplied to it either by creditors or by the owner. Therefore, the total claims of the creditors plus the claim of the owner equal the total assets of the business.

The equality of assets on the one hand and of the claims of the creditors and the owner on the other hand is expressed in the following **accounting equation**:

The accounting equation

$$\text{Assets} = \text{Liabilities} + \text{Owner's Equity}$$
$$\$300,000 = \$80,000 + \$220,000$$

The amounts listed in the equation were taken from the balance sheet illustrated on page 14. The balance sheet is simply a detailed statement of this equation. To illustrate this relationship, compare the balance sheet of Vagabond Travel Agency with the above equation.

To emphasize that the owner's equity is a *residual claim,* secondary to the claims of creditors, it is often helpful to transpose the terms of the equation, as follows:

Alternative form of the accounting equation

$$\text{Assets} - \text{Liabilities} = \text{Owner's Equity}$$
$$\$300,000 - \$80,000 = \$220,000$$

Notice that if a business has liabilities *in excess* of its assets, the owner's equity will be a *negative* amount.

Every business transaction, no matter how simple or how complex, can be expressed in terms of its effect on the accounting equation. A thorough understanding of the equation and some practice in using it are essential to the student of accounting.

Regardless of whether a business grows or contracts, this equality between the assets and the claims against the assets is always maintained. Any increase in the amount of total assets is necessarily accompanied by an equal increase on the other side of the equation, that is, by an increase in either the liabilities or the owner's equity. Any decrease in total assets is necessarily accompanied by a corresponding decrease in liabilities or owner's equity. The continuing equality of the two sides of the balance sheet can best be illustrated by taking a brand-new business as an example and observing the effects of various transactions upon its balance sheet.

THE EFFECTS OF BUSINESS TRANSACTIONS: AN ILLUSTRATION

To illustrate basic accounting concepts and procedures, we will use the example of a small auto repair business. (We will continue this example throughout our first four chapters.)

LO 5: Indicate the effects of business transactions upon the accounting equation and the balance sheet.

The Business Entity   Assume that Michael McBryan, an experienced auto mechanic, opens his own automotive repair business, called Overnight Auto Service. A distinctive feature of Overnight's operations is that all repair work is done at night. This strategy offers customers the convenience of dropping off their cars in the evening and picking them up the following morning.

Operating at night also enables Overnight to minimize its labour costs. Instead of hiring full-time employees, Overnight offers part-time work to mechanics who already have "day jobs" at major automobile dealerships. This eliminates the need for costly employee training programs and also such payroll "fringe benefits" as group health insurance and employees' pension plans.[7]

Overnight's Accounting Policies   McBryan has taken several courses in accounting and will maintain Overnight's accounting records himself. He knows that small businesses such as his are not required to prepare formal financial statements, but he prepares them anyway. If Overnight is successful, McBryan plans to open many more locations. Thus, he anticipates needing to raise substantial amounts of capital from investors and creditors. He believes that the financial history provided by a series of monthly financial statements will be very helpful in attracting investment capital.

The Company's First "Transaction"   McBryan officially started Overnight on November 1, 1999. On that date, he opened a bank account in the name of the business, into which he deposited *$80,000* of his personal savings.

This transaction provided Overnight with its first asset—Cash—and also created the initial owner's equity in the business entity. A balance sheet showing the company's financial position after this initial transaction follows:

Beginning balance sheet of a new business

OVERNIGHT AUTO SERVICE
Balance Sheet
November 1, 1999

Assets		Owner's Equity	
Cash	$80,000	Michael McBryan, capital	$80,000

Overnight's next two transactions involved the acquisition of a suitable site for its business operations.

Purchase of an Asset for Cash   Representing the business, McBryan negotiated with both Megacity and the Metropolitan Transit Authority (MTA) to purchase an abandoned bus garage. (The MTA owned the garage, but the city owned the land.)

On November 3, Overnight purchased the land from the city for *$52,000 cash.* This transaction had two immediate effects upon the company's financial position: first, Overnight's cash was reduced by $52,000; and second, the company acquired a new asset—Land. The company's financial position following this transaction was:

---

[7]These benefits usually are associated only with full-time employment.

Balance sheet totals unchanged by purchase of land for cash

OVERNIGHT AUTO SERVICE Balance Sheet November 3, 1999			
Assets		**Owner's Equity**	
Cash	$28,000	Michael McBryan, capital	$80,000
Land	52,000		
Total	$80,000	Total	$80,000

Purchase of an Asset and Financing Part of the Cost On November 5, Overnight purchased the abandoned garage building from Metropolitan Transit Authority for **$36,000.** Overnight made a cash down payment of **$6,000** and issued a 90-day non-interest-bearing note payable for the **$30,000** balance owed.

As a result of this transaction, Overnight had (1) $6,000 less cash; (2) a new asset, Building, which cost $36,000; and (3) a new liability, Note Payable, in the amount of $30,000. This transaction is reflected in the following balance sheet:

Totals increased equally by debt incurred in acquiring asset

OVERNIGHT AUTO SERVICE Balance Sheet November 5, 1999			
Assets		**Liabilities & Owner's Equity**	
Cash	$ 22,000	**Liabilities:**	
Land	52,000	Notes payable ...	$ 30,000
Building	36,000	**Owner's equity:**	
		Michael McBryan,	
		capital	80,000
Total	$110,000	Total	$110,000

Purchase of an Asset "On Account" On November 17, Overnight purchased tools and automotive repair equipment from Snap-On Tools Corp. The purchase price was **$13,800,** due within 60 days, resulting in an increase in a new asset—Tools and equipment—and a new liability—Accounts payable—of $13,800. After this purchase, Overnight's financial position was as follows:

Totals increased equally by purchase of tools and equipment on credit

OVERNIGHT AUTO SERVICE Balance Sheet November 17, 1999			
Assets		**Liabilities & Owner's Equity**	
Cash	$ 22,000	**Liabilities:**	
Land	52,000	Notes payable ...	$ 30,000
Building	36,000	Accounts payable .	13,800
Tools and equipment ..	13,800	Total liabilities ...	$ 43,800
		Owner's equity:	
		Michael McBryan,	
		capital	80,000
Total	$123,800	Total	$123,800

Sale of an Asset   After taking delivery of the new tools and equipment, Overnight found that it had purchased more than it needed. Ace Towing, a neighbouring business, offered to buy the excess items. On November 20, Overnight sold some of its new tools to Ace for **$1,800,** a price equal to Overnight's cost.[8] Ace made no down payment, but agreed to pay the amount due within 45 days. This transaction caused an increase in a new asset—Accounts Receivable—of $1,800 and a corresponding decrease in another asset—Tools and Equipment. A balance sheet as of November 20 appears below:

OVERNIGHT AUTO SERVICE			
Balance Sheet			
November 20, 1999			
Assets		**Liabilities & Owner's Equity**	
Cash	$ 22,000	*Liabilities:*	
Accounts receivable .	1,800	Notes payable . . .	$ 30,000
Land	52,000	Accounts payable .	13,800
Building	36,000	Total liabilities . . .	$ 43,800
Tools and equipment . .	12,000	*Owner's equity:*	
		Michael McBryan,	
		capital	80,000
Total	$123,800	Total	$123,800

No change in totals by sale of equipment at cost

Collection of an Account Receivable   On November 25, Overnight received $600 from Ace Towing as partial settlement of its account receivable from Ace. This transaction caused an increase in Overnight's cash, but a decrease of the same amount in accounts receivable. In essence, this transaction merely converts one asset into another of equal value; there is no change in the amount of total assets. After this transaction, Overnight's financial position may be summarized as follows:

OVERNIGHT AUTO SERVICE			
Balance Sheet			
November 25, 1999			
Assets		**Liabilities & Owner's Equity**	
Cash	$ 22,600	*Liabilities:*	
Accounts receivable .	1,200	Notes payable . . .	$ 30,000
Land	52,000	Accounts payable .	13,800
Building	36,000	Total liabilities . . .	$ 43,800
Tools and equipment . .	12,000	*Owner's equity:*	
		Michael McBryan,	
		capital	80,000
Total	$123,800	Total	$123,800

Totals unchanged by collection of a receivable

---

[8]Sales of assets at prices above or below cost result in gains or losses. Such transactions are discussed in later chapters.

Payment of a Liability   On the last day of November, Overnight made a partial payment of $6,800 on its account payable to Snap-On Tools. This transaction reduced Overnight's cash and accounts payable by the same amount, leaving total assets and the total of liabilities plus owner's equity "in balance." Overnight's balance sheet at November 30 appears below:

OVERNIGHT AUTO SERVICE _Balance Sheet_ November 30, 1999				
Assets		**Liabilities & Owner's Equity**		
Cash	$ 15,800	**Liabilities:**		
Accounts receivable .	1,200	Notes payable . . .	$ 30,000	
Land	52,000	Accounts payable .	7,000	
Building	36,000	Total liabilities . . .	$ 37,000	
Tools and equipment . .	12,000	**Owner's equity:**		
		Michael McBryan,		
		capital	80,000	
Total	$117,000	Total	$117,000	

Both totals decreased by paying a liability

November was a month devoted exclusively to organizing the business and not to income-producing activities. Overnight will begin regular business operations in December (and in Chapter 3).

Effects of These Business Transactions Upon the Accounting Equation

The balance sheet is a detailed expression of the accounting equation:

$$\textbf{Assets = Liabilities + Owner's Equity}$$

The accounting equation summarizes a balance sheet

In the preceding pages, we have illustrated the effects of Overnight's November transactions upon the balance sheet. Let us now illustrate the effects of these transactions upon the accounting equation.

To review, Overnight's transactions during November were as follows:

Nov. 1   Michael McBryan started the business by depositing $80,000 in a company bank account.

Nov. 3   Purchased land for $52,000, paying cash.

Nov. 5   Purchased a building for $36,000, paying $6,000 in cash and issuing a note payable for the remaining $30,000.

Nov. 17   Purchased tools and equipment on account, $13,800.

Nov. 20   Sold some of the tools at a price equal to their cost, $1,800, collectible within 45 days.

Nov. 25   Received $600 in partial collection of the account receivable from the sale of tools.

Nov. 30   Paid $6,800 in partial payment of an account payable.

The following table shows the effects of these transactions upon the accounting equation. The effects of each transaction are shown in black. Notice that the "balances," shown in blue, are the amounts appearing in

Overnight's balance sheets on pages 20–23. Notice also that the accounting equation *always* remains "in balance."

	Cash	+	Accounts Receivable	+	Land	+	Building	+	Tools and Equipment	=	Notes Payable	+	Accounts Payable	+	Michael McBryan, Capital
			Assets							=			**Liabilities**	+	**Owner's Equity**
Nov. 1	$80,000									=					$80,000
Balances	$80,000									=					$80,000
Nov. 3	−52,000				+$52,000					=					
Balances	$28,000				$52,000					=					$80,000
Nov. 5	−6,000						+$36,000			=	+$30,000				
Balances	$22,000				$52,000		$36,000			=	$30,000				$80,000
Nov. 17									+$13,800	=			+$13,800		
Balances	$22,000				$52,000		$36,000		$13,800	=	$30,000		$13,800		$80,000
Nov. 20			+$1,800						−1,800	=					
Balances	$22,000		$1,800		$52,000		$36,000		$12,000	=	$30,000		$13,800		$80,000
Nov. 25	+600		−600							=					
Balances	$22,600		$1,200		$52,000		$36,000		$12,000	=	$30,000		$13,800		$80,000
Nov. 30	−6,800									=			−6,800		
Balances	$15,800		$1,200		$52,000		$36,000		$12,000	=	$30,000		$7,000		$80,000

FORMS OF BUSINESS ORGANIZATIONS

LO 6: Describe the three forms of business organizations.

In Canada, a business enterprise may be organized as a *sole proprietorship,* a *partnership,* or a *corporation.* Generally accepted accounting principles apply to the financial statements of all three forms of organization.

Sole Proprietorships

A **sole proprietorship** is an unincorporated business owned by one person. The owner also usually runs the business. For example, Overnight Auto Service, the company used in our illustration, is a sole proprietorship owned and managed by Michael McBryan. Creating a sole proprietorship requires no authorization from a governmental agency other than obtaining a business licence from the local authority, such as the city. Proprietorships are the most common form of business organization, particularly for retail stores, farms, restaurants, and professional practices such as medicine, law, and public accounting.

From an accounting viewpoint, a sole proprietorship is regarded as a business entity *separate from the other financial affairs of its owner.* This enables the owner and others to measure the financial position and performance of the business separately. From the legal viewpoint, however, a sole proprietorship is *not an entity separate from its owner.* It merely represents one of the proprietor's financial activities. Thus, the assets and liabilities of the business legally belong to the proprietor. If the business becomes insolvent, creditors can force the owner to sell his or her personal assets to pay the business debt. This is commonly known as *unlimited personal liability.*

Similarly, under income tax laws, the owner, not the proprietorship, is subject to income taxes. Thus, the financial statements of a sole proprietorship business do not show income taxes.

The continuing existence of a sole proprietorship depends on the owner. It can be terminated at the discretion, or with the retirement or death, of the owner.

Partnerships[9]

A **partnership** is an unincorporated business owned by two or more persons, called partners. It is created by an agreement among the partners. Thus, it requires a minimum of formality. The partners jointly manage the business. Partnerships are common for small businesses and professional practices such as law, medicine, and public accounting. Some partnerships can be quite large.

CASE IN POINT	The public accounting firm of Price Waterhouse, founded in 1865, began in England as a partnership between Samuel Price and Edwin Waterhouse. As the firm grew, qualified members of its professional staff were admitted to the partnership. It recently merged with Coopers & Lybrand, another international accounting firm. Today, this new firm PricewaterhouseCoopers has thousands of partners and billions of dollars in revenue.

From an accounting viewpoint, a partnership is a business entity *separate* from the other financial affairs of the partners. This makes possible the separate evaluation of the financial position and performance of the partnership business. From a legal viewpoint, the partnership is not an entity separate from its partners. The partners jointly owned the partnership assets and are personally responsible for its debts. Thus, the partners have unlimited personal liability.[10]

Under income tax laws, the partners, rather than the partnership, are subject to income taxes. Therefore, the financial statements of a partnership business do not show income taxes.

From a legal standpoint, an "old" partnership is terminated and a "new" one created whenever there is a change in partners. Practically, however, a partnership agreement can make the change in partners a routine event without affecting its continuing existence.

Corporations

A **corporation** is a *legal entity,* having an existence separate and distinct from that of its owners. These owners are called **shareholders** and their ownership is evidenced by transferable shares of capital stock. As a separate legal entity, a corporation owns its assets, is liable for its debts, and pays its

---

[9]The topic of partnerships, including limited partnerships will be fully covered in Chapter 13.
[10]An exception is "limited partners" in a limited partnership, which will be covered fully in Chapter 13, as indicated in footnote 9.

income taxes. The shareholders are not personally liable for the debts of their corporation and can lose no more than the amounts invested in the corporation—a concept known as limited liability. From an accounting viewpoint, a corporation is also an entity separate from its shareholders.

The formation of a corporation requires some legal formality such as obtaining a certificate of incorporation or a corporate charter from the federal or provincial government. A corporation has perpetual existence until it is legally dissolved.

Corporations are run by salaried professional managers, not by their shareholders.[11] However, the control of the corporation rests with the shareholders.

Summary Comparison of Forms of Business Organization

Based on the discussions on the three forms of business organization thus far, their characteristics can be summarized as follows:

Characteristics of Forms of Business Organizations			
	Sole Proprietorship	Partnership	Corporation
1. Legal status	Not a separate legal entity	Not a separate legal entity	Separate legal entity
2. Liability of owners for business debts	Personal liability for business debts	Personal liability for partnership debts	No personal liability for corporate debts
3. Accounting status	Separate entity	Separate entity	Separate entity
4. Tax status	Income taxable to owner	Income taxable to partners	Files a corporate tax return and pays income taxes on its earnings
5. Persons with managerial authority	Owner	Every partner	Hired professional managers
6. Continuity of the business	Entity ceases at the discretion or with retirement or death of owner	New partnership is formed with a change in partners	Indefinite existence

Reporting Ownership Equity in the Balance Sheet

Assets and liabilities are presented in the same manner in the balance sheets for all three forms of business organization. The key difference is in the ownership equity. For a sole proprietorship, there is one item under owner's equity, the owner's capital. A partnership has two or more capital accounts under the partners' equity. For a corporation, the ownership equity is called **shareholders' equity** and it has two items: **capital stock** and **retained earnings**; the former represents the shareholders' original

---

[11]In many cases, the managers and shareholders are one and the same. That is, managers may own stock, and shareholders may be hired into management roles. Ownership of stock, however, does not **automatically** give the shareholder managerial authority.

investment in exchange for the capital stock, the latter represents the increase in shareholders' equity as a result of profitable operations.[12]

The three methods of reporting ownership equity in the balance sheet are illustrated below:

Ownership equity as reported in a balance sheet

In a Sole Proprietorship

Owner's equity:
Dale Nelson, capital . . . . $ 60,000

In a Partnership

Partners' equity:
Pamela Barnes, capital $60,000
Scott Davis, capital   35,000
Total partners' equity . . . . $ 95,000

In a Corporation

Shareholders' equity:
Capital stock $1,000,000
Retained earnings   928,000
Total shareholders' equity $1,928,000

THE USE OF FINANCIAL STATEMENTS BY OUTSIDERS

Most "outside" decision makers use financial statements in making ***investment or credit decisions***—that is, in selecting those companies in which they will invest resources, or to which they will extend credit. For this reason, financial statements are designed primarily to meet the needs of creditors and investors.[13] Two factors of concern to creditors and investors are the ***solvency*** and ***profitability*** of a business organization.

Creditors are interested in **solvency**—the ability of the business to pay its debts as they come due. Business concerns that are able to pay their debts promptly are said to be ***solvent.*** In contrast, a company that finds itself unable to meet its obligations as they fall due is called ***insolvent.*** Solvency is critical to the very survival of a business organization—a business that becomes insolvent may be forced into bankruptcy by its creditors. Once bankrupt, a business may be forced by the courts to stop its operations, sell its assets (for the purpose of paying its creditors), and end its existence.

For a sole proprietorship, creditors are interested in the solvency of both the business and its owner. This is because the owner is responsible for the debts of the business.

Investors also are interested in the solvency of a business organization, but they are even more interested in its **profitability**. A business is profitable when its revenue exceeds its expenses for an accounting period. Thus, ***profitable operations increase the value of the owners' equity*** in the business. A company that continually operates unprofitably will eventually exhaust its resources and be forced out of existence. Therefore, most users

---

[12]If the business operates ***unprofitably,*** retained earnings can become a ***negative*** amount, indicating the extent to which the unprofitable operations have ***decreased*** the shareholders' equity. The implications of negative retained earnings are discussed in Chapter 14.

[13]In this context, ***creditors*** include everyone to whom the business owes money. One may become a creditor of a business either by lending it money or by providing goods and services with payment due at a later date. ***Investors,*** on the other hand, are those persons having or considering an ***ownership*** interest in the organization.

of financial statements study these statements carefully for clues to the company's solvency and future profitability.

The Short Run Versus the Long Run   In the short run, solvency and profitability may be independent of each other. A business may be operating profitably, but nevertheless run out of cash and thereby become insolvent. On the other hand, a company may operate unprofitably during a given year yet have enough cash to pay its bills and remain solvent.

Over a longer term, however, the goals of solvency and profitability go hand in hand. If a business is to survive, it must remain solvent and, in the long run, it must operate profitably.

LO 7: Use a balance sheet to evaluate the solvency of an organization.

Evaluating Short-Term Solvency   One key indicator of short-term solvency is the relationship between an entity's *liquid* assets and the liabilities requiring payment *in the near future.* By studying the nature of a company's assets, and the amounts and due dates of its liabilities, users of financial statements often may anticipate whether the company is likely to have difficulty in meeting its upcoming obligations. This simple type of analysis meets the needs of many *short-term* creditors. Evaluating long-term solvency is a more difficult matter and is discussed in later chapters.

In studying financial statements, users should *always* read the accompanying notes and the auditors' report.

The Need for Adequate Disclosure

The concept of adequate **disclosure** is an important generally accepted accounting principle. Adequate disclosure means that users of financial statements are informed of any facts *necessary for the proper interpretation* of the statements. Adequate disclosure may be made either in the body of the financial statements, or in *notes* accompanying the statements.

Among the events that require disclosure are significant financial events occurring *after* the balance sheet date, but before the financial statements have been issued to outsiders. For an example, let us refer to the December 31, 1999 balance sheet of Vagabond Travel Agency, illustrated on page 14. Assume that on January 4, *2000,* the building owned by Vagabond is completely destroyed by a tornado. As the building existed at the end of 1999, it properly is included in the balance sheet date of December 31. However, users of this balance sheet need to be informed that the building *no longer exists.* The destruction of this building should be disclosed as a *subsequent event* in a note accompanying the financial statements, such as the following:

"Notes" to the statements contain vital information

Note 7: Events occurring subsequent to the balance sheet date
On January 4, 2000, a building shown in the balance sheet at $90,000 was destroyed by a tornado. The Company does not insure against this type of loss. The financial effects of this loss will be reflected in the Company's 2000 financial statements.

Subsequent events can have significant effect on the company's financial position and operations. Thus, such disclosure is essential to ensure a proper understanding of the company's future prospects.

CASE IN POINT

Hudson's Bay Company, for the year ended January 31, 1998, disclosed in a note to its financial statements: On February 27, 1998 the Company acquired all of the outstanding shares of Kmart Canada Co., which operates discount department stores in Canada, for a consideration of approximately $260 million. This amount does not include costs of acquisition that might be incurred for employee terminations, store closures, professional fees, and other related costs.

Similarly, *BCE Inc.* disclosed the following in a note to its December 31, 1997 financial statements: On January 5, 1998, BCE purchased 6 million outstanding Class A Subordinate Voting Shares of CGI Group Inc. (CGI) at $22.98 per share [for a total of $137,880,000], thereby increasing BCE's consolidated equity ownership from 24% to approximately 34%. . . . The agreement in principle would result in the transferring of some 2,300 employees of Bell Canada [a wholly-owned subsidiary] to CGI. The agreement in principle is subject to due diligence, the completion of definitive agreement, regulatory and other required approval, and is expected to close by June 30, 1998. Accordingly, the impact of this transaction on BCE's financial statements is subject to uncertainty and cannot be reasonably determined at this time. . . .

In addition to important "subsequent events," many other situations may require disclosure in notes to the financial statements. Examples include lawsuits against the company, due dates of major liabilities, assets pledged as collateral to secure loans, amounts receivable from officers or other "insiders," and contractual commitments requiring large future cash outlays.

CASE IN POINT

Bank of Montreal disclosed in a note to its December 31, 1997 financial statement the lawsuit relating to a multi-billion dollar mining fraud: Nesbitt Burns Inc., an indirect subsidiary of the Bank of Montreal, has been named a defendant in several class and individual actions in Canada and a class action in the United States of America brought on behalf of shareholders of Bre-X Minerals Ltd. ("Bre-X"). Other defendants named in one or more of these actions include Bre-X, officers and directors of Bre-X, ... The actions are largely based on allegations of negligence, misrepresentation and breaches of the *Securities Exchange Act of 1934* (U.S. only), in conjunction with the sale of Bre-X securities. . . . Based upon information presently available, counsel for Nesbitt Burns Inc. are not in a position to express an opinion as to the likely outcome of any of these actions. Management is of the view that the company has strong defences and will vigorously defend against all such action.

On the other hand, Canadian Pacific Limited disclosed the following commitments in a note to its financial statements: At December 31, 1997, commitments for capital expenditure amounted to $726.6 million and minimum payments under operating leases and gas pipeline transportation agreements were estimated at $3,373.1 million in the aggregate, ...

There is no comprehensive list of the items and events that may require disclosure. As a general rule, a company should disclose any financial facts that an intelligent person would consider ***necessary to the proper interpretation*** of the financial statements. Events that clearly are unimportant ***do not*** require disclosure.

The Reliability of Financial Statements

LO 8: Identify factors contributing to the reliability of financial statements.

Why should decision makers outside an organization regard financial statements as being fair and reliable? We already have identified three factors: (1) companies' internal control structures, (2) the concept of adequate disclosure, and (3) audits performed by independent accounting firms. In Canada, corporate and securities laws provide additional assurance as to the reliability of financial statements. These laws require that the financial statements of publicly owned companies be audited and prepared in conformity with generally accepted accounting principles, including the concept of adequate disclosure. Any person who ***knowingly causes such financial statements to be misleading*** may be held financially responsible for the losses incurred by anyone relying upon the statements. These laws apply to the management of the company issuing the statements and also to the independent auditors.

Management's Interest in Financial Statements

The management of a business organization is vitally concerned with the financial position of the business, and also with its profitability. Therefore, management is anxious to receive financial statements as frequently and as quickly as possible, so that it may take action to improve areas of weak performance. Most large organizations provide managers with financial statements on at least a monthly basis.

However, managers have a special interest in the ***annual*** financial statements, as these are the statements most widely used by decision makers outside of the organization. For example, if creditors view the year-end balance sheet as "strong," they will be more willing to extend credit to the business than if they regard the company's financial position as weak.

A strong balance sheet is one that shows relatively little debt, and large amounts of liquid assets relative to the liabilities due in the near future. Management can—and does—take steps to make the year-end balance sheet look as strong as possible. For example, cash purchases of assets may be delayed so that large amounts of cash will be on hand at the balance sheet date. Liabilities due in the near future may be paid, or replaced with longer-term liabilities.

These actions are called **window dressing**—legitimate measures taken by management to make a business look as strong as possible at the balance sheet date. Users of year-end balance sheets should realize that while these statements are "fair" and "reliable," they do not necessarily describe the "typical" financial position of the business. In its annual financial statements, almost every company tries to "put its best foot forward."

Many creditors, therefore, regard monthly balance sheets as providing a more typical picture of a company's financial position.

Competence, Integrity, and Professional Judgment

The preparation of accounting reports is not a mechanical task that can be performed by machine or even by well-trained clerical personnel. A characteristic common to all recognized professions—such as medicine, law, and accounting—is the need for individual practitioners to resolve many problems with their own ***professional judgment.*** The problems encountered in the practice of a profession are often complex, and the specific circumstances unique. Consequently, no written set of rules exists to provide answers in every situation.

LO 9: Discuss the importance of professional judgment and ethical conduct in accounting practice.

In preparing the financial statements of a large business organization, the company's accountants and its independent auditors must make many "judgment calls." For example:

- Which accounting principles are appropriate for the specific business?
- What constitutes "adequate" disclosure?
- At what point should a business in financial difficulties cease to be viewed as a going-concern?
- What types of investigative procedures are necessary to assure auditors that a company's financial statements represent a fair presentation?
- Which efforts by management represent legitimate window dressing, and which are inappropriate actions that would make the financial statements misleading?

Unfortunately, judgmental decisions ***always involve some risk of error.*** Some errors in judgment result from carelessness or inexperience on the part of the decision makers. However, others occur simply because future events did not work out as had been anticipated.

If the public is to have confidence in the judgment of professional accountants, these accountants first must demonstrate that they possess the characteristics of ***competence*** and ***integrity.***

Professional Competence   Professional competence means the possession of adequate technical training and proficiency in accountancy. Such training and proficiency is attained in qualifying for a professional designation such as Chartered Accountant (CA), Certified General Accountant (CGA), or Certified Management Accountant (CMA). To ensure continuing competence, professional accountants in public practice are required to take appropriate professional development courses and are subject to practice inspection. Practice inspection involves the review of the **public accountant's** work on auditing and accounting engagements by an independent external party.

Integrity and Ethics   *Integrity* means honesty and a strong commitment to **ethical conduct**—doing the "right thing." For a professional accountant, integrity is just as important as competence. However, it is far more difficult to test or enforce.

Organizations of professional accountants have taken steps to encourage and enforce integrity within the profession. For example, professional organizations have developed **codes of professional ethics** for their members.[14] These codes are intended to help professional accountants fulfill their professional obligations with integrity. Violation of these codes may cause a public accountant to lose his or her professional designation and licence to practise public accounting.

One concept found in all professional codes of ethics for accountants is that accountants must ***never knowingly be associated with misleading accounting information.*** In fact, a professional accountant should ***resign his or her position*** rather than become involved in the preparation or distribution of misleading information.

Of course, the basic concept of ethical conduct—acting with honour and integrity—***applies to management*** as well as to professional accountants.

The users of financial statements should recognize that the reliability of these statements is affected by the ***competence, integrity,*** and ***professional judgment*** of the management, accountants, and auditors involved in the financial reporting process. But as we have previously stated, audited financial statements—and the accounting profession—have established an impressive track record of reliability. More than any other factor, the competence and integrity of professional accountants ensure the fairness and reliability of financial statements.

CASE IN POINT   A national survey of a large number of business people on the ethical conducts of sixteen professional and business groups ranks accountants first, followed by dentists and doctors. The others include corporate officers, lawyers, realtors, union leaders, newspaper reporters, and politicians.

Professional Accountants and Top Corporate Executives

LO 10: Describe the relationship between professional accountants and top corporate executives.

While most professional accountants devote their career to public, management, and government accounting, many have become top corporate executives. The chairpersons and presidents of many large and well-known corporations in Canada have a professional accounting designation. These top executives run the leading corporations in almost all industries—banking, commercial, manufacturing, airline, insurance, publication, brewery, mining, and real estate. Thus, a background in accounting can be a stepping stone to top management.

---

[14]In accounting, codes of professional ethics have been developed by the institutes of chartered accountants, the certified general accountants' associations, and the societies of certified management accountants.

CASE IN POINT

In recent years, some of these well-known top corporate executives with a professional accounting background included: Laurent Beaudoin, FCA*, chairman and CEO (chief executive officer) of Bombardier; Paul Beeston, FCA, president of the Toronto Blue Jays; Grant Billing, CA, president and CEO of Norcen Energy Resources; W. Michael Brown, CA, president of Thomson Corp.; John Cleghorn, FCA, chairman of Royal Bank of Canada; Gordon Cummings, FCMA, CEO of Alberta Wheat Pool; Dominic D'Allesandro, FCA, president and CEO of Manulife Financial; Douglas W. Dodds, FCMA, chairman and CEO of Schneider Corporation; Kevin Benson, CA, president and CEO of Canadian Airlines International; Peter Godsoe, CA, chairman and CEO of Bank of Nova Scotia; Gordan Gray, FCA, chairman of Royal LePage; George Myhal, CA, president and CEO of Trilon Financial; Paul Ivanier, Ph.D., CA, president and CEO of Ivaco; Lucille Johnstone, CGA, president and COO (chief operating officer) of Rivtow Straits; Robert Kelly, FCA, vice-chairman of T-D Bank; David W. Kerr, CA, chairman and CEO of Noranda Inc.; Brian MacNeill, CA, president and CEO of IPL Energy Inc.; Wayne McLeod, FCA, vice-chairman and president, CCL Industries; Jean Neveu, CA, president and CEO of Quebecor Inc.; Bob Nicholson, CA, president of Toronto Argonauts (Canadian Football League); Guylaine Saucier, FCA, chair, Canadian Broadcasting Corporation; Fredric Tomczyk, CA, president and CEO of London Insurance Group; Victor Zaleschuk, CA, president and CEO of Canadian Occidental Petroleum.

---

*The "F" preceding the professional designation CA, CGA, or CMA means "Fellow," which is awarded to the members for their outstanding service and the distinction they brought to the profession.

*Supplemental Topic

CAREERS IN ACCOUNTING

THE ACCOUNTING PROFESSION

LO 11: Describe various career opportunities in accounting.

In Canada, there are three major professional accounting organizations: the provincial Institutes (in Quebec, Order) of Chartered Accountants, Societies of Management Accountants and Certified General Accountants' Association (in Quebec, Professional Corporation). The national organizations of these three accounting bodies are the Canadian Institute of Chartered Accountants, the Society of Management Accountants of Canada, and the Certified General Accountants' Association of Canada. Members of these organizations receive their respective professional designations as chartered accountants (CAs), certified management accountants (CMAs), and certified general accountants (CGAs). The Institutes of Chartered Accountants place more emphasis on public accounting, the Societies of Management Accountants are primarily interested in management accounting, and the Certified General Accountants are interested in management as well as public accounting. In terms of career opportunities, accounting may be divided into four broad areas: (1) public accounting, (2) management accounting, (3) governmental accounting, and (4) accounting education.

Public Accounting

Public accounting firms are organizations that offer a variety of accounting services to the public. These firms vary in size from one-person practices to large, international organizations with thousands of professional accountants.

Most of the people in public accounting are **chartered accountants (CAs).** Thus, public accounting firms often are called **CA firms.** The specific requirements regarding the right to practise public accounting vary among provinces. In some provinces, such as Ontario and Nova Scotia, only chartered accountants have the automatic privilege to practise public accounting. In other provinces, such as Alberta and British Columbia, the practice of public accounting is open only to members of the professional accounting organizations.

The primary services offered by CA firms include auditing, income tax, and management advisory services.

We have already discussed the role of independent audits in the financial reporting process. For many years, auditing has been the principal function of public accountants. Today, however, tax work and management consulting are separate areas of specialization that are rapidly growing in importance.

Providing **management advisory services** is, perhaps, the fastest growing area in public accounting. The advisory services extend well beyond tax planning and accounting matters; public accountants advise management on such diverse issues as international mergers, manufacturing processes, and the introduction of new products. The entry of public accountants into the field of management consulting reflects the fact that **financial considerations enter into every business decision.**

Management Accounting

In contrast to the public accountant who serves many clients, the management (or managerial) accountant works for one enterprise. Management accountants develop and interpret accounting information designed specifically to meet the various needs of management.

The chief accounting officer of an organization usually is called the **controller**, in recognition of the fact that one basic purpose of accounting data is to aid in controlling business operations. The controller is part of the top management team, which is responsible for running the business, setting its objectives, and seeing that these objectives are achieved.

In addition to developing information to assist managers, management accountants are responsible for operating the company's accounting system, including the recording of transactions and the preparation of financial statements, tax returns, and other accounting reports. As the responsibilities of management accountants are so broad, many areas of specialization have developed. Among the more important are the following:

Financial Forecasting   A financial forecast (or budget) is a plan of financial operations for some **future** period. Actually, forecasting is much like financial reporting, except that the accountant is estimating future outcomes, rather than measuring past results. A forecast provides each department of a business with financial goals. Comparison of the results actually achieved with these forecast amounts is one widely used means of evaluating departmental performance.

Cost Accounting   Knowing the cost of each business operation and of each manufactured product is essential to the efficient management of a business. Determining the per-unit cost of business activities and of manufactured products, and interpreting this cost data, comprise a specialized field called **cost accounting.**

Internal Auditing   Large organizations usually maintain a staff of **internal auditors.** Internal auditors are charged with studying the internal control structure and evaluating the efficiency of many different aspects of the company's operations. As employees, internal auditors are not "independent" of the organization. Therefore, they **do not** perform independent audits of the company's financial statements.

Careers in managerial accounting often lead to positions in top management—just as do careers in public accounting.

Governmental Accounting

Governmental agencies use accounting information in allocating their resources and in controlling their operations. Therefore, the need for management accountants is similar to that in business organizations.

The accounting standards used in government differ significantly from those in the business world, because earning a profit is not an objective of government. Universities, hospitals, churches, and other **not-for-profit** institutions also follow a pattern of accounting similar to that of governmental agencies.

Accounting Education

Many accountants, including your instructor and the authors of this book, have chosen to pursue careers in accounting education. A position as an accounting faculty member offers opportunities for research and consulting, and an unusual degree of freedom in developing individual skills. Accounting educators contribute to the accounting profession in many ways. One, of course, lies in effective teaching; another, in publishing significant research findings; and a third, in influencing top students to pursue careers in accounting.

What About Bookkeeping?

Some people think that the work of professional accountants consists primarily of bookkeeping. Actually, it doesn't. In fact, many professional accountants do **little or no** bookkeeping.

Bookkeeping is the clerical side of accounting—the recording of routine transactions and day-to-day record keeping. Such tasks are performed primarily by computers and skilled clerical personnel, not by "accountants."[15]

Professional accountants are involved more with the **interpretation and use** of accounting information than with its actual preparation. Their work includes evaluating the efficiency of operations, resolving complex financial reporting issues, forecasting the results of future operations, auditing, tax planning, and designing efficient accounting systems. There is very little that is "routine" about the work of a professional accountant.

A person might become a proficient bookkeeper in a few weeks or months. To become a professional accountant, however, is a far greater challenge. It requires years of study, experience, and an on-going commitment to "keeping current."

We will illustrate and explain a number of bookkeeping procedures in this text, particularly in the next several chapters. But teaching bookkeeping skills is **not** our goal; the primary purpose of this text is to develop your abilities to **understand and use** accounting information in today's business world.

Accounting as a "Stepping-Stone"

We have mentioned that many professional accountants leave their accounting careers for key positions in management or administration. An accounting background is invaluable in such positions, because top management works continuously with issues defined and described in accounting terms and concepts.

An especially useful stepping-stone is experience in public accounting. Public accountants have the unusual opportunity of getting an "inside look" at many different business organizations.

---

[15]Some public accountants do "keep books" for a number of small businesses. But they also may serve their clients in many other ways, such as preparing tax returns, tax planning, and acting as financial advisors.

End-of-Chapter Review

Key Terms Introduced or Emphasized in Chapter 1

Note to Students: Each chapter includes a glossary explaining the key accounting terms introduced or emphasized. You should review these glossaries carefully; an understanding of accounting terminology is an essential step in the study of accounting. These terms will appear frequently in later chapters, in problem material, and in examination questions. (Because of the broad and introductory nature of Chapter 1, this glossary is longer than those in later chapters.)

Accounting (*p.3*) Accounting is the process of identifying, measuring, recording, interpreting, and communicating the results of economic activities.

Accounting equation (*p.19*) Assets are equal to the sum of liabilities plus owner's equity (A = L + OE). This equation is reflected in the format of the balance sheet.

Accounting Standards Board (*p.13*) A board of the CICA that is responsible for issuing recommendations with respect to matters of accounting standards. The board's recommendations, which are contained in the *CICA Handbook,* are recognized as an authoritative source of generally accepted accounting principles.

Accounting system (*p.7*) The personnel, procedures, records, forms, and devices used by an organization in developing and communicating accounting information.

Annual report (*p.10*) A document issued annually by publicly owned corporations to their shareholders. Includes audited financial statements for several years, as well as nonfinancial information about the company and its operations.

Assets (*p.15*) Economic resources owned by an entity.

Auditing (*p.9*) Performing an investigation enabling the auditors to express an independent opinion (auditors' report) as to the fairness of a set of financial statements.

Auditors' report (*p.9*) A report containing the professional opinion of a public accounting firm as to the fairness of the financial statements.

Balance sheet (*p.6*) The financial statement showing the financial position of an entity by summarizing its assets, liabilities, and owner's equity at one specific date.

Business entity (*p.15*) An economic unit that controls resources, incurs obligations, and engages in business activities. It is also called accounting entity.

Canadian Institute of Chartered Accountants (CICA) (*p.13*) The national organization of chartered accountants (CAs) that carries on extensive research and is influential in developing and improving accounting standards and practices.

Capital stock (*p.26*) Transferable units of ownership in a corporation.

Cash flow statement (*p.7*) A financial statement summarizing the cash receipts and cash payments in the time period covered by the income statement.

Code of professional ethics (*p.32*) Formal guidelines developed by professional organizations to assist members in conducting their practices in a manner consistent with their obligations to society.

Controller (*p.35*) The chief accounting officer within an organization.

Corporation (*p.25*) A business organized as a separate legal entity, with ownership divided into transferable shares of capital stock.

Cost principle (*p.16*) The widely used principle of accounting for assets at their original cost to the current owner.

Creditor (*p.17*) A lender; an entity to which money is owed.

Disclosure ("adequate") (*p.28*) The accounting principle of providing with financial statements any financial facts necessary for the proper *interpretation* of those statements.

Ethical conduct (*p.31*) Doing "the right thing." Acting with honour and integrity, even at the sacrifice of personal advantage.

Fair (*p.9*) A term used by accountants to describe a set of financial statements that are complete, not misleading, and prepared in conformity with generally accepted accounting principles. Auditors express their opinions as to the "fairness" of financial statements.

Financial accounting (*p.4*) The development and use of accounting information describing the financial position of an entity and the results of its operations.

Financial position (*p.5*) The financial resources and obligations of an organization, as described in a balance sheet.

Financial reporting (*p.6*) The process of periodically providing "general-purpose" financial information (such as financial statements) to persons *outside* the business organization.

Financial statements (*p.6*) Four related accounting reports that concisely summarize the current financial position of an entity and the results of its operations for the preceding year (or other time period).

Generally accepted accounting principles (GAAP) (*p.12*) The accounting concepts, measurement techniques, and standards of presentation used in financial statements. Examples include the cost principle and objectivity principle.

Going-concern assumption (*p.16*) An assumption by accountants that a business will operate indefinitely unless specific evidence to the contrary exists, such as impending bankruptcy.

Income statement (*p.7*) A financial statement indicating the profit (or loss) of a business over a period of time, usually a year.

Internal control (*p.9*) All measures used within an organization to assure management that the organization is operating in accordance with management's policies and plans.

Liabilities (*p.17*) Debts or obligations of an entity that have arisen from past transactions. The claims of **creditors** against the assets of a business.

Objectivity principle (*p.8*) Accountants' tendency to base accounting measurements upon dollar amounts that are factual and subject to independent verification.

Owner's equity (*p.18*) The excess of assets over liabilities. The amount of the owner's investment in a business, including profits from successful operations that have been retained in the business.

Partnership (*p.25*) An unincorporated business owned by two or more persons voluntarily associated as partners.

Profitability (*p.27*) An increase in owner's equity resulting from successful business operations. (This concept is discussed further in Chapter 3.)

Public Accountant (*p.31*) An independent professional accountant who offers auditing and other accounting services to clients.

Publicly owned corporations (*p.6*) Corporations in which members of the general public may buy or sell shares of capital stock.

Retained earnings (*p.26*) The portion of the owner's equity in a corporation that has accumulated as a result of profitable business operations.

Shareholders (*p.25*) Owners of capital stock in a corporation; hence, the owners of the corporation.

Shareholders' equity (*p.26*) The **owners' equity** in an entity organized as a corporation.

Sole proprietorship (*p.24*) An unincorporated business owned by one person.

Solvency (*p.27*) Having the financial ability to pay debts as they become due.

Stable-dollar assumption (*p.16*) An assumption by accountants that the dollar is a stable unit of measure, like the kilometre or the litre. A simplifying assumption that permits adding or subtracting dollar amounts originating in different time periods. Unfortunately, the assumption technically is incorrect and may distort accounting information during periods of severe inflation.

Statement of owner's equity (*p.7*) A financial statement summarizing the changes in owner's equity occurring in a business organized as a sole proprietorship. Covers the same period of time as does the income statement.

Statement of retained earnings (*p.7*) A financial statement explaining certain changes in the amount of the owners' investment in the business organized as a corporation. (Appears in lieu of a statement of owner's equity.)

Transactions (*p.8*) Events that cause an immediate change in the financial position of an entity and that can be measured objectively in monetary terms. In current practice, transactions serve as the basis for recording financial activity.

Window dressing (*p.30*) Legitimate measures taken by management to make a business look as strong as possible at the balance sheet date.

DEMONSTRATION PROBLEM

The accounting data (listed alphabetically) for Crystal Auto Wash at September 30, 19__, are shown below. The figure for Don Johnson, capital, is not given but it can be determined when all the available information is assembled in the form of a balance sheet.

Accounts payable	$14,000	Land	$68,000
Accounts receivable	800	Machinery & equipment	65,000
Building	52,000	Notes payable	
Cash	9,200	(due in 30 days)	29,000
Don Johnson, capital	?	Salaries payable	3,000
		Supplies	400

INSTRUCTIONS

a. Prepare a balance sheet at September 30, 19___.

b Does this balance sheet indicate that the company is in a strong financial position? Explain briefly.

SOLUTION TO DEMONSTRATION PROBLEM

a.

CRYSTAL AUTO WASH Balance Sheet September 30, 19___			
Assets		**Liabilities & Owner's Equity**	
Cash	$ 9,200	*Liabilities:*	
Accounts receivable . . .	800	Notes payable	$ 29,000
Supplies	400	Accounts payable . . .	14,000
Land	68,000	Salaries payable	3,000
Building	52,000	Total liabilities	$ 46,000
Machinery &		*Owner's equity:*	
equipment	65,000	Don Johnson,	
		capital	149,400
Total	$195,400	Total	$195,400

*Computed as total assets, $195,400 – total liabilities, $46,000 = Don Johnson, capital, $149,400

b.   The balance sheet indicates that Crystal Auto Wash is in a ***very weak*** financial position. The highly "liquid" assets—cash and receivables—total only $10,000, but the company has ***$46,000*** in debts due in the near future. Based upon this balance sheet, the company appears to be insolvent.†

Self-Test Questions

The answers to these questions appear on page 55. ***Note:*** In order to review as many chapter concepts as possible, some self-test questions include ***more than one*** correct answer. In these cases, you should indicate ***all*** of the correct answers.

1. Almost ***everyone*** will benefit from a basic understanding of accounting terms and concepts, as this knowledge will enable them to: (Select the single ***best*** answer.)
   a. Become professional accountants.
   b. Act in an ethical manner.
   c. Better understand economic activities.
   d. Prepare their own income tax returns.

2. A "set" of financial statements: (Indicate all correct answers.)
   a. Is intended to assist users in evaluating the financial position, profitability, and future prospects of an entity.
   b. Is intended to assist Revenue Canada in determining the amount of income taxes owed by a business organization.

---

†Perhaps the company can generate enough cash from its daily operations to pay its debts. A balance sheet does not indicate the ***rate*** at which cash flows into the business. A recent ***cash flow statement*** would be useful in making a more complete analysis of the company's financial position. Also, as this business is organized as a sole proprietorship, creditors may look to the personal solvency of the owner, Don Johnson. He is personally liable for the debts of the business entity.

    c. Includes "notes" disclosing items necessary for the proper interpretation of the statements.

    d. Is intended to assist investors and creditors in making decisions involving the allocation of economic resources.

3. Generally accepted accounting principles: (Indicate all correct answers.)

    a. Include only the official pronouncements of the standard-setting organizations, such as the CICA.

    b. May include customary accounting practices in widespread use even if not mentioned specifically in official pronouncements.

    c. Eliminate the need for professional judgment in the preparation of financial statements.

    d. Change and evolve as business organizations enter into new forms of business activity.

4. Which of the following statements is **not** consistent with generally accepted accounting principles relating to asset valuation?

    a. Assets are originally recorded in accounting records at their cost to the business entity.

    b. Subtracting total liabilities from total assets indicates what the owner's equity in the business is worth under current market conditions.

    c. Accountants assume that assets such as office supplies, land, and buildings will be used in business operations, rather than sold at current market prices.

    d. Accountants prefer to base the valuation of assets upon objective, verifiable evidence rather than upon appraisals or personal opinion.

5. Arrowhead Boat Shop purchased a truck for $12,000, making a down payment of $5,000 cash and signing a $7,000 note payable due in 60 days. (Indicate all correct answers.)

    a. Total assets increased by $12,000.

    b. Total liabilities increased by $7,000.

    c. From the viewpoint of a short-term creditor, this transaction makes the business less solvent.

    d. This transaction had no immediate effect upon the owner's equity in the business.

6. A transaction caused a $10,000 **decrease** in both total assets and total liabilities. This transaction could have been:

    a. Purchase of a delivery truck for $10,000 cash.

    b. An asset with a cost of $10,000 was destroyed by fire.

    c. Repayment of a $10,000 bank loan.

    d. Collection of a $10,000 account receivable.

7. Which of the following factors contribute to the **reliability** of the information contained in financial statements? (Indicate all correct answers.)

    a. The competence and integrity of professional accountants.

    b. An audit required by corporate and securities laws.

    c. Systems of internal control.

    d. The concept of adequate disclosure.

8. Which of the following statements relating to the role of professional judgment in the financial reporting process are valid? (Indicate all correct answers.)

    a. Different accountants may evaluate similar situations differently.

    b. The determination of which items should be "disclosed" in notes to financial statements requires professional judgment.

    c. Once a complete list of generally accepted accounting principles is prepared, judgment need no longer enter into the financial reporting process.

    d. The possibility always exists that professional judgment later may prove to have been incorrect.

9. During the current year, the assets of Rankin Green increased by $29,000, and the liabilities decreased by $7,000. If the owner's equity in the business is $79,000 at the end of the year, the owner's equity at the beginning of the year must have been:
    a. $57,000
    b. $43,000
    c. $115,000
    d. $101,000

10. Which of the following statements are characteristic of most unincorporated businesses, such as sole proprietorships and partnerships? (Indicate all correct answers.)
    a. Although the owners have limited lives, the business entity is assumed to be a going concern.
    b. The business entity does not pay income taxes on its earnings.
    c. If the business fails, the owners' potential losses are limited to the amounts of their equity.
    d. Owners do not receive dividends, but may withdraw assets from the business at will.

ASSIGNMENT MATERIAL

Discussion Questions

One objective of these questions is to give you an opportunity to demonstrate and develop your **communication skills.** Therefore, we ask that you answer each question in your own words.

1. In broad general terms, what is the basic purpose of accounting?

2. Why is a knowledge of accounting terms and concepts useful to persons other than professional accountants?

3. What is **public information?** What does this concept have to do with financial reporting?

4. In general terms, what does a set of **financial statements** describe? Identify the specific statements and other information that comprise a complete **set** of financial statements.

5. Are financial statements the **only means** by which decision makers outside of management obtain information about the financial position, profitability, and future prospects of a business?

6. Define the term **business transaction.** Give several examples of business transactions, and several examples of important events in the life of a business that **do not** qualify as "transactions." What is the relationship between business transactions and the information contained in financial statements?

7. Explain briefly why each of the following groups is interested in the financial statements of a business.
    a. Creditors.
    b. Potential investors.
    c. Labour unions.

8. What is the basic purpose of **internal control?**

9. Which is more useful to potential investors, a company's *financial statements* for the current year or its *annual report?* Explain.

10. How do accounting principles become "generally accepted"?

11. Identify those factors that make the corporate form of business organization attractive to investors who will not participate personally in management of the business.

12. Explain briefly the concept of the *business entity.*

13. State briefly the purpose and content of a balance sheet. Does a balance sheet show how much a business is currently worth? Explain.

14. Why is owner's equity considered to be a *residual claim* to the assets of a business organization? Can the owner's equity in a business be a *negative* amount? Explain.

15. The owner's equity in a business arises from what two sources? What two ways can cause decreases in owner's equity?

16. State the accounting equation in two alternative forms.

17. Why are the total assets shown in a balance sheet always equal to the total of the liabilities and the owner's equity?

18. Can a business transaction cause one asset to increase without affecting any other asset, liability, or the owner's equity?

19. Give examples of business transactions that would:
    a. Cause one asset to increase and another asset to decrease, with no effect upon liabilities or owner's equity.
    b. Cause both total assets and liabilities to increase, with no effect upon owner's equity.

20. Assume that a business becomes insolvent. Can the owner (or owners) of the business be held personally liable for the debts of the business? Give separate answers assuming that the business is organized as (a) a sole proprietorship, (b) a partnership, and (c) a corporation.

21. What are the main differences between the balance sheet of a sole proprietorship or partnership and a corporation?

22. One objective of every business is to operate profitably. What other primary objective must be met for a business to survive? Explain.

23. What is meant by the term *adequate disclosure?* Give several examples of items that may require "disclosure" in financial statements.

24. Describe three factors that contribute to the *reliability* of financial statements.

25. What is meant by the phrase "a *strong* balance sheet"?

26. Describe the term *window dressing.* Why should users of financial statements be aware of this concept? Explain.

*27. Identify four broad areas of *career opportunities* in accounting.

*28. What are the principal types of services rendered by public accountants?

Exercises

EXERCISE 1-1
Users of Accounting
Information
(LO 2)

Boeing Company is the largest manufacturer of commercial aircraft in the United States and is a major employer in Seattle, Washington. Explain why each of

---

**Supplemental Topic, "Careers in Accounting."*

the following individuals or organizations would be interested in financial information about the company.
a. **California Public Employees' Retirement System**, one of the world's largest pension funds.
b. **China Airlines**, a rapidly growing airline serving the Pacific Rim.
c. Henry James, a real estate investor considering building apartments in the Seattle area.
d. Boeing's top management.
e. **International Aerospace Machinists**, a labour union representing many Boeing employees.

EXERCISE 1-2
Accounting Terminology
(LO 2, 3, 8)

Listed below are twelve technical accounting terms emphasized in this chapter.

Audit	*Insolvent*	*Financial reporting*
Assets	*Profitable*	*Financial statements*
Liabilities	*Owner's equity*	*CICA*
Unlimited personal liability	*GAAP*	*Balance sheet*

Each of the following statements may (or may not) describe one of these technical terms. For each statement, indicate the term described, or answer "None" if the statement does not correctly describe any of the terms.
a. Obligations of an entity arising from past transactions.
b. Accounting reports describing the financial position, profitability, and cash transactions of a business entity.
c. Being able to meet financial obligations as they come due.
d. The owner is **personally liable** for all debts of the business.
e. Assets minus liabilities.
f. The "ground rules" for presenting information in financial statements.
g. The financial statement indicating the profitability of the business for a period of time.
h. An investigation by independent public accountants intended to assure outsiders of the fairness of a company's financial statements.
i. The organization primarily responsible for developing new accounting principles by issuing recommendations.
j. The process of distributing general-purpose financial information to persons outside a business organization.
k. Economic resources owned by an entity.

EXERCISE 1-3
What Is Financial Reporting?
(LO 2)

A major focus of this course is the process of financial reporting.
a. What is meant by the term **financial reporting?**
b. What are the principal accounting reports involved in the financial reporting process? In general terms, what is the purpose of these reports?
c. Do all business entities engage in financial reporting? Explain.
d. How does society benefit from the financial reporting process?

EXERCISE 1-4
Generally Accepted Accounting Principles
(LO 2)

Generally accepted accounting principles play an important role in financial reporting.
a. What is meant by the phrase "generally accepted accounting principles"?
b. What are the major sources of these principles?
c. Is there a comprehensive list of generally accepted accounting principles? Explain.
d. What types of accounting reports are prepared in conformity with generally accepted accounting principles?

EXERCISE 1-5
The Nature of Assets and Liabilities
(LO 3)

a. Define assets. Give three examples of assets other than cash that might appear in the balance sheet of (1) **Air Canada** and (2) a professional sports team, such as the **Toronto Blue Jays**

b. Define liabilities. Give three examples of liabilities that might appear in the balance sheet of (1) **Air Canada** and (2) a professional sports team, such as the **Toronto Blue Jays**

EXERCISE 1-6
Preparing a Balance Sheet
(LO 3)

The night manager of Majestic Limousine Service, who had no accounting background, prepared the following balance sheet for the company at February 28, 2000. The dollar amounts were taken directly from the company's accounting records and are correct. However, the balance sheet contains a number of errors in its headings, format, and the classification of assets, liabilities, and owner's equity.

> **MAJESTIC LIMO**
> **Manager's Report**
> **8 PM Thursday**
>
> | Assets | | Owner's Equity | |
> |---|---|---|---|
> | J. Snow, capital . . . | $162,000 | Accounts receivable . . . | $ 78,000 |
> | Cash . . . . | 69,000 | Notes payable . . . . . . | 288,000 |
> | Building . . . . | 80,000 | Supplies . . . . | 14,000 |
> | Automobiles . . . . | 165,000 | Land . . . . | 70,000 |
> | | | Accounts payable . . . . | 26,000 |
> | | $476,000 | | $476,000 |

Prepare a corrected balance sheet. Include a proper heading.

EXERCISE 1-7
Preparing a Balance Sheet
(LO 3)

The balance sheet items of the Perez Company as of December 31, 2000, are shown below in random order. You are to prepare a balance sheet for the company, using a similar sequence for assets as in the illustrated balance sheet on page 14. You must compute the amount for Eduardo Perez, capital.

Land	$90,000	Office equipment	$ 10,200
Accounts payable	43,800	Building	210,000
Accounts receivable	56,700	Eduardo Perez, capital	?
Cash	36,300	Notes payable	213,600

EXERCISE 1-8
Using the Accounting Equation
(LO 5)

Compute the missing amount in each of the following three lines.

	Assets	= Liabilities +	Owner's Equity
a.	$558,000	$342,000	?
b.	?	562,500	$375,000
c.	307,500	?	142,500

EXERCISE 1-9
The Accounting Equation
(LO 5)

A number of business transactions carried out by Green River Farms are shown below:
a. Borrowed money from a bank.
b. Sold land for cash at a price equal to its cost.
c. Paid a liability.
d. Returned for credit some of the office equipment previously purchased on credit but not yet paid for.
e. Sold land for cash at a price in excess of cost.
f. Purchased a computer on credit.
g. The owner invested cash in the business.
h. Purchased office equipment for cash.
i. Collected an account receivable.

Indicate the effects of each of these transactions upon the total amounts of the company's assets, liabilities, and owner's equity. Organize your answer in tabular form, using the column headings shown below and the code letters **I** for increase, **D** for decrease, and **NE** for no effect. The answer for transaction (a) is provided as an example:

Transaction	Assets	=	Liabilities	+	Owner's Equity
(a)	I		I		NE

EXERCISE 1-10
Effects of Business Transactions
(LO 5)

For each of the following categories, state concisely a transaction that will have the required effect on the elements of the accounting equation.
a. Increase an asset and increase a liability.
b. Decrease an asset and decrease a liability.
c. Increase one asset and decrease another asset.
d. Increase an asset and increase owner's equity.
e. Increase one asset, decrease another asset, and increase a liability.

EXERCISE 1-11
Factors Contributing to Solvency
(LO 7)

Explain whether each of the following balance sheet items increases, reduces, or has no direct effect upon a company's short-term solvency. Explain your reasoning.
a. Cash.
b. Accounts payable.
c. Accounts receivable.
d. M. Tsung, capital.

EXERCISE 1-12
Audits of Financial Statements
(LO 8)

The annual financial statements of all large, publicly owned corporations are audited.
a. What is an audit of financial statements?
b. Who performs these audits?
c. What is the basic purpose of an audit?

EXERCISE 1-13
Professional Judgment
(LO 9)

Professional judgment plays a major role in the practice of accounting.
a. In general terms, explain why judgment enters into the accounting process.
b. Identify three situations in which accountants must rely upon their professional judgment, rather than upon official rules.

*EXERCISE 1-14
Careers in Accounting
(LO 11)

Four accounting majors, Maria Acosta, Kenzo Nakao, Helen Martin, and Anthony Mandella, recently graduated from Central University and began professional accounting careers. Acosta entered public accounting, Nakao became a managerial accountant with IBM, Martin joined a governmental agency, and Mandella (who had completed a graduate program) became an accounting faculty member.

Assume that each of the four graduates was successful in his or her chosen career. Identify the types of accounting *activities* in which each of these graduates might find themselves specializing several years after graduation.

Problems

PROBLEM 1-1
Preparing a Balance Sheet and Evaluating Solvency
(LO 3, 7)

Listed below in random order are the items to be included in the balance sheet of Mystery Mountain Lodge at December 31, 2000:

Equipment	$ 29,200		Buildings	$450,000
Land	425,000		Stanley Gardner, capital	-?-
Accounts payable	54,800		Cash	21,400
Accounts receivable	10,600		Furnishings	58,700
Salaries payable	33,500		Snowmobiles	15,400
Interest payable	12,000		Notes payable	620,000

---

*Supplemental Topic, "Careers in Accounting."

INSTRUCTIONS

a. Prepare a balance sheet at December 31, 2000. Include a proper heading and organize your balance sheet similar to the illustration on page 14. (After "Buildings," you may list the remaining assets in any order.) You will need to compute the amount to be shown for owner's equity.

b. Assume that no payment is due on the notes payable until 2003. Does this balance sheet indicate that the company is in a strong financial position as of December 31, 2000? Explain briefly.

PROBLEM 1-2
Interpreting the Effects of Business Transactions
(LO 5)

Six transactions of Horizon Moving Company are summarized below in equation form, with each of the six transactions identified by a letter. For each of the transactions (a) through (f) you are to write a separate sentence explaining the nature of the transaction. For example, the explanation of transaction *a* could be as follows: Purchased delivery equipment for cash at a cost of $3,200.

	Cash	+	Accounts Receivable	+	Land	+	Building	+	Delivery Equipment	=	Accounts Payable	+	P. Youngblood, Capital
									Assets		**Liabilities**	+	**Owner's Equity**
Balances	$26,000		$39,000		$45,000		$110,000		$36,000		$42,000		$214,000
(a)	−3,200								+3,200				
Balances	$22,800		$39,000		$45,000		$110,000		$39,200		$42,000		$214,000
(b)	+900		−900										
Balances	$23,700		$38,100		$45,000		$110,000		$39,200		$42,000		$214,000
(c)	−3,500								+13,500		+10,000		
Balances	$20,200		$38,100		$45,000		$110,000		$52,700		$52,000		$214,000
(d)	−14,500										−14,500		
Balances	$5,700		$38,100		$45,000		$110,000		$52,700		$37,500		$214,000
(e)	+15,000												+15,000
Balances	$20,700		$38,100		$45,000		$110,000		$52,700		$37,500		$229,000
(f)									+2,100		+2,100		
Balances	$20,700		$38,100		$45,000		$110,000		$54,800		$39,600		$229,000

PROBLEM 1-3
Recording the Effects of Transactions
(LO 5)

Nova Communications was organized on December 1 of the current year, and had the following account balances at December 31, listed in tabular form.

	Cash	+	Land	+	Building	+	Office Equipment	=	Notes Payable	+	Accounts Payable	+	C. Sagan, Capital
			Assets					=		**Liabilities**		+	**Owner's Equity**
Balances	$37,000		$95,000		$125,000		$51,250		$80,000		$28,250		$200,000

Early in January, the following transactions were carried out by Nova Communications:

1. C. Sagan, the owner, deposited $25,000 of personal funds into the business's bank account.
2. Purchased land and a small office building for a total price of $90,000, of which $35,000 was the value of the land and $55,000 was the value of the building. Paid $22,500 in cash and signed a note payable for the remaining $67,500.

3. Bought several computer systems on credit for $8,500 (30-day open account).
4. Obtained a loan from Scotia Bank in the amount of $10,000. Signed a note payable.
5. Paid the $28,250 account payable owed as of December 31.

INSTRUCTIONS

a. List the December 31 balances of assets, liabilities, and owner's equity in tabular form shown.
b. Record the effects of each of the five transactions in the format illustrated on page 24. Show the totals for all columns after each transaction.

PROBLEM 1-4
An Alternate Problem on Recording the Effects of Transactions
(LO 5)

The items making up the balance sheet of Triad Truck Rental at December 31 are listed below in tabular form similar to the illustration of the accounting equation on page 24.

	Assets				=	Liabilities		+	Owner's Equity
	Cash +	Accounts Receivable +	Trucks +	Office Equipment =		Notes Payable +	Accounts Payable +		Bill Foreman, Capital
Balances	$9,500	$8,900	$58,000	$3,800		$20,000	$5,200		$55,000

During a short period after December 31, Triad Truck Rental had the following transactions:
1. Bought office equipment at a cost of $2,700. Paid cash.
2. Collected $4,000 of accounts receivable.
3. Paid $3,200 of accounts payable.
4. Borrowed $10,000 from a bank. Signed a note payable for that amount.
5. Purchased a truck for $30,500. Paid $15,000 cash and signed a note payable for the balance.
6. Bill Foreman, the owner, invested $20,000 cash in the business.

INSTRUCTIONS

a. List the December 31 balances of assets, liabilities, and owner's equity in tabular form as shown above.
b. Record the effects of each of the six transactions in the tabular arrangement illustrated above. Show the totals for all columns after each transaction.

PROBLEM 1-5
Preparing a Balance Sheet; Effects of a Change in Assets
(LO 3, 5)

HERE COME THE CLOWNS! is the name of a travelling circus owned by Red Costello. The ledger accounts of the business at June 30, 2000 are listed below in alphabetical order.

Accounts payable	$ 26,100	Notes payable	$180,000
Accounts receivable	7,450	Notes receivable	9,500
Animals	189,060	Props and equipment	89,580
Cages	24,630	Red Costello, capital	337,230
Cash	?	Salaries payable	9,750
Costumes	31,500	Tents	63,000
		Trucks & wagons	105,840

INSTRUCTIONS

a. Prepare a balance sheet by using these items and computing the amount of cash at June 30, 2000. Organize your balance sheet similar to the one illustrated on page 14. (After "Accounts receivable," you may list the remaining assets in any order.) Include a proper balance sheet heading.
b. Assume that late in the evening of June 30, after your balance sheet had been prepared, a fire destroyed one of the tents, which had cost $14,300. The tent was not insured. Explain what changes would be required in your June 30 balance sheet to reflect the loss of this asset.

PROBLEM 1-6
Preparing a Balance Sheet—a
Second Problem
(LO 3, 5)

Shown below in random order is a list of balance sheet items for Red River Farms at September 30, 2000:

Land	$550,000	Fences & gates	$ 33,570
Barns and sheds	78,300	Irrigation system	20,125
Notes payable	530,000	Cash	16,710
Accounts receivable	22,365	Livestock	120,780
Citrus trees	76,650	Farm machinery	42,970
Accounts payable	77,095	Hollis Roberts, capital	?
Property taxes payable	9,135	Wages payable	1,820

INSTRUCTIONS

a. Prepare a balance sheet by using these items and computing the amount for Hollis Roberts, capital. Use a sequence of assets similar to that illustrated on page 14. (After "Barns and sheds" you may list the remaining assets in any order.) Include a proper heading for your balance sheet.

b. Assume that on September 30, immediately after this balance sheet was prepared, a tornado completely destroyed one of the barns. This barn had a cost of $23,800, and was not insured against this type of disaster. Explain what changes would be required in your September 30 balance sheet to reflect the loss of this barn.

PROBLEM 1-7
Preparing a Balance Sheet;
Effects of Business
Transactions; Evaluating
Financial Position
(LO 3, 5, 7)

The balance sheet items for The Julian Bakery (arranged in alphabetical order) were as follows at August 1, 19__. (You are to compute the missing figure for owner's equity.)

Accounts payable	$16,200	Julian Lee, capital	$?
Accounts receivable	11,260	Land	$67,000
Building	84,000	Notes payable	74,900
Cash	6,940	Salaries payable	8,900
Equipment & fixtures	44,500	Supplies	7,000

During the next two days, the following transactions occurred:

Aug. 2   Lee invested an additional $25,000 in the business. The accounts payable were paid in full. (No payment was made on the notes payable or income taxes payable.)

Aug. 3   Equipment was purchased at a cost of $7,200 to be paid within 10 days. Supplies were purchased for $1,250 cash from a restaurant supply centre that was going out of business. These supplies would have cost $1,890 if purchased through normal channels.

INSTRUCTIONS

a. Prepare a balance sheet at August 1, 19—.
b. Prepare a balance sheet at August 3, 19—.
c. Assume the note payable does not come due for several years. Is The Julian Bakery in a stronger financial position on August 1 or on August 3? Explain briefly.

PROBLEM 1-8
Preparing a Balance Sheet;
Effects of Business
Transactions; Evaluating
Financial Position
(LO 3, 5, 7)

The balance sheet items of The Original Malt Shop (arranged in alphabetical order) were as follows at the close of business on September 30, 2000:

Accounts payable	$ 8,500	Land	$55,000
Accounts receivable	1,250	Kay Martin, capital	54,090
Building	45,500	Notes payable	?
Cash	7,400	Supplies	3,440
Furniture & fixtures	20,000		

Throughout October, the business will be closed for remodelling. The transactions occurring during the first week of October were:

Oct. 3   Martin invested an additional $30,000 cash in the business. The accounts payable were paid in full. (No payment was made on the notes payable.)

Oct. 6 More furniture was purchased on account at a cost of $18,000, to be paid within 30 days. Supplies were purchased for $1,000 cash from a restaurant supply centre that was going out of business. These supplies would have cost $1,875 if purchased under normal circumstances.

INSTRUCTIONS

a. Prepare a balance sheet at September 30, 2000. (You are to compute the missing figure for notes payable.)
b. Prepare a balance sheet at October 6, 2000.
c. Assume the note payable does not come due for several years. Is the Original Malt Shop in a stronger financial position on September 30 or on October 6? Explain briefly.

PROBLEM 1-9
Preparing a Balance Sheet;
Discussion and Application of
Accounting Principles
(LO 3, 4, 5)

Helen Berkeley is the founder and manager of Old Town Playhouse. The business needs to obtain a bank loan to finance the production of its next play. As part of the loan application, Berkeley was asked to prepare a balance sheet for the business. She prepared the following balance sheet, which is arranged correctly, but contains several errors with respect to certain accounting principles.

OLD TOWN PLAYHOUSE
Balance Sheet
September 30, 19___

Assets		Liabilities & Owner's Equity	
Cash	$ 21,900	**Liabilities:**	
Accounts receivable . .	132,200	Accounts payable . . .	$ 6,000
Props and costumes . .	3,000	Salaries payable	29,200
Theatre building	27,000	Total liabilities	$35,200
Lighting equipment . . .	9,400	**Owner's equity:**	
Automobile	15,000	Helen Berkeley,	
		capital	50,000
Total	$208,500	Total	$85,200

In discussions with Berkeley and by reviewing the accounting records of Old Town Playhouse, you discover the following facts:

1. The amount of cash, $21,900, includes $15,000 in the company's bank account, $1,900 on hand in the company's safe, and $5,000 in Berkeley's personal savings account.
2. The accounts receivable, listed as $132,200, includes $7,200 owed to the business by Artistic Tours. The remaining $125,000 is Berkeley's estimate of future ticket sales from September 30 through the end of the year (December 31).
3. Berkeley explains to you that the props and costumes were purchased several days ago for $18,000. The business paid $3,000 of this amount in cash and issued a note payable to Actors' Supply Co. for the remainder of the purchase price ($15,000). As this note need not be paid until January of next year, it was not included among the company's liabilities. However, the $3,000 payment was recorded.
4. Old Town Playhouse rents the theatre building from Kievits International at a rate of $3,000 a month. The $27,000 shown in the balance sheet represents the rent paid through September 30 of the current year. Kievits International acquired the building seven years ago at a cost of $135,000.
5. The lighting equipment was purchased on September 26 at a cost of $9,400, but the stage manager says that it isn't worth a dime.

6. The automobile is Berkeley's classic 1978 Jaguar, which she purchased two years ago for $9,000. She recently saw a similar car advertised for sale at $15,000. She does not use the car in the business, but it has a personalized licence plate that reads "PLAHOUS."
7. The accounts payable include business debts of $3,900 and the $2,100 balance of Berkeley's personal VISA card.
8. Salaries payable includes $25,000 offered to Mario Dane to play the lead role in a new play opening next December and also $4,200 still owed to stage hands for work done through September 30.
9. When Berkeley founded Old Town Playhouse several years ago, she invested $20,000 in the business. However, Live Theatre, Inc., recently offered to buy her business for $50,000. Therefore, she listed this amount as her equity in the above balance sheet.

a. Prepare a corrected balance sheet for Old Town Playhouse at September 30, 19__.
b. For each of the nine numbered items above, explain your reasoning in deciding whether or not to include the items in the balance sheet and in determining the proper dollar valuation.

Hollywood Scripts is a service-type enterprise in the entertainment field, and its owner, William Pippin, has only a limited knowledge of accounting. Pippin prepared the balance sheet below, which, although arranged satisfactorily, contains certain errors with respect to certain accounting principles.

HOLLYWOOD SCRIPTS
Balance Sheet
November 30, 19__

Assets		Liabilities & Owner's Equity	
Cash	$ 5,150	*Liabilities:*	
Notes receivable	2,700	Notes payable	$ 67,000
Accounts receivable . .	2,450	Accounts payable . .	35,805
Land	70,000	Total liabilities	$102,805
Building	54,320	*Owner's equity:*	
Office furniture	8,850	William Pippin,	
Other assets	22,400	capital	63,065
Total	$165,870	Total	$165,870

In discussion with Pippin and by inspection of the accounting records, you discover the following facts:

1. The amount of cash, $5,150, includes $3,400 in the company's bank account, $540 on hand in the company's safe, and $1,210 in Pippin's personal savings account.
2. One of the notes receivable in the amount of $500 is an IOU that Pippin received in a poker game several weeks ago. The IOU is signed by "B.K.," whom Pippin met at the game, but has not heard from since.
3. The asset "Land" was acquired at a cost of $39,000 but was increased to a valuation of $70,000 when a friend of Pippin offered to pay that much for it if Pippin would move the building off the lot.
4. Office furniture includes $2,900 for a Persian rug for the office purchased on November 20. The total cost of the rug was $9,400. The business paid $2,900 in cash and issued a note payable to Zoltan Carpet for the balance due ($6,500).

As no payment on the note is due until January, this debt is not included in the liabilities above.

5. Also included in the amount for office furniture is a computer that cost $2,525 but is not on hand because Pippin gave it to his daughter to use at the university.

6. The "Other assets" of $22,400 represents the total amount of income taxes Pippin has paid over a period of years. Pippin believes the income tax law to be unconstitutional, and a friend who attends law school has promised to help Pippin recover the taxes paid as soon as he passes the bar exam.

7. The accounts payable include business debts of $32,700 and the $3,105 balance owed on Pippin's personal Mastercard.

INSTRUCTIONS

a. Prepare a corrected balance sheet at November 30, 19__.

b. For each of the seven numbered items above, use a separate numbered paragraph to explain whether the treatment followed by Pippin is in accordance with generally accepted accounting principles.

PROBLEM 1-11
Forms of Business Organizations
(LO 6)

Versatile Company has assets of $850,000 and liabilities of $460,000.

a. Prepare the ownership equity section of Versatile's balance sheet under each of the following *independent* assumptions:

1. The business is organized as a sole proprietorship, owned by Julia Adams.

2. The business is organized as a partnership, owned by Julia Adams and Paul Cormier. Adams' equity amounts to $240,000.

3. The business is a corporation with 25 shareholders, each of whom originally invested $10,000 in exchange for shares of the company's capital stock. The remainder of the shareholders' equity has resulted from profitable operation of the business.

b. Assume that you are a loan officer at Royal Bank. Versatile has applied to your bank for a large loan to finance the development of new products. Is it likely to matter to a lender whether Versatile is organized as a sole proprietorship, a partnership, or a corporation? Explain.

c. In whose balance sheet would you expect to find income taxes payable, the sole proprietorship, partnership, or corporation? Explain.

Analytical and Decision Problems and Cases

A&D 1-1
Content of a Balance Sheet
(LO 3, 4)

You are to prepare a balance sheet for a *hypothetical* business entity of your choosing (or specified by your instructor). Include in your balance sheet the types of assets and liabilities that you think the entity might have, and show these items at what you believe would be realistic dollar amounts. (*Note:* The purpose of this assignment is to help you visualize the types of assets and liabilities relating to the operations of a specific type of business. You should complete this assignment *without* referring to an actual balance sheet for this type of business.)

A&D 1-2
Accounting Principles and Asset Valuation
(LO 4)

The following cases relate to the valuation of assets. Consider each case independently:

a. World-Wide Travel Agency has office supplies costing $1,700 on hand at the balance sheet date. These supplies were purchased from a supplier that does not give cash refunds. World-Wide's management believes that the company could sell these supplies for no more than $500 if it were to advertise them for sale. However, the company expects to use these supplies and to purchase more when they are gone. In its balance sheet, the supplies were valued at $500.

b. Zenith Corporation purchased land in 1955 for $20,000. In 2000, it purchased a similar parcel of land for $300,000. In its 2000 balance sheet, the company valued these two parcels of land at a combined value of $320,000.

c. At December 30, 2000, Lenier, Inc., purchased a computer system from a mail-order supplier for $14,000. The retail value of the system—according to the mail-order supplier—was $20,000. On January 7, however, the system was stolen during a burglary. In its December 31, 2000 balance sheet, Lenier showed this computer system at $14,000 and made no reference to its retail value or to the burglary.

INSTRUCTIONS

In each case, indicate the appropriate balance sheet valuation of the asset under generally accepted accounting principles. If the valuation assigned by the company is incorrect, briefly explain the accounting principles that have been violated. On the other hand, if the valuation is correct, identify the accounting principles that justify this valuation.

A&D 1-3
Using a Balance Sheet
(LO 3, 4, 7, 8)

Obtain from the library the ***annual report*** of a well-known company (or a company specified by your instructor). From the balance sheet, notes to the financial statements, and auditors' report, answer the following:

a. What public accounting firm audited the company's financial statements, and did the auditors consider the financial statements a "fair" presentation?

b. Select three items in the notes accompanying the financial statements and explain briefly the importance of these items to people making decisions about investing in, or extending credit to, this company.

c. Assume that you are a lender, and this company has asked to borrow an amount of cash equal to 10% of its total assets, to be repaid in 90 days. Would you consider this company to be a good credit risk? Explain.

A&D 1-4
Reliability of Financial
Statements
(LO 8)

In the early 1980s, **Chrysler Corporation** was in severe financial difficulty and desperately needed large loans if the company were to survive. What factors prevented Chrysler from simply providing potential lenders with misleading financial statements, making the company look like a risk-free investment?

A&D 1-5
Using a Balance Sheet in
Business Decisions
(LO 6, 7)

King Company and Yonge Company are in the same line of business and both were recently organized, so it may be assumed that the recorded costs for assets are close to current market values. Balance sheets for the two companies are as follows.

KING COMPANY
Balance Sheet
July 31, 19__

Assets		Liabilities & Owner's Equity	
Cash	$ 4,800	Liabilities:	
Accounts receivable . .	10,600	Notes payable	
Land	96,000	(due in 60 days) . . .	$ 23,400
Building	60,000	Accounts payable . .	43,200
Office equipment	12,000	Total liabilities	$ 66,600
		Owner's equity:	
		Susan King, capital . . .	116,800
Total	$183,400	Total	$183,400

```
                        YONGE COMPANY
                         Balance Sheet
                          July 31, 19__

            Assets                    Liabilities & Owner's Equity

Cash . . . . . . . . . . . .   $ 18,000   Liabilities:
Accounts receivable  . .         28,000      Notes payable
Land . . . . . . . . . . . .     37,200         (due in 60 days) . . .  $ 12,400
Building  . . . . . . . . .      38,000      Accounts payable  . .        10,600
Office equipment  . . . .         1,200         Total liabilities  . . . .  $ 23,000
                                           Owner's equity:
                                              Charles Yonge,
                                                 capital  . . . . . . . .     99,400
Total  . . . . . . . . . . .   $122,400   Total  . . . . . . . . . . .  $122,400
```

INSTRUCTIONS

a. Assume that you are a banker and that each company has applied to you for a 90-day loan of $16,000. Based solely on the balance sheets, which is the more favourable prospect? Explain fully.

b. Assume that you are an investor considering the purchase of one or both of the companies. Both Susan King and Charles Yonge have indicated to you that they would consider selling their respective businesses. In either transaction you would assume the existing liabilities. For which business would you pay the higher price? Explain fully. (It is recognized that for either decision, additional information would be useful, but you are to reach your decisions on the basis of the information available.)

c. Assume that Susan King has much greater personal assets than Charles Yonge and that, while both King and Yonge have other business operations, the total profits from all the other unrelated business operations are far greater for King than Yonge. Would such assumptions change your answers to part (**a**) and (**b**)? Explain fully.

A&D 1-6
Application of Accounting Principles and Business Concepts; Preparing a Balance Sheet for a Corporation
(LO 4, 6)

Anna Jones and John Innes own all the capital stock of Property Management Corporation. Both shareholders also work full time in the business. The company performs management services for apartment house owners, including finding tenants, collecting rents, and doing maintenance and repair work.

When the business was organized early this year, Jones and Innes invested a total of $60,000 to acquire the capital stock. At December 31, a partial list of the corporation's balance sheet items included cash of $16,800, office equipment of $26,100, accounts payable of $36,700, and income taxes payable of $12,900. Additional information on financial position and operations is as follows:

1. Earlier this year the corporation purchased an office building from Jones at a price of $48,000 for the land and $69,000 for the building. Jones had acquired the property several years ago at a cost of $26,000 for the land and $52,000 for the building. At December 31, Jones and Innes estimated that the land was worth $49,000 and the building was worth $78,000. The corporation owes Jones a $54,000 note payable in connection with the purchase of the property.

2. While working, Jones drives her own automobile, which cost $22,600. Innes uses a car owned by the corporation, which cost $20,200.

3. One of the apartment houses managed by the company is owned by Innes. The cost to Innes was $100,000 for the land and $190,000 for the building, but the total market value was at least $380,000.

4. Company records show a $1,900 account receivable from Innes's relatives and $23,400 accounts receivable from other clients.
5. Innes has a $20,000 bank account in the same bank used by the corporation. He explains that if the corporation should run out of cash, it may use that $20,000 and repay him later.
6. Company records have not been properly maintained, and the amount of retained earnings is not known.

INSTRUCTIONS

a. For each of the above items numbered **1** through **5,** explain your reasoning in deciding whether or not to include the items on the balance sheet and in determining the proper dollar valuation.
b. Prepare a balance sheet for the business entity Property Management Corporation at December 31, 19__.
c. Even though Innes and Jones invested an equal amount in the business, Innes feels that he is taking a greater risk than Jones should the business fail. Innes's concern is based on the fact that he has more personal assets than Jones. Explain whether Innes's concern is justified.

A&D 1-7
Selecting a Form of Business Organization
(LO 6)

Interview the owners of two local small businesses. One business should be organized as a corporation and the other as either a sole proprietorship or a partnership. Inquire as to:

- **Why** this form of entity was selected.
- Have there been any unforeseen complications with this form of entity?
- Is the form of entity likely to be changed in the foreseeable future? And if so, why?

(***Note:*** All interviews are to be conducted in accordance with the guidelines discussed in the *Preface* of this book.)

A&D 1-8
"Nonfinancial" Information
(LO 1, 2)

In 1987, **The Procter & Gamble Company (P&G)** discovered Olestra, a new synthetic food oil that greatly reduces the fat content and calories in potato chips and other fried foods. The company spent more than 25 years and $275 million in developing this product, according to *Maclean's*. The product is believed to have great market potential, and in 1996 the U.S. Food and Drug Administration approved its use and sale.

INSTRUCTIONS

a. In 1987, would the discovery of Olestra and its future sales potential have been recorded in P&G's accounting records and reflected in the company's financial statements?
b. How did investors, creditors, and other interested people learn of this discovery and its potential benefit to P&G?

A&D 1-9
Ethics and "Window Dressing"
(LO 1, 4, 5, 7, 8, 9)

The date is November 18, 2000. You are the chief executive officer of Flowerhill Software—a publicly owned company that is currently in financial difficulty. Flowerhill needs large new bank loans if it is to survive.

You have been negotiating with several banks, but each has asked to see your 2000 financial statements, which will be dated December 31. These statements will, of course, be audited. You are now meeting with other corporate officers to discuss the situation, and the following suggestions have been made:
1. "We are planning to buy WordMaster Software for $8 million cash in December. The owners of WordMaster are in no hurry; if we delay this acquisition until January, we'll have $8 million more cash at year-end. That should make us look a lot more solvent."
2. "At year-end, we'll owe accounts payable of about $18 million. If we were to show this liability in our balance sheet at half that amount—say, $9 million—

no one would know the difference. We could report the other $9 million as shareholders' equity and our financial position would appear much stronger."

3. "We owe Delta Programming $5 million, due in 90 days. I know some people at Delta. If we were to sign a note to pay them 8% interest, they'd let us postpone this debt for a year or more."

4. "We own land that cost us $2 million, but today is worth at least $6 million. Let's show it at $6 million in our balance sheet, and that will increase our total assets and our shareholders' equity by $4 million."

INSTRUCTIONS

Separately evaluate each of these four proposals. Your evaluations should consider ethical and legal issues as well as accounting issues.

Answers to Self-Test Questions

1. c   2. a, c, d   3. b, d   4. b   5. b, c, d   6. c   7. a, b, c, d   8. a, b, d
9. b   10. a, b, d

CHAPTER 2

Changes in Financial Position

Many historians believe that writing was invented for the purpose of communicating accounting information. The principles of our "modern" system of double-entry accounting first were explained in print by Luca Pacioli, an Italian mathematician. Pacioli was a friend of Leonardo da Vinci; his book, *Summa de Arithmetica . . . ,* was published in 1494.

Three hundred years later, Johann von Goethe, perhaps the most influential writer of the late 18th century, described Pacioli's system as something of timeless beauty and simplicity—one of the greatest achievements of the human intellect. Goethe was right. Even now—in a world of computers, databases, and international business activities—Pacioli's simple principles still apply.

1. Discuss the role of accounting records in an organization.
2. Describe a ledger account and a ledger.
3. State the rules of debit and credit for balance sheet accounts.
4. Explain the double-entry system of accounting.
5. Explain the purpose of a journal and its relationship to the ledger.
6. Prepare journal entries to record common business transactions.
7. Prepare a trial balance and explain its uses and limitations.
8. Discuss the basic steps of the accounting cycle in both manual and computer-based accounting systems.

The Role of Accounting Records

LO 1: Discuss the role of accounting records in an organization.

Businesses do not prepare new financial statements after every transaction. Rather, they accumulate the effects of individual business transactions in their **accounting records.** Then, at regular intervals, the data in these records are used to prepare financial statements, income tax returns, and other types of accounting reports.

But the need for accounting reports is not the only reason businesses maintain accounting records. Managers and employees of the business frequently use these records for such purposes as:

1. Establishing **accountability** for the assets and/or transactions under an individual's control.
2. Keeping track of routine business activities—such as the amounts of money in company bank accounts, amounts due from credit customers, amounts owed to suppliers.
3. Obtaining detailed information about a particular transaction.
4. Evaluating the efficiency and performance of various departments within the organization.
5. Maintaining documentary evidence of the company's business activities. (For example, tax laws require companies to maintain accounting records supporting the amounts reported in tax returns.)

The Upcoming Series of "Accounting System" Chapters   Chapter 2 is the first of five chapters exploring various aspects of accounting systems. In this chapter, we explain the **double-entry** system of accounting and illustrate the "flow" of data through basic accounting records. Our examples are based upon the November transactions of Overnight Auto Service, which we described in Chapter 1. These transactions affect only the balance sheet. Business transactions that also affect the income statement are discussed in Chapters 3 and 4. In Chapters 5 and 6, we will broaden our discussion to include merchandising activities, more advanced accounting systems, and internal control.

THE LEDGER

LO 2: Describe a ledger account and a ledger.

An accounting system includes a separate record for each item that appears in the balance sheet. For example, a separate record is kept for the asset cash, showing all increases and decreases in cash resulting from the many transactions in which cash is received or paid. A similar record is kept for every other asset, every liability, and for owner's equity.

The record used to keep track of the increases and decreases in a single balance sheet item is termed a ledger account, or simply an **account**. The entire group of accounts is kept together in an accounting record called a **ledger**.[1]

In manual accounting systems, each ledger account is maintained on a separate page of columnar paper. These pages are kept in a loose-leaf binder (or in a tray), which serves as the ledger. (This format explains why accounting records traditionally have been described as the company's "books.") In computer-based systems, of course, the ledger accounts are maintained on disc.

The Use of Ledger Accounts

A ledger account is a means of accumulating in one place all the information about changes in a specific asset, a liability, or owner's equity. For example, a ledger account for the asset cash provides a record of the amount of cash receipts, cash payments, and the current cash balance. By maintaining a Cash account, management can keep track of the amount of cash available for meeting payrolls and for making current purchases of assets or services. This record of cash is also useful in planning future operations and in advance planning of applications for bank loans.

In its simplest form, an account has only three elements: (1) a title, consisting of the name of the particular asset, liability, or owner's equity; (2) a left side, which is called the *debit* side; and (3) a right side, which is called the *credit* side. This form of account, illustrated below and on the following page, is called a *T account* because of its resemblance to the letter T. More complete forms of accounts will be illustrated later.

A "T" account—a ledger account in its simplest form

Title of Account	
Left or Debit Side	Right or Credit Side

Debit and Credit Entries

An amount recorded on the left or debit side of an account is called a **debit**, or a *debit entry;* an amount entered on the right or credit side is called a **credit**, or a *credit entry.* Accountants also use the words debit and credit as verbs. The act of recording a debit in an account is called *debiting* the account; the recording of a credit is called *crediting* the account.

Students beginning a course in accounting often have erroneous notions about the meanings of debits and credits. For example, they may view credits as more desirable than debits. Such connotations have no validity in the field of accounting. Accountants use *debit* to mean an entry on the left-hand side of an account and *credit* to mean an entry on the right-hand side. Thus, debit and credit simply mean left and right, without any hidden or subtle implications.

---

[1]The ledger also includes an account for each item appearing in the income statement. Income statement accounts are discussed in Chapter 3.

To illustrate the recording of debits and credits in an account, let us go back to the five cash transactions of Overnight Auto Service, described in Chapter 1. When these cash transactions are recorded in the Cash account, the *receipts* are listed in vertical order on the *debit side* of the account and the *payments* are listed on the *credit side.* The dates of the transactions may also be listed, as shown in the following illustration:

Cash transactions entered
in ledger account

Cash			
Nov. 1	*80,000*	*Nov. 3*	*52,000*
Nov. 25	*600*	*Nov. 5*	*6,000*
		Nov. 30	*6,800*
80,600		*64,800*	
Nov. 30 Balance 15,800			

Each debit and credit entry in the Cash account represents a cash receipt or a cash payment. The amount of cash owned by the business at a given date is equal to the *balance* of the account on that date. For example, the balance of the cash account on November 3 is $28,000 ($80,000 − $52,000). This daily balance is useful in managing cash in the business (an account with such **running balance** is shown on page 65).

Determining the Balance of a T Account   The balance of a ledger account is the difference between the debit and credit entries in the account. If the debit total exceeds the credit total, the account has a *debit balance;* if the credit total exceeds the debit total, the account has a *credit balance.*

In our illustrated Cash account, a "dotted rule" has been drawn across the account following the last cash transaction recorded in November. The total cash receipts (debits) recorded in November amount to $80,600, and the total cash payments (credits) amount to $64,800. These totals, called **footings**, are entered in small-size figures just above the rule. (Notice that these totals are written to the left of the regular money columns so that they will not be mistaken for debit or credit entries.) By subtracting the credit total from the debit total ($80,600 − $64,800), we determine that the Cash account has a debit balance of *$15,800* on November 30.

This debit balance is entered in the debit side of the account just below the rule. In effect, the horizontal rule creates a "fresh start" in our T account, with the month-end balance representing the *net result* of all the previous debit and credit entries. The Cash account now shows the amount of cash owned by the business on November 30. In a balance sheet prepared at this date, Cash in the amount of $15,800 would be listed as an asset.

Debit Balances in Asset Accounts   In the preceding illustration of a cash account, increases were recorded on the left or debit side of the account and decreases were recorded on the right or credit side. The increases were greater than the decreases and the result was a debit balance in the account.

All asset accounts ***normally have debit balances.*** It is hard to imagine an account for an asset such as land having a credit balance, as this would indicate that the business had disposed of more land than it had ever acquired. (For other assets, such as cash in the bank, it is possible to acquire a credit balance due to overdraft—but such balances are only ***temporary.***)

The fact that assets are located on the ***left*** side of the balance sheet is a convenient means of remembering the rule that an increase in an asset is recorded on the ***left*** (debit) side of the account, and also that an asset account normally has a debit ***(left-hand)*** balance.

	Any Asset Account	
(Asset accounts normally have debit balances)	Debit *(representing an increase)*	Credit *(representing a decrease)*

Credit Balances in Liability and Owner's Equity Accounts   Increases in liability and owner's equity accounts are recorded by credit entries and decreases in these accounts are recorded by debits. The relationship between entries in these accounts and their position on the balance sheet may be summed up as follows: (1) liabilities and owner's equity belong on the ***right*** side of the balance sheet, (2) an increase in a liability or an owner's equity account is recorded on the ***right*** (credit) side of the account, and (3) liability and owner's equity accounts normally have credit ***(right-hand)*** balances.

Any Liability Account Or Owner's Equity Account		
Debit *(representing a decrease)*	Credit *(representing an increase)*	(Liability and owner's equity accounts normally have credit balances)

Concise Statement of the Debit and Credit Rules   The use of debits and credits to record changes in assets, liabilities, and owner's equity may be summarized as follows:

Debit and credit rules

Asset Accounts	Liability & Owner's Equity Accounts
Normally have debit balances. Thus, increases are recorded by debits and decreases are recorded by credits.	*Normally have credit balances. Thus, increases are recorded by credits and decreases are recorded by debits.*

Double-Entry Accounting—The Equality of Debits and Credits

The rules for debits and credits are designed so that *every transaction is recorded by equal dollar amounts of debits and credits.* The reason for this equality lies in the relationship of the debit and credit rules to the accounting equation:

$$\text{Assets} = \text{Liabilities} + \text{Owner's Equity}$$
$$\text{Debit balances} = \text{Credit balances}$$

If this equation is to remain in balance, any change in the left side of the equation (assets) *must be accompanied by an equal change* in the right-hand side (either liabilities or owner's equity). According to the debit and credit rules that we have just described, increases in the left side of the equation (assets) are recorded by *debits,* while increases in the right side (liabilities and owner's equity) are recorded by *credits.*

LO 4: Explain the double-entry system of accounting.

This system is often called **double-entry accounting**. The phrase "double-entry" refers to the need for both *debit entries* and *credit entries,* equal in dollar amount, to record every transaction. Virtually every business organization uses the double-entry system regardless of whether the company's accounting records are maintained manually or by computer. In addition, the double-entry system allows us to measure net income at the same time we record the effects of transactions upon the balance sheet accounts. (The measurement of net income is discussed in Chapter 3.)

Double-entry accounting is not a new idea. The system has been in use for more than 600 years. The first systematic presentation of the double-entry system appears in a mathematics textbook written by Luca Pacioli, a friend of Leonardo da Vinci. This text was published in 1494—just two years after Columbus discovered America. Although Pacioli wrote the first textbook on this subject, surviving accounting records show that double-entry accounting had already been in use for at least 150 years.

Recording Transactions in Ledger Accounts: An Illustration

The use of debits and credits for recording transactions in ledger accounts now will be illustrated using the November transactions of Overnight Auto Service. Each transaction will first be analyzed in terms of increases and decreases in assets, liabilities, and owner's equity. Then we shall follow the debit and credit rules in entering these increases and decreases in T accounts. Asset accounts will be shown on the left side of the page; liability and owner's equity accounts on the right side. For convenience in following the transactions into the ledger accounts, both the debit and credit entries in the *transaction under discussion* are shown in *blue* type. Entries relating to earlier transactions appear in *black* type.

Nov. 1   Michael McBryan, the owner, invested $80,000 cash in the business.

Owner invests cash in the business

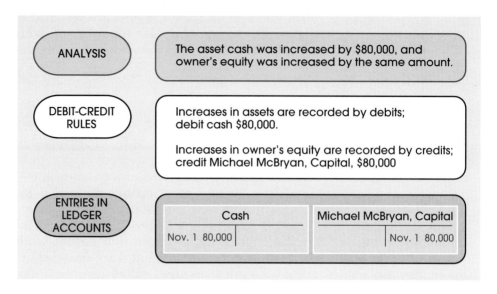

Nov. 3   Representing Overnight, McBryan negotiated with both Mega-city and Metropolitan Transit Authority (MTA) to purchase an abandoned bus garage. (The city owned the land, but the MTA owned the building.) On November 3, Overnight Auto Service purchased the land from the city for $52,000 cash.

Purchase of an asset for cash

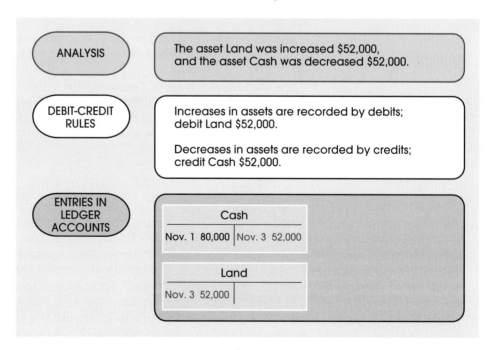

Nov. 5   Overnight completed the acquisition of its business location by purchasing the abandoned old garage building from the MTA. The purchase price was $36,000; Overnight made a $6,000 cash

down payment and issued a 90-day, non-interest-bearing note payable for the remaining $30,000.

Purchase of an asset, making a small down payment

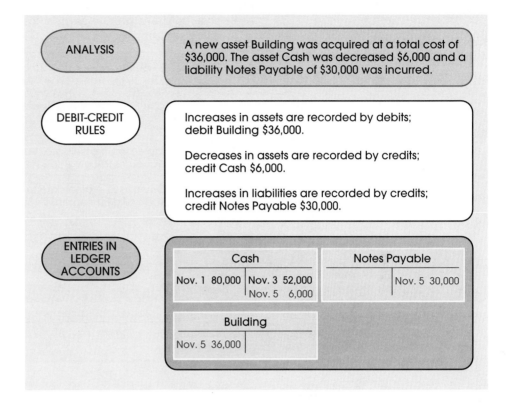

Nov. 17   Overnight purchased tools and equipment on account (also referred to as "on credit") from Snap-On Tools Corp. The purchase price was $13,800, due in 60 days.

Credit purchase of an asset

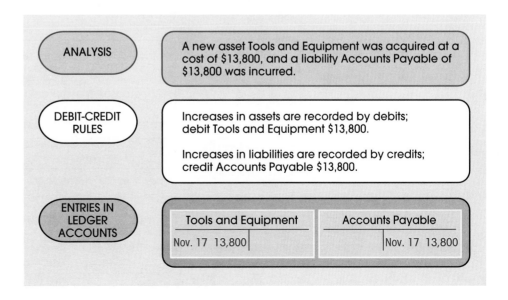

Nov. 20   Overnight found that it had purchased more tools than it needed. On November 20, it sold the excess tools on account to Ace Towing at a price of $1,800. The tools were sold at a price equal to their cost, so there was no gain or loss on this transaction.

Credit sale of an asset
(with no gain or loss)

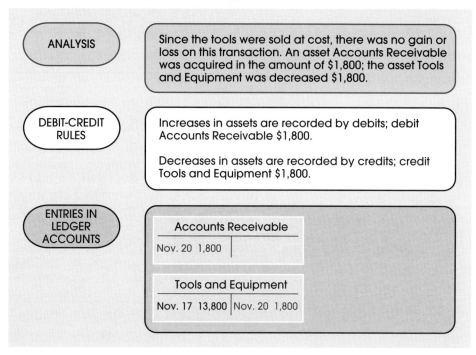

| ANALYSIS | Since the tools were sold at cost, there was no gain or loss on this transaction. An asset Accounts Receivable was acquired in the amount of $1,800; the asset Tools and Equipment was decreased $1,800. |

| DEBIT-CREDIT RULES | Increases in assets are recorded by debits; debit Accounts Receivable $1,800.

Decreases in assets are recorded by credits; credit Tools and Equipment $1,800. |

ENTRIES IN LEDGER ACCOUNTS

Accounts Receivable
Nov. 20 1,800

Tools and Equipment
Nov. 17 13,800 | Nov. 20 1,800

Nov. 25   Overnight received $600 in partial collection of the account receivable from Ace Towing.

Collection of an account receivable

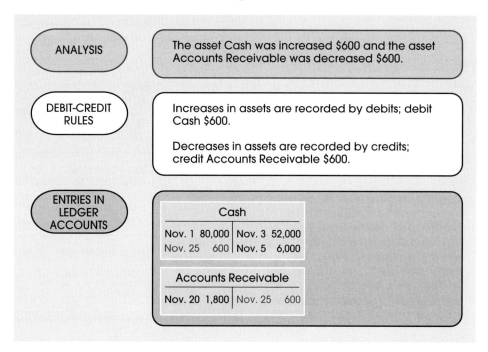

| ANALYSIS | The asset Cash was increased $600 and the asset Accounts Receivable was decreased $600. |

| DEBIT-CREDIT RULES | Increases in assets are recorded by debits; debit Cash $600.

Decreases in assets are recorded by credits; credit Accounts Receivable $600. |

ENTRIES IN LEDGER ACCOUNTS

Cash
Nov. 1 80,000 | Nov. 3 52,000
Nov. 25   600 | Nov. 5   6,000

Accounts Receivable
Nov. 20 1,800 | Nov. 25   600

Nov. 30   Overnight made a $6,800 partial payment of its account payable to Snap-On Tools Corp.

Payment of an account payable

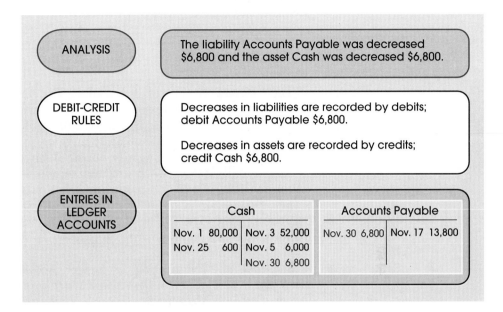

| ANALYSIS | The liability Accounts Payable was decreased $6,800 and the asset Cash was decreased $6,800. |

| DEBIT-CREDIT RULES | Decreases in liabilities are recorded by debits; debit Accounts Payable $6,800.

Decreases in assets are recorded by credits; credit Cash $6,800. |

ENTRIES IN LEDGER ACCOUNTS

Cash			Accounts Payable	
Nov. 1 80,000	Nov. 3 52,000		Nov. 30 6,800	Nov. 17 13,800
Nov. 25 600	Nov. 5 6,000			
	Nov. 30 6,800			

Running Balance Form of Accounts

T accounts are widely used in the classroom and in accounting textbooks, because they provide a concise conceptual picture of the financial effects of a business transaction. In actual practice, however, most businesses prefer to use the **running balance** form of ledger account. This form of account has special columns for recording additional information, as illustrated below with the Cash account of Overnight:

Ledger account—running balance form

Cash					Account No. 1
Date	Explanation	Ref	Debit	Credit	Balance
1999					
Nov. 1			80000		80000
3				52000	28000
5				6000	22000
25			600		22600
30				6800	15800

The **Date** column shows the date of the transaction—which is not necessarily the same as the date the entry is recorded in the account. The **Explanation** column is needed only for unusual items, and in many companies it is seldom used. The **Ref** (Reference) column is used to list the page number of the journal in which the transaction is recorded, thus making it possible to trace ledger entries back to their source. (The use of a *journal* is explained later in this chapter.) In the *Balance* column of the account, the new balance is entered each time the account is debited or credited. Thus the current balance of the account can always be observed at a glance. As noted earlier, such daily balance is useful in managing cash in the business.

The "Normal" Balance of an Account   The running balance form of ledger account does not indicate specifically whether the balance of the account is a debit or credit balance. However, this causes no difficulty because we know that asset accounts normally have debit balances and that accounts for liabilities and owner's equity normally have credit balances.

Occasionally an asset account may temporarily acquire a credit balance, either as the result of an accounting error or because of an unusual transaction. For example, an account receivable may acquire a credit balance because of overpayment by a customer. However, a credit balance in the Building account could be created only by an accounting error.

Sequence and Numbering of Ledger Accounts   Accounts are usually arranged in the ledger in *financial statement order,* that is, assets first, followed by liabilities, owner's equity, revenue, and expenses. The number of accounts needed by a business will depend upon its size, the nature of its operations, and the extent to which management and regulatory agencies want detailed classification of information. An identification number is assigned to each account. A **chart of accounts** is a listing of the account titles and account numbers being used by a particular business.

In the following list of accounts, many possible account numbers have been skipped; these numbers are held in reserve so that additional accounts can be inserted in any section of the ledger. In this illustration, the numbers from 1 to 29 are used exclusively for asset accounts; numbers from 30 to 49 are reserved for liabilities; and numbers in the 50s signify owners' equity accounts. (Revenue and expense will be discussed in Chapter 3.) The balance sheet accounts used thus far in our Overnight Auto Service illustration are numbered as shown in the following *chart of accounts:*

Account Title	Account No.
Assets:	
Cash	1
Accounts receivable	4
Land	20
Building	22
Tools and equipment	25
Liabilities:	
Notes payable	30
Accounts payable	32
Owner's equity:	
Michael McBryan, capital	50

In large businesses with hundreds or thousands of accounts, a more elaborate numbering system is used. Some companies use an eight- or ten-digit number for each ledger account; each of the digits carries special significance as to the classification of the account.

Sequence of Asset Accounts   As shown in all the balance sheets we have illustrated, cash is listed first among the assets. It is followed by such assets as marketable securities, short-term notes receivable, accounts receivable, inventories of merchandise, and supplies. These are the most common examples of current assets. The term *current assets* includes cash and those assets that will quickly be converted into cash or used up in operations. Next on the balance sheet come the relatively permanent assets used in the business (often called *plant assets*). Of this group, land is listed first and is followed by buildings. After these two items, any order is acceptable for other assets used in the business, such as automobiles, furniture and fixtures, computers, office equipment, store equipment, etc.

THE JOURNAL

LO 5: Explain the purpose of a journal and its relationship to the ledger.

In our preceding discussion, we recorded business transactions directly in the company's ledger accounts. We did this in order to stress the effects of business transactions upon the individual asset, liability, and owner's equity accounts appearing in the company's balance sheet. In an actual accounting system, however, the information about each business transaction is initially recorded in an accounting record called the **journal**. After the transaction has been recorded in the journal, the debit and credit changes in the individual accounts are entered in the ledger. Since the journal is the accounting record in which transactions are *first recorded,* it is sometimes called the *book of original entry.*

The journal is a chronological (day-by-day) record of business transactions. The information recorded about each transaction includes the date of the transaction, the debit and credit changes in specific ledger accounts, and a brief explanation of the transaction. At convenient intervals, the debit and credit amounts recorded in the journal are transferred *(posted)* to the accounts in the ledger. The updated ledger accounts, in turn, serve as the basis for preparing the balance sheet and other financial statements.

Why Use a Journal?

Since it is technically possible to record transactions directly in the ledger, why bother to maintain a journal? The answer is that the unit of organization for the journal is the *transaction,* whereas the unit of organization for the ledger is the *account.* By having both a journal and a ledger, we achieve several advantages that would not be possible if transactions were recorded directly in ledger accounts:

1. *The journal shows all information about a transaction in one place and also provides an explanation of the transaction.* In a journal entry, the debits and credits for a given transaction are recorded together, but when the transaction is recorded in the ledger, the debits and credits are entered in different accounts. Since a ledger may

contain hundreds of accounts, it would be very difficult to locate all the facts about a particular transaction by looking in the ledger. The journal is the record that shows the complete story of a transaction in one entry.

2. ***The journal provides a chronological record of all the events in the life of a business.*** If we want to look up the facts about a transaction of some months or years back, all we need is the date of the transaction in order to locate it in the journal.

3. ***The use of a journal helps to prevent errors.*** If transactions were recorded directly in the ledger, it would be very easy to make errors such as omitting the debit or the credit, or entering the debit twice or the credit twice. Such errors are not likely to be made in the journal, since the offsetting debits and credits appear together for each transaction.

The General Journal: Illustration of Entries

Many businesses maintain several types of journals. The nature of operations and the volume of transactions in the particular business determine the number and type of journals needed. The simplest type of journal is called a **general journal** and is shown on the next page. A general journal has only two money columns, one for debits and the other for credits; it may be used for recording any type of transaction.

LO 6: Prepare journal entries to record common business transactions.

The process of recording a transaction in a journal is called ***journalizing*** the transaction. To illustrate the use of the general journal, we shall now journalize the November transactions of Overnight Auto Service.

Efficient use of a general journal requires two things: (1) ability to analyze the effect of a transaction upon assets, liabilities, and owner's equity and (2) familiarity with the standard form and arrangement of journal entries. Our primary interest is in the analytical phase of journalizing; the procedural steps can be learned quickly by observing the following points in the illustration of journal entries:

1. The year, month, and day of the first entry on the page are written in the date column. The year and month need not be repeated for subsequent entries until a new page or a new month is begun.

2. The name of the account to be debited is written for the first line of the entry and is customarily placed at the extreme left next to the date column. The amount of the debit is entered on the same line in the ***left-hand*** money column.

3. The name of the account to be credited is entered on the line below the debit entry and is ***indented,*** that is, placed about 1 centimetre to the right of the date column. The amount credited is entered on the same line in the ***right-hand*** money column.

4. A brief explanation of the transaction begins on the line immediately below the last account credited. This explanation includes any data needed to identify the transaction, such as the name of the customer or supplier. The explanation is not indented.

5. A blank line should be left after each entry. This spacing causes each journal entry to stand out clearly as a separate unit and makes the journal easier to read.

6. An entry that includes more than one debit or more than one credit (such as the entry on November 5) is called ***compound journal entry.***

Regardless of how many debits or credits are contained in a compound journal entry, *all the debits* are entered *before any credits* are listed.

7. The LP (ledger page) column just to the left of the debit money column is left blank at the time of making the journal entry. When the debits and credits are later transferred to ledger accounts, the numbers of the ledger accounts will be listed in this column to provide a convenient cross-reference with the ledger.

Journal entries for November transactions of Overnight Auto Service

GENERAL JOURNAL				Page 1	
Date	Account Titles and Explanation	LP	Debit	Credit	
1999					
Nov. 1	Cash	1	80000		
	Michael McBryan, Capital	50		80000	
	Owner invested cash in the business.				
3	Land	20	52000		
	Cash	1		52000	
	Purchased land for business site.				
5	Building	22	36000		
	Cash	1		6000	
	Notes Payable	30		30000	
	Purchased building from MTA. Paid part cash; balance payable within 90 days.				
17	Tools and Equipment	25	13800		
	Accounts Payable	32		13800	
	Purchased tools and equipment on credit from Snap-On Tools Corp. Due in 60 days.				
20	Accounts Receivable	4	1800		
	Tools and Equipment	25		1800	
	Sold unused tools and equipment at cost to Ace Towing. Sales price due within 60 days.				
25	Cash	1	600		
	Accounts Receivable	4		600	
	Collected part of account receivable from Ace Towing.				
30	Accounts Payable	32	6800		
	Cash	1		6800	
	Made partial payment of the liability to Snap-on Tools Corp.				

In journalizing transactions, remember that the **exact title** of the ledger accounts to be debited and credited should be used. For example, in recording the purchase of tools and equipment for cash, **do not** make a journal entry debiting "Tools and Equipment Purchased" and crediting "Cash Paid Out." There are no ledger accounts with such titles. The proper journal entry would consist of a debit to **Tools and Equipment** and a credit to **Cash.**

A familiarity with the general journal form of describing transactions is just as essential to the study of accounting as a familiarity with plus and minus signs is to the study of mathematics. The journal entry is a **tool** for **analyzing** and **describing** the impact of various transactions upon a business entity. The ability to describe a transaction in journal entry form requires an understanding of the nature of the transaction and its effects upon the financial position of the business.

Posting Journal Entries to the Ledger Accounts

We have made the point that transactions are recorded **first** in the journal. Ledger accounts are updated **later,** through a process called **posting**. (In a computerized system, posting may occur instantaneously, rather than "later.") So, posting simply means **updating the ledger accounts** for the effects of the transactions recorded in the journal.

In addition, posting involves recording the date of the transaction in the ledger and creating a "cross-reference" between the entries in the ledger accounts and the related journal entry. In a manual accounting system, the complete posting process includes the following steps for each account title named in the journal entry:

1. Locate the corresponding account in the ledger and enter the date of the transaction.
2. Enter in the appropriate column the dollar amount being debited or credited to the ledger account.
3. In the **Ref** (posting reference) column of the ledger account, enter the **page number of the journal** from which the entry is being posted. (This creates a cross-reference between the ledger to the journal, enabling anyone using the ledger to find more information about a particular entry.)
4. Return to the journal; in the **LP** (ledger page) column, enter the **account number** of the ledger account to which the entry was posted. (The presence or absence of this account number shows at a glance which journal entries have been posted, and which have not.)

The posting of Overnight's first journal entry is illustrated in the following diagram:

Posting a transaction from journal to ledger accounts

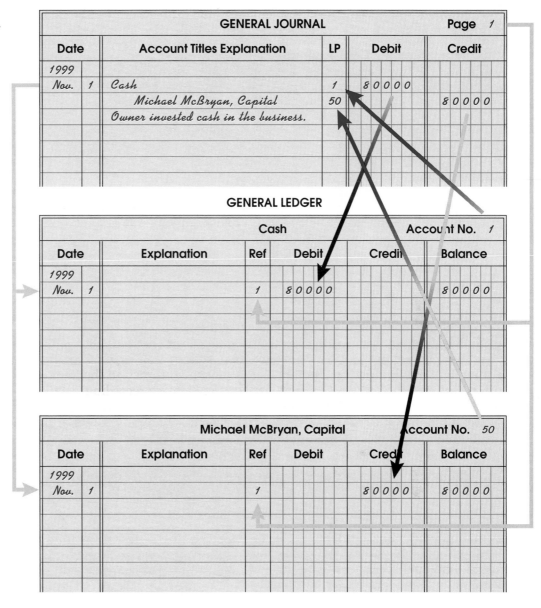

Notice that no new information is recorded during the posting process. Posting involves copying into the ledger accounts information that *already has been recorded in the journal.* In manual accounting systems, this can be a tedious and time-consuming process; but in computer-based systems, it usually is done instantly and automatically. In addition, computerized posting greatly reduces the risk of errors.

Ledger Accounts After Posting After all the November transactions have been posted, Overnight's ledger appears as shown below. The accounts are arranged in the ledger in the same order as in the balance sheet—that is, assets first, followed by liabilities and owner's equity.

To conserve space in this illustration, several ledger accounts appear on a single page. In actual practice, however, each account occupies a separate page in the ledger.

Ledger showing November transactions

	Cash		Account No. 1			
Date	Explanation	Ref	Debit	Credit	Balance	
1999						
Nov. 1		1	8 0 0 0 0		8 0 0 0 0	
3		1		5 2 0 0 0	2 8 0 0 0	
5		1		6 0 0 0	2 2 0 0 0	
25		1	6 0 0		2 2 6 0 0	
30		1		6 8 0 0	1 5 8 0 0	

	Accounts Receivable		Account No. 4			
Date	Explanation	Ref	Debit	Credit	Balance	
1999						
Nov. 20		1	1 8 0 0		1 8 0 0	
25		1		6 0 0	1 2 0 0	

	Land		Account No. 20			
Date	Explanation	Ref	Debit	Credit	Balance	
1999						
Nov. 3		1	5 2 0 0 0		5 2 0 0 0	

	Building		Account No. 22			
Date	Explanation	Ref	Debit	Credit	Balance	
1999						
Nov. 5		1	3 6 0 0 0		3 6 0 0 0	

Tools and Equipment					Account No.	25
Date	Explanation	Ref	Debit	Credit	Balance	
1999						
Nov. 17		1	1 3 8 0 0		1 3 8 0 0	
20		1		1 8 0 0	1 2 0 0 0	

Notes Payable					Account No.	30
Date	Explanation	Ref	Debit	Credit	Balance	
1999						
Nov. 5		1		3 0 0 0 0	3 0 0 0 0	

Accounts Payable					Account No.	32
Date	Explanation	Ref	Debit	Credit	Balance	
1999						
Nov. 17		1		1 3 8 0 0	1 3 8 0 0	
30		1	6 8 0 0		7 0 0 0	

Michael McBryan, Capital					Account No.	50
Date	Explanation	Ref	Debit	Credit	Balance	
1999						
Nov. 1		1		8 0 0 0 0	8 0 0 0 0	

THE TRIAL BALANCE

LO 7: Prepare a trial balance and explain its uses and limitations.

Since equal dollar amounts of debits and credits are entered in the accounts for every transaction recorded, the sum of all the debits in the ledger must be equal to the sum of all the credits. If the computation of account balances has been accurate, it follows that the total of the accounts with debit balances must be equal to the total of the accounts with credit balances.

Before using the account balances to prepare a balance sheet, it is desirable to *prove* that the total of accounts with debit balances is in fact equal to the total of accounts with credit balances. This proof of the equality of debit and credit balances is called a **trial balance**. A trial balance is a two-column schedule listing the names and balances of all the accounts *in the order in which they appear in the ledger;* the debit balances are listed in the left-hand column and the credit balances in the right-hand column. The totals of the two columns should agree. A trial balance taken from Overnight's ledger follows.

OVERNIGHT AUTO SERVICE Trial Balance November 30, 1999		
Cash	$ 15,800	
Accounts receivable	1,200	
Land	52,000	
Building	36,000	
Tools and equipment	12,000	
Notes payable		$ 30,000
Accounts payable		7,000
Michael McBryan, capital		80,000
	$117,000	$117,000

Trial balance at month-end proves ledger is in balance

Uses and Limitations of the Trial Balance

The trial balance provides proof that the ledger is in balance. The agreement of the debit and credit totals of the trial balance gives assurance that:

1. Equal debits and credits have been recorded for all transactions.
2. The debit or credit balance of each account has been correctly computed.
3. The addition of the account balances in the trial balance has been correctly performed.

Suppose that the debit and credit totals of the trial balance do not agree. This situation indicates that one or more errors have been made. Typical of such errors are (1) the posting of a debit as a credit, or vice versa; (2) arithmetic mistakes in determining account balances; (3) clerical errors in copying account balances into the trial balance; (4) listing a debit balance in the credit column of the trial balance, or vice versa; and (5) errors in addition of the trial balance.

The preparation of a trial balance does ***not*** prove that transactions have been correctly analyzed and recorded in the proper accounts. If, for example, a receipt of cash were erroneously recorded by debiting the Land account instead of the Cash account, the trial balance would still balance. Also, if a transaction were completely omitted from the ledger, the error would not be disclosed by the trial balance. In brief, ***the trial balance proves only one aspect of the ledger, and that is the equality of debits and credits.***

Despite these limitations, the trial balance is a useful device. It not only provides assurance that the ledger is "in balance," but it also serves as a convenient stepping-stone for the preparation of financial statements. As explained in Chapter 1, the balance sheet is a formal statement showing the financial position of the business, intended for distribution to managers, owners, bankers, and various outsiders. The trial balance, on the other hand, is merely an informal ***working paper,*** useful to the accountant but not intended for distribution to others. The balance sheet and other financial statements can be prepared more conveniently from the trial balance than directly from the ledger, especially if there are a great many ledger accounts.

THE ACCOUNTING CYCLE: AN INTRODUCTION

LO 8: Describe the basic steps of the accounting cycle in both manual and computer-based accounting systems.

The sequence of accounting procedures used to record, classify, and summarize accounting information is often termed the **accounting cycle**. The accounting cycle begins with the initial recording of business transactions and concludes with the preparation of formal financial statements summarizing the effects of these transactions upon the assets, liabilities, and owner's equity of the business. The term *cycle* indicates that these procedures must be repeated continuously to enable the business to prepare new, up-to-date financial statements at reasonable intervals.

At this point, we have illustrated a complete accounting cycle as it relates to the preparation of a balance sheet for a service-type business with a manual accounting system. The accounting procedures discussed to this point may be summarized as follows:

1. ***Record transaction in the journal.*** As each business transaction occurs, it is entered in the journal, thus creating a chronological record of events. This procedure completes the recording step in the accounting cycle.
2. ***Post to ledger accounts.*** The debit and credit changes in account balances are posted from the journal to the ledger. This procedure classifies the effects of the business transactions in terms of specific asset, liability, and owner's equity accounts.
3. ***Prepare a trial balance.*** A trial balance proves the equality of the debit and credit entries in the ledger. The purpose of this procedure is to verify the accuracy of the posting process and the computation of ledger account balances.
4. ***Prepare financial statements.*** At this point, we have discussed only one financial statement—the balance sheet. This statement shows the financial position of the business at a specific date. The preparation of financial statements summarizes the effects of business transactions occurring through the date of the statements and completes the accounting cycle.

In the next section of this chapter, and throughout this book, we will extend our discussion to include computer-based accounting systems. In Chapter 3, we will expand the accounting cycle to include the measurement of business income and the preparation of an income statement.

Manual and Computer-Based Systems: A Comparison

In our preceding discussion, we have assumed the use of a manual accounting system, in which all the accounting procedures are performed manually by the company's accounting personnel. You may wonder about the relevance of such a discussion in an era when even many small businesses use computer-based accounting systems. However, the concepts and procedures involved in the operation of manual and computer-based accounting systems are ***essentially the same.*** The differences are largely a question of whether specific procedures require human attention, or whether they can be performed automatically by machine, based on programs stored in the computer.

Computers can be programmed to perform mechanical tasks with great speed and accuracy. For example, they can be programmed to read data, to perform mathematical computations, and to rearrange data into any desired format. However, computers cannot think. Therefore, they are not able to *analyze* business transactions. Without human guidance, computers cannot determine which events should be recorded in the accounting records, or which accounts should be debited and credited to record an unusual event. With these abilities and limitations in mind, we will explore the effects of computer-based systems upon the basic accounting cycle.

Recording Business Transactions   The recording of transactions requires two steps. First, the transaction must be *analyzed* to determine whether it should be recorded in the accounting records and, if so, which accounts should be debited and credited and for what dollar amounts. Second, the transaction must be *physically entered* (recorded) in the accounting system. As computers do not know which transactions should be recorded or how to record them properly, these two functions must be performed by accounting personnel in both manual and computerized systems.

Differences do exist, however, in the manner in which data are physically entered into manual and computer-based systems. In manual systems, the data are entered in the form of handwritten journal entries. In a computer-based system, the data will be entered through a keyboard, an optical scanner, or other input device. Also, data entered into a computer-based system need *not* be arranged in the format of a journal entry. The data often are entered into a *database,* instead of a journal.

What Is a Database?   A **database** is a warehouse of information stored within a computer system. The purpose of the database is to allow information that will be used for several different purposes to be entered into the computer system *only once.* Data are originally entered into the database. Then, as data are needed, the computer refers to the database, selects the appropriate data, and arranges them in the desired format.

The information that must be entered into the database is the same as that contained in a journal entry—the date, the accounts to be debited and credited, the dollar amounts, and an explanation of the transaction. However, this information need not be arranged in the format of a journal entry. For example, in a database, accounts usually are identified by number, rather than by title. Also, short codes—such as "D" or "C"—may be used to indicate whether an account should be debited or credited. Once information has been entered in the database, the computer, based on the instructions in the computer programs prepared by someone with accounting knowledge, can arrange this information into any desired format, such as journal entries, ledger accounts, and financial statements.

Posting to Ledger Accounts   Posting merely copies existing information from one accounting record to another—a function that easily can be performed by a computer. In a computer-based system, data posted to the ledger accounts come directly from the database, rather than from the journal.

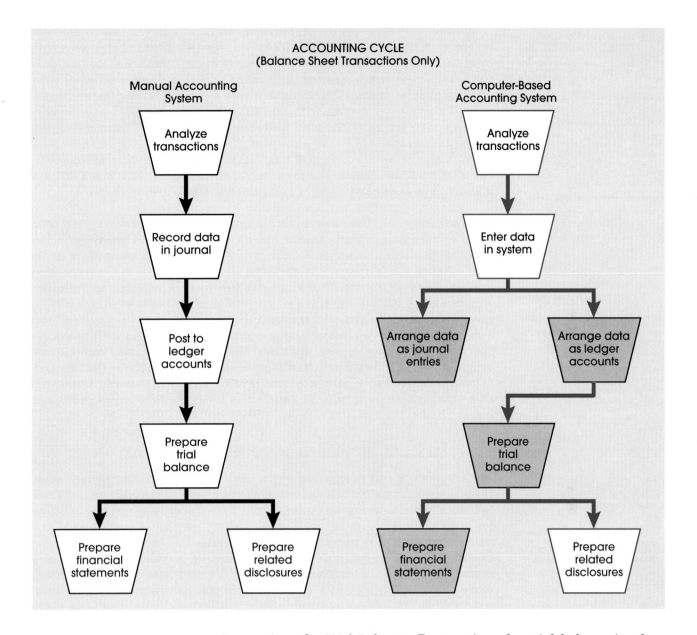

ACCOUNTING CYCLE
(Balance Sheet Transactions Only)

Manual Accounting System

Analyze transactions

Record data in journal

Post to ledger accounts

Prepare trial balance

Prepare financial statements

Prepare related disclosures

Computer-Based Accounting System

Analyze transactions

Enter data in system

Arrange data as journal entries

Arrange data as ledger accounts

Prepare trial balance

Prepare financial statements

Prepare related disclosures

Preparation of a Trial Balance   Preparation of a trial balance involves three steps: (1) determining the balances of ledger accounts, (2) arranging the account balances in the format of a trial balance, and (3) adding up the trial balance columns and comparing the column totals. All these functions involve information already contained in the accounting system and can be performed by the computer.

Preparation of Financial Statements and Related Disclosures   The preparation of a balance sheet and of the related disclosures are two very different tasks. The balance sheet—like the trial balance—consists of account titles and dollar amounts taken directly from the ledger. Hence, a balance sheet may be prepared automatically in a computer-based system.

Making the appropriate *disclosures* to accompany a set of financial statements, however, is a very different matter. Determining the items to be disclosed and wording the appropriate notes to the financial statements are tasks requiring *professional judgment.* Therefore, appropriate disclosures cannot be prepared automatically by a computer; they must be prepared carefully by people with *sound judgment,* as well as extensive knowledge of generally accepted accounting principles and financial reporting requirements.

At this point, our discussion of financial statements is limited to the preparation of a balance sheet. The preparation of an income statement involves additional procedures that will be discussed in the following chapter.

In Summary ... Computers can eliminate the need for copying and rearranging information that already has been entered into the system. They also can perform mathematical computations. In short, computers eliminate most of the "paper work" involved in the operation of an accounting system. However, they *do not* eliminate the need for accounting personnel who can analyze business transactions and explain these events in conformity with generally accepted accounting principles.

The differences in manual and computer-based systems with respect to the accounting procedures discussed in this chapter are summarized graphically in the flowcharts on the preceding page. Functions that are performed by accounting personnel are printed on a white background, and tasks that can be performed automatically by the computer are printed on a grey shaded background.

JOURNALS, LEDGERS, AND ACCOUNTING EDUCATION

In this chapter, our discussion of journals and ledgers has focused upon the simplest forms of these accounting records—a manually maintained "general" journal and T accounts. While these records might be sufficient for a very small business, most organizations use more complicated and more efficient types of journals and ledgers. An increasing number of organizations use computer-based accounting systems. Even when a manual system is in use, the recording of transactions can be done much more quickly in "special journals" than in the two-column general journal.[2] The formats of accounting software differ somewhat from one package to the next; also, the formats of special journals vary from one company to the next.

However, general journal entries and T accounts *illustrate the effects of transactions upon the financial position of a business* more clearly than do accounting software displays or entries in special journals. Despite their limited use in accounting practice, general journal entries and T accounts remain the preferred method of illustrating the effects of business transactions in accounting classrooms and accounting textbooks.

---

[2]Special journals are journals designed to record *one particular type* of transaction quickly and efficiently. By having several different kinds of special journals, a business may be able to record efficiently *all* types of transactions that *occur frequently.* Special journals will be discussed further in Chapter 6 and in Appendix B.

As a student, you should view general journal entries and T accounts as ***tools for analyzing transactions and illustrating their financial effects,*** not elements of actual accounting systems. Remember, our primary goal in this course is to develop your ability to ***understand and use*** accounting information, not to train you in record-keeping procedures.[3]

The Usefulness of Journals and Ledgers to Managers

Managers continually make use of the information contained in the accounting records. For example, to obtain information about a specific business transaction, managers may refer to the journal entry in which the transaction was recorded. To learn the current balance in such critical accounts as Cash, Accounts Receivable, and Accounts Payable, managers look to the ledger. Managers need not wait until financial statements are issued to obtain financial information about the business. They may obtain this information whenever they need it—often through desktop computers with "read only" access to the company's accounting system.[4]

In contrast, investors, creditors, and other outsiders ***do not*** have direct access to a company's accounting records. They obtain financial information about the business only ***periodically***—when financial statements are issued.[5]

---

[3]Although the format of accounting records varies from one business to the next, a student who understands the basic concepts of double-entry accounting should have little trouble in learning to understand and use the accounting records of any specific organization.

[4]"Read only" is an internal control that allows users of a specific computer terminal to read data, but not to alter the data or input new data into the system.

[5]Certain financial events may be disclosed to outsiders between financial statement dates, through such media as press conferences. Still, managers have far more timely access to most accounting information than do outside decision makers.

*Supplemental Topic

SOME TIPS ON RECORD-KEEPING PROCEDURES

Locating Errors

In our text illustration, the trial balance is always in balance. Every accounting student soon discovers in working problems, however, that errors are easily made that prevent trial balances from balancing. The lack of balance may be the result of a single error or a combination of several errors. An error may have been made in adding the trial balance columns or in copying the balances from the ledger accounts. If the preparation of the trial balance has been accurate, then the error may lie in the accounting records, either in the journal or in the ledger accounts. What is the most efficient approach to locating the error or errors? There is no single technique that will give the best results every time, but the following procedures, done in sequence, will often save considerable time and effort in locating errors.

1. Prove the addition of the trial balance columns by adding these columns in the opposite direction from that previously followed.
2. If the error does not lie in addition, next determine the exact amount by which the schedule is out of balance. The amount of the discrepancy is often a clue to the source of the error. If the discrepancy is **divisible by 9,** this suggests either a **transposition** error or a **slide.** For example, assume that the Cash account has a balance of $2,175, but in copying the balance into the trial balance the figures are **transposed** and written as $2,157. The resulting error is $18, and like all transposition errors is **divisible by 9.** Another common error is the **slide,** or incorrect placement of the decimal point, as when $2,175.00 is copied as $21.75. The resulting discrepancy in the trial balance will also be an amount **divisible by 9.**

   To illustrate another method of using the amount of a discrepancy as a clue to locating the error, assume that the asset account Office Supplies has a **debit** balance of $420, but that it is erroneously listed in the **credit** column of the trial balance. This will cause a discrepancy of two times $420, or **$840,** in the trial balance totals. Such errors as recording a debit in a credit column are not uncommon. Thus, after determining the difference in the trial balance totals, you should scan the columns for an amount equal to **one-half** of the discrepancy. Also scan the journal for an amount **equal** to the discrepancy. Perhaps this amount has not been posted.
3. Compare the amounts in the trial balance with the balances in the ledger. Make sure that each ledger account balance has been included in the correct column of the trial balance.
4. Recompute the balance of each ledger account.
5. Trace all postings from the journal to the ledger accounts. As this is done, place a check mark in the journal and in the ledger after each figure verified. When the operation is completed, look through the journal and the ledger for unchecked amounts. In tracing postings, be alert

not only for errors in amount but also for debits entered as credits, or vice versa.

Odds and Ends

Dollar signs are not used in journals or ledgers. Some accountants use dollar signs in trial balances; some do not. In this book, dollar signs are used in trial balances. Dollar signs should always be used in the balance sheet, the income statement, and other formal financial reports. In the balance sheet, for example, a dollar sign is placed by the first amount in each column and also by the final amount or total. Many accountants also place a dollar sign by each subtotal or other amount listed below an underlining. In the published financial statements of large corporations, the use of dollar signs is often limited to the first and last figures in a column.

When dollar amounts are being entered in the columnar paper used in journals and ledgers, commas and decimal points are not needed. On unruled paper, commas and decimal points should be used. Most of the problems and illustrations in this book are in even dollar amounts. In such cases the cents column can be left blank or, if desired, zeros or dashes may be used. A dollar amount that represents a final total within a schedule is underlined by a double rule.

End-of-Chapter Review

Key Terms Introduced or Emphasized in Chapter 2

Account *(p.58)* A record used to summarize all increases and decreases in a particular asset, such as Cash, or any other type of asset, liability, owner's equity, revenue, or expense.

Accountability *(p.57)* The condition of being held responsible for one's actions by the existence of an independent record of those actions. Establishing accountability is a major goal of accounting records and of internal control procedures.

Accounting cycle *(p.75)* The sequence of accounting procedures applied in recording, classifying, and summarizing accounting information. The cycle begins with the occurrence of business transactions and concludes with the preparation of financial statements. This concept will be expanded in later chapters.

Chart of accounts *(p.66)* This chart lists the ledger account titles and account numbers that are used by a particular business.

Credit *(p.58)* An amount entered on the right-hand side of a ledger account. A credit is used to record a decrease in an asset or an increase in a liability or in owner's equity.

Database *(p.76)* A storage centre of information within a computer-based accounting system. The idea behind a database is that data intended for a variety of uses may be entered into the computer system only once, at which time the information is stored in the database. Then, as the information is needed, the computer can retrieve it from the database and arrange it in the desired format.

Debit *(p.58)* An amount entered on the left-hand side of a ledger account. A debit is used to record an increase in an asset or a decrease in a liability or in owner's equity.

Double-entry accounting *(p.61)* A system of recording every business transaction with equal dollar amounts of both debit and credit entries. As a result of this system, the accounting equation always remains in balance; in addition, the system makes possible the measurement of net income and also the use of error-detecting devices such as a trial balance.

Footing *(p.59)* The total of amounts in a column.

General journal *(p.68)* The simplest type of journal, it has only two money columns—one for credits and one for debits. This journal may be used for all types of transactions, which are later posted to the appropriate ledger accounts.

Journal *(p.67)* A chronological record of transactions, showing for each transaction the debits and credits to be entered in specific ledger accounts. The simplest type of journal is called a general journal.

Ledger *(p.58)* A loose-leaf book, tray, or other record containing all the separate accounts of a business.

Posting *(p.70)* The process of transferring information from the journal to individual accounts in the ledger.

Trial balance *(p.73)* A two-column schedule listing the names and the debit or credit balances of all accounts in the ledger.

DEMONSTRATION PROBLEM

Stadium Parking was organized on July 2 to operate a parking lot near a new sports arena. The following transactions occurred during July prior to the company beginning its regular business operations.

July 2 Sylvia Snyder opened a bank account in the name of the business with a deposit of $50,000 cash.

July 3 Purchased land to be used as the parking lot for a total price of $140,000. A cash down payment of $28,000 was made and a note payable was issued for the balance of the purchase price.

July 5 Purchased a small portable building for $9,000 cash. The purchase price included installation of the building on the parking lot.

July 12   Purchased office equipment on credit from Suzuki & Co. for $3,000.

July 28   Paid $2,000 of the amount owed to Suzuki & Co.

The account titles and account numbers used by Stadium Parking to record these transactions are

Cash	1	Notes payable	30
Land	20	Accounts payable	32
Building	22	Sylvia Snyder, capital	50
Office equipment	25		

INSTRUCTIONS

a. Prepare journal entries for the month of July.

b. Post to ledger accounts of the three-column running balance form.

c. Prepare a trial balance at July 31.

SOLUTION TO DEMONSTRATION PROBLEM

a.

GENERAL JOURNAL						Page 1
Date		Account Titles and Explanation	LP	Debit		Credit
20__						
July	2	Cash	1	50000		
		Sylvia Snyder, Capital	50			50000
		Owner invested cash to begin business.				
	3	Land	20	140000		
		Cash	1			28000
		Notes Payable	30			112000
		Purchased land. Paid part cash and				
		issued a note payable for the balance.				
	5	Building	22	9000		
		Cash	1			9000
		Purchased a small portable building				
		for cash.				
	12	Office Euipment	25	3000		
		Accounts Payable	32			3000
		Purchased office equipment on credit				
		from Suzuki & Co.				
	28	Accounts Payable	32	2000		
		Cash	1			2000
		Paid part of account payable to				
		Suzuki & Co.				

b.   **GENERAL LEDGER**

Cash								Account No.	1
Date	**Explanation**	**Ref**	**Debit**	**Credit**	**Balance**
20__					
July 2		1	50000		50000
3		1		28000	22000
5		1		9000	13000
28		1		2000	11000

Land								Account No.	20
Date	**Explanation**	**Ref**	**Debit**	**Credit**	**Balance**
20__					
July 3		1	140000		140000

Building								Account No.	22
Date	**Explanation**	**Ref**	**Debit**	**Credit**	**Balance**
20__					
July 5		1	9000		9000

Office Equipment								Account No.	25
Date	**Explanation**	**Ref**	**Debit**	**Credit**	**Balance**
20__					
July 12		1	3000		3000

Notes Payable								Account No.	30
Date	**Explanation**	**Ref**	**Debit**	**Credit**	**Balance**
20__					
July 3		1		112000	112000

Accounts Payable					Account No. 32
Date	Explanation	Ref	Debit	Credit	Balance
20__					
July 12		1		3000	3000
28		1	2000		1000

Sylvia Snyder, Capital					Account No. 50
Date	Explanation	Ref	Debit	Credit	Balance
20__					
July 2		1		50000	50000

c.

STADIUM PARKING Trial Balance July 31, 20__		
	Debit	Credit
Cash	$ 11,000	
Land	140,000	
Building	9,000	
Office equipment	3,000	
Notes payable		$112,000
Accounts payable		1,000
Sylvia Snyder, capital		50,000
	$163,000	$163,000

Self-Test Questions

Answers to these questions appear on page 102.

1. According to the rules of debit and credit for balance sheet accounts:
   a. Increases in asset, liability, and owner's equity accounts are recorded by debits.
   b. Decreases in asset and liability accounts are recorded by credits.
   c. Increases in asset and owner's equity accounts are recorded by debits.
   d. Decreases in liability and owner's equity accounts are recorded by debits.

2. Which of the following statements about accounting procedures is **not** correct?
   a. The journal shows in one place all the information about specific transactions, arranged in chronological order.
   b. A ledger account shows in one place all the information about changes in a specific asset or liability, or in owner's equity.
   c. Posting is the process of transferring debit and credit changes in account balances from the ledger to the journal.
   d. The end product of the accounting cycle consists of formal financial statements, such as the balance sheet and the income statement.

3. On March 31, the ledger for Regal Dry Cleaning consists of the following:

Cleaning Equipment	$27,800	Accounts Receivable	$21,000
Accounts Payable	15,700	Cash	6,900
R. Temple, Capital	20,000	Salaries Payable	9,600
Office Equipment	2,000	Notes Payable	22,500
Automobile	7,500	Cleaning Supplies	2,600

In a trial balance prepared on March 31, the total of the credit column is:
a. $67,800   **b.** $93,100   **c.** $25,300   **d.** $65,300

4. Sunset Tours has a $3,500 account receivable from the Del Mar Rotary. On January 20, the Rotary makes a partial payment of $2,100 to Sunset Tours. The journal entry made on January 20 by Sunset Tours to record this transaction includes:
   a. A debit to the Cash Received account of $2,100.
   b. A credit to the Accounts Receivable account of $2,100.
   c. A debit to the Cash account of $1,400.
   d. A debit to the Accounts Receivable account of $1,400.

5. The following journal entry was made in Dixie Stores' accounting records:

Cash	12,000	
Notes Receivable	48,000	
Land		60,000

This transaction:
a. Involves the purchase of land for $60,000.
b. Involves a $12,000 cash payment.
c. Involves the sale of land for $60,000.
d. Causes an increase in total assets of $12,000.

ASSIGNMENT MATERIAL

Discussion Questions

1. Baker Construction is a small business owned and managed by Tom Baker. The company has 21 employees, few creditors, and no investor other than Tom Baker. Thus, like many small businesses, it has no obligation to issue financial statements to creditors or investors. Under these circumstances, is there any reason for this company to maintain accounting records?

2. In its simplest form, an account has only three elements or basic parts. What are these three elements?

3. At the beginning of the year, the Office Equipment account of Pacific Coast Airlines had a debit balance of **$126,900.** During the year, debit entries of **$23,400** and credit entries of **$38,200** were posted to the account. What was the balance of this account at the end of the year? (Indicate debit or credit balance.)

4. What relationship exists between the position of an account on the balance sheet and the rules for recording increases in that account?

5. State briefly the rules of debit and credit as applied to asset accounts. As applied to liability and owner's equity accounts.

6. Does the term ***debit*** mean increase and the term ***credit*** mean decrease? Explain.

7. What requirement is imposed by the double-entry system in the recording of any business transaction?

8. Explain precisely what is meant by each of the phrases listed below. Whenever appropriate, indicate whether the left or right side of an account is affected and whether an increase or decrease is indicated.
   a. A debit of $200 to the Cash account.
   b. A debit of $600 to Accounts Payable.
   c. A credit of $50 to Accounts Receivable.
   d. A debit to the Land account.
   e. Credit balance.
   f. Credit side of an account.

9. For each of the following transactions, indicate whether the account in parentheses should be debited or credited, and ***give the reason*** for your answer.
   a. Purchased land for cash. (Cash)
   b. Sold an old, unneeded typewriter on 30-day credit. (Office Equipment)
   c. Obtained a loan of $30,000 from a bank. (Cash)
   d. Purchased a copying machine on credit, promising to make payment in full within 30 days. (Accounts Payable)
   e. Jan Williams began the business of Williams Word Processing by depositing $25,000 in a bank account in the name of the business. (Jan Williams, Capital)

10. For each of the following accounts, state whether it is an asset, a liability, or owner's equity; also state whether it would normally have a debit or a credit balance: (a) Office Equipment, (b) P. Cook, Capital, (c) Accounts Receivable, (d) Accounts Payable, (e) Cash, (f) Notes Payable, (g) Land.

11. Why is a journal sometimes called the ***book of original entry?***

12. Compare and contrast a ***journal*** and a ***ledger.***

13. What is a ***compound*** journal entry?

14. Since it is possible to record the effects of business transactions directly in ledger accounts, why is it desirable for a business to maintain a journal?

15. What purposes are served by a trial balance?

16. In preparing a trial balance, an accounting student listed the balance of the Office Equipment account in the credit column. This account had a balance of $2,450. What would be the amount of the discrepancy in the trial balance totals? Explain.

17. List the following five items in a logical sequence to illustrate the flow of accounting information through a manual accounting system:
   a. Debits and credits posted from journal to ledger
   b. Preparation of a trial balance
   c. Information entered in the journal
   d. Preparation of financial statements
   e. Occurrence of a business transaction

18. Which step in the recording of transactions requires greater understanding of accounting principles: (a) the entering of transactions in the journal or (b) the posting of entries to ledger accounts?

19. List the procedures in the ***accounting cycle*** as described in this chapter.

20. What is a **database?** How does a database relate to the preparation of journal entries and ledger accounts in a computer-based system?

*21. Are dollar signs used in journal entries? In ledger accounts? In trial balances? In financial statements?

Exercises

EXERCISE 2-1
Accounting Terminology
(LO 1, 2, 3, 4, 5, 7, 8)

Listed below are nine technical accounting terms introduced in this chapter:

Database	*Ledger*	*Account*
Double-entry	*Posting*	*Credit*
Journal	*Trial balance*	*Debit*

Each of the following statements may (or may not) describe one of these technical terms. For each statement, indicate the accounting term described, or answer "none" if the statement does not correctly describe any of the terms.

a. The accounting record in which transactions are initially recorded in a manual accounting system.

b. Information stored in a computer-based accounting system that can be arranged into any desired format.

c. A device that proves the equality of debits and credits posted to the ledger.

d. The accounting record from which a trial balance is prepared.

e. The system of accounting in which all transactions are recorded both in the journal and in the ledger.

f. An entry on the left-hand side of a ledger account.

g. The process of transferring information from a journal to the ledger.

EXERCISE 2-2
Double-Entry and the
Accounting Equation
(LO 3, 4)

A number of transactions are described below in terms of the balance sheet accounts debited and credited:

1. Debit Cash, credit Accounts Receivable.
2. Debit Accounts Payable, credit Cash.
3. Debit Cash, credit Tom Hill, Capital.
4. Debit Equipment, credit Accounts Payable.
5. Debit Land, credit Cash and Notes Payable.
6. Debit Accounts Payable, credit Equipment.

a. Indicate the effects of each transaction upon the elements of the accounting equation, using the code letters *I* for increase, *D* for decrease, and *NE* for no effect. Organize your answer in tabular form using the column headings shown below. The answer for transaction **1** is provided as an example.

Transaction	Assets	=	Liabilities	+	Owner's Equity
1	NE		NE		NE

b. Write a one-sentence description of each transaction.

EXERCISE 2-3
Double-Entry Accounting:
Debit and Credit Rules
(LO 3, 4)

Analyze separately each of the following transactions, using the format illustrated at the end of the exercise. In each situation, explain the debit portion of the transaction before the credit portion.

a. On April 2, Michele Corti organized a company to conduct business under the name of Vagabond Travel Services; she opened a bank account in the company name with a deposit of $90,000 cash.

b. On April 11, the company purchased an office building in an industrial park for a total price of $224,000, of which $126,000 was applicable to the land and

---

Supplemental Topic, "Some Tips on Record-Keeping Procedures."

$98,000 to the building. A cash down payment of $56,000 was made and a note payable was issued for the balance of the purchase price.

c. On April 21, office equipment was purchased on account from ADR Company at a price of $5,900. The account payable was to be paid on May 2.

d. On April 29, a portion of the office equipment purchased on April 21 was found to be defective and was returned to ADR Company. ADR Company agreed that Vagabond Travel Services would not be charged for the defective equipment, which had cost $870.

e. On May 21, the remaining liability to ADR Company was paid in full.

Note: The type of analysis to be made is shown by the following illustration, using transaction *a* as an example:

a. (1) The asset Cash was increased. Increases in assets are recorded by debits. Debit Cash, $90,000.

(2) The owner's equity was increased. Increases in owner's equity are recorded by credits. Credit Michele Corti, Capital.

EXERCISE 2-4
T Accounts; Preparation of Trial Balance
(LO 3, 4, 7)

The first five transactions of Beaumont Consulting are described below.

1. On June 8, Travis Brooks opened a bank account in the name of his new business, Beaumont Consulting, by making a bank deposit of $95,000.
2. On June 12, land was acquired for $43,000 cash.
3. On June 14 a prefabricated building was purchased from E-Z Built Corporation at a cost of $47,900. A cash payment of $15,400 was made and a note payable was issued for the balance.
4. On June 20, office equipment was purchased at a cost of $8,600. A cash down payment of $1,600 was made, and it was agreed that the balance should be paid within 30 days.
5. On June 26, $6,500 of the amount due E-Z Built Corporation was paid. (Ignore interest expense.)

a. Enter the above transactions in T accounts drawn on ordinary notebook paper. Label each debit and credit with the number identifying the transaction.
b. Prepare a trial balance at June 30.

EXERCISE 2-5
Effects of Debits and Credits on Ledger Account Balances; Trial Balance
(LO 3, 4, 7)

The first six transactions of Cycle Scene Tour Agency appear in the following T accounts.

Cash					Office Equipment		
(1)	60,000	(2)	20,000	(3)	20,000	(4)	3,000
(6)	1,300	(5)	15,000				

Accounts Receivable					Notes Payable		
(4)	3,000	(6)	1,300			(2)	100,000

Land					Accounts Payable		
(2)	72,000			(5)	15,000	(3)	20,000

Building					Michel LeMond, Capital		
(2)	48,000					(1)	60,000

a. For each of the six transactions in turn, indicate the type of accounts affected (asset, liability, or owner's equity) and whether the account was increased or decreased. Arrange your answers in the form illustrated for transaction **1**, shown here as an example.

	Account(s) Debited		Account(s) Credited	
Transaction	Type of Account(s)	Increase or Decrease	Type of Account(s)	Increase or Decrease
(1)	Asset	Increase	Owner's equity	Increase

b. Write a brief description of each transaction.
c. Prepare a trial balance for Cycle Scene Tour Agency after these six transactions. Assume the date is January 10, 20__.

EXERCISE 2-6
Recording Transactions in a Journal
(LO 3, 4, 6)

Enter the following selected transactions in the two-column journal for Fraser Appliance Centre. Include a brief explanation of the transaction as part of each journal entry.

Oct. 1   The owner, Mark Fraser, invested an additional $80,000 cash in the business.

Oct. 5   Purchased an adjacent vacant lot for use as parking space. The price was $102,000 of which $30,600 was paid in cash; a note payable was issued for the balance.

Oct. 15   Issued a cheque for $976 in full payment of an account payable to Hampton Supply Co.

Oct. 18   Borrowed $30,000 cash from the bank by signing a 90-day note payable.

Oct. 23   Collected an account receivable of $2,900 from a customer, Jocelyn Scott.

Oct. 30   Acquired office equipment from Tower Company for $6,200. Made a cash down payment of $1,500; balance to be paid within 30 days.

EXERCISE 2-7
Journal Entries to Illustrate Effects of Transactions
(LO 3, 4, 6)

Prepare general journal entries to illustrate the effects of each of the following transactions upon the financial statements of Seacoast Airline. You are to determine appropriate account titles.

Jan. 4   Purchased two seaplanes from Scout Aircraft at a total cost of $825,000. Paid $425,000 in cash and signed a note payable to National Bank for the remainder.

Jan. 8   Purchased spare parts for the new planes from Breckwoldt Aviation. The parts cost $15,200, and were purchased on account.

Jan. 12   Issued a note payable in the amount of $375,000 to Earl Scoggins, the owner of Scoggins' Flight School, in exchange for a parcel of waterfront land and a floating aircraft hangar in Conception Bay. The current value of the land is appraised at $235,000, and of the floating hangar, $140,000.

Jan. 15   Returned to Breckwoldt Aviation $2,400 of the aircraft parts purchased on January 8. The return of these parts reduced by $2,400 the amount owed to Breckwoldt.

Feb. 2   Paid the remaining balance owed to Breckwoldt Aviation from the purchase on January 8.

Follow up: What was the overall effect of the *January 4* transaction upon total assets of Seacoast Airlines? Indicate type of overall effect (increase, decrease, or no effect) as well as dollar amount.

EXERCISE 2-8
Relationship between Journal and Ledger Accounts
(LO 3, 4, 5, 6)

Transactions are recorded *first* in a journal and *then* posted to ledger accounts. In this exercise, however, your understanding of the relationship between journal and ledger is tested by asking you to study some ledger accounts and determine the journal entries that probably were made by the company's accountant to produce these ledger entries. The following accounts show the first six transactions of the Gutierrez Construction Company. Prepare a journal entry (including written explanation) for each transaction.

Cash				Vehicle		
Nov. 1	120,000	Nov. 8	33,600	Nov. 30	9,400	
		Nov. 25	12,000			

Land			Notes Payable		
Nov. 8	70,000		Nov. 25	12,000	Nov. 8	95,000

Building			Accounts Payable		
Nov. 8	58,600		Nov. 21	480	Nov. 15	3,200

Office Equipment				Joe Gutierrez, Capital		
Nov. 15	3,200	Nov. 21	480		Nov. 1	120,000
					Nov. 30	9,400

EXERCISE 2-9
Preparing a Trial Balance
(LO 7)

Using the information in the ledger accounts presented in Exercise 2-8, prepare a trial balance for Gutierrez Construction Company at November 30, 19__.

EXERCISE 2-10
Uses and Limitations of a Trial Balance
(LO 7)

Some of the following errors would cause the debit and credit columns of the trial balance to have unequal totals. For each of the four paragraphs, write a statement explaining whether the error would cause unequal totals in the trial balance. Each paragraph is to be considered independently of the others.
  a. An account receivable in the amount of $625 was collected in full. The collection was recorded by a debit to Cash for $625 and a debit to Accounts Payable for $625.
  b. An account payable was paid by issuing a cheque for $495. The payment was recorded by debiting Accounts Payable $495 and crediting Accounts Receivable $495.
  c. A payment of $390 to a creditor was recorded by a debit to Accounts Payable of $390 and a credit to Cash of $39.
  d. A $520 payment for a new typewriter was recorded by a debit to Office Equipment of $52 and a credit to Cash of $52.

EXERCISE 2-11
Uses and Limitations of a Trial Balance
(LO 7)

The trial balance prepared by Design Solutions, at June 30 was not in balance. In searching for the error, an employee discovered that a transaction for the purchase of a laptop computer on credit for $1,580 had been recorded by a *debit* of $1,580 to the Office Equipment account and a *debit* of $1,580 to Accounts Payable. The credit column of the incorrect trial balance has a total of $129,640.
  In answering each of the following five questions, explain fully the reasons underlying your answer and state the dollar amount of the error if any.

a. Was the Office Equipment account overstated, understated, or correctly stated in the trial balance?
b. Was the total of the debit column of the trial balance overstated, understated, or correctly stated?
c. Was the Accounts Payable account overstated, understated, or correctly stated in the trial balance?
d. Was the total of the credit column of the trial balance overstated, understated, or correctly stated?
e. How much was the total of the debit column of the trial balance before correction of the error?

EXERCISE 2-12
Steps in the Accounting Cycle; Computerized Accounting Systems
(LO 8)

Various steps and decisions involved in the accounting cycle are described in the seven lettered statements below. Indicate which of these procedures are mechanical functions that can be performed by machine in a computerized accounting system, and which require the judgment of people familiar with accounting principles and concepts.
a. Decide whether or not events should be recorded in the accounting records.
b. Determine which ledger accounts should be debited and credited to describe specific business transactions.
c. Arrange recorded data in the format of journal entries.
d. Arrange recorded data in the format of ledger accounts.
e. Prepare a trial balance.
f. Prepare financial statements (a balance sheet).
g. Evaluate the debt-paying ability of one company relative to another.

EXERCISE 2-13
Manual versus Computer-based Systems
(LO 8)

For each of the following steps in the accounting cycle, explain whether the step requires human judgment, or whether it can be performed automatically by a computer in a computer-based accounting system.
a. Record transactions as they occur.
b. Post recorded data to ledger accounts.
c. Prepare a trial balance.
d. Prepare a balance sheet and related disclosures.

EXERCISE 2-14
Different Uses for Journals and Ledgers
(LO 1, 5)

Briefly explain the usefulness of journal entries and of ledger accounts:
a. In the operation of an accounting system.
b. From the viewpoint of business managers who are **not** personally responsible for maintaining accounting records or preparing their company's financial statements.
c. From the viewpoint of an accounting student or an accounting instructor (assuming **general** journal entries and T accounts).

Problems

PROBLEM 2-1
Recording Transactions in a Journal
(LO 2, 3, 4, 6)

TKO Entertainment is a sole proprietorship that owns and operates a chain of movie theatres. Selected business transactions of the company during April 1999 are listed below.

April 1   Purchased cleaning supplies on account from Janitorial Supply Co., $5,000. Payment due within 60 days, to be paid in two equal instalments of $2,500.

April 3   Purchased projection equipment for cash from Video Concepts, $5,900.

April 5 Returned to Video Concepts a projector purchased on April 3, because the lens was defective. The projector had cost TKO $1,954; Video Concepts agreed to refund TKO's purchase price within 5 days.

April 10 Received the $1,954 refund from Video Concepts.

April 12 The owner, Herb Geffen, invested an additional $200,000 cash in the business.

April 15 Purchased the Village Theatre for $630,000, paying $150,000 in cash and issuing a note payable for the balance of the purchase price. The assets included in the purchase price, and their values at August 15, were as follows:

Land	*$170,000*
Building	*365,000*
Equipment	*95,000*

April 26 Paid the first instalment owed to Janitorial Supply Co. from April 1 purchase.

INSTRUCTIONS

a. Prepare journal entries to record the above transactions. Select the appropriate account titles from the following chart of accounts:

Cash	*Land*	*Notes payable*
Accounts receivable	*Building*	*Accounts payable*
Cleaning supplies	*Equipment*	*Herb Geffen, Capital*

b. What impact did the April 15 transaction have on the financial position of TKO Entertainment? (Indicate direction and dollar effect of this transaction on TKO's assets, liabilities, and owner's equity.)

PROBLEM 2-2
Recording Transactions in a
Journal: A Second Problem
(LO 2, 3, 4, 6)

Louis Dixon, a dentist, resigned from his position with a large dental group in order to begin his own pediatric dental practice. The practice was organized as a sole proprietorship, called Louis Dixon Pediatric Dentistry. The business transactions during September while the new venture was being organized are listed below.

Sept. 1 Dixon opened a bank account in the name of the business by depositing $50,000 cash, which he had saved over a number of years.

Sept. 10 Purchased a small office building located on a large lot for a total price of $182,400, of which $106,000 was applicable to the land and $76,400 to the building. A cash payment of $36,500 was made and a note payable was issued for the balance of the purchase price.

Sept. 15 Purchased a microcomputer system from Computer Stores, Inc., for $4,680 cash.

Sept. 19 Purchased office furnishings and dental equipment from Turnkey Operations, Inc., at a cost of $5,760, of which $1,760 was for office furnishings. A cash down payment of $960 was made, the balance to be paid in three equal instalments due September 28, October 28, and November 28. The purchase was on open account and did not require signing of a promissory note.

Sept. 26 A $280 monitor in the microcomputer system purchased on September 15 stopped working. The monitor was returned to Computer Stores, Inc., which promised to refund the $280 within five days.

Sept. 28   Paid Turnkey Operations, Inc., $1600 cash as the first instalment due on the account payable for office furnishings and dental equipment.

Sept. 30   Received $280 cash from Computer Stores, Inc., in full settlement of the account receivable created on September 26.

INSTRUCTIONS

a. Prepare journal entries to record the above transactions. Select the appropriate account titles from the following chart of accounts:

Cash	*Office furnishings*
Accounts receivable	*Dental equipment*
Land	*Notes payable*
Building	*Accounts payable*
Computer system	*Louis Dixon, capital*

b. What impact did the Sept. 10 transaction have on the financial position of the company? (Indicate direction and dollar effect of this transaction on the proprietorship's assets, liabilities, and owner's equity.)

PROBLEM 2-3
Analyzing Transactions and
Preparing Journal Entries
(LO 2, 3, 4, 6)

Lars Retton is the founder and owner of North Coast Gymnastics, a youth gymnastics training facility. A few of the company's business transactions occurring during July are described below:

1. On July 2, collected cash of $700 from accounts receivable.
2. On July 7, purchased gymnastics equipment for $2,175, paying $500 in cash and charging the remainder on the company's 30-day account at Weider Fitness Co.
3. On July 9, returned to Weider Fitness Co. $200 of gymnastics equipment that was not needed. The return of this equipment reduced by $200 the amount owed to Weider Fitness Co.
4. On July 25, Retton made an additional investment in North Coast Gymnastics by depositing $5,000 cash in the company bank account.
5. On July 31, paid the remaining $1,475 owed to Weider Fitness Co.

INSTRUCTIONS

a. Prepare an analysis of each of the above transactions. The form of analysis to be used is as follows, using transaction **1** as an example.

   1(a) The asset Cash was increased. Increases in assets are recorded by debits. Debit Cash, $700.

    (b) The asset Accounts Receivable was decreased. Decreases in assets are recorded by credits. Credit Accounts Receivable, $700.

b. Prepare journal entries, including explanations, for the above transactions.

PROBLEM 2-4
Analyzing Transactions and
Preparing Journal Entries
(LO 2, 3, 4, 6)

The U-R Choice Rental was organized to rent trailers, tools, and other equipment to its customers. The organization of the business began on May 1, and the following transactions occurred in May before the company began regular operations on June 1.

1. On May 1, Susan Kennedy opened a bank account in the name of her new company with a deposit of $120,000 cash.
2. On May 3, the company bought land for use in its operations at a total cost of $75,000. A cash down payment of $15,000 was made, and a note payable (payable within 90 days without interest) was issued for the balance.
3. On May 5, a movable building was purchased for $82,000 cash and installed on the lot.
4. On May 10, equipment was purchased on credit from Ace Tool Company at a cost of $16,100. The account payable was to be paid within 30 days. (The asset account is entitled Rental Equipment.)
5. On May 31, a cash payment of $20,000 was made in partial settlement of the note payable issued on May 3.

INSTRUCTIONS

a. Prepare an analysis of each of the above transactions. The form of analysis to be used is as follows, using transaction **1** above as an example:

   1. a. The asset Cash was increased. Increases in assets are recorded by debits. Debit Cash, $120,000.

      b. The owner's equity was increased. Increases in owner's equity are recorded by credits. Credit Susan Kennedy, Capital, $120,000.

b. Prepare journal entries for the above five transactions. Include an explanation as a part of each journal entry.

PROBLEM 2-5
Analyzing and Describing Transactions
(LO 2, 3, 4, 6)

The following transactions were recorded by Handan Stores:

GENERAL JOURNAL				Page 1
May	1	Furniture and Fixtures	3,450	
		Accounts Payable		3,450
	8	Cash	10,000	
		Helen Longon, Capital		10,000
	18	Store Equipment	38,000	
		Cash		18,000
		Notes Payable		20,000
	20	Cash	7,000	
		Accounts Receivable		7,000
	22	Notes Payable	8,000	
		Store Equipment		8,000

INSTRUCTIONS

a. Write an explanation for each of the journal entries.
b. Prepare an analysis of each of the transactions in the format illustrated in the chapter.

PROBLEM 2-6
Preparing a Trial Balance and a Balance Sheet
(LO 7)

Environmental Services is a weather forecasting service that provides information to growers and dealers in perishable commodities. Its ledger account balances at November 30 are as shown in the following alphabetical list.

Accounts payable	$ 6,810	Land	$ 92,200
Accounts receivable	9,540	Notes payable	115,000
Automobiles	21,500	Notes receivable	2,400
Building	104,300	Office furniture	10,820
Carly McKay, Capital	149,930	Office supplies	850
Cash	12,950	Property Taxes Payable . . .	2,045
Computers	15,270	Salaries payable	3,325
Computer software	3,480	Technical library	3,800

INSTRUCTIONS

a. Prepare a trial balance with the accounts arranged in financial statement order. Include a proper heading for your trial balance.
b. Prepare a balance sheet. Include a subtotal for total liabilities.
c. Explain the difference in purpose between a trial balance and a balance sheet.

PROBLEM 2-7
Short "Cycle" Problem—Posting to Ledger Accounts; Preparing a Trial Balance and a Balance Sheet
(LO 5, 7, 8)

After several years of working as sous-chef at Helenann, a five-star restaurant in Windsor, Cindy Black had saved enough money to open her own gourmet restaurant, to be known as Onyx. During July, while organizing the business, Black prepared the following journal entries to record the first week's transactions. She has not posted these entries to ledger accounts. The ledger account numbers to be used are: Cash 1, Supplies 9, Land 20, Building 22, Kitchen Equipment 25, Notes Payable 30, Accounts Payable 31, and Cindy Black, Capital 50.

GENERAL JOURNAL					Page 1
19__ July	2	Cash . . . . Cindy Black, Capital . . . . Investment in business by owner.		50,000	50,000

	2	Land . . . .
		Building . . . .
		    Cash . . . .
		    Notes Payable . . . .
		Purchased land and building to be
		used as a restaurant.
				60,000
				43,400
					25,850
					77,550

	3	Kitchen Equipment . . . . Accounts Payable . . . . Bought equipment on credit from ProChef, Inc.		4,680	4,680
	3	Supplies . . . . Accounts Payable . . . . Bought supplies from HB Restaurant Supply.		1,260	1,260
	5	Accounts Payable . . . . Kitchen Equipment . . . . Returned defective equipment to ProChef, Inc. for credit on account.		725	725
	7	Accounts Payable . . . . Cash . . . . Made partial payment of liability to HB Restaurant Supply.		630	630
	7	Accounts Payable . . . . Cash . . . . Made payment of liability to ProChef, Inc.		3,955	3,955

INSTRUCTIONS

a. Post the journal entries to ledger accounts of the three-column running balance form.

b. Prepare a trial balance at July 7 from the ledger accounts completed in part **a.**

c. Prepare a balance sheet at July 7, 19__.

PROBLEM 2-8
Preparing Journal Entries,
Posting, and Preparing a Trial
Balance
(LO 1–8)

Joseph Hyla formed a business entity to provide bus service for a fee to public and private schools in the Walnut Creek area. The business is organized as a sole proprietorship, called Walnut Creek Transportation Services. The transactions during July, while the new business was being organized, are listed below.

July 2   Hyla opened a bank account in the name of the business with a deposit of $211,500 cash.

July 3   The new company purchased land and a building at a cost of $120,000, of which $72,000 was regarded as applicable to the land and $48,000 to the building. The transaction involved a cash payment of $30,000 and the issuance of a note payable for the balance of the purchase price.

July 5   Purchased 6 new minibuses at $40,500 each from Fleet Sales Company. Paid $76,500 cash, and agreed to pay $80,000 by July 31 and the remaining balance by August 15. The liability is viewed as an account payable.

July 7   Sold one of the buses at cost to YMCA Camping Services. The buyer paid $15,000 in cash and agreed to pay the balance within 30 days.

July 8   Upon inspection, one of the buses was found to be defective and was returned to Fleet Sales Company. The amount payable to this creditor was thereby reduced by $40,500.

July 20   Purchased office equipment at a cost of $2,400 cash.

July 31   Issued a cheque for $80,000 in partial payment of the liability to Fleet Sales Company.

The account titles and the account numbers used by the company are as follows:

Cash	10	Buses	22
Accounts receivable	11	Notes payable	31
Land	16	Accounts payable	32
Building	17	Joseph Hyla, capital	50
Office equipment	20		

INSTRUCTIONS

a. Journalize the July transactions.
b. Post to ledger accounts. Use the running balance form of ledger account.
c. Prepare a trial balance at July 31, 19___.
d. Does the company have sufficient cash at July 31 to pay the balance owed to Fleet Sales Company on August 15? Based solely upon the information provided in the problem data, will the business have sufficient cash by August 15 to pay the amount owed Fleet Sales Company? Explain briefly.

PROBLEM 2-9
Preparing Journal Entries,
Posting, and Preparing a Trial
Balance: A Second Problem
(LO 1–8)

In April, licensed real estate broker Joan Windsor organized a sole proprietorship, Windsor Property Management, to provide management services for the owners of apartment buildings. The organizational period extended throughout April and included the transactions listed below.

April 1   Joan Windsor opened a bank account in the name of the business with a deposit of $40,000 cash.

April 4   Purchased land and an office building for a price of $175,000, of which $100,000 was considered applicable to the land and $75,000 attributable to the building. A cash down payment of $35,000 was made and a note payable for $140,000 was issued for the balance of the purchase price.

April 7   Purchased office equipment on credit from Eaton Office Equipment, $6,350, due in 30 days.

April 9   A copier (cost $895), which was part of the April 7 purchase of office equipment, proved defective and was returned for credit to Eaton Office Equipment.

April 17   Sold one-fourth of the land acquired on April 4 to Ace Parking Lots at a price of $25,000. This price is equal to the cost for this portion of the land, so there is no gain or loss on this transaction. Received a $5,000 cash down payment from Ace Parking Lots and a note receivable in the amount of $20,000, due in four monthly instalments of $5,000 each, beginning on April 30. (Ignore interest.)

April 28   Paid $1,600 in partial settlement of the liability to Eaton.

April 30   Received cash of $5,000 as partial collection of the note receivable from Ace Parking Lots.

The account titles and account numbers to be used are:

Cash	1	Office equipment	25
Notes receivable	5	Notes payable	31
Land	21	Accounts payable	32
Building	23	Joan Windsor, capital	51

INSTRUCTIONS

a. Prepare journal entries for the month of April.
b. Post to ledger accounts of the three-column running balance form.
c. Prepare a trial balance at April 30, 19__.
d. Assume that Windsor Property Management is scheduled to make a $10,000 instalment payment on the note payable on May 15. Based solely upon the information in the problem data and in prior parts of your solution, will the company have sufficient cash to make this $10,000 payment? Explain.

PROBLEM 2-10
The Accounting Cycle: a Comprehensive Problem
(LO 1–8)

Forum Broadcasting was organized in May 20__ to operate as a local television station. The account titles and numbers used by the sole proprietorship are:

Cash	11	Telecasting equipment	24
Accounts receivable	15	Film library	25
Supplies	19	Notes payable	31
Land	21	Accounts payable	32
Building	22	Daniel Chung, capital	51
Transmitter	23		

The transactions for May 20__, were as follows:

May 1   Daniel Chung deposited $350,000 cash in a bank account in the name of the business, Forum Broadcasting.

May 3   The new company purchased the land, building, and telecasting equipment previously used by a local television station that had gone bankrupt. The total purchase price was $325,000, of which $120,000 was attributable to the land, $95,000 to the building, and the remainder to the telecasting equipment. The terms of the purchase required a cash payment of $200,000 and the issuance of a note payable for the balance; the note payable is due in 3 years.

May 5   Purchased a transmitter at a cost of $225,000 from AC Mfg. Co., making a cash down payment of $75,000. The balance, in the form of a note payable, was to be paid in monthly instalments, of $12,500, beginning May 15. (Interest expense is to be ignored.)

May 9   Purchased a film library at a cost of $50,000 from Modern Film Productions, making a down payment of $15,000 cash, with the balance on account, payable in 30 days.

May 12   Bought supplies costing $3,190, paying cash.

May 15   Paid $12,500 to AC Mfg. Co. as the first monthly payment on the note payable created on May 5. (Interest expense is to be ignored.)

May 25   Sold part of the film library to City College; cost was $8,900 and the selling price also was $8,900. City College agreed to pay the full amount in 30 days.

INSTRUCTIONS

a. Prepare journal entries for the month of May.
b. Post to ledger accounts of the three-column running balance form.
c. Prepare a trial balance at May 31, 20__.
d. Prepare a balance sheet at May 31, 20__.

e. Based upon your answers to parts **a** through **d** and information presented in the problem data, does it appear the business will have sufficient cash to pay liabilities as they come due in June? Explain.

PROBLEM 2-11
The Accounting Cycle: A Second Problem
(LO 1–8)

After playing several seasons of professional football, George Harris had saved enough money to start a business, to be called Number One Auto Rental. The transactions during March while the new business was being organized are listed below:

Mar. 2   George Harris invested $140,000 cash in the business by making a deposit in a bank account in the name of the new company.

Mar. 4   The new company purchased land and a building at a cost of $120,000, of which $72,000 was regarded as applicable to the land and $48,000 to the building. The transaction involved a cash payment of $41,500 and the issuance of a note payable for the balance. The note is due in 5 years.

Mar. 5   Purchased 10 new automobiles at $17,200 each from Fleet Sales Company. Paid $40,000 cash; the balance, in the form of a note payable, is to be paid in 4 monthly instalments of $33,000 each, beginning March 15. (Interest expense to be ignored.)

Mar. 7   Sold an automobile at cost to Harris's father-in-law, Howard Facey, who paid $2,400 in cash and agreed to pay the balance within 60 days.

Mar. 8   One of the automobiles was found to be defective and was returned to Fleet Sales Company. The amount payable to this creditor was thereby reduced by $17,200.

Mar. 15   Paid $33,000 to Fleet Sales Company as the first monthly payment on note payable created on March 4. (Interest expense to be ignored.)

Mar. 20   Purchased office equipment on credit; total cost, $4,000, due in 30 days.

The account titles and the account numbers used by the company are as follows:

Cash	10	Automobiles	22
Accounts receivable	11	Notes payable	31
Land	16	Accounts payable	32
Building	17	George Harris, capital	50
Office equipment	20		

INSTRUCTIONS

a. Journalize the March transactions.
b. Post to ledger accounts. Use the running balance form of ledger account.
c. Prepare a trial balance at March 31, 20__.
d. Prepare a balance sheet at March 31, 20__.
e. Based upon your answers to parts **a** through **d** and information presented in the problem data, does it appear the business will have sufficient cash to pay liabilities as they come due in April? Explain.

Analytical and Decision Problems and Cases

A&D 2-1
The Role of Accounting Records
(LO 1)

Interview someone familiar with the accounting system in a small local business, such as a restaurant or a retail store. (Interviews should be planned and conducted in accordance with the instructions given in the Preface to this textbook.)

INSTRUCTIONS

a. Does this business have any obligation to furnish financial statements to creditors or investors who are not actively involved in management? Explain briefly.

b. List specific types of accounting information that this business has either a legal or ethical obligation to develop within its accounting system. (***Note:*** We recognize the overlap between legal and ethical obligations. We ***do not*** ask you to distinguish between these categories.)

A&D 2-2
Reconstructing Journal Entries;
Understanding Accounting
Records and Concepts
(LO 2, 3, 4, 5, 6)

John Church, a friend of yours, ran into your office one morning, almost out of breath. You knew right away that John needed help.

YOU: Hi, John, what's up?

JOHN: You wouldn't believe what happened to me last night. I was in my office getting information from the books that my bookkeeper prepared for me, free of charge, before she left for a job abroad. You know, the journal and the ledger. Then I had to go to an emergency meeting, so I brought them with me. When I got home, I couldn't find either of them. I must have lost them somewhere.

YOU: What did you want to get from these books?

JOHN: I wanted to find the cash balance from the journal. As you know, I started organizing my landscaping consulting business early this month and I ordered some business cards and stationery. I wanted to find out whether I had enough cash to pay for them next month. I wanted to get everything ready to start operating the business then. Also, I wanted to look at the ledgers to make sure that all transactions were recorded.

YOU: How can I help?

JOHN: I want you to reconstruct these records for me.

YOU: Fine, but I need more information.

JOHN: I managed to put a few items together in this thing called a balance sheet before I went to the meeting. (The following is what John gave you.)

JOHN CHURCH LANDSCAPING CONSULTING
Balance Sheet
October 29, 1999

Assets		Liabilities	
Accounts receivable . . . $450		*Liabilities:*	
		Notes payable $17,500	
		Accounts payable 5,000	
		Total liabilities $22,500	
		Owner's equity	
		Owner's capital 50,000	
		Total $72,500	

YOU: Where did you get this information?

JOHN: Well, I got the assets and liability amounts from the journal and I know the exact amount that I put into the business, the cash and the land.

YOU: This is a good start. What else?

JOHN: Remember the land I bought a few years ago for $50,000? Well, I sold half of it for $30,000 cash. I took $5,000 to pay off the mortgage and put the rest in the business account. Then, I bought a small building from a construction company. I got a fantastic deal. This company wanted to get rid of it quickly, so I got it moved to the land for just

$35,000! Oh, yes, because I had to put the building somewhere, I put the other half of the land into the business. Now back to the building. I paid half in cash and the other half with a bank loan. The bank thought the building was worth at least $50,000 and was willing to lend me that amount.

YOU: Is this it?

JOHN: No, I paid for half of the office equipment that I ordered because the company didn't have enough in stock. I also bought some office supplies for cash.

YOU: Did you use any of the supplies and what happened to the other half of the office equipment?

JOHN: No, none of the supplies has been used. The other half of the office equipment arrived two days ago and because I didn't get all of it at one time, the company let me pay for it next month. Yesterday, I let Zhang Huang, the owner of Five Corner Travel Agency down the street, have one-third of the office supplies at cost. He really liked them and will pay me back in two weeks. Well, that is all I can remember.

INSTRUCTIONS

Based on the above information, answer the following:

a. Reconstruct the journal entries.

b. Comment on John Church's understanding or misunderstanding of the journal, ledger, and accounting concept.

A&D 2-3
Computer-based Accounting Systems
(LO 2, 4, 5)

Bill Gates is planning to create a computer-based accounting system for small businesses. His system will be developed from a database program and will be suitable for use on personal computers.

The idea underlying database software is that data needed for a variety of uses is entered into the database only once. The computer is programmed to arrange this data into any number of desired formats. In the case of Gates' accounting system, the company's accounting personnel must enter the relevant information about each business transaction into the database. The program that Gates plans to write will then enable the computer operator to have the information arranged by the computer into the formats of (1) journal entries (with written explanations), (2) three-column running balance form ledger accounts, (3) a trial balance, and (4) a balance sheet.

INSTRUCTIONS

a. Identify the relevant information about each business transaction that the company's accounting personnel must enter into the database to enable Gates' program to prepare the four types of accounting records and statements described above.

b. As described in this chapter, the accounting cycle includes the steps of (1) analyzing and recording business transactions, (2) posting the debit and credit amounts to ledger accounts, (3) preparing a trial balance, and (4) preparing financial statements (at this stage, only a balance sheet). Indicate which of these functions can be performed automatically by Gates' computer program and which must still be performed by the company's accounting personnel.

A&D 2-4
Preparing Balance Sheets and an Introduction to Measuring Income
(Prelude to Chapter 3)

Brooke Lowell, a college student with several summers' experience as a guide on bicycle camping trips and with savings of $3,200 from her last summer's earnings of $4,800, decided to go into business for herself. On June 1, Lowell organized Point Pelee Bicycle Tours by depositing $2,000 of personal savings in a bank account in the name of the business. Also on June 1, the business borrowed an additional $3,500 cash from John Lowell (Brooke's uncle) by issuing a three-year note payable. To help the business get started, John Lowell agreed that no interest would be charged on the loan. The following transactions were also carried out by the business on June 1:

1. Bought a number of bicycles at a total cost of $6,500; paid $2,500 cash and agreed to pay the balance within 60 days.
2. Bought camping equipment at a cost of $3,200, payable in 60 days.
3. Bought supplies for cash, $650.

After the close of the season on September 1, Lowell asked another student, Tom Cummings, who had taken a course in accounting, to help determine the financial position of the business.

The only record Lowell had maintained was a chequebook with memorandum notes written on the cheque stubs. From this source Cummings discovered that Lowell had invested an additional $1,000 of savings in the business on July 2, and also that the accounts payable arising from the purchase of the bicycles and camping equipment had been paid in full. A bank statement received from the bank on September 1 showed a balance on deposit of $2,990.

Lowell informed Cummings that all cash received by the business had been deposited in the bank and all bills had been paid by cheque immediately upon receipt; consequently, as of September 1 all bills for the season had been paid. However, nothing had been paid on the note payable.

The bicycles and camping equipment were all in excellent condition at the end of the season and Lowell planned to resume operations the following summer. In fact, she had already accepted reservations from many customers who wished to return.

Cummings felt that some consideration should be given to the wear and tear on the bicycles and equipment, but he agreed with Lowell that for the present purpose the bicycles and equipment should be listed in the balance sheet at the original cost. The supplies remaining on hand had cost $75 and Lowell felt that these supplies could be used next summer.

Cummings suggested that two balance sheets be prepared, one to show the condition of the business on June 1 and the other showing the condition on September 1. He also recommended to Lowell that a complete set of accounting records be established.

INSTRUCTIONS

a. Use the information in the first paragraph (including the three numbered transactions) as a basis for preparing a balance sheet dated June 1, 20___.
b. Prepare a balance sheet at September 1, 20___. (Because of the incomplete information available, it is not possible to determine the amount of cash at September 1 by adding cash receipts and deducting cash payments throughout the season. The amount on deposit as reported by the bank at September 1 is to be regarded as the total cash belonging to the business at that date.)
c. Determine the change in owner's equity and the sources of this change. Explain whether you consider the business to be successful. Also comment on the cash position at the beginning and end of the season.

Answers to Self-Test Questions

1. d   2. c   3. a ($15,700 + $20,000 + $9,600 + $22,500)   4. b   5. c

LITTLE BEAR RAILROAD, INC.

An introduction to the accounting process.

Note to students: Accountants often find themselves confronted with situations different from anything they have encountered before. They resolve these situations by doing research and by applying their knowledge of basic accounting concepts. One objective of this problem is to demonstrate these challenging aspects of accounting.

Based upon the accounting concepts introduced in Chapters 1 and 2, you should be able to "reason out" a solution to this problem. If you prefer a more research-oriented approach, you might look up "Intangible assets," "Capital stock: issuance of," and "Unincorporated business, incorporation of" in the index of this textbook. Whichever approach you take, *be prepared to discuss your conclusions in class!*

Those of you who find this type of problem interesting may be well-suited to a career in accounting.

For many years Kim-Chung (K-C) Jones has owned and operated the Little Bear Railroad, a narrow gauge railroad operating inside a national park. The Little Bear operates for only eight months each year—April 1 through November 30—offering park visitors a 22-kilometre scenic tour of the area. The train consists of a woodburning locomotive and three passenger cars. Until March 1999, the business had been organized as a sole proprietorship.

In March, prior to opening for the 1999 season, Jones decided to reorganize the business as Little Bear Railroad, Inc., a corporation. The following events occurred as the new corporation was being organized:

Mar. 1   Jones transferred into the new corporation all of the assets and liabilities of the Little Bear Railroad; in exchange for which the corporation issued 100,000 shares of capital stock (assumed issuance price, $1,000,000). The business assets and liabilities, and their value at March 1, were as follows:

Cash	$ 48,000
Accounts receivable	8,600
Supplies	4,900
Spare parts	10,400
Buildings	170,000
Equipment & rolling stock	415,000
Roadbed, track, & ties	250,000
Notes payable (due in 2005)	300,000
Accounts payable	6,900

In addition to the assets and liabilities listed above, Jones also transferred into the corporation a permanent "right-of-way" allowing the railroad to operate on specific portions of the national park's land. (Notice that the railroad owns no land; the land upon which it operates is part of the national park.) Jones acquired the right-of-way from Parks Canada many years ago at a cost of $100,000. However, this asset was considered to be worth $400,000 at the date that Jones transferred it into the new corporation.

Mar. 4 Jones sold 10% of her capital stock in the corporation to Adrian Wong-Boren, a relative, for $115,000 cash.

Mar. 10 The corporation borrowed $100,000 cash from Pine City Bank to provide capital for expanding its operations. A note payable was issued, due in 90 days. (Ignore interest charges.)

Mar. 12 Signed an agreement with Jay Gould Construction Limited, which is to build a three-kilometre extension of roadbed and track within Little Bear's right-of-way through the park. Work will begin on April 1 and is to be completed by August 15, 1999. The total cost will be $240,000, payable in thirds as each kilometre of track is completed.

Mar. 15 The corporation purchased a replica of an 1865 steam-driven locomotive and an original 1898 dining car from The Spud, a narrow-gauge railroad in Regina that had gone bankrupt. The purchase price was $380,000; Little Bear Railroad, Inc., paid $90,000 in cash and issued a note payable for the balance. The note, payable to Quality Trust, is due in one year.

INSTRUCTIONS

a. Prepare all general journal entries necessary through March 15 to record these events in the accounting records of the new corporation. (Not all of these events require journal entries.)

b. Post to ledger accounts of the three-column form. (You are to create the company's ledger by assigning names and numbers to an appropriate number of ledger accounts.)

c. Prepare a trial balance at March 15, 1999.

d. Prepare a balance sheet at March 15, 1999. Also, draft a note accompanying this balance sheet to disclose the company's contractual commitment to Jay Gould Construction Limited.

e. Assume that you are a loan officer at TD Bank. Little Bear Railroad, Inc., wants to borrow from your bank the $240,000 to pay for the three-kilometre extension of its track. The corporation intends to repay this loan in one year. Based solely upon the available information, does the corporation appear to be a reasonably good credit risk? Explain the reasons for your conclusion.

CHAPTER 3

Measuring Business Income and Completing the Accounting Cycle

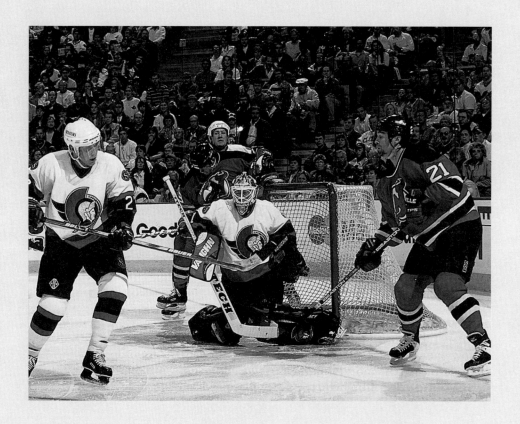

Net income is *not* an amount of "money" received. Rather, it is a *measure of economic performance.*

In some ways, net income is to the business world what *goals* are to a hockey game—it indicates which companies are coming out ahead, and which are losing ground. And as in hockey, it's difficult to follow the game if you don't know the score.

1. Explain the nature of net income, revenue, expenses, and the time period principle.
2. Apply the *realization* (*recognition*) and *matching* principles in recording revenue and expenses.
3. Explain *why* revenues are recorded with credits and expenses are recorded with debits.
4. Explain the nature of *adjusting entries and record supplies expense.*

5. Define and record depreciation (also called amortization)* expense.
6. Prepare statements of income and of owner's equity. Explain how these statements relate to the balance sheet.
7. Explain the purposes of *closing entries;* prepare these entries.
8. Describe steps in the *accounting cycle.*
9. Distinguish between the *accrual basis* and the *cash basis* of accounting.

WHAT IS NET INCOME?

LO 1: Explain the nature of net income, revenue, expenses, and the time period principle.

In Chapter 1, we stated that a basic objective of every business is to earn a profit, or net income. Why? The answer lies in the very definition of **net income:** *an increase in owner's equity resulting from the profitable operation of the business.* The opposite of net income, a *decrease* in owner's equity resulting from unprofitable operation of the business, is termed a **net loss**

If you were to organize a business of your own, you would do so with the hope and expectation that the business would produce a net income, thereby increasing your ownership equity. Individuals who invest in the capital stock of a large corporation also expect the business to earn a net income that will increase the value of their investment.

Notice that net income does not consist of cash or any other specific asset. Rather, net income is a *computation* of the overall effects of many business transactions upon *owner's equity.* The increase in owner's equity resulting from profitable operations usually is accompanied by an increase in total assets, though not necessarily an increase in cash. In some cases, however, an increase in owner's equity is accompanied by a decrease in total liabilities. The effects of earning net income upon the basic accounting equation are illustrated below:

Net income is not an asset—it's an *increase in owner's equity*

> *Assets = Liabilities + Owner's Equity*
>
> *Increase = Decrease – Increase*
>
> *Either (or both) of these effects occur as net income is earned . . .* *. . . but this is what "net income" really means.*

---

*While section 3060 of the *CICA Handbook* uses the term "amortization" to encompass the commonly used terms "depreciation" and "depletion," it indicates that the latter two terms may also be used. In practice, the terms "depreciation" and "depletion" are still most widely used. These two terms are used in all four examples (four companies from four industries) cited in the most recent CICA's *Financial Reporting in Canada* (Twenty-second Edition, 1997). Accordingly, the terms "depreciation" and "depletion" are used in this text.

Our point is that net income represents an ***increase in owner's equity*** and has no direct relationship to the types or amounts of assets on hand. Even a business earning a net income may run short of cash and become insolvent.

In the balance sheet, the changes in owner's equity resulting from profitable or unprofitable operations are reflected in the balance of the ***owner's capital account.*** The assets of the business organization appear in the ***assets*** section of the balance sheet.

The Income Statement: A Preview

An **income statement** is a one-page financial statement that summarizes the profitability of the business entity over a specified period of time. In this statement, net income is determined by comparing for the time period: (1) the ***sales price*** of the goods sold and services rendered by the business with (2) the ***cost*** to the business of the goods and services used up in business operations. The technical accounting terms for these components of ***net income*** are ***revenue*** and ***expenses.*** Therefore, accountants say that net income is equal to ***revenue minus expenses,*** as shown in the following income statement.

An income statement has two basic sections— revenue and expenses— that lead to the computation of net income

OVERNIGHT AUTO SERVICE		
Income Statement		
For the Month Ended December 31, 1999		
Revenue:		
Repair service revenue		$10,380
Expenses:		
Advertising expense	$ 830	
Wages expense	4,900	
Supplies expense	400	
Depreciation expense: building	150	
Depreciation expense: tools and equipment	200	6,480
Net income		$ 3,900

When we measure the net income earned by a business we are measuring its economic performance—its success or failure as a business enterprise. The owner, managers, and major creditors are anxious to see the latest available income statement and thereby judge how well the company is doing. If the business is organized as a corporation, the shareholders and prospective investors also will be keenly interested in each successive income statement.

Later in this chapter we will show how this income statement is developed from the accounting records of Overnight Auto Service. For the moment, however, this illustration will assist us in discussing some of the basic concepts involved in measuring business income.

Income Must Be Related to a Specified Period of Time   Notice that our sample income statement covers a ***period of time***—namely, the month of December. A balance sheet shows the financial position of a business at a ***particular date.*** An income statement, on the other hand, shows the results of business operations over a span of time. We cannot evaluate net income unless it is associated with a specific time period. For example, if an executive says, "My business earns a net income of $10,000," the profitability of the business is unclear. Does it earn $10,000 per week, per month, or per year?

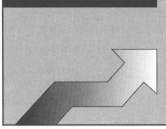

CASE IN POINT The late J. Paul Getty, one of the world's first billionaires, was once interviewed by a group of business students. One of the students asked Getty to estimate the amount of his income. As the student had not specified a time period, Getty decided to have some fun with his audience and responded, "About $11,000 . . ." He paused long enough to allow the group to express surprise over this seemingly low amount, and then completed his sentence, ". . . an hour." (Incidentally, $11,000 per hour, 24 hours per day, amounts to about $100 million per year.)

Accounting Periods The period of time covered by an income statement is termed the company's **accounting period**. To provide the users of financial statements with timely information, net income is measured for relatively short accounting periods of equal length. This concept, called the **time period principle**, is one of the generally accepted accounting principles that guide the interpretation of financial events and the preparation of financial statements.

The length of a company's accounting period depends upon how frequently managers, investors, and other interested people require information about the company's performance. Every business prepares annual income statements, and most businesses prepare quarterly and monthly income statements as well. (Quarterly statements cover a three-month period and are prepared by all large corporations for distribution to their shareholders.)

The 12-month accounting period used by an entity is called its **fiscal year**. The fiscal year used by most companies coincides with the calendar year and ends on December 31. Some businesses, however, elect to use a fiscal year that ends on some other date. It may be convenient for a business to end its fiscal year during a slack season rather than during a time of peak activity.

CASE IN POINT The Walt Disney Company ends its fiscal year on September 30. Why? For one reason, September and October are relatively slow months at Disney's theme parks. For another, September financial statements provide timely information about the preceding summer, which is the company's busiest season.

As another example, many department stores, including The Bay, Kmart, and Zellers end their fiscal years on January 31—after the rush of the holiday season.

Let us now explore the meaning of the accounting terms *revenue* and *expenses.*

Revenue

Revenue *is the price of goods sold and services rendered during a given accounting period.* Earning revenue causes owner's equity to increase. When a business renders services or sells merchandise to its customers, it usually receives cash or acquires an account receivable from the customer. The inflow of cash and receivables from customers increases the total assets of the company; on the other side of the accounting equation, the liabilities do not change, but owner's equity increases to match the increase in total assets. Thus revenue is the **gross increase in owner's equity** resulting from operation of the business.

Various account titles are used to describe different types of revenue. For example, Overnight records its revenue in an account entitled **Repair Services Revenue.** A business that sells merchandise rather than services, uses the term **Sales** to describe its revenue. In the professional practices of physicians, public accountants, and lawyers, revenue usually is called **Fees Earned.** A real estate office, however, might call its revenue **Commissions Earned.**

A professional sport team might have separate revenue accounts for **Ticket Sales, Concessions Revenue,** and **Revenue from Television Contracts.** Another type of revenue common to most businesses is **Interest Revenue** (or Interest Earned), stemming from the interest earned on bank deposits, notes receivable, and interest-bearing investments.

The Realization (Recognition) Principle: When to Record Revenue   We have defined revenue as *the price of goods sold and services rendered during a given accounting period.* Thus, revenue earned by selling merchandise is recognized *when the goods are sold.* Revenue earned by rendering services to customers is recognized in the period in which the *services are rendered.*

To illustrate, assume that on July 25, KGPO Radio contracts with Rancho Ford to run two hundred 1-minute radio advertisements during August. KGPO runs these ads in August and receives full payment from Rancho Ford on September 6. In which month should KGPO recognize this advertising revenue—July, August, or September?

LO 2: Apply the realization (recognition) and matching principles in recording revenue and expenses.

The answer is in **August**—the month in which KGPO *rendered the services* that earned the revenue.[1] In summary, revenue is recognized *when it is earned,* without regard to when payment is received. This concept is called the **realization (recognition) principle**.

Because of the realization (recognition) principle, revenue represents the **value of goods sold and services rendered** during the accounting period, not the amount of cash received.

---

[1]Some readers may wonder what would happen if some of the ads were aired in August and others in September. In this case, KGPO should recognize an **appropriate portion** of the advertising revenue in August, and the remainder in September. The accounting procedures for allocating revenue between accounting periods are discussed and illustrated in the next chapter.

Expenses

Expenses *are the costs of the goods and services used up in the process of earning revenue.* Incurring an expense causes a *decrease in owner's equity.* The related changes in the accounting equation can be either (1) a decrease in assets, or (2) an increase in liabilities. An expense reduces assets if payment occurs at the time that the expense is incurred. If the expense will not be paid until later, as, for example, the purchase of advertising services on account, the recording of the expense will be accompanied by an increase in liabilities.

Examples of expenses include the cost of employees' salaries, advertising, rent, utilities, and the gradual wearing-out (depreciation) of such assets as buildings, automobiles, and office equipment. All these costs are necessary to attract and serve customers and thereby earn revenue. Expenses are often called the "costs of doing business," that is, the cost of the various activities necessary to carry on a business.

The Matching Principle: When to Record Expenses   A significant relationship exists between revenue and expenses. Expenses are incurred for the *purpose of producing revenue.* In measuring net income for a period, revenue should be offset by *all the expenses incurred in producing that revenue.* This concept of offsetting expenses against revenue on a basis of "cause and effect" is called the **matching principle**

Timing is an important factor in matching (offsetting) revenue with the related expenses. For example, in preparing monthly income statements, it is important to offset this month's expenses against this month's revenue. We should not offset this month's expenses against last month's revenue because there is no cause and effect relationship between the two.

To illustrate the matching principle, assume that the salaries earned by sales personnel serving customers during July are not paid until early August. In which month should these salaries be regarded as an expense? The answer is *July,* because this is the month in which the sales personnel's services *helped to produce revenue.*

We previously explained that revenue and cash receipts are not one and the same thing. Similarly, expenses and cash payments are not identical. The cash payment for an expense may occur before, after, or in the same period that an expense helps to produce revenue. In deciding when to record an expense, the critical question is *"In what period does this expenditure help to produce revenue?"* not "When does the cash payment occur?"

Expenditures Benefiting More Than One Accounting Period   Many expenditures made by a business benefit two or more accounting periods. Fire insurance policies, for example, usually cover a period of 12 months. If a company prepares monthly income statements, a portion of the cost of such a policy should be allocated to insurance expense each month that the policy is in force. In this case, apportionment of the cost of the policy by months is an easy matter. If the 12-month policy costs $2,400, for example, the insurance expense for each month amounts to $200 ($2,400 cost ÷ 12 months).

Not all transactions can be so precisely divided by accounting periods. The purchase of a building, furniture and fixtures, machinery, a type-writer, or an automobile provides benefits to the business over all the years in which such an asset is used. No one can determine in advance exactly how many years of service will be received from such long-lived assets. Nevertheless, in measuring the net income of a business for a period of one year or less, the accountant must *estimate* what portion of the cost of the building and other long-lived assets is applicable to the cur-rent year. Since the allocations of these costs are estimates rather than precise measurements, it follows that income statements should be regarded as useful *approximations* of net income rather than as absolutely exact measurements.

For some expenditures, such as those for advertising or employee train-ing programs, it is not possible to estimate objectively the number of accounting periods over which revenue is likely to be produced. In such cases, generally accepted accounting principles require that the expenditure be charged *immediately to expense.* This treatment is based upon the accounting principle of **objectivity** and the concept of **conservatism**. Accountants require *objective evidence* that an expenditure will produce revenue in future periods before they will view the expenditure as creating an asset. When this objective evidence does not exist, they follow the con-servative practice of recording the expenditure as an expense. *Conser-vatism,* in this context, means applying the accounting treatment that results in the *lowest* (most conservative) estimate of net income for the cur-rent period.

Debit and Credit Rules for Revenue and Expense

LO 3: Explain why revenues are recorded with credits and expenses are recorded with debits.

We have stressed that revenue increases owner's equity and that expenses decrease owner's equity. The debit and credit rules for record-ing revenue and expenses in the ledger accounts are a natural extension of the rules for recording changes in owner's equity. The rules previously stated for recording increases and decreases in owner's equity were as follows:

- *Increases* in owner's equity are recorded by *credits.*
- *Decreases* in owner's equity are recorded by *debits.*

This rule is now extended to cover revenue and expense accounts:

- *Revenue* increases owner's equity; therefore revenue is recorded by a *credit.*
- *Expenses* decrease owner's equity; therefore expenses are recorded by *debits.*

Ledger Accounts for Revenue and Expenses   During the course of an accounting period, a great many revenue and expense transactions occur in the average business. To classify and summarize these numer-ous transactions, a separate ledger account is maintained for each major type of revenue and expense. For example, almost every business maintains accounts for Advertising Expense, Wages (or Salaries) Expense, and Depreciation Expense. At the end of the period, all the advertising expenses appear as debits in the Advertising Expense account. The debit balance of this account represents the total advertising expense of the period and is listed as one of the expense items in the income statement.

Revenue accounts are usually much less numerous than expense accounts. A small business such as Overnight Auto Service (our continuing illustration) may have only one or two types of revenue. Even a very large business may show only two or three types of revenue in its income statement.[2]

Investments and Withdrawals by the Owner

The owner of an unincorporated business may at any time invest assets or withdraw assets from the business. These "investment transactions" cause changes in the amount of owner's equity, but they are **not** considered revenue or expenses of the business.

Investments of assets by the owner are recorded by debiting the asset accounts and crediting the owner's capital account. This transaction is not viewed as revenue, because the business has not sold any merchandise or rendered any service in exchange for the assets received.

The income statement of a sole proprietorship does not include any salary expense representing the managerial services rendered by the owner. One reason for not including a salary to the owner-manager is that individuals in such positions are able to set their salaries at any amount they choose. The use of an unrealistic salary to the proprietor would tend to destroy the usefulness of the income statement for measuring the profitability of the business. Thus, accountants regard the owner-manager as working to earn the **entire net income** of the business, rather than as working for a salary.

Even though the owner does not technically receive a salary, he or she usually makes withdrawals of cash from time to time for personal use. These withdrawals reduce the assets and owner's equity of the business, but they are **not** expenses. Expenses are incurred for the purpose of **generating revenue,** and withdrawals by the owner do not have this purpose.

Withdrawals could be recorded by debiting the owner's capital account. However, a clearer record is created if a separate **drawing account** is debited. (In our Overnight Auto Service example, we will use an account entitled Michael McBryan, Drawing to record withdrawals by the owner.)

---

[2]These businesses maintain more revenue accounts than their income statements suggest. They maintain separate accounts for each type of revenue, and also for each branch or division within the company. For financial reporting purposes, however, the balances in these accounts are combined into a few very broad categories.

Debits to the owner's drawing account result from such transactions as:

1. Withdrawals of cash.
2. Withdrawals of other assets. The owner of a clothing store, for example, may withdraw merchandise for his or her personal use. The amount of the debit to the drawing account would be for the cost of the goods that were withdrawn.
3. Payment of the owner's personal bills out of company funds.

As investments and withdrawals by the owner are not classified as revenue and expenses, they are not included in the income statement. Instead, they are summarized in the statement of owner's equity, which will be discussed later in this chapter.

The debit-credit rules for revenue, expense, and withdrawals by the owner are summarized below:

Debit-Credit rules related to effect on owner's equity

Owner's Equity	
Decreases recorded by Debits	*Increases recorded by Credits*
Expenses decrease owner's equity *Expenses are recorded by Debits*	*Revenue increases owner's equity* *Revenue is recorded by a Credit*
Drawings reduce owner's equity *Drawings are recorded by Debits*	

Recording Revenue and Expense Transactions: An Illustration

In Chapters 1 and 2, we discussed the transactions relating to the creation of Overnight Auto Service in November, 1999. We will now continue this example into December—the first month of Overnight's regular business operations.

But first let us explain a few practical "limitations" on Overnight's activities. Most auto repair businesses render services to a great many customers. They sell parts as well as services. To keep our illustration short, we will assume that Overnight has only *two* customers in December: Airport Shuttle Service and Harbour Cab Co. We also assume that both of these customers purchase the parts used in the maintenance of their vehicles from an independent supplier. Thus, Overnight earns all of its revenue in December from *rendering services,* not from sales of parts or other merchandise. (Sales of merchandise will be discussed in Chapter 5.)

Overnight's transactions in December are described below, along with an analysis of each transaction and illustrations of the entries made in the company's accounting records:

Incurred an expense,
paying cash

Dec. 1   Paid *Daily Tribune* $360 cash for newspaper advertising to be run during December.

ANALYSIS

The cost of advertising was an expense.

The asset Cash was decreased.

DEBIT-CREDIT RULES

Expenses decrease owner's equity and are recorded by debits; debit Advertising Expense $360.

Decreases in assets are recorded by credits; credit Cash $360.

JOURNAL ENTRY

Dec. 1   Advertising Expense 360
                  Cash 360

ENTRIES IN LEDGER ACCOUNTS

Cash		
Nov. 30 Bal. 15,800	Dec. 1	360

Advertising Expense	
Dec. 1	360

Incurred an expense to be
paid later

Dec. 2   Purchased radio advertising from KRAM to be aired in December. The cost was $470, payable within 30 days.

ANALYSIS

The cost of advertising was an expense.

The liability Accounts Payable was incurred.

DEBIT-CREDIT RULES

Expenses decrease owner's equity and are recorded by debits; debit Advertising Expense $470.

Increases in liabilities are recorded by credits; credit Accounts Payable $470.

JOURNAL ENTRY

Dec. 2   Advertising Expense 470
                  Accounts Payable 470

ENTRIES IN LEDGER ACCOUNTS

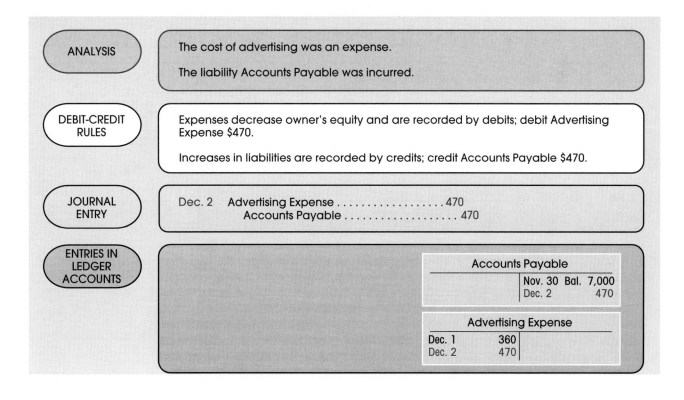

Accounts Payable	
Nov. 30 Bal. 7,000	
Dec. 2	470

Advertising Expense	
Dec. 1	360
Dec. 2	470

When a purchase clearly benefits future accounting periods, it's an asset, not an expense

Dec. 4 Purchased various shop supplies (such as grease, solvents, nuts, and bolts) from NAPA Auto Parts; cost $1,400, due in 30 days. These supplies are expected to meet Overnight's needs for **three or four months.**

ANALYSIS	As these supplies will last for several accounting periods, they are an asset, not an expense of December.[3] A liability was incurred.
DEBIT-CREDIT RULES	Increases in assets are recorded by debits; debit Shop Supplies $1,400. Increases in liabilities are recorded by credits; credit Accounts Payable $1,400.
JOURNAL ENTRY	Dec. 4 Shop Supplies . . . . .1,400 Accounts Payable 1,400

ENTRIES IN LEDGER ACCOUNTS

Shop Supplies		
Nov. 30 Bal.	0	
Dec. 4	1,400	

Accounts Payable		
	Nov. 30 Bal.	7,000
	Dec. 2	470
	Dec. 4	1,400

Revenue earned and collected

Dec. 15 Collected $4,980 cash for repairs made to vehicles of Airport Shuttle Service.

ANALYSIS	The asset Cash was increased. Revenue was earned.
DEBIT-CREDIT RULES	Increases in assets are recorded by debits; debit Cash $4,980. Revenue increases owner's equity and is recorded by a credit; credit Repair Service Revenue $4,980.
JOURNAL ENTRY	Dec. 15 Cash . . . . 4,980 Repair Service Revenue 4,980

ENTRIES IN LEDGER ACCOUNTS

Cash		
Nov. 30 Bal.15,800	Dec. 1	360
Dec. 15 4,980		

Repair Service Revenue		
	Dec. 15	4,980

---

[3]If the supplies are expected to be used within the **current** accounting period, their cost is debited directly to the Supplies Expense account, rather than to an asset account.

A withdrawal of assets by the owner reduces owner's equity—but it's not an "expense"

Dec. 23   Michael McBryan, the owner, withdrew $3,100 cash from the company's bank account for his personal use.

| ANALYSIS | Withdrawals of assets by the owner reduce owner's equity. |
| | The asset Cash was decreased. |

| DEBIT-CREDIT RULES | Decreases in owner's equity are recorded by debits; debit Michael McBryan, Drawing for $3,100. |
| | Decreases in assets are recorded by credits; credit Cash $3,100. |

| JOURNAL ENTRY | Dec. 23   Michael McBryan, Drawing ....3,100 |
| | Cash.................................3,100 |

ENTRIES IN LEDGER ACCOUNTS

Cash			
Nov. 30 Bal.	15,800	Dec. 1	360
Dec. 15	4,980	Dec. 23	3,100

Michael McBryan, Drawing	
Dec. 23	3,100

An investment by the owner is one of the two sources of owner's equity (the other is net income)

Dec. 29   McBryan found that he did not need all of the cash he had withdrawn on December 23, so he redeposited $1,000 in Overnight's bank account.

| ANALYSIS | The asset Cash was increased. |
| | The owner's equity in the business was increased. |

| DEBIT-CREDIT RULES | Increases in assets are recorded by debits; debit Cash $1,000. |
| | Increases in owner's equity are recorded by credits; credit Michael McBryan, Capital, $1,000. |

| JOURNAL ENTRY | Dec. 29   Cash.................................1,000 |
| | Michael McBryan, Capital..............1,000 |

ENTRIES IN LEDGER ACCOUNTS

Cash			
Nov. 30 Bal.	15,800	Dec. 1	360
Dec. 15	4,980	Dec. 23	3,100
Dec. 29	1,000		

Michael McBryan, Capital	
Nov. 30 Bal.	80,000
Dec. 29	1,000

Revenue earned but not yet collected

Dec. 31 Billed Harbour Cab Co. $5,400 for maintenance and repair services rendered during December. The agreement with Harbour Cab calls for payment to be received by January 10.

| ANALYSIS | An asset, Accounts Receivable, was acquired. |
| | Revenue was earned. |

| DEBIT-CREDIT RULES | Increases in assets are recorded by debits; debit Accounts Receivable $5,400. |
| | Revenue increases owner's equity and is recorded by a credit; credit Repair Service Revenue $5,400. |

JOURNAL ENTRY

Dec. 31   Accounts Receivable 5,400
              Repair Service Revenue 5,400

ENTRIES IN LEDGER ACCOUNTS

Accounts Receivable			Repair Service Revenue		
Nov. 30 Bal. 1,200				Dec. 15	4,980
Dec. 31 5,400				Dec. 31	5,400

Incurred an expense, paying cash

Dec. 31 Paid all employees' wages for December, $4,900.

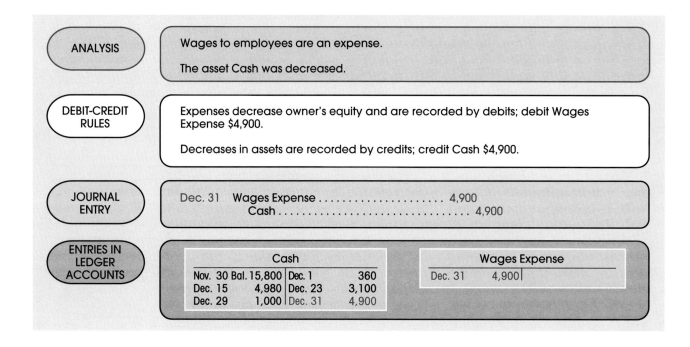

| ANALYSIS | Wages to employees are an expense. |
| | The asset Cash was decreased. |

| DEBIT-CREDIT RULES | Expenses decrease owner's equity and are recorded by debits; debit Wages Expense $4,900. |
| | Decreases in assets are recorded by credits; credit Cash $4,900. |

JOURNAL ENTRY

Dec. 31   Wages Expense 4,900
              Cash 4,900

ENTRIES IN LEDGER ACCOUNTS

Cash				Wages Expense	
Nov. 30 Bal. 15,800	Dec. 1	360		Dec. 31	4,900
Dec. 15 4,980	Dec. 23	3,100			
Dec. 29 1,000	Dec. 31	4,900			

The Journal

In our illustration, journal entries were shown in a very abbreviated form. The actual entries made in Overnight's journal appear below. Notice that these "formal" journal entries include short **explanations** of the transaction, which include such details as the terms of credit transactions and the names of customers and creditors.

Journal entries contain more information than just dollar amounts

Date		Account Titles and Explanation	LP	Debit	Credit
GENERAL JOURNAL					**Page 2**
1999 Dec.	1	Advertising Expense . . . . 　　　Cash . . . . Purchased newspaper advertising from Daily Tribune *to run in December.*	70 1	360	 360
	2	Advertising Expense . . . . 　　　Accounts Payable . . . . Purchased radio advertising on account from KRAM; payment due in 30 days.	70 32	470	 470
	4	Shop Supplies . . . . 　　　Accounts Payable . . . . Purchased shop supplies on account from NAPA; payment due in 30 days.	6 32	1,400	 1,400
	15	Cash . . . . 　　　Repair Service Revenue . . . . Repair services rendered to Airport Shuttle.	1 60	4,980	 4,980
	23	Michael McBryan, Drawing . . . . 　　　Cash . . . . Owner withdrew cash from business.	52 1	3,100	 3,100
	29	Cash . . . . 　　　Michael McBryan, Capital . . . . Owner invested cash in the business	1 50	1,000	 1,000
	31	Accounts Receivable . . . . 　　　Repair Service Revenue . . . . Billed Harbour Cab for services rendered in December.	4 60	5,400	 5,400
	31	Wages Expense . . . . 　　　Cash . . . . Paid all wages for December.	72 1	4,900	 4,900

The column headings at the top of the illustrated journal page *(Date, Account Titles and Explanation, LP, Debit,* and *Credit)* are seldom used in practice. They are included here as an instructional guide but will be omitted from some of the later illustrations of journal entries.

The Ledger

After the posting of these December transactions, Overnight's ledger accounts appear as shown on the following page. To conserve space, we illustrate these accounts in "T account" form, rather than the running balance

THE LEDGER

Asset Accounts

Cash — 1

Nov. 1	80,000	Nov. 3	52,000
Nov. 25	600	Nov. 5	6,000
		Nov. 30	6,800
Nov. 30 Bal.		Dec. 1	15,800
Dec. 15	4,980	Dec. 23	3,100
Dec. 29	1,000	Dec. 31	4,900

Bal. $13,420

Accounts Receivable — 4

Nov. 20	1,800	Nov. 25	600
Nov. 30 Bal.	1,200		
Dec. 31	5,400		

Bal. $6,600

Shop Supplies — 6

Dec. 4	1,400		

Bal. $1,400

Land — 20

Nov. 3	52,000		
Nov. 30 Bal.	52,000		

Bal. $52,000

Building — 22

Nov. 5	36,000		
Nov. 30 Bal.	36,000		

Bal. $36,000

Tools and Equipment — 25

Nov. 17	13,800	Nov. 20	1,800
Nov. 30 Bal.	12,000		

Bal. $12,000

Liability and Owner's Equity Accounts

Notes Payable — 30

		Nov. 5	30,000
		Nov. 30 Bal.	30,000

Bal. $30,000

Accounts Payable — 32

Nov. 30	6,800	Nov. 17	13,800
		Nov. 30 Bal.	7,000
		Dec. 2	470
		Dec. 4	1,400

Bal. $8,870

Michael McBryan, Capital — 50

		Nov. 1	80,000
		Nov. 30 Bal.	80,000
		Dec. 29	1,000

Bal. $81,000

Michael McBryan, Drawing — 52

Dec. 23	3,100		

Bal. $3,100

Repair Service Revenue — 60

		Dec. 15	4,980
		Dec. 31	5,400

Bal. $10,380

Advertising Expense — 70

Dec. 1	360		
Dec. 2	470		

Bal. $830

Wages Expense — 72

Dec. 31	4,900		

Bal. $4,900

form used in Chapter 2. But for convenience, we show in **black** the **December 31 balance** of each account. (Debit balances appear to the left of the account, credit balances appear to the right. We do not include the balances **within** the accounts, because some of them will be **adjusted** in the next step in the accounting cycle.)

The accounts in this illustration appear in **financial statement order**—that is, balance sheet accounts first (assets, liabilities, and owner's equity), followed by income statement accounts (revenue and expenses). The sequence of accounts within the balance sheet categories was explained in Chapter 2. Within the categories of revenue and expense, accounts may be listed in any order.

The Trial Balance

A trial balance prepared from Overnight's ledger at December 31 is shown below.

OVERNIGHT AUTO SERVICE Trial Balance December 31, 1999		
Cash	$ 13,420	
Accounts receivable	6,600	
Shop supplies	1,400	
Land	52,000	
Building	36,000	
Tools and equipment	12,000	
Notes payable		$ 30,000
Accounts payable		8,870
Michael McBryan, capital		81,000
Michael McBryan, drawing	3,100	
Repair service revenue		10,380
Advertising expense	830	
Wages expense	4,900	
	$130,250	$130,250

A trial balance proves the equality of debits and credits—but it also gives you a "feel" for how the business stands. But wait—there's more to consider

This trial balance proves the equality of the debit and credit entries in the company's ledger. Notice that the trial balance now contains income statement accounts as well as balance sheet accounts.

ADJUSTING ENTRIES: THE NEXT STEP IN THE ACCOUNTING CYCLE

LO 4: Explain the nature of adjusting entries and record supplies expense.

We will now see that there is more to the measurement of business income than merely recording transactions. Many transactions affect the revenue or expenses of **two or more** accounting periods. For example, a business may purchase equipment that will last for many years, an insurance policy that covers 12 months, or—as Overnight has done—enough supplies to last for several months.

Initially, the costs of such items are recorded as **assets,** because they will benefit the business in future accounting periods. Over time, these assets are **used up,** and their costs **become expenses** of the periods in which the goods or services are used.

How do businesses allocate the costs of such assets to expense over a span of several accounting periods? The answer is by making **adjusting entries** at the end of each accounting period. The purpose of these entries is to assign to each accounting period the appropriate amounts of revenue and expense. These entries "adjust" the balances of various ledger accounts—hence the name, ***adjusting entries.***

There are several different types of adjusting entries, some affecting expenses and others affecting revenue. In fact, a business may make a dozen or more adjusting entries in each period. To keep our illustration short, we will assume that Overnight's accounts require only three adjusting entries at December 31, all of which involve the recognition of expenses. Other types of adjusting entries, including those affecting revenue, will be discussed and illustrated in Chapter 4.

Shop Supplies: An Asset That Turns into an Expense

On December 4, Overnight purchased for $1,400 a quantity of shop supplies expected to last for three or four months. At the date of purchase, this $1,400 cost was debited to an asset account (Shop Supplies), because it was expected to ***benefit future accounting periods.*** But as these supplies are ***used,*** this asset gradually ***becomes an expense.*** This concept is illustrated in the following diagram:

As an asset is "used up," it becomes an expense

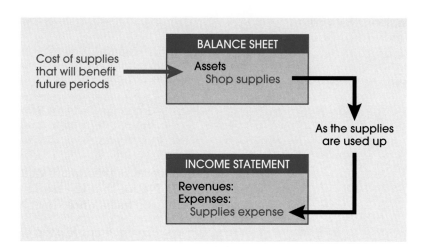

Assume that during December, ***$400*** worth of Overnight's shop supplies was used in business operations, and that approximately ***$1,000*** worth remains on hand—available for use in future periods. The $400 of supplies ***used*** during December should be ***recognized as expense*** in that month; the $1,000 in supplies ***still on hand*** should appear in the December 31 balance sheet as an ***asset.***

To transfer the cost of the supplies used during the month from the asset account to an expense account, Overnight will make the following ***adjusting entry*** at December 31:

GENERAL JOURNAL					Page 3
Date		Account Titles and Explanation	LP	Debit	Credit
1999 Dec.	31	Supplies Expense . . . . Shop Supplies . . . . To recognize as expense the cost of shop supplies used in December.	74 6	400	400

The adjusting entry to recognize supplies used up as an expense

The idea of shop supplies being used up over several months is easy to understand. But did you know the same concept applies to assets such as buildings, automobiles, and even railroad tracks?

The Concept of Depreciation

LO 5: Define and record depreciation (also called amortization) expense.

Depreciable assets are ***physical objects*** that retain their size and shape, but eventually wear out or become obsolete. They are not physically consumed, as are assets such as supplies, but nonetheless their economic usefulness is "used up" over time. Examples of depreciable assets include buildings and all types of equipment, fixtures, furnishings—and even railroad tracks. Land, however, is ***not*** viewed as a depreciable asset, as it has an ***unlimited*** useful life.

Each period, a portion of a depreciable asset's usefulness ***expires.*** Therefore, a corresponding portion of its cost is recognized as ***depreciation expense.***

What Is Depreciation (Amortization)?   In accounting, the term **depreciation** means the ***systematic allocation of the cost of a depreciable asset to expense*** over the asset's useful life. This process is illustrated below:

Depreciation: A process of allocating the cost of a depreciable asset to expense

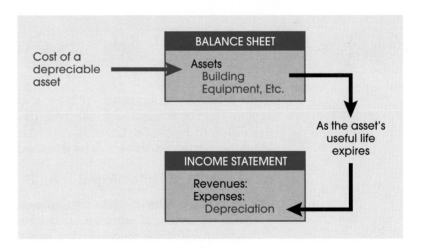

Notice the similarity of this diagram to that on the previous page.

Depreciation ***is not*** an attempt to record changes in the asset's market value. In the short run, the market value of some depreciable assets may even increase, but the process of depreciation continues anyway. The rationale for depreciation lies in the ***matching principle.*** Our goal is to offset a reasonable portion of the asset's cost against revenue in each period of the asset's **useful life**

Depreciation expense occurs continuously over the life of the asset, but there are no daily "depreciation transactions." Therefore, **_adjusting entries_** are needed at the end of each accounting period to transfer an appropriate amount of the asset's cost to depreciation expense.

Depreciation Is Only an Estimate   The "appropriate amount" of depreciation expense is **_only an estimate._** After all, we cannot look at a building or a piece of equipment and determine precisely how much of its economic usefulness has expired during the current period.

The most widely used means of estimating periodic depreciation expense is the **straight-line method**. Under the straight-line approach, an **_equal portion_** of the asset's cost is allocated to depreciation expense in every period of the asset's estimated useful life. The formula for computing depreciation expense by the straight-line method is:[4]

$$\text{Depreciation expense (per period)} = \frac{\text{Cost of the asset}}{\text{Estimated useful life}}$$

The use of an **_estimated useful life_** is the major reason why depreciation expense is **_only an estimate._** In most cases, management does not know in advance exactly how long the asset will remain in use.

CASE IN POINT   How long does a building last? For purposes of computing depreciation expense, most companies estimate about 30 to 40 years. But the Empire State Building was built in 1931, and it's not likely to be torn down anytime soon. And how about Windsor Castle or the CN Tower? While these are not "typical" examples, they illustrate the difficulty in estimating in advance just how long depreciable assets may remain in use.

In their financial statements, most companies determine depreciation expense by the straight-line method. In income tax returns, however, they use different methods. Alternatives to the straight-line method of computing depreciation expense will be discussed in Chapter 10.

Recording Depreciation Expense: An Illustration

Overnight Auto Service owns two categories of depreciable assets: its building, and its tools and equipment. Because these categories of assets have different useful lives, depreciation must be computed separately for each category. Overnight elects to compute depreciation expense by the straight-line method.

Depreciation on the Building   Overnight purchased its building for $36,000. Because the building was old, McBryan estimates that it has a

---

[4]At this point in our discussion, we are ignoring any possible **_residual value_** that might be recovered upon disposal of the asset. Residual values are discussed in Chapter 10.

remaining useful life of only 20 years. Thus, Overnight will recognize annual depreciation expense equal to 1/20 of the building's cost, or **$1,800** ($36,000 cost ÷ 20-year estimated useful life). On a monthly basis, the depreciation expense amounts to **$150** ($36,000 cost ÷ 240 months).

The adjusting entry to record depreciation on this building for the month of December appears below:

Adjusting entry to record depreciation of the building

GENERAL JOURNAL					Page 3
Date		Account Titles and Explanation	LP	Debit	Credit
1999 Dec.	31	Depreciation Expense: Building	76	150	
		Accumulated Depreciation: Building . .	23		150
		To record one month's depreciation on building (cost, $36,000, divided by estimated useful life, 240 months, equals $150 per month).			

The **Depreciation Expense** account will appear in Overnight's income statement for December, along with the other expenses for the month. The **Accumulated Depreciation** account will appear in the balance sheet as a deduction from the balance of the Building account, as shown below:

Showing accumulated depreciation in the balance sheet

OVERNIGHT AUTO SERVICE
Partial Balance Sheet
December 31, 1999

Assets

Cash		$13,420
Accounts receivable		6,600
Shop supplies		1,000
Land		52,000
Building	$36,000	
Less: Accumulated depreciation	150	35,850

The end result of crediting the Accumulated Depreciation: Building account is much the same as if the credit had been made to the Building account; that is, the net amount shown on the balance sheet for the building is reduced from $36,000 to $35,850. Although the credit side of a depreciation entry **could** be made directly to the asset account, it is customary and more efficient to record such credits in a separate account entitled **Accumulated Depreciation.** The original cost of the asset and the total amount of depreciation recorded over the years can more easily be determined from the ledger when separate accounts are maintained for the asset and for the accumulated depreciation.

Accumulated Depreciation: Building is an example of a **contra-asset account**, because it has a credit balance and is offset against an asset account (Building) to produce the proper balance sheet amount for the asset.

Depreciation on the Tools and Equipment Overnight also must record depreciation on its tools and equipment. These assets cost $12,000, and management estimates that they will remain in service for about 5 years.

Thus, the monthly depreciation expense amounts to **$200** ($12,000 cost ÷ 60 months). The adjusting entry to recognize this monthly expense is:

Adjusting entry to record depreciation of tools and equipment

GENERAL JOURNAL					Page 3
Date		Account Titles and Explanation	LP	Debit	Credit

1999
Dec.
	31	*Depreciation Expense: Tools and Equipment*
		    Accumulated Depreciation: Tools and
		        Equipment . . . .
		To record depreciation on tools and
		equipment ($12,000 ÷ 60 months).
			78
			
			26
				200	
					
					200

Similar adjusting entries to recognize depreciation expense on the building and tools and equipment will be made each month throughout the assets' useful lives. Once the assets have become "fully depreciated," that is, their total cost has been recognized as depreciation expense, the recognition of depreciation will stop. (We did not recognize depreciation on these assets in November, because Overnight had not yet begun its regular business operations. Depreciation begins when the assets are **placed in use** for the intended business purpose.)

Depreciation Is a "Noncash" Expense   We have made the point that net income does **not** represent an inflow of cash or any other asset. Rather, it is a **computation** of the overall effect of certain business transactions upon owner's equity. The computation and recognition of depreciation expense illustrate this point.

As depreciable assets "expire," owner's equity declines; but **there is no corresponding cash outlay** in the current period. For this reason, depreciation often is called a "noncash expense." Often it represents the **largest difference** between net income and the cash flows (receipts and payments) resulting from business operations.

The Adjusted Trial Balance

After all the necessary adjusting entries have been journalized and posted, an **adjusted trial balance** is prepared to prove that the ledger is still in balance. It also provides a complete listing of the account balances to be used in preparing the financial statements. The following adjusted trial balance differs from the trial balance shown on page 121 because it includes several new account titles, and the balances in some existing accounts have been "adjusted."

Once an adjusted trial balance has been prepared, the process of recording changes in financial position for this accounting period is complete. **Financial statements are prepared directly from the adjusted trial balance.**

Every account in the adjusted trial balance contains its end-of-the-period balance, **with the exception of the owner's capital account.** During the accounting period, many transactions affecting owner's equity were not recorded directly in the owner's capital account. Rather, these transactions were recorded in the various revenue and expense accounts, or in the owner's drawing account. Therefore, the balance in the owner's capital account shown in the adjusted trial balance is **not** completely up to date. This will not cause a problem; as we prepare a "set" of financial statements, the amount of the owner's equity at the *end* of the period will become apparent.

Adjusted trial balance—accounts affected by end-of-period adjusting entries are shown in black

OVERNIGHT AUTO SERVICE Adjusted Trial Balance December 31, 1999		
Cash	$ 13,420	
Accounts receivable	6,600	
Shop supplies	1,000	
Land	52,000	
Building	36,000	
Accumulated depreciation: building		$ 150
Tools and equipment	12,000	
Accumulated depreciation: tools and equipment .		200
Notes payable		30,000
Accounts payable		8,870
Michael McBryan, capital		81,000
Michael McBryan, drawing	3,100	
Repair service revenue		10,380
Advertising expense	830	
Wage expense	4,900	
Supplies expense	400	
Depreciation expense: building	150	
Depreciation expense: tools and equipment	200	
	$130,600	$130,600

Let us now look at the process of preparing a set of financial statements directly from the amounts listed in the adjusted trial balance.

PREPARING A "SET" OF FINANCIAL STATEMENTS

LO 6: Prepare statements of income and of owner's equity. Explain how these statements relate to the balance sheet.

Now that Overnight Auto Service has been operating for a month, managers and outside parties will want to know more about the company than just its financial position. They will want to know the ***results of operations***—whether the month's activities have been profitable or unprofitable. To provide this additional information, we will prepare a more complete set of financial statements, consisting of an income statement, a statement of owner's equity, and a balance sheet.[5] These statements are illustrated on the following page.

The Income Statement

The revenue and expenses shown in the income statement are taken directly from the company's adjusted trial balance. Overnight's income statement for December shows that revenue exceeded the expenses for the month, thus producing a net income of $3,900. Bear in mind, however, that our measurement of net income is not absolutely accurate or precise, because of the ***assumptions and estimates*** in the accounting process.

An income statement has certain limitations. Remember that the amounts shown for depreciation expense are based upon ***estimates*** of the

---

[5]A complete set of financial statements also includes a cash flow statement, which will be illustrated and discussed in Chapter 19.

Income statement for
December . . .

OVERNIGHT AUTO SERVICE
Income Statement
For the Month Ended December 31, 1999

Revenue:		
Repair service revenue		$10,380
Expenses:		
Advertising expense	$ 830	
Wages expense	4,900	
Supplies expense	400	
Depreciation expense: building . .	150	
Depreciation expense: tools and		
equipment	200	6,480
Net income		$ 3,900

Net income
increases
owner's equity

. . . a statement of owner's
equity . . .

OVERNIGHT AUTO SERVICE
Statement of Owner's Equity
For the Month Ended December 31, 1999

Michael McBryan, capital, Nov. 30, 1999	$ 80,000	
Add: **Net income for December**	3,900	
Additional investment by owner	1,000	
Subtotal	$ 84,900	
Less: Withdrawals by owner	3,100	
Michael McBryan, capital, Dec. 31, 1999	$ 81,800	

The ending
balance of
owner's equity
appears in the
balance sheet

. . . and the month-end
balance sheet (in report
form)

OVERNIGHT AUTO SERVICE
Balance Sheet
December 31, 1999

Assets

Cash		$ 13,420
Accounts receivable		6,600
Supplies		1,000
Land		52,000
Building	$36,000	
Less: Accumulated depreciation . .	150	35,850
Tools and equipment	$12,000	
Less: Accumulated depreciation . .	200	11,800
Total assets		$120,670

Liabilities & Owner's Equity

Liabilities:		
Notes payable		$ 30,000
Accounts payable		8,870
Total liabilities		$ 38,870
Owner's equity:		
Michael McBryan, capital, Dec. 31, 1999 . . .		81,800
Total liabilities & owner's equity		$120,670

useful lives of the company's building and office equipment. Also, the income statement includes only those events that have been *evidenced by business transactions.* Perhaps during December, Overnight's advertising has caught the attention of many potential customers. A good "customer base" is certainly an important step toward profitable operations. However, the development of a customer base is not reflected in the income statement because its value cannot be measured *objectively* until actual transactions take place. Despite these limitations, the income statement is of vital importance and indicates that the new business has been profitable during its first month of operation.

Alternative titles for the income statement include *statement of earnings, statement of operations,* and *profit and loss statement.* However, *income statement* is one of the two most popular terms for this important financial statement.[6] In summary, we can say that an income statement is used to summarize the *operating results* of a business by matching the revenue earned during a given time period with the expenses incurred in obtaining that revenue.

The Statement of Owner's Equity

The **statement of owner's equity** summarizes the increases and decreases during the accounting period in the amount of owner's equity. Increases result from earning net income and from additional investments by the owner; decreases result from net losses and from withdrawals of assets by the owner.

The owner's equity at the beginning of the period ($80,000) may be obtained from the ledger or from the balance sheet of the preceding period. As we have just illustrated, the amount of net income or net loss for the period is determined in the company's *income statement.* Additional investments by the owner may be determined by reviewing the credit column of the owner's capital account in the ledger. Withdrawals during the period are indicated by the balance in the owner's drawing account. By adjusting the beginning amount of owner's equity for the increases and decreases occurring during the period, we are able to determine the owner's equity at the end of the period. This amount, *$81,800* in our example, will also appear in the company's December 31 balance sheet.

The Balance Sheet

The balance sheet lists the amounts of the company's assets, liabilities, and owner's equity at the *end* of the accounting period. The balances of the asset and liability accounts are taken directly from the adjusted trial balance on page 127. The amount of owner's equity at the end of the period, $81,800, was determined in the *statement of owner's equity.*

---

[6]Clarence Byrd and Ida Chen, *Financial Reporting in Canada,* Twenty-second Edition (CICA, Toronto, 1997), p. 77. The other term is "statement of earnings."

Previous illustrations of balance sheets have been arranged in *account form*—that is, with assets on the left and liabilities and owner's equity on the right. The illustration on page 128 is arranged in *report form,* with the liabilities and owner's equity sections listed below rather than to the right of the asset section. Both the account form and the report form of balance sheet are widely used, with the latter being far more popular.[7]

Relationship Among the Financial Statements

A set of financial statements becomes easier to understand if we recognize that the income statement, statement of owner's equity, and balance sheet all are *related to one another.* These relationships are emphasized by the arrows in the right-hand margin of our illustration on page 128.

The balance sheet prepared at the end of the preceding period and the one prepared at the end of the current period both include the amount of owner's equity at the respective balance sheet dates. The statement of owner's equity summarizes the *changes* in owner's equity occurring between these two balance sheet dates. The income statement explains in greater detail the change in owner's equity resulting from profitable—or unprofitable—operation of the business. Thus, the income statement and the statement of owner's equity provide informative links between successive balance sheets.

CLOSING THE "TEMPORARY" EQUITY ACCOUNTS

LO 7: Explain the purposes of closing entries; prepare these entries.

As previously stated, revenue *increases* owner's equity, and expenses and withdrawals by the owner *decrease* owner's equity. If the only financial statement that we needed was a balance sheet, these changes in owner's equity could be recorded directly in the owner's capital account. However, owners, managers, investors, and others need to know amounts of specific revenues and expenses, and the amount of net income earned in the period. Therefore, we maintain separate ledger accounts to measure each type of revenue and expense, and the owner's drawings.

The revenue, expense, and drawing accounts are called *temporary* accounts, or *nominal* accounts, because they accumulate the transactions of *only one accounting period.* At the end of this accounting period, the changes in owner's equity accumulated in these temporary accounts are transferred into the owner's capital account, through a temporary clearing account called **Income Summary**. This process serves two purposes. First, it *updates the balance of the owner's capital account* for changes in owner's equity occurring during the accounting period. Second, it *returns the balances of the temporary accounts to zero,* so that they are ready for measuring the revenue, expenses, and drawings of the next accounting period.

---

[7]Ibid., p. 46.

The owner's capital account and other balance sheet accounts are called **permanent** or **real** accounts, because their balances continue to exist beyond the current accounting period. The process of transferring the balances of the temporary accounts into the owner's capital account is called **closing** the accounts. The journal entries made for the purpose of closing the temporary accounts are called **closing entries**.

Revenue and expense accounts are **closed** at the end of each accounting period by **transferring their balances** to an account called **Income Summary.** When the credit balances of the revenue accounts and the debit balances of the expense accounts have been transferred into this account, the balance of this Income Summary will be the **net income** or **net loss** for the period. If the revenue (credit balances) exceeds the expenses (debit balances), the Income Summary account will have a credit balance representing net income. Conversely, if expenses exceed revenue, the Income Summary will have a debit balance representing net loss. This is consistent with the rule that increases in owner's equity are recorded by credits and decreases are recorded by debits. The balance in the **Income Summary** account is then closed by transferring its balance to the owner's capital account.

It is common practice to close the accounts only once a year, but for illustration, we will demonstrate the closing of the accounts of Overnight Auto Service at December 31 after only one month of business operations.

Closing Entries for Revenue Accounts

Revenue accounts have credit balances. Therefore, closing a revenue account means transferring its credit balance to the Income Summary account. This transfer is accomplished by a journal entry debiting the revenue account in an amount equal to its credit balance, with an offsetting credit to the Income Summary account. The debit portion of this closing entry returns the balance of the revenue account to zero; the credit portion transfers the former balance of the revenue account into the Income Summary account.

The only revenue account of Overnight Auto Service is Repair Service Revenue, which had a credit balance of $10,380 at December 31. The closing entry is as follows:

GENERAL JOURNAL					Page 3
Date		Account Titles and Explanation	LP	Debit	Credit
1999 Dec.	31	Repair Service Revenue . . . . Income Summary . . . . To close the Repair Service Revenue account.	60 53	10,380	10,380

Closing a revenue account

After this closing entry has been posted, the two accounts affected will appear as follows. A few details of account structure have been omitted to simplify the illustration; a directional arrow has been added to show the transfer of the $10,380 balance of the revenue account into the Income Summary account.

Repair Service Revenue					60	Income Summary					53
Date	Expl.	Ref	Debit	Credit	Balance	Date	Expl.	Ref	Debit	Credit	Balance
Dec. 15		2		4,980	4,980	Dec. 31	Revenue	3		10,380	10,380
31		2		5,400	10,380						
31	To close	3	10,380		–0–						

Closing Entries for Expense Accounts

Expense accounts have debit balances. Closing an expense account means transferring its debit balance to the Income Summary account. The journal entry to close an expense account, therefore, consists of a credit to the expense account in an amount equal to its debit balance, with an offsetting debit to the Income Summary account.

There are five expense accounts in the ledger of Overnight Auto Service. Five separate journal entries could be made to close these five expense accounts, but the use of one *compound journal entry* is an easier, time-saving method of closing all five expense accounts. A compound journal entry is an entry that includes debits to more than one account or credits to more than one account.

Closing the various expense accounts by use of a compound journal entry

GENERAL JOURNAL				Page 3	
Date		Account Titles and Explanation	LP	Debit	Credit
1999					
Dec.	31	Income Summary	53	6,480	
		Advertising Expense	70		830
		Wages Expense	72		4,900
		Supplies Expense	74		400
		Depreciation Expense: Building	76		150
		Depreciation Expense: Tools and			
		Equipment	78		200
		To close the expense accounts.			

After this closing entry has been posted, the Income Summary account has a credit balance of *$3,900,* and the five expense accounts have zero balances, as shown on the following page.

Expense accounts have zero balances after closing entries have been posted

Advertising Expense						Account No. 70
Date		Explanation	Ref	Debit	Credit	Balance
1999 Dec.	1		2	360		360
	2		2	470		830
	31	To close	3		830	-0-

Wages Expense						Account No. 72
Date		Explanation	Ref	Debit	Credit	Balance
1999 Dec.	31		2	4,900		4,900
	31	To close	3		4,900	-0-

Supplies Expense						Account No. 74
Date		Explanation	Ref	Debit	Credit	Balance
1999 Dec.	31		3	400		400
	31	To close	3		400	-0-

Depreciation Expense: Building						Account No. 76
Date		Explanation	Ref	Debit	Credit	Balance
1999 Dec.	31		3	150		150
	31	To close	3		150	-0-

Depreciation Expense: Tools and Equipment						Account No. 78
Date		Explanation	Ref	Debit	Credit	Balance
1999 Dec.	31		3	200		200
	31	To close	3		200	-0-

Income Summary						Account No. 53
Date		Explanation	Ref	Debit	Credit	Balance
1999 Dec.	31	Revenue	3		10,380	10,380
	31	**Expenses**	3	**6,480**		3,900

Closing the Income Summary Account

The five expense accounts have now been closed and the total amount of $6,480 formerly contained in these accounts appears in the debit column of the Income Summary account. The revenue of $10,380 earned during December appears in the credit column of the Income Summary account. Since the credit entry of $10,380 representing December revenue is larger than the debit of $6,480 representing December expenses, the account has a credit balance of $3,900—the net income for December.

The net income of $3,900 earned during December causes the owner's equity to increase. The *credit* balance of the Income Summary account is, therefore, transferred to the owner's equity account by the following closing entry:

Net income increases the owner's equity

		GENERAL JOURNAL			Page 3
Date		Account Titles and Explanation	LP	Debit	Credit
1999 Dec.	31	Income Summary . . . . Michael McBryan, capital . . . . To close the Income Summary account for December by transferring the net income to the owner's capital account.	53 50	3,900	 3,900

After this closing entry has been posted, the Income Summary account has a zero balance, and the net income for December will appear as an increase or credit entry in the owner's capital account, as shown below.

Income Summary account is closed to the owner's capital account

		Income Summary				Account No. 53
Date		Explanation	Ref	Debit	Credit	Balance
1999 Dec.	31 31 31	Revenue Expenses To close	3 3 3	 6,480 3,900	10,380	10,380 3,900 –0–

		Michael McBryan, Capital				Account No. 50
Date		Explanation	Ref	Debit	Credit	Balance
1999 Nov. Dec.	1 29 31	Investment by owner Additional investment by owner Net income for December	1 2 3		80,000 1,000 3,900	80,000 81,000 84,900

In our illustration the business has operated profitably with revenue in excess of expenses. Not every business is so fortunate: if the expenses of a business are larger than its revenue, the Income Summary account will have a debit balance, representing a *net loss* for the accounting period. In that case, the closing of the Income Summary account requires a debit to the owner's capital account and an offsetting credit to the Income Summary account. The owner's equity will, of course, be reduced by the amount of the loss debited to the capital account.

Note that the Income Summary account is used only at the end of the period *when the accounts are being closed.* The Income Summary account has no entries and no balance except during the process of closing the accounts at the end of the accounting period.

Closing the Owner's Drawing Account

As explained earlier in this chapter, withdrawals of cash or other assets by the owner are not considered an expense of the business and, therefore, are not a factor in determining the net income for the period. Since drawings by the owner do not constitute an expense, the owner's drawing account is closed not into the Income Summary account but directly to the owner's capital account. The following journal entry serves to close the drawing account in the ledger of Overnight Auto Service at December 31.

Drawing account is closed into the owner's capital account

GENERAL JOURNAL					Page 3
Date		**Account Titles and Explanation**	**LP**	**Debit**	**Credit**

1999 Dec.	31	Michael McBryan, Capital . . . .
		    Michael McBryan, Drawing . . . .
		    To close the owner's drawing account
			50
			52
				3,100	3,100

After this closing entry has been posted, the drawing account will have a zero balance, and the amount withdrawn by McBryan during December will appear as a deduction or debit entry in his capital account.

Michael McBryan, Drawing						Account No. 52	
Date		**Explanation**	**Ref**	**Debit**	**Credit**	**Balance**
1999 Dec.	23	Withdrawal	2	3,100		3,100
	31	To close	3		*3,100*	–0–

One account now shows the total equity of the owner

Michael McBryan, Capital						Account No. 50	
Date		**Explanation**	**Ref**	**Debit**	**Credit**	**Balance**
1999 Nov.	1	Investment by owner	1		80,000	80,000
Dec.	29	Additional investment by owner	2		1,000	81,000
	31	Net income for December	3		3,900	84,900
	31	To close drawing account	3	3,100		81,800

Summary of the Closing Process

Let us now summarize the process of closing the accounts.

1. Close the various **revenue** accounts by transferring their balances into the Income Summary account.
2. Close the various **expense** accounts by transferring their balances into the Income Summary account.
3. Close the **Income Summary account** by transferring its balance into the owner's capital account.
4. Close the owner's **drawing** account into the owner's capital account. (The balance of the owner's capital account in the ledger will now be the same as the amount of owner's equity appearing in the balance sheet.)

The closing of the accounts may be illustrated graphically by use of T accounts as follows:

Flowchart of the closing process

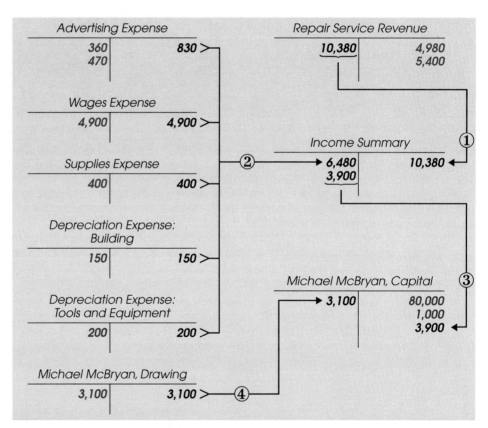

After-Closing Trial Balance

After the revenue and expense accounts have been closed, it is desirable to prepare an **after-closing trial balance**, which will consist of balance sheet accounts **only**. There is always the possibility that an error in posting the closing entries may have upset the equality of debits and credits in the ledger. The after-closing trial balance is prepared from the ledger. It gives assurance that the accounts are in balance and ready for the recording of the transactions of the new accounting period. The after-closing trial balance of Overnight Auto Service follows:

OVERNIGHT AUTO SERVICE After-Closing Trial Balance December 31, 1999		
Cash	$ 13,420	
Accounts receivable	6,600	
Shop supplies	1,000	
Land	52,000	
Building	36,000	
Accumulated depreciation: building		$ 150
Tools and equipment	12,000	
Accumulated depreciation: tools and equipment		200
Notes payable		30,000
Accounts payable		8,870
Michael McBryan, capital		81,800
	$121,020	$121,020

Only the balance sheet accounts remain open

THE COMPLETE ACCOUNTING CYCLE

LO 8: Describe the steps in the accounting cycle.

In Chapter 2, we introduced the concept of the **accounting cycle**. Our illustration, however, was limited to transactions affecting the balance sheet. Now we have explained and illustrated a **complete** accounting cycle—from the initial recording of transactions to the preparation of a "set" of financial statements.

The steps comprising this cycle are listed below:

1. ***Journalize (record) transactions.*** Enter all transactions in the journal, thus creating a chronological record of events.
2. ***Post to ledger accounts.*** Post debits and credits from the journal to the proper ledger accounts, thus creating a record classified by accounts.
3. ***Prepare a trial balance.*** Prove the equality of debits and credits in the ledger.
4. ***Make end-of-period adjustments.*** Draft adjusting entries in the general journal, and post to ledger accounts.
5. ***Prepare an adjusted trial balance.*** Prove again the equality of debits and credits in the ledger. (***Note:*** These are the amounts used in the preparation of financial statements.)
6. ***Prepare financial statements and appropriate disclosures.*** An income statement shows the results of operation for the period. A statement of owner's equity shows changes in owner's equity during the period. A balance sheet shows the financial position of the business at the end of the period. Financial statements should be accompanied by ***notes*** disclosing facts necessary for the proper ***interpretation*** of those statements.
7. ***Journalize and post the closing entries.*** The closing entries "zero" the revenue, expense, and drawing accounts, making them

ready for recording the events of the next accounting period. These entries also bring the balance in the owner's capital account up-to-date.

8. ***Prepare an after-closing trial balance.*** This step ensures that the ledger remains in balance after posting of the closing entries.

The Accrual Basis of Accounting

LO 9: Distinguish between the accrual basis and the cash basis of accounting.

The policy of recognizing revenue in the accounting records when it is ***earned,*** and recognizing expenses when the related goods or services are ***used,*** is called the **accrual basis** of accounting. The purpose of accrual accounting is to measure the profitability of the ***economic activities conducted*** during the accounting period.

The most important concept involved in accrual accounting is the ***matching principle.*** Revenue is offset with all of the expenses incurred in generating that revenue, thus providing a measure of the overall profitability of the economic activity.

An alternative to the accrual basis is something called **cash basis** accounting. Under cash basis accounting, revenue is recognized when cash is collected from the customer, rather than when the company sells goods or renders services. Expenses are recognized when payment is made, rather than when the related goods or services are used in business operations.

The cash basis of accounting measures the amounts of cash received and paid out during the period, but it does ***not*** provide a good measure of the ***profitability of activities*** undertaken during the period.

CASE IN POINT Airlines sell many tickets weeks or even months ***in advance*** of scheduled flights. Yet many expenses relating to a flight—such as salaries of the flight crew and the cost of fuel used—may not be paid until ***after*** the flight has occurred. Thus, the cash basis often would fail to "match" in one accounting period both the revenue and all expenses relating to specific flights.

Generally accepted accounting principles usually ***require*** use of the accrual basis in measuring revenue, expenses, and net income. However, the cash basis is generally acceptable (and advantageous) in individuals' ***income tax returns.*** (Remember that income tax rules often differ from financial reporting requirements.)

In this textbook, we will emphasize the ***accrual basis*** of accounting. Accrual basis accounting is used by virtually all businesses that distribute their financial statements to investors, shareholders, creditors, and other decision makers outside of the business organization.

The Usefulness of Revenue and Expense Data to Managers

The revenue and expense data used by managers in planning and controlling business operations differ significantly from the income statements used by outsiders. Outsiders usually receive income statements on either a quarterly or an annual basis. Managers, on the other hand, need information about daily, weekly, and monthly performance. Also, the income statements distributed to investors and creditors describe the profitability of the business *viewed as a whole.* Managers need to know the revenue and expenses relating to *specific departments* within the organization.

In summary, the revenue and expense information used by managers generally covers much shorter time periods and is more detailed than the information contained in a formal income statement. For example, the manager of a large department store might receive a sales report every morning, showing separately the revenue earned by each sales department in the store on the preceding day.

The revenue and expense reports prepared daily or weekly for use by managers show only *selected* revenue and expenses—usually those items that are under the *direct control* of individual managers. Thus, revenue and expense reports usually do not contain all of the information necessary to determine net income.

Managers may compare the revenue and expenses of individual departments with such standards as past performance, budgeted performance for the current and future periods, and the performance of other departments. Their basic goal is to see how well each department within the business is performing.

SOME CONCLUDING REMARKS

The Accounting Cycle in Perspective

We view the accounting cycle as an efficient means of introducing basic accounting terms, concepts, processes, and reports. This is why we introduce it early in the course.

But, please, do not confuse familiarity with this sequence of procedures with a knowledge of *accounting.* The accounting cycle is but one accounting process—and a relatively simple one at that.

Computers have freed accountants today to focus upon the more *analytical* aspects of their discipline. These include, for example:

- Determining the information needs of decision makers
- Designing systems to provide the information quickly and efficiently
- Evaluating the efficiency of operations throughout the organization
- Assisting decision makers in interpreting accounting information
- Auditing (confirming the reliability of accounting information)
- Forecasting the probable results of future operations
- Tax planning

We will emphasize such topics in our remaining chapters.

But let us first repeat a very basic point from Chapter 1: The need for some familiarity with accounting concepts and processes is not limited to individuals planning careers in accounting. Today, an understanding of accounting information and of the business world go hand in hand. You cannot know much about one without understanding quite a bit about the other.

A Look Back at Overnight: Was December a "Good Month"?

We have stressed the importance to every individual of an ability to ***interpret*** accounting information. So how should we interpret Overnight's net income of $3,900 in December? Was it impressive? About what we might have expected? Or was it disappointing?

As stated in this chapter, a sole proprietorship does not recognize salary expense for services provided to the business by its owner. Nor does it recognize interest expense on the equity capital that the owner has provided. Thus, the net income of a proprietorship represents the owner's financial compensation for three factors:

1. Personal services rendered to the business
2. Capital provided to the business
3. Assuming the ***risks of ownership*** (As we pointed out in Chapter 1, the owner of a sole proprietorship has ***unlimited personal liability*** for the debts of the business. Thus, the owner faces potential financial losses ***in excess*** of his or her equity in the business.)

Evaluating Business Income: A Short Example   Assume that if McBryan were not running his own business, he could earn a salary of $4,000 per month managing another garage. We will also assume that by investing in the stock market, he could earn an average annual return of, say, 12% on his $80,000 in equity capital. This return would amount to a monthly return of about 1%, or $800. Thus, instead of owning Overnight, McBryan might be earning about $4,800 per month, substantially more than the $3,900 net income from the business and without assuming the risks inherent in owning a sole proprietorship.

Of course, many proprietors take great pride in "being their own boss"— often, the satisfaction of running the business more than compensates for the loss of a potentially higher income as an employee.

Remember also that this is Overnight's ***first month*** of business operations. Most businesses ***incur net losses*** while they are "just getting started." By anyone's standards, a business that earns a profit in its first month of operations is off to an impressive start.

Evaluating the profitability of any business, however, requires more than the results of a single month. Among the most important considerations is the ***trend*** of earnings over time. This trend of earnings is then compared to the trend of the salary and investment income to determine whether it is better to stay in business. Of course, the owners must personally judge whether the excess of the earnings from the business over the salary and investment income is worth the risk involved. Evaluating the adequacy of net income is a topic we will revisit in future chapters.

End-of-Chapter Review

Key Terms Introduced or Emphasized in Chapter 3

Accounting cycle (*p.137*) The sequence of accounting procedures applied every period in recording transactions and preparing financial statements. These procedures begin with journalizing transactions, include adjusting and closing the accounts, and conclude with preparation of an after-closing trial balance.

Accounting period (*p.109*) The span of time covered by an income statement. One year is the accounting period for much financial reporting, but financial statements are also prepared by companies for each quarter of the year and also for each month.

Accrual basis of accounting (*p.138*) Calls for recording revenue in the period in which it is earned and recording expenses in the period in which they are incurred. The effect of events on the business is recognized as services are rendered or consumed rather than when cash is received or paid.

Accumulated depreciation (*p.125*) A contra-asset account shown as a deduction from the related asset account in the balance sheet. Depreciation taken throughout the useful life of an asset is accumulated in this account.

Adjusted trial balance (*p.126*) A listing of all ledger account balances after the amounts have been changed to include the adjusting entries made at the end of the period.

Adjusting entries (*p.122*) Entries required at the end of the period to update the accounts before financial statements are prepared. Adjusting entries serve to apportion transactions properly between the accounting periods affected and to record any revenue earned or expenses incurred that have not been recorded prior to the end of the period.

After-closing trial balance (*p.136*) A trial balance prepared after all closing entries have been made. Consists only of accounts for assets, liabilities, and owner's equity.

Cash basis of accounting (*p.138*) Revenue is recorded when received in cash and expenses are recorded in the period in which cash payment is made. Does not lead to a logical measurement of net income.

Closing entries (*p.131*) Journal entries made at the end of the period for the purpose of closing temporary accounts (revenue, expense, and owner's drawing accounts) and transferring balances to the owner's capital account.

Conservatism (*p.112*) The traditional accounting practice of resolving uncertainty by choosing the solution that leads to the lower (more conservative) amount of income being recognized in the current accounting period. This concept is designed to avoid overstatement of financial strength or earnings.

Contra-asset account (*p.125*) An account with a credit balance that is offset against or deducted from an asset account to produce the proper balance sheet valuation for the asset.

Depreciable assets (*p.123*) Physical objects with a limited life. The cost of these assets is gradually recognized as depreciation expense.

Depreciation (Amortization) (*p.123*) The systematic allocation of the cost of an asset to expense during the periods of its useful life.

Drawing account (*p.113*) The account used to record the withdrawals of cash or other assets by the owner. Closed at the end of the period by transferring its balance to the owner's capital account.

Expenses (*p.111*) The costs of the goods and services used up in the process of obtaining revenue.

Fiscal year (*p.109*) Any 12-month accounting period adopted by a business.

Income statement (*p.108*) A financial statement summarizing the results of operations of a business by matching its revenue and related expenses for a particular accounting period. Shows the net income or net loss.

Income Summary account (*p.130*) The temporary clearing account in the ledger to which revenue and expense accounts are closed at the end of the period. The balance (credit balance for a net income, debit balance for a net loss) is transferred to the owner's capital account.

Matching principle (*p.111*) The generally accepted accounting principle that determines when expenses should be recorded in the accounting records. The revenue earned during an accounting period is matched (offset) with the expenses incurred in generating this revenue.

Net income (*p.107*) An increase in owner's equity resulting from profitable operations. Also, the excess of revenue earned over the related expenses for a given period.

Net loss (*p.107*) A decrease in owner's equity resulting from unprofitable operations.

Objectivity principle (*p.112*) Accountants' preference for using dollar amounts that are relatively "factual"— as opposed to merely matters of personal opinion. Objective measurements can be verified.

Realization (Recognition) principle (*p.110*) The generally accepted accounting principle that determines when revenue should be recorded in the accounting records. Revenue is realized when services are rendered to customers or when goods sold are delivered to customers.

Revenue (*p.110*) The price of goods sold and services rendered by a business.

Statement of owner's equity (*p.129*) A financial statement summarizing the increases and decreases in owner's equity during an accounting period.

Straight-line method of depreciation (*p.124*) The widely used approach of recognizing an **equal amount** of depreciation expense in each period of a depreciable asset's useful life. (Alternatives to this method are discussed in Chapter 10.)

Time period principle (*p.109*) To provide the users of financial statements with timely information, net income is measured for relatively short accounting periods of equal length. The period of time covered by an income statement is termed the company's accounting period.

Useful life (*p.123*) The period of time that a depreciable asset is expected to be useful to the business. This is the period over which the cost of the asset is allocated to depreciation expense.

DEMONSTRATION PROBLEM

Riley Insurance Agency was organized on September 1, 20__. Assume that the accounts are closed and financial statements prepared each month. The company occupies rented office space but owns office equipment estimated to have a useful life of 5 years from date of acquisition, September 1. The trial balance for Riley Insurance Agency at November 30 is shown below.

RILEY INSURANCE AGENCY Trial Balance November 30, 20__		
Cash	$ 6,565	
Accounts receivable	17,050	
Office supplies	500	
Office equipment	18,000	
Accumulated depreciation: office equipment		$ 600
Accounts payable		1,260
Pat Riley, Capital		35,000
Pat Riley, Drawing	2,500	
Commissions earned		15,555
Advertising expense	1,400	
Salaries expense	2,600	
Rent expense	3,800	
	$52,415	$52,415

Riley estimates that only about **$300** worth of office supplies remain on hand at November 30.

a. Prepare adjusting entries at November 30 to reflect the office supplies used in November and depreciation expense for the month.

b. Prepare an **adjusted** trial balance at November 30, 20__.

c. Prepare an income statement and statement of owner's equity for the month, and a balance sheet in report form at November 30, 20__.

SOLUTION TO DEMONSTRATION PROBLEM

a. Adjusting entries:

	GENERAL JOURNAL			
Date	Account Titles and Explanation	LP	Debit	Credit
20__ Nov. 30	Supplies Expense . . . . Office Supplies . . . . To recognize cost of supplies used in November ($500 – $300 left).		200	200

30	Depreciation Expense: Office Equipment . .
	    Accumulated Depreciation: Office
	        Equipment . . . .
	To record depreciation for November
	($18,000 ÷ 60 months).
			300	300

b.

RILEY INSURANCE AGENCY Adjusted Trial Balance November 30, 20__		
Cash	$ 6,565	
Accounts receivable	17,050	
Office supplies	300	
Office equipment	18,000	
Accumulated depreciation: office equipment		$ 900
Accounts payable		1,260
Pat Riley, Capital		35,000
Pat Riley, Drawing	2,500	
Commissions earned		15,555
Advertising expense	1,400	
Salaries expense	2,600	
Rent expense	3,800	
Supplies expense	200	
Depreciation expense: office equipment	300	
	$52,715	$52,715

c.

RILEY INSURANCE AGENCY Income Statement For the Month Ended November 30, 20__		
Revenue:		
Commissions earned		$15,555
Expenses:		
Advertising expense	$ 1,400	
Salaries expense	2,600	
Rent expense	3,800	
Supplies expense	200	
Depreciation expense: office equipment	300	8,300
Net income		$ 7,255

RILEY INSURANCE AGENCY
Statement of Owner's Equity
For the Month Ended November 30, 20__

Pat Riley, capital, Oct. 31, 20__	$35,000
Add: Net income for the month	7,255
Subtotal	$42,255
Less: Withdrawals by owner	2,500
Pat Riley, capital, Nov. 30, 20__	$39,755

RILEY INSURANCE AGENCY
Balance Sheet
November 30, 20__

Assets

Cash		$ 6,565
Accounts receivable		17,050
Office supplies		300
Office equipment	$18,000	
Less: Accumulated depreciation	900	17,100
Total assets		$41,015

Liabilities & Owner's Equity

Liabilities:	
Accounts payable	$ 1,260
Owner's equity:	
Pat Riley, capital	39,755
Total liabilities & owner's equity	$41,015

Self-Test Questions

Answers to these questions appear on page 164.

1. Identify any of the following statements that correctly describe net income. (Indicate all correct answers.) Net income:
   a. Is computed in the income statement, appears in the statement of owner's equity, and increases owner's equity in the balance sheet.
   b. Is equal to revenue minus expenses.
   c. Is computed in the income statement, appears in the statement of owner's equity, and increases the amount of cash shown in the balance sheet.
   d. Can be determined using the account balances appearing in an adjusted trial balance.

2. Which of the following are based upon the realization (recognition) principle and the matching principle? (Indicate all correct answers.)
   a. Adjusting entries.
   b. Closing entries.
   c. The accrual basis of accounting.
   d. The measurement of net income under generally accepted accounting principles.

3. Which of the following explains the debit and credit rules relating to the recording of revenue and expenses?
   a. Expenses appear on the left side of the balance sheet and are recorded by debits; revenue appears on the right side of the balance sheet and is recorded by credits.
   b. Expenses appear on the left side of the income statement and are recorded by debits; revenue appears on the right side of the income statement and is recorded by credits.
   c. The effects of revenue and expenses upon owner's equity.
   d. The realization (recognition) principle and the matching principle.

4. The entry to recognize **depreciation expense:** (Indicate all correct answers.)
   a. Is an application of the matching principle.
   b. Is a closing entry.
   c. Usually includes an offsetting credit either to Cash or to Accounts Payable.
   d. Is an adjusting entry.

5. In the accounting cycle: (Indicate all correct answers.)
   a. Closing entries are made before adjusting entries.
   b. Financial statements may be prepared as soon as an adjusted trial balance is complete.
   c. The owner's capital account is not up-to-date until closing entries have been posted.
   d. Adjusting entries are made before financial statements are prepared.

6. The balance in the owner's capital account of Dayton Company at the beginning of the year was $65,000. During the year, the company earned revenue at $430,000 and incurred expenses of $360,000, the owner withdrew $50,000 in assets, and the balance of the Cash account increased by $10,000. At year-end, the company's net income and the year-end balance in the owner's capital account were, respectively:
   a. $20,000 and $95,000   c. $60,000 and $75,000
   b. $70,000 and $95,000   d. $70,000 and $85,000

Use the following information in questions **7** and **8.**

Accounts appearing in the trial balance of Siyuen Plumbing at May 31 are listed below in alphabetical order:

Accounts payable	$2,450	Equipment	$16,200
Accounts receivable	3,100	Insurance expense	1,000
Accumulated depreciation:		J. T. Golden, capital	11,000
equipment	8,100	J. T. Golden, drawing	2,100
Advertising expense	150	Other expenses	900
Cash	2,900	Service revenue	4,800

No adjusting entry has yet been made to record depreciation expense of $270 for the month of May.

7. The balance of J. T. Golden's capital account appearing in the May 31 balance sheet should be:
   a. $11,650   b. $8,630   c. $11,380   d. Some other amount

8. In an **after-closing** trial balance prepared at May 31, the total of the credit column will be:
   a. $26,620   b. $22,200   c. $13,830   d. Some other amount

ASSIGNMENT MATERIAL

Discussion Questions

1. Explain the effect of operating profitably upon the balance sheet of a business entity.

2. Does net income represent a supply of cash that could be withdrawn by the owner of a business? Explain.

3. What is the meaning of the term *revenue?* Does the receipt of cash by a business indicate that revenue has been earned? Explain.

4. What is the meaning of the term *expenses?* Does the payment of cash by a business indicate that an expense has been incurred? Explain.

5. A service enterprise performs services in the amount of $500 for a customer in May and receives payment in June. In which month is the $500 of revenue recognized? What is the journal entry to be made in May and the entry to be made in June?

6. When do accountants consider revenue to be realized? What basic question about recording revenue in accounting records is answered by the *realization (recognition) principle?*

7. Late in March, Classic Auto Painters purchased paint on account, with payment due in 60 days. The company used the paint to paint customers' cars during the first three weeks of April. Late in May, the company paid the paint store from which the paint had been purchased. In which month should Classic Auto Painters recognize the cost of this paint as expense? What generally accepted accounting principle determines the answer to this question?

8. In what accounting period does the *matching principle* indicate that an expense should be recognized?

9. Explain the rules of debit and credit with respect to transactions recorded in revenue and expense accounts.

10. Supply the appropriate term (debit or credit) to complete the following statements.
    a. The owner's capital account and revenue accounts are increased by _____ entries.
    b. Asset accounts and expense accounts are increased by _____ entries.
    c. Liability accounts and owner's equity accounts are decreased by _____ entries.

11. What is the *purpose* of adjusting entries? When are they made, and what is being "adjusted" by adjusting entries?

12. Why does any company that owns equipment or buildings need to make adjusting entries at the end of every accounting period?

13. Does a well-prepared income statement provide an exact measurement of net income for the period, or does it represent merely an approximation of net income? Explain.

14. How does depreciation expense differ from other operating expenses?

15. What is meant by the *straight-line* method of determining depreciation expense? Is the amount of depreciation expense determined under this method an estimate or an exact amount? Explain.

16. When should a business **begin** depreciating a depreciable asset? When should depreciation of a depreciable asset **cease?**

17. All ledger accounts belong in one of the following five groups: asset, liability, owners' equity, revenue, and expense. For each of the following accounts, state the group in which it belongs. Also indicate whether the normal balance would be a debit or a credit.
    a. Building
    b. Depreciation Expense
    c. Accumulated Depreciation: Building
    d. Fees Earned
    e. Notes Payable
    f. Telephone Expense
    g. Charles Scott, Capital
    h. Supplies Expense
    i. Charles Scott, Drawing

18. For each of the following financial statements, indicate whether the statement relates to a particular date or to a period of time:
    a. Balance sheet
    b. Income statement
    c. Statement of owner's equity

19. Briefly describe the content and format of an income statement and of a statement of owner's equity.

20. Explain the relationships among the three financial statements discussed in this chapter—that is, the income statement, the statement of owner's equity, and the balance sheet.

21. Which of the following accounts are closed at the end of the accounting period?

Cash	Donna Jackson, drawing
Fees earned	Donna Jackson, capital
Income summary	Accumulated depreciation
Accounts payable	Accounts receivable
Telephone expense	Depreciation expense

22. Supply the appropriate term (debit or credit) to complete the following statements.
    a. When a business is operating **profitably,** the journal entry to close the Income Summary account will consist of a _____ to that account and a _____ to the owner's capital account.
    b. When a business is operating at a **loss,** the journal entry to close the Income Summary account will consist of a _____ to that account and a _____ to the owner's capital account.
    c. The journal entry to close the owner's drawing account consists of a _____ to that account and a _____ to the owner's capital account.

23. Bill Foreman owns and operates a video rental business organized as a sole proprietorship, which generated a net income of $30,000 for the year. Foreman has heard "through the grapevine" that the manager of a competing video rental store makes an annual salary of $27,000. What factors should Foreman consider in evaluating the adequacy of his business's net income?

24. How does the accrual basis of accounting differ from the cash basis of accounting? Which gives a more accurate picture of the profitability of a business? Explain.

Exercises

EXERCISE 3-1
Accounting Terminology
(LO 1, 2, 5, 7, 9)

Listed below are twelve technical accounting terms introduced in this chapter:

Net Income	*Accounting period*	*Depreciation*
Realization	*Accrual basis of accounting*	*Expenses*
Revenue	*Cash basis of accounting*	*Income statement*
Drawing	*Closing entries*	*Matching*

Each of the following statements may (or may not) describe one of these technical terms. For each statement, indicate the accounting term described, or answer "None" if the statement does not correctly describe any of the terms.

a. The generally accepted accounting principle used in determining when to recognize revenue.

b. Recognizing revenue when it is earned and expenses when the related goods or services are used in the effort to obtain revenue.

c. The systematic allocation of the cost of a long-lived asset, such as a building or equipment, to expense over the useful life of the asset.

d. The procedures for transferring the balances of the revenue, expense, Income Summary, and owner's drawing accounts into the owner's capital account.

e. The cost of goods and services used up in the process of earning revenue.

f. The span of time covered by an income statement.

g. An increase in owner's equity as a result of earning revenue and incurring expenses.

h. A decrease in owner's equity not reported in the income statement.

i. The generally accepted accounting principle used in determining when expenses should be offset against revenue.

EXERCISE 3-2
Effects of Transactions on the Accounting Equation
(LO 1, 2, 4, 6, 9)

Dante Trucking Co. closes its accounts at the end of each month. Among the events occurring in *November* were the following:

a. Purchased on account enough office supplies to last several months.

b. Hauled freight for a credit customer; payment due December 10.

c. Paid Truck Service Centre for repairs to trucks performed in October. (In October, Dante Trucking had received and properly recorded the invoice for these repairs.)

d. Collected in full the amount due from a credit customer for hauling done in October.

e. Received a bill from Apex Truck Stops for fuel used in November. Payment due December 15.

f. Purchased two new trucks on November 30, paying part cash and issuing a note payable for the balance. The trucks are first scheduled for use on December 3.

g. Prepared an adjusting entry to record depreciation on trucks used for operations in November.

h. Prepared an adjusting entry to recognize as expense the cost of office supplies used in November.

Indicate the effects that each of these transactions will have upon the following six *total amounts* in the company's financial statements for the month of *November*. Organize your answer in tabular form, using the column headings shown below, and use the code letters *I* for increase, *D* for decrease, and *NE* for no effect. The answer to transaction (**a**) is provided as an example.

	Income Statement			Balance Sheet		
Transaction	*Revenue*	*– Expenses*	*= Net Income*	*Assets*	*= Liabilities +*	*Owner's Equity*
a	*NE*	*NE*	*NE*	*I*	*I*	*NE*

EXERCISE 3-3
Effects of Transactions; the
Accounting Equation
(LO 1, 6)

A number of transactions of Taiwu Steamship Lines are described below in terms of the accounts debited and credited:
1. Debit Wages Expense, credit Cash.
2. Debit Accounts Receivable, credit Freight Revenue.
3. Debit N. Stravros, Drawing, credit Cash.
4. Debit Depreciation Expense: Ships; credit Accumulated Depreciation: Ships.
5. Debit Repairs Expense, credit Accounts Payable.
6. Debit Cash, credit Accounts Receivable.
7. Debit Accounts Payable, credit Cash.
8. Debit Office Supplies Expense, credit Office Supplies.

a. Indicate the effects of each transaction upon the elements of the income statement and the balance sheet. Use the code letters *I* for increase, *D* for decrease, and *NE* for no effect. Organize your answer in tabular form using the column headings shown below. The answer for transaction 1 is provided as an example.

	Income Statement			Balance Sheet		
Transaction	Revenue −	Expenses =	Net Income	Assets =	Liabilities +	Owner's Equity
1	NE	I	D	D	NE	D

b. Write a one-sentence description of each transaction.

EXERCISE 3-4
Relationship between Net
Income and Owner's Equity
(LO 1, 6)

Total assets and total liabilities of The Fontaine Gallery as shown by the balance sheets at the beginning and end of the year were as follows:

	Beginning of Year	End of Year
Assets	$285,000	$370,000
Liabilities	90,000	125,000

Compute the net income or net loss from operations for the year in each of the following independent cases:
a. Fontaine made no withdrawals during the year and no additional investments.
b. Fontaine made no withdrawals but made an additional capital investment of $40,000.
c. Fontaine made withdrawals of $30,000 but made no additional investments.
d. Fontaine made withdrawals of $40,000 and made an additional capital investment of $15,000.
e. Fontaine made no withdrawals, but made an additional capital investment of $75,000.

EXERCISE 3-5
Relationship between Net
Income and Owner's Equity
(LO 1, 6)

Supply the missing figure in the following independent cases:
a. Owner's equity at beginning of year $115,000
   Net income for the year . . . . −?−
   Owner's drawings during the year 34,000
   Owner's equity at end of year 132,800
b. Owner's equity at beginning of year 96,500
   Net income for the year 28,200
   Owner's drawings during the year . . . . −?−
   Owner's equity at end of year 98,700
c. Owner's equity at beginning of year . . . . −?−
   Net income for the year 189,400
   Owner's drawings during the year 106,000
   Owner's equity at end of year 532,900

d.	Owner's equity at beginning of year	83,000
	Additional investment by owner during the year	15,000
	Net income for the year	26,800
	Owner's drawing during the year	19,000
	Owner's equity at end of year	–?–
e.	Owner's equity at beginning of year	362,500
	Additional investment by owner during the year	76,000
	Net income for the year	–?–
	Owner's drawings during the year	30,000
	Owner's equity at end of year	469,100

EXERCISE 3-6
Heading of an Income Statement
(LO 6)

On January 14, 2000 the accountant for Wrightwood Design Company prepared an income statement for the fiscal year ended December 31, 1999. The accountant used the following heading on this financial statement:

WRIGHTWOOD, INC.
Income Statement
January 14, 2000

a. Identify any errors in this heading.
b. Prepare a corrected heading.

EXERCISE 3-7
When Is Revenue Realized?
(LO 2, 9)

The following transactions were carried out during the month of May by M. Palmer and Company, a firm of design architects. For each of the five transactions, you are to state whether the transaction represented revenue to the firm during the month of May. Give reasons for your decision in each case.
a. M. Palmer invested an additional $15,000 cash in the business.
b. Collected cash of $2,400 from an account receivable. The receivable originated in April from services rendered to a client.
c. Borrowed $12,800 from Century Bank to be repaid in three months.
d. Earned $83 interest on a company bank account during the month of May. No withdrawals were made from this account in May.
e. Completed plans for guest house, pool, and spa for a client. The $5,700 fee for this project was billed to the client in May, but will not be collected until June 25.

EXERCISE 3-8
When Are Expenses Incurred?
(LO 2, 9)

During March, the activities of Evergreen Landscaping included the following transactions and events. Which of these items represent expenses in March? Explain.
a. Purchased a copying machine for $2,750 cash. (Consider only the asset purchase in your answer.)
b. Paid $192 for gasoline purchases for a delivery truck during March.
c. Paid $2,280 salary to an employee for time worked during March.
d. Paid a lawyer $560 for legal services rendered in January.
e. The owner withdrew $1,800 from the business for personal use.
f. Supplies used up during the month of March had a cost of approximately $725. No supplies were purchased during March as the company had several months' requirements on hand at the end of February.

EXERCISE 3-9
Preparing Journal Entries for Revenue and Expenses
(LO 2, 3, 4, 5, 9)

Shown below are selected transactions of the law firm of Rodenberry & Associates. The firm closes its accounts at the end of each calendar year.

Mar. 19 Drafted a trust agreement for Patrick Stewart. Sent Stewart an invoice for $1,200 requesting payment within 30 days. (The appropriate revenue account is entitled Legal Fees Earned.)

May 15 Owner Jean Rodenberry withdrew $6,000 from the business for personal use.

May 31 Received a bill from Lawyers' Delivery Service for process service during the month of May, $2,050. Payment due by June 10. (The appropriate expense account is entitled Process Service Expense.)

June 10 Paid the amount due on the May 31 invoice from Lawyers' Delivery Service.

Dec. 31 Made a year-end adjusting entry to record depreciation expense on the firm's law library, $5,100.

Dec. 31 Made adjusting entry to recognize as expense the cost of supplies used during the fourth quarter of the firm's fiscal year, $3,750. (Supplies are purchased in bulk and recorded as assets when purchased.)

a. Prepare journal entries to record the transactions in the firm's accounting records.

b. What is the effect of the May 15 transaction upon the firm's net income? What is the effect of this transaction upon the owner's equity of the firm?

EXERCISE 3-10
Adjusting Entry for
Depreciation; Balance Sheet
Presentation
(LO 5)

Aquino Pharmacy acquired a delivery truck at a cost of $14,400. Estimated life of the truck is four years. Management of Aquino Pharmacy elects to use the straight-line method of depreciation for vehicles.

a. State the amount of depreciation expense per year and per month. Give the adjusting entry to record depreciation on the truck at the end of the first month, and explain where the accounts involved would appear in the financial statements.

b. Assume the delivery truck was acquired on Sept. 1, 1999, and that this vehicle is the only delivery truck owned by the business. Show how this truck would be reported in Aquino Pharmacy's balance sheet at December 31, 1999.

c. Compare the amount credited to Accumulated Depreciation in the adjusting entry in part **a** to the Accumulated Depreciation reported in the balance sheet at December 31, 1999 (part **b**). Are these two amounts the same? Explain briefly.

EXERCISE 3-11
Adjusting Entries for
Depreciation and Supplies
Expense
(LO 4, 5)

TRC Graphics, a sole proprietorship, adjusts and closes its books each month. On May 31, 1999, **before** adjusting entries are recorded, the trial balance for TRC Graphics is as shown:

TRC GRAPHICS Trial Balance May 31, 1999		
	Debit	Credit
Cash	$10,500	
Accounts Receivable	3,000	
Supplies	2,250	
Equipment	30,000	
Accumulated Depreciation: Equipment		$ 6,500
Accounts Payable		2,500
T. R. Cummings, Capital		23,750
T. R. Cummings, Drawing	2,500	
Fees Earned		24,000
Supplies Expense	600	
Salaries Expense	4,000	
Rent Expense	2,400	
Utilities Expense	1,500	
	$56,750	$56,750

The equipment was purchased in 1998 and has an estimated useful life of five years. TRC Graphics estimates that supplies on hand at May 31, 1999, total approximately $1,900.

a. Compute the amount of depreciation expense on the equipment for May. Give the adjusting entry to record depreciation on the equipment at the end of May.

b. Compute supplies expense for May. Give the adjusting entry to record supplies expense for the month of May.

c. What is the amount of net income or loss reported in TRC Graphics' income statement for the month of May? Show computation.

d. As of the end of May, how long had TRC Graphics used the equipment in business operations? Show computation.

EXERCISE 3-12
Prepare an Income Statement and a Statement of Owner's Equity
(LO 4, 5, 6)

The following account balances, among others, appeared in the adjusted trial balance of Cortes Painting Contractors at December 31, 2000. Cortes closes its books annually at December 31.

Eduard Cortes, Capital,		Salaries Expense	$66,800
December 31, 1999	$ 27,200	Rent Expense	9,600
Eduard Cortes, Drawing . .	18,000	Advertising Expense	3,200
Painting Fees Earned	163,300	Depreciation Expense:	
Paint & Supplies Expense . .	27,500	Painting Equipment	1,200
Accumulated Depreciation:		Insurance Expense	12,000
Painting Equipment	3,000	Painting Equipment	7,200

a. From the above account balances, prepare first an income statement and then a statement of owner's equity for Cortes Painting Contractors for the year ended December 31, 2000. Include the proper headings on both financial statements.

b. What is the estimated useful life of the painting equipment owned by Cortes Painting Contractors? How long has Cortes used this equipment as of December 31, 2000? Explain your answers.

EXERCISE 3-13
Preparing Closing Entries
(LO 7)

Prepare the year-end closing entries for Cortes Painting Contractors, using the data given in Exercise *3-12*. Use four separate entries. Indicate the balance in the owner's capital account that should appear in the balance sheet dated December 31, 2000.

EXERCISE 3-14
Financial Statement Relationships
(LO 1, 6)

Shown below is a list of abbreviated terms, each representing an element of financial statements.

Term	Explanation
REV	Revenue of the period
EXP	Expenses of the period
NI	Net Income for the period
DRW	Drawings by the owner during the period
INV	Additional investment by the owner during the period
OE_{BEG}	Owner's equity, beginning of the period
OE_{END}	Owner's equity, end of the period

Shown below are five incomplete formulas describing interrelationships among the elements of financial statements. You are to complete the right-hand side of each formula by adding or subtracting the appropriate terms from the list provided above. (The number of question marks indicates the number of terms needed to complete each formula.)

a. $NI = REV$ (+ or − ?)

b. $EXP = REV$ (+ or − ?)

c. $REV = EXP$ (+ or − ?)

d. $OE_{END} = OE_{BEG}$ (+ or − ? and ? and ?)

e. $OE_{BEG} = OE_{END}$ (+ or − ? and ? and ?)

f. $NI = OE_{END} - OE_{BEG}$ (+ or − ? and ?)

EXERCISE 3-15
The Accounting Cycle
(LO 8)

Listed below *in random order* are the eight steps comprising a complete accounting cycle.

a. Prepare a trial balance.
b. Journalize and post the closing entries.
c. Prepare financial statements and appropriate disclosures.
d. Post transaction data to the ledger.
e. Prepare an adjusted trial balance.
f. Make end-of-period adjusting entries.
g. Journalize transactions.
h. Prepare an after-closing trial balance.

a. List these eight steps in the logical sequence in which they would be performed.
b. Indicate which of these steps are mechanical functions that can be performed by machine in a computerized accounting system, and which require the judgment of people familiar with accounting principles and concepts.

Problems

PROBLEM 3-1
Journal Entries and Effect on Balance Sheet and Net Income
(LO 1, 2, 3, 9)

City Flights provides transportation by helicopter between a major airport and various business centres of a large city. Among the ledger accounts used by the company are the following:

Cash	*Passenger fare revenue*
Accounts payable	*Advertising expense*
Aircraft	*Fuel expense*
Accounts receivable	*Rent expense*
O. Wright, capital	*Repair & maintenance expense*
O. Wright, drawing	*Salaries expense*

Some of the January transactions of City Flights are listed below.

Jan. 3   Paid $3,520 rent for hangar space during January.

Jan. 4   Placed advertising in local newspapers for publication during January. The agreed price of $860 was payable within 10 days after the end of the month.

Jan. 15   Cash receipts from passengers for the first half of January amounted to $23,160.

Jan. 15   O. Wright, the owner, withdrew $7,500 cash for personal use.

Jan. 16   Paid salaries to employees for services rendered in first half of January, $13,200.

Jan. 25   Provided transportation for executives of the Hurley Corporation. A long-time credit customer. Sent bill for $470, due within 30 days.

Jan. 29   Received a bill from Western Oil Limited for fuel used in January, amounting to $4,340, and payable by February 10.

Jan. 31   Paid $3,372 to Stevens Motors for repair and maintenance work during January.

INSTRUCTIONS

a. Prepare a journal entry (including an explanation) for each of the above transactions.
b. Describe the effect of the January 29 transaction involving fuel used in January upon each of the following: assets, liabilities, owner's equity, and net income. For each of the four items, indicate whether the transaction caused an increase, decrease, or no effect.

PROBLEM 3-2
Journal Entries and Effect on Balance Sheet and Net Income
(LO 1, 2, 3, 9)

Computer Resources provides consulting and systems design services on both a cash and credit basis. Credit customers are required to pay within 30 days from date of billing. Among the ledger accounts used by the company are the following:

Cash   *J. Markham, drawing*
Accounts receivable   *Consulting fees earned*
Office equipment   *Advertising expense*
J. Markham, capital   *Rent expense*
Accounts payable   *Salaries expense*

Among the June transactions were the following:

June 1   Provided consulting services to Arden Publications, a credit customer. Sent bill for $3,280.

June 2   Paid rent for June, $1,650.

June 3   Purchased office equipment with estimated life of 5 years for $3,100 cash.

June 10   Provided consulting for Quinn Veterinary Hospital and collected in full the charge of $1,020.

June 15   Newspaper advertising to appear on June 18 was arranged at a cost of $610. Received bill from *Tribune* requiring payment within 30 days.

June 18   Received payment in full of the $3,280 account receivable from Arden Publications for our services on June 1.

June 20   James Markham, owner of Computer Resources, withdrew $5,500 cash from the business for personal use.

June 30   Paid salaries of $6,800 to employees for services rendered during June.

INSTRUCTIONS

a. Prepare a journal entry (including explanation) for each of the above transactions.

b. How does the transaction on June 20 (withdrawal by owner in the amount of $5,500) affect net income of the company for June? What is the immediate impact of this transaction upon the assets, liabilities, and owner's equity of Computer Resources? (For each of these three items, state increase, decrease, or no effect.)

PROBLEM 3-3
Analyzing Transactions and Preparing Journal Entries
(LO 1, 2, 3, 9)

Garwood Marine is a boat repair yard. During August its transactions included the following:

1. On August 1, paid rent for the month of August, $4,400.

2. On August 3, at request of Kiwi Insurance, Inc., made repairs on boat of Michael Fay. Sent bill for $5,620 for services rendered to Kiwi Insurance, Inc.

3. On August 9, made repairs to boat of Dennis Conner and collected in full the charge of $2,830.

4. On August 14, received an invoice for an advertisement in *Yachting World* to be published in issue of August 16 at cost of $165, payment to be made within 30 days.

5. On August 25, received a cheque for $5,620 from Kiwi Insurance, Inc., representing collection of the receivable of August 3.

6. On August 26, made repairs on the vessel *Independent* totalling $1,890. Collected $400 cash; balance due within 30 days.

7. On August 30, sent cheque to *Yachting World* in payment of the liability incurred on August 14.

8. On August 31, Barbara Garwood, owner of Garwood Marine, withdrew $7,600 for personal use.

INSTRUCTIONS

a. Write an analysis of each transaction. An example of the type of analysis desired is as follows:
  1. a. Rent is an operating expense. Expenses are recorded by debits. Debit Rent Expense, $4,400.
     b. The asset Cash was decreased. Decreases in assets are recorded by credits. Credit Cash, $4,400.
b. Prepare a journal entry (including explanation) for each of the above transactions.
c. Transactions 1, 7, and 8 all involve cash payments, yet only one of these transactions is recorded an expense. Describe three situations in which a cash payment would ***not*** involve recognition of an expense.

PROBLEM 3-4
Analyzing Transactions and Preparing Journal Entries
(LO 1, 2, 3, 9)

The July transactions of Canyon Ridge Dental Group, a sole proprietorship, included the following:
1. On July 2, paid rent for the month of July, $2,400.
2. On July 3, provided check-ups, x-rays, and fluoride treatments for six members of the Devane family. Sent the bill for $710 for services rendered to the Safeguard Insurance Company Dental Plan.
3. On July 9, provided emergency dental services to D. Reginald and collected in full the charge of $860.
4. On July 14, purchased some special supplies to be used for the next two weeks at cost of $350. Paid $100 cash, balance due within 30 days.
5. On July 25, received a $710 payment from Safeguard Insurance Company representing collection of the receivable of July 3.
6. On July 31, Greg Toolson, owner of the practice, withdrew $11,800 for personal use.
7. On July 31, obtained a loan from bank. Received $15,000 cash and signed a note payable for that amount.
8. On July 31, received bill from Southwest Gas & Electric for power used in July amounting to $621, payable by August 15.

INSTRUCTIONS

a. Write an analysis of each transaction. An example of the type of analysis desired is as follows for transaction (1) above.
  1. a. Rent is an operating expense. Expenses are recorded by debits. Debit Rent Expense, $2,400.
     b. The asset Cash was decreased. Decreases in assets are recorded by credits. Credit Cash, $2,400.
b. Prepare a journal entry (including explanation) for each of the above transactions.
c. Examine the transactions above involving receipt of cash. Does receipt of cash always involve recording revenue? Describe three situations in which a cash receipt would ***not*** involve immediate recognition of revenue.

PROBLEM 3-5
Preparing Journal Entries, Posting, and Preparing a Trial Balance
(LO 1, 2, 3, 4, 5, 8, 9)

In June 1999, Pat Campbell organized a company to provide crop dusting services. The company, called Campbell Crop Dusting, began operations immediately. Transactions during the month of June were as follows:

June 1 Campbell deposited $60,000 cash in a bank account in the name of the business.

June 2 Purchased a crop-dusting aircraft from Utility Aircraft for $220,000. Made a $40,000 cash down payment and issued a note payable for $180,000.

June 4 Paid Red Bridge Airport $2,500 to rent office and hangar space for the month.

June 15 Billed customers $8,320 for crop dusting services rendered during the first half of June.

June 15 Paid $5,880 salaries to employees for services rendered during the first half of June.

June 18 Paid Hannigan's Hangar $1,890 for maintenance services.

June 25 Collected $4,910 of the amounts billed to customers on June 15.

June 30 Billed customers $16,450 for crop dusting services rendered during the second half of the month.

June 30 Paid $6,000 salaries to employees for services rendered during the second half of June.

June 30 Received a fuel bill from Henry's Feed & Fuel for $2,510 of aircraft fuel purchased during June. This amount is due by July 10.

June 30 Campbell withdrew $2,000 cash from the business for personal use.

The account titles and numbers used by Campbell Crop Dusting were:

Cash	1	Pat Campbell, drawing	45
Accounts receivable	5	Crop dusting revenue	51
Aircraft	15	Maintenance expense	61
Notes payable	31	Fuel expense	62
Accounts payable	32	Salaries expense	63
Pat Campbell, capital	40	Rent expenses	64

INSTRUCTIONS

Based on the foregoing transactions:

a. Prepare journal entries. (Number journal pages to permit cross reference to ledger.)

b. Post to ledger accounts. (Number ledger accounts to permit cross reference to journal.) Enter ledger account numbers in the LP column of the journal as the posting work is done.

c. Prepare a trial balance at June 30, 1999.

d. Using the trial balance at June 30, 1999 (part **c**), compute each of the following at June 30, 1999: total assets, total liabilities, total owner's equity. Are these amounts the figures that would be reported for assets, liabilities, and owner's equity in the balance sheet at June 30, 1999? Explain your answer briefly.

PROBLEM 3-6
Adjusted Trial Balance, Part I—
Preparing Financial Statements
and Explaining the Concept of
Income
(LO 1, 4, 5, 6)

Environmental Solutions prepares financial statements and closes its accounts at the end of each calendar year. The following *adjusted* trial balance was prepared at December 31, 2000.

ENVIRONMENTAL SOLUTIONS
Adjusted Trial Balance
December 31, 2000

Cash	$ 42,750	
Notes receivable	12,740	
Accounts receivable	65,090	
Supplies	5,300	
Land	196,000	
Building	126,000	
Accumulated depreciation: building		$ 33,600
Office equipment	33,600	
Accumulated depreciation: office equipment		13,440
Notes payable		112,000
Accounts payable		22,680
Frank L. Adams, capital, December 31, 1999		230,300
Frank L. Adams, drawing	70,000	
Consulting fees earned		487,200
Advertising expense	31,500	
Insurance expense	38,720	
Utilities expense	15,040	
Salaries expense	245,280	
Supplies expense	9,640	
Depreciation expense: building	4,200	
Depreciation expense: office equipment	3,360	
	$899,220	$899,220

INSTRUCTIONS

a. Prepare an income statement and a statement of owner's equity for the year ended December 31, 2000.
b. Prepare a balance sheet (in report form) as of December 31, 2000.
c. What was the estimated useful life used by Environmental Solutions in setting the depreciation rate for the building? Approximately how long has Environmental Solutions been using the building in its operations? Show computation.
d. Adams' 15-year-old son Ansel is trying to understand what the net income of the business represents. He feels that net income less withdrawals by the owner should be available as cash. He compares Environmental Solutions' 2000 net income, less withdrawals by owner, to the cash reported in the balance sheet and asks what happened to the rest of the net income.

   Explain the concept of net income to Ansel Adams, including in your answer an explanation of where the undistributed net income from 2000 (and prior years) "ended up."

PROBLEM 3-7
Adjusted Trial Balance, Part II—
Preparing Closing Entries
(LO 7)

Using the data shown in the adjusted trial balance in Problem **3-6:**
a. Prepare journal entries to close the accounts.
b. Does the amount of net income or net loss appear in the closing entries? Explain fully.

PROBLEM 3-8
Preparing Financial Statements
from an Adjusted Trial Balance
(LO 1, 4, 5, 6)

NP Enterprises operates several miniature golf courses, all of which are located on rented land within city parks. Shown below is the company's **adjusted** trial balance at December 31, 2000. The company closes its accounts at the end of each calendar year.

```
                          NP ENTERPRISES
                        Adjusted Trial Balance
                         December 31, 2000

Cash  . . . . . . . . . . . . . . . . . . . . . . . . . . . .  $   41,100
Accounts receivable  . . . . . . . . . . . . . . .          7,800
Buildings . . . . . . . . . . . . . . . . . . . . . .      180,000
Accumulated depreciation: buildings  . . . . . . . .                      $   36,000
Golf course structures . . . . . . . . . . . . . . . .     270,000
Accumulated depreciation: golf course structures  .                          90,000
Accounts payable . . . . . . . . . . . . . . . .                              23,100
Salaries payable . . . . . . . . . . . . . . . .                               6,900
Nick Palmer, capital (December 31, 1999) . . . . . .                         331,560
Nick Palmer, drawing  . . . . . . . . . . . . . . .         75,000
Admissions revenue . . . . . . . . . . . . . . . .                           576,000
Advertising expense . . . . . . . . . . . . . . .          45,000
Rent expense  . . . . . . . . . . . . . . . . . . . .     108,000
Repairs expense  . . . . . . . . . . . . . . . . .         15,600
Salaries expense . . . . . . . . . . . . . . . . .       237,000
Light & power expense  . . . . . . . . . . . . . .        13,500
Depreciation expense: buildings  . . . . . . . . . . .     18,000
Depreciation expense: golf course structures . . . .      45,000
Insurance expense  . . . . . . . . . . . . . . . . .        7,560
                                                        $1,063,560   $1,063,560
```

INSTRUCTIONS

a. Prepare an income statement and a statement of owner's equity for the year ended December 31, 2000.

b. Prepare a balance sheet (in report form) as of December 31, 2000.

c. Is 2000 the first year of operations for NP Enterprises? Support your answer.

d. Assume that Nick Palmer invested $300,000 to start NP Enterprises. Does the difference between the owner's capital at December 31, 2000, and this $300,000 initial investment equal the amount of profits generated by the business since inception? Explain briefly.

PROBLEM 3-9
Preparing Closing Entries from an Adjusted Trial Balance
(LO 7)

Using the adjusted trial balance presented in Problem **3-8:**

a. Prepare journal entries to close the accounts. Use four entries.

b. Assume that in the following year, NP Enterprises again had $576,000 of admissions revenue, but that expenses increased to $600,000. Assuming that the revenue account and all the expense accounts had been closed into the Income Summary account at December 31, prepare a journal entry to close the Income Summary account.

PROBLEM 3-10
Preparing Closing Entries
(LO 7)

During the absence of the regular accountant of Vanderpool Consulting, a new employee, Doug Webb, prepared the closing entries from the ledger accounts for the year 20__. Webb has very little understanding of accounting and the closing entries he prepared were not satisfactory in several respects. The entries by Webb were:

Entry 1

```
Professional Fees Earned  . . . . . . . . . . . . . . . . . . . . . .   273,600
Accumulated Depreciation: Building  . . . . . . . . . . . . . .        25,600
Accounts Payable  . . . . . . . . . . . . . . . . . . . . . . . . .    86,400
Salaries Payable  . . . . . . . . . . . . . . . . . . . . . . . . . .    9,200
       Income Summary  . . . . . . . . . . . . . . . . . . . . . .                394,800
To close accounts with credit balances.
```

Entry 2

Income Summary	160,800	
Salaries Expense		96,400
Al Vanderpool, drawing		36,000
Advertising Expense		12,800
Depreciation Expense: Building		6,400
Insurance Expense		9,200
To close accounts with debit balances.		

Entry 3

Al Vanderpool, Capital	234,000	
Income Summary		234,000
To close the owner's capital account.		

INSTRUCTIONS

a. For each entry, identify any errors that Webb made.

b. Prepare four correct closing entries.

c. Using the information presented above (and considering your answers to parts **a** and **b**), compute net income or net loss of Vanderpool Consulting for the year 20__. Show computation.

PROBLEM 3-11
End-of-period Adjusting and Closing Procedures; Preparing Financial Statements
(LO 4–9)

The operations of Hempstead Realty consist of obtaining listings of houses being offered for sale by owners, advertising these houses, and showing them to prospective buyers. The company earns revenue in the form of commissions. The building and office equipment used in the business were acquired on January 1 of the current year and were immediately placed in use. Useful life of the building was estimated to be 30 years and that of the office equipment five years. The company closes its accounts monthly; on March 31 of the current year, the trial balance is as follows:

HEMPSTEAD REALTY
Trial Balance
March 31, 20__

Cash	$ 29,750	
Accounts receivable	7,500	
Office supplies	850	
Land	30,000	
Building	90,000	
Accumulated depreciation: building		$ 500
Office equipment	21,000	
Accumulated depreciation: office equipment . . .		700
Accounts payable		14,750
M. Valentino, capital		126,650
M. Valentino, drawing	4,500	
Commissions earned		50,000
Advertising expense	900	
Automobile rental expense	500	
Salaries expense	7,000	
Telephone expense	600	
	$192,600	$192,600

INSTRUCTIONS

From the trial balance and supplementary data given, prepare the following as of March 31, 20__.

a. Adjusting entries for depreciation during March of building and of office equipment.

b. Adjusting entry to recognize as expense the cost of office supplies used in March. At the end of March, the supplies on hand are estimated to have a cost of $500.

      c. Adjusted trial balance.

      d. Income statement and a statement of owner's equity for the month of March, and a balance sheet at March 31 in report form. Assume no additional investments by owner during March.

      e. Closing entries.

      f. After-closing trial balance.

PROBLEM 3-12
Complete Accounting Cycle
(LO 1–9)

April Stein, M.D., after completing her medical education, established her own practice on May 1. The following transactions occurred during the first month.

May 1	Stein opened a bank account in the name of the practice, April Stein, M.D., by making a deposit of $12,000.
May 1	Paid office rent for May, $1,700.
May 2	Purchased office equipment for cash, $7,200.
May 3	Purchased medical equipment from Niles Medeq, Inc., at a cost of $9,000. A cash down payment of $1,000 was made and a note payable was issued for the remaining $8,000.
May 4	Retained by Western Hospital to be on call for emergency service at a monthly fee of $1,600. The fee for May was collected in cash.
May 15	Excluding the retainer of May 4, fees earned during the first 15 days of the month amounted to $2,800, of which $600 was in cash and $2,200 was in accounts receivable.
May 15	Paid office salary for the first half of May, $1,600.
May 16	Dr. Stein withdrew $975 for personal use.
May 19	Treated Michael Tracy at Western Hospital's emergency department for minor injuries received in an accident.
May 27	Treated Cynthia Knight (a tourist without medical insurance), who paid $25 cash for an office visit and who agreed to pay $35 on June 1 for laboratory medical tests completed May 27.
May 31	Excluding the treatment of Cynthia Knight on May 27, fees earned during the last half of month amounted to $4,900, of which $300 was in cash and $4,600 was in accounts receivable.
May 31	Paid office salary for the second half of month, $1,600.
May 31	Received a bill from McGraw Medical Supplies in the amount of $640 representing the amount of medical supplies used during May.
May 31	Paid utilities for the month, $300.

OTHER INFORMATION

Dr. Stein estimated the useful life of medical equipment at 3 years and of office equipment at 5 years. The account titles to be used and the account numbers are as follows:

Cash	10	April Stein, drawing	41
Accounts receivable	13	Income summary	45
Medical equipment	20	Fees earned	49
Accumulated depreciation: medical equipment	21	Medical supplies expense	50
		Rent expense	51
Office equipment	22	Salaries expense	52
Accumulated depreciation: office equipment	23	Utilities expense	53
Notes payable	30	Depreciation expense: medical equipment	54
Accounts payable	31	Depreciation expense: office equipment	55
April Stein, capital	40		

INSTRUCTIONS

a. Journalize the above transactions. (Number journal pages to permit cross reference to ledger.)

b. Post to ledger accounts. (Use running balance form of ledger account. Number ledger accounts to permit cross reference to journal.)

c. Prepare a trial balance at May 31, 20__.

d. Prepare adjusting entries to record depreciation for the month of May and post to ledger accounts.

e. Prepare an adjusted trial balance.

f. Prepare an income statement and a statement of owner's equity for the month of May, and a balance sheet in report form at May 31. (As this is a new business, the first line in the statement of owner's equity should be: "Initial investment by owner, May 1, 20__, $12,000.")

g. Prepare closing entries and post to ledger accounts.

h. Prepare an after-closing trial balance.

i. Dr. Stein is disappointed in her first month's earnings, as she had expected to earn a net income of $90,000 from her practice during the first year. Based upon the transactions you have recorded in May, assess her prospects of achieving that goal. Explain your reasoning.

PROBLEM 3-13
The Accounting Cycle; a
Comprehensive Problem
(LO 1-9)

On November 1, 19__, Joseph Hawke organized Global Transport to provide transportation of office and household furniture. During November the following transactions occurred:

Nov. 1   Hawke deposited $400,000 cash in a bank account in the name of the business.

Nov. 2   Purchased land for $170,000 and building for $360,000, paying $130,000 cash and signing a $400,000 note payable to Secure Mortgage Company bearing interest at 9%.

Nov. 3   Purchased six new moving vans from Willis Motors at a total cost of $432,000. A cash down payment of $200,000 was made and a note payable was issued for the balance of the purchase price. This note is due in 60 days and does not call for payment of interest.

Nov. 6   Purchased office equipment for cash, $24,000.

Nov. 6   Moved furniture for DBO Adertising Agency from Vancouver to Toronto for $12,975. Collected $7,275 in cash, balance to be paid within 30 days.

Nov. 9   Moved furniture for various clients for $28,500. Collected $7,500 in cash, balance to be paid within 30 days.

Nov. 15   Paid salaries to employees for the first half of the month, $17,400.

Nov. 25   Moved furniture for various clients for a total of $25,525. Cash collected in full.

Nov. 30   Salaries expense for the second half of November amounted to $13,250; paid in full.

Nov. 30   Received a gasoline bill for the month of November from Lucier Oil Company in the amount of $17,500, to be paid by December 10.

Nov. 30   Received bill of $1,250 for repair work on vans during November by Newport Repair Company.

Nov. 30   Paid $5,000 to Secure Mortgage Company. This $5,000 payment included $3,000 interest expense for November and $2,000 reduction in the balance of the note payable issued on November 2.

Nov. 30   Hawke withdrew $4,000 cash from the business for his personal use.

Hawke estimated the useful life of the building at 20 years, the vans at 4 years, and the office equipment at 10 years. The account titles to be used and the account numbers are as follows:

Cash	1	Joseph Hawke, capital	40
Accounts receivable	3	Joseph Hawke, drawing	41
Land	11	Income summary	50
Building	12	Moving service revenue	60
Accumulated depreciation:		Salaries expense.	70
building	13	Gasoline expense	71
Vans	15	Repairs & maintenance expense	72
Accumulated depreciation: vans	16	Interest expense	73
Office equipment	18	Depreciation expense: building	74
Accumulated depreciation: office		Depreciation expense: vans	75
equipment	19	Depreciation expense: office	
Notes payable	30	equipment	76
Accounts payable	31		

a. Prepare journal entries. (Number journal pages for cross reference to ledger.)
b. Post to ledger accounts. (Number ledger accounts for cross reference to journal.)
c. Prepare a trial balance at November 30, 19__.
d. Prepare adjusting entries to record depreciation for November and post to ledger accounts.
e. Prepare an adjusted trial balance.
f. Prepare an income statement and a statement of owner's equity for November, and a balance sheet at November 30, 19__, in report form.
g. Prepare closing entries and post to ledger accounts.
h. Prepare an after-closing trial balance of November 30, 19__.
i. Hawke's estimate of 4 years for the useful lives of the moving vans is too short. Such vehicles normally last 12 years or more. Explain the effects of Hawke's depreciating these vehicles over 4 years instead of 12 upon Global's (1) reported net income in November and (2) cash flows for the month.
j. To start Global, Hawke gave up a salaried position in which he earned $60,000 per year. Also, the $400,000 that he used to start Global had been previously invested in a mutual fund earning an annual return of 9%. Does it appear that starting Global will prove financially rewarding to Hawke, or would he have been better off keeping his old job? Explain your reasoning.

Analytical and Decision Problems and Cases

The realization (recognition) principle determines when a business should recognize revenue. Listed below are three common business situations involving revenue. After each situation, we give two alternatives as to the accounting period (or periods) in which the business might recognize this revenue. Select the appropriate alternative by applying the realization (recognition) principle, and explain your reasoning.
a. Airline ticket revenue: most airlines (Air Canada, Canadian Airlines) sell tickets well before the scheduled date of the flight. (Period ticket sold, period of flight)
b. Sales on account: in June 1999, a Toronto based furniture store had a big sale featuring "no payments until 2000." (Period furniture sold; periods that payments are received from customers)
c. Magazine subscriptions revenue: most magazine publishers (Maclean Hunter, Canadian Business Media) sell subscriptions for future delivery of the magazine. (Period subscription sold; periods that magazines are mailed to customers)

A&D 3-2
Expense Recognition
(LO 2, 9)

As a basis for deciding when to recognize expense, we have discussed the ***matching principle,*** the need for ***objective evidence*** to recognize the existence of an asset, and the concept of ***conservatism.*** Shown below are three costs that ultimately become expenses. Each situation is followed by two alternatives as to when the business might record this expense. Select the appropriate alternative based upon the principles described above, and explain your answer.

a. Computers: most businesses own them, and they are expensive. Due to the rapid advances in technology, it is very difficult to estimate in advance how long the business will keep them. (Period computers purchased; periods in the estimated useful life)

b. Advertising: **Apple Computer** launched the Macintosh with an expensive television advertising campaign. The Macintosh line has been a major source of revenue for Apple ever since. (Period in which advertising was done; periods in estimated production life of the original model Macintosh)

c. Interest expense: on some loans, the borrower does not pay any interest until the end of the loan. This practice is very common on short-term loans, such as 60 or 90 days, but may also occur in some special types of long-term borrowing. (Periods comprising the life of the loan; period in which interest is paid)

A&D 3-3
Accrual Accounting;
Relationship of Depreciation
Expense to Cash Outlays
(LO 4, 5, 9)

The Dark Room is a business that develops film within one hour, using a large and expensive developing machine. The business is organized as a sole proprietorship and operates in rented quarters in a large shopping centre. Sharon Douglas, owner of The Dark Room, plans to retire and has offered the business for sale. A typical monthly income statement for The Dark Room appears below:

Revenue:		
Fees earned		*$8,900*
Operating expenses:		
Wages	*$1,600*	
Rent	*1,850*	
Supplies	*920*	
Depreciation: developing machine	*1,510*	
Miscellaneous	*460*	*6,340*
Net income		*$2,560*

Revenue is received in cash at the time that film is developed. The wages, rent, supplies, and miscellaneous expenses are all paid in cash on a monthly basis. Douglas explains that the developing machine, which is 12 months old and is fully paid for, is being depreciated over a period of five years. She is using this estimated useful life because she believes that faster and more efficient machines will probably be available at that time. However, if the business does not purchase a new machine, the existing machine should last for 10 years or more.

Dave Berg, a friend of yours, is negotiating with Douglas to buy The Dark Room. Berg does not have enough money to pay the entire purchase price in cash. However, Douglas has offered to accept a note payable from Berg for a substantial portion of the purchase price. The note would call for 18 monthly payments in the amount of $2,500, which would pay off the remainder of the purchase price as well as the interest charges on the note. Douglas points out that these monthly payments can be made "out of the monthly earnings of the business."

Berg comes to you for advice. He feels that the sales price asked by Douglas is very reasonable, and that the owner-financing makes this an excellent opportunity. However, he is worried about turning over $2,500 of the business's earnings to Douglas each month. Berg states, "This arrangement will only leave me with about $60 each month. I figure that my family and I need to take about $1,200 out of the business each month just to meet our living expenses." Also, Berg is concerned about the depreciation expense. He does not understand when or to whom the depreciation expense must be paid, or how long this expense will continue.

INSTRUCTIONS

a. Explain to Berg the nature of depreciation expense, including when this expense is paid and what effect, if any, it has upon monthly cash expenditures.
b. Advise Berg as to how much cash the business will generate each month. Will this amount enable Berg to pay $2,500 per month to the former owner and still withdraw $1,200 per month to meet his personal living expenses?
c. Caution Berg about the need to replace the developing machine. Briefly discuss when this expenditure might occur and how much control, if any, Berg has over the timing and dollar amount of this expenditure.

A&D 3-4
A Good Buy?
(LO 1, 2, 9)

Lisome Mody, owner of a small business called Imports from Shanghai, has accepted a salaried position overseas and is trying to interest Jane McKay in buying the business. Mody describes the operating results of the business as follows: "The business has been in existence for only 18 months, but the growth trend is very impressive. Just look at these figures."

	Cash collections from customers
First six-month period	*$120,000*
Second six-month period	*160,000*
Third six-month period	*180,000*

"I think you'll agree those figures show real growth," Mody concluded.

McKay then asked Mody whether sales were made only for cash or on both a cash and credit basis. Mody replied as follows:

"At first we sold both for cash and on open account. In the first six months we made total sales of $200,000 and 70% of those sales were made on credit. We had $80,000 of accounts receivable at the end of the first six-month period."

"During the second six-month period, we tried to discourage selling on credit because of the extra paper work involved and the time required to follow up on slow-paying customers. Our sales on credit in that second six-month period amounted to $70,000, and our total accounts receivable were down to $60,000 at the end of that period."

"During the third six-month period we made sales only for cash. Although we prefer to operate on a cash basis only, we did very well at collecting receivables. We collected in full from every customer to whom we ever sold on credit and we don't have a dollar of accounts receivable at this time."

INSTRUCTIONS

a. Jane McKay has come to you for advice. She is unsure whether the use of cash collections from customers is the best basis for evaluating the "growth trend" of the business and wants your comment on it. She also asks you to provide her with an alternative analysis to determine whether Mody's business is a good buy and whether the "cash sales only" policy has been beneficial.
b. Based upon your analysis in **a,** advise Jane McKay on whether she should buy Mody's business and whether the "cash sales only" policy has been beneficial.

Answers to Self-Test Questions

1. a, b, and d   **2.** a, c, and d   **3.** c   **4.** a and d   **5.** b, c, and d   **6.** d   **7.** c
8. b

CHAPTER 4

Year-End!

Closing out the old year and ringing in the new! It's a tradition everywhere—but for accountants, it takes much longer than one night. Year-end is our "busy season." There is much to be done—adjusting and closing the accounts, financial statements, audits, annual reports, income tax returns, next year's budget—and everyone wants the work "done yesterday."

1. Identify annual accounting activities that make year-end the "busy season."
2. Explain the purpose of adjusting entries.
3. Describe and prepare the four basic types of adjusting entries.
4. Explain the concept of *materiality*.
5. Explain the concept of *adequate disclosure* and the closing of accounts.
6. Explain how *interim* financial statements are prepared in a business that closes its accounts only at year-end.
*7. Prepare a work sheet and explain its usefulness.

THE "BUSY SEASON"

LO 1: Identify annual accounting activities that make year-end the "busy season."

Accounting is an ongoing, year-round activity. Decision makers need—and accountants provide—up-to-date accounting information on a daily basis. But the end of a company's *fiscal year* is an especially busy time. Most companies close their accounts only once each year—at their fiscal year-end. And there is much to be done—taking inventory,[1] making adjusting entries, preparing financial statements, drafting the *notes* that accompany the statements, preparing income tax returns, finalizing next year's budgets, and, perhaps, undergoing an audit.

Publicly owned companies—those with shares listed on a stock exchange—have obligations to release annual and quarterly information to their shareholders and also to the public. These companies don't just "prepare financial statements"; they publish *annual reports.*

An annual report includes comparative financial statements for several years and a wealth of other information about the company's financial position, business operations, and future prospects. But before these reports are issued, the financial statements must be *audited* by a firm of public accountants. Thus, both the company's accountants and the public accountants are under great time pressure to get their work done and the annual report issued as soon as possible. A copy of the annual report is sent to each shareholder; copies also are available to the general public upon request.

Publicly owned companies also must file their audited financial statements and other information with securities commissions. And then there are the income tax returns—provincial and federal.

Many businesses expect their accounting departments to develop comprehensive *budgets* for the coming fiscal year. These budgets show in detail the planned financial operations of every department within the organization, usually on a month-by-month basis. They are used throughout the year—both to coordinate the activities of different departments and as a basis for evaluating departmental performance. Much of the planning involved in the budgeting process is done well before year-end. Nonetheless, the work generally becomes much more intense as the new year approaches.

As explained in Chapter 3, a company's fiscal year *need not* coincide with the calendar year. Some companies elect to end their fiscal year during a seasonal "low point" in business activity. However most companies *do*

---

*Supplemental Topic, "The Work Sheet."

[1]Many companies that sell merchandise take a complete physical inventory at year-end. The phrase "taking inventory" means counting all of the merchandise on hand and determining its cost. This accounting procedure will be discussed further in Chapter 5.

end their fiscal year on December 31. Thus, many accountants refer to the months of December through March as the "busy season."

Our goal in these few paragraphs is only to *identify* the annual accounting activities that often take place around year-end. We cannot adequately discuss all of these activities in a single chapter. Thus, in Chapter 4 we focus upon *end-of-period adjusting entries* and the *preparation of financial statements.* Taking inventory, audits, and annual reports are addressed in later chapters.

ADJUSTING ENTRIES: A CLOSER LOOK

LO 2: Explain the purpose of adjusting entries.

The *realization (recognition) principle,* as explained in Chapter 3, requires that revenue be recognized and recorded in the period it is earned. The *matching principle* stresses that expenses are incurred in order to produce revenue. To measure net income for an accounting period, we must "match" or compare the revenue earned during the period with the expenses incurred to produce that revenue. At the end of an accounting period, adjusting entries are needed so that all revenue *earned* is reflected in the accounts regardless of whether it has been collected. Adjusting entries are also needed for expenses to assure that all expenses *incurred* are matched against the revenue of the current period, regardless of when cash payment of the expense occurs.

Thus, adjusting entries help in achieving the goals of accrual accounting—recording revenue when it is *earned* and recording expenses when the related goods and services are *used.* The realization (recognition) principle and the matching principle are key elements of accrual accounting. Adjusting entries are a technique of applying these principles to transactions that affect two or more accounting periods.

Transactions may affect two or more accounting periods because the life of a business is divided into a series of relatively short accounting periods, for example, a quarter or a year. This is done for the purpose of measuring income and financial position of a business on a timely basis. Thus, it enables decision makers to compare the financial statements of successive accounting periods and to identify significant trends.

We introduced **adjusting entries** in Chapter 3, using as examples the entries to record supplies expense and depreciation expense. Now, let's look into other types of expenses and revenue that also require adjustments at the end of the accounting period.

Types of Adjusting Entries

The exact number of adjustments needed at the end of each accounting period depends upon the nature of the company's business activities. However, most adjusting entries fall into one of five general categories. We will focus on the following *four* in this chapter:[2]

---

[2]A fifth category of adjusting entries consists of adjustments to the balance sheet valuation of certain assets, such as marketable securities and accounts receivable. Valuation adjustments are explained and illustrated in later chapters.

LO 3: Describe and prepare the four basic types of adjusting entries.

1. ***Entries to apportion recorded costs.*** A cost that will benefit more than one accounting period usually is recorded by debiting an asset account. In each period that benefits from the use of this asset, an adjusting entry is made to allocate a portion of the asset's cost to expense.
2. ***Entries to apportion unearned revenue.*** A business may collect in advance for services to be rendered to customers in future accounting periods. In the period in which these services are actually rendered, an adjusting entry is made to record the portion of the revenue earned during the period.
3. ***Entries to record unrecorded expenses.*** An expense may be incurred in the current accounting period even though no bill has yet been received and payment will not occur until a future period. Such unrecorded expenses are recorded by an adjusting entry made at the end of the period.
4. ***Entries to record unrecorded revenue.*** Revenue may be earned during the current period, but not yet billed to customers or recorded in the accounting records. Such unrecorded revenue is recorded by making an adjusting entry at the end of the period.

Adjusting entries bridge the gap between the dates upon which transactions occur, and the periods in which revenue is ***earned*** and expenses are ***incurred.*** Each type of adjusting entry is directly related either to ***past or future transactions.*** These relationships are summarized in the "time-line" diagram on the following page.

Characteristics of Adjusting Entries

It will be helpful to keep in mind two important characteristics of all adjusting entries. First, every adjusting entry ***involves the recognition of either revenue or expense.*** Revenue and expenses represent changes in owners' equity. However, owner's equity cannot change by itself; there also must be a corresponding change in either assets or liabilities. ***Thus, every adjusting entry affects both an income statement account*** (revenue or expense) ***and a balance sheet account*** (asset or liability).

Second, adjusting entries are based upon the concepts of accrual accounting, ***not upon monthly bills or month-end transactions.*** No one sends us a bill saying, "Depreciation expense on your building amounts to $500 this month." Yet, we must be aware of the need to estimate and record depreciation expense if we are to measure net income properly for the period. Making adjusting entries requires a greater understanding of accrual accounting concepts than does the recording of routine business transactions. In many businesses, the adjusting entries are made by the company's controller or by a professional accountant, rather than by the regular accounting staff.

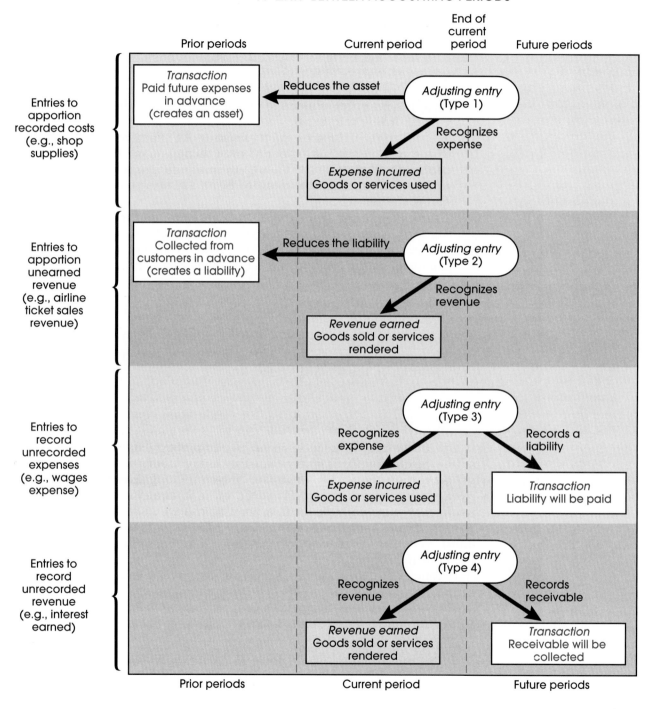

ADJUSTING ENTRIES:
A "LINK" BETWEEN ACCOUNTING PERIODS

Year-End at Overnight Auto Service

To illustrate the various types of adjusting entries, we will again use our example involving Overnight Auto Service. We will skip ahead to December 31, **2000**—the end of the company's first complete year of operations. This will enable us to illustrate the preparation of *annual* financial statements, rather than statements that cover only a single month.

In Chapter 3, we assumed that Overnight adjusted and closed its accounts at the *end of each month.* This allowed us to keep our first illustration short, but closing the accounts every month is *not* a common business practice. Most companies *adjust* their accounts every month, but make closing entries *only at year-end.* We will assume that Overnight has been following this approach throughout 2000.

The company's *unadjusted* trial balance as of December 31, 2000 appears below.

OVERNIGHT AUTO SERVICE Trial Balance December 31, 2000		
Cash	$ 27,950	
Accounts receivable	6,500	
Shop supplies	1,800	
Unexpired insurance	3,000	
Land	52,000	
Building	36,000	
Accumulated depreciation: building		$ 1,800
Tools and equipment	15,000	
Accumulated depreciation: tools and equipment		2,950
Notes payable		40,000
Accounts payable		2,690
Unearned rent revenue		6,000
Michael McBryan, capital		81,000
Michael McBryan, drawing	44,800	
Repair service revenue		161,460
Advertising expense	3,900	
Wages expense	56,800	
Supplies expense	6,900	
Depreciation expense: building	1,650	
Depreciation expense: tools and equipment	2,200	
Utilities expense	19,400	
Insurance expense	15,000	
Interest expense	3,000	
	$295,900	$295,900

When temporary accounts are closed only at year-end, their balances represent the year-to-date

Because Overnight now closes its accounts only at year-end, the balances in the revenue, expense, and owner's drawing accounts represent the activities of the *entire year,* rather than those of a single month. But Overnight last *adjusted* its accounts on November 30; therefore, it is still necessary to make adjusting entries for the month of December.

In the next few pages we illustrate several transactions, as well as the related adjusting entries. Both are shown in the format of general journal entries. To help distinguish between transactions and adjusting entries, transactions will be shown in *blue;* and adjusting entries will be printed in *black.*

Apportioning Recorded Costs

When a business makes an expenditure that will benefit more than one accounting period, the amount usually is debited to an asset account. At the end of each period benefiting from this expenditure, an adjusting entry is made to transfer an appropriate portion of the cost from the asset account to an expense account. This adjusting entry reflects the fact that part of the asset has been used up—or become expense—during the current accounting period.

An adjusting entry to apportion a recorded cost consists of a debit to an expense account and a credit to an asset account (or a contra-asset account). Examples of these adjustments include the entries to record depreciation expense and to apportion the costs of **prepaid expenses.**

Prepaid Expenses   Payments in advance are often made for such items as insurance, rent, and office supplies. If the advance payment (or prepayment) will benefit more than just the current accounting period, the cost *represents an asset* rather than an expense. The cost of this asset will be allocated to expense in the accounting periods in which the services or the supplies are used. In summary, *prepaid expenses are assets;* they become expenses only as the goods or services are used up.

Shop Supplies   To illustrate, consider Overnight's accounting policies for shop supplies. As supplies are purchased, their cost is debited to the asset account, Shop Supplies. It is not practical to make journal entries every few minutes as supplies are used. Instead, an estimate is made of the supplies remaining on hand at the end of each month; the supplies that are not on hand are assumed to have been used.

Prior to making adjusting entries at December 31, the balance in Overnight's Shop Supplies account is $1,800. Assume that at December 31, McBryan estimates there are about $1,200-worth of shop supplies remaining on hand. This suggests supplies costing about $600 have been *used* in December; thus, the following *adjusting entry* is made:

Transferring the cost of supplies used from the asset account to expense	Dec. 31 Supplies Expense	600	
	Shop Supplies		600
	Shop supplies used in December.		

This adjusting entry serves two purposes: (1) it charges to expense the cost of supplies used in December, and (2) it reduces the balance of the Shop Supplies account to $1,200—the amount of supplies estimated to be on hand at December 31.

Insurance Policies   Insurance policies also are a prepaid expense. These policies provide a service, insurance protection, over a specific period of time. As the time passes, the insurance policy *expires*—that is, it is "used up" in business operations.

To illustrate, assume that on February 1, Overnight purchased for $18,000 a one-year insurance policy providing comprehensive liability insurance and insurance against fire and damage to customers' vehicles while in Overnight's facilities. This expenditure (a *transaction*) was debited to an asset account, as shown below:

Purchase 12 months of
insurance coverage

Feb. 1	*Unexpired Insurance*	*18,000*	
	Cash		*18,000*
	Purchased an insurance policy providing coverage for the next 12 months.		

This $18,000 expenditure provides insurance coverage for a period of one year. Therefore, $\frac{1}{12}$ of this cost, or $1,500, is recognized as insurance expense every month. The insurance expense for the month of December is recorded by the following ***adjusting entry*** at month-end:

Cost of insurance
coverage expiring in
December

Dec. 31	*Insurance Expense*	*1,500*	
	Unexpired Insurance		*1,500*
	Insurance expense for December.		

Notice the similarities between the ***effects*** of this adjusting entry and the one that we previously made for shop supplies. In both cases, the entries transfer to expense that portion of an asset that was "used up" during the period.

Recording Prepayments Directly in the Expense Accounts   In our illustration, payments for shop supplies and for insurance covering more than one period were debited to asset accounts. However, some companies follow an alternative policy of debiting such prepayments directly to an expense account, such as Supplies Expense. At the end of the period, the adjusting entry then would be to debit Shop Supplies and credit Supplies Expense for the cost of supplies that had ***not*** been used.

This alternative method leads to the ***same results*** as does the procedure used by Overnight. Under either approach, the cost of supplies used during the current period is treated as an ***expense,*** and the cost of supplies still on hand is carried forward in the balance sheet as an ***asset.***

In this text, we will follow Overnight's practice of recording prepayments in asset accounts and then making adjustments to transfer these costs to expense accounts as the assets expire. This approach correctly describes the ***conceptual flow of costs*** through the elements of financial statements. That is, a prepayment ***is*** an asset that later becomes an expense. The alternative approach is used widely in practice only because it is an efficient "short-cut," which standardizes the recording of transactions and may reduce the number of adjusting entries needed at the end of the period. Remember, our goal in this course is to develop your ability to ***understand and use*** accounting information, not to train you in alternative bookkeeping procedures.

Depreciation of Building   The recording of depreciation expense at the end of an accounting period provides another example of an adjusting entry that ***apportions a recorded cost.*** The adjusting entry to record depreciation on Overnight's building is the same every month throughout the building's estimated useful life (20 years). This entry, essentially the same as illustrated in Chapter 3, is:

The adjusting entry for
monthly depreciation on
the building

Dec. 31	*Depreciation Expense: Building*	*150*	
	Accumulated Depreciation: Building		*150*
	Monthly depreciation on building ($36,000 ÷ 240 mo.).		

The monthly depreciation expense is based upon the following facts: the building cost $36,000, and has an estimated useful life of 20 years (240 months). Under the ***straight-line*** method of depreciation, the cost assumed to expire each month is ¹⁄₂₄₀ of $36,000, or $150.[3]

Accountants often use the term **book value** (or ***carrying value***) to describe the net valuation of an asset in a company's accounting records. For depreciable assets, such as buildings and equipment, book value is equal to the cost of the asset, less the related amount of accumulated depreciation. After Overnight has posted its December adjusting entries, the accumulated depreciation on the building will total ***$1,950*** (the unadjusted balance of $1,800 plus the $150 recognized in December). Thus, the book value of the building is ***$34,050*** ($36,000 − $1,950).

Book value is of significance primarily for accounting purposes. It represents costs that will be offset against the revenue of future periods. Also, it gives users of financial statements an indication of the age of a company's depreciable assets. But book value is ***not*** intended to represent the asset's ***current market value.*** Remember, balance sheets are based primarily upon ***costs,*** rather than estimated market values.

Depreciation on Tools and Equipment   Overnight depreciates its tools and equipment over a period of five years (60 months), using the straight-line method. The December 31 trial balance shows that the company owns tools and equipment that cost $15,000. Therefore, the adjusting entry to record December's depreciation expense is:

Monthly depreciation on tools and equipment—why is it higher than last year?

Dec. 31	Depreciation Expense: Tools and Equipment	250	
	Accumulated Depreciation: Tools and		
	Equipment		250
	Monthly depreciation on tools and equipment		
	($15,000 ÷ 60 months = $250/mo.).		

Some readers may remember that Overnight recognized only $200 in depreciation expense on tools and equipment in December of 1999. If the company is using the straight-line method, why might the amount of monthly depreciation expense have ***increased?*** The answer is quite basic—Overnight now owns more tools and equipment than it did in 1999.

What is the book value of Overnight's tools and equipment at December 31, 2000? If you said ***$11,800,*** you're right.[4]

Apportioning Unearned Revenue

In some instances, customers may ***pay in advance*** for services to be rendered in later accounting periods. For example, a football team collects much of its revenue in advance through the sale of season tickets. Health clubs collect in advance by selling long-term membership contracts. Airlines sell many of their tickets well in advance of a scheduled flight.

---

[3]The straight-line method of depreciation was introduced in Chapter 3; alternative methods are discussed in Chapter 10. Once a business selects a depreciation method, it should apply that method ***consistently*** throughout the asset's useful life.
[4]Cost, $15,000 less accumulated depreciation that, after the December 31 adjusting entry, amounts to $3,200.

For accounting purposes, amounts collected in advance ***do not represent revenue,*** because these amounts have ***not yet been earned.*** Amounts collected from customers in advance are recorded by debiting the Cash account and crediting an ***unearned revenue*** account. **Unearned revenue** also may be called ***deferred revenue.***

When a company collects money in advance from its customers, it has an ***obligation*** to render services in the future. Therefore, the balance of an unearned revenue account is considered to be a liability; ***it appears in the liability section of the balance sheet, not in the income statement.*** Unearned revenue differs from other liabilities because it usually will be settled by rendering services, rather than by making payment in cash. In short, it will be ***worked off*** rather than ***paid off.*** Of course if the business is unable to render the service, it must discharge this liability by refunding money to its customers.

CASE IN POINT

The largest liability in the balance sheet of Air Canada is "Advance ticket sales." This account, with a balance of $400 million, represents unearned revenue resulting from the sale of tickets for future flights. Most of this unearned revenue will be earned as the future flights occur. Some customers, however, will change their plans and will return their tickets to Air Canada for a cash refund.

When the company renders the services for which customers have paid in advance, it is working off its liability to these customers and is earning the revenue. At the end of the accounting period, an adjusting entry is made to transfer an appropriate amount from the unearned revenue account to a revenue account. This adjusting entry consists of a debit to a liability account (unearned revenue) and a credit to a revenue account.

To illustrate these concepts, assume that on December 1, Harbour Cab Co. agreed to rent space in Overnight's building to provide indoor storage for some of its cabs. The agreed-upon rent is $2,000 per month, and Harbour paid for the first three months in advance. The journal entry to record this ***transaction*** on December 1 was:

An "advance"—it's not revenue, it's a liability

Dec. 1	Cash	6,000	
	Unearned Rent Revenue		6,000
	Collected in advance from Harbour Cab for rental of storage space for 3 months		

Remember that Unearned Rent Revenue is a ***liability*** account, ***not a revenue account.*** Overnight will earn rental revenue ***gradually*** over a three-month period as it provides storage facilities to Harbour Cab. At the end of each of these three months, Overnight will make an ***adjusting entry*** transferring $2,000 from the Unearned Revenue account to an "Earned" Revenue account, which will appear in Overnight's income statement. The first in this series of monthly transfers will be made at December 31 with the following adjusting entry:

An adjusting entry showing that some unearned revenue has now been earned

Dec. 31	Unearned Rent Revenue	2,000	
	Rent Revenue Earned		2,000
	Portion of rent received in advance from Harbour		
	Cab that was earned in December ($6,000 ÷ 3 mo.).		

After this adjusting entry has been posted, the Unearned Rent Revenue account will have a $4,000 credit balance. This balance represents Overnight's obligation to render $4,000-worth of services over the next two months and will appear in the liability section of the company's balance sheet. The Rent Revenue Earned account will appear in Overnight's income statement.

Recording Advance Collections Directly in the Revenue Accounts   We have stressed that amounts collected from customers in advance represent *liabilities,* not revenue. However, some companies follow an accounting policy of crediting these advance collections directly to revenue accounts. The adjusting entry then should consist of a debit to the revenue account and a credit to the unearned revenue account for the portion of the advance payments *not yet earned.* This alternative accounting practice leads to the same results as does the method used in our illustration.

In this text, we will follow the originally described practice of crediting advance payments from customers to an unearned revenue account.

Recording Unrecorded Expenses

This type of adjusting entry recognizes expenses that will be paid in *future* transactions; therefore, no cost has yet been recorded in the accounting records. Salaries of employees and interest on borrowed money are common examples of expenses that accumulate from day to day, but that usually are not recorded until they are paid. These expenses are said to **accrue** over time, that is, to grow or to accumulate. At the end of the accounting period, an adjusting entry should be made to record any expenses that have accrued, but that have not yet been recorded. Since these expenses will be paid at a future date, the adjusting entry consists of a debit to an expense account and a credit to a liability account. We shall now use the example of Overnight Auto Service to illustrate this type of adjusting entry.

Accrual of Wages (or Salaries) Expense   Overnight pays its employees every other Tuesday. This month, however, ends on a *Sunday*—two days before the next scheduled payday. Thus, Overnight's employees have worked for more than a week in December *for which they have not yet been paid.*

Time cards indicate that since the last payroll date, Overnight's employees have worked a total of 130 hours. Including payroll taxes, Overnight's wage expense averages about $15 per hour. Therefore, at December 31, the company owes its employees approximately *$1,950* for work performed in December.[5] The following adjusting entry should be made to record this amount both as wages expense of the current period and as a liability:

Wages owed as of month-end

Dec. 31	*Wages Expense*	*1,950*	
	Wages Payable		*1,950*
	To accrue wages owed to employees, but unpaid as of month-end.		

This adjusting entry increases Overnight's wages expense for 2000 and also creates a liability—wages payable—that will appear in the December 31 balance sheet.

On Tuesday, January 2, Overnight will pay its regular biweekly payroll. Let us assume that this payroll amounts to, say, $2,397. In this case, the entry to record payment will be as follows:[6]

Payment of wages earned in two accounting periods

2001

Jan. 2	*Wages Expense*	*447*	
	Wages Payable	*1,950*	
	Cash		*2,397*
	Biweekly payroll, $1,950 of which had been accrued at December 31.		

Accrual of Interest Expense   In November, *1999,* Overnight purchased its building, an abandoned bus garage, from Metropolitan Transit Authority. Overnight issued a $30,000 short-term note payable for much of the purchase price.

Unfortunately, Overnight has never been able to arrange long-term financing on the old garage building. Instead, it has had to arrange a series of short-term loans—usually only three to six months in term. The proceeds of each new loan are used to repay the "old" loan that is coming due.

The facts surrounding the most recent of these short-term loans are as follows: On November 30, Overtime borrowed $40,000 from National Bank. This loan is to be repaid in three months (on February 28), along with interest computed at the annual rate of 9%. The entry made on November 30 to record this borrowing transaction appears below:

Nov. 30	*Cash*	*40,000*	
	Notes Payable		*40,000*
	Borrowed cash from National Bank, issuing a 9% $40,000 note payable, due in three months.		

---

[5]In preparing a formal payroll, wages and payroll taxes must be computed "down to the last cent." But this is not a payroll; it is an amount to be used in the company's financial statements. Therefore, a reasonable estimate will suffice. The accounting principle of **materiality** is discussed later in this chapter.

[6]In this illustration, we do not address the details associated with payroll taxes and amounts withheld. These topics are discussed in the *Supplemental Topic* at the end of Chapter 11.

On February 28, Overnight must pay the bank **$40,900.** This represents the $40,000 amount borrowed, **plus $900 interest** ($40,000 $\times$ .09 $\times$ $\frac{3}{12}$).[7] The $900 interest charge covers a period of **three months.** Although no payment will be made until February 28, interest expense is **incurred** at the rate of $300 per month, as shown below:

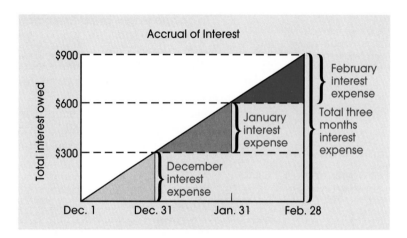

The following adjusting entry is made at December 31 to charge December operations with one month's interest expense and also to record the amount of interest owed to the bank at month-end:

Adjusting entry for interest expense incurred through Dec. 31

Dec. 31   *Interest Expense* *300*
           Interest Payable *300*
           Interest expense accrued during December
           on note payable ($40,000 $\times$ .09 $\times$ $\frac{1}{12}$).

This entry increases the amount of interest expense recognized during the year from $3,000 (unadjusted trial balance on page 171) to **$3,300,** the amount that will appear in Overnight's 2000 income statement. Both the $300 in interest payable, and also the $40,000 note payable to National Bank will appear as **liabilities** in December 31 balance sheet.

Overnight will make an adjusting entry recognizing another $300 in interest expense on January 31 of the coming year. The entry at February 28 to record repayment of this loan, including $900 in interest charges, will be as follows:

Payment of interest expense incurred over several months

2001
Feb. 28   *Notes Payable* *40,000*
            Interest Payable *600*
            Interest Expense *300*
                Cash *40,900*
            Repaid $40,000 note payable, to National Bank,
            including $900 in interest charges, of which, $600
            was accrued for December and January.

---

[7]To simplify the interest calculation for demonstration purposes, the months rather than the days are used and thus the three days of grace for a note payable are not included.

Notice that only *$300* of the total interest charge is recognized as expense in February. Through the process of adjusting entries, we have spread the total $900 interest charge over the three months in which this expense was incurred.

Recording Unrecorded Revenue

A business may earn revenue during the current accounting period but not bill the customer until a future accounting period. This situation is likely to occur if additional services are being performed for the same customer, in which case the bill might not be prepared until all services are completed. Any revenue that has been *earned but not recorded* during the current accounting period should be recorded at the end of the period by means of an adjusting entry. This adjusting entry consists of a debit to an account receivable and a credit to the appropriate revenue account. The term *accrued revenue* often is used to describe revenue that has been earned during the period but that has not been recorded prior to the closing date.

To illustrate this type of adjusting entry, assume that in December, Overnight entered into an agreement to perform routine maintenance on several vans owned by Airport Shuttle Service. Overnight agreed to maintain these vans for a flat fee of $1,500 per month, payable on the fifteenth of each month.

No entry was made to record the signing of this agreement, because no services had yet been rendered. Overnight began rendering services on *December 15,* but the first monthly payment will not be received until January 15. Therefore, Overnight should make the following adjusting entry at December 31 to record the revenue *earned* from Airport Shuttle during the month:

Adjusting entry recognizing revenue earned, but not yet billed or collected

Dec. 31	**Accounts Receivable**	**750**	
	Repair Service Revenue		**750**
	To recognize revenue from services rendered on Airport Shuttle maintenance contract during December. Account is settled on the 15th of each month.		

The collection of the first monthly fee from Airport Shuttle will occur in the next accounting period (January 15, to be exact). Of this $1,500 cash receipt, half represents collection of the receivable recorded on December 31; the other half represents revenue earned in January. Thus, the entry to record the receipt of $1,500 from Airport Shuttle on January 15 will be:

Entry to record collection of accrued revenue

2001			
Jan. 15	Cash	*1,500*	
	Accounts Receivable		750
	Repair Service Revenue		750
	Collected from Airport Shuttle for van maintenance, Dec. 15 thru Jan. 15.		

The net result of the December 31 adjusting entry has been to divide the revenue from maintenance of Airport Shuttle's vans between December and January in proportion to the services rendered during each month.

Adjusting Entries and Accounting Principles

Adjusting entries are **tools** by which accountants apply the **realization (recognition)** and **matching** principles. Through these entries, revenues are recognized as they are **earned,** and expenses are recognized as the related goods and services are **used.**

Another generally accepted accounting principle also plays a major role in the making of adjusting entries—the concept of **materiality**

The Concept of Materiality

LO 4: Explain the concept of materiality.

The term **materiality** refers to the **relative importance** of an item or an event. An item is "material" if knowledge of the item might reasonably **influence the decisions** of users of financial statements. Accountants must be sure that all material items are properly reported in financial statements.

However, the financial reporting process should be **cost effective**—that is, the value of the information should exceed the cost of its preparation. By definition, the accounting treatment accorded to **immaterial** items is of **little or no consequence to decision makers.** Therefore, accountants do not waste time accounting for immaterial items; these items may be handled in the **easiest and most convenient manner.**

In summary, the concept of materiality allows accountants to use estimated amounts and even to ignore other accounting principles if the results of these actions **do not have a "material effect"** upon the financial statements. Materiality is one of the most important generally accepted accounting principles; you will encounter applications of this concept throughout the study of accounting.

Materiality and Adjusting Entries   The concept of materiality enables accountants to shorten and simplify the process of making adjusting entries in several ways. For example:

1. Businesses purchase many "assets" that have a very low cost, or that will be consumed quickly in business operations. Examples include wastebaskets, lightbulbs, and janitorial supplies. The materiality concept permits charging such purchases **directly to expense accounts,** rather than to asset accounts. This treatment conveniently eliminates the need for an adjusting entry at the end of the period to transfer a portion of these costs from an asset account to expense. This accounting "short-cut" is acceptable as long as the cost of the **unused** items on hand at the end of the period is "immaterial."

2. Some expenses, such as telephone bills and utility bills, may be charged to expense as the bills are **paid,** rather than as the services are used. Technically this treatment violates the **matching principle.** However, accounting for utility bills on a cash basis is very convenient, as the monthly cost of utility service is not even known until the utility bill is received. Under this "cash basis" approach, one month's utility bill is charged to expense each month. Although the bill charged to expense is actually the **prior** month's bill, the resulting "error" in the financial statements is not likely to be material.

3. Adjusting entries to accrue unrecorded expenses or unrecorded revenue may be ignored if the dollar amounts are immaterial.

4. If the amount of error is not likely to be material, adjusting entries may be based on ***estimates.*** For example, on page 172 we illustrate an adjusting entry allocating part of the $1,800 balance in the Supplies account to expense. The amount of supplies used during the period ($600) was based upon an ***estimate*** of the supplies still on hand ($1,200). This $1,200 estimate is an "educated guess"; no one actually counts all of the shop supplies on hand and looks up their cost. The adjusting entry recording accrued wages payable also was based upon an estimate, not a detailed calculation.

Materiality Is a Matter of Professional Judgment   Whether or not a specific item or event is "material" is a matter of ***professional judgment.*** In making these judgments, accountants consider several factors.

First, what constitutes a "material amount" varies with the size of the organization. For example, a $1,000 expenditure may be material in relation to the financial statements of a small business, but not to the statements of a large corporation such as Shell Canada.[8] There are no official rules as to what constitutes a "material amount," but most accountants would consider amounts of less than 2 or 3% of net income to be ***immaterial,*** unless there were other factors to consider.

One such "other factor" is the ***cumulative effect*** of numerous "immaterial" events. Each of a dozen items may be immaterial when considered by itself. When viewed together, however, the ***combined effect*** of all twelve items may be material.

Finally, materiality depends upon the ***nature*** of the item, as well as its dollar amount. Assume, for example, that several managers systematically have been stealing money from the company that they manage. Shareholders probably would consider this fact important even if the dollar amounts were small in relation to the company's total resources.

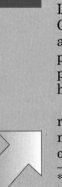

CASE IN POINT   *The Globe and Mail* reported on April 8, 1998 the following lawsuit: Hedy Lamarr, a glamorous movie star of the 1930s and 1940s, is suing Corel Corp. for damage in excess of $15,000 (U.S.) in a Florida circuit court. She alleges that Corel has profited from the use of her likeness in a stylized picture on the cover of CorelDraw 8 (Corel's flagship graphic software product) and on Corel's Web site. She also alleges that Corel's actions have disturbed her peace of mind and violated her privacy.

Corel is one of the 500 largest companies in Canada, with assets and revenue of $233 million and $359 million respectively. Is this lawsuit material enough to be disclosed in the financial statement? Reach your own conclusion and check it with Corel's annual financial statements.

*Maclean's reported on December 14, 1998 that the lawsuit was settled and that the original claim was for $23 million. However, details of the settlement were not released.

---

[8]This point is emphasized by the fact that Shell Canada rounds the dollar amounts shown in its financial statements to the nearest $1 million. This rounding of financial statement amounts is, in itself, an application of the materiality concept.

Note to students: In the assignment material accompanying this textbook, you are to consider all dollar amounts to be material, unless the problem specifically raises the question of materiality.

Effects of the Adjusting Entries

We now have discussed eight separate adjusting entries that Overnight will make at December 31. These entries appear below in the format of journal entries. (Overnight also recorded many transactions throughout the month of December. The company's December transactions are not illustrated, but were accounted for in the manner described in Chapters 2 and 3.)

Adjusting entries are recorded only at the end of the period

GENERAL JOURNAL				Page 26	
Date		Account Titles and Explanation	LP	Debit	Credit
2000 Dec.	31	Supplies Expense . . . . Shop Supplies . . . . Shop supplies used during December ($1,800 − $1,200).		600	600
	31	Insurance Expense . . . . Unexpired Insurance . . . . Insurance expense for December ($18,000 ÷ 12).		1,500	1,500
	31	Depreciation Expense: Building . . . . . . Accumulated Depreciation: Building . Monthly depreciation on building ($36,000 ÷ 240 mo.).		150	150
	31	Depreciation Expense: Tools and Equipment . . . . Accumulated Depreciation: Tools and Equipment . . . . Monthly depreciation on tools and equipment ($15,000 ÷ 60 mo.).		250	250
	31	Unearned Rent Revenue . . . . Rent Revenue Earned . . . . Portion of rent received in advance from Harbour Cab that was earned in December ($6,000 ÷ 3 mo.).		2,000	2,000
	31	Wages Expense . . . . Wages Payable . . . . To accrue wages owed to employees, but unpaid as of month-end.		1,950	1,950
	31	Interest Expense . . . . Interest Payable . . . . Interest expense accrued during December on note payable ($40,000 × .09 × 1/12).		300	300
	31	Accounts Receivable . . . . Repair Service Revenue . . . . To recognize revenue from services rendered on Airport Shuttle maintenance contract during December (1/2 × $1,500).		750	750

After these adjustments are posted to the ledger, Overnight's ledger accounts will be up-to-date (except for the balance in the owner's capital account). The company's **adjusted trial balance** at December 31, 2000, appears as follows. (For emphasis, those accounts affected by the month-end adjusting entries are shown in ***black.***)

	OVERNIGHT AUTO SERVICE Adjusted Trial Balance December 31, 2000	
Cash	$ 27,950	
Accounts receivable	7,250	
Shop supplies	1,200	
Unexpired insurance	1,500	
Land	52,000	
Building	36,000	
Accumulated depreciation: building		$ 1,950
Tools and equipment	15,000	
Accumulated depreciation: tools and equipment .		3,200
Notes payable		40,000
Accounts payable		2,690
Wages payable		1,950
Interest payable		300
Unearned rent revenue		4,000
Michael McBryan, capital*		81,000
Michael McBryan, drawing	44,800	
Repair service revenue		162,210
Rent revenue earned		2,000
Advertising expense	3,900	
Wages expense	58,750	
Supplies expense	7,500	
Depreciation expense: building	1,800	
Depreciation expense: tools and equipment	2,450	
Utilities expense	19,400	
Insurance expense	16,500	
Interest expense	3,300	
	$299,300	$299,300

Balance sheet accounts ← (Cash through Unearned rent revenue)

Statement of owner's equity accounts ← (Michael McBryan, capital / drawing)

Income statement accounts ← (Repair service revenue through Interest expense)

The capital still must be updated for transactions recorded in the revenue, expense, and drawing accounts. Closing entries serve this purpose.

PREPARING THE STATEMENTS

As explained in Chapter 3, the income statement, statement of owner's equity and balance sheet can be prepared ***directly from the amounts listed in the adjusted trial balance.*** (For illustrative purposes, we have made marginal notes beside the adjusted trial balance indicating which accounts appear in which financial statements.) Overnight's financial statements for the year-ended December 31, 2000 are illustrated on the following page.

Data taken directly from the adjusted trial balance

OVERNIGHT AUTO SERVICE
Income Statement
For the Year Ended December 31, 2000

Revenue:		
Repair service revenue		$162,210
Rent revenue earned		2,000
Total revenue		$164,210
Expenses:		
Advertising	$ 3,900	
Wages	58,750	
Supplies	7,500	
Depreciation: building	1,800	
Depreciation: tools and equipment	2,450	
Utilities	19,400	
Insurance	16,500	
Interest	3,300	113,600
Net income		$ 50,610

Net income also appears in the statement of owner's equity

OVERNIGHT AUTO SERVICE
Statement of Owner's Equity
For the Year Ended December 31, 2000

Michael McBryan, capital, Dec. 31, 1999	$ 81,000
Add: **Net income**	50,610
Subtotal	$131,610
Less: Withdrawals	44,800
Michael McBryan, capital, Dec. 31, 2000	$ 86,810

The ending balance in the owner's capital account also appears in the balance sheet

OVERNIGHT AUTO SERVICE
Balance Sheet
December 31, 2000

Assets

Cash		$ 27,950
Accounts receivable		7,250
Shop supplies		1,200
Unexpired insurance		1,500
Land		52,000
Building	$36,000	
Less: Accumulated depreciation	1,950	34,050
Tools and equipment	$15,000	
Less: Accumulated depreciation	3,200	11,800
Total assets		$135,750

Liabilities & Owner's Equity

Liabilities:	
Notes payable	$ 40,000
Accounts payable	2,690
Wages payable	1,950
Interest payable	300
Unearned rent revenue	4,000
Total liabilities	$ 48,940
Owner's equity:	
Michael McBryan, capital	86,810
Total liabilities & owner's equity	$135,750

The income statement is prepared first, because the amount of net income appears in the statement of owner's equity. The statement of owner's equity, in turn, determines the amount of owner's capital appearing in the balance sheet.

Drafting the "Notes" That Accompany Financial Statements

LO 5: Explain the concept of adequate disclosure and the closing of accounts.

To the users of financial statements, **adequate disclosure** is perhaps the most important accounting principle. This principle simply means that financial statements should be accompanied by any information necessary for the statements to be *interpreted properly.*

Most disclosures appear within the several pages of **notes** (or *footnotes*) that accompany the financial statements. Drafting these notes can be one of the most challenging tasks confronting accountants at the end of the period. The content of these notes often cannot be drawn directly from the accounting records. Rather, drafting these notes requires an *in-depth understanding* of the company and its operations, of accounting principles, and of how decision makers interpret and use accounting information.

Two items always disclosed in the notes to financial statements are the accounting methods in use and the due dates of major liabilities. Thus, Overnight's 2000 financial statements should include the following notes:

Note 1: Depreciation policies
Depreciation expense in the financial statements is computed by the straight-line method. Estimated useful lives are 20 years for the building and 5 years for tools and equipment.

Note 2: Maturity dates of liabilities
The Company's notes payable consist of a single obligation that matures on February 28 of the coming year. The maturity value of this note, including interest charges, will amount to $40,900.

The second note should be of great importance to users of Overnight's financial statements. Where is the company going to get the money to pay this note in only two months? It certainly doesn't have enough liquid resources on hand at December 31. Therefore, Overnight must either refinance this loan, or come up with lots of cash—fast.

What Types of Information Must Be Disclosed?

There is no comprehensive list of the information that should be disclosed in financial statements. The "adequacy" of disclosure is based upon a combination of official rules, tradition, and accountants' *professional judgment.*

As a general rule, a company should disclose any facts that an intelligent person would consider necessary for the statements to be *interpreted properly.* In addition to accounting methods in use and the due dates of major liabilities, businesses may need to disclose such matters as:

- Lawsuits pending against the business.
- Scheduled plant closings.

- Governmental investigations into the safety of the company's products or the legality of its pricing policies.
- Significant events occurring **after** the balance sheet date, but before the financial statements are actually issued.
- Specific customers that account for a large portion of the company's business.
- Unusual transactions or conflicts of interest between the company and its key officers.

Let us stress again that **there is no comprehensive list of items that must be disclosed.** Throughout this course, we will identify and discuss many items that may require disclosure in financial statements.

In some cases, companies must even disclose information that could have a **damaging effect** upon the business. For example, a manufacturer may need to disclose that it is being sued by customers who have been injured by its products. The fact that a disclosure might prove embarrassing—or even damaging to the business—is **not** a valid reason for keeping the information "secret." The concept of adequate disclosure demands a **good faith effort** by management to keep the users of financial statements informed about the company's operations.

Companies are **not** required to disclose information that is immaterial, or that does not have a direct **financial** impact upon the business. For example, a company is not required by generally accepted accounting principles to disclose the resignation, firing, or death of a key executive. Of course, companies often **do** disclose such "nonfinancial" events on a voluntary basis.

Disclosures that accompany financial statements should be limited to **facts** and **reasonable estimates.** They should not include **optimistic speculation** that cannot be substantiated.

For a realistic look at the types of disclosure made by a publicly owned corporation, we refer readers to the notes to the consolidated financial statements of Loblaw Companies Limited that appear at the end of this textbook.

Closing the Accounts

Accountants sometimes use the phrase "closing the accounts" to describe **all** of the year-end procedures. But technically, closing the accounts refers only to one specific step in the accounting cycle. This step consists of closing (or transferring) the balances of all revenue, expense, and drawing accounts into the owner's capital account.

Closing accounts is not at all difficult—balances are simply transferred from one account to another. In a computer-based system, this is done with the touch of a button. Overnight, however, has a manual accounting system. The entries to close its revenue and expense accounts, as well as the owner's drawing account, at December 31, 2000, are illustrated below:

Closing entries derived from the adjusted trial balance

GENERAL JOURNAL					Page 27
Date		Account Titles and Explanation	LP	Debit	Credit
2000 Dec.	31	Repair Service Revenue		162,210	
		Rent Revenue Earned		2,000	
		Income Summary			164,210
		To close the revenue accounts.			
	31	Income Summary		113,600	
		Advertising Expense			3,900
		Wages Expense			58,750
		Supplies Expense			7,500
		Depreciation Expense: Building . . .			1,800
		Depreciation Expense: Tools and			
		Equipment			2,450
		Utilities Expense			19,400
		Insurance Expense			16,500
		Interest Expense			3,300
		To close the expense accounts.			
	31	Income Summary		50,610	
		Michael McBryan, Capital			50,610
		To close the Income Summary account.			
	31	Michael McBryan, Capital		44,800	
		Michael McBryan, Drawing			44,800
		To close the owner's drawing account.			

After these entries are posted, the revenue, expense, and drawing accounts will have "zero" balances and be ready for use in measuring the activities of the coming year.

As the final step in its accounting cycle, Overnight will prepare an after-closing trial balance:

The balances in the "temporary" equity accounts have been closed into the owner's capital account

OVERNIGHT AUTO SERVICE After-Closing Trial Balance December 31, 2000		
Cash	$ 27,950	
Accounts receivable	7,250	
Shop supplies	1,200	
Unexpired insurance	1,500	
Land	52,000	
Building	36,000	
Accumulated depreciation: building		$ 1,950
Tools and equipment	15,000	
Accumulated depreciation: tools and equipment .		3,200
Notes payable		40,000
Accounts payable		2,690
Wages payable		1,950
Interest payable		300
Unearned rent revenue		4,000
Michael McBryan, capital		86,810
	$140,900	$140,900

In comparison with the adjusted trial balance, an after-closing trial balance contains only *balance sheet* accounts. Also, the Michael McBryan, Capital account has a new balance. Through the closing of the revenue, expense, and drawing accounts, the owner's capital account has been brought up-to-date.

A Last Look at Overnight: Was 2000 a "Good Year"?

In Chapter 3, we briefly evaluated Overnight after its first month of operations. Let us now consider the financial results of its first fiscal year.

Evaluating Profitability   In 2000, Overnight earned net income of just over *$50,600.* The owner of a small business often evaluates the company's net income in light of his or her alternative financial opportunities.

We assumed in Chapter 3 that if McBryan did not own his own business, he could earn an annual salary of about $48,000 managing another auto service. We also assumed he could earn a return of 12% (about $9,700) if his equity in Overnight had been invested in the stock market. Thus, instead of owning Overnight, McBryan might have earned around $58,000 in 2000—probably with less risk, shorter hours, and fewer headaches. Based on this comparison, the business would not be considered successful for McBryan.

But in evaluating profitability, the real question is not only how the business *did,* but also how it is *likely to do* in the future. If Overnight were in, say, its fifth year of operations, we would view the current level of profitability as inadequate. But this is Overnight's *first* year of operations. Many businesses sustain losses in their early years. To earn a substantial profit in the first year indicates *excellent potential.*

Notice also the $2,000 in revenue earned in December by renting storage space to Harbour Cab. There probably are few additional expenses associated with this revenue. Thus, this agreement alone may increase Overnight's net income by $20,000 or more in the coming year. Thus, the net income of Overnight for next year would be about $70,000, much more than the $58,000 from salary and investment that McBryan would make. In addition, if Harbour stores its cabs in Overnight's garage, Overnight becomes the likely candidate for performing any necessary maintenance and repairs. So, it is quite probable that McBryan's business will be a successful one in the second year.

The operating results over the next couple of years are likely to "tell the story." If Overnight's profits fall, McBryan probably will not consider the business a success. But if the business remains at the second year level of $70,000 or more, it would provide him with an income far above what he might earn in a salaried position. This is why investors—and business owners—consider the *trend* in profitability more important than the results of a given year. However, as mentioned in Chapter 3, McBryan must also consider whether the extra earnings over the salary and investment income is worth the risk involved.

Evaluating Solvency   Solvency, at least in the short term, may be independent of profitability. And in the short term, Overnight has potential cash flow problems.

In the very near future, Overnight may be confronted with the need to make two major cash expenditures. Notice that the company's insurance policy expires at the end of January. Based upon last year, this could require about an $18,000 cash outlay, due around February 1. Next, Overnight's $40,000 note payable comes due at the end of February. Together, these cash outlays could amount to nearly $60,000—an amount well in excess of the company's liquid assets (cash and receivables).

Overnight probably can handle the cost of a new insurance policy, but not repayment of the note. If the bank will not renew this loan, McBryan may be forced to close Overnight's doors and liquidate its assets. Thus, McBryan's business appears to be "at the mercy of the bank."[9]

McBryan can solve this problem if he is able to replace the short-term notes payable, which frequently require refinancing, with a long-term mortgage loan. In our opinion, this should be among his top business priorities.

Focusing Management's Attention   One of the primary uses of accounting information is in ***directing management's attention*** to problems and opportunities. We have mentioned the opportunity inherent in the new rental agreement with Harbour Cab. Management also should review the income statement to determine whether any expenses appear to be excessive.

Because McBryan is an experienced mechanic, we will assume Overnight's wages expense is in line with current market rates. But our attention immediately is drawn to the amounts of insurance expense and utilities expense. We do not know that either expense is excessive, but both appear to offer at least a ***potential*** for significant savings.

In renewing Overnight's insurance policy, McBryan should seek competitive quotes from several companies. Perhaps comparable insurance is available for substantially less than $18,000 per year.

With respect to the utilities expense (which averages $1,600 per month), McBryan should consider such factors as:

- Is the lighting system efficient? (Especially important, as the lights are on all night.)
- Is the heating system efficient and is the building adequately insulated? (Also important, as the heating system often may run all night.)

At first glance, these items may seem small and unimportant. But if Overnight could have cut these expenses by 20%, its net income for 2000 would have been ***$7,480*** [20% × ($19,400 + $18,000)] ***higher.*** Overnight's net income then would have ***exceeded*** what McBryan could expect to earn working for a salary—and that would have "made his year!"

Preparing Financial Statements Covering Different Periods of Time

Many businesses prepare financial statements every quarter, as well as at year-end. In addition, they may prepare financial statements covering other time periods, such as one month, or the year-to-date.

---

[9]The owner of a sole proprietorship is ***personally*** liable for the debts of the business. Therefore, lenders' decisions usually are based upon the solvency of the ***proprietor,*** not that of the business entity. If McBryan has substantial resources and good credit, he should have little trouble in renewing this short-term note. But if he has limited resources and large personal debts, the bank probably would ***not*** renew the loan.

LO 6: Explain how interim financial statements are prepared in a business that closes its accounts only at year-end.

When a business closes its accounts only at year-end, the revenue, expense, and owner's drawing accounts have balances representing the activities of the **year-to-date.** Thus, at **June 30,** these account balances represent the activities recorded over the past six months. Year-to-date financial statements can be prepared directly from an adjusted trial balance. But how might this business prepare **interim financial statements** covering only the month of June? Or the quarter (three months) ended June 30?

The answer is by doing a little **subtraction.** As an example, assume that the adjusted balance in Overnight's Repair Service Revenue account at the ends of the following months was as shown below:

Revenue amounts are for the year-to-date

March 31 (end of the first quarter)	$38,000
May 31	67,000
June 30	80,000

At each date, the account balance represents the revenue earned since January 1. Thus, the March 31 balance represents three months' revenue; the May 31 balance, five months' revenue; and the June 30 balance, the revenue earned over a period of six months.

To prepare an income statement for the **six months** ended June 30, we simply use the June 30 balance in the revenue account—**$80,000.** But to prepare an income statement for the **month** ended June 30, we would have to subtract from the June 30 balance of this account its balance as of May 31. The remainder, **$13,000,** represents the amount of revenue recorded in the account during June ($80,000 − $67,000 = $13,000).

To prepare an income statement for the **quarter** ended June 30, we would subtract from the June 30 balance in this revenue account its balance as of March 31. Thus, the revenue earned during the second quarter (April 1 through June 30) amounts to **$42,000** ($80,000 − $38,000).

This process of subtracting prior balances from the current balance is repeated for each revenue and expense account, and also for the owner's drawing account.

This sounds like a bigger job than it really is. There are only about ten or fifteen accounts involved, and in a computerized system, the entire process is done automatically. Even in a manual system, a person using a "10-key" adding machine can complete this process in a few minutes.

No such computations are required for the balance sheet accounts. A balance sheet always is based upon the account balances **at the balance sheet date.** Therefore, a June 30 balance sheet looks exactly the same **regardless** of the time period covered by the other financial statements.

*Supplemental Topic

THE WORK SHEET

LO 7: Prepare a work sheet and explain its usefulness.

A **work sheet** illustrates in one place the relationships between the unadjusted trial balance, proposed adjusting entries, and the financial statements. A work sheet is prepared at the end of the period, but **before** the adjusting entries are formally recorded in the accounting records. It is not a formal "step" in the accounting cycle. Rather, it is the "scratch pad" upon which accountants work out the details of the proposed end-of-period adjustments. It also provides them with a preview of how the financial statements will look.

A work sheet for Overnight Auto Service at December 31, 2000 is illustrated on the following page.

Isn't This Really a "Spreadsheet"?

Yes. The term "work sheet" is a holdover from the days when these schedules were prepared manually on large sheets of columnar paper. Today, most work sheets are prepared on a computer using spreadsheet software, such as *Lotus 1-2-3*™ or *Excel*™, or with **general ledger software** such as *Peachtree*™ or *Dac-Easy*™.

Since the work sheet is just the accountant's scratch pad, it often isn't printed out in "hard copy"—it may exist only on a computer screen. But the concept remains the same; the work sheet displays **in one place** the unadjusted account balances, proposed adjusting entries, and financial statements as they will appear if the proposed adjustments are made.

What's It Used For?

A work sheet serves several purposes. It allows accountants to **see the effects** of adjusting entries without actually entering these adjustments in the accounting records. This makes it relatively easy for them to correct errors or make changes in estimated amounts. It also enables accountants and management to preview the financial statements before the final drafts are developed. Once the work sheet is complete, it serves as the source for recording adjusting and closing entries in the accounting records and also for preparing financial statements.

Another important use of the work sheet is in the preparation of **interim financial statements.** Interim statements are financial statements developed at various points **during** the fiscal year. Most companies close their accounts only once each year. Yet they often need to develop quarterly or monthly financial statements. Through the use of a work sheet, they can develop these interim statements **without** having to formally adjust and close their accounts.

™Registered trademarks of the respective manufacturers.

OVERNIGHT AUTO SERVICE
Work Sheet
For the Year Ended December 31, 2000

	Trial Balance Dr	Trial Balance Cr	Adjustments* Dr	Adjustments* Cr	Adjusted Trial Balance Dr	Adjusted Trial Balance Cr	Income Statement Dr	Income Statement Cr	Balance Sheet Dr	Balance Sheet Cr
Balance sheet accounts:										
Cash	27,950				27,950				27,950	
Accounts receivable	6,500		(h) 750		7,250				7,250	
Shop supplies	1,800			(a) 600	1,200				1,200	
Unexpired insurance	3,000			(b) 1,500	1,500				1,500	
Land	52,000				52,000				52,000	
Building	36,000				36,000				36,000	
Accumulated depreciation: building		1,800		(c) 150		1,950				1,950
Tools and equipment	15,000				15,000				15,000	
Accumulated depreciation: tools & equip.		2,950		(d) 250		3,200				3,200
Notes payable		40,000				40,000				40,000
Accounts payable		2,690				2,690				2,690
Unearned rent revenue		6,000	(e) 2,000			4,000				4,000
Michael McBryan, capital		81,000				81,000				81,000
Michael McBryan, drawing	44,800				44,800				44,800	
Wages payable				(f) 1,950		1,950				1,950
Interest payable				(g) 300		300				300
	295,900	295,900								
Income statement accounts:										
Repair service revenue		161,460		(h) 750		162,210		162,210		
Advertising expense	3,900				3,900		3,900			
Wages expense	56,800		(f) 1,950		58,750		58,750			
Supplies expense	6,900		(a) 600		7,500		7,500			
Depreciation expense: building	1,650		(c) 150		1,800		1,800			
Depreciation expense: tools & equip.	2,200		(d) 250		2,450		2,450			
Utilities expense	19,400				19,400		19,400			
Insurance expense	15,000		(b) 1,500		16,500		16,500			
Interest expense	3,000		(g) 300		3,300		3,300			
Rent revenue earned				(e) 2,000		2,000		2,000		
			7,500	7,500	299,300	299,300	113,600	164,210	185,700	135,090
Net income							50,610			50,610
Totals							164,210	164,210	185,700	185,700

*Adjustments:

(a) Shop supplies used in December.
(b) Portion of insurance cost expiring in December.
(c) Depreciation on building for December.
(d) Depreciation of tools and equipment for December.
(e) Earned one-third of rent revenue collected in advance from Harbour Cab.
(f) Unpaid wages owed to employees at December 31.
(g) Interest payable accrued during December.
(h) Repair service revenue earned in December but not yet billed.

The Mechanics: How It's Done

Whether done manually or on a computer, the preparation of a work sheet involves five basic steps. We first will describe these steps as if the work sheet were being prepared manually. Afterward, we will explain how virtually all of the mechanical steps can be performed automatically by a computer.

1. Enter the ledger account balances in the Trial Balance columns. The work sheet begins with an unadjusted trial balance—that is, a listing of the ledger account balances at the end of the period *prior* to making any adjusting entries. In our illustration, the unadjusted trial balance appears in *blue.*

   Notice our inclusion of the captions "Balance Sheet accounts" and "Income Statement accounts." These captions are optional, but they help clarify the relationships between the ledger accounts and the financial statements. (Hint: A few lines should be left blank immediately below the last Balance Sheet account. It is often necessary to add a few more accounts during the adjusting process. Additional income statement accounts can be added on the lines below the trial balance totals.)

2. Enter the adjustments in the Adjustments columns. The next step is the most important: Enter the appropriate end-of-period adjustments in the Adjustments columns. In our illustration, these adjustments appear in *black.*

   Notice that each adjustment includes both debit and credit entries, which are linked together by the small "key letters" appearing to the left of the dollar amount. Thus, adjusting entry *a* consists of a $600 debit to Supplies Expense and a $600 credit to Shop Supplies. Just as individual adjusting entries involve equal debit and credit amounts, so the totals of the debit and credit Adjustment columns should be equal.

   Sometimes the adjustments require adding accounts to the original trial balance. (The three ledger account titles printed in *black* were added during the adjusting process.)

3. Prepare an adjusted trial balance. Next, an adjusted trial balance is prepared. The balances in the original trial balance *(blue)* are adjusted for the debit or credit amounts in the adjustments columns *(black).* This process of horizontal addition or subtraction is called *cross-footing.* The adjusted trial balance is totalled to determine that the accounts remain in balance.

   At this point, the entire work sheet is virtually complete. We have emphasized that financial statements are prepared *directly from the adjusted trial balance.* Thus, we have only to arrange these accounts into the format of financial statements. For this reason, we show the adjusted trial balance amounts in *blue*—both in the Adjusted Trial Balance columns and when these amounts are *extended* (carried forward) into the financial statement columns.

4. Extend the adjusted trial balance amounts into the appropriate "financial statement" columns. The "balance sheet accounts"—assets, liabilities, and owner's equity—are extended into the Balance Sheet columns; income statement amounts, into the Income Statement columns. (The "Balance Sheet" and "Income Statement" captions in the original trial balance should simplify this procedure. Notice each amount is extended to one and only one column. Also, the account retains the same debit or credit balance as shown in the adjusted trial balance.)

5. Total the financial statement columns; determine and record net income or net loss. The final step in preparing the work sheet consists of totalling

the income statement and balance sheet columns and then bringing each set of columns "into balance." These tasks are performed on the bottom three lines of the work sheet. In our illustration, the amounts involved in this final step are shown in *grey.*

When the Income Statement and Balance Sheet columns are first totalled, the debit and credit columns will not agree. But each set of columns should be "out-of-balance" by the *same amount*—and that amount should be the amount of net income or net loss for the period.

Let us briefly explain *why* both sets of columns initially are out-of-balance by this amount. First consider the Income Statement columns. The credit column contains the revenue accounts, and the debit column, the expense accounts. The difference, therefore, represents the net income (net loss) for the period.

Now consider the Balance Sheet columns. All of the balance sheet amounts are shown at up-to-date amounts *except* for the owner's capital account, which still contains the balance from the *beginning* of the period. To bring the owner's capital account up-to-date, we must add net income and subtract any drawings. The drawings already appear in the Balance Sheet debit column. So what's the only thing missing? The net income (or net loss) for the period.

To bring both sets of columns into balance, we enter the net income (or net loss) on the next line. The same amount will appear in both the Income Statement columns and the Balance Sheet columns. But in one set of columns it appears as a debit, and in the other, it appears as a credit.[1] After this amount is entered, each set of columns should "balance."

Computers Do the "Pencil-Pushing"   When a work sheet is prepared by computer, accountants perform only *one* of the steps listed above—*entering the adjustments.* The computer automatically lists the ledger accounts in the form of a trial balance. After the accountant has entered the adjustments, it automatically computes the adjusted account balances and completes the work sheet. (Once the adjusted balances are determined, completing the work sheet involves nothing more than putting these amounts in the appropriate column and determining the column totals.)

"What If . . .:" A Special Application of Work Sheet Software

We have discussed a relatively simple application of the work sheet concept—illustrating the effects of proposed *adjusting entries* upon account balances. But the same concept can be applied to proposed *future transactions.* The effects of the proposed transactions simply are entered in the "Adjustments" columns. Thus, without disrupting the accounting records, accountants can prepare schedules showing how the company's financial statements might be affected by such events as a merger with another company, a 15% increase in sales volume, or the closure of a plant.

There is a tendency to view work sheets as mechanical and "old-fashioned." This is not at all the case. Today, the mechanical aspects are handled entirely by computer. The real purpose of a work sheet is to show quickly and efficiently how specific events or transactions will affect the financial statements. This isn't bookkeeping—it's *planning.*

---

[1] To bring the Income Statement columns into balance, net *income* is entered in the *debit column.* This is because the credit column (revenue) exceeds the debit column (expenses). But in the balance sheet, net income is an element of owner's equity, which is represented by a credit. In event of a net *loss,* this situation reverses.

End-of-Chapter Review

Key Terms Introduced or Emphasized in Chapter 4

Accrue *(p.176)* To grow or accumulate over time, for example, interest expense.

Adequate disclosure *(p.185)* The generally accepted accounting principle of providing with financial statements any information that users need to properly interpret those statements.

Adjusted trial balance *(p.183)* A schedule showing the balances in ledger accounts *after* end-of-period adjusting entries have been posted. The amounts shown in the adjusted trial balance are carried directly into financial statements.

Adjusting entries *(p.168)* Entries made at the end of the accounting period for the purpose of recognizing revenue and expenses that are not properly measured as a result of journalizing transactions as they occur.

Book value *(p.174)* The net amount at which an asset appears in financial statements. For depreciable assets, book value represents cost minus accumulated depreciation. Also called *carrying value.*

General ledger software *(p.191)* Computer software used for recording transactions, maintaining journals and ledgers, and preparing financial statements. Also includes spreadsheet capabilities for showing the effects of proposed adjusting entries or transactions upon the financial statements without actually recording these entries in the accounting records.

Immaterial *(p.180)* Something of little or no consequence. Immaterial items may be accounted for in the most *convenient* manner, without regard to other theoretical concepts.

Interim financial statements *(p.190)* Financial statements prepared for periods of less than one year (includes monthly and quarterly statements).

Matching (principle) *(p.180)* The accounting principle of offsetting revenue with the expenses incurred in producing that revenue. Requires recognition of expenses in the periods that the goods and services are *used* in the effort to produce revenue.

Materiality *(p.180)* The relative importance of an item or amount. Items significant enough to influence decisions are said to be *material.*

Notes (accompanying financial statements) *(p.185)* Supplemental disclosures which accompany financial statements. These notes provide users with various types of information considered necessary for the proper interpretation of the statements.

Prepaid expenses *(p.172)* Assets representing advance payment of the expenses of future accounting periods. As time passes, adjusting entries are made to transfer the related costs from the asset account into an expense account.

Realization (recognition principle) *(p.180)* The accounting principle that governs the timing of revenue recognition. Basically, the principle indicates that revenue should be recognized in the period in which it is *earned.*

Unearned revenue *(p.175)* An obligation to deliver goods or render services in the future, stemming from the receipt of advance payment.

Work sheet *(p.191)* A multi-column schedule showing the relationships among the current account balances (a trial balance), proposed adjusting entries or transactions, and the financial statements that would result if these adjusting entries or transactions were recorded. Used both at the end of the accounting period as an aid to preparing financial statements, and for planning purposes.

DEMONSTRATION PROBLEM

Reed Geophysical Consulting formally adjusts and closes its accounts only at year-end. (Interim financial statements are prepared from work sheets, but the adjustments are not recorded in the accounting records.) At December 31, 2000, the balances in the ledger accounts *prior to making adjusting entries for the year* were as follows:

REED GEOPHYSICAL CONSULTING Trial Balance December 31, 2000		
Cash	$ 19,140	
Consulting fees receivable	23,400	
Prepaid rent	3,300	
Prepaid dues and subscriptions	960	
Supplies	1,300	
Equipment	40,000	
Accumulated depreciation: equipment		$ 7,200
Notes payable		5,000
Unearned consulting fees		35,650
Glen Reed, capital		47,040
Glen Reed, drawing	63,000	
Consulting fees earned		90,860
Salaries expense	16,900	
Telephone expense	2,550	
Rent expense	11,000	
Miscellaneous expenses	4,200	
	$185,750	$185,750

OTHER DATA

a. For the first 11 months of the year, office rent had been charged to the Rent Expense account at a rate of $1,000 per month. On December 1, however, the company signed a new rental agreement and paid three months' rent in advance at a rate of $1,100 per month. This advance payment was debited to the Prepaid Rent account.

b. Dues and subscriptions expired during the year in the total amount of $710.

c. An estimate of supplies on hand was made at December 31; the estimated cost of the unused supplies was $450.

d. The useful life of the equipment has been estimated at 10 years from date of acquisition. (Remember no depreciation expense has been recorded in the accounting records for the current year.)

e. Accrued interest on notes payable amounted to $100 at year-end.

f. Consulting services valued at $32,550 were rendered during the year for clients who had made payment in advance.

g. It is the custom of the firm to bill clients only when consulting work is completed or, in the case of prolonged engagements, at six-month intervals. At December 31, engineering services valued at $3,000 had been rendered to clients but not yet billed. No advance payments had been received from these clients.

h. Reed Geophysical has only one salaried employee. The salary owed to this individual as of December 31 amounted to $1,200.

INSTRUCTIONS

a. Prepare the adjusting entries, in the format of journal entries, at December 31, 2000.

***b.** Prepare a work sheet for the year ended December 31, 2000.

SOLUTION TO DEMONSTRATION PROBLEM

a. Adjusting entries

	GENERAL JOURNAL			Page 328
Date	**Account Title and Explanation**	**LP**	**Debit**	**Credit**
2000	*(a)*			
Dec. 31	Rent Expense		1,100	
	Prepaid Rent			1,100
	Rent expense for December (1/3 × $3,300)			
	(b)			
31	Dues and Subscriptions Expense		710	
	Prepaid Dues and Subscriptions			710
	Dues and subscriptions expenses for the year			
	(c)			
31	Supplies Expense		850	
	Supplies			850
	Supplies used for the year ($1,300 − $450)			
	(d)			
31	Depreciation Expense: Equipment		4,000	
	Accumulated Depreciation: Equipment			4,000
	Depreciation expense for the year			
	($40,000 ÷ 10)			
	(e)			
31	Interest Expense		100	
	Interest Payable			100
	Accrued interest on notes payable			
	(f)			
31	Unearned Consulting Fees		32,550	
	Consulting Fees Earned			32,550
	Consulting services rendered for clients			
	who paid in advance			
	(g)			
31	Consulting Fees Receivable		3,000	
	Consulting Fees Earned			3,000
	Consulting services rendered but not billed			
	(h)			
31	Salaries Expense		1,200	
	Salaries Payable			1,200
	Salaries earned but not paid			

Supplemental Topic, "The Work Sheet."

b. Work Sheet

REED GEOPHYSICAL CONSULTING
Work Sheet
For the Year Ended December 31, 2000

	Trial Balance Dr	Trial Balance Cr	Adjustments* Dr	Adjustments* Cr	Adjusted Trial Balance Dr	Adjusted Trial Balance Cr	Income Statement Dr	Income Statement Cr	Balance Sheet Dr	Balance Sheet Cr
Balance sheet accounts:										
Cash	19,140				19,140				19,140	
Consulting fees receivable	23,400		(g) 3,000		26,400				26,400	
Prepaid rent	3,300			(a) 1,100	2,200				2,200	
Prepaid dues and subscriptions	960			(b) 710	250				250	
Supplies	1,300			(c) 850	450				450	
Equipment	40,000				40,000				40,000	
Accumulated depreciation: equipment		7,200		(d) 4,000		11,200				11,200
Notes payable		5,000				5,000				5,000
Unearned consulting fees		35,650	(f) 32,550			3,100				3,100
Glen Reed, capital		47,040				47,040				47,040
Glen Reed, drawing	63,000				63,000				63,000	
Interest payable				(e) 100		100				100
Salaries payable				(h) 1,200		1,200				1,200
Income statement accounts:										
Consulting fees earned		90,860		(f) 32,550 (g) 3,000		126,410		126,410		
Salaries expense	16,900		(h) 1,200		18,100		18,100			
Telephone expense	2,550				2,550		2,550			
Rent expense	11,000		(a) 1,100		12,100		12,100			
Miscellaneous expense	4,200				4,200		4,200			
	185,750	185,750								
Dues and subscriptions expense			(b) 710		710		710			
Supplies expense			(c) 850		850		850			
Depreciation expense: equipment			(d) 4,000		4,000		4,000			
Interest expense			(e) 100		100		100			
			43,510	43,510	194,050	194,050	42,610	126,410	151,440	67,640
Net income							83,800			83,800
Totals							126,410	126,410	151,440	151,440

*Adjustments:
(a) Rent expense for December (1/3 × $3,300).
(b) Dues and subscriptions expense for year.
(c) Supplies used for year ($1,300 − $450 = $850).
(d) Depreciation expense for year ($40,000 ÷ 10 = $4,000)
(e) Accrued interest on notes payable.
(f) Consulting services performed for clients who paid in advance.
(g) Services rendered but not billed.
(h) Salaries earned but not paid.

198

Self-Test Questions

The answers to these questions appear on page 221.

1. For a publicly owned company, indicate which of the following accounting activities are likely to occur at or shortly after year-end. (More than one answer may be correct.)
   a. Preparing of income tax returns.
   b. Adjusting and closing the accounts.
   c. Drafting disclosures that accompany the financial statements.
   d. An audit of the financial statements by a firm of public accountants.

2. The purpose of adjusting entries is to:
   a. Adjust the Owner's Capital account for the revenue, expense, and drawings recorded during the accounting period.
   b. Adjust daily the balances in asset, liability, revenue, and expense accounts for the effects of business transactions.
   c. Apply the realization (recognition) principle and the matching principle to transactions affecting two or more accounting periods.
   d. Prepare revenue and expense accounts for recording the transactions of the next accounting period.

3. Before month-end adjustments are made, the January 31 trial balance of Rover Excursions contains revenue of $27,900 and expenses of $17,340. Adjustments are necessary for the following items:
   —portion of prepaid rent applicable to January, $2,700.
   —depreciation for January, $1,440.
   —portion of fees collected in advance earned in January, $3,300.
   —fees earned in January, not yet billed to customers, $1,950.

   Net income in Rover Excursions' January income statement is:
   a. $10,560   b. $17,070   c. $7,770   d. Some other amount

4. The public accounting firm auditing Mason Street Recording Studios found that owner's equity was understated and liabilities were overstated. Which of the following errors could have been the cause?
   a. Making the adjusting entry for depreciation expense twice.
   b. Failure to record interest accrued on a note payable.
   c. Failure to make the adjusting entry to record revenue that had been earned, but not yet billed to clients.
   d. Failure to record the earned portion of fees received in advance.

5. The concept of ***materiality:*** (Indicate all correct answers.)
   a. Requires that financial statements are accurate to the nearest dollar, but need not show cents.
   b. Is based upon what users of financial statements are thought to consider important.
   c. Permits accountants to ignore other generally accepted accounting principles in certain situations.
   d. Permits accountants to use the easiest and most convenient means of accounting for events that are ***immaterial.***

6. Indicate those items for which generally accepted accounting principles ***require*** disclosure in notes accompanying the financial statements. (More than one answer may be correct.)
   a. A large lawsuit was filed against the company two days ***after*** the balance sheet date.
   b. The depreciation method in use, given that several different methods are acceptable under generally accepted accounting principles.

    c. Whether small but long-lived items—such as electric pencil sharpeners and hand-held calculators—are charged to asset accounts or to expense accounts.

    d. As of year-end, the chief executive officer had been hospitalized because of chest pains.

7. Ski West adjusts its accounts at the end of each month, but closes them only at the end of each calendar year (December 31). The ending balances in the Equipment Rental Revenue account and the Cash account in February and March appear below.

	Feb. 28	Mar. 31
Cash	$14,200	$26,500
Equipment rental revenue	12,100	18,400

Ski West prepares financial statements showing separately the operating results of each month. In the financial statements prepared for the month ended March 31, Equipment Rental Revenue and Cash should appear as follows:

    a. Equipment Rental Revenue, $18,400; Cash, $26,500

    b. Equipment Rental Revenue, $18,400; Cash, $12,300

    c. Equipment Rental Revenue, $6,300; Cash, $26,500

    d. Equipment Rental Revenue, $6,300; Cash, $12,300

*8. A work sheet can be used for all of the following purposes *except:*

    a. Showing accountants and management how proposed adjusting entries and transactions will affect the financial statements.

    b. Developing end-of-period adjusting entries prior to actually recording these adjustments in the accounting records.

    c. Reducing to a single page the presentation of financial information within the company's annual report.

    d. Preparing interim financial statements without actually adjusting or closing the accounts.

ASSIGNMENT MATERIAL

Discussion Questions

1. Identify three or more accounting activities that take place primarily at year-end, as opposed to uniformly throughout the year.

2. What is the purpose of making adjusting entries? Your answer should relate adjusting entries to the goals of accrual accounting.

3. Do all transactions involving revenue or expenses require adjusting entries at the end of the accounting period? If not, what is the distinguishing characteristic of those transactions that do require adjusting entries?

4. Do adjusting entries affect income statement accounts, balance sheet accounts, or both? Explain.

5. Why does the recording of adjusting entries require a better understanding of the concepts of accrual accounting than does the recording of routine revenue and expense transactions occurring throughout the period?

---

*Supplemental Topic, "The Work Sheet."

6. Why does the purchase of a one-year insurance policy four months ago give rise to insurance expense in the current month?

7. If services have been rendered to customers during the current accounting period but no revenue has been recorded and no bill has been sent to the customers, why is an adjusting entry needed? What types of accounts should be debited and credited by this entry?

8. What is meant by the term **unearned revenue?** Where should an unearned revenue account appear in the financial statements? As the work is done, what happens to the balance of an unearned revenue account?

9. The weekly payroll for employees of Ryan Company, who work a five-day week, amounts to $20,000. All employees are paid up-to-date at the close of business each Friday. If December 31 falls on Thursday, what year-end adjusting entry is needed?

10. At year-end the adjusting entry to reduce the Unexpired Insurance account by the amount of insurance premium applicable to the current period was accidentally omitted. Which items in the income statement will be in error? Will these items be overstated or understated? Which items in the balance sheet will be in error? Will they be overstated or understated?

11. Briefly explain the concept of **materiality.** If an item is not material, how is the item treated for financial reporting purposes?

12. In Chapter 1, assets were defined as economic resources owned by a business and expected to benefit future business operations. By this definition, the gasoline in the tank of a business automobile, unused typewriter ribbons, and even ballpoint pens are actually "assets." Why, then, are purchases of such items routinely charged directly to expense?

13. Explain the accounting principle of **adequate disclosure.**

14. Briefly describe the content of the **notes** that accompany financial statements.

*15. Explain several purposes that may be served by preparing a work sheet (or using computer software that achieves the goals of a work sheet).

Exercises

EXERCISE 4-1
Accounting Terminology
(LO 1–5)

Listed below are nine technical accounting terms used in this chapter:

Unrecorded revenue	*Adjusting entries*	*Accrued expenses*
Adequate disclosure	*Closing entries*	*Book value*
Unearned revenue	*Materiality*	*Prepaid expenses*

Each of the following statements may (or may not) describe one of these technical terms. For each statement, indicate the accounting term described, or answer "None" if the statement does not correctly describe any of the terms.

a. The net amount at which an asset is carried in the accounting records as distinguished from its market value.

b. An accounting concept that may justify departure from other accounting principles for purposes of convenience and economy.

c. The accounting principle intended to assist users in **interpreting** financial statements.

d. Revenue earned during the current accounting period but not yet recorded or billed, which requires an adjusting entry at the end of the period.

---

*Supplemental Topic, "The Work Sheet."

e. Entries made at the end of the period to achieve the goals of accrual accounting by recording revenue when it is earned and by recording expenses when the related goods and services are used.

f. A type of account credited when customers pay in advance for services to be rendered in the future.

g. A balance sheet category used for reporting advance payments of such items as insurance, rent, and office supplies.

h. Entries made during the accounting period to correct errors in the original recording of complex transactions.

EXERCISE 4-2
Effects of Adjusting Entries
(LO 2, 3)

Security Service Company adjusts its accounts at the end of the month. On November 30, adjusting entries are prepared to record:

a. Depreciation expense for November.

b. Interest expense that has accrued during November.

c. Revenue earned during November that has not yet been billed to customers.

d. Salaries payable to company employees that have accrued since the last payday in November.

e. The portion of the company's prepaid insurance that has expired during November.

f. Earning a portion of the amount collected in advance from a customer, Harbour Restaurant.

Indicate the effect of each of these adjusting entries upon the major elements of the company's financial statements—that is, upon revenue, expenses, net income, assets, liabilities, and owner's equity. Organize your answer in tabular form, using the column headings shown below and the symbols **I** for increase, **D** for decrease, and **NE** for no effect. The answer for adjusting entry **a** is provided as an example.

	Income Statement			Balance Sheet		
Adjusting Entry	Revenue −	Expenses =	Net Income	Assets =	Liabilities +	Owner's Equity
a	NE	I	D	D	NE	D

EXERCISE 4-3
Preparing Adjusting Entries for Recorded Costs and Recorded Revenue
(LO 2, 3)

The Outlaws, a professional football team, prepare financial statements on a monthly basis. Football season begins in August, but in July the team engaged in the following transactions:

a. Paid $1,500,000 to SkyDome as advance rent for use of its facilities for the five-month period from August 1 through December 31. This payment was debited to the asset account, Prepaid Rent.

b. Collected $2,560,000 cash from sales of season tickets for the team's eight home games. This amount was credited to Unearned Ticket Revenue.

During the month of August, The Outlaws played one home game and two games on the road. Their record was two wins, one loss.

Prepare the two adjusting entries required at August 31 to apportion this recorded cost and recorded revenue.

EXERCISE 4-4
Preparing Adjusting Entries for Unrecorded Revenue and Expenses
(LO 2, 3)

The law firm of Dale & Clark prepares its financial statements on a monthly basis. Among the items requiring adjustment at December 31 are the following:

1. Salaries to staff lawyers are paid on the fifteenth day of each month. Salaries accrued since December 15 amount to $17,800 and have not yet been recorded.

2. The firm is defending J. R. Stone in a civil lawsuit. The agreed-upon legal fees are $2,100 per day while the trial is in progress. The trial has been in progress for nine days during December and is not expected to end until late January.

No legal fees have yet been billed to Stone. (Legal fees are recorded in an account entitled Legal Fees Earned.)

a. Prepare the two adjusting entries required at December 31 to record the accrued salaries expense and the accrued legal fees revenue.

b. Assume that salaries paid to staff lawyers on January 15 amount to $35,000 for the period December 15 through January 15. How much of this amount is considered salaries expense of *January?* (Although not required, you may wish to prepare the journal entry at January 15 to record payment of staff lawyers.)

c. Assume that on January 29, Dale & Clark receives $60,900 from J. R. Stone in full settlement of legal fees for services in the civil lawsuit. What portion of this amount constitutes revenue earned in *January?* (Although not required, you may wish to prepare the journal entry at January 29 to record receipt of the $60,900.)

EXERCISE 4-5
Distinction Between Adjusting and Closing Process
(LO 2, 3, 5)

When Torretti Company began business on August 1, it purchased a one-year fire insurance policy and debited the entire cost of $7,200 to Unexpired Insurance. Torretti *adjusts* its accounts at the end of each month, and *closes* its books at the end of the year.

a. Give the ***adjusting entry*** required at December 31 with respect to this insurance policy.

b. Give the ***closing entry*** required at December 31 with respect to insurance expense. Assume that this policy is the only insurance policy Torretti had during the year.

c. Compare the dollar amount appearing in the December 31 adjusting entry (part **a**) with that in the closing entry (part **b**). Are the dollar amounts the same? Why or why not? Explain.

EXERCISE 4-6
Get Your Tickets Early
(LO 3)

When **Air Canada** sells tickets for future flights, it debits cash and credits an account entitled Advance Ticket Sales. With respect to this Advance Ticket Sales account:

a. What does the balance of the account represent? Where should the account appear in Air Canada's financial statements?

b. Explain the activity that normally ***reduces*** the balance of this account. Can you think of any ***other*** transaction that would reduce this account?

EXERCISE 4-7
Preparing Various Adjusting Entries
(LO 2, 3)

Hill Company adjusts its accounts at the end of each month. Prepare the adjusting entries required at December 31 based on the following information.

a. A bank loan had been obtained on December 1. Accrued interest on the loan at December 31 amounts to $1,050. No interest expense has yet been recorded.

b. Depreciation of office equipment is based on an estimated life of five years. The balance in the Office Equipment account is $24,000; no change has occurred in the account during the year.

c. Interest revenue earned on government bonds during December amounts to $750. This accrued interest revenue has not been recorded or received as of December 31.

d. On December 31, an agreement was signed to lease a truck for 12 months beginning January 1 at a rate of 35 cents a kilometre. Usage is expected to be 2,000 kilometres per month and the contract specifies a minimum payment equivalent to 18,000 kilometres a year.

e. The company's policy is to pay all employees up-to-date each Friday. Since December 31 fell on Monday, there was a liability to employees at December 31 for one day's pay amounting to $2,800.

What's the effect?   Assume that *prior* to making December 31 adjusting entries, Hill Company's net income was $129,350. Compute net income *after* December adjustments have been recorded. Show your work.

EXERCISE 4-8
Notes Payable and Interest
(LO 2, 3)

Ventura Company adjusts its accounts *monthly* and closes its accounts on December 31. On October 31, 1999, Ventura Company signed a note payable and borrowed $120,000 from a bank for a period of six months at an annual interest rate of 9%.

a. How much is the total interest expense over the life of the note? How much is the monthly interest expense? (Assume equal amounts of interest expense each month.)

b. In the company's annual balance sheet at December 31, 1999, what is the amount of the liability to the bank?

c. Prepare the journal entry to record issuance of the note payable on October 31, 1999.

d. Prepare the adjusting entry to accrue interest on the note at December 31, 1999.

e. Assume the company prepared a balance sheet at March 31, 2000. State the amount of the liability to the bank at this date.

EXERCISE 4-9
Relationship of Adjusting Entries to Business Transactions
(LO 2, 3)

Among the ledger accounts used by Glenwood Speedway are the following: Prepaid Rent, Rent Expense, Unearned Admissions Revenue, Admissions Revenue, Prepaid Printing, Printing Expense, Concessions Receivable, and Concessions Revenue. For each of the following items, write first the journal entry (if one is needed) to record the external transaction and second the adjusting entry, if any, required on May 31, the end of the fiscal year.

a. On May 1, borrowed $300,000 cash from National Bank by issuing a 12% note payable due in three months.

b. On May 1, paid rent for six months beginning May 1 at $30,000 per month.

c. On May 2, sold season tickets for a total of $910,000 cash. The season includes 70 racing days: 20 in May, 25 in June, and 25 in July.

d. On May 4, an agreement was reached with Snack-Bars, Inc., allowing that company to sell refreshments at the track in return for 10% of the gross receipts from refreshment sales.

e. On May 6, schedules for the 20 racing days in May and the first 10 racing days in June were printed and paid for at a cost of $12,000.

f. On May 31, Snack-Bars, Inc., reported that the gross receipts from refreshment sales in May had been $165,000 and that the 10% owed to Glenwood Speedway would be remitted on June 10.

Something to Consider   Assume that the May 1 payment of $180,000 rent was properly recorded as Prepaid Rent, but that the May 31 adjusting entry for this item was inadvertently omitted. What is the effect, if any, of this omission on Glenwood's financial statements at May 31? (Specifically consider the financial statement elements Revenue, Expense, Net Income, Assets, Liabilities, and Owner's Equity at May 31; indicate whether each would be overstated, understated, or not affected by the omission.)

EXERCISE 4-10
Concept of Materiality
(LO 4)

The concept of materiality is a generally accepted accounting principle.

a. Briefly explain the concept of materiality.

b. Is $2,500 a "material" dollar amount? Explain.

c. Describe two ways in which the concept of materiality may save accountants time and effort in making adjusting entries.

EXERCISE 4-11
Materiality: a Specific Application at Year-End
(LO 4)

The income statement of Maritimes Airlines for a recent year is reproduced below. Assume you learn that $100,000 of the fuel and oil charged to expense in 2000 actually had been on hand in the company's storage tanks at year-end. Would you consider this to be a "material" error in the company's financial statements? Explain fully.

MARITIMES AIRLINES
Consolidated Statement of Income
For the Year Ended December 31, 2000
(In thousands)

Operating revenues:

Passenger	$ 973,568
Freight	18,771
Other	22,713
Total operating revenues	$1,015,052

Operating expenses:

Salaries, wages, and benefits	$ 301,066
Fuel and oil	168,579
Maintenance and repairs	75,842
Agency commissions	61,362
Aircraft rentals	21,636
Landing fees and other rentals	51,902
Depreciation	72,343
Other operating expenses	164,696
Total operating expenses	$ 917,426
Operating income	$ 97,626

Other expenses (income):

Interest expense (net of amounts capitalized)	$ 23,269
Interest income	(16,637)
Nonoperating gains, net	(19,988)
Total other expenses (income)	$ (13,356)
Income before income taxes	$ 110,982
Provision for income taxes	39,424
Net income	$ 71,558

EXERCISE 4-12
Accounting Principles
(LO 2, 4, 5 & Review)

For each of the situations described below, indicate the generally accepted accounting principle that is being *violated.* Choose from the following principles:

Matching	*Materiality*
Cost	*Realization*
Objectivity	*Adequate disclosure*

If you do not believe that the practice violates any of these principles, answer "None," and explain.

a. The financial statements include no mention of a large lawsuit filed against the company, because the suit has not been settled as of year-end.
b. The bookkeeper of a large metropolitan auto dealership depreciates the $7.20 cost of metal wastebaskets over a period of 10 years.
c. A small commuter airline recognizes no depreciation expense on its aircraft because the planes are maintained in "as good as new" condition.
d. Palm Beach Hotel recognizes room rental revenue on the date that a reservation is received. For the winter season, many guests make reservations as much as a year in advance.

EXERCISE 4-13
Interim Results
(LO 6)

Paradise Inn ends its fiscal year on April 30. The business adjusts its accounts monthly, but closes them only at year-end (April 30). The "busy season" in Paradise—in terms of tourist trade—is from November 1 through March 31.

Sam Morse, owner of the Paradise Inn, has learned to keep a "close eye" on two accounts in his accounting systems—Guest Revenue and Cash. The balances of these accounts at the ends of each of the last five months appear below:

	Feb. 28	Jan. 31	Dec. 31	Nov. 30	Oct. 31
Guest revenue	$460,000	$384,000	$304,000	$229,000	$175,000
Cash	142,000	105,000	65,000	31,500	4,500

On February 28, Morse prepares an income statement and balance sheet for his inn. You are to indicate the amounts that should be shown in these statements for (1) Guest revenue, and (2) Cash, assuming that these statements are prepared for:

a. The ***month*** ended February 28.

b. The "busy season to date"—that is, October 31 through February 28.

In terms of guest revenue and net increase in cash, which has been Paradise Inn's "best month"? (Indicate the dollar amounts.)

*EXERCISE 4-14
What Were the Adjustments?
(LO 3, 7)

Shown below are the Trial Balance and Adjusted Trial Balance columns of the work sheet prepared for Fisher Insurance Agency for the month ended January 31, 2000.

	Trial Balance Dr	Trial Balance Cr	Adjusted Trial Balance Dr	Adjusted Trial Balance Cr
Balance sheet accounts:				
Cash	$ 4,980		$ 4,980	
Commissions receivable	3,000		3,850	
Office supplies	600		240	
Office equipment	6,600		6,600	
Accumulated depreciation: office equipment		$ 2,420		$ 2,530
Accounts payable		1,660		1,660
Salaries payable				550
Unearned commissions		400		190
Pat Fisher, capital		12,300		12,300
Pat Fisher, drawing	1,000		1,000	
Income statement accounts:				
Commissions earned		6,900		7,960
Salaries expense	6,000		6,550	
Rent expense	1,500		1,500	
Office supplies expense			360	
Depreciation expense: office equipment			110	
	$23,680	$23,680	$25,190	$25,190

By comparing the two trial balances shown above, it is possible to determine which accounts have been adjusted. You are to prepare the adjusting journal entries that must have been made to cause these changes in account balances. Include an explanation as part of each adjusting entry.

*EXERCISE 4-15
Preparing Financial Statements from an Adjusted Trial Balance
(LO 7)

From the adjusted trial balance columns of the work sheet shown in Exercise 4-14, prepare an income statement and a statement of owner's equity for Fisher Insurance Agency for the month ended January 31, 2000, and also a balance sheet (in report form) at January 31, 2000. Assume that Pat Fisher made no additional investment in the business during January.

*Supplemental Topic, "The Work Sheet."

Problems

PROBLEM 4-1
Preparing Adjusting Entries
(LO 2, 3)

Alta Sequoia Resort adjusts its accounts **monthly** and closes its accounts annually. Most guests of the resort pay at the time they check out, and the amounts collected are credited to Rental Revenue. A few guests pay in advance for rooms, and these amounts are credited to Unearned Rental Revenue at the time of receipt. The following information is available as a source for preparing adjusting entries at December 31.

a. Salaries earned by employees but not yet recorded or paid amount to $7,900.

b. As of December 31, Alta Sequoia has earned $11,075 rental revenue from current guests who will not be billed until they are ready to check out.

c. On November 1, a suite of rooms was rented to a corporation for six months at a monthly rental of $3,200. The entire six months' rent of $19,200 was collected in advance and credited to Unearned Rental Revenue.

d. A limousine to carry guests to and from the airport had been rented beginning December 19 from Transport Rentals, Inc., at a daily rate of $120. No rental payment has yet been made. (The limousine has been rented for 13 days in December.)

e. A six-month loan in the amount of $30,000 had been obtained on December 1. Interest is to be computed at a rate of 10% per year and is payable when the loan is due. No interest has been paid and no interest expense has been recorded.

f. Depreciation on the resort's buildings is based upon an estimated useful life of 30 years. The original cost of the buildings was $1,755,000. Alta Sequoia uses the straight-line method.

g. In December, Alta Sequoia Resort entered into an agreement to host the annual symposium of ACE (Academics for a Clean Environment) in April of next year. The resort expects to earn rental revenue of at least $45,000.

h. A one-year fire insurance policy had been purchased on September 1. The premium of $7,200 for the entire life of the policy had been paid on September 1 and recorded as Unexpired Insurance.

INSTRUCTIONS

a. For each of the above lettered paragraphs, draft a separate adjusting journal entry (including explanation) if the information indicates that an adjusting entry is needed.

b. As of December 31, how much of the $19,200 received on November 1 has been earned by Alta Sequoia? Is this amount the same as the amount of revenue recognized in your adjusting entry for item **c**? Explain.

PROBLEM 4-2
Preparing Adjusting Entries
(LO 2, 3)

Silver Spur Ranch, a dude ranch and resort, adjusts its accounts **monthly** and closes its accounts annually on December 31. Most guests of the ranch pay at the time they check out, and the amounts collected are credited to Rental Revenue. The following information is available as a source for preparing adjusting entries at December 31.

a. Among the assets owned by Silver Spur is an investment in government bonds in the face amount of $175,000. Accrued interest receivable on the bonds at December 31 was computed to be $875. None of the interest has yet been received.

b. A 12-month bank loan in the amount of $90,000 had been obtained on November 1. Interest is to be computed at an annual rate of 10% and is payable when the loan becomes due.

c. Depreciation on a station wagon owned by the ranch was based on a four-year life. The vehicle had been purchased new on September 1 of the current year at a cost of $25,200. Silver Spur uses the straight-line method of depreciation.

d. Management of the ranch signed an agreement on December 28 to lease a truck from Ace Motors for a period of 6 months beginning January 1 at a rate of 20 cents per kilometre, with a clause providing for a minimum monthly charge of $400.

e. Salaries earned by employees but not yet recorded or paid amounted to $9,900 at the end of the year.

f. As of December 31, Silver Spur has earned $12,500 rental revenue from current guests who will not be billed until they are ready to check out.

g. A portion of land owned by Silver Spur had been leased on August 1 of the current year to a service station operator at a yearly rental rate of $18,000. Six months' rent was collected in advance at the date of the lease and credited to Unearned Rental Revenue.

h. A bus to carry guests to and from town and the airport had been rented early on December 10 at a daily rate of $50. No rental payment has been made, although Silver Spur has had use of the bus for 22 days in December.

INSTRUCTIONS

a. For each of the above lettered paragraphs, draft a separate adjusting journal entry (including explanation) if the information indicates that an adjusting entry is needed.

b. What is the amount of interest expense recognized *during the year* on the $90,000 bank loan obtained on November 1?

c. Compute the *book value* of the station wagon described in item **c** (above) as of December 31.

PROBLEM 4-3
Preparing Adjusting Entries from a Trial Balance
(LO 2, 3)

On April 1, 2000, Pat Hamilton, a lawyer, opened her own legal practice, to be known as the Law Office of Pat Hamilton. The business adjusts its accounts at the end of each month. The following trial balance was prepared at April 30, 2000, *after one month* of operations:

LAW OFFICE OF PAT HAMILTON Trial Balance April 30, 2000		
Cash	$10,060	
Legal fees receivable	—0—	
Unexpired insurance	3,000	
Prepaid office rent	4,800	
Office supplies	1,460	
Office equipment	26,400	
Accumulated depreciation: office equipment		$—0—
Notes payable		16,000
Interest payable		—0—
Salaries payable		—0—
Unearned retainer fees		16,020
Pat Hamilton, capital		20,000
Pat Hamilton, drawing	4,000	
Legal fees earned		1,580
Salaries expense	2,680	
Miscellaneous expense	1,200	
Office rent expense	—0—	
Office supplies expense	—0—	
Depreciation expense: office equipment	—0—	
Interest expense	—0—	
Insurance expense	—0—	
	$53,600	$53,600

OTHER DATA

a. No interest has yet been paid on the note payable. Accrued interest at April 30 amounts to $180.

b. Salaries earned by the office staff but not yet recorded or paid amounted to $3,470 at April 30.

c. Many clients are asked to make an advance payment for the legal services to be rendered in future months. These advance payments are credited to the

Unearned Retainer Fees account. During April, $7,700 of these advances were earned by the business.

d. Some clients are not billed until all services relating to their matter have been rendered. As of April 30, services priced at $4,780 had been rendered to these clients but had not yet been recorded in the accounting records.

e. A professional liability insurance policy was purchased on April 1. The premium of $3,000 for the first six months was paid and recorded as Unexpired Insurance.

f. The business rents an office at a monthly rate of $1,600. On April 1, three months' rent was paid in advance and charged to the Prepaid Office Rent account.

g. Office supplies on hand at April 30 amounted to $1,100.

h. The office equipment was purchased on April 1 and is being depreciated over an estimated useful life of 10 years.

INSTRUCTIONS

a. Prepare the adjusting entries required at April 30.

b. Determine the amount of net income to be reported in the company's income statement for the month ended April 30, 2000.

PROBLEM 4-4
Preparing Adjusting Entries from a Trial Balance
(LO 2, 3)

Nick Charles operates a private investigating business called Nick Charles Investigations. Some clients are required to pay in advance for the company's services, while others are billed after the services have been rendered. Advance payments are credited to an account entitled Unearned Retainer Fees, which represents unearned revenue. The business adjusts its accounts each month and closes its accounts at the end of the year. At March 31, the end of the first quarter, the trial balance appeared as follows:

NICK CHARLES INVESTIGATIONS		
Trial Balance		
March 31, 19__		
Cash	$ 17,150	
Fees receivable	37,800	
Unexpired insurance	1,600	
Prepaid rent	5,400	
Office supplies	1,050	
Office equipment	17,100	
Accumulated depreciation: office equipment		$ 5,700
Accounts payable		3,900
Unearned retainer fees		24,000
Nick Charles, capital		45,300
Nick Charles, drawing	3,200	
Fees earned		33,320
Depreciation expense	570	
Rent expense	3,000	
Office supplies expense	450	
Insurance expense	800	
Telephone expense	1,200	
Travel expense	3,400	
Salaries expense	19,500	
	$112,220	$112,220

OTHER DATA

a. The useful life of the office equipment was estimated at five years.

b. Fees of $8,400 were earned during the month by performing services for clients who had paid in advance.

c. Salaries earned by employees during the month but not yet recorded or paid amounted to $1,665.

d. On March 1, the business moved into a new office and paid the first three months' rent in advance.

e. Investigative services rendered during the month but not yet collected or billed to clients amounted to $3,900.

f. Office supplies on hand March 31 amounted to $700.

g. On January 1, $2,400 was paid as the premium for six months' liability insurance.

INSTRUCTIONS

a. Prepare the adjusting entries required at March 31. (Use the straight-line method for depreciation.)

b. Determine the amount of net income to be reported in the company's income statement for the quarter ended March 31, 19__.

c. Did the monthly rent of Nick Charles Investigations increase or decrease as a result of the move to a new office on March 1? Explain your answer.

PROBLEM 4-5
Analysis of Adjusted Data;
Preparing Adjusting Entries
(LO 2, 3)

Sea Cat, Inc., operates a large catamaran that takes tourists at several island resorts on diving and sailing excursions. The company adjusts its accounts at the end of each month. Selected account balances appearing on the June 30 **adjusted** trial balance are as follows:

Prepaid rent	$ 6,000	
Unexpired insurance	1,400	
Catamaran	46,200	
Accumulated depreciation: catamaran		$9,240
Unearned passenger revenue		825

OTHER DATA

a. The catamaran is being depreciated over a 10-year estimated useful life, with no residual value.

b. The unearned passenger revenue represents tickets good for future rides sold to a resort hotel for $15 per ticket on June 1. During June, 145 of the tickets were used.

c. Six months' rent had been prepaid on June 1.

d. The unexpired insurance is a 12-month fire insurance policy purchased on March 1.

INSTRUCTIONS

a. Determine

1. The age of the catamaran in months

2. How many $15 tickets for future rides were sold to the resort hotel on June 1

3. The monthly rent expense

4. The original cost of the 12-month fire insurance policy

b. Prepare the adjusting entries that were made on June 30.

PROBLEM 4-6
Adjusting Entries
(LO 3)

Selected accounts with their normal balances from the December 31 trial balance and adjusted trial balance of Dante Consulting are as follows:

	Trial Balance	Adjusted Trial Balance
Cash	$ 8,200	$ 8,200
Prepaid rent	2,100	—0—
Office supplies	780	180
Equipment	30,000	30,000
Notes payable	90,000	90,000
Salaries payable	—0—	970
Unearned consulting fees	4,800	2,300
Kitty Moore, Drawing	26,500	26,500
Consulting fees earned	76,500	79,600
Salaries expense	15,700	16,670
Telephone expense	3,200	3,200
Rent expense	10,000	12,100
Office supplies expense	—0—	600
Depreciation expense: equipment	—0—	1,000
Interest Expense	—0—	800

INSTRUCTIONS

Prepare all the adjusting entries (with explanations) that you can derive from the two trial balances.

PROBLEM 4-7
Closing Entries
(LO 5)

Siu Zhang, owner of Oralco Enterprise, wants you to help her close the books because the part-time bookkeeper has suddenly left the company. She manages to obtain the following information from the bookkeeper's drawers (the accounts are in alphabetical order).

	December 31 (Year-end)	
	Trial Balance	Adjusted Trial Balance
Accounts payable	$ 2,300	$ 2,600
Accounts receivable	7,800	8,800
Accumulated depreciation: equipment .	3,000	5,000
Cash	1,900	1,900
Depreciation expense: equipment	—0—	2,000
Equipment	30,000	30,000
Interest expense	—0—	720
Interest payable	—0—	720
Management fees earned	208,000	232,900
Office supplies expense	300	900
Prepaid rent	5,000	2,500
Rent expense	27,500	30,000
Salaries expense	126,200	129,500
Siu Zhang, drawing	49,800	49,800
Telephone expense	2,800	3,180
Unearned management fees	26,900	3,000

INSTRUCTIONS

Prepare the closing entries (with explanations) based on the information provided by Zhang.

PROBLEM 4-8
Interim Financial Statements
(LO 5, 6)

Guardian Insurance Agency adjusts its accounts monthly, but closes them only at the end of the calendar year. Shown below are the adjusted balances of the revenue and expense accounts at September 30 of the current year, and at the ends of two earlier months:

	Sept. 30	Aug. 31	June 30
Commissions earned	$144,000	$128,000	$90,000
Advertising expense	28,000	23,000	15,000
Salaries expense	36,000	32,000	24,000
Rent expense	22,500	20,000	15,000
Depreciation expense	2,700	2,400	1,800

a. Prepare a "three-column income statement," showing net income for three separate time periods, all of which end on September 30. Use the format illustrated below. Show supporting computations for the amounts of revenue reported in the first two columns.

GUARDIAN INSURANCE AGENCY
Income Statement
For the Following Time Periods in 19__

	Month Ended Sept. 30	Quarter Ended Sept. 30	9 Months Ended Sept. 30
Revenue:			
Commissions earned	$____(1)	$____(2)	$____
Expenses:			

b. Briefly explain how you determined the dollar amounts for each of the three time periods. Would you apply the same process to the balances in Guardian's balance sheet accounts? Explain.

c. Assume that Guardian adjusts **and closes** its accounts at the end of **each month.** Briefly explain how you then would determine the revenue and expenses that would appear in each of the three columns of the income statement prepared in part **a.**

*PROBLEM 4-9
Format of a Work Sheet
(LO 5, 6, 7)

Shown below are the first 4 columns of a 10-column work sheet to be prepared for Westhaven Executive Golf Course for the month ended October 31, 2000. The golf course operates on land rented from the city.

WESTHAVEN EXECUTIVE GOLF COURSE
Work Sheet
For the Month Ended October 31, 2000

	Trial Balance		Adjustments*	
	Dr	Cr	Dr	Cr
Balance sheet accounts:				
Cash	20,900			
Unexpired insurance	7,200			(a) 800
Prepaid rent	18,000			(b) 6,000
Equipment	24,000			
Accumulated depreciation:				
equipment		7,600		(c) 400
Notes payable		10,000		
Unearned greens' fees revenue ...		6,400	(d) 2,200	
Walter Nelson, capital		38,200		
Walter Nelson, drawing	5,900			
Salaries payable				(e) 1,900
Interest payable				(f) 100
Income statement accounts:				
Greens' fees revenue		26,400		(d) 2,200
Salaries expense	8,600		(e) 1,900	
Water expense	1,200			
Advertising expense	600			
Repairs and maintenance				
expense	1,500			
Miscellaneous expense	700			
	88,600	88,600		
Insurance expense			(a) 800	
Rent expense			(b) 6,000	
Depreciation expense: equipment ..			(c) 400	
Interest expense			(f) 100	
			11,400	11,400

*Adjustments
(a)   Insurance expiring in October.
(b)   Prepaid rent applicable to October.
(c)   Depreciation for the month.
(d)   Portion of revenue collected in advance but earned during October.
(e)   Salaries owed to employees but unpaid as of month-end.
(f)   Accrued interest on notes payable at October 31.

_____

Supplemental Topic, "The Work Sheet."

INSTRUCTIONS

a. Prepare a 10-column work sheet utilizing the trial balance and adjustments shown above in the first 4 columns.

b. What is the amount reported for owner's capital in Westhaven's **balance sheet** at October 31, 2000? Show computation.

c. Assume that Westhaven Executive Golf Course has been operating for several years and has a fiscal year ending December 31. How often does Westhaven **adjust** its accounts? When did Westhaven last **close** its accounts? Can you determine from the above work sheet **how often** Westhaven **closes** its accounts? Support your answers.

*PROBLEM 4-10
Preparing a Work Sheet
(LO 3, 5, 7)

Kent Cinema adjusts its accounts **each month.** Kent Cinema closes its accounts at the end of each quarter and has a fiscal year ending December 31. At July 31, the trial balance and other information below were available for adjusting the accounts:

KENT CINEMA
Trial Balance
July 31, 19__

Cash	$ 20,000	
Prepaid film rental	31,200	
Land	80,000	
Building	168,000	
Accumulated depreciation: building		$ 10,500
Projection equipment	36,000	
Accumulated depreciation: projection equipment		3,000
Notes payable		190,000
Accounts payable		4,400
Unearned admissions revenue (YMCA)		1,000
Li Trong, capital		103,400
Li Trong, drawing	3,500	
Admissions revenue		36,900
Salaries expense	8,700	
Light and power expense	1,800	
	$349,200	$349,200

OTHER DATA

a. Film rental expense for the month is $15,200. However, the film rental expense for several months had been paid in advance.

b. The building is being depreciated over a period of 20 years.

c. The projection equipment is being depreciated over a period of 5 years.

d. At July 31, accrued interest payable on the note payable amounts to $1,650. No entry has yet been made to record interest expense for the month of July.

e. Kent Cinema allows the local YMCA to bring children attending summer camp to the movies on any weekday afternoon for a fixed fee of $500 per month. On May 28, the YMCA made a $1,500 advance payment covering the months of June, July, and August.

f. Kent Cinema receives a percentage of the revenue earned by Tastie Corporation, the concessionaire operating the snack bar. For snack bar sales in July, Tastie owes Kent Cinema $2,250, payable on August 10. No entry has yet been made to record this concessions revenue.

g. Salaries owed to employees, but not recorded or paid as of July 31 amount to $1,500.

_____

Supplemental Topic, "The Work Sheet."

INSTRUCTIONS

a. Prepare a 10-column work sheet utilizing the trial balance and adjusting data provided. Include at the bottom of the work sheet a brief explanation keyed to each adjusting entry.
b. Kent Cinema has been operating throughout the year and adjusts its accounts *monthly.* Why does no depreciation expense appear in the above unadjusted trial balance as of July 31? Would you expect this situation to recur in the unadjusted trial balance at August 31? Explain briefly.

*PROBLEM 4-11
Preparing a Work Sheet,
Financial Statements, and
Adjusting and Closing Entries
(LO 3, 5, 7)

Island Hopper is an airline providing passenger and freight service among some Pacific islands. The accounts are adjusted and closed each month. At June 30 the trial balance shown below was prepared from the ledger.

ISLAND HOPPER Trial Balance June 30, 2000		
Cash	$ 23,600	
Accounts receivable	7,200	
Prepaid rent	9,600	
Unexpired insurance	21,000	
Aircraft	1,200,000	
Accumulated depreciation: aircraft		$ 380,000
Notes payable		600,000
Advance ticket sales		60,000
Mary Earhart, capital		230,850
Mary Earhart, drawing	7,000	
Freight revenue		130,950
Fuel expense	53,800	
Salaries expense	66,700	
Maintenance expense	12,900	
	$1,401,800	$1,401,800

OTHER DATA

a. The aircraft is being depreciated by the straight-line method over a period of 10 years.
b. During June, $38,650 of the advance ticket sales was earned by the airline.
c. Salaries earned by employees but not yet recorded or paid amount to $3,300 at June 30.
d. Accrued interest on notes payable amounts to $5,000 at June 30 and has not yet been recorded. Interest is paid monthly, within 10 days of the end of the month. The $600,000 note payable matures on December 31, 2003.
e. One of Island Hopper's regular customers is Pacific Trading. The airline keeps track of the weight of shipments carried for the trading company during the month and sends a bill shortly after month-end. No entry has yet been made to record $4,600 earned in June carrying freight for Pacific Trading.
f. Three months' rent had been prepaid on May 1.
g. On April 1, a 12-month insurance policy had been purchased.

INSTRUCTIONS

a. Prepare a work sheet for the month ended June 30, 2000.

_____

*Supplemental Topic, "The Work Sheet."

b. Prepare an income statement for the month, a statement of owner's equity for the month, and a balance sheet at June 30, 2000.

c. Draft two notes to accompany Island Hopper's financial statements at June 30, 2000. The first should disclose depreciation methods in use and depreciable lives of assets being depreciated. The second should disclose due dates of major liabilities.

d. Prepare adjusting and closing entries.

Analytical and Decision Problems and Cases

A&D 4-1
Working for the Competition
(LO 1)

This case focuses upon the following question: *Is it ethical for a public accountant (or a public accounting firm) to provide similar accounting and auditing services to companies that compete directly with one another?*

INSTRUCTIONS

a. *Before* doing any research, discuss this question as a group. Identify potential arguments on *each side* of the issue.

b. Arrange an interview with a practising (or retired) public accountant. Learn the accounting profession's position on this issue, and discuss the various arguments developed in part **a.** (*Note:* All interviews are to be conducted in accordance with the guidelines in the *Preface* of this textbook.)

c. Develop your "group's position" on this issue, and be prepared to explain it in class. Explain why you have chosen to overlook the conflicting arguments developed in part **a.** (If your group is not in agreement, dissenting members may draft a "dissenting opinion.")

A&D 4-2
Accrual Accounting—An
Application
(LO 2)

Air Canada credits the proceeds from advance passenger and cargo sales to an account entitled Advance Ticket Sales. The company's recent annual reports show the following trend in the balance of this account over a three-year period:

	1997	1996	1995
Advance ticket sales (in millions)	$400	$270	$215

The first note accompanying the financial statements, entitled *"Significant Accounting Policies,"* includes the following disclosure:

Airline passenger and cargo sales are recognized as operating revenues when the transportation is provided. The value of unused transportation is included in current liabilities.

INSTRUCTIONS

a. Why does Air Canada recognize this sales revenue when transportation is provided, rather than when proceeds are received?

b. Should Air Canada recognize flight expenses, such as aircraft fuel and flight crew's salaries, in the period that flights occur or the period in which tickets are sold? Explain.

c. What does the balance in the Advance Ticket Sales account represent?

d. How does Air Canada normally discharge this liability?

e. Explain the most probable reason for the increase in the amount of this liability from year to year.

f. Based solely upon the trend in the amount of this liability, would you expect the annual amounts of passenger and cargo revenue earned by the airlines to be increasing or decreasing over this three-year period? Explain.

A&D 4-3
Adjusting Entries
(LO 2, 3)

The purpose of this problem is to help you understand the need for adjusting entries in a specific business situation. You are to prepare examples of "typical" adjusting entries that might be made at the end of an accounting period by a company that owns and operates a large hotel. You are to decide upon the types of assets, liabilities, revenue, and expenses that might be involved in these entries. Prepare two examples of **each of the four basic types of adjusting entries.** Thus, you will prepare a total of eight adjusting entries.

You need not include dollar amounts—simply enter **"xxx"** in the debit and credit columns. However, your written explanations of each entry should describe specific facts that make the adjustment necessary. For example, one adjusting entry that a hotel might make to apportion unearned revenue is shown below:

a. Examples of adjusting entries to apportion recorded revenue:

(1) *Unearned Banquet Revenue*	*xxx*	
Banquet Revenue		*xxx*

To recognize revenue earned this period from catering the Canadian Football League awards banquet in the hotel. The League had paid for this banquet in an earlier accounting period.

A&D 4-4
Adjusting Entries: An Alternative to A&D 4-3
(LO 2, 3)

This problem is an alternative to A&D 4-3. You are to follow the same instructions as in A&D 4-3, but use a large **law firm** as the business entity. Also, you are to prepare only **one** example of each of the four basic types of adjusting entries.

A&D 4-5
Should This Be Adjusted?
(LO 2, 3)

Property Management Professionals provides building management services to owners of office buildings and shopping centres. The company closes its accounts at the **end of the calendar year.** The manner in which the company has recorded several transactions occurring during 1999 is described below:

a. On September 1, received advance payment from a shopping centre for property management services to be performed over the three-month period beginning September 1. The entire amount received was credited directly to a **revenue** account.

b. On December 1, received advance payment from the same customer described in part **a** for services to be rendered over the three-month period beginning December 1. This time, the entire amount received was credited to an **unearned** revenue account.

c. Rendered management services for many customers in December. Normal procedure is to record revenue on the date the customer is billed, which is early in the month after the services have been rendered.

d. On December 15, made full payment for a one-year insurance policy that goes into effect on January 1, 2000. The cost of the policy was debited to Unexpired Insurance.

e. Numerous purchases of equipment were debited to asset accounts, rather than to expense accounts.

f. Payroll expense is recorded when employees are paid. Payday for the last two weeks of December falls on January 2, 2000.

INSTRUCTIONS

For each item above, explain whether an adjusting entry is needed at **December 31, 1999,** and state the reasons for your answer. If you recommend an adjusting entry, explain the effects this entry would have upon assets, liabilities, owner's equity, revenue, and expense in the 1999 financial statements.

A&D 4-6
What To Adjust?
(LO 2, 3)

Gisele Little, a recent university graduate, decided to start a formal wear and costume rental business. Thus, on August 1, Gisele withdrew $2,000 from her savings account and deposited it in a bank account in the name of her business, Little's Place. To obtain more capital to finance the acquisition of the needed tuxedos, gowns, and costumes, as well as furniture and fixtures, Gisele borrowed $8,000 from her mother and deposited the cash in the bank account of the business.

August 1 was a very busy day for Gisele. She rented a store from Handnoral Property Management. Handnoral would give Gisele a better deal if she paid rent in advance every three months. Gisele accepted the offer and paid $2,700 to Handnoral. On the same day, she purchased furniture and fixtures for $6,000, paying $1,000 cash and signing a one-year note payable for the balance at an annual interest rate of 6%, payable at maturity. The furniture and fixtures were estimated to have a useful life of five years. To obtain a volume discount, Gisele purchased two months of office supplies on account for $300. Also, Gisele purchased tuxedos, gowns, and costumes from Designer Fashions Limited for $8,400, paying $3,000 cash and agreeing to pay the balance in 60 days. The management of Designer Fashions told Gisele that these items would have a useful life of seven years.

To attract business, Gisele advertised extensively in local newspapers and weekly magazines. On August 3, she paid $1,800 for the advertisements to ensure there would be adequate and equal promotion for two months.

Apparently, the advertisements paid off. Revenue for the first two weeks of operation was $2,600, all paid in cash. In addition, on August 16, the Theatre Players Group paid $2,500 to rent some costumes for a month for the performances in a local casino. The costumes will be returned on September 16.

On Monday, August 28, Gisele hired a part-time employee to help with the increasing volume of business for $250 for a five-day work week. The first week's salary is payable on Friday, September 1.

The business continued to grow. The last two weeks' revenue was $5,200, of which $1,200 was in cash, $3,000 on account, and $1,000 yet to be billed. Feeling that the first month had been a success, Gisele withdrew $1,500 cash from the business. To ensure that she would have sufficient cash to make payments in September, Gisele called the utilities company to find out when she would be paying utilities for August. Gisele was happy to find out that she owed only $230 and it would not be due until early September.

INSTRUCTIONS

Prepare the necessary adjusting entries at August 31.

*A&D 4-7
Completing a Work Sheet
(LO 7)

An unexpected virus attacked the microcomputer system of Gaffar Management Services. As a result, Alice Gaffar, the owner, is left with the partially completed work sheet on the following page and asks for your assistance.

INSTRUCTIONS

Complete the work sheet for Alice Gaffer.

Supplemental Topic, "The Work Sheet."

GAFFAR MANAGEMENT SERVICES
Work Sheet
For the Month Ended June 30, 2000

	Trial Balance		Adjustments		Income Statement		Balance Sheet	
	Debit	Credit	Debit	Credit	Debit	Credit	Debit	Credit
Balance sheet accounts:								
Cash	15,485						12,610	
Management fees receivable							15,785	
Prepaid rent							800	
Unexpired insurance				800			450	
Office supplies	1,080							
Office equipment	9,600							
Accumulated depreciation: office equipment								300
Notes payable		890						8,000
Accounts payable		3,700						
Unearned management fees		23,715						1,700
Alice Gaffar, capital								
Alice Gaffar, drawing							2,250	
Salaries payable				290				290
Interest payable				300 ⎱				60
Income statement accounts:								
Management fees earned						25,580		
Rent expense					1,600			
Salaries expense					1,260			
Telephone expense	1,260							
Insurance expense			450		380			
Office supplies expense			380					
Depreciation expense: office equipment			100					
Interest expense			60					
Net income								7,240
					25,580	25,580		7,240

A&D 4-8
The Concept of Materiality
(LO 4)

The concept of materiality is one of the most basic generally accepted accounting principles.
a. Answer the following questions:
   1. Why is the materiality of a transaction or an event a matter of professional judgment?
   2. What criteria should accountants consider in determining whether a transaction or an event is "material"?
   3. Does the concept of materiality mean that financial statements are not precise, down to the last dollar? Does this concept make financial statements less useful to most users?
b. **Avis Rent-a-Car** purchases a large number of cars each year for its rental fleet. The cost of any individual automobile is immaterial to Avis, which is a very large corporation. Would it be acceptable for Avis to charge the purchase of automobiles for its rental fleet directly to expense, rather than to an asset account? Explain.

A&D 4-9
Materiality in Practice
(LO 4)

During the current year, East-West Airlines earned net income of $50 million from total revenue of $350 million. The company services primarily cities in Canada, but also has service to several foreign countries. Three events are described below, along with the treatment accorded to these events in the company's financial statements.
a. During the year, the company purchased $5 million in spare parts to be used in aircraft maintenance. All of these purchases were charged immediately to Maintenance Expense. No adjusting entry was made at year-end to reflect approximately $50,000 in spare parts remaining on hand, because the amount was considered immaterial.
b. The company's internal auditors discovered that the vice president of in-flight services had embezzled $100,000 from the airlines by authorizing payments to a fictitious supplier of in-flight meals. The vice president was fired, and criminal charges currently are pending against her, as is a civil lawsuit to recover the embezzled funds. In the income statement, this $100,000 loss was deducted from revenue as part of the Flight Operations Expenses, which totalled more than $200 million. No special disclosures were made, because the amount of the embezzlement was considered immaterial.
c. Shortly after year-end, the company suspended all flight operations to a particular foreign country as a result of political unrest. These flights provided approximately 2% of the company's net income during the current year. Cancellation of service to this country was not disclosed in notes to the current year's financial statements, because operations of the current year were not affected.

INSTRUCTIONS

Explain whether in your own judgment you concur or disagree with the treatment accorded to these events by East-West in its current financial statements. If you recommend a different financial statement presentation, explain why you do. In each case, indicate whether or not you consider the item "material," and explain your reasons. Consider each of these three situations *independently* of the others.

A&D 4-10
Adequate Disclosure
(LO 5)

Listed below are five independent cases that may—or may not—require disclosure in the notes that accompany financial statements.
a. Mandella Construction uses the "percentage-of-completion" method to recognize revenue on long-term construction contracts. This is one of two acceptable methods of accounting for such projects. Over the life of the project, both methods produce the same results; but the annual results may differ substantially.
b. One of the most popular artists at Spectacular Comics is leaving the company and going to work for a competitor.
c. Shortly after the balance sheet date, but before the financial statements are issued, one of Coast Foods' two processing plants was damaged by a tornado. The plant will be out of service for at least three months.

d. The management of Soft Systems believes that the company has developed systems software that will make *Windows* virtually obsolete. If they are correct, the company's profits could increase by 10-fold or more.

e. College Property Management (CPM) withheld a $500 security deposit from students who, in violation of their lease, kept a dog in their apartment. The students have sued CPM for this amount in small claims court.

INSTRUCTIONS

For each case, explain what, if any, disclosure is required under generally accepted accounting principles. Explain your reasoning.

A&D 4-11
A Sure Thing?
(LO 2)

Adam Peitou is interested in buying Foxie's, an aerobic dance studio. He has come to you for help in interpreting the company's financial statements and to seek your advice about purchasing the business.

Foxie's has been in operation for one year. The business is a sole proprietorship owned by Sandy Beech. Foxie's rents the building in which it operates, as well as all of its exercise equipment. As the business is small, Beech has maintained the accounting records on a cash basis. She has prepared the following income statement and balance sheet from these cash basis records at December 31, the year-end date:

Income Statement

Revenue:		
Membership fees	*$150,000*	
Membership dues	*30,000*	*$180,000*
Expenses:		
Rent	*$ 18,000*	
Wages	*52,000*	
Advertising	*20,000*	
Miscellaneous	*15,000*	*105,000*
Net income		*$ 75,000*

Balance Sheet

Assets

Cash	*$ 25,000*

Liabilities & Owner's Equity

Sandy Beech, capital	*$ 25,000*

Beech is offering to sell Foxie's for the balance of her capital account—$25,000. Peitou is very enthusiastic and states, "How can I go wrong? I'll be paying $25,000 to buy $25,000 cash, and I'll be getting a very profitable business that generates large amounts of cash in the deal."

In a meeting with you and Peitou, Beech makes the following statement: "This business has been very good to me. In the first year of operations, I've been able to withdraw $50,000 in cash. Yet the business is still quite solvent—it has lots of cash and no debts."

You ask Beech to explain the difference between membership fees and membership dues. She responds, "Foxie's is an exclusive club. We cater only to members. This year, we sold 500 five-year memberships. Each membership requires the customer to pay $300 cash in advance and to pay dues of $10 per month for five years. I credited the advance payments to the Membership Fees account and credited the $10 monthly payments to Membership Dues. Thus, all the revenue is hard cash—no 'paper profits' like you see in so many businesses."

You then enquire as to when these five-year memberships were sold. Beech responds, "On the average, these memberships are only six months old. No members have dropped out, so Foxie's should continue receiving dues from these people for another four and one-half years, thus assuring future profitability. Another beneficial factor is that the company hasn't sold any new memberships in the last several months. Therefore, I think that the company could discontinue its advertising and further increase future profitability. Since further advertising may not produce any new members, the $3,000 television commercial for early next year, for which I have paid, is really worthless and I have included it in the $20,000 advertising expense of this year."

INSTRUCTIONS

a. Prepare a revised income statement and balance sheet based on generally zaccepted accounting principles.
b. Assume that none of the 500 members drop out of Foxie's during the next year, and that the business sells no new memberships. What would be the amount of the company's expected cash receipts? Assuming that advertising expense is discontinued but that other expenses remain the same, what would be the expected amount of cash payments for the coming year?
c. Use the information in your analysis in parts **a** and **b** to draft a letter to Peitou advising him on the wisdom of purchasing Foxie's for $25,000.

Answers to Self-Test Questions

1. a, b, c, d   **2.** c   **3.** d $11,670 ($27,900 − $17,340 − $2,700 − $1,440 + $3,300 + $1,950)   **4.** d   **5.** b, c, d   **6.** a, b   **7.** c   *8. c

---

Supplemental Topic, "The Work Sheet."

FRIEND WITH A TRUCK

A comprehensive accounting cycle problem.

On September 1, 19__, Anthony Ferrara organized a business called Friend With A Truck for the purpose of operating an equipment rental yard. The new business was able to begin operations immediately by purchasing the assets and taking over the location of Rent-It, an equipment rental company that was going out of business.

Friend With A Truck uses the following chart of accounts:

Cash	1	Anthony Ferrara, Capital	30
Accounts Receivable	4	Anthony Ferrara, Drawing	35
Prepaid Rent	6	Income Summary	40
Unexpired Insurance	7	Rental Fees Earned	50
Office Supplies	8	Salaries Expense	60
Rental Equipment	10	Maintenance Expense	61
Accumulated Depreciation:		Utilities Expense	62
Rental Equipment	12	Rent Expense	63
Notes Payable	20	Office Supplies Expense	64
Accounts Payable	22	Depreciation Expense: Rental	
Interest Payable	25	Equipment	65
Salaries Payable	26	Interest Expense	66
Unearned Rental Fees	29		

The company closes its accounts and prepares financial statements at the end of each month. During September, the company entered into the following transactions:

Sept. 1   Anthony Ferrara deposited $100,000 cash in a bank account in the name of the business, Friend With A Truck.

Sept. 1   Paid $9,000 to Shapiro Realty as three months' advance rent on the rental yard and office formerly occupied by Rent-It.

Sept. 1   Purchased for $180,000 all the equipment formerly owned by Rent-It. Paid $70,000 cash and issued a one-year note payable for $110,000, plus interest at the annual rate of 9%. The equipment is estimated to have a useful life of 10 years.

Sept. 4   Purchased office supplies on account from Modern Office Co., $1,630. Payment due in 30 days. (These supplies are expected to last for several months.)

Sept. 8   Received $10,000 cash from McBryan Construction as advance payment on rental equipment.

Sept. 12   Paid salaries for the first two weeks in September, $3,600.

Sept. 15 Excluding the McBryan advance, equipment rental fees earned during the first 15 days of September amounted to $6,100, of which $5,300 was received in cash.

Sept. 17 Purchased on account from Earth Movers, Inc., $340 in parts needed immediately to repair a rental tractor. Payment is due in 10 days.

Sept. 23 Collected $210 of the accounts receivable recorded on September 15.

Sept. 25 Rented a backhoe to Mission Landscaping at a price of $100 per day, to be paid when the backhoe is returned. Mission Landscaping expects to keep the backhoe for about two or three weeks.

Sept. 26 Paid biweekly salaries, $3,600.

Sept. 27 Paid the account payable to Earth Movers, Inc., $340.

Sept. 28 Anthony Ferrara withdrew $2,000 cash from the business to pay the rent on his personal residence.

Sept. 29 Friend With A Truck (Anthony Ferrara) was named, along with Mission Landscaping and Collier Construction, as a co-defendent in a $25,000 lawsuit filed on behalf of Kevin Davenport. Mission Landscape had left the rented backhoe in a fenced construction site owned by Collier Construction. After working hours on September 26, Davenport had climbed the fence to play on parked construction equipment. While playing on the backhoe, he fell and broke his arm. The extent of legal and financial responsibility for this accident, if any, cannot be determined at this time.

Sept. 29 Purchased a 12-month public-liability insurance policy for $2,700. This policy protects the company against liability for injuries and property damage caused by its equipment. However, the policy goes into effect on October 1, and affords no coverage for the injuries sustained by Kevin Davenport on September 26.

Sept. 30 Received a bill from Universal Utilities for the months of September, $270. Payment is due in 30 days.

Sept. 30 Equipment rental fees earned during second half of September and received in cash amounted to $8,450.

The information available on September 30 is as follows: the company uses the straight-line method of depreciation; the office supplies on hand are estimated at $1,100; $4,840 of the advance payment from McBryan Construction has been earned; Mission Landscaping owed five days of rental; salaries earned by employees since the last payroll are $900.

INSTRUCTIONS

 a. Journalize the above transactions.
 b. Post to ledger accounts. (Use running balance form of ledger accounts. Enter numbers of journal pages and ledger accounts to complete the cross-referencing between the journal and ledger.)
*c. Prepare a 10-column work sheet for the month ended September 30, 19__.

---

*Supplemental Topic, "The Work Sheet."

   d. Prepare an income statement and a statement of owner's equity for the month of September, and a balance sheet (in report form) as of September 30.

   e. Prepare required disclosures to accompany the September 30 financial statements of Friend With A Truck. Your solution should include a separate note addressing each of the following areas: (1) depreciation policy, (2) maturity dates of major liabilities, and (3) potential liability due to pending litigation.

   f. Prepare adjusting and closing entries and post to ledger accounts.

   g. Prepare an after-closing trial balance as of September 30.

PART 2

The Business World

An understanding of accounting information and of business decisions go hand in hand. You can't know much about one without understanding the other.

CHAPTER 5

Accounting for Merchandising Activities; Classified Financial Statements

North America is the land of creative merchandising. It is the birthplace of television shopping channels, mail-order catalogues, and membership warehouse clubs. Merchandising businesses range in size from sidewalk vendors to corporate giants. Every successful merchandising business makes extensive use of accounting information. It keeps track of inventory—what's in stock, which products are the "best sellers," and when to buy more merchandise. It also keeps track of the amounts owed to each supplier and due from each credit customer. And it keeps a sharp eye on the trends in net sales, gross profit, and net income. Because accounting is the "language of business," it is also the language of buying and selling.

1. Describe the operating cycle of a merchandising company.
2. Explain the purpose of subsidiary ledgers.
3. Account for purchases and sales of merchandise in a perpetual inventory system.
4. Account for cash discounts, merchandise returns, transportation costs, sales tax, and goods and services tax.
5. Explain the operation of a periodic inventory system.

6. Discuss factors to be considered in selecting an inventory system.
7. Prepare a classified balance sheet. Compute the current ratio and amount of working capital.
8. Identify two standards for comparison widely used in evaluating financial ratios and prepare a classified income statement.
9. Analyze an income statement; evaluate the adequacy of net income.

MERCHANDISING COMPANIES

In the preceding chapters we have illustrated the accounting cycle for organizations that render *services* to their customers. Merchandising companies, in contrast, earn their revenue by selling *goods.*

The goods that a merchandising company sells to its customers are called **inventory** (or merchandise). Thus, the inventory of an automobile dealership consists of automobiles and trucks offered for sale, whereas the inventory of a grocery store consists of a wide variety of food items. In most cases, inventory is a relatively "liquid" asset—that is, it usually will be sold within a few weeks or months. For this reason, the asset inventory appears near the top of the balance sheet, immediately below accounts receivable.

The Operating Cycle of a Merchandising Company

LO 1: Describe the operating cycle of a merchandising company.

The series of transactions through which a business generates its revenue and its cash receipts from customers is called the **operating cycle.** The operating cycle of a merchandising company consists of the following basic transactions: (1) purchases of merchandise; (2) sales of the merchandise, often on account; and (3) collection of the accounts receivable from customers. As the word *cycle* suggests, this sequence of transactions repeats continuously. Some of the cash collected from the customer is used to purchase more merchandise, and the cycle begins anew.

This continuous sequence of merchandising transactions is illustrated in the diagram on the following page.

Merchandising Activities Compared with Manufacturing Most merchandising companies purchase their inventories from other business organizations in a *ready-to-sell* condition. Companies that *manufacture* their inventories, such as General Motors, Alcan Aluminium, and Bombardier, are called *manufacturers,* rather than merchandisers. The operating cycle of a manufacturing company is longer and more complex than that of a merchandising company, because the first transaction—purchasing merchandise—is replaced by the many transactions involved in manufacturing the merchandise.

The operating cycle
repeats continuously

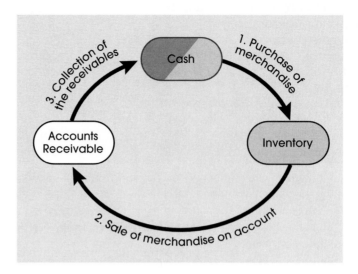

Our examples and illustrations in this chapter are limited to companies that purchase their inventory in a ready-to-sell condition. The basic concepts, however, also apply to manufacturers.

Retailers and Wholesalers   Merchandising companies include both retailers and wholesalers. A ***retailer*** is a business that sells merchandise directly to the public. Retailers may be large or small; they vary in size from giant department store chains, such as The Bay, Sears, and Wal-Mart, to small neighbourhood businesses, such as gas stations and convenience stores. In fact, more businesses engage in retail sales than in any other types of business activity.

The other major type of merchandising company is the ***wholesaler.*** Wholesalers buy large quantities of merchandise from several different manufacturers and then resell this merchandise to many different retailers. As wholesalers do not sell directly to the public, even the largest wholesalers are not well known to most consumers. Nonetheless, wholesaling is a major type of merchandising activity.

The concepts discussed in the remainder of this chapter apply equally to retailers and to wholesalers.

Income Statement of a Merchandising Company

Selling merchandise introduces a new and major cost of doing business: the ***cost*** to the merchandising company of the goods that it resells to its customers. This cost is termed the **cost of goods sold.** In essence, the cost of goods sold is an ***expense;*** however, this item is of such importance to a merchandising company that it is shown separate from other expenses in the income statement.

A ***highly condensed*** income statement for a merchandising business is shown on the next page. In comparison with the income statement of a service-type business, the new features of this statement are the inclusion of the ***cost of goods sold*** and a subtotal called **gross profit.**

Condensed income
statement for a merchan-
dising company

COMPUTER BARN
Condensed Income Statement
For the Year Ended December 31, 2000

Net sales	*$900,000*
Less: Cost of goods sold	540,000
Gross profit	$360,000
Less: Expenses	270,000
Net income	$ 90,000

Net sales represent the *sales price* of merchandise sold to customers during the period, less sales returns and allowances, and sales
discounts. The cost of goods sold, on the other hand, represents the *cost*
incurred by the merchandising company in purchasing these goods
(that were sold) from the company's suppliers. The difference between
revenue from sales and the cost of goods sold is called *gross profit* (or
gross margin).

Gross profit is a useful means of measuring the profitability of sales
transactions, but it does *not* represent the overall profitability of the business. A merchandising company has many expenses *other than* the cost of
goods sold. Examples include salaries, rent, advertising, and depreciation.
The company only earns a net income if its gross profit exceeds the sum of
these other expenses.

What Accounting Information Does a Merchandising Company Need?

Before we illustrate how a merchandising company accounts for the transactions in its operating cycle, let us consider the basic *types of information* that the company's accounting system should develop. The company
needs accounting information that will (1) meet its financial reporting
requirements, (2) serve the needs of company personnel in conducting daily
business operations, and (3) meet any special reporting requirements, such
as information required by tax authorities for income, sales, and goods and
services.

To meet its financial reporting requirements, a merchandising company
must measure and record its revenue from sales transactions, and also the
cost of goods sold. (Other types of revenue and expenses must also be
recorded, but this is done in the same manner as in a service-type business.)
In addition, the accounting system must provide a complete record of the
company's assets and liabilities.

The information appearing in financial statements is highly summarized. For example, the amount shown as accounts receivable in a balance sheet represents the *total* accounts receivable at the balance sheet
date. Managers and other company employees need *much more
detailed* accounting information than that provided in financial statements. In billing customers, for example, the company's billing clerks
need to know the amount receivable from *each credit customer.* In
addition, the accounting system must provide the billing clerks with the
dates and amounts of all charges and payments affecting each customer's account.

In most respects, the information needed for income, sales, and goods and services tax purposes parallels that used in the financial statements. Differences between income tax rules and financial reporting requirements will be discussed in later chapters.

Let us now see how the accounting system of a merchandising company meets the company's needs for financial information.

General Ledger Accounts

Up to now, we have been recording transactions only in **general ledger** accounts. These general ledger accounts are used in preparing financial statements and other accounting reports that **summarize** the financial position of a business and the results of its operations.

Although general ledger accounts provide a useful **overview** of a company's financial activities, they do not provide much of the detailed information needed by managers and other company employees in daily business operations. This detailed information is found in accounting records called **subsidiary ledgers.**

Subsidiary Ledgers: A Source of More Detail

LO 2: Explain the purpose of subsidiary ledgers.

A subsidiary ledger shows separately the individual items that comprise the balance of a general ledger account. For example, an **accounts receivable subsidiary ledger** contains a **separate account for each credit customer.** If the company has 500 credit customers, there will be 500 separate accounts in the accounts receivable subsidiary ledger. The balances of these 500 subsidiary ledger accounts add up to the balance in the Accounts Receivable account in the general ledger.

An accounts receivable subsidiary ledger contains all the information about a specific customer, including the amounts due, the dates and amounts of credit sales and past payments, the dates that payments are due, the credit limit, and the customer's billing address. In fact, each subsidiary account provides a **complete history** of the credit transactions between the company and a particular credit customer.

Most businesses maintain several different subsidiary ledgers, each providing details about the composition of a different general ledger account. A general ledger account that summarizes the content of a subsidiary ledger is called a **controlling account** (or control account).

For convenience, the word "subsidiary" often is omitted in describing a specific subsidiary ledger. Thus, an accounts receivable subsidiary ledger might simply be called the accounts receivable ledger (or customers ledger).

Subsidiary Ledgers Needed for Merchandising Transactions   In addition to a subsidiary ledger for accounts receivable, every merchandising company also maintains an **accounts payable subsidiary ledger,** showing the amount owed to each creditor. Many merchandising companies also maintain an **inventory subsidiary ledger,** with a separate account for each type of merchandise that the company sells. Thus, the inventory ledger of a large department store contains thousands of accounts. Each of these accounts shows for ***one type of product*** the quantities, per-unit costs, and total costs of all units purchased, sold, and currently "in inventory."

The diagram on the next page shows the relationship between several subsidiary ledgers and the related controlling accounts in the general ledger.

Other Types of Subsidiary Ledgers   In this chapter, we discuss the subsidiary ledgers for inventory, accounts payable, and accounts receivable. However, subsidiary ledgers also are maintained for many other general ledger accounts. The following schedule lists some of the general ledger accounts usually supported by a subsidiary ledger:

Controlling Account in the General Ledger	Unit of Organization within the Subsidiary Ledger
Cash	Each bank account
Notes receivable	Each note receivable
Accounts receivable	Individual credit customers
Inventory	Each type of product offered for sale
Plant assets	Each asset (or group of similar assets)
Notes payable	Each note payable
Accounts payable	Each creditor
Capital stock (only in a business organized as a corporation)	Each shareholder (this ledger shows each shareholder's name, address, and the number of shares owned)
Sales (or any revenue account)	Each department, branch location, or product line
Cost of goods sold	Same organization as the sales ledger
Any expense account	Each department incurring this type of expense

Subsidiary ledgers are intended to meet the information needs of the company's ***managers and employees.*** These accounting records are ***not*** used in the preparation of financial statements, nor are they usually made available to persons outside of the business organization.

Posting to Subsidiary Ledger Accounts   Any transaction that affects the balance of a subsidiary ledger account ***also*** affects the balance of the related controlling account. Thus, entries affecting subsidiary ledger accounts must be ***posted twice***—once to the subsidiary ledger account and once to the controlling account in the general ledger.

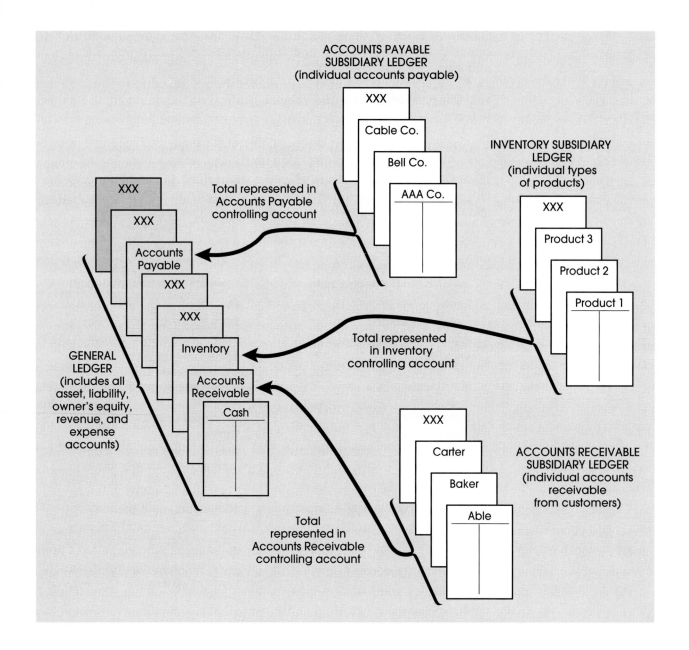

To illustrate, assume that on July 12 Hillside Company collects a $1,000 account receivable from L. Brown, a credit customer. This transaction is illustrated below in the form of a general journal entry:

GENERAL JOURNAL					
Date		Account Titles and Explanation	LP	Debit	Credit
July	12	*Cash*		*1,000*	
		Accounts Receivable (L. Brown) . . .			*1,000*
		Collected an account receivable.			

Assume that in the general ledger the account number for the Cash account is **101** and the account number of the Accounts Receivable controlling account is **120.** Hillside also maintains an accounts receivable subsidiary ledger, in which customers' accounts are arranged alphabetically. (We will assume that the company has only one bank account and, therefore, does not maintain a subsidiary ledger for cash.)

Our original journal entry is **repeated** below, along with the appropriate posting references included in the LP (Ledger Page) column:

Notice the "double posting" of the credit entry

GENERAL JOURNAL					
Date		Account Titles and Explanation	LP	Debit	Credit
July	12	Cash	101	1,000	
		Accounts Receivable (L. Brown) . . .	120/✓		1,000
		Collected an account receivable.			

The account numbers **101** and **120** entered in this column indicate that the entry has been posted to both the Cash account and the Accounts Receivable controlling account in the general ledger. The check mark (✓) indicates that the credit portion of the entry also has been posted to the account for L. Brown in the accounts receivable subsidiary ledger.

(In working homework assignments in this text, you often are asked to describe the effects of business transactions in the form of general journal entries. You should **not** include posting references in these entries unless you actually have posted the data to ledger accounts.)

Reconciling Subsidiary Ledgers with the Controlling Account   Periodically, accountants **reconcile** a subsidiary ledger with the controlling account—that is, they determine that the sum of the subsidiary ledger account balances **does,** in fact, equal that of the controlling account.

Reconciling a subsidiary ledger is an **internal control procedure** that may bring to light certain types of errors. For example, this procedure should detect a failure to post a transaction to the subsidiary ledger or a mechanical error in computing an account balance. Unfortunately, it does **not** provide assurance that all transactions were posted to the **correct account** within the subsidiary ledger. If a debit or credit entry is posted to the wrong account in the subsidiary ledger, the subsidiary ledger and controlling account will remain "in balance." These types of posting errors are difficult to detect and are one reason why individuals and businesses that purchase merchandise on account should review carefully the monthly statements that they receive from their suppliers.

Subsidiary Ledgers in Computer-Based Systems   At first, it may seem that maintaining subsidiary ledgers with hundreds or thousands of separate accounts would involve a great deal of work. However, business organizations big enough to require large subsidiary ledgers use computer-based accounting systems. In a computer-based accounting system, subsidiary ledger accounts and general ledger accounts are posted **automatically** as transactions are recorded. In addition, the computer automatically reconciles the subsidiary ledgers with the controlling accounts. Thus, no significant effort is required of accounting personnel to maintain subsidiary ledgers in a computer-based system.[1]

Two Approaches Used in Accounting for Merchandising Transactions

Either of two approaches may be used in accounting for merchandising transactions: (1) a ***perpetual inventory system*** or (2) a ***periodic inventory system.*** In past decades, both systems were in widespread use. Today, however, most large businesses (and many smaller ones) use perpetual systems. Periodic systems are used primarily in small businesses with manual accounting systems.

PERPETUAL INVENTORY SYSTEM

LO 3: Account for purchases and sales of merchandise in a perpetual inventory system.

In a **perpetual inventory system,** merchandising transactions are recorded ***as they occur.*** The system draws its name from the fact that the accounting records are kept perpetually up-to-date. Purchases of merchandise are recorded by debiting an asset account entitled Inventory. When merchandise is sold, two entries are necessary: one to recognize the ***revenue earned*** and the second to recognize the related ***cost of goods sold.***[2] This second entry also reduces the balance of the Inventory account to reflect the sale of some of the company's inventory.

A perpetual inventory system includes an ***inventory subsidiary ledger.*** This ledger provides company personnel with up-to-date information about each type of product that the company sells, including the per-unit cost and the number of units purchased, sold, and currently on hand.

To illustrate the perpetual inventory system, we will follow specific items of merchandise through the operating cycle of Computer Barn, a retail store. The transactions comprising this illustration are as follows:

Sept. 1 Purchased 10 Regent CX-21 computer monitors on account from Okawa Wholesale Co. The monitors cost $600 each, for a total of $6,000; payment is due in 30 days.

Sept. 7 Sold 2 monitors on account to RJ Travel Agency at a retail sales price of $1,000 each, for a total of $2,000. Payment is due in 30 days.

Oct. 1 Paid the $6,000 account payable to Okawa Wholesale Co.

Oct. 7 Collected the $2,000 account receivable from RJ Travel Agency.

In addition to a general ledger, Computer Barn maintains separate subsidiary ledgers for accounts receivable, inventory, and accounts payable.

---

[1]The maintenance of subsidiary ledgers was one of the earliest applications of computers in the business world. For a large organization, the time savings in this area alone may justify the cost of a computer-based accounting system. Prior to the use of computers, large business organizations employed many clerical workers for the sole purpose of posting transactions to subsidiary ledger accounts.

[2]In some perpetual systems, only the number of ***units*** sold is recorded at the time of sale, and the dollar costs are entered at a later date—perhaps monthly. Such variations in perpetual systems are discussed in Chapter 9.

Purchases of Merchandise   Purchases of inventory are recorded at cost. (The effect of cash discounts on cost will be introduced in a later section.) Thus, Computer Barn records its purchase of the 10 computer monitors on September 1 as follows:

Purchase of merchandise: the start of the cycle

```
Inventory . . . . . . . . . . . . . . . . . . . . . . . . . . . . . . . .   6,000
        Accounts Payable (Okawa Wholesale Co.) . . . . . . . . . . .            6,000
Purchased 10 Regent CX-21 computer monitors for $600 each;
payment due in 30 days.
```

The data contained in this entry are posted to the general ledger *and also to the subsidiary ledgers.* First, the entry is posted to the Inventory and Accounts Payable controlling accounts in the general ledger. The debit to Inventory also is posted to the Regent CX-21 Monitors account in the inventory subsidiary ledger.[3] The quantity of monitors purchased (10) and the per-unit cost ($600) also are recorded in this subsidiary ledger account. (This subsidiary ledger account is illustrated on page 236.)

The credit to Accounts Payable also is posted to the account for Okawa Wholesale Co. in Computer Barn's accounts payable subsidiary ledger.

Sales of Merchandise   The revenue earned in a sales transaction is equal to the *sales price* of the merchandise and is credited to a revenue account entitled *Sales.* Except in rare circumstances, sales revenue is considered "realized" when the merchandise is *delivered to the customer,* even if the sale is made on account. Therefore, Computer Barn will recognize the revenue from the sale to RJ Travel Agency on September 7, as shown below:

Entries to record a sale . . .

```
Accounts Receivable (RJ Travel Agency)  . . . . . . . . . . . . .   2,000
        Sales . . . . . . . . . . . . . . . . . . . . . . . . . . . . .            2,000
Sold 2 Regent CX-21 monitors for $1,000 each; payment due
in 30 days.
```

The *matching principle* requires that revenue be matched (offset) with all of the costs and expenses incurred in producing that revenue. Therefore, a *second journal entry* is required at the date of sale to record the cost of goods sold.

. . . and the related cost of goods sold

```
Cost of Goods Sold . . . . . . . . . . . . . . . . . . . . . . . . .   1,200
        Inventory  . . . . . . . . . . . . . . . . . . . . . . . . . . .            1,200
To transfer the cost of 2 Regent CX-21 monitors ($600 apiece)
from Inventory to the Cost of Goods Sold account.
```

Notice that this second entry is based upon the *cost* of the merchandise to Computer Barn, not upon its retail sales price. The per-unit cost of the Regent monitors ($600) was determined from the inventory subsidiary ledger (see page 236).

---

[3]In journal entries, it is common practice to indicate specific suppliers and customers using a parenthetic note following the account title "Accounts Payable" or "Accounts Receivable." Similar notations usually are *not* used with the Inventory account, because *many different types of products* may be purchased or sold in a single transaction. The detailed product information used in posting to the inventory ledger is found in the *invoice* (bill) which the seller sends to the buyer.

Both of the journal entries relating to this sales transaction are posted to Computer Barn's general ledger. In addition, the $2,000 debit to Accounts Receivable (first entry) is posted to the account for RJ Travel Agency in the accounts receivable subsidiary ledger. The credit to Inventory (second entry) also is posted to the Regent CX-21 Monitors account in the inventory subsidiary ledger (see below).

Payment of Accounts Payable to Suppliers   The payment to Okawa Wholesale Co. on October 1 is recorded as follows:

Payment of an account payable

Accounts Payable (Okawa Wholesale Co.) *6,000*
      Cash *6,000*
Paid account payable.

Both portions of this entry are posted to the general ledger. In addition, payment of the account payable is entered in the Okawa Wholesale Co. account in the Computer Barn's accounts payable subsidiary ledger.

Collection of Accounts Receivable from Customers   On October 7, collection of the account receivable from RJ Travel Agency is recorded as follows:

Collection of an account receivable

Cash *2,000*
      Accounts Receivable (RJ Travel Agency) *2,000*
Collected an account receivable.

Both portions of this entry are posted to the general ledger; the credit to Accounts Receivable also is posted to the RJ Travel Agency account in the accounts receivable subsidiary ledger.

Collection of the cash from RJ Travel Agency completes Computer Barn's operating cycle with respect to these two units of merchandise.

The Inventory Subsidiary Ledger   An inventory subsidiary ledger includes a separate account (or "inventory card") for each type of product in the company's inventory. Computer Barn's subsidiary inventory record for Regent monitors is illustrated below:

Inventory subsidiary ledger account

Item	Regent CX-21			Primary supplier	Okawa Wholesale Co.				
Description	21″ Grey scale monitor			Secondary supplier	Forbes Importers, Inc.				
Location	Storeroom 2			Inventory level: Min: 2		Max: 10			

	Purchased			Sold			Balance		
Date	Units	Unit Cost	Total	Units	Unit Cost	Cost of Goods Sold	Units	Unit Cost	Total
Sept. 1	10	$600	$6,000				10	$600	$6,000
7				2	$600	$1,200	8	$600	$4,800

When Regent CX-21 monitors are purchased, the quantity, unit cost, and total cost are entered in this subsidiary ledger account. When any of these monitors are sold, the number of units, unit cost, and total cost of the units sold also are recorded in this subsidiary ledger account. After each purchase or sales transaction, the "Balance" columns are updated to show the quantity, unit cost, and total cost of the monitors still on hand.[4]

An inventory ledger provides useful information to a variety of company personnel. A few examples of the company personnel who utilize this information on a daily basis are listed below:

- ***Sales managers*** use the inventory ledger to see at a glance which products are selling quickly and which are not.
- ***Accounting personnel*** use these records to determine the unit costs of merchandise sold.
- ***Sales personnel*** use this subsidiary ledger to determine the quantities of specific products currently on hand and the physical location of this merchandise.
- ***Employees responsible for ordering merchandise*** refer to the inventory ledger to determine when specific products should be reordered, the quantities to order, and the names of major suppliers.

When a ***physical inventory*** is taken, management uses the inventory ledger to determine on a product-by-product basis whether ***inventory shrinkage*** has been reasonable or excessive.

OTHER TRANSACTIONS RELATING TO PURCHASES

LO 4: Account for cash discounts, merchandise returns, transportation costs, sales tax, and goods and services tax.

In the preceding section, purchases of merchandise are recorded at cost. Now, let's see how cost may be affected by such factors as cash discounts and transportation charges. Also, the issue of purchased merchandise returned to suppliers is addressed.

Credit Terms and Cash Discounts

Manufacturers and wholesalers normally sell merchandise ***on account.*** The credit terms are stated in the seller's bill, or ***invoice.*** One common example of credit terms is "net 30 days," or "n/30," meaning full payment is due in 30 days. Another common form of credit terms is "10 eom," meaning payment is due 10 days after the end of the month in which the purchase occurred.

Manufacturers and wholesalers usually allow their customers 30 or 60 days in which to pay for credit purchases. Frequently, however, sellers offer their customers a small discount to encourage earlier payment.

Perhaps the most common credit terms offered by manufacturers and wholesalers are ***"2/10, n/30."*** This expression is read "2, 10, net 30," and means that full payment is due in 30 days, but that the buyer may take a ***2% discount*** if payment is made within 10 days. The period during which the discount is available is termed the ***discount period.*** Because the discount provides an incentive for the customer to make an early cash payment, it is called a ***cash discount.*** Buyers, however, often refer to these discounts as ***purchase discounts,*** while sellers frequently call them ***sales discounts.***

---

[4]In our illustration, all of the Regent monitors were purchased on the same date and have the same unit cost. Often a company's inventory of a given product includes units acquired at several ***different*** per-unit costs. This situation is addressed in Chapter 9.

Most well-managed companies have a policy of taking advantage of all cash discounts available on purchases of merchandise.[5] These companies initially record purchases of merchandise at the **net cost**—that is, the invoice price **minus** any available discount. After all, this is the amount that the company expects to pay.

To illustrate, assume that on November 3 Computer Barn purchases 100 spreadsheet programs from PC Products. The cost of these programs is $100 each, for a total of $10,000. However, PC Products offers credit terms of 2/10, n/30. If Computer Barn pays for this purchase within the discount period, it will have to pay only **$9,800,** or 98% of the full invoice price. Therefore, Computer Barn will record this purchase as follows:

Purchase recorded at net cost

Inventory	*9,800*	
Accounts Payable (PC Products)		*9,800*
To record purchase of 100 spreadsheet programs at net cost		
($100 × 98% × 100 units).		

The debit and credit are posted to the controlling and subsidiary accounts for inventory and accounts payable respectively for $9,800. If the invoice is paid within the discount period, Computer Barn simply records payment of a $9,800 account payable.

Through oversight or carelessness, Computer Barn might fail to make payment within the discount period. In this event, Computer Barn must pay PC Products the entire invoice price of **$10,000,** rather than the recorded liability of $9,800. The journal entry to record payment **after the discount period**—on, say, December 3—is:

Recording the loss of a cash discount

Accounts Payable (PC Products)	*9,800*	
Purchase Discounts Lost	*200*	
Cash		*10,000*
To record payment of invoice after expiration of discount		
period.		

The debit to accounts payable is posted to both the controlling and subsidiary accounts.

Notice that the additional $200 paid because the discount period has expired is debited to an account entitled Purchase Discounts Lost. Purchase Discounts Lost is an **expense account.** The only benefit to Computer Barn from this $200 expenditure was a **20-day delay** in paying an account payable. Thus, the lost purchase discount is basically a **finance charge,** similar to interest expense. In an income statement, finance charges usually are classified as nonoperating expenses.

The fact that purchase discounts **not taken** are recorded in a separate expense account is the primary reason why a company should record purchases of merchandise at **net cost** (the **net cost method.**) The use of a Pur-

---

[5]The terms 2/10, n/30 offer the buyer a 2% discount for sending payment 20 days before it is otherwise due. Saving 2% over only 20 days is equivalent to earning an annual rate of return of more than 36% (2% × 365/20 = 36.5%). Thus, taking cash discounts represents an excellent investment opportunity. Most companies take advantage of all cash discounts, even if they must borrow from a bank the cash necessary to make payment within the discount period.

chase Discounts Lost account immediately brings to management's attention any failure to take advantage of the cash discounts offered by suppliers.

Recording Purchases at Gross Invoice Price   As an alternative to recording purchases at net cost, some companies record merchandise purchases at the **gross** (total) invoice **price** (the **gross price method**). If payment is made within the discount period, these companies must record the amount of the purchase discount **taken.**

To illustrate, assume that Computer Barn followed a policy of recording purchases at gross invoice price. The entry on November 3 to record the purchase from PC Products would have been:

Purchase recorded at gross price

Inventory	*10,000*	
Accounts Payable (PC Products)		*10,000*
To record purchase of 100 spreadsheet programs at gross invoice price ($100 × 100 units).		

The postings for this entry are exactly the same as the net cost method except for the amount.

If payment is made within the discount period, Computer Barn will discharge this $10,000 account payable by paying only $9,800. The entry will be:

Buyer records discounts taken

Accounts Payable (PC Products)	*10,000*	
Cash		*9,800*
Purchase Discounts Taken		*200*
Paid a $10,000 invoice within the discount period; taking a 2% purchase discount.		

The debit to accounts payable is posted to both the controlling and subsidiary accounts. **Purchase Discounts Taken** is treated as a reduction in the cost of goods sold.

Both the net cost and gross price methods are widely used and produce substantially the same results in financial statements.[6] A shortcoming in the gross price method, however, is that it does **not** direct management's attention to discounts lost. Instead, these lost discounts are "buried" in the costs assigned to inventory. For this reason, we recommend the net cost method.

Returns of Unsatisfactory Merchandise

On occasion, a purchaser may find the purchased merchandise unsatisfactory and want to return it to the seller for a refund. Most sellers permit such returns.

To illustrate, assume that on November 9 Computer Barn returns to PC Products five of the spreadsheet programs purchased on November 3, because these programs were not properly labelled. As Computer Barn has not yet paid for this merchandise, the return will reduce the amount that Computer Barn owes PC Products. The gross invoice price of the returned merchandise was $500 ($100 per program). Remember, however, that Computer Barn records purchases at **net cost.** Therefore, these spreadsheet

---

[6]The net cost method values the ending inventory at net cost, whereas the gross cost method shows this inventory at gross invoice price. This difference, however, is **immaterial.**

programs are carried in Computer Barn's inventory subsidiary ledger at a per-unit cost of *$98,* or $490 for the five programs being returned. The entry to record this purchase return is:

Return is based upon
recorded acquisition cost

Accounts Payable (PC Products) *490*
     Inventory *490*
*Returned 5 defective spreadsheet programs to supplier. Net cost
of the returned items, $490 ($100 × 98% × 5 units).*

The reduction in accounts payable and inventory must be posted to the controlling as well as the subsidiary ledger accounts.

Transportation Costs on Purchases

The purchaser sometimes may pay the costs of having the purchased merchandise delivered to its premises. Transportation costs relating to the *acquisition* of inventory or any other asset are *not expenses* of the current period; rather, these charges are *part of the cost of the asset* being acquired.[7] If the purchaser is able to associate transportation costs with specific products, these costs should be debited directly to the Inventory account as part of the "cost" of the merchandise.

Often, many different products arrive in a single shipment. In such cases, it may be impractical for the purchaser to determine the amount of the total transportation cost that is applicable to each product. For this reason, many companies follow the convenient policy of debiting all transportation costs on inbound shipments of merchandise to an account entitled *Transportation-in.* The dollar amount of transportation-in usually is too small to show separately in the financial statements. Therefore, this amount is merely included in the amount reported in the income statement as cost of goods sold. At the end of the period, the Transportation-in account is closed into the Income Summary in the same manner as the Cost of Goods Sold account.

This treatment of transportation costs is not entirely consistent with the *matching principle.* Some of the transportation costs may apply to merchandise still in inventory rather than to goods sold during the current period. We have mentioned, however, that transportation costs are relatively small in dollar amount. The accounting principle of *materiality,* therefore, usually justifies accounting for these costs in the most convenient manner.

OTHER TRANSACTIONS RELATING TO SALES

Credit terms and merchandise returns also affect the amount of sales revenue earned by the seller. To the extent that credit customers take advantage of cash discounts or return merchandise for a refund, the seller's revenue is reduced. Thus, revenue shown in the income statement of a merchandising concern is often called *net sales.* The following partial income statement illustrates this relationship:

---

[7]The "cost" of an asset includes all reasonable and necessary costs of getting the asset to an appropriate location ready for sale or putting it into usable condition.

What is "net sales"?

COMPUTER BARN Partial Income Statement For the Year Ended December 31, 2000			
Sales			*$912,000*
Less: Sales returns and allowances	*$8,000*		
Sales discounts	*4,000*	*12,000*	
Net sales		*$900,000*	

As we stated earlier in the chapter, the details of this computation seldom are shown in an actual income statement. The normal practice is to begin the income statement with the amount of net sales, as shown on page 229.

Sales Returns and Allowances

Most merchandising companies allow customers to obtain a refund by returning any merchandise considered to be unsatisfactory. If the merchandise has only minor defects, customers sometimes agree to keep the merchandise if an ***allowance*** (reduction) is made in the sales price.

Under the perpetual inventory system, two entries are needed to record the sale of merchandise: one to recognize the revenue earned and the other to transfer the cost of the merchandise from the Inventory account to Cost of Goods Sold. If some of the merchandise is returned, both of these entries are partially reversed.

First, let us consider the effects upon revenue of granting either a refund or an allowance. Both refunds and allowances have the effect of nullifying previously recorded sales and reducing the amount of revenue earned by the business. The journal entry to reduce sales revenue as the result of a sales return (or allowance) is shown below:

A sales return reverses recorded revenue . . .

Sales Returns and Allowances	*200*	
Accounts Receivable (or Cash)		*200*

Customer returned merchandise purchased on account for $200.
Allowed customer full credit for returned merchandise.

Sales Returns and Allowances is a **contra-revenue account**—that is, it is deducted from gross sales as a step in determining net sales.

Why use a separate Sales Returns and Allowances account rather than merely debiting the Sales account? The answer is that using a separate contra-revenue account enables management to see both the total amount of sales ***and also*** the amount of sales returns and allowances. The relationship between these amounts gives management an indication of customer satisfaction with the merchandise.

If merchandise is returned by the customer, a second entry is made to remove the cost of this merchandise from the Cost of Goods Sold account and restore it to the inventory records. This entry is:

. . . and the recorded cost of goods sold.

Inventory	*160*	
Cost of Goods Sold		*160*

To restore in the Inventory account the cost of merchandise
returned by a customer.

Notice that this entry is based upon the **cost** of the returned merchandise to the seller, **not upon its sales price.** (This entry is not necessary when a sales **allowance** is granted to a customer who keeps the merchandise.)

Special accounts are maintained in the inventory subsidiary ledger for returned merchandise. Often this merchandise will be returned to the supplier or sold to a damaged-goods "liquidator" rather than again being offered for sale to the company's regular customers.[8]

Sales Discounts

We have explained that sellers frequently offer cash discounts, such as 2/10, n/30, to encourage their customers to make early payments for purchases on account.

Sellers and buyers account for cash discounts quite differently. To the seller, the "cost" associated with cash discounts is not the discounts **lost** when payments are delayed, but rather the discounts **taken** by customers that do pay within the discount period. Therefore, sellers design their accounting systems to measure the sales discounts **taken** by their customers. To achieve this goal, the seller records the sale and the related account receivable at the **gross** (full) invoice price.

To illustrate, assume that Computer Barn sells merchandise to Susan Hall for $1,000, offering terms of 2/10, n/30. The sales revenue is recorded at the full invoice price, as shown below:

Sales are recorded at the gross sales price	*Accounts Receivable (Susan Hall)*	*1,000*
	Sales	*1,000*
	Sold merchandise on account. Invoice price, $1,000; terms, 2/10, n/30.	

If Hall makes payment after the discount period has expired, Computer Barn merely records the receipt of $1,000 cash in full payment of this account receivable. If Hall pays **within** the discount period, however, she will pay only **$980** to settle her account. In this case, Computer Barn will record the receipt of Hall's payment as follows:

Seller records discounts taken by customers	*Cash*	*980*
	Sales Discounts	*20*
	Accounts Receivable (Susan Hall)	*1,000*
	Collected a $1,000 account receivable from a customer who took a 2% discount for early payment.	

The debit and credit to accounts receivable in these two entries must be posted to both the controlling and subsidiary accounts.

Sales Discounts is another contra-revenue account. In computing net sales, sales discounts are deducted from gross sales along with any sales returns and allowances. (If the customer has returned part of the merchandise, a discount may be taken only on the gross amount owed **after** the return.)

---

[8]An inventory of returned merchandise should not be valued in the accounting records at a cost that exceeds its **net realizable value.** The possible need to write down the carrying value of inventory is discussed in Chapter 9.

Contra-revenue accounts have much in common with expense accounts; both are deducted from gross revenue in determining net income, and both have debit balances. Thus, contra-revenue accounts (Sales Returns and Allowances and Sales Discounts) are closed into the Income Summary account *in the same manner as expense accounts.*

Delivery Expenses

If the seller incurs any costs in delivering merchandise to the customer, these costs are debited to an expense account entitled Delivery Expense. In an income statement, delivery expense is classified as a regular operating expense, not as part of the cost of goods sold.

Accounting for Sales and Goods and Services Taxes

Sales and goods and services taxes are levied by the provincial and federal governments on retail sales.[9] These taxes actually are imposed upon the consumer, not upon the seller. For example, the goods and services tax (known as GST) of 7% is levied by the federal government on the final consumer. However, businesses have to first pay the GST on their purchases and later receive full credit for the GST on their sales to consumers. The GST applies to almost all the goods sold and services rendered. Thus, the seller must collect the tax, file tax returns at times specified by law, and remit the taxes owed on all reported sales.

For cash sales, these taxes are collected from the customer at the time of the sales transaction. For credit sales, they are included in the amount charged to the customer's account. The liability to the governmental unit for sales and goods and services taxes may be recorded at the time the sale is made as shown in the following journal entry:

Sales tax recorded at time of sale		
Cash (or Accounts Receivable)	*1,150*	
Provincial Sales Tax Payable		*80*
Goods and Services Tax Payable		*70*
Sales		*1,000*

To record sales of $1,000 subject to 7% goods and services tax and 8% provincial tax.

This approach requires separate credit entries to the Provincial Sales Tax Payable and Goods and Services Tax Payable accounts for each sale. At first glance, this may seem to require an excessive amount of bookkeeping. However, today's electronic cash registers can be programmed to record automatically these tax liabilities at the time of each sale.

An Alternative Approach to Sales and Goods and Services Taxes   Instead of recording the sales and goods and services tax liability at the time of sale, some businesses prefer to credit the Sales account with the entire amount collected, including the taxes, and to make an adjustment at the end of each period to reflect the taxes payable. For example, suppose that the total recorded sales for the period under this method were $345,000. Since the

---

[9]The Maritime provinces combined these taxes and called the single tax "harmonized sales tax."

Sales account includes both the sales price and the sales and goods and services taxes (of 15%), it is apparent that $345,000 is **115%** of the actual sales figure. Actual sales are $300,000 (computed $345,000 ÷ 1.15), and the amount of taxes due is $45,000. (Proof: 15% of $300,000 = $45,000.) The entry to record the liability for sales taxes would be

<table>
<tr><td>Sales tax recorded as adjustment of sales</td><td>*Sales* . . . .</td><td align="right">*45,000*</td><td></td></tr>
<tr><td></td><td>   *Provincial Sales Tax Payable* . . . .</td><td></td><td align="right">*24,000*</td></tr>
<tr><td></td><td>   *Goods and Services Tax Payable* . . . .</td><td></td><td align="right">*21,000*</td></tr>
</table>

To remove sales tax of 8% and goods and services tax of 7% on $300,000 of sales from the Sales account, and record as a liability.

This second approach is widely used in businesses that do not use electronic devices for recording sales transactions.

If some of the products being sold are not subject to sales and goods and services taxes, the business must keep separate records of taxable and non-taxable sales.

Taking a Physical Inventory

The basic characteristic of the perpetual inventory system is that the Inventory account is **continuously updated** for all purchases and sales of merchandise. Over time, however, normal inventory shrinkage usually causes some discrepancies between the quantities of merchandise shown in the inventory records and the quantities actually on hand. **Inventory shrinkage** refers to unrecorded decreases in inventory resulting from such factors as breakage, spoilage, employee theft, and shoplifting.

In order to ensure the accuracy of their perpetual inventory records, most businesses take a **complete physical count** of the merchandise on hand at least once a year. This procedure is called **taking a physical inventory,** and it usually is performed at year-end.

Once the quantity of merchandise on hand has been determined by a physical count, the per-unit costs in the inventory ledger accounts are used to determine the total cost of the inventory. The Inventory controlling account and also the accounts in the inventory subsidiary ledger then are **adjusted** to the quantities and dollar amounts indicated by the physical inventory.

To illustrate, assume that at year-end the Inventory controlling account and inventory subsidiary ledger of Computer Barn both show an inventory with a cost of **$72,200.** A physical count, however, reveals that some of the merchandise listed in the accounting records is missing; the items actually on hand have a total cost of **$70,000.** Computer Barn would make the following adjusting entry to correct its Inventory controlling account:

<table>
<tr><td>Adjusting for inventory shrinkage</td><td>*Cost of Goods Sold* . . . .</td><td align="right">*2,200*</td><td></td></tr>
<tr><td></td><td>   *Inventory* . . . .</td><td></td><td align="right">*2,200*</td></tr>
</table>

To adjust the perpetual inventory records to reflect the results of the year-end physical count.

Computer Barn also will adjust the appropriate accounts in its inventory subsidiary ledger to reflect the quantities indicated by the physical count.

Reasonable amounts of inventory shrinkage are viewed as a normal cost of doing business and simply are debited to the Cost of Goods Sold account, as illustrated above.[10]

Closing Entries in a Perpetual Inventory System

As explained and illustrated in Chapter 3, revenue and expense accounts are *closed* at the end of each accounting period. A merchandising business with a perpetual inventory system makes closing entries that parallel those of a service-type business. The Sales account is a revenue account and is closed into the Income Summary along with other revenue accounts. The Cost of Goods Sold account is closed into the Income Summary in the same manner as the other expense accounts.

PERIODIC INVENTORY SYSTEM

A **periodic inventory system** is an ***alternative*** to a perpetual inventory system. In a periodic inventory system, no effort is made to keep up-to-date records of either the inventory or the cost of goods sold. Instead, these amounts are determined only "periodically"—usually at the end of each year.

Operation of a Periodic Inventory System

LO 5: Explain the operation of a periodic inventory system.

A traditional periodic inventory system operates as follows. When merchandise is purchased, its cost is debited to an account entitled **Purchases,** rather than to the Inventory account. When merchandise is sold, an entry is made to recognize the sales revenue, but ***no entry*** is made to record the cost of goods sold or to reduce the balance of the Inventory account. As the inventory records are not updated as transactions occur, there is no inventory subsidiary ledger.

The foundation of the periodic inventory system is the taking of a ***complete physical inventory*** at year-end. This physical count determines the amount of inventory appearing in the balance sheet. The cost of goods sold for the entire year then is determined by a short computation.

Data for an Illustration   To illustrate, assume that Special Occasions, a party supply store, has a periodic inventory system. At December 31, 2000, the following information is available:

1. The inventory on hand at the end of *1999* cost *$14,000.*
2. During *2000,* purchases of merchandise for resale to customers totalled $136,000, of which $6,000 was returned for credit.
3. Inventory on hand at the end of *2000* cost *$12,000.*

The inventories at the ends of 1999 and 2000 were determined by taking a complete physical inventory at (or very near) each year-end. (Because the Inventory account was not updated as transactions occurred during 2000, it still shows a balance of $14,000—the inventory on hand at the *beginning* of the year.)

---

[10]If a large inventory shortage is caused by an event such as a fire or theft, the cost of the missing or damaged merchandise may be debited to a special loss account, such as Fire Loss. In the income statement, a loss is deducted from revenue in the same manner as an expense.

The $136,000 cost of merchandise purchased during 2000 was recorded in the Purchases account.

Recording Purchases of Merchandise   Special Occasions made many purchases of merchandise and returned some of the merchandise from time to time during 2000. The entries to record the first of these purchases and returns are illustrated below:

Jan. 6	Purchases	*2,000*	
	Accounts Payable (Paper Products Co.)		*2,000*
	Purchased inventory on account; payment		
	due in 30 days.		

Jan. 8	Accounts Payable (Paper Products Co.)	*300*	
	Purchase Returns and Allowances		*300*
	Returned unsatisfactory merchandise for credit.		

These two entries were posted to the Purchases, Accounts Payable, and Purchase Returns and Allowances accounts in the general ledger. The credit and debit portions also were posted to the account for Paper Products Co. in Special Occasions' accounts payable subsidiary ledger. The debit to Purchases and credit to Purchase Returns and Allowances were ***not*** "double-posted," as there is ***no inventory subsidiary ledger*** in a periodic system.

Computing the Cost of Goods Sold   The year-end inventory is determined by taking a complete physical count of the merchandise on hand. Once the ending inventory is known, the cost of goods sold for the entire year can be determined by a short computation. This computation is shown below, using the 2000 data for Special Occasions:

Computation of the cost of goods sold

Inventory (beginning of the year) (1)	*$ 14,000*
Add: Purchases ($136,000 − $6,000 returns and allowances) (2)	*130,000*
Cost of goods available for sale	*$144,000*
Less: Inventory (end of the year) (3)	*12,000*
Cost of goods sold	*$132,000*

Recording Inventory and the Cost of Goods Sold   Special Occasions has now determined its inventory at the end of 2000 and its cost of goods sold for the year. But neither of these amounts has yet been recorded in the company's accounting records.

In a periodic system, the ending inventory and the cost of goods sold are recorded during the company's year-end ***closing procedures.*** (The term "closing procedures" refers to the making of end-of-period adjusting and closing entries.) These procedures are illustrated in Appendix A, which follows this chapter.

A Short-Cut System for Businesses with Little Inventory

Some businesses maintain very little inventory, yet still sell substantial amounts of merchandise. This situation is especially likely to arise if the inventory is highly perishable. For example, restaurants, flower shops, and fish markets maintain very little inventory. In any given month, these businesses usually purchase approximately the same amount of merchandise as they sell.

Such businesses often follow a policy of debiting the Cost of Goods Sold account when merchandise is purchased. This approach enables a company to prepare monthly income statements without taking a physical inventory *or* recording separately the cost of each sales transaction. If the amount of inventory on hand at year-end is material in dollar amount, a physical count is made. The Inventory account then is adjusted to reflect this physical count, with an offsetting debit or credit to the Cost of Goods Sold.

This "short-cut" approach appeals to small businesses with manual accounting systems because very little record keeping is required. However, this approach does *not* produce satisfactory results if the size of the company's inventory *fluctuates* significantly from month to month. Also, this short-cut system does not provide management with the benefits of an inventory subsidiary ledger.

Despite these limitations, this system works well in some small businesses. Also, some large businesses use this system in accounting for insignificant components of their inventory. A department store, for example, may use this system in its candy department, its cafeteria, and in accounting for low-cost products such as shoelaces and novelty items.

Our objective in describing this modified periodic system is not to illustrate the accounting practices of fish markets and flower shops. Rather, it is to make a very basic point: generally accepted accounting principles *do not* specify how a business should maintain its accounting records. Every business should use an accounting system that meets the company's specific needs for accounting information as *efficiently* as possible.

Comparison of Perpetual and Periodic Inventory Systems

Perpetual systems are used when management needs information throughout the year about inventory levels and gross profit. Periodic systems are used when the primary goals are to develop annual data and to minimize record-keeping requirements. One business often uses *different inventory systems* in accounting for *different types of merchandise.*

Who Uses Perpetual Systems?   When management or employees *need up-to-date information about inventory levels and gross profit,* there is no substitute for a perpetual inventory system. Almost all manufacturing companies use perpetual systems. These businesses need current information to coordinate their inventories of direct (raw) materials with their production schedules. Most large merchandising companies—and many small ones—also use perpetual systems.

In the days when all accounting records were maintained by hand, businesses that sold many types of low-cost products had no choice but to use *periodic* inventory systems. A Wal-Mart store, for example, may sell several

CASE IN POINT

The Bay, Wal-Mart, Price Club, Sears, and many other retailers use electronic cash registers called point-of-sale terminals. These registers read bar codes (a pattern of thick and thin vertical bars) attached to each item of merchandise. The bar code identifies the product to the company's computer, which instantly records the sale and updates the computer-based perpetual inventory records.

Notice that no accounting personnel are directly involved in recording sales transactions or maintaining the inventory records. Transactions are recorded automatically as the cashier passes an electronic scanner over the bar-coded merchandise.

thousand items *per hour.* Imagine the difficulty of keeping a perpetual inventory system up-to-date if the records were maintained by hand. But with today's **point-of-sale terminals** and **bar coded merchandise,** many high-volume retailers now use perpetual inventory systems.

Perpetual inventory systems are not limited to businesses with point-of-sale terminals. Many small businesses with manual accounting systems also use perpetual inventory systems. However, these businesses may update their inventory records on a weekly or a monthly basis, rather than at the time of each sales transaction.

Whether accounting records are maintained manually or by computer, most businesses use perpetual inventory systems in accounting for products with a *high per-unit cost.* Examples include automobiles, heavy machinery, electronic equipment, home appliances, and jewellery. Management has a greater interest in keeping track of inventory when the merchandise is expensive. Also, sales volume usually is low enough that a perpetual system can be used even if accounting records are maintained by hand.

Who Uses Periodic Systems? Periodic systems are used when the need for current information about inventories and sales *does not justify the cost* of maintaining a perpetual system. In a small retail store, for example, the owner may be so familiar with the inventory that formal perpetual inventory records are unnecessary. Most businesses—large and small—use periodic systems for inventories that are *immaterial* in dollar amount, or when management has little interest in the quantities on hand.

As stated previously, businesses that sell many low-cost items and have manual accounting systems sometimes have no choice but to use the periodic method.

Selecting an Inventory System

Accountants—and business managers—often must select an inventory system appropriate for a particular situation. Some of the factors usually considered in these decisions are listed in the table on the next page.

The Trend in Today's Business World Advances in technology are quickly extending the use of perpetual inventory systems to more businesses and

LO 6: Discuss factors to be considered in selecting an inventory system.

Factors Suggesting a Perpetual Inventory System	Factors Suggesting a Periodic Inventory System
Large company with professional management.	Small company, run by owner.
Management and employees want information about items in inventory and the quantities in which specific products are selling.	Accounting records of inventories and specific product sales are not needed in daily operations. Such information is developed primarily for use in annual income tax returns.
Items in inventory have a high per-unit cost.	Inventory consists of many different kinds of low-cost items.
Low volume of sales transactions or a computerized accounting system, (*i.e.,* point-of-sale terminals).	High volume of sales transactions and a manual accounting system. Lack of full-time accounting personnel.
Merchandise stored in multiple locations or in warehouses separate from the sales sites.	All merchandise stored at the sales site (*i.e.,* in the store).

more types of inventory. This trend is certain to continue. Throughout this textbook, you may assume that a ***perpetual inventory system*** is in use unless we specifically state otherwise.

CLASSIFIED FINANCIAL STATEMENTS

Most business organizations prepare **classified financial statements,** meaning that items with certain characteristics are placed together in a group, or "classification." The purpose of these classifications is to ***develop useful subtotals*** that will assist users of the statements in evaluating the company's solvency, profitability, and future prospects. These classifications and subtotals are standardized throughout most businesses, thus assisting decision makers in comparing the financial statements of different companies.

A Classified Balance Sheet

LO 7: Prepare a classified balance sheet . . .

In a classified balance sheet, assets usually are presented in three groups: (1) current assets, (2) plant and equipment,[11] and (3) other assets. Liabilities are classified into two categories: (1) current liabilities and (2) long-term

---

[11]Section 3060 of the *CICA Handbook* uses the general term "capital assets" to encompass three groups of long-term assets: property, plant, and equipment; intangible assets; and natural resources. Since each of these three groups of assets is usually presented separately in the financial statements, it is more descriptive to use the specific terms "property, plant, and equipment," "intangible assets," and "natural resources." Also, these three specific terms are most widely used in published financial statements. In the four examples (four companies from four different industries) cited by the 1997 edition of *Financial Reporting in Canada,* published by the CICA, two use the terms "property, plant, and equipment" and the other two use "property and equipment" and "fixed assets" respectively.

liabilities. A classified balance sheet for Computer Barn is illustrated below:

A classified balance sheet

COMPUTER BARN Balance Sheet December 31, 2000			
Assets			
Current assets:			
Cash			$ 30,000
Marketable securities			11,000
Notes receivable			5,000
Accounts receivable			60,000
Inventory			70,000
Prepaid expenses			4,000
Total current assets			$180,000
Plant and equipment:			
Land		$151,000	
Building	$120,000		
Less: Accumulated depreciation	9,000	111,000	
Fixtures & equipment	$ 45,000		
Less: Accumulated depreciation	27,000	18,000	
Total plant and equipment			280,000
Other assets:			
Land held as a future building site			170,000
Total assets			$630,000
Liabilities & Owner's Equity			
Current Liabilities:			
Notes payable (due in 6 months)			$ 20,000
Accounts payable			65,000
Sales, goods and services taxes payable			3,000
Salaries payable			8,000
Unearned revenue and customer deposits			4,000
Total current liabilities			$100,000
Long-term liabilities:			
Mortgage payable (due in 15 years)			210,000
Total liabilities			$310,000
Owner's equity:			
Pat O'Brien, capital			320,000
Total liabilities & owner's equity			$630,000

Using a Classified Balance Sheet in Evaluating Solvency

The classifications **current assets** and **current liabilities** are especially useful to short-term creditors in evaluating the immediate debt-paying ability, or ***solvency,*** of the business entity. This is an extension of the topic on solvency that was briefly introduced in Chapters 1 and 4.

Current Assets   Current assets are relatively "liquid" resources; this category includes cash, investments in marketable securities, receivables, inventories, and prepaid expenses. To qualify as a current asset, an asset must be capable of ***being converted into cash*** within a relatively short period of time, without interfering with normal business operations.[12]

---

[12]Prepaid expenses are not actually "converted" into cash, but they ***substitute*** for cash by eliminating the need to make certain future cash payments.

The time period in which current assets are expected to be converted into cash is usually one year. If a company requires more than a year to complete its normal operating cycle, however, the **length of the operating cycle** is used as the time period defining current assets. Thus, **inventory** and **accounts receivable from customers** normally are classified as current assets, even if the conversion of these assets into cash will not be completed within one year.[13]

In a balance sheet, current assets are listed in order of liquidity (the closer an asset is to becoming cash, the greater its liquidity.) Thus, cash always is listed first among the current assets, followed by marketable securities, receivables, inventory, and prepaid expenses.

Current Liabilities   Current liabilities are **existing debts** that must be paid within the **same time period** used in defining current assets. Among the most common current liabilities are notes payable (due within one year), accounts payable, unearned revenue, and accrued expenses, such as salaries payable and interest payable. In the balance sheet, notes payable usually are listed first, followed by accounts payable; other types of current liabilities may be listed in any sequence.

The **relationship** between current assets and current liabilities is more important than the total dollar amount in either category. Current liabilities must be paid in the near future, and the money to pay these liabilities usually comes—in large part—from the conversion of current assets into cash. Thus, decision makers evaluating the solvency of a business often compare the relative amounts of current assets and current liabilities.

The Current Ratio

The most widely used measure of short-term debt-paying ability is the **current ratio.** The reader of a balance sheet may compute this ratio by **dividing** total current assets by total current liabilities.

LO 7: . . . Compute the current ratio and amount of working capital.

In the balance sheet of Computer Barn illustrated previously, current assets amount to $180,000 and current liabilities total $100,000, indicating a current ratio of **1.8 to 1** ($180,000 ÷ $100,000 = 1.8). A current ratio of 1.8 to 1 means that the company's current assets are 1.8 times as large as its current liabilities.

The higher the current ratio, the more solvent the company appears to be. Many bankers and other short-term creditors traditionally have believed that a retailer should have a current ratio of at least 2 to 1 to qualify as a good credit risk. By this standard, Computer Barn comes up a little short; the company probably would **not** receive a top

---

[13]The time period used in defining current assets is one year or the length of the operating cycle, whichever is **longer.** Most businesses have operating cycles far shorter than one year. However, companies that sell merchandise on long-term instalment contracts or that manufacture products such as ships may have operating cycles requiring several years to complete. The user of financial statements should recognize that the current assets of such companies are converted into cash **much more slowly** than are the current assets of most businesses.

credit rating from a bank or other short-term creditor that applied this criterion.

Working Capital

Working capital is another measurement often used to express the relationship between current assets and current liabilities. Working capital is the *excess* of current assets over current liabilities.[14] Our illustrated balance sheet indicates that at the end of 2000, Computer Barn has working capital of *$80,000* ($180,000 − $100,000).

The amount of working capital that a company needs to remain solvent varies with the size of the organization and the nature of its business activities. An analyst familiar with the nature of a company's operations usually can determine from the amount of working capital whether the company is in a sound financial position or is soon likely to encounter financial difficulties.

Evaluating Financial Ratios

We caution users of financial statements *against* placing much confidence in general rules, such as "a current ratio should be at least 2 to 1." To interpret any financial ratio properly, the decision maker must first understand the characteristics of the company and the industry in which it operates.

Retailers and wholesalers, for example, tend to have lower current ratios than do manufacturing companies. Service-type businesses—which have no inventory—generally have lower current ratios than merchandising or manufacturing companies. Large businesses with highly reliable sources of revenue and cash receipts are able to operate with lower current ratios than are small companies with less stable earnings.

CASE IN POINT   Large telephone companies are regarded within the business community as pillars of financial strength. Yet these companies usually do not have high current ratios. Such financially sound companies as Bell Canada, British Columbia Telephone, New Brunswick Telephone, and Maritime Telephone and Telegraph often operate with current ratios of much less than 1 to 1.

Although a high current ratio is one indication of strong debt-paying ability, an extremely high ratio—say, 4 or 5 to 1—may indicate that *too much* of the company's resources are "tied up" in current assets. In maintaining such a highly liquid position, the company may be using its financial resources inefficiently.

---

[14]A company with current liabilities in excess of its current assets has a *negative* amount of working capital. Negative working capital does *not* necessarily mean that a company is insolvent. Any company with a current ratio of less than 1 to 1 has a negative amount of working capital.

LO 8: Identify two standards for comparison widely used in evaluating financial ratios, and prepare a classified income statement.

Standards for Comparison   We have seen that Computer Barn has a current ratio of 1.8 to 1. What standards for comparison are commonly used in evaluating such a statistic?

Users of financial information generally use two criteria in evaluating the reasonableness of a financial ratio. One criterion is the **trend** in the ratio over a period of years. By reviewing this trend, the analyst is able to determine whether a company's performance or financial strength is improving or deteriorating. Second, an analyst compares a company's financial ratios with the ratios of **similar companies** and also with **industry-wide averages.** These comparisons assist the analyst in evaluating a particular ratio in light of the company's current business environment.

In summary, ratios are useful tools; but they can be interpreted properly only by individuals who understand the characteristics of the company and its environment.

Publicly owned corporations issue **annual reports** providing a great deal of information about the company, including comparative financial data for several years, and a discussion and analysis by management of the company's financial condition and the results of its recent operations. Financial information about **entire industries** is available through a number of financial publications and on-line computer data bases.

Usefulness and Limitations of Ratios Analysis   A financial ratio expresses the relationship of one quantity or amount relative to another. Most users of financial statements find that certain ratios assist them in quickly evaluating the financial position, profitability, and future prospects of a business. A comparison of key ratios for several successive years may indicate whether the business is becoming stronger or weaker. Ratios also provide a means of comparing quickly the financial strength and profitability of different companies.

Users of financial statements should recognize, however, that ratios have several limitations. For example, management may enter into year-end transactions that temporarily improve key ratios. To illustrate, the balance sheet of Computer Barn includes current assets of $180,000 and current liabilities of $100,000, resulting in a current ratio of **1.8 to 1.** What would happen if shortly before year-end, management were to use $20,000 of the company's cash to pay off accounts payable? This transaction would reduce current assets to $160,000 and current liabilities to $80,000. However, it would also increase the company's year-end current ratio to a more impressive **2 to 1** ($160,000 ÷ $80,000 = 2).

Financial statement ratios contain the same limitations as do the dollar amounts used in financial statements. For example, assets usually are valued at historical cost rather than at current market value. Also, financial statement ratios express only **financial** relationships. They give no indication of a company's progress in achieving nonfinancial goals, such as creating new jobs or protecting the environment. A thorough analysis of the future prospects of any business involves more than merely computing and comparing financial ratios.

The Owner's Responsibility for Debts of the Business

As discussed in Chapters 1 and 4, accountants view a business entity as separate from the other economic activities of the business owner (or owners). The law, however, draws an important distinction between corporations and unincorporated business organizations.

Under the law, the owners of **unincorporated** businesses (sole proprietorships and partnerships) are **personally liable** for any and all debts of the business organization. Therefore, creditors of unincorporated businesses often base their lending decisions upon the solvency of the business **owners** rather than upon the financial position of the business itself.

If a business is organized as a **corporation,** however, the owners (shareholders) are **not** personally responsible for the debts of the business. Creditors may look **only to the business entity** in seeking payment of their claims. Thus, the solvency of the business entity becomes much more important if the business is organized as a corporation.

Small Corporations and Loan "Guarantees"   Often small corporations do not have sufficient financial resources to qualify for credit. In such cases, creditors may require that one or more of the company's shareholders personally guarantee (or "co-sign") specific debts of the business entity. By co-signing debts of the corporation, individual shareholders become personally liable for the debt if the corporation fails to make payment.

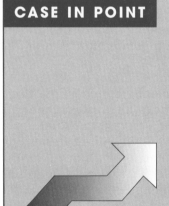

CASE IN POINT   A small, family-owned wholesale business was organized as a corporation. To operate efficiently, the business needed to purchase merchandise on account. However, the corporation had so few liquid assets that suppliers were unwilling to extend credit. To obtain credit for the business, a major shareholder pledged his vacation home—a condominium on the Hawaiian island of Maui—to secure the company's debt to a particular supplier. With this additional security, the supplier allowed the business to purchase large quantities of merchandise on account.

Unfortunately, however, the small wholesale business became insolvent and was forced into bankruptcy. Not only did the owners' equity in this business become worthless, but one shareholder also lost his vacation home to the company's creditors.

Classifications in an Income Statement

An income statement may be prepared in either the **multiple-step** or the **single-step** format. The multiple-step income statement is more useful in illustrating accounting concepts and has been used in all of our illustrations thus far. A multiple-step income statement for Computer Barn is illustrated below:

A multiple-step income
statement

COMPUTER BARN Income Statement For the Year Ended December 31, 2000			
Net sales			$900,000
Less: Cost of goods sold (including transportation-in)			540,000
Gross profit			$360,000
Less: Operating expenses:			
Selling expenses:			
Sales salaries and commissions	$78,800		
Advertising	42,000		
Delivery service	14,200		
Depreciation: store equipment	9,000		
Other selling expenses	6,000		
Total selling expenses		$150,000	
General & administrative expenses:			
Administrative & office salaries	$73,000		
Utilities	6,500		
Depreciation: building	8,500		
Other general & administrative expenses . .	11,000		
Total general & administrative expenses		99,000	
Total operating expense			249,000
Operating income			$111,000
Less (add): Nonoperating items:			
Interest expense		$23,000	
Purchase discounts lost		1,200	
Interest revenue		(3,200)	21,000
Net income			$ 90,000

This income statement also is ***classified,*** meaning that revenue and expenses have been classified into several categories. (For comparative purposes, this income statement is illustrated in single-step format on page 258.)

Multiple-Step Income Statements

LO 9: Analyze an income statement; evaluate the adequacy of net income

The **multiple-step income statement** draws its name from the ***series of steps*** in which costs and expenses are deducted from revenue. As a first step, the cost of goods sold is deducted from sales revenue to determine the subtotal ***gross profit.*** As a second step, operating expenses are deducted to obtain a subtotal called **operating income** (or income from operations). As a final step, "nonoperating" items are taken into consideration to arrive at ***net income.***

Notice that the income statement is divided into four major sections: (1) revenue, (2) cost of goods sold, (3) operating expenses, and (4) nonoperating items. Multiple-step income statements are noted for their numerous sections and the development of significant subtotals.

The Revenue Section   The revenue section of an income statement usually contains only one line, entitled ***Net sales.*** Net sales represents the balance in the sales revenue account, less some minor adjustments for transactions such as refunds made to customers.

The *trend* in net sales from period to period is considered by many users of financial statements to be a key indicator of a company's future prospects. Increasing sales suggest the probability of larger profits in future periods. Declining sales, on the other hand, may provide advance warning of financial difficulties.

In our economy, most prices increase over time. The *average* increase in prices during the year is called the *rate of inflation.* Because of inflation, a company's total dollar sales may increase somewhat from year-to-year without any increase in the quantity of merchandise sold. If a company is selling more merchandise each year, its net sales usually increase *faster* than the rate of inflation.

The Cost of Goods Sold Section   The *matching principle* requires that revenue be offset by the costs and expenses incurred in generating that revenue. Therefore, revenue from sales must be offset by the cost to the merchandising business of acquiring the goods that it sells. The cost of goods sold usually is shown as a single amount in the income statement.

Gross Profit: A Key Subtotal   Gross profit is the *difference* between the sales revenue earned during the period and the *cost* to the business of the merchandise it has sold. In evaluating the performance of a merchandising company, many analysts find it useful to express the gross profit as a *percentage* of net sales. This percentage is called the **gross profit rate.** In 2000, Computer Barn has an average gross profit rate of *40%* (gross profit, $360,000, divided by net sales, $900,000, equals 40%).

By computing the gross profit rate earned in successive accounting periods, users of financial statements may gain insight into the strength of the company's products in the marketplace. A rising gross profit rate usually means that demand for the company's products is strong enough that the company has been able to increase its sales prices.[15] A declining gross profit rate, on the other hand, generally indicates a weakness in demand for the company's products.

In evaluating the rate of gross profit earned by a particular company, the users of the financial statements should consider the rate earned by the company in prior periods and also the gross profit rates earned by other companies in the same industry. In most merchandising companies, the gross profit rate remains reasonably consistent from one period to the next.

Gross profit rates usually lie between 30% and 50% of net sales, depending upon the type of merchandise sold. The gross profit rate usually is lowest on fast-moving merchandise, such as groceries, and highest on low-volume goods, such as fine jewellery.

The Operating Expense Section   Operating expenses are incurred for the purpose of *producing revenue.* These expenses often are subdivided into functional classifications, such as *selling expenses* and *general and administrative expenses.* Subdividing operating expenses

---

[15]An alternative explanation could be that the company is reducing its cost of goods sold relative to its selling prices. Reductions in the cost of goods sold are more likely to occur in companies that *manufacture* their inventories than in merchandising companies.

into functional classifications aids management and other users of the statements in evaluating different aspects of the company's operations separately.

The classification of operating expenses into subcategories is a common practice, but it is *not required* under generally accepted accounting principles. Also, the categories into which operating expenses are classified often vary from one company to the next.

Operating Income: Another Key Subtotal   Operating income (or income from operations) shows the relationship between revenue *earned from customers* and expenses incurred in *producing this revenue.* In effect, operating income measures the profitability of a company's *basic business operations* and "leaves out" other types of revenue and expenses.

Nonoperating Items   Revenue and expenses that are not directly related to the company's primary business activities are listed in a final section of the income statement following the determination of operating income.

Two significant "nonoperating items" are interest expense and corporate income taxes expense. Interest expense stems from the manner in which assets are *financed,* not the manner in which these assets are *used* in business operations. Corporate income taxes are not viewed as operating expenses because paying income taxes does not help produce revenue.[16]

Any nonoperating revenue, such as interest revenue earned on investments, also is listed in this section of the income statement.

Net Income   Most equity investors—that is, the owners—consider net income (or net loss) to be the most important figure in the income statement. This amount represents the overall increase (or decrease) in owners' equity resulting from business operations during the period.

Single-Step Income Statements

With its several classifications and subtotals, a multiple-step income statement highlights significant relationships. For this reason, it is widely used in accounting textbooks and in classroom illustrations. However, many large corporations use a *single-step* format in the income statements appearing in their annual reports.

The **single-step** format **income statement** takes its name from the fact that all costs and expenses are deducted from total revenue in a single step. No subtotals are shown for gross profit or for operating income, although the statement provides investors with enough information to compute these subtotals on their own. The 2000 income statement of Computer

---

[16]Only those businesses organized as corporations are subject to corporate income taxes. Because Computer Barn (the company used in our example) is organized as a sole proprietorship, no income taxes expense appears in the company's income statement.

Barn, previously illustrated in the multiple-step format, is rearranged below in the single-step format:

A single-step income statement

COMPUTER BARN Income Statement For the Year Ended December 31, 2000		
Revenue:		
Net sales		$900,000
Interest earned		3,200
Total revenue		$903,200
Costs and expenses:		
Cost of goods sold	$540,000	
Selling expenses	150,000	
General & administrative expenses	99,000	
Interest expense	23,000	
Purchase discounts lost	1,200	
Total costs and expenses		813,200
Net income		$ 90,000

Evaluating the Adequacy of Net Income

Should the $90,000 net income of Computer Barn be viewed as excellent, fair, or poor performance for a business of this size? First, notice that Computer Barn is organized as a ***sole proprietorship.*** In an unincorporated business, no "salary expense" is deducted for the value of the personal services rendered to the business by the owner.[17] Any amounts paid to the owner are recorded as "withdrawals." Thus, the net income of a sole proprietorship represents, in part, compensation to the owner for the time and effort devoted to running the business.

The owner of a business also may have a substantial amount of money invested in the business in the form of owner's equity. Thus, the net income of the business also represents the owner's "return" on this financial investment.

Finally, the net income of a business should be adequate to compensate the owner for taking significant ***risks.*** Some studies show that more than half of all new businesses fail in their first year. Remember, in an unincorporated business, the owners are ***personally liable*** for the debts of the business. Therefore, if an unincorporated business sustains large losses, the owner can lose more than the amount of his or her equity investment. In fact, the owner can lose almost everything he or she owns.

As discussed in Chapters 3 and 4, the net income of an unincorporated business should be sufficient to compensate the owner for three factors: (1) personal services rendered to the business, (2) a return on capital invested, and (3) the degree of financial risk that the owner is taking. Using these criteria, let us now appraise the adequacy of the $90,000 net income of Computer Barn.

---

[17]The reason for omitting the owner's "salary" from the expenses is that the owner could set this salary at any desired level. An unrealistic salary to the owner, whether too high or too low, would lessen the usefulness of the income statement as a measure of the earning power of the business.

Assume that Pat O'Brien, the owner of Computer Barn, works full time in the business. Also assume that if he were not running his own business, he could earn a salary of $50,000 per year managing a similar store.

Also notice that O'Brien has $320,000 invested in Computer Barn as of the end of the year. Let us assume that this also was the average amount of his ownership equity throughout the year. If this money had been invested in savings bonds and similar securities, O'Brien might have earned investment income of, say, $25,000.

Thus, the two factors of the owner's personal services and financial investment indicate a need for the company to earn at least $75,000 per year to be considered successful. As the business actually earned $90,000, it has provided a $15,000 "cushion" to compensate O'Brien for the risk involved in owning this type of business. Since the business is a sole proprietorship, O'Brien must also consider the risk of being personally liable for the business debts if the business fails.

Whether or not $15,000 is adequate compensation for these risks depends upon the degree of risk involved in this type of business activity, the amount of O'Brien's personal assets, and O'Brien's personal attitude toward risk taking.

Remember, Computer Barn's profitability in the current year is no guarantee that the business will remain profitable in future years. By looking at the *trend* in net income over a period of several years, O'Brien can see whether the business is becoming consistently more or less profitable, that is, whether it has been consistently successful.

Evaluating the Net Income of a Corporation   If Computer Barn were organized as a corporation, both the amount of net income for the year and our evaluation of this net income would have been somewhat different. First, as mentioned in Chapter 1, profitable corporations incur the expense of corporate income taxes, whereas unincorporated businesses do not. Also, corporations record as expenses all salaries paid to employees, even if these employees are owners (shareholders) of the business. Thus, if Computer Barn were organized as a corporation, its net income would have been lower by the amount of O'Brien's salary and the income taxes expense for the period. On the other hand, we then could ignore the value of O'Brien's personal services in evaluating the adequacy of the company's net income.

Shareholders tend to evaluate the net income of a corporation only in terms of (1) the amount of their financial investment and (2) the degree of risk that they are taking. Remember, however, that shareholders usually are exposed to *less* financial risk than are the owners of an unincorporated business, as they are ***not personally liable*** for the debts of the business entity.

We will discuss specific techniques for evaluating the adequacy of a corporation's earnings in later chapters.

End-of-Chapter Review

Key Terms Introduced or Emphasized in Chapter 5

Bar codes (*p.248*) A label (consisting of a pattern of thick and thin vertical bars) that is attached to items of merchandise. The bar code can be "read" by an optical scanner, thus allowing sales transactions to be recorded quickly at **point-of-sale terminals.**

Classified financial statements (*p.249*) Financial statements in which similar items are arranged in groups; subtotals are shown to assist users in analyzing the statements.

Contra-revenue account (*p.241*) A debit balance account that is offset against revenue in the revenue section of the income statement. Examples include Sales Discounts and Sales Returns and Allowances.

Controlling account (*p.230*) A general ledger account that summarizes the content of a specific subsidiary ledger.

Cost of goods sold (*p.228*) The cost to a merchandising company of the goods that it has sold to its customers during the period.

Current assets (*p.250*) Cash and other assets that can be converted into cash within one year or the operating cycle (whichever is longer) without interfering with normal business operations.

Current liabilities (*p.250*) Existing liabilities that must be paid within one year or the operating cycle (whichever is longer).

Current ratio (*p.251*) Current assets divided by current liabilities. A measure of short-term debt-paying ability.

Gross profit (*p.228*) Net sales revenue minus the cost of goods sold.

Gross profit rate (*p.256*) Gross profit expressed as a percentage of net sales.

Inventory (*p.227*) Any type of merchandise intended for resale to customers.

Inventory shrinkage (*p.244*) The loss of merchandise through such causes as shoplifting, breakage, and spoilage.

Multiple-step income statement (*p.255*) An income statement in which the cost of goods sold and expenses are subtracted from revenue in a series of steps, thus producing a number of useful subtotals.

Net sales (*p.229*) Gross sales revenue less sales returns and allowances and minus sales discounts; usually the first figure shown in an income statement.

Operating cycle (*p.227*) The repeating sequence of transactions by which a business generates its revenue and cash receipts from customers.

Operating income (*p.255*) A subtotal in an income statement representing the revenue earned from customers less only those expenses incurred for the purpose of generating that revenue.

Periodic inventory system (*p.245*) An alternative to the perpetual inventory system that eliminates the need for recording the cost of goods sold as sales occur. However, the amounts of inventory and the cost of goods sold are not known until a complete physical inventory is taken at year-end.

Perpetual inventory system (*p.234*) A system of accounting for merchandising transactions in which the Inventory and Cost of Goods Sold accounts are kept perpetually up-to-date.

Point-of-sale (POS) terminals (*p.248*) Electronic cash registers used for computer-based processing of sales transactions. The POS terminal identifies each item of merchandise from its **bar code** and then automatically records the sale and updates the computer-based inventory records. These terminals permit the use of perpetual inventory systems in many businesses that sell a high volume of low-cost merchandise.

Single-step income statement (*p.257*) An income statement in which the cost of goods sold and all expenses are combined and deducted from total revenue in a single step.

Subsidiary ledger (*p.230*) A ledger containing separate accounts for each of the items making up the balance of a controlling account in the general ledger. The total of the account balances in a subsidiary ledger is equal to the balance in the general ledger controlling account.

Taking a physical inventory (*p.244*) The procedure of counting all merchandise on hand and determining its cost.

Working capital (*p.252*) Current assets minus current liabilities. A measure of short-run debt-paying ability.

DEMONSTRATION PROBLEM

Whitby Wholesale Corporation sold 100 pairs of Excel-Elegant ladies boots to Boot Hill, a chain of retail stores. The sales price was $5,000 ($50 per pair), with terms of 2/10, n/30. United Express charged $162 to deliver this merchandise to Boot Hill's stores; these charges were split evenly between the buyer and seller and were paid in cash.

Boot Hill returned 10 pairs of these boots to Whitby Wholesale because they were the wrong style. Whitby Wholesale agreed to accept this return and credit Boot Hill's account for the full invoice price. Boot Hill then paid the remaining balance within the discount period.

Both companies use a perpetual inventory system.

INSTRUCTIONS

a. Record this sequence of transactions in the general journal of Whitby Wholesale Corporation. The company records sales at the full invoice price; these boots had cost Whitby Wholesale $32 per pair.

b. Record this sequence of transactions in the general journal of Boot Hill. The company records purchases of merchandise at *net cost* and uses a Transportation-in account in recording transportation charges on inbound shipments.

c. Explain what information in **a** and **b** should be posted to subsidiary ledger accounts.

d. If a periodic, rather than a perpetual inventory, system is used, would the answers to **a** and **b** be different? How?

SOLUTION TO DEMONSTRATION PROBLEM

General Journal

a. Journal entries by Whitby Wholesale Corporation:

Accounts Receivable (Boot Hill)	5,000	
Sales		5,000
Sold merchandise on account; terms, 2/10, n/30.		
Cost of Goods Sold	3,200	
Inventory		3,200
To record cost of merchandise sold ($32/pr. × 100 pr. Excel-Elegant ladies boots).		
Delivery Expense	81	
Cash		81
Paid delivery charges on outbound shipment.		
Sales Returns and Allowances	500	
Accounts Receivable (Boot Hill)		500
Customer returned merchandise with a sales price of $500.		
Inventory	320	
Cost of Goods Sold		320
Reduce cost of goods sold for cost of returned merchandise ($32/pr. × 10 pr. Excel-Elegant ladies boots).		
Cash	4,410	
Sales Discounts	90	
Accounts Receivable (Boot Hill)		4,500
Collected amount due from credit sale to Boot Hill, less $500 return and less 2% cash discount on remaining $4,500 balance ($4,500 × 2% = $90).		

b. Journal entries by Boot Hill:

Inventory	4,900	
Accounts Payable (Whitby Wholesale Corp.)		4,900
Purchased 100 pairs of Excel-Elegant ladies boots on		
account; terms, 2/10, n/30. Net cost, $4,900, $49 per pair		
($50, less 2%).		
Transportation-in	81	
Cash		81
Paid transportation charges in inbound shipment.		
Accounts Payable (Whitby Wholesale Corp.)	490	
Inventory		490
Returned 10 pairs of Excel-Elegant ladies boots to supplier.		
(Net cost, $49 per pair × 10 pairs = $490.)		
Accounts Payable (Whitby Wholesale Corp.)	4,410	
Cash		4,410
Paid within discount period balance owed to Whitby		
Wholesale Corp. ($4,900 − $490 = $4,410).		

c. In **a,** the debits and credits to Accounts Receivable and Inventory should be posted to the accounts receivable and inventory subsidiary ledger accounts respectively.

In **b,** the debits and credits to Inventory and Accounts Payable should be posted to the inventory and accounts payable subsidiary ledger accounts respectively.

d. Yes, the answers to **a** and **b** would be different. For **a,** the two entries involving the cost of goods sold would not be required. For **b,** the debit and credit to Inventory would be changed to a debit to Purchases and a credit to Purchase Returns and Allowances.

Self-Test Questions

Answers to these questions appear on page 282.

1. Mark and Amanda Carter own an appliance store and a restaurant. The appliance store sells merchandise on a 12-month instalment plan; the restaurant sells only for cash. Which of the following statements are true? (More than one answer may be correct.)
   a. The appliance store has a longer operating cycle than the restaurant.
   b. The appliance store probably uses a perpetual inventory system, whereas the restaurant probably uses a periodic system.
   c. Both businesses require subsidiary ledgers for accounts receivable and inventory.
   d. Both businesses probably have subsidiary ledgers for accounts payable.

2. Which of the following types of information are found in subsidiary ledgers, but **not** in the general ledger? (More than one answer may be correct.)
   a. Total cost of goods sold for the period.
   b. The quantity of a particular product sold during the period.
   c. The dollar amount owed to a particular creditor.
   d. The portion of total current assets that consists of cash.

3. Marietta Corporation uses a **perpetual** inventory system. The company sells merchandise costing $3,000 at a sales price of $4,300. In recording this transaction, Marietta will make all of the following entries **except:**

a. Credit Sales, $4,300.
b. Credit Inventory, $4,300.
c. Debit Cost of Goods Sold, $3,000.
d. Credit one or more accounts in the inventory subsidiary ledger for amounts totalling $3,000.

4. Fashion House uses a ***perpetual*** inventory system. At the beginning of the year, inventory amounted to $50,000. During the year, the company purchased merchandise for $230,000, and sold merchandise costing $245,000. A physical inventory taken at year-end indicated shrinkage losses of $4,000. ***Prior*** to recording these shrinkage losses, the year-end balance in the company's Inventory account was:
a. $31,000
b. $35,000
c. $50,000
d. Some other amount.

5. Best Hardware uses a ***periodic*** inventory system. Its inventory was $38,000 at the beginning of the year and $40,000 at the end. During the year, Best made purchases of merchandise totalling $107,000. Identify all of the correct answers:
a. To use this system, Best must take a complete physical inventory twice each year.
b. Prior to making adjusting and closing entries at year-end, the balance in Best's Inventory account is $38,000.
c. The cost of goods sold for the year is $109,000.
d. As sales transactions occur, Best makes no entries to update its inventory records or record the cost of goods sold.

6. The two basic approaches to accounting for inventory and the cost of goods sold are the ***perpetual*** inventory system and the ***periodic*** inventory system. Indicate which of the following statements are correct. (More than one answer may be correct.)
a. Most large merchandising companies and manufacturing businesses use periodic inventory systems.
b. As a practical matter, a grocery store or a large department store could not maintain a perpetual inventory system without the use of point-of-sale terminals.
c. In a periodic inventory system the cost of goods sold is not determined until a complete physical inventory is taken.
d. In a perpetual inventory system, the Cost of Goods Sold account is debited promptly for the cost of merchandise sold.

7. Two of the lawnmowers sold by Garden Products Co. are the LawnMaster and the Mark 5. LawnMasters sell for $250 apiece, which results in a 35% gross profit rate. Each Mark 5 costs Garden Products $300 and sells for $400. Indicate all correct answers.
a. The dollar amount of gross profit is greater on the sale of a Mark 5 than a LawnMaster.
b. The gross profit rate is higher on Mark 5s than on LawnMasters.
c. Garden makes more gross profit by selling one Mark 5 than by selling one LawnMaster.
d. Garden makes more gross profit by selling $2,000 worth of Mark 5s than $2,000 worth of LawnMasters.

8. Big Brother, a retail store, purchased 100 television sets from Krueger Electronics on account at a cost of $200 each. Krueger offers credit terms of 2/10,

n/30. Big Brother uses a perpetual inventory system and records purchases at **net cost.** Big Brother determines that 10 of these television sets are defective and returns them to Krueger for full credit. In recording this return, Big Brother will:

a. Debit Sales Returns and Allowances.
b. Debit Accounts Payable, $1,960.
c. Debit Cost of Goods Sold, $1,960.
d. Credit Inventory, $2,000.

ASSIGNMENT MATERIAL

Discussion Questions

1. Describe the operating cycle of a merchandising company.

2. Compare and contrast the merchandising activities of a wholesaler and a retailer.

3. The income statement of a merchandising company includes a major type of cost that does not appear in the income statement of a service-type business. Identify this cost and explain what it represents.

4. During the current year, Green Bay Company earned a gross profit of $350,000, whereas New England Company earned a gross profit of only $280,000. Does this mean that Green Bay is more profitable than New England? Explain.

5. Thornhill Company's income statement shows gross profit of $432,000, cost of goods sold of $638,000, and other expenses totalling $390,000. Compute the amounts of (a) revenue from sales (net sales) and (b) net income.

6. Explain the need for subsidiary ledgers in accounting for merchandising activities.

7. All Night Auto Parts, Inc., maintains subsidiary ledgers for accounts receivable, inventory, and accounts payable. Explain in detail what information from the following journal entry should be posted, and to which subsidiary and general ledger accounts.

   Inventory *420*
        Accounts Payable (Boss Automotive) *420*
   Purchased 12 Boss LoadMaster II shock absorbers. Cost,
   $35 per unit.

8. What is meant by the phrase "reconciling a subsidiary ledger"? In general terms, what is the purpose of this procedure?

9. Define the term **inventory shrinkage.** How is the amount of inventory shrinkage determined in a business using a perpetual inventory system, and how is this shrinkage recorded in the accounting records?

10. Briefly contrast the accounting procedures in **perpetual** and **periodic** inventory systems.

11. Miracle Home Cleanser uses a **periodic** inventory system. During the current year the company purchased merchandise with a cost of $55,000. State the cost of goods sold for the year under each of the following alternative assumptions:

    a. No beginning inventory; ending inventory $3,500.
    b. Beginning inventory $10,000; no ending inventory.
    c. Beginning inventory $2,000; ending inventory $7,200.
    d. Beginning inventory $8,000; ending inventory $1,400.

12. Evaluate the following statement: "Without electronic point-of-sale terminals, it simply would not be possible to use perpetual inventory systems in businesses that sell large quantities of many different products."

13. Define the term ***gross profit rate.*** Explain several ways in which management might improve a company's overall profit rate.

14. How does a balance arise in the Purchase Discounts Lost account? Why does management pay careful attention to the balance (if any) in this account?

15. European Imports pays substantial freight charges to obtain inbound shipments of purchased merchandise. Should these freight charges be debited to the company's Delivery Expense account? Explain.

16. Outback Sporting Goods purchases merchandise on terms of 4/10, n/60. The company has a "line of credit" that enables it to borrow money as needed from Northern Bank at an annual interest rate of 13%. Should Outback pay its suppliers within the 10 day discount period if it must draw on its line of credit (borrow from Northern Bank) to make these early payments? Explain.

17. TireCo is a retail store in a province that has a sales tax of 8%, in addition to the goods and services tax of 7%. Would you expect to find sales tax expense and sales and goods and services taxes payable in TireCo's financial statements? Explain.

18. A seller generally records sales at the full invoice price, but the buyer often records purchases at ***net cost.*** Explain the logic of the buyer and seller recording the transaction at different amounts.

19. Berlasty Company uses the periodic inventory system and maintains its accounting records on a calendar-year basis. Does the beginning or the ending inventory figure appear in the ledger account on December 31?

20. Compute the amount of cost of goods sold, given the following account balances: beginning inventory $48,000, purchases $100,800, purchase returns and allowances $5,400, and ending inventory $43,200.

21. What is the basic purpose of ***classifications*** in financial statements?

22. What is the basic characteristic of ***current assets?*** Many retail stores regularly sell merchandise on "instalment plans," calling for payments over a period of 24 or 36 months. Do such receivables qualify as current assets? Explain.

23. Madison Corporation has current assets of $570,000 and current liabilities of $300,000. Compute the current ratio and the amount of working capital.

24. Identify two criteria that users of financial statements often use in evaluating the reasonableness of the financial ratios of a particular company.

25. Briefly describe the extent of a business owner's personal liability for the debts of (a) an unincorporated business and (b) a corporation.

26. Describe the format of a multiple-step income statement and that of a single-step income statement.

27. Define the term ***gross profit rate.*** Explain two factors that may cause a company's gross profit rate to increase.

28. How does interest expense differ from normal operating expenses such as advertising and salaries? How is interest expense presented in a multiple-step income statement?

29. Distinguish between *operating income* and *net income.*

30. Identify the three basic factors for which the net income of a sole proprietorship compensates the owner.

Exercises

EXERCISE 5-1
Accounting Terminology
(LO 1, 2, 3, 5, 7, 9)

Listed below are nine technical accounting terms introduced in this chapter.

Perpetual inventory system *Periodic inventory system* *Classified financial statements*

Gross profit *Current ratio* *Subsidiary ledger*

Cost of goods sold *Working capital* *Operating income*

Each of the following statements may (or may not) describe one of these technical terms. For each statement, indicate the term described, or answer "None" if the statement does not correctly describe any of the terms.

a. Current assets plus current liabilities.

b. An item deducted from revenue in the income statement of a merchandising company that *does not appear* in the income statement of a service-type business.

c. Revenue earned from customers, less expenses relating directly to the production of this revenue.

d. An approach to accounting for inventory and determining the cost of goods sold that is based upon complete annual physical counts of the inventory.

e. An accounting record providing details about the individual items comprising the balance of a controlling account.

f. The difference between the sales price and the cost of all merchandise sold during the period.

g. An approach to accounting for inventory and the cost of goods sold that produces up-to-date accounting records, including an inventory subsidiary ledger.

EXERCISE 5-2
Effects of Basic Merchandising Transactions
(LO 3)

Shown below are selected transactions of Marston's, a retail store that uses a perpetual inventory system:

a. Purchased merchandise on account.

b. Recognized the revenue from a sale of merchandise on account. (Ignore the related cost of goods sold.)

c. Recognized the cost of goods sold relating to the sale in transaction **b.**

d. Collected in cash the account receivable from the customer in transaction **b.**

e. Following the taking of a physical inventory at year-end, made an adjusting entry to record a normal amount of inventory shrinkage.

Indicate the effects of each of these transactions upon the elements of the company's financial statements shown below. Organize your answer in tabular form, using the column headings shown below. (Notice that the cost of goods sold is shown separately from all other expenses.) Use the code letters *I* for increase, *D* for decrease, and *NE* for no effect.

	Income Statement				Balance Sheet		
	Net Sales	− Cost of Goods Sold	− All Other Expenses	= Net Income	Assets	= Liabilities	+ Owner's Equity
Transaction *a*							

EXERCISE 5-3
Subsidiary Ledgers
(LO 2)

Listed below are eight typical merchandising transactions of Everyday Auto Parts, a retail auto supply store.

a. Purchased merchandise from Acme Wholesale on account.
b. Paid an account payable to a supplier.
c. Sold merchandise for cash.
d. Sold merchandise on account.
e. Collected an account receivable from a customer.
f. Returned merchandise to a supplier, receiving credit against the amount owed.
g. Gave a cash refund to a customer who returned merchandise.
h. Reduced the account receivable from a credit customer who returned merchandise.

Among the accounting records of Everyday Auto Parts are subsidiary ledgers for inventory, accounts receivable, and accounts payable. For each of the eight transactions, you are to indicate any subsidiary ledger (or ledgers) to which the transaction would be posted. Use the codes below:

Inv = Inventory subsidiary ledger
AR = Accounts receivable subsidiary ledger
AP = Accounts payable subsidiary ledger

Also indicate whether each posting causes the balance in the subsidiary ledger account to *increase* or *decrease*. Organize your answer in tabular form as illustrated below. The answer for transaction **a** is provided as an example.

Transaction	Subsidiary Ledger	Effect upon Subsidiary Account Balance
a	Inv	Increase
	AP	Increase

EXERCISE 5-4
Posting to Subsidiary Ledgers
(LO 2)

In addition to a general ledger, LeatherWorks maintains subsidiary ledgers for accounts receivable, inventory, and accounts payable (the company does not maintain a subsidiary ledger for cash). Two entries appearing in the company's journal are illustrated, along with the posting references that have been entered in the LP column:

GENERAL JOURNAL

Accounts Titles and Explanation	LP	Debit	Credit
Inventory	130/✓	2,500	
Accounts Payable (Pucci, Inc.)	✓		2,500
Purchased 50 shoulder bags from Pucci, Inc., @ $50; payment due in 30 days.			
Cash	101	6,000	
Accounts Receivable (The Bag Man)	105		6,000
Collected an account receivable.			

a. Based upon the posting references shown, explain in detail the accounts to which the debit and credit portions of each journal entry apparently have been posted.
b. Does it appear that the posting of each entry has been completed properly? Explain. (Assume that illustrated account numbers are correct.)

EXERCISE 5-5
Perpetual Inventory System
(LO 3)

Caliente Products uses a perpetual inventory system. On January 1 the Inventory account had a balance of $93,500. During the first few days of January the following transactions occurred:

Jan. 2   Purchased 100 novelty XT phones on credit from Bell Company for $6,300.

Jan. 3   Sold 200 Seamaster watches for cash, $19,000. The cost of the watches was $12,500.

a. Prepare entries in general journal form to record the above transactions.
b. What was the balance of the Inventory account at the close of business January 3?

EXERCISE 5-6
Taking a Physical Inventory
(LO 4)

Electronics Warehouse uses a perpetual inventory system. At year-end, the Inventory account has a balance of $314,000, but a physical count shows that the merchandise on hand has a cost of only $309,100.
a. Explain the probable reason(s) for this discrepancy.
b. Prepare the journal entry required in this situation.
c. Indicate all the accounting records to which your journal entry in part **b** should be posted.

EXERCISE 5-7
Periodic Inventory Systems
(LO 5)

Hanson's Gift Shop uses a periodic inventory system. At the end of 2000, the accounting records include the following information:

Inventory (as of December 31, 1999)	$ 8,700
Net sales	160,400
Purchases, less returns and allowances	81,500

A complete physical inventory taken at December 31, 2000 indicates merchandise costing **$6,400** remains in stock.
a. How were the amounts of beginning and ending inventory determined?
b. Compute the amount of the cost of goods sold in 2000.
c. Prepare a partial income statement showing the shop's gross profit for the year.

EXERCISE 5-8
Relationships within Periodic Inventory Systems
(LO 1, 5)

This exercise stresses the relationships between the information recorded in a periodic inventory system and the basic elements of an income statement. Each of the five lines represents a separate set of information. You are to copy the table and fill in the missing amounts. A net loss in the right-hand column is to be indicated by placing brackets around the amount, as for example, in line **e** (25,000).

	Net Sales	Beginning Inventory	Net Purchases	Ending Inventory	Cost of Goods Sold	Gross Profit	Expenses	Net Income or (Loss)
a.	300,000	95,000	130,000	44,000	?	119,000	90,000	?
b.	600,000	90,000	340,000	?	330,000	?	?	25,000
c.	700,000	230,000	?	185,000	490,000	210,000	165,000	?
d.	900,000	?	500,000	150,000	?	260,000	300,000	?
e.	?	260,000	?	255,000	660,000	225,000	?	(25,000)

EXERCISE 5-9
Selecting an Appropriate Inventory System
(LO 6)

Select a specific merchandising business in your area. Briefly describe the nature of the business, and indicate whether you think a perpetual or a periodic inventory system is more appropriate. ***Explain your reasoning and be prepared to discuss your answer in class.*** (Notice that you are not asked to determine the type of inventory system actually in use.)

EXERCISE 5-10
Cash Discounts
(LO 4)

Key Imports sold merchandise to Marine Systems for $8,000, offering terms of 2/10, n/30. Marine Systems paid for the merchandise within the discount period. Both companies use perpetual inventory systems.

a. Prepare journal entries in the accounting records of Key Imports to account for this sale and the subsequent collection. Assume the original cost of the merchandise to Key Imports had been $4,800.

b. Prepare journal entries in the accounting records of Marine Systems to account for the purchase and subsequent payment. Marine Systems records purchases of merchandise at **net cost.**

c. Assume that because of a change in personnel, Marine Systems failed to pay for this merchandise within the discount period. Prepare the journal entry in the accounting records of Marine Systems to record payment **after** the discount period.

EXERCISE 5-11
Net Sales and Gross Profit
(LO 4, 9)

Glamour, Inc., is a retail store. In 2000, the company had gross sales revenue of $2,490,000, cost of goods sold of $1,248,000, sales returns and allowances of $59,000, and sales discounts of $31,000.

Compute for the year (a) net sales, (b) gross profit, and (c) gross profit rate. Show supporting computations.

EXERCISE 5-12
Returned Merchandise
(LO 4)

College Bookstore returned certain merchandise that it had purchased from McGraw-Hill. McGraw-Hill allowed the bookstore full credit for this return against the account receivable from the bookstore.

The returned merchandise had been purchased by College Bookstore for $7,000, terms 2/30, n/90. College Bookstore records purchases of merchandise **net** of any available cash discounts.

Prepare journal entries to record the return of this merchandise in the accounting records of (a) College Bookstore and (b) McGraw-Hill. (Assume that the cost of the merchandise to McGraw-Hill had been $5,600.)

EXERCISE 5-13
Accounting for Sales and Goods and Services Taxes
(LO 4)

Trophy Shop operates in a province in which an 8% sales tax and a 7% goods and services tax are levied on all products handled by the store. On cash sales, the salesclerks include these taxes in the amount collected from the customer and ring up the entire amount on the cash register without recording separately the tax liability. On credit sales, the customer is charged for the list price of the merchandise plus the taxes, and the entire amount is debited to Accounts Receivable and credited to the Sales account. On sales of less than one dollar, the tax collected is rounded to the nearest cent.

These taxes must be remitted to the government authorities periodically. At March 31 the Sales account showed a balance of $332,235 for the three-month period ended March 31.

a. What are the amounts of sales tax and goods and services tax owed at March 31?

b. Give the journal entry to record the sales tax and goods and services tax liabilities in the accounting records.

EXERCISE 5-14
Gross Profit Rate
(LO 9)

Shown below is selected information from the recent annual reports of two well-known retailers. (Dollar amounts are stated in millions.)

	Kmart	Toys "R" Us
Net sales	$37,724	$7,169
Cost of goods sold	28,485	?
Gross profit	?	?
Gross profit rate	?%	30.7%

a. Copy this table, filling in the missing amounts and percentages. (Round dollar amounts to the nearest million, and percentages to the nearest tenth of one percent.)

b. Based upon this data, comment upon the relative sales volume and gross profit margins of each company. Is this data consistent with your knowledge (or impression) of these two retailers?

EXERCISE 5-15
A Quick Look at IBM's Current Position
(LO 7)

A balance sheet of **IBM** contained the following items among others. (Dollar amounts are stated in millions.)

Cash and cash equivalents	$ 7,687
Marketable securities (current asset)	450
Notes & accounts receivable—trade, net of allowances	16,515
Sales-type leases receivable	5,721
Other accounts receivables	931
Inventories	5,870
Prepaid expenses and other current assets	3,521
Taxes (payable)	3,029
Short-term debt	12,957
Accounts payable	4,767
Compensation and benefits	2,950
Deferred income (Future taxes)	3,640
Other accrued expenses and liabilities	6,657
Long-term debt	9,872
Shareholders' equity	21,628

INSTRUCTIONS

a. From the above information, compute the amount of IBM's current assets and the amount of its current liabilities.
b. How much working capital does IBM have?
c. Compute the current ratio to the nearest tenth of a percent.

EXERCISE 5-16
Recognition of Industry Characteristics
(LO 7, 8)

Reebok is a manufacturer of popular athletic footware. **Maritime Telephone & Telegraph** is one of the largest telephone companies in the Maritimes. Both companies are solvent and profitable. Which company would you expect to have the higher current ratio? Which company do you believe has the greater debt-paying ability? Explain fully the reasons for your answers.

EXERCISE 5-17
Logical Gross Profit Relationships
(LO 9)

Several factors must be considered in interpreting a company's gross profit rate.
a. Companies such as **Lotus Development** and **Microsoft** usually enjoy a higher gross profit rate on sales of a particular software product when it is first introduced than they do in later years. Why?
b. For each of the following pairs of businesses, indicate which you would expect to have the highest gross profit rate. Briefly explain the reasons for your answer.
  1. A grocery store, or a retail furniture store.
  2. **The Bay** (a chain of department stores), or **Zellers** (a chain of discount stores).

Problems

PROBLEM 5-1
Perpetual Inventory System and Performance Evaluation
(LO 1, 3, 8, 9)

Indian Lake Lumber Co. is the only lumberyard in Beaumont, a remote mountain town and popular ski resort. Some of Indian Lake's transactions during 2000 are as follows:

Nov. 5   Sold lumber on account to Dally Construction Co., $39,600. The inventory subsidiary ledger shows the cost of this merchandise to Indian Lake was $26,140.

Nov. 9   Purchased lumber on account from Pine Valley Mill, $108,000.

Dec. 5   Collected in cash the $39,600 account receivable from Dally Construction Co.

Dec. 9   Paid the $108,000 owed to Pine Valley Mill.

Dec. 31 Company personnel counted the inventory on hand and determined its cost to be $965,130. The accounting records, however, indicate inventory of $974,360 and a cost of goods sold of $3,268,330. The physical count of the inventory was observed by the company's auditors and is considered correct.

INSTRUCTIONS

a. Prepare journal entries to record these transactions and events in the accounting records of Indian Lake Lumber Co. (The company uses a perpetual inventory system.)

b. Prepare a partial income statement showing the company's gross profit for the year. (Net sales for the year amount to $4,966,000.)

c. Indian Lake purchases lumber at the same wholesale prices as other lumber companies. Due to its remote mountain location, however, the company must pay between $90,000 and $100,000 per year in extra transportation charges to receive delivery of its purchased lumber. (These additional charges are included in the amount shown as cost of goods sold.)

Assume that an index of key business ratios in your library shows retail lumberyards of Indian Lake's approximate size (in total assets) average net sales of $5,000,000 per year and a gross profit rate of **27%**.

Is Indian Lake Lumber Co. able to pass its extra transportation costs on to its customers? Does the company appear to suffer or benefit financially from its remote location? Explain your reasoning and support your conclusions with specific accounting data comparing the operations of Indian Lake Lumber Co. with the industry averages.

PROBLEM 5-2
Perpetual Inventory System and an Inventory Subsidiary Ledger
(LO 1, 2, 3)

Facts-by-FAX sells facsimile machines, copiers, and other types of office equipment. On May 10, the company purchased for the first time a new "plain-paper" fax manufactured by Mitsui Corporation. Transactions relating to this product during May and June were as follows:

May 10 Purchased five P-500 facsimile machines on account from Mitsui Corporation, at a cost of $560 each. Payment due in 30 days.

May 23 Sold four P-500 facsimile machines on account to Foster & Cole, stockbrokers; sales price, $900 per machine. Payment due in 30 days.

May 24 Purchased an additional seven P-500 facsimile machines on account from Mitsui. Cost, $560 per machine; payment due in 30 days.

June 9 Paid $2,800 cash to Mitsui Corporation for the facsimile machines purchased on May 10.

June 19 Sold two P-500 facsimile machines to Tri-County Realty for cash. Sales price, $950 per machine.

June 22 Collected $3,600 from Foster & Cole in full settlement of the credit sale on May 23.

INSTRUCTIONS

a. Prepare journal entries to record these transactions in the accounting records of Facts-by-FAX. (The company uses a perpetual inventory system.)

b. Post the appropriate information from these journal entries to an inventory subsidiary ledger account like the one illustrated in this chapter.

c. How many Mitsui P-500 facsimile machines were in inventory on May 31? From what accounting record did you obtain the answer to this question?

d. Describe the types of information contained in any inventory subsidiary ledger account and explain how this information may be useful to various company personnel in conducting daily business operations.

PROBLEM 5-3
The Periodic Inventory System
(LO 5, 6)

Mountain Mabel's is a small general store located just outside of Point Pelee National Park. The store uses a periodic inventory system. Every January 1, Mabel and her husband close the store and take a complete physical inventory. Last year, the inventory amounted to $5,200; this year it totalled $3,800. During the current year, the business recorded sales of $125,000 and purchases of $62,000.

INSTRUCTIONS
a. Compute the cost of goods sold for the current year.
b. Explain why a small business such as this might use the periodic inventory system.
c. Explain some of the **disadvantages** of the periodic system to a larger business, such as a Sears store.

PROBLEM 5-4
Comparison of Inventory Systems
(LO 3, 5, 6)

Halleys' Space Scope sells state-of-the-art telescopes to individuals and organizations interested in studying the solar system. At December 31 last year, the company's inventory amounted to $90,000. During the first week of January this year, the company made only one purchase and one sale. These transactions were as follows:

Jan. 2   Sold one telescope costing $28,000 to Eastern University for cash, $40,000.

Jan. 5   Purchased merchandise on account from Solar Optics, $18,500. Terms, net 30 days.

INSTRUCTIONS
a. Prepare journal entries to record these transactions assuming that Halley's Space Scope uses the perpetual inventory system.
b. Compute the balance of the Inventory account on January 6.
c. Prepare journal entries to record the two transactions assuming that Halley's Space Scope uses the periodic inventory system.
d. Compute the cost of goods sold for the first week of January assuming use of a periodic inventory system. Use your answer to part **b** as the ending inventory.
e. Which inventory system do you believe that a company such as Halley's Space Scope would probably use? Explain your reasoning.

PROBLEM 5-5
Comparison of Inventory Systems
(LO 1, 3, 5, 6)

STAR-TRACK sells satellite tracking systems for receiving television broadcasts from communications satellites in space. At December 31, 1999, the company's inventory amounted to $44,000. During the first week in January 2000, STAR-TRACK made only one purchase and one sale. These transactions were as follows:

Jan. 3   Sold a tracking system to Mystery Mountain Resort for $20,000 cash. The system consisted of 7 different devices, which had a total cost to STAR-TRACK of $11,200.

Jan. 7   Purchased two Model 400 and four Model 800 satellite dishes from Space Technology Corp. The total cost of this purchase amounted to $10,000; terms 2/10, n/30.

STAR-TRACK records purchases of merchandise at net cost. The company has full-time accounting personnel and uses a manual accounting system.

INSTRUCTIONS
a. Briefly describe the operating cycle of a merchandising company.
b. Prepare journal entries to record these transactions assuming that STAR-TRACK uses a perpetual inventory system.
c. Explain what information in part **b** should be posted to subsidiary ledger accounts.
d. Compute the balance in the Inventory controlling account at Jan. 7.
e. Prepare journal entries to record the two transactions, assuming that STAR-TRACK uses a **periodic** inventory system.
f. Compute the cost of goods sold for the first week of January, assuming use of the periodic system. As the amount of ending inventory, use your answer to part **d**.
g. Which type of inventory system do you think STAR-TRACK should use? Explain your reasoning.

PROBLEM 5-6
Cash Discounts and
Merchandise Returns
(LO 3, 4)

21st Century Sound purchased 50 compact disc players from Advance Technology at a price of $200 apiece. The terms of the sale were 2/10, n/30. 21st Century didn't like the colour of two of the disc players and returned them immediately to the seller. 21st then paid for the remaining 48 disc players within the discount period.

INSTRUCTIONS

a. Record this sequence of transactions in the general journal of 21st Century. The company uses a perpetual inventory system and records purchases of merchandise at ***net cost.***
b. Record this sequence of transactions in the general journal of Advanced Technology. Advance uses a perpetual inventory system and records sales transactions at the full invoice price. (Assume the cost of the disc players to Advance was $105 each.)

PROBLEM 5-7
Comparison of Net Cost and
Gross Price Methods
(LO 3, 4)

Fedders TV uses a perpetual inventory system. Shown below are three recent merchandising transactions:

June 10   Purchased 10 U-Vision 15″ televisions from Shogun Electronics on account. Invoice price, $250 per unit, for a total of $2,500. The terms of purchase were 2/10, n/30.

June 15   Sold 1 of these televisions for $400 cash.

June 20   Paid the account payable to Shogun within the discount period.

INSTRUCTIONS

a. Prepare journal entries to record these transactions assuming that Fedders records purchases of merchandise at:
   1. Net cost.
   2. Gross invoice price.
b. Assume that Fedders did ***not*** pay Shogun within the discount period, but instead paid the full invoice price on July 10. Prepare journal entries to record this payment assuming that the original liability had been recorded at:
   1. Net cost.
   2. Gross invoice price.
c. Assume that you are evaluating the efficiency of Fedder's bill-paying procedures. Which accounting method—net cost or gross invoice price—provides you with the most ***useful*** information? Explain.

PROBLEM 5-8
Effects of Merchandising
Transactions
(LO 1, 3, 4)

Beacon Hill Medical Supply sells medical supplies to other businesses, such as drugstores and hospitals. Selected merchandising transactions are listed below:
a. Paid air freight charges in order to receive overnight delivery of purchased merchandise needed immediately.
b. Paid transportation charges to deliver merchandise to a customer.
c. Returned defective merchandise to a supplier, receiving full credit against amounts currently owed.
d. Paid an account payable to a merchandise supplier within the discount period.
e. Paid an account payable to a merchandise supplier after the discount period had expired.
f. A credit customer returned merchandise because its customer had cancelled the order. Gave the customer full credit on its account receivable.
g. Collected an account receivable from a customer making payment within the discount period.
h. Collected an account receivable from a customer making payment after the discount period had expired.

To interpret properly the effects of these transactions upon Beacon Hill's financial statements, you first must be familiar with some of the company's accounting policies:

• Beacon Hill uses a perpetual inventory system.
• All purchases are recorded ***net*** of available cash discounts.

- Transportation costs on inbound shipments of merchandise are debited to a Transportation-in account, which in the income statement is combined with the cost of goods sold.
- All credit sales are made on terms 2/10, n/30 and are recorded at the full invoice price.
- The liability for sales and goods and services taxes payable is recorded at the time of sale.

INSTRUCTIONS

Indicate the effects of each of these transactions upon the following elements of the company's financial statements. Organize your answer in tabular form, using the following column headings. (Notice that the cost of goods sold is shown separately from all other expenses.) Use the code letters **I** for increase, **D** for decrease, and **NE** for no effect.

	Income Statement				Balance Sheet		
Transaction	Net Sales	− Cost of Goods Sold	− All Other Expenses	= Net Income	Assets	= Liabilities	+ Owner's Equity
a							

PROBLEM 5-9
Merchandising Transactions—
A Short Comprehensive
Problem
(LO 3, 4)

Riviera Fashions, a wholesaler, regularly sells merchandise on account to Caroline's, a chain of retail stores. Among the transactions between these companies are the following:

Mar. 3   Sold 1,000 Puregold cashmere sweaters to Caroline's on account, terms, 2/10, n/30. These sweaters had cost Riviera Fashions $32 each; the sales price to Caroline's was $50 per sweater.

Mar. 5   Caroline's returned 100 of the sweaters because they were the wrong colour. Riviera Fashions always allows such returns.

Mar. 13   Caroline's paid within the discount period the remaining amount owed to Riviera Fashions, after allowing for the purchase return on Mar. 5.

Both companies use perpetual inventory systems. Caroline's records purchases of merchandise at **net cost.**

INSTRUCTIONS

a. Prepare journal entries to record these transactions in the accounting records of Riviera Fashions.
b. Prepare journal entries to record these transactions in the accounting records of Caroline's.
c. Assume that Caroline's had not paid the remaining balance of its account payable to Riviera Fashions until April 2. Record this payment after the discount period in:
  1. The accounting records of Riviera Fashions.
  2. The accounting records of Caroline's.
d. Explain the benefit of recording merchandise purchases at **net cost.**

PROBLEM 5-10
A Comprehensive Problem
(LO 1-6, 9)

Medical Equipment Corp. (MEC) sells x-ray machines and other medical equipment to hospitals. At December 31, 2000, MEC's inventory amounted to $480,000. During the first week in January 2001, the company made only one purchase and one sale. These transactions were as follows:

Jan. 2   Purchased an I-2 x-ray machine and an E-10 ultra-sound scanner from Son-X. The total cost of these machines was $60,000, terms 3/10, n/60.

Jan. 6 Sold three different types of machines on account to Mercy Hospital. The total sales price was $90,000, terms 5/10, n/90. The total cost of these three machines to MEC was $55,800.

MEC has a full-time accountant and a computer-based accounting system. It records sales at the gross sales price and purchases at net cost, and maintains subsidiary ledgers for accounts receivable, inventory, and accounts payable.

INSTRUCTIONS

a. Briefly describe the operating cycle of a merchandising company. Identify the assets and liabilities directly affected by this cycle.
b. Prepare journal entries to record these transactions, assuming that MEC uses a perpetual inventory system.
c. Explain the information in part **b** that should be posted to subsidiary ledgers accounts.
d. Compute the balance in the Inventory controlling account at the close of business on Jan. 6.
e. Prepare journal entries to record the two transactions assuming that MEC uses a ***periodic*** inventory system.
f. Compute the cost of goods sold for the first week of January assuming use of the periodic system. (Use your answer to part **d** as the ending inventory.)
g. Which type of inventory system do you think MEC would most likely use? Explain your reasoning.
h. Compute the gross profit rate on the January 6 sales transaction.

PROBLEM 5-11
Computing Current Ratio and Working Capital; Evaluating Solvency
(LO 7)

Some of the accounts appearing in the year-end financial statements of Diet Frozen Dinners (a corporation) appear below. This list includes all of the company's current assets and current liabilities.

Sales	*$1,980,000*
Accumulated depreciation: equipment	*370,000*
Notes payable (due in 90 days)	*80,000*
Cash	*47,600*
Capital stock	*150,000*
Marketable securities	*175,040*
Accounts payable	*125,430*
Mortgage payable (due in 15 years)	*320,000*
Salaries payable	*7,570*
Interest payable	*4,600*
Accounts receivable	*230,540*
Inventory	*179,600*
Unearned revenue	*10,000*
Unexpired insurance	*4,500*

INSTRUCTIONS

a. Prepare a partial balance sheet for Diet Frozen Dinners consisting of the current asset section and the current liability section ***only***. Select the appropriate items from the above list.
b. Compute the current ratio and the amount of working capital. Explain how each of these measurements is computed. State with reasons whether you consider the company to be in a strong or weak current position.

PROBLEM 5-12
Classified Financial Statements and Financial Ratios
(LO 7, 8, 9)

Westport Department Store has advertised for an accounting student to work in its accounting department during the summer, and you have applied for the job. To determine whether you are familiar with the content of classified financial statements, the controller of Westport has developed the following problem based upon the store's operations in the year ended December 31, 2000:

Available information (dollar amounts in thousands):

Net sales	$10,000
Net income	?
Current liabilities	2,000
Selling expenses	1,000
Long-term liabilities	1,600
Total assets (and Total liabilities & shareholder's equity)	6,800
Shareholders' equity	?
Gross profit	?
Cost of goods sold	7,000
Current assets	4,000
Income taxes expense and other nonoperating items	220
Operating income	?
General and administrative expenses	980
Plant and equipment	2,600
Other assets	?

INSTRUCTIONS

a. Using the captions given above, prepare for Westport Department Store a condensed:
   1. Classified balance sheet at December 31, 2000.
   2. Multiple-step income statement for the year ended December 31, 2000.
   (***Note:*** Your financial statements should include only as much detail as these captions permit. For example, the first asset listed in your balance sheet will be "Current assets . . . $4,000." Notice also that this company is a corporation and that "shareholders' equity" is to be summarized in the balance sheet as a single dollar amount.)

b. Using the classified financial statements developed in part **a,** compute the following:
   1. Current ratio
   2. Working capital
   3. Gross profit rate for 2000

PROBLEM 5-13
Classified Income Statement
(LO 8)

Sharon Carpio is very happy about her new business, S. Carpio Company. The operations for the first year have been fantastic and she is going to show the financial statements to her banker to get some money to finance another store. However, she cannot locate the income statement for the year ended December 31, 2001. Fortunately, she remembers from her accounting courses that the following information may help.

Sales	689,200	
Interest revenue	2,800	
Income summary		692,000
To close the revenue accounts		

Income summary	572,280	
Cost of goods sold		329,520
Transportation-in		14,700
Advertising expense		20,800
Delivery expense		19,500
Depreciation: Store equipment		8,000
Sales salaries expense		72,080
Miscellaneous selling expense		1,690
General office salaries expense		63,900

Depreciation expense: office building	18,000
Utilities expense	9,210
Insurance expense	2,300
Office supplies expense	1,900
Interest expense	9,780
Purchase discount lost	900

To close the Cost of Goods Sold account and other
expense accounts

Income summary	119,720	
Sharon Carpio, capital		119,720

To close the Income Summary account

Sharon Carpio, capital	78,000	
Sharon Carpio, drawing		78,000

To close the owner's drawing account

INSTRUCTIONS

Prepare a classified income statement.

Analytical and Decision Problems and Cases

A&D 5-1
What Would You Expect?
(LO 6)

In each of the following situations, indicate whether you would expect the business to use a periodic inventory system or a perpetual inventory system. Explain the reasons for your answer.

a. The Frontier Shop is a small retail store that sells boots and western clothing. The store is operated by the owner, who works full time in the business, and by one part-time salesclerk. Sales transactions are recorded on an antique cash register. The business uses a manual accounting system, which is maintained by ACE Bookkeeping Service. At the end of each month, an employee of ACE visits The Frontier Shop to update its account records, prepare sales tax and goods and services tax returns, and perform other necessary accounting services.

b. Allister's Corner is an art gallery in Yorkville in Toronto. All accounting records are maintained manually by the owner, who works in the store on a full-time basis. The store sells three or four paintings each week, at sales prices ranging from about $5,000 to $50,000 per painting.

c. A publicly owned corporation publishes about 200 titles of college and university-level textbooks. The books are sold to college and university bookstores throughout the country. Books are distributed to these bookstores from four central warehouses, located in Vancouver, Toronto, Montreal, and Halifax.

d. Toys-4-You operates a national chain of 86 retail toy stores. The company has a "state-of-the-art" computerized accounting system. All sales transactions are recorded on electronic point-of-sale terminals. These terminals are tied into a central computer system that provides the national headquarters with information about the profitability of each store on a weekly basis.

e. Mr. Jingles is an independently owned and operated ice cream truck.

f. TransComm is a small company that sells very large quantities of a single product. The product is a low-cost, 3.5 inch, double-sided, double-density computer floppy disc, manufactured by a large company overseas. Sales are made only in large quantities, primarily to chains of computer stores and large discount stores. This year, the average sales transaction has amounted to $14,206 worth of merchandise. All accounting records are maintained by a full-time employee using commercial accounting software and a personal computer.

A&D 5-2
Hey, You! Put That Back!
(LO 5, 8, 9)

Village Hardware is a retail store selling hardware, small appliances, and sporting goods. The business follows a policy of selling all merchandise at exactly twice the amount of its cost to the store and uses a *periodic* inventory system.

At year-end, the following information is taken from the accounting records:

Net Sales	*$400,000*
Inventory, January 1	*40,000*
Purchases	*205,000*

A physical count indicates merchandise costing $34,000 is on hand at December 31.

INSTRUCTIONS

a. Prepare a partial income statement showing computation of the gross profit for the year.

b. Upon seeing your income statement, the owner of the store makes the following comment: "Inventory shrinkage losses are really costing me. If it weren't for shrinkage losses, the store's gross profit would be 50% of net sales. I'm going to hire a security guard and put an end to shoplifting once and for all."

   Determine the amount of loss from inventory "shrinkage" stated (1) at cost, and (2) at retail sales value.

c. Assume that Village Hardware could virtually eliminate shoplifting by hiring a security guard at a cost of $1,500 per month. Would this strategy be profitable? Explain your reasoning.

A&D 5-3
What Information Is Really Needed?
(LO 1, 2, 3, 5, 6)

Always Fresh is a fish market operating on the pier in the Halifax harbour; it sells fresh fish by the kilogram, and also fish sandwiches. All sales are made for cash. Every day, the market buys for cash a few hundred kilograms of "whatever looks good" directly from incoming fishing boats. At closing time, it sells any leftover inventory to Best Friend, a cannery that makes pet food.

a. Would Always Fresh benefit from using a perpetual inventory system? Explain.

b. Briefly discuss the company's needs (if any) for subsidiary ledgers for inventory, accounts receivable, and accounts payable.

c. Describe accounting procedures for recording purchases and sales that you believe will efficiently meet this company's needs.

A&D 5-4
Out of Balance
(LO 2)

Marcus Dean works in the accounts payable department of Artistic Furniture, a large retail furniture store. At month-end, Dean's supervisor assigned him the task of reconciling the accounts payable subsidiary ledger with the controlling account.

Dean found that the balance of the controlling account was $4,500 higher than the sum of the subsidiary ledger accounts. He traced this error to a transaction occurring early in the month. Artistic had purchased $9,400 in merchandise on account from Appalachian Woods, a regular supplier. The transaction had been recorded correctly in Artistic's journal, and posted correctly to the Inventory and Accounts Payable accounts in the general ledger. The $9,400 credit to Accounts Payable, however, had erroneously been posted as **$4,900** to the Appalachian Woods account in Artistic's accounts payable subsidiary ledger.

Artistic uses its subsidiary ledger as the basis for making payment to its suppliers. In the middle of the month, Artistic had sent a cheque to Appalachian in the amount of $4,900. This $4,900 payment was recorded and posted correctly to both the general and subsidiary ledger accounts. Thus, at the end of the month the subsidiary ledger account for Appalachian Woods had a "zero" balance.

Dean learned that Appalachian had failed to detect Artistic's error. The month-end statement from Appalachian simply said "Account Paid in full." Therefore, Dean proposed the following "correcting entry" to bring Artistic's controlling account into balance with the subsidiary ledger and the supplier's month-end statement:

| Accounts Payable . . . . | 4,500 | |
| Miscellaneous Revenue . . . . | | 4,500 |

To reduce Accounts Payable controlling account for unpaid
amount that was not rebilled by the supplier.

This entry is to be posted to the general ledger accounts, but not to the accounts payable subsidiary ledger.

INSTRUCTIONS

a. Will the proposed correcting entry bring the Accounts Payable controlling account into agreement with the accounts in the subsidiary ledger?
b. Identify and discuss any ethical considerations that you see in this situation, and suggest an appropriate course of action.

A&D 5-5
Group Assignment with
Business Community
Involvement
(LO 3, 5, 6)

Identify one local business that uses a perpetual inventory system, and another that uses a periodic system. Interview an individual in each organization who is familiar with the inventory system and the recording of sales transactions. (Interviews are to be planned and conducted in accordance with the instructions in the Preface of this textbook.)

INSTRUCTIONS

Separately for each business organization:
a. Describe the procedures used in accounting for sales transactions, keeping track of inventory levels, and determining the cost of goods sold.
b. Explain the reasons offered by the person interviewed as to *why* the business uses this type of system.
c. Indicate whether your group considers the system in use appropriate under the circumstances. If not, recommend specific changes. ***Explain your reasoning.***

A&D 5-6
Journal Entries for Additional
Merchandising Transactions
(LO 4)

David Walters, owner of Major Cosmos, is quite upset that his bookkeeper has misplaced all the accounting records for July, the first month of operation. Fortunately, the following account balances at July 31 are available from one of his files:

Cash	$ 600
Accounts receivable	1,500
Accounts payable	490
Sales	9,800
Sales returns & allowances	800
Sales discounts	60
Purchases	4,508
Purchase returns & allowances	588
Transportation-in	182
Selling and general expenses	930

Even though Major Cosmos prefers cash sales, the July sales, after returns and allowances, were equally divided between cash and credit. Of the credit sales, two-thirds were collected during the month and the customers were given a 2% discount of $60. Sales returns and allowances for July amounted to $800, all of which were related to credit sales. All purchases were for credit; $588 of which were returned to suppliers because of defects. Major Cosmos used the net cost to record its purchase and paid its accounts payable promptly to take advantage of the 2% discount from its suppliers. The transportation-in and selling and general expenses were all paid in cash.

David Walters wonders whether you, an accounting student, would be able to reconstruct the journal entries in summary form, for the month of July, based on the above information.

INSTRUCTIONS

Prepare all the journal entries (including explanations) in a general journal format, to summarize the business transactions for July.

A&D 5-7
Evaluating Debt-Paying Ability
(LO 7, 8)

You are a loan officer with Martindale Bank. Dan Scott owns two successful restaurants, each of which has applied to your bank for a $250,000 one-year loan for the purpose of opening a second location. Condensed balance sheets for the two business entities are shown below:

RIVERSIDE STEAK RANCH
Balance Sheet
December 31, 2000

Assets		*Liabilities & Shareholders' Equity*	
Current assets	$ 75,000	Current liabilities	$ 30,000
Plant and equipment . . .	300,000	Long-term liabilities	200,000
		Capital stock	100,000
		Retained earnings	45,000
		Total liabilities &	
Total assets	$375,000	shareholders' equity . . .	$375,000

THE STOCKYARDS
Balance Sheet
December 31, 2000

Assets		*Liabilities & Owner's Equity*	
Current assets	$ 24,000	Current liabilities	$ 30,000
Plant and equipment . . .	301,000	Long-term liabilities	200,000
		Dan Scott, Capital	95,000
		Total liabilities &	
Total assets	$325,000	owner's equity	$325,000

Both restaurants are popular and have been successful over the last several years. Riverside Steak Ranch has been slightly more profitable, but the operating results for the two businesses have been quite similar. You think that either restaurant's second location should be successful. On the other hand, you know that restaurants are a very "faddish" type of business, and that their popularity and profitability can change very quickly.

Dan Scott is one of the wealthiest people in Alberta. He made a fortune—estimated at more than $60 million—as the founder of Micro Time, a highly successful manufacturer of computer software. Scott now is retired and spends most of his time at Second Life, his huge cattle ranch. Both of his restaurants are run by experienced professional managers.

INSTRUCTIONS

a. Compute the current ratio and working capital of each business entity.
b. Based upon the information provided in this case, which of these businesses do you consider to be the better credit risk? Explain fully.
c. What simple measure might you insist upon that would make the other business as good a credit risk as the one you identified in part **b?** Explain.

A&D 5-8
Strategies to Improve the
Current Ratio
(LO 7)

Home Improvement Centres owns a chain of nine retail stores that sell building materials, hardware, and garden supplies. In early October, the company's current ratio is 1.7 to 1. This is about normal for the company but is lower than the current ratios of several large competitors. Management feels that to qualify for the best credit terms from its suppliers, the company's year-end balance sheet should indicate a current ratio of at least 2 to 1.

INSTRUCTIONS

a. Indicate whether taking each of the following actions would increase or decrease the company's current ratio. Explain your reasoning.

1. Pay some of the company's current liabilities.
2. Purchase large amounts of inventory on account.
3. Offer credit customers a special discount if they pay their account balance prior to year-end.

b. Propose several other **legitimate** steps that management might take to increase the company's current ratio prior to year-end.

A&D 5-9
What Am I Getting Myself Into?
(LO 7)

Megan DeLong, an experienced engineer, is considering buying Taichung Engineering Company at year-end from its current owner, Jack Peterson. Taichung Engineering Company, a sole proprietorship, has been a profitable business, earning about $70,000 to $75,000 each year. DeLong is certain she could operate the business just as profitably. The principal activity of the business has been the performance of engineering studies for government agencies interested in the development of air and water pollution control programs.

Peterson has agreed to sell the business for "what he has in it"—namely, $200,000. DeLong comes to you with the balance sheet of Taichung Engineering Company, which follows, and asks your advice about buying the business.

TAICHUNG ENGINEERING COMPANY
Balance Sheet
December 31, 19__

Assets		Liabilities & Owner's Equity	
Cash	$ 40,500	Notes Payable	$ 60,000
Government contract		Accounts payable	20,600
receivable	110,000	Wages payable	5,400
Other contracts		J. Peterson, capital	200,000
receivable	21,500		
Equipment			
(net of depreciation) . .	76,000		
Patents	38,000	Total liabilities & owner's	
Total assets	$286,000	equity	$286,000

DeLong immediately points out, as evidence of the firm's solvency, that the current ratio for Taichung Engineering is 2 to 1. In discussing the specific items on the balance sheet, you find that the patents were recently purchased by Taichung, and DeLong believes them to be worth their $38,000 cost. The notes payable liability consists of one note to the manufacturer of the equipment owned by Taichung, which Peterson had incurred five years ago to finance the purchase of the equipment. The note becomes payable, however, in February of the coming year. The accounts payable all will become due within 30 to 60 days.

Since DeLong does not have enough cash to buy Peterson's equity in the business, she is considering the following terms of purchase: (1) Peterson will withdraw all the cash from the business, thus reducing his equity to $159,500, (2) Peterson will also keep the $110,000 receivable from the government, leaving his equity in the business at $49,500, and (3) by borrowing heavily, DeLong thinks she can raise $49,500 in cash, which she will pay to Peterson for his remaining equity. DeLong will assume the existing liabilities of the business.

INSTRUCTIONS

DeLong wants you to write her a memorandum explaining what problems she may encounter if she purchases the business as planned. (Support your answer with proper analyses.)

A&D 5-10
Decisions, Decisions!
(LO 9)

Helen Honanda, Bob Lamiken, and Susan Kowzanski are enjoying their class reunion at Laukudini U. The following conversation follows after reminiscing about their good old days on campus:

SUSAN: Helen, how's your restaurant business?

HELEN: It is doing quite well. My business has been consistently making a net income of $150,000 a year and my equity in the business is only $400,000.

BOB: You probably are a millionaire now.

HELEN: Well, not yet, because I have to pay income tax on this income and have a lot of personal expenses, even though I don't own a house or a car. I have saved $120,000, which is invested in a very safe portfolio of bonds and treasury bills, earning me a 6% annual return.

SUSAN: As an investment banker, I can tell that this is a very reasonable rate of return on this kind of investment. If you need any advice on investing your money, just let me know.

HELEN: Good. I have been thinking recently about whether I should remain in business or work for someone. I have just been offered a job for $100,000 a year managing a similar restaurant.

SUSAN: How much can you get for selling your restaurant?

HELEN: I have received an offer of $500,000 for my equity in the business and I think it is very reasonable.

SUSAN: I will help you invest the $500,000 in very safe securities for a 6% annual return. If you want to remain in the same risk category as your restaurant business, I can get you 11% a year on your $500,000 investment.

BOB: Helen, is your business organized as a sole proprietorship or corporation?

HELEN: As a sole proprietorship because I don't like the extra formalities of a corporation.

BOB: As a lawyer, I can help you in the legal aspects of selling your business. As you probably know, there are advantages to a corporate form of business, especially when you have a sizeable amount of personal assets.

HELEN: It is certainly nice to have helpful friends like you two. I really appreciate it and will let you know.

INSTRUCTIONS

a. Discuss whether the business has been successful.
b. Advise Helen Honanda whether she should sell her business and accept the job offer. Your answer should include the relevant factors that Honanda should consider.

Answers to Self-Test Questions

1. a, b, d   2. b, c   3. b   4. b   5. b, d   6. b, c, d   7. a, c   8. b

MORE ABOUT A PERIODIC INVENTORY SYSTEM

The purpose of this appendix is to explain in greater detail the operation of a *periodic* inventory system. As indicated in the text, virtually all large organizations are *perpetual* inventory systems. However, periodic systems are used in a number of smaller companies—particularly those that use manual accounting systems.

LEARNING OBJECTIVES

1. Explain the characteristics, advantages, and disadvantages of a periodic inventory system.
2. Account for merchandising transactions using a periodic inventory system.

3. Prepare closing entries for a business using a periodic inventory system, including the entry to "reopen" the inventory account.

Characteristics of a Periodic Inventory System

A periodic inventory system is an ***alternative*** to a perpetual inventory system. The basic characteristics of a periodic system are:

LO 1: Explain the characteristics, advantages, and disadvantages of a periodic inventory system.

1. During an accounting period no entries are made in the Inventory account to record the cost of merchandise purchased or sold. Purchases are recorded by debiting an account called ***Purchases.*** When merchandise is sold, the revenue is recorded, but no entry is made to record the cost of goods sold. Thus, the balance in the Inventory account remains ***unchanged*** throughout the year, and the accounting records do not indicate the cost of goods sold.
2. At the end of each year, a complete ***physical inventory*** is taken. The merchandise on hand is counted, and its cost is determined. (The procedures for assigning per-unit costs to the items in inventory are discussed in Chapter 9.)
3. As stated above, the cost of goods sold is ***not recorded*** as individual sales transactions occur. Rather, the cost of goods sold for the entire year is determined at year-end by a computation such as the one that follows:

Inventory, beginning of the year (per last year's physical count) . . .	*$ 10,000*
Add: Purchases	*140,000*
Cost of goods available for sale during the year	*$150,000*
Less: Ending inventory (per this year's physical count)	*12,000*
Cost of goods sold	*$138,000*

Advantages and Disadvantages of a Periodic System   As compared with a perpetual inventory system, a periodic inventory system has one advantage: no entries are required to record the cost of goods sold relating to individual sales transactions. The disadvantage is that the accounting records do not indicate the amount of inventory on hand, or the cost of goods sold, until a complete physical inventory is taken.

Taking a complete physical inventory is both inconvenient and costly. Therefore, a physical inventory usually is taken only at year-end. Thus, a periodic inventory system is well suited to the preparation of annual financial statements, but not to preparing financial statements for shorter periods, such as quarters or months.

Another shortcoming of the periodic system is the lack of an inventory subsidiary ledger. As stated in Chapter 5, an inventory subsidiary ledger indicates by type of product the costs and quantities of merchandise sold during the period and currently in inventory. This information—absent in a periodic inventory system—is useful to management in developing marketing strategies and in deciding what products to purchase, when to reorder merchandise, and the quantities of merchandise to be purchased.

In order to manage inventories in an efficient manner, and also to meet their quarterly reporting obligations, most publicly owned companies use perpetual inventory systems. Also, most businesses with point-of-sale terminals or computerized inventory accounting systems use the perpetual approach. For a small business with a manual accounting system, however, the fact that a periodic system requires less record keeping than does a perpetual system may outweigh all other considerations.

In businesses in which accounting records are maintained manually by the owner, or by a professional accountant who provides service to the business on a weekly or monthly basis, a periodic inventory system may be the **only** practical means of accounting for inventory.

Operation of a Periodic Inventory System

In a periodic inventory system, the amount of inventory on hand at the end of each accounting period is determined by physical count. The inventory at the end of one accounting period also represents the **beginning inventory** of the following period.

In summary, a periodic inventory system requires that a complete physical inventory be taken at the end of each accounting period. Annual financial statements may be prepared by taking inventory at the end of the fiscal year. The preparation of monthly financial statements, however, would require monthly inventories.[1]

Purchases of Merchandise   Under a periodic inventory system, the cost of merchandise purchased for resale is recorded by debiting an account entitled **Purchases,** as shown below:

LO 2: Account for merchandising transactions using a periodic inventory system.

---

[1]In Chapter 9, we discuss several **estimating** techniques that may be used in preparing monthly or quarterly financial statements. If inventory (and the cost of goods sold) are based upon such estimating techniques, this fact should be disclosed in the financial statements.

Purchases	*1,960*	
* Accounts Payable (Beta Wholesale Co.)*		*1,960*
Purchased merchandise on account; gross price, $2,000;		
terms 2/10, n/30 ($2,000, less 2% = $1,960.).		

Purchases may be recorded either at the gross invoice price, or at net price—that is, net of available cash discounts. We will record purchases at the ***net*** cost.

Other Accounts Included in the Cost of Goods Sold   In our preceding illustration, we used only three items in computing the cost of goods sold: beginning inventory, purchases, and ending inventory. In most cases, however, two additional accounts are involved in this computation: Purchase Returns and Allowances, and Transportation-in.

Purchase Returns and Allowances   When merchandise purchased from suppliers is found to be unsatisfactory, the goods may be returned or a request may be made for an allowance on the price. A return of goods to the supplier is recorded as follows:

Journal entry for return of goods to supplier

Accounts Payable (Beta Wholesale Co.)	*196*	
* Purchase Returns and Allowances*		*196*
To reduce liability to Beta Wholesale Co. by the cost of goods		
returned for credit.		

Assuming that the purchase had been recorded at net cost, the purchase return also should be recorded at the net cost of the merchandise.

The Purchase Returns and Allowances account may be viewed as a reduction in the cost of purchases made during the period. It is preferable to credit this "contra-purchases" account when merchandise is returned to a supplier rather than crediting the Purchases account directly. Together, these two accounts show both the total amount of purchases and the amount of cost adjustments and returns. Management is interested in the percentage relationship between goods purchased and the portion of these goods that must be returned. Returning merchandise is time-consuming and expensive and also may result in a loss of sales opportunities. Excessive returns may suggest a need to find more reliable suppliers.

Transportation-in   Transportation charges relating to merchandise are accounted for in the same manner in periodic and perpetual inventory systems. The freight charges paid on ***inbound*** shipments are debited to an account entitled ***Transportation-in,*** which is added to the cost of goods sold. Delivery costs on ***outbound*** shipments are debited to Delivery Expense, which is classified as a selling expense.

Purchase Discounts   We follow the policy of recording purchases at their net cost. Under this net method, the amount paid to the supplier will be equal to the recorded liability, assuming that payment will be made within the discount period. If payment is not made until after the discount period has expired, the purchaser must pay the gross invoice price. The additional amount paid is debited to an account entitled ***Purchase Discounts Lost,***

an expense account representing a form of interest expense. We strongly recommend this net method, as it focuses management's attention upon any failures to take advantage of available cash discounts.[2]

Accounting for Sales Transactions

Accounting for sales transactions is the same under periodic and perpetual inventory systems, with one notable exception. In a periodic system, no entries are made transferring costs from the Inventory account to the Cost of Goods Sold account.

To illustrate, assume that Farrow's Bait & Tackle Shop sells merchandise on account to South Shore Marina for $1,200; terms, 2/10, net/30. South Shore finds $200 worth of this merchandise defective and returns it to Farrow's immediately. South Shore then pays for the remainder of these goods within the discount period. Farrow's should record the original sales transaction as shown below:

Accounts Receivable (South Shore Marina)	*1,200*	
Sales		*1,200*
To record credit sale, terms 2/10, n/30.		

Notice that ***only one entry*** is needed to record a sale. The primary advantage of a periodic inventory system is that it is not necessary to record the cost of goods sold relating to individual sales transactions. (As in a perpetual inventory system, sales usually are recorded at the ***gross*** invoice price, not at the net amount.)

Farrow's would record the sales return by South Shore as follows:

Sales Returns and Allowances	*200*	
Accounts Receivable (South Shore Marina)		*200*
Credit customer returned defective merchandise.		

Again, only one entry is necessary. Under a periodic inventory system, no entry is made to update the Inventory account or to adjust the cost of goods sold.

Following this sales return, South Shore owes Farrow's $1,000. If South Shore pays within the discount period, however, it may take a 2% cash discount. The entry to record the collection of this account receivable within the discount period is:

Cash	*980*	
Sales Discounts	*20*	
Accounts Receivable (South Shore Marina)		*1,000*
To record collection of account receivable within the discount period.		

Both Sales Returns & Allowances and Sales Discounts are ***contra-revenue*** accounts, which are deducted from gross sales revenue as a step in

---

[2]An alternative approach is to record purchases at the gross invoice price. If payment is made within the discount period, the buyer will then pay the supplier less than the recorded amount of the liability. This "cost savings" is credited to an account called Purchase Discounts Taken. Purchase Discounts Taken is a contra-purchases account, similar to Purchase Returns and Allowances. In terms of net income, the "gross method" and "net method" produce essentially the same results.

determining net sales. These debit balance accounts reduce the revenue of a specific time period. At the end of the period, they are closed into the Income Summary along with the company's expense accounts.

Income Statement for a Company Using a Periodic Inventory System

To pull together the concepts discussed in this appendix, let us look at a detailed income statement of a business using a periodic inventory system.

Olympic Sporting Goods is a small retail store organized as a sole proprietorship and operated by Robert Riley. The business has no external reporting responsibilities, other than determining its annual income for inclusion in Riley's personal income tax return. Also, Riley works in the store on a daily basis and is intimately familiar with the inventory on hand. Thus, Olympic Sporting Goods is able to meet Riley's needs for accounting information with a periodic inventory system. The company's 2000 income statement is illustrated below:

OLYMPIC SPORTING GOODS
Income Statement
For the Year Ending December 31, 2000

Notice the computation of the cost of goods sold

Revenue:			
Sales			$627,000
Less: Sales returns and allowances		$ 12,000	
Sales discounts		5,000	17,000
Net sales			$610,000
Cost of goods sold:			
Inventory, Jan. 1		$ 60,000	
Purchases	$375,000		
Less: Purchase returns and allowances	10,000		
Net purchases	$365,000		
Add: Transportation-in	11,000		
Delivered cost of purchases		376,000	
Cost of goods available for sale		$436,000	
Less: Inventory, Dec. 31		70,000	
Cost of goods sold			366,000
Gross profit			$244,000
Operating expenses:			
Selling expenses:			
Sales salaries	$ 74,000		
Advertising	29,000		
Delivery service	7,000		
Depreciation	6,000		
Total selling expenses		$116,000	
General and administrative expenses:			
Office salaries	$ 55,000		
Utilities	2,100		
Depreciation	2,000		
Total general and administrative expenses		59,100	
Total operating expenses			175,100
Income from operations			$ 68,900
Nonoperating expenses:			
Purchase discounts lost		$ 1,000	
Interest expense		8,200	9,200
Net income			$ 59,700

Work Sheet for a Merchandising Business

In Chapter 4, we illustrated the preparation of a work sheet as a means of organizing the data used in making adjusting and closing entries and in preparing financial statements. A merchandising business using a periodic inventory system also may elect to prepare a work sheet. In fact, it is small businesses with periodic inventory systems and manual accounting records that are the most likely to actually prepare such a schedule.[3]

In most respects, a work sheet prepared by a merchandising company with a periodic inventory system parallels the work sheet explained and illustrated in Chapter 4. There are, however, a few new features—namely, the Inventory account and other accounts used in recording merchandising transactions. As an illustration, a year-end work sheet for Olympic Sporting Goods is illustrated on the following page. For emphasis, the new types of accounts included in this work sheet are shown in **black.**

Trial Balance Columns   The trial balance columns are prepared by listing the account balances in the ledger at December 31, **prior** to making adjusting and closing entries. The Inventory account, however, is **not** up-to-date; its $60,000 balance represents the inventory at the **beginning of the year.** (A distinctive feature of the periodic inventory system is that the Inventory account is **not** updated throughout the year for purchases and sales of merchandise.)

Adjustment Columns and Adjusted Trial Balance   The adjustments required in a merchandising company at the end of the period are similar to those of a service business. In our illustration, we assume that the only adjustment needed at December 31 is an entry to record depreciation expense for the year.

The merchandising accounts (shown in black) usually do not require adjustment. Therefore, their balances are extended directly from the Trial Balance columns to the Adjusted Trial Balance columns.

Income Statement Columns   The accounts used in the determination of net income are extended from the Adjusted Trial Balance columns into the Income Statement columns. These are the revenue accounts, expense accounts, and **all accounts used in the computation of the cost of goods sold.**

Notice that the $60,000 balance in the Inventory account is extended into the **Income Statement** debit column, instead of the Balance Sheet debit column. This is because the $60,000 balance in this account represents the inventory at the **beginning** of the year. At year-end, the beginning inventory is **no longer an asset;** rather, it has become **part of the cost of goods sold.** The cost of goods sold, of course, is offset against revenue in the income statement.

---

[3]Remember that a work sheet is **not** an essential step in the accounting cycle. In essence, it is "scratch paper," upon which an accountant may work out certain entries before making entries in the accounting records. You should regard the work sheets in this text as illustrations of accounting **processes,** not of accounting documents. In practice, accountants often perform the illustrated processes **without** first preparing a work sheet.

Note the treatment of
the beginning and the
ending inventories

OLYMPIC SPORTING GOODS
Work Sheet
For the Year Ended December 31, 2000

	Trial Balance		Adjustments*		Adjusted Trial Balance		Income Statement		Balance Sheet	
	Dr	Cr	Dr	Cr	Dr	Cr	Dr	Cr	Dr	Cr
Balance sheet accounts:										
Cash	19,400				19,400				19,400	
Accounts receivable	48,300				48,300				48,300	
Inventory	60,000				60,000		60,000	70,000	70,000	
Land	52,000				52,000				52,000	
Building	160,000				160,000				160,000	
Accumulated depreciation: building		56,000		(a) 8,000		64,000				64,000
Notes payable		82,000				82,000				82,000
Accounts payable		55,000				55,000				55,000
Robert Riley, capital		115,000				115,000				115,000
Robert Riley, drawing	26,000				26,000				26,000	
Income statement accounts:										
Sales		627,000				627,000		627,000		
Sales returns and allowances	12,000				12,000		12,000			
Sales discounts	5,000				5,000		5,000			
Purchases	375,000				375,000		375,000			
Purchase returns and allowances		10,000				10,000		10,000		
Transportation-in	11,000				11,000		11,000			
Sales salaries	74,000				74,000		74,000			
Advertising expense	29,000				29,000		29,000			
Delivery service	7,000				7,000		7,000			
Office salaries	55,000				55,000		55,000			
Utilities expense	2,100				2,100		2,100			
Purchase discounts lost	1,000				1,000		1,000			
Interest expense	8,200				8,200		8,200			
	945,000	945,000								
Depreciation expense: building			(a) 8,000		8,000		8,000			
			8,000	8,000	953,000	953,000	647,300	707,000	375,700	316,000
Net income							59,700			59,700
Totals							707,000	707,000	375,700	375,700

Explanatory footnote keyed to adjustments
*Adjustment
(a) Depreciation of building for the year.

Treatment of the Inventory Account   The most unique element of this work sheet is the treatment accorded to the Inventory account. As we have explained, the $60,000 beginning balance is extended into the Income Statement debit column, not into the Balance Sheet columns. Now, however, it is time to **update** the Inventory account to show the $70,000 **ending inventory,** as determined by a physical inventory taken at year-end.

Updating the Inventory account requires **two entries** in the work sheet. Notice that the cost of the ending inventory appears both in the **Income Statement credit column** and in the **Balance Sheet debit column.** (For emphasis, these two entries are shown in **grey.**)

Let us briefly explain the reasoning behind these entries. The cost of the ending inventory is entered into the Balance Sheet debit column because this amount will appear in the December 31 balance sheet. The amount also is entered into the Income Statement credit column because, in a periodic inventory system, the amount of ending inventory **enters into the determination of net income.**

In a periodic inventory system, the cost of goods sold is determined by **subtracting ending inventory** from the total of beginning inventory, purchases, and transportation-in. By entering the ending inventory in the Income Statement **credit** column, we in effect are **deducting** it from the sum of the beginning inventory, purchases, and transportation-in, all of which were extended into the Income Statement **debit** column.

One of the functions of the Income Statement columns is to bring together all of the accounts involved in determining the cost of goods sold. The accounts with debit balances are the beginning Inventory, Purchases, and Transportation-in; these accounts total $446,000. Against this total the two credit items of Purchase Returns & Allowances, $10,000, and ending Inventory, $70,000, are offset. The three accounts with debit balances exceed the total of the two credit balances by **$366,000;** this amount is the **cost of goods sold,** as shown in the income statement for Olympic Sporting Goods, which appeared earlier.

Completing the Work Sheet   When all the accounts on the work sheet have been extended into the Income Statement or Balance Sheet columns, the final four columns are totalled. The net income is computed, and the work sheet completed in the same manner as illustrated in Chapter 4 for a service business.

Financial Statements

The work to be done at the end of the period is much the same for a merchandising business as for a service-type firm. First, the work sheet is completed; then, financial statements are prepared from the data in the work sheet; next, the adjusting and closing entries are entered in the journal and posted to the ledger accounts; and finally, an after-closing trial balance is prepared. This completes the annual accounting cycle.

The income statement presented earlier was prepared from the Olympic Sporting Goods work sheet. Note particularly the arrangement of items in the cost of goods sold section of the income statement; this portion of the income statement illustrates many of the essential accounting concepts covered in this appendix.

Closing Entries

LO 3: Prepare closing entries for a business using a periodic inventory system, including the entry to "reopen" the inventory account.

In a **perpetual** inventory system, the Cost of Goods Sold account simply is closed along with the company's expense accounts. In a **periodic** inventory system, a single Cost of Goods Sold account is not used throughout the accounting period. Instead, separate ledger accounts are maintained for the various components of the cost of goods sold, each of which is closed at year-end. The major new elements in the closing process for a merchandising business using a periodic inventory system are the entries showing the **elimination** of the beginning inventory and the **recording** of the ending inventory.

The beginning inventory is "cleared out" of the Inventory account by a debit to Income Summary and a credit to Inventory. A separate entry could be made for this purpose, but we can save time by making one **compound entry** that debits the Income Summary account with the balance of the beginning inventory and with the balances of all temporary accounts having debit balances.

The **temporary** accounts are those that appear in the income statement, including those which enter into the computation of the cost of goods sold. As the name suggests, the temporary accounts are used to accumulate temporarily the increases and decreases in owner's equity resulting from operation of the business. The entry to close the beginning inventory and income statement accounts with debit balances is illustrated below. (For emphasis, the accounts relating specifically to merchandising transactions are shown in black.)

Closing beginning inventory and income statement accounts with debit balances

Dec. 31 Income Summary	647,300	
Inventory (Jan. 1)		60,000
Sales Returns and Allowances		12,000
Sales Discounts		5,000
Purchases		375,000
Transportation-in		11,000
Sales Salaries		74,000
Advertising Expense		29,000
Delivery Service		7,000
Office Salaries		55,000
Utilities Expense		2,100
Purchase Discounts Lost		1,000
Interest Expense		8,200
Depreciation Expense: Building		8,000
To close out the beginning inventory and the income statement accounts with debit balances.		

The preceding closing entry closes all the operating expense accounts, as well as the accounts used to accumulate the cost of goods sold. It also closes the accounts for Sales Returns and Allowances and for Sales Discounts, as well as Purchase Discounts Lost. After this first closing entry, the Inventory account has a zero balance. Therefore, it is time to record in this account the new inventory of $70,000 determined by a physical count at December 31.

To bring the ending inventory into the accounting records after the physical inventory on December 31, we could make a separate entry debiting Inventory and crediting the Income Summary account. It is more convenient, however, to combine this step with the closing of the Sales account and any other income statement accounts having credit balances, as illustrated in the following closing entry:

<table>
<tr><td>Closing income statement accounts with credit balances and recording ending inventory</td><td>Dec. 31</td><td>Inventory (Dec. 31) ....</td><td>70,000</td><td></td></tr>
<tr><td></td><td></td><td>Sales ....</td><td>627,000</td><td></td></tr>
<tr><td></td><td></td><td>Purchase Returns and Allowances ....</td><td>10,000</td><td></td></tr>
<tr><td></td><td></td><td>   Income Summary ....</td><td></td><td>707,000</td></tr>
<tr><td></td><td></td><td>To record the ending inventory and to close all income statement accounts with credit balances.</td><td></td><td></td></tr>
</table>

In this entry, we "close" the Sales account and the Purchase Returns and Allowances account, as each of these accounts will have a **zero balance** after the closing entry is posted. On the other hand, the Inventory account had been "closed" in the **preceding** entry, which transferred its entire balance into the Income Summary account. Therefore, debiting the Inventory account for the amount of the ending inventory should be viewed as **"reopening"** the Inventory account.

The remaining closing entries serve to transfer the balance of the Income Summary account to the owner's capital account and to close the drawing account, as follows:

<table>
<tr><td>Closing the Income Summary account and Owner's Drawing account</td><td>Dec. 31</td><td>Income Summary ....</td><td>59,700</td><td></td></tr>
<tr><td></td><td></td><td>   Robert Riley, Capital ....</td><td></td><td>59,700</td></tr>
<tr><td></td><td></td><td>To close the Income Summary account.</td><td></td><td></td></tr>
<tr><td></td><td>Dec. 31</td><td>Robert Riley, Capital ....</td><td>26,000</td><td></td></tr>
<tr><td></td><td></td><td>   Robert Riley, Drawing ....</td><td></td><td>26,000</td></tr>
<tr><td></td><td></td><td>To close the drawing account.</td><td></td><td></td></tr>
</table>

After the preceding four closing entries have been posted to the ledger, the only ledger accounts left with dollar balances will be balance sheet accounts. An after-closing trial balance should be prepared to prove that the ledger is in balance after the year-end entries to adjust and close the accounts have been recorded and posted.

Record-Keeping Requirements in a Periodic System

At first glance, the more complex closing procedures may seem to negate the basic advantage of a periodic inventory system—that is, a reduction in the amount of required record keeping. However, recording the cost of goods sold relating to each sales transaction may require dozens, scores, or hundreds of entries **each day.** In contrast, the end-of-the-year closing procedures for a periodic inventory system involve only two additional elements: "closing out" the beginning inventory and "reopening" the Inventory account at the proper ending inventory amount. As closing procedures are usually handled by experienced accountants, use of a periodic system adds only a couple of minutes to the closing process.

ASSIGNMENT MATERIAL

Problems

PROBLEM A-1
Journal Entries for
Merchandising Transactions

Runners' World deals in a wide variety of low-priced merchandise and uses a periodic inventory system. The company's accounting policies call for recording credit sales at the gross invoice price, but recording purchases at net cost. The following is a partial list of the transactions occurring during May:

May 2	Purchased merchandise (running shoes) on credit from MinuteMan Shoes, $9,500. Terms, 2/10, n/30.
May 3	Paid freight charges of $45 on the shipment of merchandise purchased from MinuteMan Shoes.
May 4	Upon unpacking the shipment from MinuteMan, discovered that some of the shoes were the wrong style. Returned these shoes, which had a gross invoice price of $400 ($392 net cost) to MinuteMan and received full credit.
May 9	Sold merchandise on account to Harbour Castle Spa Hotel, $4,100. Terms, 2/10, n/30.
May 11	Paid $22 freight charges on the outbound shipment to Harbour Castle Spa Hotel.
May 12	Paid MinuteMan Shoes within the discount period the remaining amount owed for the May 2 purchase, after allowing for the purchase return on May 4.
May 16	Sold merchandise on account to Holiday Sportswear, $2,755. Terms, 2/10, n/30.
May 19	Received payment from Harbour Castle Spa Hotel within the discount period in full settlement of the May 9 sale.
May 21	Holiday Sportswear returned $650 of the merchandise it had purchased on May 16. Runners' World has a policy of accepting all merchandise returns within 30 days of the date of sale without question. Full credit was given to Holiday for the returned merchandise.

INSTRUCTIONS

Prepare journal entries to record each of these transactions in the accounting records of Runners' World. Include a written explanation for each journal entry.

PROBLEM A-2
Preparing an Income
Statement and Closing Entries

Listed below are the amounts relating to the income statement of Leather Bandit for the three-month period ended March 31, 2000:

Sales	$500,000	Inventory, Jan. 1, 2000	$170,100
Sales returns & allowances ..	15,000	Inventory, Mar. 31, 2000	
Sales discounts	7,800	(estimated)	165,000
Purchases	302,000	Operating expenses	121,400
Purchase returns & allowances	4,500	Purchase discounts lost	400
Transportation-in	1,900	Interest expense	7,500

INSTRUCTIONS

a. Compute the amount of net sales for the three-month period.
b. Compute the cost of goods sold.
c. Prepare a **_condensed_** multiple-step income statement. Show both net sales and the cost of goods sold as "one-line items," without showing the accounts used to compute these amounts. Interest expense and purchase discounts lost should be shown after determining income from operations.

d. Prepare closing entries for the period ended March 31, 2000. Only three closing entries are required as the owner, John Brown, made no withdrawals during the year.

Westport Landing is a small company maintaining its accounts on a calendar-year basis and using a periodic inventory system. A four-column schedule consisting of the first four columns of a 10-column work sheet appears below.

WESTPORT LANDING
Work Sheet
For the Year Ended December 31, 19__

	Trial Balance		Adjustments	
	Debit	Credit	Debit	Credit
Balance sheet accounts:				
Cash	6,400			
Accounts receivable	16,000			
Inventory (Jan. 1)	60,000			
Unexpired insurance	4,400			(b) 2,800
Equipment	22,000			
Accumulated depreciation:				
equipment		6,600		(a) 2,200
Accounts payable		20,400		
Jane Hill, capital		83,800		
Jane Hill, drawing	21,000			
Income statement accounts:				
Sales		529,000		
Sales returns & allowances . . .	21,000			
Sales discounts	8,000			
Purchases	361,000			
Purchase returns & allowances .		18,000		
Transportation-in	12,000			
Advertising expense	32,000			
Rent expense	25,000			
Salaries expense	68,000			
Purchase discounts lost	1,000			
	657,800	657,800		
Depreciation expense			(a) 2,200	
Insurance expense			(b) 2,800	
			5,000	5,000

The completed Adjustments columns have been included in the work sheet to minimize the detail work involved. These adjustments were derived from the following information available at December 31.

a. Depreciation expense for the year on equipment, $2,200.

b. Insurance premiums expired during the year, $2,800.

A physical inventory taken at December 31 showed the ending inventory to be $66,000.

a. Prepare a 10-column work sheet following the format illustrated in this appendix. Include at the bottom of the work sheet a legend consisting of a brief explanation keyed to each adjusting entry.

b. Prepare the two journal entries needed to adjust the accounts at December 31.

c. Prepare the necessary journal entries to close the accounts on December 31.

PROBLEM A-4
Preparing a Work Sheet,
Adjusting Entries, and Closing
Entries

Shown below is a trial balance prepared from the ledger of Western Supply at December 31, 19__. The accounts are maintained on a calendar-year basis and are adjusted and closed annually.

<table>
<tr><td colspan="3" align="center">WESTERN SUPPLY
Trial Balance
December 31, 19__</td></tr>
<tr><td>Cash ....</td><td align="right">$ 16,300</td><td></td></tr>
<tr><td>Accounts receivable ....</td><td align="right">49,200</td><td></td></tr>
<tr><td>Inventory (Jan. 1, 19__) ....</td><td align="right">62,000</td><td></td></tr>
<tr><td>Unexpired insurance ....</td><td align="right">1,800</td><td></td></tr>
<tr><td>Office supplies ....</td><td align="right">800</td><td></td></tr>
<tr><td>Land ....</td><td align="right">17,000</td><td></td></tr>
<tr><td>Building ....</td><td align="right">60,000</td><td></td></tr>
<tr><td>Accumulated depreciation: building ....</td><td></td><td align="right">$ 2,400</td></tr>
<tr><td>Equipment ....</td><td align="right">16,000</td><td></td></tr>
<tr><td>Accumulated depreciation: equipment ......</td><td></td><td align="right">4,800</td></tr>
<tr><td>Accounts payable ....</td><td></td><td align="right">47,900</td></tr>
<tr><td>Mary Lane, capital ....</td><td></td><td align="right">99,500</td></tr>
<tr><td>Mary Lane, drawing ....</td><td align="right">18,000</td><td></td></tr>
<tr><td>Sales ....</td><td></td><td align="right">326,000</td></tr>
<tr><td>Sales returns & allowances ....</td><td align="right">4,100</td><td></td></tr>
<tr><td>Sales discounts ....</td><td align="right">1,100</td><td></td></tr>
<tr><td>Purchases ....</td><td align="right">190,000</td><td></td></tr>
<tr><td>Purchase returns & allowances ....</td><td></td><td align="right">2,000</td></tr>
<tr><td>Purchase discounts lost ....</td><td align="right">400</td><td></td></tr>
<tr><td>Transportation-in ....</td><td align="right">4,800</td><td></td></tr>
<tr><td>Salaries and wages expense ....</td><td align="right">40,000</td><td></td></tr>
<tr><td>Property taxes expense ....</td><td align="right">1,100</td><td></td></tr>
<tr><td></td><td align="right">$482,600</td><td align="right">$482,600</td></tr>
</table>

OTHER DATA

a. Examination of policies showed $600 *unexpired* insurance on December 31.
b. Office supplies on hand at December 31 were estimated to amount to $300.
c. The building is being depreciated over a 25-year useful life. The equipment is being depreciated over a 10-year useful life.
d. Accrued salaries payable as of December 31 were $5,000.
e. Inventory of merchandise on December 31 was $44,600.

INSTRUCTIONS

a. Prepare a 10-column work sheet at December 31, 19__.
b. Prepare adjusting entries.
c. Prepare closing entries.

CHAPTER 6

Accounting Systems, Internal Control, and Audits

Accounting systems keep getting faster and easier to operate—and they provide greater amounts of useful information. Point-of-sale terminals, for example, can record merchandise sales at the rate of several thousand items per hour. They also can identify products that are selling quickly or slowly and measure departmental sales, cost of goods sold, and profit margins. And they do all of this without the need for highly trained accounting personnel. Today's accounting systems give decision makers access to a "world of information."

1. Explain why accounting systems vary from one organization to the next.
2. Define special journals and explain their usefulness.
3. Describe a database.
4. State the objectives of internal control.
5. Discuss means of achieving internal control.
6. Distinguish between employee fraud and management fraud.
7. Distinguish among audits, reviews, and compilations of financial statements.
8. Describe the nature and purpose of operational and compliance auditing.

ACCOUNTING SYSTEMS

LO 1: Explain why accounting systems vary from one organization to the next.

An **accounting system** consists of the personnel, procedures, devices, forms, and records used by an organization to (1) develop accounting information, and (2) communicate this information to decision makers. The design and capabilities of these systems vary greatly from one organization to the next. In very small businesses, the accounting system may consist of little more than a cash register, a chequebook, and an annual trip to an income tax preparer. In large businesses, an accounting system includes computers, highly trained personnel, and accounting reports that affect the daily operations of every department. But in every case, the basic purpose of the accounting system remains the same: ***to meet the organization's needs for accounting information as efficiently as possible.***

Many factors affect the structure of the accounting system within a particular organization. Among the most important are (1) the company's ***needs for accounting information,*** and (2) the ***cost*** of producing accounting information.

Determining Information Needs

The types of accounting information that a company must develop vary with such factors as the size of the organization, whether it is publicly owned, and the philosophy of management. The need for some types of accounting information may be prescribed by law. For example, income tax regulations require every business to have an accounting system that can measure the company's taxable income and explain the nature and source of every item in the company's income tax return. Corporate and securities laws require publicly owned companies to prepare financial statements in conformity with generally accepted accounting principles. These statements must be filed with the regulatory authorities and distributed to shareholders.

Other types of accounting information are required as matters of practical necessity. For example, every business needs to know the amounts receivable from each customer and the amounts owed to each creditor.

Although much accounting information clearly is essential to business operations, management still has many choices as to the types and amount of accounting information to be developed. For example, should the accounting system of a department store measure separately the sales of each department and of different types of merchandise? The answer to such questions depends upon **_how useful_** management considers the information to be, and also the **_cost_** of developing the information.

The Cost of Producing Accounting Information

Accounting systems should be **cost effective**—that is, the value of the information produced should exceed the cost of producing it. Management has no choice but to produce the types of accounting reports required by law. In other cases, however, management may use **_cost effectiveness_** as the criterion for deciding whether or not to produce the information.[1]

In recent years, the development and installation of computer-based accounting systems have increased greatly the types and amount of accounting information that can be produced in a cost-effective manner.

Basic Functions of an Accounting System

In developing information about the financial position of a business and the results of its operations, every accounting system performs the following basic functions:

1. **_Identify, measure, and record_** the effects of business transactions.
2. **_Classify_** the effects of similar transactions in a manner that permits determination of the various **_totals_** and **_subtotals_** useful to management and used in accounting reports.
3. **_Summarize, interpret, and communicate_** the data contained in the system to decision makers.

The differences in accounting systems arise primarily in the manner and speed with which these functions are performed.

In our illustrations, we often assume the use of a simple manual accounting system. In this system, transactions are recorded in a general journal and classified in both general and subsidiary ledger accounts. Such a system is useful in illustrating basic accounting concepts, but it is too slow and cumbersome to meet the needs of most business organizations. In a large business, transactions may occur at a rate of several hundred or several thousand per hour. To keep pace with such a rapid flow of accounting information, these companies must use accounting systems that are largely computer-based.

Many small businesses continue to use manual accounting systems, but they modify these systems to meet their needs as efficiently as possible.

Who Designs and Installs Accounting Systems?

The design and installation of accounting systems is a specialized field. It involves not just accounting, but expertise in management, information systems, marketing, and—in many cases—computer programming. Thus, accounting systems generally are designed and installed by a team of people with many specialized talents.

---

[1]The CICA's Accounting Standards Board specifically considers cost effectiveness in the formulation of new accounting principles. The Board also has eliminated some reporting requirements for which it viewed the cost of compliance as exceeding the benefits. See *CICA Handbook,* CICA (Toronto), section 1000.16.

Large businesses have a staff of systems analysts, internal auditors, accountants, and other professionals who work full time in designing and improving the accounting system. Medium-size companies often hire a public accounting firm to design or update their systems. Small businesses with limited resources usually purchase one of the many "packaged" accounting systems designed for small companies in their line of business. These packaged systems are available through office supply stores, computer stores, and software manufacturers.

We will now address the challenge of streamlining an accounting system to meet the needs of the organization as quickly and efficiently as possible.

Recording Transactions: The Need for Special Journals

LO 2: Define special journals and explain their usefulness.

A *journal* sometimes is called the "book of original entry" because it is the accounting record in which the effects of transactions are *first recorded.* In preceding chapters, we have used a two-column **general journal** to illustrate the recording of transactions. But journals come in many different forms.

Characteristics of a General Journal   The general journal is unique among journals because it can be used to record *any type* of business transaction. The flexibility of a general journal makes it ideal for textbook illustrations. However, this flexibility also makes the general journal a relatively *inefficient* device for recording large numbers of routine transactions.

Recording all transactions in a general journal simply is not cost effective. First, every entry in a general journal involves quite a bit of writing—a date, at least two account titles, two dollar amounts, and a written explanation. Also, if all types of business transactions are to be recorded in this journal, the person maintaining the journal must be a highly skilled accountant. For an accounting system to be cost effective, *routine transactions must be recorded by clerical personnel or by machines*—not by professional accountants.

Special Journals   Most businesses are able to speed up and simplify the recording process by designing various **special journals**. Each special journal is an accounting record or device that is designed for quickly and efficiently recording *one particular type* of transaction. The people maintaining these journals need not be experts in accounting; they need only know how to record one type of transaction.

Two concepts enter into the design of an efficient special journal. First, the person recording the transaction should have to enter *as little data as possible.* Second, the recording of transactions should be *combined with other essential business activities* in a manner that minimizes the time and effort involved in accounting functions.

"RRRrrrring!" It's a Special Journal   The old-fashioned mechanical cash register provides a familiar example of a special journal. As the salesclerk or cashier "rings up" each cash sale, the dollar amount is printed on a tape within the cash register. This tape provides a record of each sale.

Let us quickly identify some of the ways in which cash registers reduce the time and cost of recording transactions. First, notice that ***no accounting personnel*** are involved in recording the numerous cash sales. The transactions are recorded by the company's salesclerks as they accept payment from customers and make change. A business may have many cash registers. Thus, ***many people*** can participate simultaneously in the recording of transactions.

Also notice how quickly transactions are recorded. The only data that the salesclerk records on a cash register is the dollar amount of the sale. Ledger account titles and written explanations are unnecessary, because ***every*** transaction recorded on the register is a cash sale.

The use of a cash register also saves time in posting the effects of transactions to the ledger. At the end of each day, only the ***total*** appearing at the end of the register tape is posted to the ledger (as a debit to Cash and a credit to Sales). This total amount may represent the overall effects of hundreds—perhaps thousands—of individual transactions.[2]

Point-of-Sale Terminals: More Efficient Special Journals   Modern point-of-sale terminals (cash registers tied directly to computer systems) are even more efficient than the old-fashioned registers. With a point-of-sale terminal, data entry is reduced to a minimum and the need for manual posting is eliminated entirely. The salesclerk must only pass the merchandise over an optical scanner. The scanner reads a "product code" attached to the merchandise and enters the code into the computer system. Using this product code, the computer determines the cost and sales price of the merchandise from computer-based files, records the sale and the cost of goods sold, and updates both the general ledger and the inventory subsidiary ledger.

When sales are made on account, the salesclerk records the credit card number by either "reading" the credit card with the scanner or by entering the customer's credit card number into the terminal. This number identifies the customer to the computer, and the computer automatically updates the customer's account in the company's accounts receivable subsidiary ledger.

On-Line, Real-Time (OLRT) Systems

There normally is ***some delay*** between the time a transaction occurs and the time that its effects are entered in the company's ledger accounts. In manual accounting systems—and many computer-based systems—sales transactions are not posted until the end of the day. Payroll data generally are recorded only at the end of each pay period. If accounting information is required only at periodic intervals (such as month-end), these short delays may be of no consequence.

---

[2]Most cash registers also permit the recording of sales on account. Credit sales are accumulated separately on the register tape, and the daily total is posted as a debit to Accounts Receivable and a credit to Sales. In recording a credit sale, the salesclerk must record the customer's account number as well as the dollar amount of the sale. The customer's account number is needed for updating the accounts receivable subsidiary ledger.

In some cases, however, managers and employees need information that is completely up-to-date. Bank tellers, for example, often need to know the current balance in a customer's bank account. Airline ticket salespeople need up-to-date information about the number of seats still available on specific flights. Salesclerks may need to know how many units of a particular product are in stock.

An **on-line, real-time (OLRT)** accounting system has the ability to keep certain accounting records ***completely current.*** As a practical matter, OLRT systems must be computer-based. The phrase "on-line" refers to input devices and output devices with ***direct and immediate access*** to the computer-based records. "Real-time" means ***now,*** reflecting the idea that the records are up-to-date.

In an OLRT system, some types of transactions are recorded ***as they occur.*** Managers and employees then may use computer terminals to view up-to-date information. The following diagram illustrates the traditional and OLRT approaches to recording and receiving accounting information.

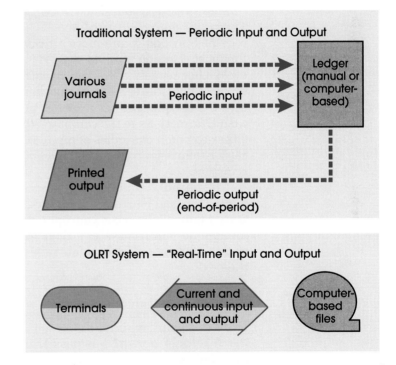

Point-of-sale terminals are examples of on-line input devices. When sales are recorded on these terminals, the general ledger and subsidiary ledger accounts may be updated immediately. Thus, managers and employees may use computer terminals to access up-to-date information about sales, inventories, and accounts receivable. (Notice that point-of-sale terminals are located on the sales floor, not in the accounting department. If transactions are to be recorded as they occur, the input devices must be located where these transactions take place.)

Even in a system with OLRT capabilities, ***not all*** accounting records are kept continuously up-to-date. Depreciation expense, for example, is recorded only at the end of each accounting period. Many other expenses, such as utility bills, are recorded only as bills are received (or as payment is made). The accounting records that are kept continuously up-to-date usually are limited to the general and subsidiary ledger accounts for cash, accounts receivable, inventory, accounts payable, cost of goods sold, and sales revenue.

Other Types of Automated Special Journals   We have emphasized the point-of-sale terminals often used in retail stores; however, many other businesses also record their routine transactions in a highly automated manner. On-line terminals are widely used by banks (for recording deposits and withdrawals) and by airlines (for recording ticket sales). The gas, electric, and water meters attached to buildings also are types of special journals. These meters automatically record the utility companies' credit sales to individual customers. In the future, such meters may become on-line input devices.

Manual Special Journals   Not all special journals are automated devices. There are many *manual* special journals, in which transactions can be recorded far faster and more efficiently than in a general journal. Perhaps the most common manual special journal is the *cheque register,* found in every chequebook. A cheque register can be used for efficiently recording every cash disbursement as the cheque is being issued. If maintained properly, the cheque register provides all of the information needed for posting cash transactions to the company's general and subsidiary ledger accounts. Other common examples of manual special journals include sales journals, cash receipts journals, purchases journals, voucher registers, and payroll registers.

In Appendix B (following this chapter) we illustrate a "typical" set of manual special journals for a merchandising business. These journals illustrate many of the basic concepts often used to increase the efficiency of a manual accounting system. Bear in mind, however, that both the number and the formats of special journals vary significantly from one business to the next.

Recording Budgeted Amounts

Up to this point, we have discussed recording in the accounting system only the results of *actual* business transactions. Many businesses also enter into their accounting system forecasts (or budgets) of the levels of activity *expected in future periods.* Often, separate budgets are developed for each department within the business. As the actual results are recorded in the system, reports are prepared showing the *differences* between the forecasts and the actual results. These reports aid managers in evaluating departmental performance.

Classifying and Storing the Recorded Data

Two methods of classifying and storing data in accounting systems are in widespread use: *ledger accounts* and *computer databases.*

Ledger Accounts

In both manual and computer-based accounting systems, the effects of business transactions are classified in terms of the company's chart of ledger accounts. A **chart of accounts** is simply a *listing* of the ledger account titles used by the business.

In designing the ledger of a given business, questions arise as to the *extent of detail* needed in the chart of accounts. For example, should one ledger account be used for advertising expense, or should separate accounts be maintained for newspaper advertising, direct mail advertising, and television advertising?

The extent of detail needed in the chart of accounts depends upon the *types of information that management considers useful.* The information appearing in financial statements and income tax returns is highly summarized. Therefore, the preparation of these types of reports does *not* require a highly detailed chart of accounts. Management, however, usually finds more detailed accounting information useful in planning and controlling business operations. For example, management may want separate information about the revenue and expenses of *each department* within the business.

The chart of revenue and expense accounts often is designed along lines of **managerial responsibility.** Thus, the chart of accounts may include separate revenue and expenses for each department (or other area of managerial responsibility). This **responsibility accounting system** provides top management with information useful in evaluating the performance of individual departments and of department managers.

A general ledger with a great many accounts would quickly become unwieldy and difficult to use. Therefore, the accounts showing a detailed "breakdown" of specific assets, liabilities, revenue, and expenses usually are placed in a *subsidiary ledger.* Only the related *controlling account* appears in the general ledger.

Database Systems

A **database** provides greater flexibility in the classification of data than even the most detailed chart of ledger accounts. When transaction data are stored in a database, they may be sorted according to a variety of criteria.

LO 3: Describe a database.

A database consists of *unclassified* data, which have not yet been grouped into categories. However, the data are accompanied by various classification *codes.* Each of these codes enables the computer quickly to classify (or "sort") the data according to different characteristics—or combinations of characteristics.

The Operation of a Database We will use the sales transactions of a department store to illustrate the concepts of a database and of "coded" transaction data. Assume that our store has several different sales departments, such as appliances, furniture, men's clothing, shoes, women's clothing, etc. Sales transactions are recorded at on-line point-of-sale terminals located in each sales department.

The first step in designing a database is to determine the alternative ways in which the transaction data might be used. This determines the *output requirements* of the system. Assume that the management of our department store wants the following types of information:

Output Requirements

1. *Continuously up-to-date general ledger accounts for Cash, Accounts Receivable, Inventory, Sales, and the Cost of Goods Sold.*
2. *Continuously up-to-date subsidiary ledgers for inventory and accounts receivable.*
3. *Daily sales reports for the store manager showing the sales of each department.*
4. *Weekly sales reports for the store's merchandise buyers showing by product the number of units sold during the week.*

To provide these types of information, the accounting system must be able to classify (or sort) sales transaction data by (1) general ledger accounts, (2) customer, (3) sales department, and (4) product.

In recording each transaction, the salesperson enters into the computer terminal a *product code* identifying each item sold. If the merchandise is sold on account, the salesperson also must enter the customer's account number in the accounts receivable subsidiary ledger. (If no customer account number is entered, the computer interprets the transaction as a cash sale.)

Very little time is required for the salesperson to enter these codes. In a computerized system, product codes can be entered automatically merely by passing the merchandise over an optical scanner. To record customers' account numbers, the salesperson may either pass the customer's credit card through an electronic device, or enter the customer's account number on a keyboard. Thus, each sales transaction can be recorded in a few seconds.

"Fields" of Information   The data sent to the computer includes several *information fields.* In our example, these fields are (1) the product code, and (2) (for credit sales) the customer's account number. Using the product code, the computer scans its files and automatically completes several other fields of information, such as sales price, unit cost, and the transaction date. All of the information fields are stored together as one "coded transaction."

Data Are Classified as Output Is Prepared   By looking at different information fields, the computer can now sort transaction data according to different criteria. Data may be classified by any field or combination of fields. For example, sales transactions may be sorted by department, by product, or by customer.

In addition, the computer can sort the data in many other ways that may prove useful to management. For example, the system in our example can generate daily information about departmental profit margins (departmental revenue, less departmental cost of goods sold). Or, it can help management evaluate the effectiveness of advertising campaigns by tracking the daily sales volume of the advertised products.

Comparison of Ledger Accounts to a Database

In a ledger-based system, the effects of transactions are classified in terms of specific ledger accounts *at the time transactions are recorded.* In a database, the effects of transactions are stored in an *unclassified format,* but are "coded" so that the computer can sort through the data and find the items that meet various criteria. Thus, data is classified as necessary to meet requests for specific types of accounting reports. The basic differences between ledger account systems and a database are illustrated below:

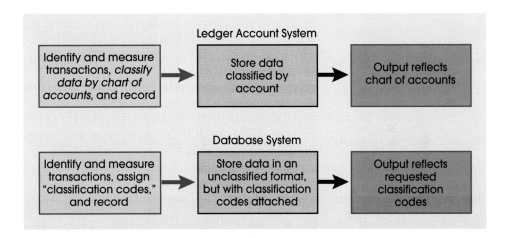

It is important to recognize that a database is *not a substitute* for a ledger. Rather, databases are used to provide management and employees with *additional information* about certain types of transactions.

To meet financial reporting requirements, the effects of all business transactions *must* be classified along the lines of a chart of ledger account. Therefore, even when a database is in use, all transaction data normally are posted to ledger accounts. Certain types of transactions *also* are entered into the database—but only those transactions that management wants to be able to sort in a variety of ways. The types of transactions entered into a database usually include only revenue, expenses, cash receipts, and cash payments.

Summarizing and Communicating Accounting Information

In general terms, the usefulness of accounting information to decision makers depends upon (1) the *relevance* of the information to the decisions at hand, (2) the *timeliness* of the information, and (3) its *reliability.* At this point, we will discuss only the first two factors—the relevance and timeliness of accounting information. The third factor—reliability—is closely related to the topics of internal control and audits of financial statements. These topics are discussed later in this chapter.

Both the relevance and timeliness of accounting information have been enhanced greatly by recent advances in the technologies of computers and communication. Database systems permit the preparation of accounting reports ***tailored to the immediate needs*** of decision makers. Computers can prepare accounting reports almost instantly. Through computer networks, electronic mail, facsimile machines, and communication satellites, these reports can be transmitted quickly anywhere in the world. In OLRT systems, decision makers may use computer terminals to access information that is ***completely current.*** Thus, advances in technology rapidly are increasing the usefulness of accounting information.

Comparison of Manual and Computer-Based Systems

In the following table, we briefly summarize the differences between a simple manual accounting system (such as the one often used in our textbook illustrations) and a modern computer-based system. Notice that both types of system perform the same basic functions. The differences lie in the ***methods and devices*** used in performing these functions.

In years ahead, accounting systems will continue performing the functions listed in the left-hand column. The means of performing these functions are likely to change, however, as technological innovations occur in the fields of computers and communication.

Basic Functions of an Accounting System	Means of Performing These Functions		
	The manual system in our illustrations	A computer-based system in a modern business	Comments on the computer-based systems
Identifying, measuring, and recording effects of transactions	General journal (all transactions)	Special journals (routine transactions) General journal (unusual transactions) Some transactions recorded using on-line input devices	Special journals may be on-line and located at transaction sites Budgeted data may be entered for comparative purposes
Classifying and storing effects of transactions	Simple chart of ledger accounts Some use of subsidiary ledgers	Detailed chart of ledger accounts and a database Extensive use of subsidiary ledger	Database allows classification in many different ways Revenue and expenses often classified along lines of managerial responsibility
Summarizing, interpreting, and communicating accounting information	Periodic printed reports	Printed reports, and computer displays Some information up-to-date and accessible on-line	On-line data may be completely current

INTERNAL CONTROL

LO 4: State the objectives of internal control.

The need for internal control is common to all organizations. The term **internal control** refers to *all measures* (policies and procedures) taken by management to ensure that the organization (1) operates efficiently and effectively, (2) produces reliable financial information, and (3) complies with applicable laws and regulations. In short, internal control consists of those measures designed to keep the business operating "on track."

Collectively, the internal control policies and procedures in place within a given organization may be described as the *internal control structure,* or the *system* of internal control.

Components of Internal Control

There are two basic components of internal control: the control environment and the control systems.[3]

The *control environment* is the collective effect of various overall factors that establish, enhance, or reduce the effectiveness of specific control policies and procedures. It reflects the overall attitude, awareness, commitment, and action of the owners, management, board of directors (for companies organized as corporations), and others concerning the importance of control and the way it is used in the organization. The control environment consists of management philosophy and operating style, the functioning of management (such as the board of directors), organizational structure, personnel policies and practices, methods of assigning authority and responsibility, management control methods, systems development methodology, the internal audit function, and management reaction to external influences.

The *control systems* are the policies and procedures used to "collect, record and process data and report the resulting information or enhance the reliability of such data and information."[4] The former is essentially the accounting system. The latter relates to the (1) proper authorization of transactions and activities, (2) appropriate segregation of duties, (3) adequate documentation and records, (4) effective safeguards over access to and use of assets and records, and (5) independent checks on performance and proper valuation of recorded amounts.

Virtually every organization—small or large—needs to establish control policies and procedures in each of these areas. The nature of these policies and procedures, however, *varies greatly* from one organization to the next. Internal control is not an "end in itself." Like an accounting system, an internal control structure should be *cost effective*—that is, the policies and procedures employed to achieve internal control should never cost more than the benefits derived.

Guidelines for Achieving Strong Internal Control

Establish Clear Lines of Responsibility   Every organization should indicate clearly the persons or departments responsible for such functions as sales, purchasing, receiving incoming shipments, paying bills, and maintaining

LO 5: Discuss means of achieving internal control.

---

[3]CICA, *CICA Handbook* (Toronto), section 5200.10
[4]Ibid., section 5200.13

accounting records. The lines of authority and responsibility can be shown in an ***organization chart.*** (A partial organization chart of a business organized as a corporation appears on the following page.) The organization chart should be supported by written job descriptions and by procedures manuals that explain in detail the authority and responsibilities of each person or department appearing in the chart.

Establish Routine Procedures for Processing Each Type of Transaction If management is to direct the activities of a business according to plan, every transaction should go through four separate steps: It should be ***authorized, approved, executed,*** and ***recorded.*** For example, consider the sale of merchandise on credit. Top management has the authority and responsibility to authorize credit sales to categories of customers who meet certain standards. The credit department is responsible for approving a credit sale of a given dollar amount to a particular customer. The transaction is executed by the shipping department, which ships or delivers the merchandise to the customer. Finally, the transaction is recorded in the accounting department by an entry debiting Accounts Receivable and crediting Sales.

Subdivision of Duties Perhaps the most important concept in achieving internal control is an appropriate subdivision—or segregation—of duties. Responsibilities should be assigned so that ***no one person or department handles a transaction completely from beginning to end.*** When duties are divided in this manner, the work of one employee serves to verify that of another and any errors that occur tend to be detected promptly.

To illustrate this concept, let us review the typical procedures followed by a wholesaler in processing a credit sale. The sales department of the company is responsible for securing the order from the customer; the credit department must approve the customer's credit before the order is filled; the stock room assembles the goods ordered; the shipping department packs and ships the goods; the billing department prepares the sales invoice; and the accounting department records the transaction.

Each department receives written evidence of the action by the other departments and reviews the documents describing the transaction to see that the actions taken correspond in all details. The shipping department, for instance, does not release the merchandise until after the credit department has approved the customer as a credit risk. The accounting department does not record the sale until it has received documentary evidence that (1) an order was received from a customer, (2) the extension of credit was approved, (3) the merchandise was shipped to the customer, and (4) a sales invoice was prepared and mailed to the customer.

Accounting Function Separate from Custody of Assets Basic to the separation of duties is the concept that an employee who has custody of an asset (or access to an asset) should not maintain the accounting record for that asset. If one person has custody of assets and also maintains the accounting records, there is both opportunity and incentive to falsify the records to conceal a shortage. However, the person with custody of the asset will not be inclined to waste it, steal it, or give it away if he or she is aware that another employee is maintaining a record of the asset.

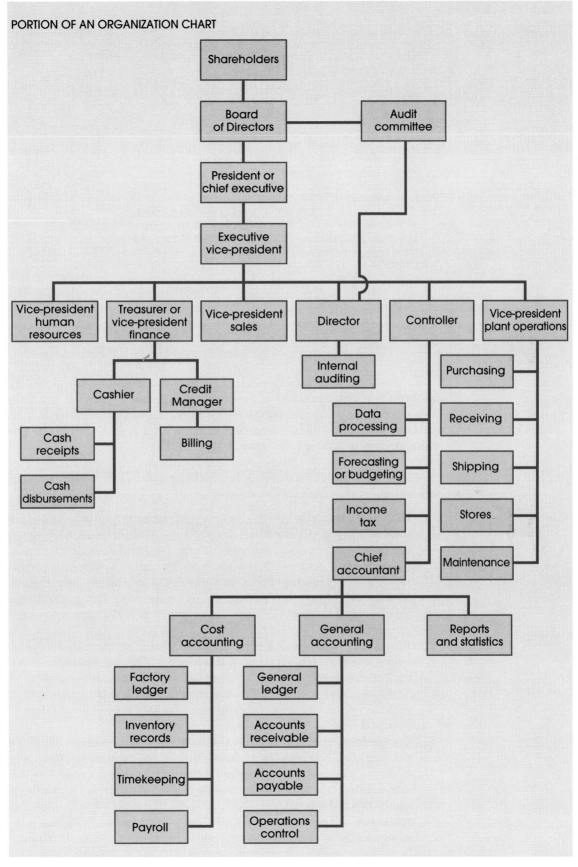

PORTION OF AN ORGANIZATION CHART

309

The following diagram illustrates how this separation of duties contributes to strong internal control.

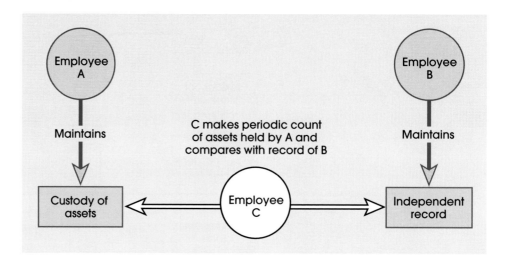

In this diagram Employee A has custody of assets and Employee B maintains an accounting record of the assets. Employee C periodically counts the assets and compares the count with the record maintained by B. This comparison should reveal any errors made by either A or B unless the two have collaborated to conceal an error or irregularity.

Other Steps Toward Achieving Internal Control   Other important internal control measures include the following:

1. *Internal auditing.* Virtually every *large* organization has an internal auditing staff. The objectives of the **internal auditors** are to monitor and improve internal control. Internal auditors test and evaluate internal controls in all areas of the organization and prepare reports to top management on their findings and recommendations. Much work of internal auditors may be described as *operational and compliance auditing.* These types of audits are discussed later in this chapter.
2. *Financial forecasts.* A plan of operations is prepared each year setting goals for each division of the business, as, for example, the expected volume of sales, amounts of expenses, and future cash balances. *Actual* results are compared with *forecast* amounts month by month. This comparison strengthens control because variations from planned results are investigated promptly.
3. *Competent personnel.* Even the best-designed internal control will not work well unless the people using it are competent. Competence of employees is in part developed through training programs, but it is also related to the policies for selection of personnel and to the adequacy of supervision.
4. *Rotation of employees.* The rotation of employees from one job assignment to another may strengthen internal control. When

employees know that another person will soon be taking over their duties, they are more likely to maintain records with care and to follow established procedures. The rotation of employees also may bring to light errors or irregularities caused by the employee formerly performing a given task.

5. ***Serially numbered documents.*** Documents such as cheques, purchase orders, and sales invoices should be serially numbered. If a document is misplaced or concealed, the break in the sequence of numbers will call attention to the missing item.

The Role of Business Documents

We have made the point that strong internal control requires subdivision of duties among the departments of the business. How does each department know that the other departments have fulfilled their responsibilities? The answer lies in the use of carefully designed ***business documents.*** Some of the more important business documents used in controlling purchases of merchandise are summarized below:

Business Document	Initiated by	Sent to
Purchase requisition Issued when quantity of goods on hand falls below established reorder point	Departmental sales managers or stores department	Original to purchasing department, copy to accounting department
Purchase order Issued when order is placed; indicates type, quantities, and prices of merchandise ordered	Purchasing department	Original to selling company (vendor, supplier), copies to department requisitioning goods, the receiving department, and the accounting department
Invoice Confirms that goods have been shipped and requests payment	Seller (supplier)	Accounting department of buying company
Receiving report Based on count and inspection of goods received	Receiving department of buying company	Original to accounting department, copies to purchasing department and to department requisitioning goods
Invoice approval form Based upon the documents listed above; authorizes payment of the purchase invoice	Accounting department of buying company	Finance department, to support issuance of cheque; returned to accounting department with a copy of the cheque

Purchase Requisition   A purchase requisition is a request from the sales department or stores department (warehousing) for the purchasing department to order merchandise. Thus, the purchasing department is not authorized to order goods *unless it has first received a purchase requisition.* A copy of the purchase requisition is sent to the accounting department.

Purchase Orders   Once a purchase requisition has been received, the purchasing department determines the lowest-cost supplier of the merchandise and places an order. This order is documented in a **purchase order**. A purchase order issued by Fairway Pro Shop to Adams Manufacturing Company is illustrated below:

A serially numbered purchase order

PURCHASE ORDER	ORDER NO. 999

FAIRWAY PRO SHOP
10 Fairway Avenue, Toronto, Ontario

TO: _Adams Manufacturing Company_   DATE _November 10, 19___

19 Union Street   SHIP VIA _Jones Truck Co._

Vancouver, B.C.   TERMS: _2/10, n/30_

PLEASE ENTER OUR ORDER FOR THE FOLLOWING:

QUANTITY	DESCRIPTION	PRICE	TOTAL
15 sets	Model S irons	$120.00	$1,800.00
50 dozen	X3Y Shur-Par golf balls	14.00	700.00
			$2,500.00

FAIRWAY PRO SHOP

BY ___DD McCarthy___

Several copies of a purchase order are usually prepared. The original is sent to the supplier; it constitutes an authorization to deliver the merchandise and to submit a bill based on the prices listed. A second copy is sent to the department that initiated the purchase requisition to show that the requisition has been acted upon. The third copy (without showing the quantity ordered) is sent to the receiving department awaiting the arrival of the goods. The final copy is sent to the accounting department of the buying company.

The issuance of a purchase order does not call for any entries in the accounting records of either the prospective buyer or seller. The company that receives an order does not consider that a sale has been made *until the merchandise is delivered.* At that point ownership of the goods changes, and both buyer and seller should make accounting entries to record the transaction.

Invoices   When a manufacturer or wholesaler receives an order for its products, it takes two actions. One is to ship the goods to the customer and the other is to send the customer an **invoice**. By the act of shipping the merchandise, the seller is giving up ownership of one type of asset, inventory; by issuing the invoice, the seller is recording ownership of another form of asset, an account receivable.

An invoice contains a description of the goods being sold, the quantities, prices, credit terms, and method of shipment. The illustration below shows an invoice issued by Adams Manufacturing Company in response to the previously illustrated purchase order from Fairway Pro Shop.

Invoice is basis for accounting entry

	INVOICE		INVOICE NO. 782

ADAMS MANUFACTURING COMPANY

19 UNION STREET

VANCOUVER, B.C.

SOLD TO: <u>Fairway Pro Shop</u>   INVOICE DATE <u>November 15, 19__</u>

<u>10 Fairway Avenue</u>   YOUR PURCHASE ORDER NO. <u>999</u>

<u>Toronto, Ontario</u>   DATE SHIPPED <u>November 15, 19__</u>

SHIPPED TO: <u>Same</u>   SHIPPED VIA <u>Jones Truck Co.</u>

TERMS <u>2/10, n/30</u>

QUANTITY	DESCRIPTION	PRICE	TOTAL
15 sets	Model S irons	$120.00	$1,800.00
50 dozen	X3Y Shur-Par golf balls	14.00	700.00
			$2,500.00

From the viewpoint of the seller, an invoice is a ***sales invoice;*** from the buyer's viewpoint it is a ***purchase invoice.*** The invoice is the basis for an entry in the accounting records of ***both*** the seller and the buyer because it evidences the ***transfer of ownership of goods.*** At the time of issuing the invoice, the selling company makes an entry debiting Accounts Receivable and crediting Sales. The buying company, however, does not record the invoice as a liability until the invoice has been approved for payment.

Receiving Report   Evidence that the merchandise has been received in good condition is obtained from the receiving department. The receiving department receives all incoming goods, inspects them as to the description (by comparing with the purchase order), quality, and condition, and determines the quantities received by counting, measuring, or weighing. The receiving department then prepares a serially numbered report for each shipment received; one copy of this **receiving report** is sent to the accounting department for use in approving the invoice for payment.

Invoice Approval Form   The approval of the invoice in the accounting department is accomplished by comparing the purchase requisition, the purchase order, the invoice, and the receiving report. Comparison of these documents establishes that the merchandise described in the invoice was actually ordered, has been received in good condition, and was billed at the prices specified in the purchase order.

The person who performs these comparisons then records the liability (debit Inventory, credit Accounts Payable) and signs an **invoice approval form** authorizing payment of the invoice by the finance department. (One type of invoice approval form, called a *voucher,* is discussed further in Chapter 7.)

As explained in Chapter 5, many companies follow a policy of recording purchases at *net cost*—that is, the invoice price less any available cash discount. This internal control policy requires the use of a Purchase Discounts Lost account that will call management's attention to any failures to take advantage of available cash discounts.

Debit and Credit Memoranda (Debit Memos, Credit Memos)   If merchandise purchased on account is unsatisfactory and is to be returned to the supplier (or if a price reduction is agreed upon), a **debit memorandum** may be prepared by the purchasing company and sent to the supplier. The debit memorandum informs the supplier that the buyer has debited (reduced) its liability to the supplier and explains the circumstances.

Upon being informed of the return of damaged merchandise (or having agreed to a reduction in price), the seller will send the buyer a **credit memorandum** indicating that the account receivable from the buyer has been credited (reduced).

Notice that issuing a credit memorandum has the same effect upon a customer's account as does receiving payment from the customer—that is, the account receivable is credited (reduced). Thus, an employee with authority to issue credit memoranda *should not be allowed to handle cash receipts from customers.* If both of these duties were assigned to the same employee, that person could abstract some of the cash collected from customers and conceal this theft by issuing fictitious credit memoranda.

Internal Control in Computer-Based Systems

Computers do not eliminate the need for internal control. In fact, most recent cases of large-scale fraud have occurred in companies with computer-based accounting systems.

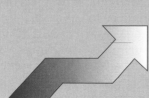

CASE IN POINT   An outside computer consultant for a major bank once used the bank's computer system to transfer $10 million of the bank's money into his personal account at another bank. The consultant's knowledge of the bank's computer system enabled him to commit this fraud. He had observed how bank employees used the computer to make legitimate transfers of funds. In addition, he had noticed that the "secret" computer codes used in these transfers were posted on the wall next to the computer terminal.

Despite the preceding CASE IN POINT, computer-based accounting systems lend themselves well to the implementation of internal control procedures. One such procedure is the use of *access codes,* or passwords, which limit access to the accounting system to authorized users. Access controls also *identify the user* responsible for each entry. (Obviously, these access codes should not be posted on the wall.)

In fact, computer-based accounting systems create many opportunities for implementing internal control procedures that might not be practical in a manual accounting system.

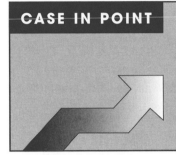

CASE IN POINT

When on-line terminals are used in recording credit sales, the salesperson enters the customer's credit card number into the system. The computer then determines whether the proposed sales transaction will cause the customer's account balance to exceed any predetermined credit limit. Also, the computer compares the customer's card number with a list of credit cards reported lost or stolen. If either of these procedures indicates that credit should not be extended to this customer, the computer immediately notifies the salesperson not to make the sale.

Limitations of Internal Control

Although internal control is highly effective in increasing the reliability of accounting data and in safeguarding assets, no internal control provides *complete* protection against fraud, theft, or errors. For example, controls based upon a subdivision of duties may be defeated—at least temporarily—by *collusion* among two or more employees. Carelessness also may cause a breakdown in internal control. Moreover, management can override internal control.

In designing internal control, the question of cost cannot be ignored. Internal control should be *cost effective.* A control that is too elaborate may entail greater expense than is justified by the protection gained.

Internal control is more difficult to achieve in a small business than in a large one. In a business with only a few employees, it may not be possible to arrange an adequate subdivision of duties. Also, such internal control features as an internal audit staff simply may not be practical.

An essential element of maintaining a reasonable degree of internal control in a small business is *active participation by the owner* in strategic control procedures. For example, the owner of a small business often is the only person authorized to sign cheques. The owner also may count the cash receipts at the end of each business day, and assume responsibility for depositing these receipts in the bank.

In summary, internal control—like an accounting system—should be *tailored to meet the specific needs of the organization.*

Prevention of Fraud

Perhaps the most highly publicized objective of internal control is the prevention of fraud. **Fraud** may be defined as the deliberate misrepresentation of facts with the *intent of deceiving* someone. If the purpose of this deception is personal gain or causing harm to another, fraud may be a criminal act. In discussing the role of the internal control in preventing acts of fraud, it is useful to distinguish between **errors** in the accounting records and **irregularities**.

Accountants use the term **_errors_** in reference to **_unintentional mistakes. Irregularities,_** on the other hand, refers to **_intentional_** mistakes, entered into accounting records or accounting reports for some fraudulent purpose. Irregularities may be further subdivided into the classifications of **employee fraud** and **management fraud**.

CASE IN POINT	The significance of fraud to Canadian business is dramatically illustrated by a recent survey of business executives made by KPMG, an international accounting firm. Some of the more significant results are summarized below:

- Fifty-six % of the businesses responding to the survey had experienced a fraud in the past year, costing over $50 million in losses.
- The most common types of fraud were misappropriation of funds, manipulation of expense accounts, and cheque forgery.
- In over 50% of the cases, **_poor internal controls_** allowed the fraud to occur.
- Internal control was the most common method in discovering fraud.

Employee Fraud

LO 6: Distinguish between employee fraud and management fraud.

Employee fraud refers to dishonest acts performed **_against the company_** by its employees. Examples of employee fraud include theft of assets, charging lower sales prices to favoured customers, receiving "kickbacks" from suppliers, overstating hours worked, "padding" expense accounts, and embezzlement. (**Embezzlement** is a theft of assets that is concealed by falsification of the accounting records.)

If one employee handles all aspects of a transaction, the danger of employee fraud increases. Studies of fraud cases suggest that individuals may be tempted into dishonest acts if given complete control of company property. Most of these persons, however, would not engage in fraud if doing so required collaboration with other employees. Thus, subdivision of duties is believed to reduce the risk of employee fraud.

In addition to subdivision of duties, the risk of employee fraud is reduced by such control procedures as investigating the backgrounds of job applicants, periodic rotation of employees to different job assignments, and frequent comparisons of assets actually on hand with the quantities shown in the accounting records.

Fidelity Bonds   No internal control can provide absolute protection against losses from dishonest employees. Therefore, many companies require that employees handling cash or other negotiable assets be **_bonded._** A **fidelity bond** is a type of insurance contract in which the bonding company agrees to reimburse an employer up to agreed dollar limits for losses caused by fraud or embezzlement by bonded employees.

Management Fraud

Management fraud refers to deliberate misrepresentations made by the ***top management*** of a business to persons **outside** of the business organization. This type of fraud often involves the issuance of fraudulent financial statements intended to mislead investors and creditors.

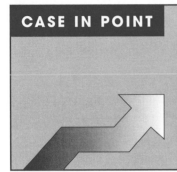

CASE IN POINT   The bankruptcy of Atlantic Acceptance Corporation Limited in 1965, then the sixth largest sales finance company in Canada, with assets of over $150,000,000, was caused mainly by management fraud. Both its assets and net income were greatly overstated over a twelve-year period. In addition, its president engaged in fraudulent actions against the company. The total loss to the shareholders and noteholders exceeded $60 million. It had a detrimental impact on the Canadian-owned finance companies because, after the Atlantic failure, they had more difficulty raising funds in the money market than the American-owned companies.

CASE IN POINT   Some years ago, the bankruptcy of Allied Crude Vegetable Oil Corporation stunned the financial world. Allied had borrowed money from 51 different companies and banks, using as collateral a huge inventory of salad oil. After the company's bankruptcy, investigators learned that much of Allied's "inventory" consisted of nothing more than forged warehouse receipts—inventory listed at $175 million in Allied's balance sheet simply did not exist.

Misuse of Company Assets   Another form of management fraud involves the misuse of company assets for the personal benefit of top management. The misuse of company assets may take many forms. Examples include excessive salaries to top managers and/or their relatives and allowing management to make extensive personal use of such company-owned assets as homes, yachts, and aircraft. Another area of possible abuse is fraudulently structured business transactions between the company and members of its top management.

The Impact of Management Fraud   Management fraud differs from employee fraud because top management is a ***willing participant*** in the fraudulent acts. A characteristic of management fraud is that management uses its position of trust and authority to ***override internal control*** and to enrich itself at the expense of the company and/or outsiders. The persons most often injured by management fraud are investors and creditors. However, the company's employees and customers and the general public also may be harmed severely.

The basic purpose of accounting is to aid decision makers in allocating and using economic resources efficiently. Cases of management fraud are far more destructive to this basic purpose than are most cases of employee fraud. The damage caused by employee fraud usually is limited to relatively small losses incurred by a specific company. Of course, these losses may be passed on to the company's customers in the form of higher prices. Seldom, however, does employee fraud force a business into bankruptcy or affect the efficient allocation of resources throughout the economy.

When the financial statements of large companies are altered to mislead investors and creditors, however, the resulting losses may be very substantial. In addition, the misallocation of economic resources may even affect the national economy.

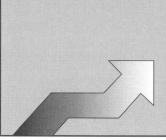

CASE IN POINT   Management fraud played a significant role in the savings and loan crisis in the United States. Some savings and loan companies falsified their accounting records and financial statements to conceal from investors and government regulators their deteriorating financial positions and management's misuse of company assets.

Ultimately, the savings and loan crisis may cost the American taxpayer—who insures deposits in these institutions—more than $500 billion. In addition, this crisis contributed to an economic recession, tax increases, the loss of many jobs, and a nationwide decline in real estate values.

Management fraud is **not** commonplace in our society. The managers and directors of most large business organizations are people of indisputable integrity. However, even a few isolated instances of management fraud can adversely affect the economy. Whenever a large publicly owned company engages in fraud, investors, creditors, and the public tend to lose confidence in the business community and the financial reporting process. This loss of confidence may create doubts and reservations that impede the efficient allocation of investment capital for many years.

Protecting Society from Management Fraud   Internal controls are not generally designed to protect outside decision makers from the possibility of management fraud. Internal controls are designed to assure *management* that the company's objectives are being met, including the generation of reliable financial information. However, top management may be able to override internal controls when it comes to reporting to individuals outside the organization.

One effective internal control over top management is active participation in the business by the company's *board of directors.* Many companies appoint an *audit committee* of the board of directors specifically to oversee the external financial reporting process of the company. In addition, an effective *internal auditing department* helps to prevent and detect management fraud, especially when it has direct access to the board of directors or its audit committee.

To engage in large-scale fraud, management generally must get lower level employees to "go along" with the scheme, often by intimidation. Specifically, many people in the company's accounting department may become aware of a large-scale fraud. Presumably, some of these people would refuse to participate in the fraud and would "blow the whistle" on a dishonest management.

Finally, *financial audits* by public accountants help to prevent and detect fraudulent financial statements before they are used by outside decision makers.

AUDITS

Audits of Financial Statements

LO 7: Distinguish among audits, reviews, and compilations of financial statements.

A **financial audit** is an examination of a company's financial statements performed by a firm of public accountants. The purpose of this audit is to provide people outside the organization with an *independent expert's opinion* as to whether the financial statements constitute a **fair presentation**. Auditors use the phrase "fair presentation" to describe financial statements that are in conformity with generally accepted accounting principles, that is, complete, unbiased, and reliable.

The Nature of a Financial Audit The financial statements of a business are *prepared by the company's management.* An audit of these financial statements is intended to bridge the "credibility gap" that otherwise might exist between the company's management and the users of these statements. For the auditors' opinion to have credibility, however, the **auditors** must (1) be independent of the company issuing the statements and of its management, and (2) have a sound basis for their opinion.

The concept of *independence* means that the auditors have no relationships with the company issuing the statements that might lessen the auditors' ability to render an unbiased opinion. Auditors not only must *be* independent; they also must *appear* to be independent of the issuing company. Otherwise, the users of financial statements may not have confidence in the auditors' report. The term **audit** describes the investigation that the auditors undertake to provide the "sound basis" for their opinion.

As part of a financial statement audit, the auditors consider and evaluate the internal control of the company issuing the statements. This evaluation gives them a "feel" for the accuracy and reliability of the information in the company's accounting system. Next, the auditors gather evidence to *substantiate every material item* appearing in the financial statements. For example, the auditors count portions of the company's inventory and compare these test counts with the company's inventory records. They also confirm some of the company's accounts receivable by verifying with customers the amounts actually owed. Auditors also perform procedures designed to determine that the statements and the accompanying notes are *complete.*

Auditors' Reports After completing the audit, the auditors express their expert opinion as to the fairness of the financial statements. This opinion is contained in the **auditors' report** that accompanies the financial statements whenever they are issued to decision makers outside of the business organization.

CASE IN POINT

Shown below is the auditors' report contained in a recent annual report of Hudson's Bay Company. The auditors, KPMG, are one of the "Big Five" international public accounting firms.*

---

*The "Big Five" are the world's five largest accounting firms. Only a large firm has the resources to audit a large corporation. Therefore, most publicly owned corporations are audited by one of the "Big Five" firms. In addition to Arthur Andersen & Co., the firms comprising the "Big Five" include (in alphabetical order): Deloitte & Touche, Ernst & Young, KPMG, and PricewaterhouseCoopers.

KPMG

AUDITORS' REPORT TO SHAREHOLDERS

We have audited the consolidated balance sheets of Hudson's Bay Company as at January 31, 1998 and January 31, 1997 and the consolidated statements of earnings, retained earnings and cash flows for the years then ended. These financial statements are the responsibility of the Company's management. Our responsibility is to express an opinion on these financial statements based on our audits.

We conducted our audits in accordance with generally accepted auditing standards. Those standards require that we plan and perform an audit to obtain reasonable assurance whether the financial statements are free of material misstatement. An audit includes examining, on a test basis, evidence supporting the amounts and disclosures in the financial statements. An audit also includes assessing the accounting principles used and significant estimates made by management, as well as evaluating the overall financial statement presentation.

In our opinion, these consolidated financial statements present fairly, in all material respects, the financial position of the Company as at January 31, 1998 and January 31, 1997 and the results of its operations and the changes in its financial position for the years then ended in accordance with generally accepted accounting principles.

KPMG

Chartered Accountants

Toronto, Canada
March 12, 1998

The illustrated report contains an **unqualified opinion**, meaning that KPMG regard Hudson's Bay's financial statements as a fair presentation. If the auditors **do not** consider the statements "fair," they modify their report to identify any shortcomings. Such modified reports are called either **qualified opinions** or **adverse opinions,** depending upon the extent of the auditors' reservations.

In practice, qualified and adverse opinions rarely are issued. Before issuing such a report, the auditors explain to management what changes should be made in the financial statements. Management usually makes these changes, as it is anxious to receive a "clean" (unqualified) auditor's report.[5]

Over many decades, audited financial statements have developed an excellent track record of reliability. Notice, however, that auditors do not **guarantee** the accuracy of financial statements. Rather, they render their professional **opinion** as to the overall "fairness" of the statements. Just as a physician may make an error in the diagnosis of a particular patient, there is always a possibility that an audit opinion may be in error.

The following diagram summarizes the relationships between the financial statements, an independent audit, and the auditors' report:

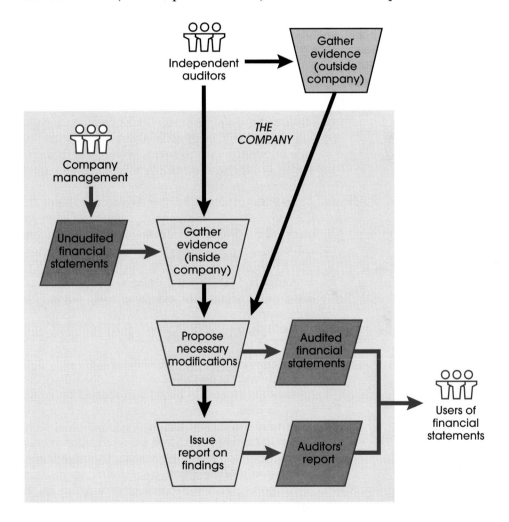

Audits and the Detection of Fraud   The primary purpose of financial audits is to determine the overall fairness of a set of financial statements, **not** to detect any and all acts of fraud. Users of financial statements should

---

[5]Securities regulatory authorities generally only accept an unqualified audit report for corporations listed on the stock exchange. See *National Policy No. 50,* issued by the provincial securities commissions.

recognize that auditors cannot guarantee that financial statements are completely free of *minor* errors and irregularities. Most audit procedures are based upon samples; it simply is not possible for the auditors to verify all of the transactions of a large organization. Therefore, there is always the possibility that errors or irregularities may exist among the transactions that were not examined by the auditors.

Auditors design their investigation (examination) to detect those errors and irregularities that are *material* in relation to the financial statements.[6] We have explained the concept of materiality in earlier chapters. With respect to financial statements, an item is material if knowledge of the item might reasonably be expected to *influence the decisions* of users of the statements.

Some cases of employee fraud, such as the theft of a few items from inventory, involve such small dollar amounts that they do not affect the overall fairness of the financial statements. An audit should not be expected to detect all such irregularities.

Any fraud of a scale that causes the financial statements to become misleading, however, is material. Such situations *should* be brought to light in the normal course of an audit. The principal purpose of an audit is to provide outsiders with assurance that the financial statements are a fair presentation. If these audited statements are misleading, the audit has failed to serve its purpose.

As explained in Chapter 1, audits are not the only factor contributing to the reliability of financial statements. Other factors include the company's internal control, accountants' and managers' personal commitments to ethical conduct, and corporate and securities laws.

Auditors' Liability to the Users of Financial Statements   If auditors perform their audit with *due professional care,* they are *not responsible* for errors or irregularities that were not detected. On the other hand, if the audit is performed in a *negligent* manner, the auditors may be held financially liable for losses sustained by users of these statements—or by the company that issued the statements.[7]

While audits do not provide an absolute guarantee of reliability, audited financial statements have established an impressive track record of reliability in comparison with unaudited accounting information. The financial statements of Allied Crude Vegetable Oil Corporation, for example, were *unaudited.* Had creditors insisted upon receiving audited financial statements prior to extending credit, the inventory shortages would have been discovered long before reaching such large amounts.

Corporate and securities laws require all publicly owned companies to have their annual financial statements audited. In dealing with nonpublic companies, creditors and investors often insist upon receiving audited financial statements before making substantial investments.

---

[6]CICA, *CICA Handbook* (Toronto), section 5135.
[7]In the context of auditors' responsibilities, *negligence* is a legal term that means failure to exercise *due professional care.*

Reviews and Compilations of Financial Statements   An audit is both time-consuming and expensive. (The cost of the audit normally is paid by the company issuing the financial statements.) All accounting information, including audited financial statements, should be *cost effective.* For this reason, many nonpublic companies have their financial statements *reviewed* or *compiled* by a public accounting firm, rather than having these statements audited.

Reviews are different from financial audits because the scope of the former is much less than that of the latter and the level of assurance is accordingly much lower. A review consists primarily of enquiry, analytical procedures, and discussion related to the financial statements. The objective of a review is to assess whether the financial statements are plausible, that is, worthy of belief. After the completion of a review, the public accountants provide a *negative assurance* on whether the financial statements are in accordance with generally accepted accounting principles. A negative assurance is the public accountants' assertion that nothing has come to their attention to cause them to believe that the financial statements are not in accordance with generally accepted accounting principles. Since a review can be performed much more quickly and is much less time consuming than an audit, its cost is a small fraction of an audit.

Public accountants also may *compile* financial statements for a small nonpublic company. **Compilations** of financial statements involve taking information from the accounting records and putting it in the form of financial statements, without performing any procedures to verify the information. While compilations provide *no assurance* to outsiders about the reliability of the financial statements, they do provide an important service to small companies that do not have accounting-trained employees.

Operational Auditing

LO 8: Describe the nature and purpose of operational and compliance auditing.

Financial audits focus primarily upon the verification of financial measurements. An **operational audit**, in contrast, focuses upon the *efficiency* and *effectiveness* of an operating unit within an organization.

An operational audit involves studying, testing, and evaluating the operating procedures and system of internal control relating to a specific unit within a larger organization. The subject of the operational audit might be the accounting department, the purchasing department, a branch office, or any other subunit within the company. The purpose of the audit is to make recommendations to management for *improving the operational efficiency and effectiveness* of the department under study. The results normally are not communicated to decision makers outside of the business organization.

Operational auditing is a rapidly growing field of specialization within accounting. Current economic pressures are forcing private companies, not-for-profit organizations, and all levels of government to reduce costs and to increase the efficiency and effectiveness of their operations. Within large organizations, operational auditing is a function of the internal audit staff.

Smaller organizations may engage public accounting firms to perform operational audits.

Compliance Auditing

An organization's operations are subject to a wide variety of laws and regulations, dealing with such matters as employee safety, environmental protection, human resource policies, and product pricing. Violations can result in huge fines and penalties that may threaten the very existence of the organization. Therefore, compliance with laws and regulations is an important concern of management of all types of organizations.

As indicated previously, compliance with laws and regulations is one of the objectives of a system of internal control. Management may obtain additional assurance by having the organization's internal or independent auditors consider these internal controls and test compliance with specific laws and regulations. These types of audits are called **compliance audits**. Compliance audits may also be performed for criteria other than laws and regulations. In auditing a particular subunit of the organization, internal auditors often perform an examination that involves both compliance and operational auditing.

Compliance audits are sometimes performed by a regulatory agency. For example, each year Revenue Canada audits the income tax returns of selected taxpayers for compliance with income tax laws and regulations. These types of audits benefit only the agency performing the audit. The results generally are *not* made available to the public or to other outside decision makers. The agency performing the audit also bears the cost of these investigations.

End-of-Chapter Review

Key Terms Introduced or Emphasized in Chapter 6

Accounting system (*p.297*) The personnel, procedures, devices, forms, and records used by an entity to develop accounting information and to communicate this information to decision makers.

Audit (*p.319*) The investigation performed by an auditor that serves as the basis for the auditor's opinion.

Auditors (*p.319*) Public accountants (also called independent auditors) who audit a company's financial statements. Being "independent" means that the public accountants have no relationships with the company issuing the statements that are likely to bias their judgments and opinion.

Auditors' report (*p.319*) The report containing the expert opinion expressed by auditors as to the fairness of financial statements.

Chart of accounts (*p.303*) A listing of the ledger accounts (and their account numbers) used by a particular business entity.

Compilation (of financial statements) (*p.323*) A service by a public accountant that involves putting the company's information in the form of financial statements, without performing any verification procedures.

Compliance audit (*p.324*) Performing an examination to determine whether an organization is violating certain criteria such as specific laws or regulations.

Cost effective (*p.298*) Having economic value in excess of its cost.

Credit memorandum (*p.314*) A document issued by the seller to a buyer indicating that the seller is reducing (crediting) its account receivable from the buyer as the result of a sales return or allowance.

Database (*p.303*) A "warehouse" within a computer system in which unclassified coded data are stored. Data in the database may be sorted and classified in any manner permitted by the classification codes attached to the data.

Debit memorandum (*p.314*) A document issued by the buyer to the seller indicating that the buyer is reducing (debiting) its account payable to the seller in connection with a purchase return or allowance.

Embezzlement (*p.316*) A theft of assets that is concealed by falsification of the accounting records.

Employee fraud (*p.316*) Fraud perpetrated against a company by one or more of its employees.

Errors (*p.316*) Unintentional mistakes; one source of erroneous accounting information. A distinction is drawn between errors and **irregularities.**

Fair presentation (*p.319*) A term used by auditors and accountants in describing financial statements that are in conformity with generally accepted accounting principles, that is, complete, unbiased, and reliable.

Fidelity bond (*p.316*) A type of insurance that reimburses an employer for losses caused by fraud or embezzlement by bonded employees.

Financial audit (*p.319*) A thorough investigation of a company's financial statements by an independent public accounting firm, conducted for the purpose of expressing an expert opinion as to the reliability and completeness (or "fairness") of the financial statements.

Fraud (*p.315*) Misrepresentation with the intent to deceive.

General journal (*p.299*) A journal that can be used for recording any type of transaction. In practice, a general journal is used only for recording those transactions that do not "fit" into any special journals. But because general journal entries clearly illustrate the effects of any type of business transaction, they are widely used in classroom and textbook illustrations.

Internal auditors (*p.310*) Professional accountants employed by an organization to continually test and evaluate internal control and to report their findings and recommendations to top management.

Internal control (*p.307*) All measures (policies and procedures) used by an organization to ensure efficient operations, compliance with management's policies and laws and regulations, and reliable accounting information. Collectively, these measures are described as ***internal control.***

Invoice (*p.313*) An itemized statement of goods being bought or sold showing the terms of sale. Serves as the basis for entries in the accounting records of both the seller and buyer because it evidences the transfer of ownership of the goods.

Invoice approval form (*p.314*) A business document prepared by the accounting department approving the recording and payment of a purchase invoice. Preliminary steps include comparison of the purchase order and receiving report with the invoice.

Irregularities (*p.316*) Intentional "mistakes" introduced into accounting information for some fraudulent purpose.

Management fraud (*p.316*) Fraud perpetrated by a company's management against outsiders. Usually involves the issuance of misleading financial statements.

On-line, real-time (OLRT) (*p.301*) A computer system in which certain accounting records are kept completely up-to-date by recording transactions as they occur.

Operational audit (*p.323*) The studying, testing, and evaluating of the efficiency and effectiveness of an operating unit within a larger organization. The purpose of an operational audit is to make recommendations to management for improving the operational efficiency and effectiveness of the unit.

Purchase order (*p.312*) A serially numbered document sent by the purchasing department of a business to a supplier for the purpose of ordering materials or services.

Receiving report (*p.313*) A form prepared by the receiving department indicating for each incoming shipment the type, quantity, and condition of goods received.

Responsibility accounting system (*p.303*) An accounting system designed to measure the performance of business units under the control of different managers.

Review (of financial statements) (*p.323*) Consisting of enquiry, analytical procedures, and discussion, resulting in a negative assurance on whether financial statements are in accordance with generally accepted accounting principles.

Special journal (*p.299*) An accounting record or device designed for recording type of transaction quickly and efficiently. A business may use many different types of special journals.

Unqualified opinion (*p.320*) A "clean" auditors' report, in which the auditors find the financial statements to constitute a fair presentation.

Self-Test Questions

The answers to these questions appear on page 336.

1. Which of the following factors is **not** a significant consideration in designing an accounting system for a business?
   a. The types of accounting information that the business is required by law to report to agencies or persons outside the organization.
   b. The cost of developing various types of accounting information.
   c. The need for subsidiary ledgers and other detailed information in conducting daily business operations.
   d. None of the above answers is correct.

2. Identify all answers that describe characteristics of special journals.
   a. Less familiarity with accounting principles is required of an employee maintaining a special journal than of an employee maintaining a general journal.
   b. The transactions best suited to special journals are routine transactions that occur frequently.
   c. For purposes of strong internal control, all special journals are located in the accounting department.
   d. Special journals are essential in an on-line, real-time accounting system.

3. In comparison with a manual accounting system, a computer-based system with point-of-sale terminals and a database should reduce greatly which of the following? (More than one answer may be correct.)
   a. The time and effort spent in recording transactions.
   b. The need for internal control.
   c. The time and effort involved in maintaining subsidiary ledger accounts.
   d. The number of ways in which transaction data may be classified in special reports to management.

4. One means of achieving internal control is an appropriate subdivision of duties. Identify all answers consistent with this concept.
   a. No one employee should handle all aspects of a transaction.
   b. Each employee's area of responsibility should be carefully defined.
   c. To the extent practicable, employees should be rotated periodically to different job assignments.
   d. Employees with custody of assets should not maintain the only accounting records relating to those assets.

5. Which of the following statements concerning internal control is **not** correct?
   a. One purpose of operational audits is to improve internal control.
   b. It is easier to achieve strong internal control in a small business than in a large one.
   c. Internal control is more effective in preventing large-scale employee fraud than in preventing large-scale management fraud.
   d. No internal control provides complete protection against errors and irregularities.

6. Parker Corporation has recently issued capital stock to the public and now must be audited annually by an independent firm of public accountants. These annual audits should eliminate the need for:
   a. Internal control.
   b. Operational audits by the company's internal auditors.
   c. Fidelity bonds on employees who handle negotiable assets.
   d. None of the above.

7. Assume that audited financial statements turn out to be misleading and investors relying upon these statements sustain losses. Which of the following best describes the auditors' potential liability for these losses?
   a. The auditors may be liable, because they have guaranteed the reliability of the statements.
   b. The auditors are not liable, as they have only issued an opinion as to the reliability of the statements.
   c. The auditors may be liable if they performed their audit in a negligent manner.
   d. The auditors may be liable, but only if the statements were misleading because of management fraud.

ASSIGNMENT MATERIAL

Discussion Questions

1. What are the basic factors affecting the design and structure of a company's accounting system?

2. Identify the sources from which an organization's accounting system may come. In other words, who designs it?

3. An accounting system should meet the specific needs of a business organization. Identify several examples of (a) information needs that are common to all publicly owned corporations and (b) accounting information that management may want developed for its own use in managing the business.

4. With respect to accounting information, define the term **cost-effective.** How does this concept affect the design and output of an accounting system?

5. Explain the unique characteristics of (a) a general journal and (b) a special journal.

6. How is it possible for cashiers using point-of-sale terminals to record cash sales by entering only a "product code" into the terminal? Why is it not necessary to enter the dollar amount of the sale and to instruct the computer to debit the Cash account and credit the Sales account?

7. Define an **on-line, real-time** accounting system. Identify several business situations in which on-line, real-time information would be useful to company personnel.

8. What is meant by the term ***responsibility accounting system?*** What are the implications of a responsibility accounting system with respect to a company's chart of ledger accounts?

9. Briefly explain the usefulness of a database.

10. Identify two general criteria (other than reliability) that affect the usefulness of an accounting report to a decision maker. How has technology affected these criteria in recent years?

11. List the three objectives of internal control.

12. List and briefly describe the two components of internal control.

13. Briefly explain the concept of ***subdivision of duties.*** How does this concept reduce the risk of errors and irregularities?

14. Suggest a control device to protect against the loss or nondelivery of invoices or other business documents that are routed from one department to another.

15. Name three business documents that are needed by the accounting department to verify that a purchase of merchandise has occurred and that payment of the invoice should be made.

16. Radio House received a shipment of 30 cellular car phones from Bund Corporation. The receiving report showed that 3 of these phones were defective and are being returned to Bund. Should Radio House issue Bund a debit memorandum or a credit memorandum when it returns this merchandise?

17. Briefly explain why a person who handles cash receipts from customers should not also have authority to issue credit memoranda for sales returns and allowances.

18. Is internal control necessary in a company with a highly reliable computer system? Explain.

19. Explain several reasons why internal control may ***fail*** to prevent certain errors or irregularities.

20. Is it usually easier to achieve strong internal control in a large business or in a very small one? Explain the reasons for your answer.

21. Distinguish between ***employee fraud*** and ***management fraud.*** Provide an example of each.

22. Describe the nature and purpose of a financial audit. Who performs these audits?

23. Do auditors guarantee the reliability of audited financial statements? If the statements should turn out to be highly misleading, can the auditors be held financially liable for the losses sustained by decision makers relying upon the statements? Explain.

24. Distinguish among an audit, a review, and a compilation of financial statements. Who performs these services? Who pays for them?

25. Describe the nature and purpose of an operational audit. Who performs these audits?

26. Explain the purpose of a compliance audit. Who performs these audits?

Exercises

EXERCISE 6-1
Accounting Terminology
(LO 2, 3, 4)

Listed below are nine technical terms related to accounting systems and/or internal control:

Internal control	Responsibility	On-line, real-time
Special journal	accounting system	system
General journal	Database	Purchase order
	Debit memorandum	Receiving report

Each of the following statements may (or may not) describe one of these technical terms. For each statement, indicate the term described, or answer "None" if the statement does not correctly describe any of the terms.

a. A chart of accounts that permits separate measurement of departmental revenue and expense.

b. A document used in verifying the unit prices in a purchase invoice.

c. A journal used in recording unusual types of transactions.

d. An element of a computer-based accounting system that enables information to be classified according to various criteria.

e. Measures intended to make all aspects of a business operate according to management's plans and policies.

f. A system in which certain accounting records are kept continuously up-to-date.

g. A business document that might be issued to conceal the theft of cash collected from a credit customer.

EXERCISE 6-2
Accounting Terminology—
Fraud and Auditing
(LO 6, 7, 8)

Listed below are nine technical terms relating to fraud and/or auditing:

Management fraud	Financial audit	Embezzlement
Employee fraud	Operational audit	Errors
Fidelity bond	Review	Irregularities

Each of the following statements may (or may not) describe one of these technical terms. For each statement, indicate the term described, or answer "None" if the statement does not correctly describe any of the terms.

a. An examination conducted by a company's internal auditors for the purpose of providing outsiders with an independent opinion upon the fairness of the company's financial statements.

b. A theft of assets that is concealed by falsification of the accounting records.

c. An investigation intended to provide negative assurance that the financial statements are in accordance with generally accepted accounting principles.

d. Intentional misstatements within financial statements that may result from employee fraud or may represent management fraud.

e. A form of insurance policy that compensates users of financial statements for losses sustained as a result of management fraud.

f. An investigation conducted for the purpose of evaluating the efficiency and effectiveness of a department or other subunit within an organization.

g. An effort to deceive outsiders through the issuance of misleading financial statements.

EXERCISE 6-3
Special Journals
(LO 2)

In every accounting system, transactions initially are recorded in some type of journal.

a. Compare and contrast basic characteristics of a **general journal** and a **special journal.**

b. Is more knowledge of accounting required to maintain a general journal or a special journal? Explain.

c. Provide several examples of special journals that you have observed in operation. Explain the nature of the transactions recorded in these journals.

d. Does a business with highly efficient special journals also need a general journal? Explain.

EXERCISE 6-4
Ledgers and Databases
(LO 3)

In computer-based accounting systems, data relating to certain types of transactions may be stored in a **database** as well as in ledger accounts.

a. Briefly distinguish between **ledger accounts** and a **database** as a means of storing and classifying data.
b. Is a database more useful in preparing financial statements or reports to management? Explain.

EXERCISE 6-5
Internal Control and Business Documents
(LO 5)

In each of the following independent cases, indicate the internal control that appears to be missing in the purchaser's invoice approval procedures.
a. Baxter Construction Company, a builder of tract homes, ordered 100 mahogany front doors from Anderson Door Company at the agreed-upon price of $79 each. In the sales invoice, Anderson erroneously listed the price of these doors at $97 each. Baxter paid the invoice total of $9,700 without detecting the error.
b. Jet Auto Parts ordered 50 Sure-Start auto batteries from Allied Battery at a price of $20 each. Allied sent Jet a sales invoice for 50 batteries at $20 but delivered only 20 batteries. Jet's accounting personnel recorded the transaction directly from the invoice, debiting Inventory and crediting Accounts Payable for $1,000.

EXERCISE 6-6
Internal Control and Fidelity Bonds
(LO 4, 5)

Strong internal control protects a company's assets against waste, fraud, and inefficient use. Fidelity bonds provide a means by which a company may recover losses caused by dishonest acts of employees. Would it be reasonable for a company to maintain strong internal control and also pay for a fidelity bond? Explain. Are fidelity bonds a satisfactory substitute for internal control? Explain.

EXERCISE 6-7
Internal Control and Fraud Prevention
(LO 4, 6)

Golden Valley Farm Supply retained a firm of public accountants to design internal controls especially for its operations. Assuming that the accounting firm has finished its work and the newly designed internal control is in use, answer fully the following:
a. Will it be possible for any type of fraud to occur without immediate detection once the new internal control is in full operation?
b. Describe two limitations inherent in internal control that prevent it from providing absolute assurance against inefficiency and fraud.

EXERCISE 6-8
Types of Audits
(LO 7, 8)

Briefly distinguish among the following types of audits: (a) a financial audit, (b) a Revenue Canada audit of a taxpayer's income tax return, and (c) the ongoing operational audits in a large business organization. You should address such issues as the basic purpose of each audit, who performs the audit, and who makes use of the auditors' findings.

EXERCISE 6-9
Responsibilities of Management and of Independent Auditors
(LO 6, 7)

The annual report of **Loblaw Companies Limited** appears at the end of this textbook. As the basis for this exercise, read the reports of management and of **KPMG**, the independent auditors. Answer the following questions, indicating the paragraph number and report in which you located each answer.
a. Who is responsible for the preparation and issuance of the company's financial statements—management or the auditors?
b. For what purposes does management say that it has established a system of internal control?
c. Identify the **internal** control to which management makes specific reference.
d. Who expresses an opinion on the company's financial statements—management, the auditors, or both—and on what basis?

Problems

PROBLEM 6-1
Accounting Systems
(LO 1, 2, 3)

Evaluate each of the following statements, indicating any areas of agreement and disagreement.

a. Transactions can be recorded more efficiently in special journals than in a general journal. Therefore, a well-designed accounting system should use only special journals.

b. The transaction data stored in a database can be arranged in the format of ledger accounts. Therefore, a business with a computer-based accounting system does not need a ledger. Whenever the balance of any ledger account is needed for any purpose, the computer can sort through the database and determine this amount.

c. In an on-line, real-time accounting system, a manager may view the up-to-the-moment balance of any ledger account from a computer terminal.

d. Advances in the technologies of computers and communications have increased the usefulness of accounting information to decision makers.

e. In recording cash sales, a cashier using a point-of-sale terminal may record a cash sale by only entering a product code that identifies the merchandise sold. This is single-entry accounting, not double-entry accounting.

PROBLEM 6-2
Purpose of a System of Internal Control
(LO 4)

Three executives of Jetlab, a small electronics firm, disagree as to their company's need for internal control. Jones argues as follows: "If we are going to spend money on fidelity bonds, it is a complete waste to duplicate that kind of protection by maintaining our own internal control." Smith disagrees and expresses the following view: "The benefits we would receive from strong internal control would go way beyond protection against fraud." Adams says: "The best internal control in my opinion is to maintain two complete but separate sets of accounting records. If all our transactions are recorded twice by different employees, the two independent sets of records and financial statements can be compared and any discrepancies investigated."

Evaluate the views expressed by each of the three executives.

PROBLEM 6-3
Internal Control Measures
(LO 5)

Listed below are several possible errors or problems that might occur in a merchandising business. Also listed are five internal control measures. You are to list the letter (**a** through **g**) designating each of these errors or problems. Beside each letter, place the number indicating the internal control measure that would prevent this type of problem from occurring. If none of the specified control measures would be effective in preventing the error or problem, place "0" after the letter.

Possible Errors or Problems

a. Paid an invoice in which the supplier had accidentally doubled the price of the merchandise.

b. Paid a supplier for goods that were delivered, but that were never ordered.

c. Purchased merchandise that turned out not to be popular with customers.

d. Several sales invoices were misplaced and the accounts receivable department is therefore unaware of the unrecorded credit sales.

e. Paid a supplier for goods that were never received.

f. The purchasing department ordered goods from one supplier when a better price could have been obtained by ordering from another supplier.

g. The cashier conceals the embezzlement of cash by reducing the balance of the Cash account.

Internal Control Measures

1. Comparison of purchase invoice with the receiving report.
2. Comparison of purchase invoice with the purchase order.
3. Separation of the accounting function from custody of assets.

4. Separation of the responsibilities for approving and recording transactions.
5. Use of serially numbered documents.
0. None of the above control procedures can effectively prevent this error or problem from occurring.

PROBLEM 6-4
Internal Control Measures—
Emphasis upon Computer-
Based Systems
(LO 5)

The lettered paragraphs below describe seven possible errors or problems that might occur in a retail business. Also listed are five internal control measures. List the letter (**a** through **g**) designating the errors or problems. Beside each letter, place the number indicating the internal control measure that should prevent this type of error or problem from occurring. If none of the specified internal control measures would effectively prevent the error or problem, place a "0" opposite the letter. Assume that a computer-based accounting system is in use.

Possible Errors or Problems

a. A salesclerk unknowingly makes a credit sale to a customer whose account has already reached the customer's prearranged credit limit.
b. The cashier of a business conceals a theft of cash by adjusting the balance of the Cash account in the company's computer-based accounting records.
c. Certain merchandise proves to be so unpopular with customers that it cannot be sold except at a price well below its original cost.
d. A salesclerk rings up a sale at an incorrect price.
e. A salesclerk uses a point-of-sale terminal to improperly reduce the balance of a friend's account in the company's accounts receivable records.
f. One of the salesclerks is quite lazy and leaves most of the work of serving customers to the other salesclerks in the department.
g. A shoplifter steals merchandise while the salesclerk is busy with another customer.

Internal Control Measures

1. Limiting the types of transactions that can be processed from point-of-sale terminals to cash sales and credit sales.
2. All merchandise has a magnetically coded label that can be read automatically by an optical scanner on a point-of-sale terminal. This code identifies to the computer the merchandise being sold.
3. Credit cards issued by the store have magnetic codes that can be read automatically by a device attached to the electronic cash register. Credit approval and posting to customers' accounts are handled by the computer.
4. The computer prepares a report with separate daily sales totals for each sales person.
5. Employees with custody of assets do not have access to accounting records.
0. None of the above control measures effectively prevents this type of error or problem from occurring.

PROBLEM 6-5
The Baker Street Diversion
(LO 5)

Printing Made Easy sells a variety of printers for use with personal computers. Last April, Arthur Doyle, the company's purchasing agent, discovered a weakness in internal control and engaged in a scheme to steal printers. Doyle issued a purchase order for 20 printers to one of the company's regular suppliers, but he included a typewritten note on company letterhead stationery requesting that the printers be delivered to 221B Baker Street, a warehouse in which Doyle had rented space.

The supplier shipped the printers to Baker Street and sent a sales invoice to Printing Made Easy. When the invoice arrived, an accounting clerk carefully complied with company policy and compared the invoice with a copy of the purchase order. After noting agreement between these documents as to quantities, prices, and model numbers, the clerk recorded the transaction in the accounting records and authorized payment of the invoice.

INSTRUCTIONS

What is the weakness in internal control discovered by the purchasing agent to enable him to commit this theft? What changes would you recommend in the company's internal documentation and invoice approval procedures to prevent such problems in the future?

PROBLEM 6-6
Internal Control in a
Computer-Based System
(LO 2, 5)

Mission Stores uses point-of-sale terminals to record its sale transactions. All merchandise bears a magnetic code number that can be read by an optical scanner. When merchandise is sold, the salesclerk passes each item over the scanner. The computer reads the code number, determines the price of the item from a master price list, and displays the price on a screen for the customer to see. After each item has been passed over the scanner, the computer displays the total amount of the sale and records the transaction in the company's accounting records.

If the transaction is a credit sale, the salesclerk enters the customer's credit card number into the register. The computer checks the customer's credit status and updates the accounts receivable subsidiary ledger.

INSTRUCTIONS

Statements **a** through **d** describe problems that may arise in a retailing business that uses manual cash registers and accounting records. Explain how the point-of-sale terminals used by Mission Stores will help reduce or eliminate these problems. If the point-of-sale terminals will not help to eliminate the problems, explain why not.
a. A salesclerk is unaware of a recent change in the price of a particular item.
b. Merchandise is stolen by a shoplifter.
c. A salesclerk fails to record a cash sale and keeps the cash received from the customer.
d. A customer buys merchandise on account using a stolen Mission Stores credit card.

PROBLEM 6-7
Types of Fraud
(LO 6)

Cases of fraud often are described either as *employee fraud* or *management fraud.*
a. Briefly distinguish between employee fraud and management fraud.
b. Identify three types of actions that constitute employee fraud.
c. Identify three types of actions that constitute management fraud.
d. Which type of fraud is likely to have the greatest impact upon the national economy? Explain the reasons for your answer.

PROBLEM 6-8
An Overview of Financial
Audits
(LO 7)

Answer each of the following questions concerning an audit of the financial statements of a publicly owned company.
a. What is the basic purpose of this type of audit?
b. Who performs the audit?
c. Why is the concept of independence important in a financial audit?
d. What consideration do these auditors give to the company's internal control?
e. To whom are the auditors' findings made available?
f. Do the auditors guarantee the reliability of the audited financial statements? If the audited statements are misleading, are the auditors held financially liable for losses incurred by people relying upon these statements? Explain.
g. Who pays for the audit?
h. Briefly distinguish between a financial audit and a "review" of financial statements by a public accounting firm.

PROBLEM 6-9
Characteristics of Financial
Audits and of Operational
Audits
(LO 7, 8)

Listed below are nine statements about auditing. Indicate whether each statement applies to *financial audits, operational audits, both,* or *neither.* Explain your reasons for each answer.
a. As part of their investigation, the auditors consider or study and evaluate internal control.

b. The auditors guarantee the reliability of the financial statements to outside decision makers.

c. The auditors' findings are communicated only to management and to Revenue Canada.

d. One major purpose of the audit is to determine compliance with generally accepted accounting principles.

e. The audit usually focuses upon a department or subunit within the organization.

f. In a large organization, these audits may be conducted continuously as part of the professional responsibilities of certain company employees.

g. If the auditors are negligent, they may be held financially liable for losses incurred by decision makers outside the organization.

h. The auditors are independent of the company and its management.

i. The basic purpose of the audit is the detection of fraud.

Analytical and Decision Problems and Cases

A&D 6-1
Internal Control in a Typical Restaurant
(LO 5)

Alice's Restaurant has a system of internal control that is similar to most restaurants. A waiter or waitress (food server) writes each customer's order on a serially numbered sales ticket. The servers give these sales tickets to the kitchen staff, which prepares the meals. While the customer is eating, the server fills in the prices on the sales ticket and leaves it at the customer's table.

When the customers are ready to leave, they present the completed sales ticket, along with the payment due, to the cashier. The cashier verifies the prices listed on the sales ticket, rings up the sale on a cash register, and gives the customer an appropriate amount of change.

A manager is always on hand observing operations throughout the restaurant. At the end of each shift, the manager determines that all of the sales tickets issued by the food servers have been collected by the cashier and computes the total dollar amount of these tickets. Next, the manager counts the cash receipts and compares this amount with the total shown on the register tape and the total developed from the serially numbered sales tickets.

INSTRUCTIONS

Identify the control procedures (if any) that prevent:

a. Food servers from providing free meals to family and friends simply by not preparing a sales ticket.

b. Food servers from undercharging favoured customers.

c. Food servers from collecting the amount due from the customer and keeping the cash for themselves.

d. The cashier from pocketing some of the customers' payments and concealing this theft by ringing up lower amounts on the cash register?

A&D 6-2
Internal Control: Another Short Case
(LO 5)

At the Uptown Theatre, the cashier is located in a box office at the front of the building. The cashier receives cash from customers and operates a ticket machine that ejects serially numbered tickets. The serial number appears on each end of the ticket. The tickets come from the printer in large rolls that fit into the ticket machine and are removed at the end of each cashier's working period.

After purchasing a ticket from the cashier, in order to be admitted to the theatre a customer must hand the ticket to a ticket taker stationed some 10 metres from the box office at the entrance to the theatre lobby. The ticket taker tears the ticket in half and returns the ticket stub to the customer. The other half of the ticket is dropped by the ticket taker into a locked box.

INSTRUCTIONS

a. Describe the internal controls present in Uptown Theatre's method of handling cash receipts.

b. What steps should be taken regularly by the theatre manager or other supervisor to make these and other internal controls work most effectively?

c. Assume that the cashier and the ticket taker decided to collaborate in an effort to abstract cash receipts. What actions might they take?

d. On the assumption made in part **c** of collaboration between the cashier and the ticket taker, what features of the control procedures would be most likely to disclose this employee fraud?

A&D 6-3
The Case of the Ethical(?)
Pharmacist
(LO 1, 6)

Susan Pico, a pharmacist, is the sole shareholder of Pico Drug Stores, a corporation that operates three small pharmacies. Pico has taken many steps to increase her company's profitability, minimize its income tax obligations, and keep its financial affairs "private." For example, she:

1. Leads people to believe that her company is less profitable than it actually is. She often makes statements such as "If things don't pick up, I may have to close one of the stores."
2. Has sold the land and building used by one store to an out-of-town investor. The company now is leasing the site from the investor, as Pico believes that leasing offers significant income tax advantages.
3. Rings up sales on a "personal" cash register, which is not used by other employees. She does not include sales recorded on this register in the company's corporate income tax returns.
4. Has hired herself as the corporation's Chief Executive Officer. She has set her salary at an amount considerably higher than that paid to any other employee. (Her salary is deductible to the corporation in determining its taxable income, although she must pay personal income taxes on this salary. She sees a high salary as providing her with an overall income tax advantage. Although her salary is substantial, it is not unreasonable in light of her skills and responsibilities.)
5. Has fired several employees "for cause"—suspicion of theft. However, the internal control is too weak to determine with any certainty whether such thefts occurred, or to specifically focus responsibility.
6. Does not show her company's financial statements to company employees or to the local bank, which holds mortgages on two of her company's stores.

INSTRUCTIONS

For each of the numbered paragraphs, explain whether you consider Pico's actions ethical. Consider each paragraph independently of the others and explain your conclusions.

A&D 6-4
The Return of the Ethical(?)
Pharmacist
(LO 1, 6)

Susan Pico, a pharmacist, is the sole shareholder of Pico Drug Stores, a corporation that operates three small pharmacies. Pico has taken many steps to increase her company's profitability, minimize its income tax obligations, and keep its financial affairs "private." For example, she:

1. Owns stock in several publicly owned pharmaceutical companies. She heavily favours the products of these companies in purchasing merchandise for her stores.
2. Advertises and sells several "generic" brands implying that they are manufactured by the same company that developed the original "brand-name" product. (Generic products often are exact imitations of brand-name products. However, they are manufactured by different companies and do not use the brand name on their labels. The manufacture and sale of generics is a widespread practice and is legal, usually because the patents protecting the brand-name products have expired.)
3. Pays several employees less than the prevailing wages for similar jobs at other companies.
4. Pays several employees in cash and leaves them "off the books." Pico withholds no income or other taxes from amounts paid to these employees, and the company pays no payroll taxes. The employees in question favour this arrangement.

5. Arranges the duties of employees who perform accounting functions so that no one employee is aware of the company's net income, or the salary that she receives from the business.
6. Asked George Miller, a licensed public accountant who maintains the corporation's accounting records and prepares its financial statements, to audit the year-end statements for half of the fee that he charges other audit clients. Miller has no financial interest in Pico Drug Stores and is not related to Susan Pico.

INSTRUCTIONS

For each of the numbered paragraphs, explain whether you consider Pico's actions ethical. Consider each paragraph independently and explain your conclusions.

A&D 6-5
Do Auditors Say What We Think They Mean?
(LO 7)

This assignment explores the responsibilities of financial statement auditors, as seen by users of financial statements and by the accounting profession.

INSTRUCTIONS

a. ***As a preliminary step***—before reading an auditors' report in detail—develop a list of ***expectations*** that you think users of audited financial statements may have concerning the auditors' responsibilities.
b. Using **KPMG's** auditors' report on page 320, discuss the following questions within your group. Summarize your findings in a written report.
   (1) What is meant by the sentence in the first paragraph: *"These financial statements are the responsibility of the Company's management"?* Does this statement limit the auditors' responsibility for conducting their audit with due professional care? Does it mean that the auditors have not assisted management in preparing the statements?
   (2) What is meant by the sentence in the second paragraph that states: *"An audit includes examining, on a test basis, evidence supporting the amounts and disclosures in the financial statements"?* Do auditors run exhaustive tests on every figure included in the statements? What role does a company's internal control play in determining the extent of the auditors' testing?
   (3) What is meant in the third paragraph by the phrase: *" . . . present fairly, in all material respects . . ."?* Does "present fairly" mean approximately the same thing as "present accurately"?
   (4) Many users of financial statements believe that an external auditors' primary responsibilities are to detect fraud and disclose all irregularities. Does the language of the report suggest that auditors have any responsibility in these areas?
c. Refer to your list of users' expectations developed in part **a.** Based on the language of the auditors' report, does the audit function appear to fulfill these expectations? If not, what disparities exist between user expectations and the auditing profession's perceptions of its role in society?
Be prepared to discuss your group's ideas in class.

Answers to Self-Test Questions

1. d   2. a, b, d   3. a, c   4. a, b, c, d   5. b   6. d   7. c

MANUAL SPECIAL JOURNALS

Special journals were introduced in Chapter 6. This Appendix expands upon that introduction with specific examples and illustrations.

The basic purpose of special journals is to record a particular type of business transaction quickly and efficiently. Some special journals are produced by machines, such as cash registers and point-of-sale terminals. Many others are handwritten accounting records. In this appendix, we illustrate and explain the use of special journals in *manual accounting systems*.

LEARNING OBJECTIVES

1. Explain why the types and formats of special journals vary from one business to the next.
2. Record transactions in special journals.
3. Design a special journal for efficiently recording a particular type of business transaction.

Why Study Manual Special Journals?

Prior to the use of computers, all accounting records were maintained manually, with the assistance of some mechanical devices such as cash registers. Today more and more businesses use computers in developing accounting information. Why, then, study the "old style" manual accounting records?

We offer several answers to this question. First, manual special journals *remain in widespread use—and probably always will.* Many individuals and small businesses rely almost entirely upon manual records for developing their accounting information. Many large businesses use manual special journals on a temporary basis—whenever their computerized systems "go down." And in some situations, it simply is more convenient to record transactions in handwriting than to use a machine. Also, you will find that the study of manual special journals will *enhance your understanding* of the operation of every accounting system—large and small.

CHEQUE REGISTER: THE MOST COMMON SPECIAL JOURNAL OF THEM ALL

Cheque registers probably outnumber all other special journals combined. A cheque register, found inside every chequebook, is a special journal for recording all of the transactions in a particular bank chequing account. Almost everyone with a chequing account maintains this type of special journal.

If a business has more than one chequing account, *a separate cheque register is maintained for each account.* When cheques are printed by computer, the computer automatically maintains a cheque register. When cheques are written "in the field," however, it often is convenient for the person issuing the cheque to record the transaction in the manual cheque register contained in the chequebook. A manual cheque register is illustrated below:

A special journal found in every chequebook

		CHEQUE REGISTER			
Date	Cheque No.	Name of Payee and Transaction Description	Amounts Deposits	Cheques	Cash Balance
Mar. 31		Balance			$9,875
Apr. 1	364	Mall Mgmt. Corp. (Store rent for April)		$2,250	(2,250) $7,625
Apr. 1	365	ADP Wholesale Co. (Invoice dated Mar. 22)		3,205	(3,205) $4,420
Apr. 1		Day's cash receipts (All cash sales)	$1,950		1,950 $6,370
Apr. 2	366	. . .			

The transactions recorded in a cheque register may be posted periodically to the company's general ledger accounts, just as are transactions recorded in a general journal. For example, the first transactions in the illustrated cheque register would be posted as a debit to Rent Expense and as a credit to Cash. Some entries—such as payment of an account payable—also are posted to subsidiary ledger accounts.

Large businesses generally post these entries promptly. Small businesses sometimes leave this task for a professional accountant who visits the business only on a monthly or quarterly basis. A special feature of a manual cheque register, however, is a column indicating the **current balance** in the chequing account. Thus, even if entries in the cheque register have not yet been posted to the general ledger, the business has an up-to-date record of the amount of cash in its chequing account.

OTHER TYPES OF SPECIAL JOURNALS

LO 1: Explain why the types and formats of special journals vary from one business to the next.

Special journals are not all alike; each is designed for recording a **specific type** of business transaction. The number and format of the special journals in use at a particular business will vary with the nature and the volume of the company's transactions.

To illustrate the design and use of special journals, let us use the common example of a small merchandising operation. Ski Chalet is a ski shop with a manual accounting system. Like many small businesses with manual accounting systems, Ski Chalet uses a **periodic inventory system.**[1]

---

[1]Characteristics of periodic inventory systems are discussed in Chapter 5. Characteristics central to this illustration are (1) purchases of merchandise are debited to a **Purchases** account, rather than to the Inventory account; and (2) no entries are made recording the cost of goods sold as sales transactions occur.

The savings of time and effort are greatest when a separate special journal is designed to record each type of transaction that *occurs frequently.* In most merchandising businesses, the vast majority of transactions (perhaps 90% to 95%) fall into four major categories: (1) sales on account, (2) purchases of merchandise on account, (3) cash receipts, and (4) cash payments. Ski Chalet uses four separate special journals for recording these types of transactions, as shown below:

Types of Transactions That Occur Frequently	Corresponding Special Journal
Sales of merchandise on account	*Sales journal*
Purchases of merchandise on account	*Purchases journal*
Cash receipts	*Cash receipts journal*
Cash payments	*Cash payments journal*

In addition to these four special journals, Ski Chalet uses a *general journal* to record any transactions that *do not fit* into one of the special journals. Examples of transactions recorded in the general journal include sales returns, end-of-period adjusting entries, and closing entries.

We will now explain and illustrate the use of each of Ski Chalet's four special journals.

Sales Journal

LO 2: Record transactions in special journals.

Ski Chalet uses its sales journal for recording only one type of transaction—*sales of merchandise on account.* If a sales transaction involves even a partial cash down payment, it is recorded in the cash receipts journal (discussed later) rather than in the sales journal.

Ski Chalet's sales journal for the month of November is illustrated below:

SALES JOURNAL					Page 8
Date	Account Receivable Debited	Invoice No.	Terms	✓	Amount
19__					
Nov 1	*Jill Adams*	*301*	*2/10, n/30*	✓	*3,000*
3	*Harold Black*	*302*	*2/10, n/30*	✓	*1,400*
10	*C. D. Early*	*303*	*net 30*	✓	*900*
18	*Terry Frost*	*304*	*10 e.o.m.*	✓	*1,280*
26	*Nordic Ski Rentals*	*305*	*2/10, n/30*	✓	*8,600*
28	*Nordic Ski Rentals*	*306*	*2/10, n/30*	✓	*430*
30	*Total for the month*				*15,610*

Notice that *special columns* are provided for recording each aspect of the sale. The data entered in each column can be quickly copied from the *sales invoice* prepared for each credit sale.

Advantages of the Sales Journal   Note that each of the six sales transactions is recorded on a single line. Each entry consists of a debit to a customer's account; the offsetting credit to the Sales account is understood without being written, because every transaction recorded in this special journal is a sale.

An entry in a sales journal ***need not include an explanation;*** if more information about the transaction is desired it can be obtained by referring to the file copy of the sales invoice. The invoice number is listed in the sales journal as part of each entry. The one-line entry in the sales journal requires much less writing than would be necessary to record a sales transaction in the general journal. Since there may be several hundred or several thousand sales transactions each month, the time saved in recording transactions in this streamlined manner becomes quite important.

Another advantage of recording transactions in special journals is that much time may be saved in posting the effects of transactions to the company's general ledger accounts.

Posting Entries from the Sales Journal   The posting of transaction data from Ski Chalet's sales journal is illustrated below:

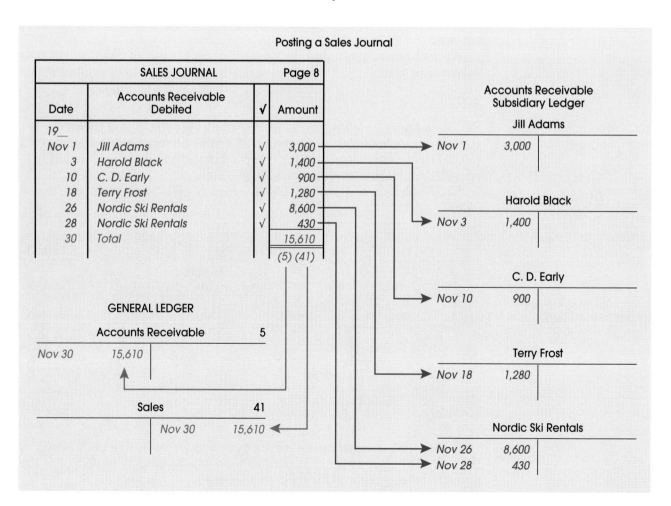

Posting a Sales Journal

Each credit sales transaction is posted promptly as a ***debit*** to the customer's account in the accounts receivable ***subsidiary ledger.*** (These postings are illustrated in **blue.**) Whenever a posting is made to a subsidiary ledger account, a check mark (✔) is placed in the sales journal posting reference column.

Use of a special journal does not save time in posting transaction data to subsidiary ledger accounts. It does, however, save great amounts of time in posting to ***general ledger*** accounts. As we have seen in Chapter 2, all entries in a ***general*** journal are posted separately to the general ledger accounts.

In the illustrated sales journal, however, every transaction is a credit sale, to be recorded as a debit to Accounts Receivable and a credit to Sales. Instead of posting each of these transactions to the general ledger separately, we wait until month-end and then post ***one amount representing all of these credit sales.***

At month-end, the Amount column in the sales journal is ***totalled.*** This total, ***$15,610,*** is posted as a debit to the Accounts Receivable controlling account in the general ledger, and also as a credit to the Sales account. (For emphasis, these postings are shown in **grey.**) The account numbers for these two general ledger accounts (5 and 41) then are placed in parentheses below the column total to show that this amount has been posted.

Notice that the amount debited to the Accounts Receivable controlling account, $15,610, is equal to the ***sum*** of the six separate amounts debited during the month to the accounts receivable subsidiary ledger.

In effect, the six credit sales transactions occurring during November were posted to the general ledger ***as one dollar amount.*** In actual practice, this one posting might represent 600, or even 6,000, separate credit sales transactions.

Purchases Journal

Ski Chalet records all of its ***purchases of merchandise on account*** in a special ***purchases journal.*** This journal is illustrated on the next page, along with arrows indicating how the transaction data are posted to accounts in the accounts payable ledger and in the general ledger.

Because Ski Chalet uses a ***periodic*** inventory system, the costs of merchandise purchased are debited to a general ledger account entitled ***Purchases*** rather than to the Inventory account.

Ski Chalet has a policy of taking advantage of all cash discounts offered by its suppliers. Therefore, purchases are recorded at ***net cost***—that is, at invoice price ***less any available cash discount.*** The two columns in the purchases journal showing the credit terms and invoice date of each purchase assist the company's accounting personnel in determining when each invoice must be paid.

This purchases journal is used in recording only one type of transaction—***purchases of merchandise on account.*** Cash purchases are recorded in the cash payments journal, not the purchases journal. When assets ***other than*** merchandise are purchased, the journal used in recording the transaction depends upon whether a cash payment is made. If

Purchases journal and . . .

. . . posting procedures

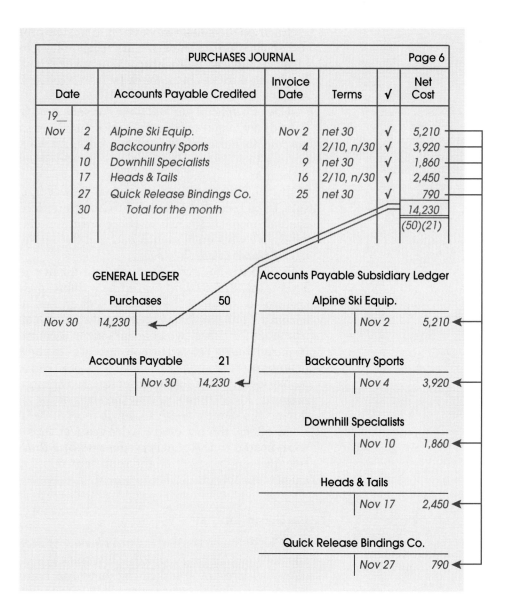

assets of this type are purchased for cash, the transaction is recorded in the cash payments journal; if the acquisition is made on account, the general journal is used.

Posting the Purchases Journal   Each credit purchase is posted immediately as a credit to the appropriate account in the accounts payable subsidiary ledger. As these postings are made, a check mark (✔) is placed in the purchases journal.

At the end of the month, the Amount column is totalled. This total—representing all credit purchases for the month—is posted to the general ledger as a debit to the Purchases account and as a credit to the Accounts Payable controlling account. The account numbers of these two general ledger accounts then are entered in parentheses just below the column total to show that these postings have been made.

Special Journals for Cash Transactions

A great many transactions involve either the receipt or the payment of cash. As shown earlier, the cash receipts and cash payments of a very small business may be summarized in a cheque register. Most businesses, however, also maintain a separate ***cash receipts journal*** and ***cash payments journal.***

When these special cash journals are in use, a cheque register is still maintained for each chequing account. However, the purpose of each cheque register is primarily to indicate the current balance in a particular chequing account. The cash receipts and cash payments journals provide more detailed information about cash transactions and are used as the basis for posting transactions to the ledger accounts.

Cash Receipts Journal

Ski Chalet's cash receipts journal is used for recording ***every transaction that involves the receipt of cash.*** Cash receipts arise from a variety of sources. Therefore, the cash receipts journal is more complicated than the "single-column" special journals that the company uses for recording credit sales and purchases on account.

Ski Chalet's most common source of cash receipts is the sale of merchandise for cash. As each cash sale is made, it is rung up on a cash register. At the end of the day, the total of the cash sales is computed by striking a total key on the register. This total is entered as cash sales in the cash receipts journal, which therefore contains one entry for each day's total cash sales.[2] For other types of cash receipts, such as the collection of an account receivable, a separate entry is made for each transaction.

The cash receipts journal illustrated on page 345 contains entries for all of the November transactions of Ski Chalet ***involving the receipt of cash.*** These transactions are described below:

Nov. 1   The owner, Loris Macor, made an additional investment in the business of $30,000 cash.

Nov. 1   Cash sales for the day totalled $1,200.

Nov. 2   Cash sales for the day totalled $910.

Nov. 8   Collected $2,940 from Jill Adams in full settlement of sales invoice no. 301. Payment received within the discount period.

Nov. 10   Sold a small portion of land not needed in the business for a total price of $27,000, receiving $7,000 cash and a note receivable for $20,000. The cost of the land was $25,000; thus, a $2,000 gain was realized on the sale.

---

[2]To conserve space, our illustration includes daily entries for cash sales only on the first two days of the month. The remaining cash sales for the month are summarized in a single entry dated November 30.

Nov. 12 Collected $1,372 from Harold Black in full settlement of sales invoice no. 302. Payment received within the discount period.

Nov. 28 Collected $500 from C. D. Early as a partial payment on sales invoice no. 303.

Nov. 30 Cash sales (since Nov. 2) totalled $18,300.

Nov. 30 Obtained a $15,000 bank loan by issuing a note payable.

Columns in a Cash Receipts Journal Notice that the illustrated cash receipts journal has several columns for recording debits and several for recording credits. Providing a separate column for debit or credit entries to a specific account *speeds up* both the recording and posting of these entries.

An entry is recorded in a special column merely by entering the dollar amount; it is not necessary to write the account title, as all entries in the column affect the same account. Also, all of the entries in a specific column have a similar effect upon the account—that is, they are either all debits or all credits. Therefore, it is not necessary to separately post each transaction to the general ledger account. Instead, all of the entries may be posted simply by posting the *column total* at the end of each month.

In designing a cash receipts journal, a separate column should be provided for any type of debit or credit entry that *occurs frequently*. For example, every cash receipt transaction includes a debit to the Cash account. Therefore, a column is provided for recording these debits. As Ski Chalet often collects its accounts receivable within the discount period, it includes a debit column for recording sales discounts taken by customers. When cash is received, the offsetting credit most often is to either Accounts Receivable or to Sales. Therefore, separate columns are provided for recording these credit entries.

In a manual journal, it usually is not practical to have more than eight or ten columns. Thus, "Other Accounts" columns must be included to accommodate entries to accounts for which there is no special column. A computerized system may (in effect) include separate columns for *every* ledger account. However, we are now focusing upon manual systems.

Using the Other Accounts Columns Notice that "Other Accounts" columns are provided on both the debit and credit sides of the journal. These columns can accommodate debit or credit entries to *any* ledger account.

Space is provided in the Other Accounts columns for writing both the name of the account and the dollar amount of the debit or credit entry. For example, the entry of November 10 in the illustrated journal shows that cash and a note receivable were received when land was sold. The amount of cash received, $7,000, simply is entered in the Cash debit column; the account title *Notes Receivable* is written in the Other Accounts debit column, along with the amount of the debit to this account ($20,000). These two debits are offset by credit entries to Land, $25,000, and Gain on Sale of Land, $2,000, in the Other Accounts column on the credit side of the ledger. (Notice that a transaction that involves several "other accounts" occupies more than one line in the cash receipts journal.)

Includes all transactions
involving receipt of cash

CASH RECEIPTS JOURNAL

Date		Explanation	Debits Cash	Debits Sales Discounts	Debits Other Accounts Name	Debits Other Accounts LP	Debits Other Accounts Amount	Account Credited	Credits Accounts Receivable ✓	Credits Accounts Receivable Amount	Credits Sales	Credits Other Accounts LP	Credits Other Accounts Amount
19__													
Nov	1	Investment by owner	30,000					Loris Macor, Capital				30	30,000
	1	Cash sales	1,200								1,200		
	2	Cash sales	910								910		
	8	Invoice 301, less 2%	2,940	60				Jill Adams	✓	3,000			
	10	Sale of land	7,000		Notes Receivable	3	20,000	{Land				11	25,000
								{Gain on Sale of Land				40	2,000
	12	Invoice 302, less 2%	1,372	28				Harold Black	✓	1,400			
	28	Invoice 303, partial											
		payment received	500					C. D. Early	✓	500			
	30	Cash sales	18,300								18,300		
	30	Obtained bank loan	15,000					Notes Payable				20	15,000
	30	Totals for the month	77,222	88			20,000			4,900	20,410		72,000
			(1)	(43)			(X)			(5)	(41)		(X)

345

Posting the Cash Receipts Journal   Three distinct posting processes are involved for the cash receipts journal:

1. As with other special journals, amounts affecting **subsidiary ledger** accounts are posted immediately. In the cash receipts journal, these entries are the credits to the accounts receivable from specific customers. A check mark (✔) is entered in the cash receipts journal as evidence that each of these entries has been posted. (For purposes of illustration, the amounts to be posted daily to subsidiary ledgers are shown in **black** type.)

2. The entries to **general ledger accounts recorded in the Other Accounts column** also should be posted daily. As these postings are made, the number of the ledger account is entered in the LP (ledger page) column of the cash receipts journal opposite the item posted. (In our illustration, amounts that should be posted immediately to general ledger accounts appear in **light blue.**)

3. At month-end, each of the debit and credit amount columns is totalled. Before any column totals are posted, it is first important to determine that the sum of the debit column totals is equal to the sum of the credit column totals. This **cross-footing** of the journal is an error-catching procedure, similar to the preparation of a trial balance.

   After the column totals have been crossfooted, any debit or credit total **relating to a specific general ledger account** is posted to that account. This posting updates the accounts for all of the individual entries recorded in the column during the month. As evidence of this month-end posting, the number of the general ledger account is entered in parentheses just below the column total. (Column totals to be posted at month-end are illustrated in **grey.**)

The totals of the Other Accounts columns are **not posted** at month-end for two reasons. First, these column totals often include entries affecting several different ledger accounts. Next, the individual amounts comprising these column totals have **already been posted,** as described in step **2,** above. The symbol **(X)** is placed below the totals of the Other Accounts columns to indicate that these amounts should not be posted.

Cash Payments Journal

Another widely used special journal is the cash payments journal, sometimes called the cash disbursements journal, in which **all payments of cash** are recorded. Among the more common of these transactions are payments of accounts payable to creditors, payment of operating expenses, and cash purchases of merchandise.

The cash payments journal illustrated on page 348 contains entries for all November transactions of Ski Chalet that required the **payment of cash.** These transactions are:

Nov. 1   Paid Powder Bowl Mall rent on store building for November, $2,400.

Nov. 2   Purchased merchandise from Uller Products for cash, $250.

Nov. 5   Bought land, $60,000, and building, $100,000, for use as a future business site. Paid cash of $35,000 to Western Limited, and signed a note payable for the $125,000 balance of the purchase price.

Nov. 17   Paid salaries of $3,600 by issuing one cheque for the entire payroll amount to Payroll Services, Inc.

Nov. 27   Paid $2,450 to Heads & Tails in full settlement of $2,500 purchase on Nov. 17, less 2% discount.

Nov. 27   Purchased merchandise from Mountain High for $800 cash.

Nov. 28   Purchased office supplies from Office World for $325, cash.

Nov. 29   Paid for newspaper advertising in *Snow Report,* $450.

Nov. 30   Paid Backcountry Sports the full $4,000 invoice amount for the purchase on Nov. 4. This invoice was inadvertently overlooked and was not paid within the discount period. (Remember, the purchase originally had been recorded at a *net* cost of $3,920.)

Notice in the illustrated cash payments journal that the two credit columns (Cash and Other Accounts) are located *to the left* of the three debit columns. Any sequence of columns is satisfactory as long as the column headings clearly indicate whether the account is being debited or credited. The Cash column often is placed first in both the cash receipts journal and the cash payments journal simply because this column is used in recording every transaction.

Good internal control over cash disbursements requires that all payments be made by cheque. The cheques are serially numbered and as each transaction is entered in the cash payments journal, the cheque number is listed in a special column provided just to the right of the date column. An unbroken sequence of cheque numbers in this column gives assurance that every cheque issued has been recorded in the accounting records.

Posting the Cash Payments Journal   The posting of the cash payments journal falls into the same phases already described for the cash receipts journal. The first phase consists of the daily posting of entries in the Accounts Payable debit column to the individual accounts of creditors in the accounts payable subsidiary ledger. Check marks (✔) are entered opposite those items to show that the posting has been made. (Amounts to be posted to the subsidiary ledger accounts are shown in **black.)**

The individual debit and credit entries in the Other Accounts columns of the cash payment journal may be posted daily or at convenient intervals during the month. As the posting of these individual items are made, the number of the ledger account debited or credited is entered in the LP (ledger page) column of the cash payments journal opposite the item posted. (Amounts to be posted to general ledger accounts on a daily basis are shown in **light blue.)**

The third phase of posting the cash payments journal is performed at the end of the month. When all the transactions of the month have been journalized, the cash payments journal is ruled as shown in our illustration, and the five money columns are totalled. The equality of debits and credits is then proved before posting.

Includes all transactions
involving payment of cash

CASH PAYMENTS JOURNAL

Date	Cheque No.	Payee	Cash	Other Accounts Name	LP	Amount	Account Debited	Accounts Payable ✓	Accounts Payable Amount	Purchases	Other Accounts LP	Other Accounts Amount
19—												
Nov 1	421	Powder Bowl Mall	2,400				Store Rent Expense				54	2,400
2	422	Uller Products	250							250		
5	423	Western Limited	35,000	Notes Payable	20	125,000	Land				11	60,000
							Building				12	100,000
17	424	Payroll Services, Inc.	3,600				Salaries Expense				53	3,600
27	425	Heads & Tails	2,450				Heads & Tails	✓	2,450			
27	426	Mountain High	800							800		
28	427	Office World	325				Office Supplies				5	325
29	428	Snow Report	450				Advertising Expense				55	450
30	429	Backcountry Sports	4,000				Backcountry Sports	✓	3,920			
							Purchase Discounts Lost				70	80
30		Totals for the month	49,275			125,000			6,370	1,050		166,855
			(1)			(X)			(21)	(50)		(X)

After the totals of the cash payments journal have been proved to be in balance, the totals of the columns for Cash, Accounts Payable, and Purchases are posted to the corresponding accounts in the general ledger. (The column totals to be posted are shown in **grey.**) The numbers of the accounts to which these postings are made are listed in parentheses just below the respective column totals in the cash payments journal. The totals of the Other Accounts columns in both the debit and credit section of this special journal are not to be posted, and the symbol *(X)* is placed below the totals of these two columns to indicate that no posting is required.

The General Journal

When all transactions involving cash or the purchase and sale of merchandise on credit are recorded in special journals, only a few types of transactions remain to be entered in the general journal. Examples include the purchase or sale of plant and equipment on credit, the return of merchandise for credit to a supplier, and the return of merchandise by customers for credit to their accounts. The general journal is also used for adjusting and closing entries at the end of the accounting period.

The following transactions of Ski Chalet during November could not conveniently be handled in any of the four special journals and were therefore entered in the general journal.

Nov. 22   A customer, Terry Frost, returned for credit $210 worth of merchandise that had been sold to her on Nov. 18.

Nov. 28   Ski Chalet returned to a supplier, Quick Release Bindings, for credit $158 worth of the merchandise purchased on Nov. 27.

Nov. 29   Purchased for use in the business, office equipment costing $3,600. Agreed to make payment within 30 days to Wolfe Computer.

Each of the above three entries includes a debit or credit to a controlling account (Accounts Receivable or Accounts Payable) and also identifies by name a particular creditor or customer. When a *controlling account* is debited or credited by a general journal entry, the debit or credit must be posted *twice:* one posting to the controlling account in the *general ledger* and another posting to a customer's account or a creditor's account in a *subsidiary ledger.* This double posting is necessary to keep the controlling account in agreement with the subsidiary ledger.

For example, in the illustrated entry of November 22 for the return of merchandise by a customer, the credit part of the entry is posted twice:

1. To the Accounts Receivable controlling account in the general ledger; this posting is evidenced by listing the account number (5) in the LP column of the general ledger.
2. To the account of Terry Frost in the subsidiary ledger for accounts receivable; this posting is indicated by the check mark (✔) placed in the LP column of the general journal.

Transactions that do not "fit" in any of the special journals

GENERAL JOURNAL					Page 4
Date		Account Titles and Explanation	LP	Debit	Credit
19__ Nov	22	Sales Returns and Allowances . . . . Accounts Receivable (Terry Frost) . . Allowed credit to customer for return of merchandise from sale of Nov. 18.	42 5/✓	210	210

	28	Accounts Payable
		    (Quick Release Bindings) . . . .
		        Purchase Returns and Allowances . .
		Returned to supplier for credit a portion of
		merchandise purchased on Nov. 27.
			21/✓
			51
				158	158

	29	Office Equipment . . . . Accounts Payable (Wolfe Computer) Purchased office equipment on 30-day credit.	14 21/✓	3,600	3,600

Showing the Source of Postings in Ledger Accounts

When a general journal and several special journals are in use, the ledger accounts should indicate the book of original entry from which each debit and credit was posted. An identifying symbol is placed opposite each entry in the reference column of the account. The symbols used in our example are:

S8	*meaning page 8 of the sales journal*
P6	*meaning page 6 of the purchases journal*
CR7	*meaning page 7 of the cash receipts journal*
CP12	*meaning page 12 of the cash payments journal*
J4	*meaning page 4 of the general journal*

The following illustration shows a typical customer's account in a subsidiary ledger for accounts receivable:

Customer: _____ C. D. Early _____			Credit terms _net 30_		
			Credit limit _$2,000_		
Date			Ref	Debit	Credit	Balance
19__ Nov	10		S8	900		900
	28		CR7		500	400

Notice that the Reference column shows the source of each debit and credit entry. Similar references are entered in general ledger accounts.

Reconciling Subsidiary Ledgers with Controlling Accounts

We have made the point that the balance in a controlling account should be equal to the sum of the balances of the subsidiary ledger accounts. Proving the equality is termed **reconciling** the subsidiary ledger with its controlling account. This process may bring to light errors in either the subsidiary ledger or in the controlling account.

The first step in reconciling a subsidiary ledger is to prepare a schedule of the balances of the subsidiary ledger accounts. For example, the balances in Ski Chalet's accounts receivable subsidiary ledger at November 30 are shown below. The total of this schedule should agree with the balance in the controlling account in the general ledger.

Schedule of Accounts Receivable
November 30, 19__

C. D. Early	$ *400*
Terry Frost	*1,070*
Nordic Ski Rentals	*9,030*
Total (per Accounts Receivable controlling account)	*$10,500*

Reconciling subsidiary ledgers with their controlling accounts is an important internal control procedure and should be performed at least once a month. This procedure may disclose such errors in the subsidiary ledger as failure to post transactions, transposition or slide errors, or mathematical errors in determining the balances of specific accounts receivable or accounts payable. However, this procedure will **not** disclose an entry that was posted to the wrong account within the subsidiary ledger.

If the subsidiary ledger and controlling account are **not** in agreement, the error may be difficult to find. The disagreement may be caused by an incorrect posting or by an error in the computation of an account balance. Thus, we may need to verify postings and recompute account balances until the error is found. Fortunately, most businesses use computer programs to maintain accounts receivable records. These programs have built-in internal control procedures that effectively prevent differences between amounts posted to the subsidiary ledger and to the related controlling account.

Variations in Special Journals

LO 3: Design a special journal for efficiently recording a particular type of business transaction.

The number of special journals used in a business, and the number of columns in these journals, depends upon the nature of the business and the volume of the various kinds of transactions. For example, a business with a large volume of merchandise returns might establish a special **sales returns and allowances journal.**

Special Journals in Perpetual Inventory Systems   The company in our illustration here used a periodic inventory system. Periodic inventory systems are used primarily in small businesses that sell a wide variety of low cost merchandise and that have manual accounting systems. Most large businesses today use **perpetual** inventory systems, in which the Inventory and Cost of Goods Sold accounts are kept up-to-date. Of course, these large companies also have computer-based accounting systems that enable them to efficiently record the cost of goods sold relating to each sales transaction.

A small business with manual accounting records can maintain a perpetual inventory system only if the company sells a **low volume** of high-cost merchandise. Examples of such businesses might include art galleries, furniture stores, and used car dealerships.

To modify the illustrated special journals for a perpetual inventory system, a few basic changes are necessary:

1. The name of the Purchases columns in the purchases journal and the cash payments journal is changed to **Inventory.** Entries in these Inventory columns should be posted daily as debits to the appropriate accounts in the inventory subsidiary ledger. At month-end, the column totals are posted to the general ledger as debits to the Inventory controlling account and as credits to the Accounts Payable controlling account.

2. A **Cost of Goods Sold column** is added to the sales journal. As sales transactions are recorded in this journal, the cost of the items sold is entered in this Cost of Goods Sold column. The individual entries in this column are posted daily as credits to the inventory subsidiary ledger. At month-end, the column total is posted to the general ledgers as a debit to the Cost of Goods Sold account and a credit to the Inventory controlling account.

3. A **Cost of Goods Sold debit column** and **Inventory credit column** are incorporated into the cash receipts journal. When cash sales of merchandise are recorded, the **cost** of the items sold is entered in each of these columns. The individual entries in the Inventory column are posted daily as credits to the inventory subsidiary ledger. At month-end, the Cost of Goods Sold column total is posted to the general ledger as a debit to the Cost of Goods Sold account; the Inventory column total is posted as a credit to the Inventory controlling account.

In Conclusion . . .   Special journals should be regarded as laboursaving devices designed to meet the needs of a particular business. Every business can benefit by using some form of special journal for recording any type of transaction that **occurs frequently.**

ASSIGNMENT MATERIAL

Problems

PROBLEM B-1
Using a Sales Journal and
Cash Receipts Journal
(LO 2)

The accounting records of Video Games, a wholesale distributor of packaged software, include a general journal and four special journals. The company maintains a general ledger and subsidiary ledgers for accounts receivable and accounts payable, and uses a periodic inventory system.

Among the general ledger accounts used by Video Games are:

Cash	10	Sales	50
Notes receivable	15	Sales returns & allowances	52
Accounts receivable	17	Sales discounts	54
Notes payable	30	Purchase returns & allowances . .	62
Accounts payable	32		

Transactions in June involving the sale of merchandise and the receipt of cash are shown below.

June 1 Sold merchandise to The Game Store for cash, $472.

June 4 Sold merchandise to Bravo Company, $8,500. Invoice no. 618; terms 2/10, n/30.

June 5 Received cash refund of $1,088 for merchandise returned to a supplier.

June 8 Sold merchandise to Micro Stores for $4,320. Invoice no. 619; terms e.o.m.

June 11 Received $2,310 cash as partial collection of a $6,310 account receivable from Olympus Company. Also received a note receivable for the $4,000 remaining balance due.

June 13 Received cheque from Bravo Company in settlement of invoice dated June 4, less discount.

June 16 Sold merchandise to Books, Etc. for $4,040. Invoice no. 620; terms 2/10, n/30.

June 16 Returned merchandise costing $960 to supplier, Software Co., for reduction of account payable.

June 20 Sold merchandise to Graphics, Inc., for $7,000. Invoice no. 621; terms 2/10, n/30.

June 21 Books, Etc. returned for credit $640 of merchandise purchased on June 16.

June 23 Borrowed $24,000 cash from a bank, signing a six-month note payable.

June 25 Received $3,332 from Books, Etc., in full settlement of invoice dated June 16, less return on June 21 and 2% discount.

June 30 Collected from Graphics, Inc., amount of invoice dated June 20, less 2% discount.

June 30 Received a 60-day note receivable for $4,320 from Micro Stores in settlement of invoice dated June 8.

INSTRUCTIONS

Record the above transactions in the appropriate journals. Use a single-column sales journal, a six-column cash receipts journal, and a two-column general journal. Foot and rule the special journals. Indicate how postings would be made by placing ledger account numbers and check marks in the appropriate columns of the journals. (You are not required to post to ledger accounts.)

PROBLEM B-2
Special Journals; Purchases and Cash Payments
(LO 2)

Poison Creek Drug Store uses a periodic inventory system and manual special journals. Among the ledger accounts used by the company are the following:

Cash	*10*	*Accounts payable*	*32*
Office supplies	*18*	*Purchases*	*60*
Land	*20*	*Purchase returns & allowances*	*62*
Building	*22*	*Salaries expense*	*70*
Notes payable	*30*	*Purchase discounts lost*	*80*

The August transactions relating to the purchase of merchandise for resale and to accounts payable are listed below along with selected other transactions. It is Poison Creek Drug's policy to record purchases of merchandise at ***net cost.***

Aug. 1 Purchased merchandise from Medco Labs at a gross invoice price of $8,450. Invoice dated today; terms 2/10, n/30.

Aug. 4 Purchased merchandise from Aluxor Products at a gross invoice price of $19,300. Invoice dated August 3; terms 2/10, n/30.

Aug. 5 Returned for credit to Medco Labs defective merchandise having an invoice price of $1,200 (net cost, $1,176).

Aug. 6 Received shipment of merchandise from Tricor Corporation and their invoice dated August 5 in amount of $14,560. Terms net 30 days.

Aug. 8 Purchased merchandise from Vita-Life, Inc., $24,480. Invoice dated today; terms net 30.

Aug. 10 Purchased merchandise from King Corporation at an invoice price of $30,000. Invoice dated August 9; terms 2/10, n/30.

Aug. 10 Issued cheque no. 631 for $7,105 to Medco Labs in settlement of balance resulting from purchase of August 1 and purchase return of August 5.

Aug. 18 Issued cheque no. 632 to Aluxor Products for $19,300, in payment of the August 3 invoice. This invoice temporarily had been misplaced, and Poison Creek failed to make payment in time to take advantage of the 2% cash discount.

Aug. 18 Issued cheque no. 633 for $29,400 to King Corporation in settlement of invoice dated August 9, less 2% discount.

Aug. 20 Purchased merchandise for cash, $1,080. Issued cheque no. 634 to Candy Corp.

Aug. 21 Bought land and building for $208,800. Land was worth $64,800, and building, $144,000. Paid cash of $36,000 and signed a promissory note for the balance of $172,800. Cheque no. 635, in the amount of $36,000, was issued to Security Co.

Aug. 23 Purchased merchandise from Novelty Products for cash, $900. Issued cheque no. 636.

Aug. 26 Purchased merchandise from Ralston Company for a gross invoice price of $32,400. Invoice dated August 26, terms 2/10, n/30.

Aug. 28 Paid cash for office supplies, $270. Issued cheque no. 637 to Super Office, Inc.

Aug. 29 Purchased merchandise from Candy Corp. for cash, $1,890. Cheque no. 638.

Aug. 31 Paid salaries for August, $17,920. Issued cheque no. 639 to National Bank, which handles the distribution of the payroll to employees. (Ignore payroll taxes.)

INSTRUCTIONS

a. Record the transactions in the appropriate journals. Use a single-column purchases journal, a five-column cash payments journal, and a two-column general journal. Foot and rule the special journals. Make all postings to the proper general ledger accounts and to the accounts payable subsidiary ledger. (For posting references in the ledgers, assume all journals are on page no. *5.*)

b. Prepare a schedule of accounts payable at August 31 to prove that the subsidiary ledger is in balance with the controlling account for accounts payable.

PROBLEM B-3
Using Special Journals to Record Cash Transactions
(LO 2)

J. D. Thomas Company wholesales furniture to interior designers and retail furniture stores. The company uses a periodic inventory system and special journals. Purchases of merchandise are recorded at *net cost* in a purchases journal.

In this problem, you are to record only the *cash transactions* of J. D. Thomas Company during October. These transactions are listed below:

Oct. 1 Issued cheque no. 734 to Furniture Trade Centre in payment of store rent for October, $2,200.

Oct. 3   Purchased office equipment for $8,400 from MicroDesk, issuing cheque no. 735 as a $1,400 cash down payment and issuing a 90-day, 10% note payable for the $7,000 balance.

Oct. 4   The owner, J. D. Thomas, invested an additional $20,000 cash in the business.

Oct. 8   Paid an account payable to Colonial House, taking the allowable 2% cash discount. Issued cheque no. 736 in the amount of $14,700.

Oct. 9   Sold merchandise for cash to Southwest Design Studios, $16,300.

Oct. 10   Received $3,600 as a partial collection of an $18,000 account receivable from Myra's Interiors. Also received a $14,400 note receivable for the uncollected balance.

Oct. 12   Received $7,742 from Furniture Gallery in settlement of our $7,900 sales invoice dated Oct. 2, less 2%.

Oct. 15   Cash sales of merchandise, $18,750.

Oct. 22   Purchased merchandise from Quebec Furniture Co. for cash, $11,200. Issued cheque no. 737.

Oct. 25   Issued cheque no. 738 in payment of account payable to Fabrics Unlimited, $6,664.

Oct. 27   Purchased merchandise from Oak World, $16,700. Issued cheque no. 739.

Oct. 29   Received cheque for $17,836 from Lambert's in settlement of our $18,200 sales invoice dated Oct. 19, less 2%.

Oct. 31   Paid monthly salaries, $8,470. Issued one cheque, no. 740, to Merchants' Bank in the full amount of these salaries. (The bank handles the distribution of the payroll to individual employees.)

Oct. 31   Paid Merchants' Bank instalment due today on a note payable. Issued cheque no. 741 in the amount of $1,630, representing $480 interest expense and a reduction in the balance of the note payable of the remaining $1,150.

INSTRUCTIONS

Enter the above transactions in either a six-column cash receipts journal or a five-column cash payments journal. Total the money columns in each journal and determine the equality of the debit and credit column totals.

PROBLEM B-4
Use of Special Journals and Subsidiary Ledgers
(LO 2)

The accounting records of Crestline Lumber Co. include a general ledger and two subsidiary ledgers, one for accounts receivable and one for accounts payable. The company uses the four special journals as well as a two-column general journal. Crestline uses the periodic inventory system and records purchases at net cost when discounts are available. All credit sales are on terms of 2/10, n/30. A partial chart of accounts for Crestline Lumber Co. is shown below:

Cash	1	Sales	60
Notes receivable	2	Sales returns & allowances	62
Accounts receivable	4	Sales discounts	64
Supplies	6	Purchases	70
Unexpired insurance	8	Purchase returns and allowances	72
Land	20	Purchase discounts lost	74
Equipment	26	Transportation-in	76
Notes payable	30	Salaries expense	80
Accounts payable	32		

The October 31 balances of the above ledger accounts appear in the partially completed work sheets accompanying the text.

The schedules of accounts receivable and accounts payable for the company at October 31, 19__, are shown below:

Schedule of Accounts Receivable October 31, 19__		Schedule of Accounts Payable October 31, 19__	
Ace Contractors	$20,800	Northwest Mills	$29,400
Reliable Builders, Inc.	18,750		
Total	$39,550		

The November transactions of the business are as follows:

Nov. 2 Purchased merchandise on account from Northwest Mills, $28,000. Invoice was dated today, terms 2/10, n/30.

Nov. 3 Sold merchandise to Ace Contractors, $16,000. Invoice no. 428.

Nov. 4 Issued cheque no. 920 to Northwest Mills for $30,000 in full payment of the invoice outstanding at October 31. Although the account payable had been initially recorded at net cost ($29,400), Crestline failed to make payment in time to take advantage of the 2% cash discount.

Nov. 5 Sold merchandise for cash, $5,600.

Nov. 6 Collected $18,375 from Reliable Builders, Inc., representing the account receivable at October 31, less 2% cash discount.

Nov. 9 Purchased supplies for cash, $875. Issued cheque no. 921 to Aero Supply Co.

Nov. 10 Purchased merchandise from Cornerbrook Gypsum, $12,500. Invoice dated November 9, terms 2/10, n/30.

Nov. 11 Sold merchandise to Mountain Homes, $21,750. Invoice no. 429.

Nov. 12 Received $36,480 from Ace Contractors, representing collection of the October 31 balance receivable, upon which the discount has lapsed, and invoice no. 428 (see Nov. 3), less 2% cash discount.

Nov. 13 Paid transportation charges of $510 on goods purchased November 10 from Cornerbrook Gypsum. Issued cheque no. 922 to Cannonball Trucking.

Nov. 16 Sold a parcel of land not needed in the business at its cost of $25,000. Received $10,000 cash and a note receivable for $15,000.

Nov. 17 Issued credit memo. no. 78 in recognition of a $1,750 sales return by Mountain Homes of some of the merchandise purchased on November 11.

Nov. 17 Sold merchandise for cash, $4,675.

Nov. 18 Issued cheque no. 923 to Empire Insurance, $1,425, in full payment of a one-year fire insurance policy.

Nov. 19 Bought merchandise for cash from Modern Tool Co., $2,625. Cheque no. 924.

Nov. 19 Issued cheque no. 925 for $12,250 to Cornerbrook Gypsum in payment of the purchase on November 10, less 2% cash discount.

Nov. 20 Received $19,600 from Mountain Homes in settlement of invoice no. 429 (Nov. 11), less sales return on Nov. 17, and less 2%.

Nov. 20 Sold merchandise on account to Ace Contractors, $13,650, invoice no. 430.

Nov. 23 Purchased merchandise from AAA Moldings for cash, $4,050, cheque no. 926.

Nov. 24 Sold goods on account to Lake Development Co., $39,950. Invoice no. 431.

Nov. 26 Purchased merchandise from Timber Products, $26,500. Invoice dated November 24, terms 2/10, n/60.

Nov. 27 Returned to Timber Products merchandise with an invoice price of $2,150. Issued debit memo. no. 42 in the amount of the recorded *net cost*, $2,107.

Nov. 30 Purchased equipment for $60,000. Issued cheque no. 927 to Electro-Lift for $10,000 as a cash down payment and issued a note payable for the $50,000 balance.

Nov. 30 Paid monthly salaries of $14,800. Issued one cheque (no. 928) to Payroll Service Co. in the amount of the entire payroll. Payroll Service Co. handles the preparation and distribution of paycheques to individual employees.

INSTRUCTIONS

a. Record the November transactions in the appropriate journals and make all individual postings to the general ledger and subsidiary ledgers. Individual postings include:
   1. All entries in the general journal.
   2. Entries in the Other Accounts columns of the cash receipts journal and the cash payments journal.
   3. All entries in any journal that affect subsidiary ledger accounts.
      In the journals, use check marks ($\checkmark$) and ledger account numbers to indicate which amounts have been posted. In the ledger accounts, use the Ref column to indicate the source of each posting. (Assume that you are using page 7 of each journal.)
b. Foot and rule the special journals and post the appropriate column totals to the general ledger. Make all appropriate posting cross-references.
c. Prepare a schedule of the individual accounts receivable at November 30 and a separate schedule of the individual accounts payable. Determine that the totals of these schedules are in agreement with the balances of the related controlling accounts in the general ledger.

Analytical and Decision Problems and Cases

A&D B-1
Designing a Special Journal
and Explaining Its Use
(LO 1, 3)

Leisure Clothing is a mail-order company that sells clothes to the public at discount prices. Recently Leisure Clothing initiated a new policy allowing a 10-day free trial on all clothes bought from the company. At the end of the 10-day period, the customer may either pay cash for the purchase or return the goods to Leisure Clothing. The new policy caused such a large boost in sales that, even after considering the many sales returns, the policy appeared quite profitable.

Leisure Clothing uses a periodic inventory system. The company's accounting system includes a sales journal, purchases journal, cash receipts journal, cash payments journal, and general journal. As an internal control procedure, an officer of the company reviews and initials every entry in the general journal before the amounts are posted to the ledger accounts. Since the 10-day free trial policy has been in effect, hundreds of entries recording sales returns have been entered in the general journal each week. Each of these entries has been reviewed and initialled by an officer of the company, and the amounts have been posted to Sales Returns & Allowances and to the Accounts Receivable controlling account in the general ledger, and also to the customer's account in the accounts receivable subsidiary ledger.

Since these sales return entries are so numerous, it has been suggested that a special journal be designed to handle them. This could not only save time in journalizing and posting the entries, but also eliminate the time-consuming individual review of each of these repetitious entries by an officer of the company.

a. How many amounts are entered in the general journal to describe a single sales return transaction? Are these amounts the same?

b. Explain why these sales return transactions are suited to the use of a special journal. Explain in detail how many money columns the special journal should have, and what postings would have to be done either at the time of the transaction or at the end of the period.

c. Assume that there were 3,000 sales returns during the month. How many postings would have to be made during the month if these transactions were entered in the general journal? How many postings would have to be made if the special journal you designed in **b** were used? (Assume a one-month accounting period.)

THE NEXT DIMENSION

The Development and Use of Accounting Information

Note: Part I of this problem *requires* use of the partially completed working papers that accompany this textbook. Part II does not require working papers.

INTRODUCTION

This problem may be started after completing the first six chapters of this text. The business in this problem is a sole proprietorship whose accounting records include a general journal and *four special journals.* Therefore, you should *familiarize yourself with the material covered in Appendix B*—Manual Special Journals. In addition, you will need to be familiar with the *Supplemental Topic* following Chapter 4, because this problem calls for the preparation of a work sheet.

This Comprehensive Problem consists of two separate parts. Part I must be completed prior to beginning Part II.

Part I   The first part of this problem is intended to "pull together" the various steps in the accounting cycle and to illustrate the "flow" of information through basic types of accounting records.

In completing this part, you act as the accountant for *THE NEXT DIMENSION* (called NEXT, for short). NEXT is a small merchandising business with a manual accounting system. You have full responsibility for maintaining the company's accounting records during the month of June, doing the necessary end-of-period work at June 30, and preparing financial statements for the month.

Part II   In the second part of this Comprehensive Problem, you are asked to answer a variety of practical business questions *using the information developed in Part I.* This part of the problem requires you to locate and use the accounting information contained within the accounting records and the financial statements. You also are expected to analyze and evaluate the information, to exercise judgment, and to explain your conclusions.

If you work this problem as a group assignment, each group member should be prepared to discuss in class all of the accounting processes performed in Part I, and all of the group's conclusions relating to Part II.

Part I: Simulation of the Accounting Cycle

1. Read the background material on pages 363–368.
2. Journalize the transactions for the month of June (pages 369–372). Make all necessary "individual postings" to the general ledger and subsidiary ledger accounts. These individual postings will include:
   a. Entries in the general journal.
   b. Entries in the Other Accounts columns of the cash receipts journal and the cash payments journal.
   c. Entries in any journal affecting accounts in the company's subsidiary ledgers (accounts receivable, accounts payable, and inventory).
   Include appropriate posting references both in the journals and in ledger accounts.

   Not all of the items described in the Events and Transactions section qualify as transactions that should be recorded in NEXT's journals. **You** must decide which events should be journalized and which should not. List on a separate sheet the date and a brief description of any item that you **do not record** in a journal and explain your reasons for not recording the event.
3. Foot and crossfoot the four special journals. Post the appropriate column totals to the general ledger accounts.

   A few "check" figures: At this stage, we provide a few check figures to help determine whether you are "on track" before you start preparing the work sheet. Prior to making adjusting entries, the following five accounts should have the balances listed below:

Cash	$136,260
Accounts receivable	51,400
Inventory	61,260
Accounts payable	133,970
Sales	208,600

   Determine that the sum of the account balances in each of the three subsidiary ledgers are equal to the balances in the controlling accounts.
4. Prepare a 10-column work sheet for the month ended June 30. (To save time, NEXT's general ledger account titles are preprinted on the partially completed working papers.) As you prepare your trial balance, you will notice that several accounts have no balances. Most of these accounts, such as Depreciation Expense, will acquire a balance **when you make adjusting entries.** It is probable, however, that one or more accounts may **never** acquire a balance in June, as NEXT simply may not have engaged in any transactions involving that account. An account with a "-0-" balance may be listed in the work sheet, but it should **not** be included in the formal financial statements. (**Note:** Briefly explain the end-of-period adjustments in your work sheet on a separate sheet to accompany the work sheet.)
5. Prepare the following financial statements for the month ended June 30, 2000:
   a. A multiple-step income statement for the month of June. Organize this statement in the format illustrated in Chapter 5. (Ledger account numbers in the **600s** designate selling expenses, ledger ac-

count numbers in the **700s** represent general and administrative expenses, and account numbers in the **800s** represent nonoperating items.)

b. A statement of owner's equity.

c. A classified balance sheet.

Also, to accompany these financial statements, draft a note that discloses the lawsuit pending against NEXT. Include the note at the bottom of the balance sheet.

6. Prepare and post the adjusting entries and closing entries.

7. Prepare an after-closing trial balance as of June 30.

8. Prepare three separate schedules showing at June 30: (1) the individual accounts receivable, (2) the individual accounts payable, and (3) the number of units, unit cost, and total cost of each type of product in inventory. Determine that the total amounts in these schedules agree with the totals of the related controlling accounts in the **after-closing** trial balance.

INSTRUCTIONS

Part II: Using the Information

Using accounting information effectively often requires the ability to **communicate** your conclusions and your reasoning to others in a clear and convincing manner. Throughout Part II of this exercise, we ask that you **explain your answers fully,** including any assumptions that you make and the basis for your conclusions.

Whenever you use quantitative information—either in computations or in support of your conclusion—clearly indicate the specific source of the information from within NEXT's accounting records or financial statements.

No accounting sheets are provided for Part II, as no schedules and few computations are required. You may answer all questions relating to Part II on ordinary notebook paper or using a word processor.

1. **Discussion of accounting policies.** Two of NEXT's accounting policies are described below:

   a. Purchase of assets (other than merchandise) costing less than $500 are charged directly to the **Supplies Expense** account, rather than to asset accounts.

   b. Utilities bills are recorded as expense in the month in which the bills are **paid,** rather than the month in which the utilities services actually are consumed.

   For each of these policies, discuss (1) the rationale for policy, (2) the distortions—if any—caused in the monthly financial statements, and (3) whether you consider the policy appropriate under the circumstances.

2. **A few preliminary computations.**

   a. An analysis of NEXT's sales by product for the last three months appears on page 374. Using the data in this analysis:

   (1) Compute separately the gross profit rate for each of the three **months.** (Round to the nearest 1/10 of 1%.)

   (2) Compute separately the gross profit rate earned on sales of each of the three products. (**Note:** The per-unit costs and sales

prices of each product remain constant over the three-month period. To achieve a degree of uniformity in students' solutions, we ask that you base your computations of gross profit rate on these **per-unit** amounts. Round computations to the nearest 1/10 of 1%.)

b. Compute NEXT's **current ratio** and the amount of its **working capital** as of May 31 and as of June 30. (Round the computation of the current ratio to one decimal place, for example, 2.1 to 1.)

3. *Using accounting information in daily business operations:*

a. On June 11, POW Stereo called and asked the dollar amount that would be required to settle its account in full by immediate payment. Determine this amount.

b. Assume that on June 24, Atlantic Auto Supply called and asked if NEXT could ship another 350 Easy Rider systems immediately. Explain to Renner the extent to which NEXT is able (or unable) to meet this request.

c. On June 29, NEXT purchased merchandise from Carnegie Acoustics at an invoice price of $34,000. Instead of the usual credit terms of 10 e.o.m., assume that Carnegie instead had offered terms of *1/10, n/60.*

(1) Specify the latest dates at which NEXT should make payment and the amounts of these payments, assuming that NEXT (a) takes advantage of the potential discount and (b) passes up the discount.

(2) Assume that NEXT does not have enough cash to make payment within the discount period but will have the money within 60 days. However, NEXT can borrow money from its bank for short periods of time, with interest computed at a rate of 9% per year (3/4% per month). Would it be advantageous for NEXT to borrow money from its bank at this interest rate in order to take advantage of the 1/10, n/60 cash discount? Explain fully.

4. *Evaluating financial position and the results of operations.* Renner has reviewed the income statements for the past three months and has noted that the amounts of net sales, gross profit, and net income have increased each month (see page 374). She also has seen your computations of NEXT's current ratio and working capital at May 31 and June 30. As a result, she is most optimistic about the company's future prospects. She states, "Not only are sales, gross profit, and net income increasing steadily, but NEXT is becoming much more solvent. Let's hope these trends continue through the summer.

"You know, I thought the bankruptcy of Home Video would hit us pretty hard, but we seem to be doing just fine without them. Now, if we can just land the Halifax Electronics Co. account. . . ."

a. Evaluate the trends in NEXT's sales, gross profit, and net income over the past three months. Do you concur with Renner's conclusions? Explain any *existing conditions* that you believe are likely to affect sales, gross profit, and net income in the months immediately ahead.

b. In this part, we ask you to evaluate the extent to which NEXT's *solvency* is increasing or decreasing from *two separate perspectives.* Explain fully the reasoning behind each of your answers.

(1) Explain whether a short-term creditor—say, *Carnegie Acoustics*—should consider NEXT more or less solvent at June 30 than it was at May 31.

(2) Now discuss the change in NEXT's solvency during June from the perspective of *Bailey Renner.* That is, is NEXT becoming more or less able to "stand on its own two feet," without additional investments of cash by Renner?

c. Assume that at the end of June, Renner receives an offer from Eastern Wholesale to buy NEXT—"lock, stock, and barrel"—for cash at a price equal to the balance in Renner's capital account. Eastern is a reputable and financially sound company.

As part of the offer, Eastern will hire Renner to manage NEXT (as a division of Eastern) at a salary of $6,000 per month (and also will retain you at your present salary). Finally, Eastern offers to assume the cost and responsibility of settling the pending litigation brought against NEXT by POW Stereo.

Evaluate the effect that accepting this offer is likely to have upon Renner's monthly income over the next several months. (If Renner does *not* accept the offer, her monthly income will consist of the net income earned by NEXT, plus interest on her money market fund. The money market fund yields about 6% per year [or ½% per month].)

Based upon the information available in this case, make an overall recommendation to Renner as to whether she should seriously consider Eastern's offer. Explain your reasoning.

GENERAL BACKGROUND

NEXT is a wholesaler. The company is organized as a sole proprietorship and is owned by Bailey Renner, who works full time in the business.

Until recently, NEXT sold a single product—SuperScreen television sets, manufactured by Home Video, Inc. In April, Home Video declared bankruptcy and ceased operations, leaving NEXT with only a small inventory of SuperScreen televisions and no source of additional merchandise.

Fortunately, Renner was able to make arrangements quickly with Carnegie Acoustics for NEXT to become the regional wholesaler of Carnegie's two lines of popular stereo speaker systems.

The Company's Products . . .

The two Carnegie speaker systems sold by NEXT are:

Easy Riders   A system for cars and trucks
MegaMites   A system of very small—but "big sound"—speakers for homes and offices

NEXT also is continuing to sell its remaining inventory of SuperScreen televisions.

Its Accounting Policies . . .

Note to the student: As NEXT's chief accountant, you are expected to adhere to NEXT's accounting policies. Become sufficiently familiar with these policies so that you are able to apply them as you record transactions.

Recording Purchases of Merchandise   NEXT maintains a ***perpetual*** inventory system and records purchases of merchandise at ***net cost.*** If payment is not made within the discount period, the additional amount that must be paid is charged to account no. 812, Purchase Discounts Lost. (Home Video, Inc., offered terms of 2/10 n/30. Carnegie Acoustics, however, offers ***no*** cash discounts. Its credit terms are ***10 eom***—meaning that full payment is due on the tenth day of the month following the credit purchase.)

All purchases are F.O.B. destination (that is, title to the merchandise passes to NEXT at destination), and purchases therefore are recorded on the date that the merchandise is ***received*** by NEXT.

Recording Sales of Merchandise   As a wholesaler, NEXT sells only to other businesses, not to the general public. Sales normally are made on account, with credit terms of ***2/10, n/30.*** Sales are recorded at gross invoice prices; if customers pay within the discount period, any cash discounts allowed the customers are debited to account no. 404, Sales Discounts.

All sales are recorded on the date the merchandise is shipped.

Freight Charges   NEXT usually does not pay the freight charges on its inbound shipments (purchases) and, therefore, does not have a separate Transportation-in account in its ledger. On occasion, the company does pay the extra freight charges involved in "rush" orders. Such expenditures are charged directly to the Cost of Goods Sold account.

Freight charges on ***outbound*** shipments (sales) are charged to account no. 620, Freight Expense. To maintain a strong customer relationship, NEXT has a policy of paying the freight charges for all outbound shipments.

Purchases of Assets Other Than Merchandise   Purchases of assets other than merchandise in which the total transaction amount is ***less than $500*** are charged directly to Supplies Expense (account no. 628). If the amount of the transaction is ***$500 or more,*** the cost of the purchased items is debited to an appropriate ***asset*** account. (All purchases of merchandise are debited to the Inventory account and are entered in the inventory subsidiary records, regardless of dollar amount.)

Monthly Utilities Bills   For convenience, all utilities bills (telephone, gas, and electric) are charged to expense at the date that ***payment is made,*** rather than by making adjusting entries at the end of each month.

Accounting Period The company adjusts and closes its accounts at the end of each month.

. . . And Its Accounting Records

The accounting records appearing in this exercise include the company's general journal, four special journals, general ledger, and separate subsidiary ledgers for accounts receivable, accounts payable, and inventory.

Bailey Renner, the owner of the business, personally signs all cheques and maintains a cheque register showing the daily balance in the company's chequing account. As you are not responsible for maintaining the cheque register, it is not included in this exercise.

Journals NEXT uses manual special journals in recording (1) sales on account, (2) purchases of merchandise on account, (3) cash receipts, and (4) cash payments. In addition, the company maintains a conventional general journal for recording other types of transactions.

The columnar structures of the four special journals appear on the following page. These journals are similar to those illustrated in Appendix B of the textbook but contain the following modifications:

1. Because NEXT uses a perpetual inventory system, the ***sales journal*** contains ***two*** money columns. In addition to the column used for recording the amount of sales revenue from each sales transaction, a column has been added for recording the ***cost of goods sold.*** (You must determine the cost of goods sold from the unit costs appearing in the inventory subsidiary ledger.)

   Each of the two money columns is accompanied by a separate posting reference column. Check marks are entered in these posting reference columns as the individual amounts are posted to the appropriate subsidiary ledger accounts. (The sales price is posted as a debit to the customer's account in the ***accounts receivable*** subsidiary ledger. The cost of goods sold is posted as a credit to the appropriate account in the ***inventory*** subsidiary ledger.)

   At month-end, the two money columns in the sales journal are totalled and are posted to the appropriate accounts in the ***general*** ledger.

2. All purchases of merchandise are made on account and are recorded in a one-column ***purchases journal.*** Because NEXT has a perpetual inventory system, however, individual transaction amounts are posted immediately as both a debit to the inventory subsidiary ledger and as a credit to the accounts payable subsidiary ledger. Because of this "double posting," the purchases journal also contains two posting reference columns.

   At month-end, the column total of the purchases journal is debited to the ***Inventory*** account, rather than to the Purchases account that is often used in a periodic inventory system.

3. As all sales are made on account, the ***cash receipts journal*** does not have a "sales" column. If an occasional cash sale were to occur, the transaction would be recorded using the "other accounts" columns.

CASH RECEIPTS JOURNAL

Date	Account Credited	Credits				Debits					Explanation
		Accounts Receivable		Other Accounts		Sales Discounts	Cash	Other Accounts			
		✓	Amount	LP	Amount			Name	LP	Amount	

CASH PAYMENTS JOURNAL

Date	Ch. No.	Payee	Account Debited	Debits				Credits			
				Accounts Payable		Other Accounts		Cash	Other Accounts		
				✓	Amount	LP	Amount		Name	LP	Amount

SALES JOURNAL

Date	Account Receivable Debited	Invoice No.	A/R ✓	Invoice Amount	Inventory ✓	Cost of Goods Sold

PURCHASES JOURNAL

Date	Account Payable Credited	Invoice Date	Terms	Inventory ✓	A/P ✓	Net Cost

Ledgers   The chart of accounts for NEXT's general ledger appears both in the May 31 after-closing trial balance on page 368 and also at the beginning of the partially completed working papers for this problem. (Partially completed work sheets for problems are available as a supplement to the text.) The accounts in each of the three subsidiary ledgers are arranged in alphabetical order, and their balances at May 31 are as shown in the schedules in the next section.

Balances at the Beginning of June

The general ledger accounts used by NEXT are shown in the after-closing trial balance at May 31, which appears on the following page. (The May 31 balances also appear in the general ledger accounts of the partially completed work sheets.) For convenience, all account balances and transaction amounts are stated in even dollars.

The subsidiary ledger accounts used in this exercise (and their balances at May 31) are as follows:

Accounts Receivable:

Atlantic Auto Supply	$ 13,200
Electric City	17,800
POW Stereo	55,000
Stereo Depot	16,400
The Buzzer	–0–
Total (per controlling account)	$102,400

Accounts Payable:

Carnegie Acoustics	$195,000
Express Transport Co.	4,075
Home Video, Inc.	102,900
Total (per controlling account)	$301,975

	Quantity	Unit Cost	Total Cost
Inventory:			
Easy Rider Speaker Systems	500	$ 68	$34,000
MegaMite Speaker Systems	300	93	27,900
SuperScreen TVs	30	1,029	30,870
Total (per controlling account)			$92,770

		Debit	Credit
	THE NEXT DIMENSION **After-Closing Trial Balance** **May 31, 2000**		
101	Cash	$ 156,230	
103	Notes receivable		
104	Accounts receivable	102,400	
106	Interest receivable		
108	Inventory	92,770	
110	Unexpired insurance	120	
112	Prepaid advertising	2,750	
113	Supplies	2,800	
120	Land	370,000	
122	Buildings	450,000	
123	Accumulated depreciation: buildings		$ 52,500
130	Warehouse equipment	42,000	
131	Accumulated depreciation: warehouse equipment		19,600
132	Office equipment	18,000	
133	Accumulated depreciation: office equipment		2,100
201	Notes payable (due Nov. 20, 2001)		300,000
205	Accounts payable		301,975
210	Salaries payable		
212	Interest payable		750
301	Bailey Renner, capital		560,145
303	Bailey Renner, drawing		
305	Income summary		
401	Sales		
402	Sales returns and allowances		
404	Sales discounts		
501	Cost of goods sold		
601	Warehouse wages expense		
610	Depreciation expense: buildings		
611	Depreciation expense: warehouse equipment		
620	Freight expense		
622	Advertising expense		
624	Maintenance expense		
626	Utilities expense		
628	Supplies expense		
630	Travel and entertainment expense		
632	Inventory shrinkage losses		
701	Office salaries expense		
710	Depreciation expense: office equipment		
720	Insurance expense		
801	Interest revenue		
810	Interest expense		
812	Purchase discounts lost		
		$1,237,070	$1,237,070

NARRATIVE OF TRANSACTIONS

Events and Transactions Occurring in June

June 1 Received a cheque for $12,936 from Atlantic Auto Supply in full settlement of its account less 2% discount.

1 Purchased a round-trip ticket for Bailey Renner to fly to Halifax, Nova Scotia in early June. The purpose of this trip is for Renner to discuss with Halifax Electronics Co. the possibility of NEXT's becoming a wholesale distributor for Halifax's products. Issued cheque no. 922 to Air Canada for $398.

2 Sold 300 Easy Rider systems on account to POW Stereo. Our sales invoice no. 749, $24,000.

2 Purchased a five-day vacation-tour package of the Hawaiian Islands in mid-June. Renner plans this trip as a personal vacation and a chance to "get away" from the business. Issued cheque no. 923 to Canadian Airlines for $1,477.

3 Ordered 300 Easy Rider systems from Carnegie Acoustics at a per-unit cost of $68 (total cost, $20,400).

3 Received $17,444 cash from Electric City in full settlement of its account balance within the discount period.

4 Sold 150 MegaMite systems on account to POW Stereo. Our sales invoice no. 750, $18,000.

4 Renner received $1,200,000 in cash as her inheritance from the estate of a recently deceased relative. She invested the money in a money market fund.

5 Sold 18 SuperScreen televisions on account to The Buzzer, a chain of "sports bars." Our sales invoice no. 751, $25,200.

5 Purchased "skybox" tickets to a baseball game. The purpose of renting the skybox is to entertain NEXT's customers. Thus, the expenditure should be charged to a selling expense account (those with account numbers in the 600s). Issued cheque no. 924 to Commercial Ticket Sales for $1,200.

8 Ordered 200 MegaMite systems from Carnegie Acoustics at a per-unit cost of $93. Total cost of this purchase, $18,600.

8 Received and paid the telephone bill for May service. Issued cheque no. 925 to C & P Telephone for $206. (Telephone expense is charged to account no. 626, Utilities Expense.)

9 The 300 Easy Rider systems ordered from Carnegie on June 3 arrived and were placed in inventory. Invoice dated June 8 for $20,400, payment due 10 eom.

9 Issued cheque no. 926 to Carnegie Acoustics for $195,000 in full payment of the May 31 account balance, which is due tomorrow.

9 After returning from her trip to Halifax, Renner believes that NEXT has at least a 50-50 chance of becoming a regional distributor for Halifax Electronics Co. If NEXT wins this contract, it

should gain additional sales of about $50,000 per month, with a gross profit rate of 22%. Halifax Electronics will not make a final decision until August, however, when its contract with an existing regional distributor—one of NEXT's competitors—expires.

June 10   Issued cheque no. 927 in the amount of $105,000 to Home Video, Inc., in full settlement of the amount owed. Because of confusion surrounding the bankruptcy of Home Video, NEXT did not pay this account within the discount period. Therefore, NEXT was required to pay the gross invoice price of merchandise purchased from Home Video, rather than the net cost that NEXT had recorded in its accounting records. (Use two lines in the Cash Payments Journal in recording the debit portion of this entry.)

10   The employee who maintains the cheque register informed Renner that the issuance of the cheques to Carnegie and to Home Video had caused the company's bank account to become substantially overdrawn. Renner immediately transferred $150,000 cash from her money market fund into NEXT's chequing account.

10   Sold 350 Easy Rider systems on account to Atlantic Auto Supply. Our sales invoice no. 752, $28,000.

11   Received bill from Megacity Gas & Electric for utilities service in May; issued cheque no. 928 in full payment, $231.

11   Paid the balance owed at May 31 to Express Transport Co. for shipments to customers in May. Issued cheque no. 929 for $4,075.

11   Purchased for cash a typewriter for business use. Issued cheque no. 930 to C & D Supply Co. for $421.

12   Issued cheque no. 931 for $3,600 to Seaboard Insurance Co. in full payment for a one-year casualty insurance policy to become effective on June 16. (Debit an asset account.)

12   Received 200 MegaMite systems ordered from Carnegie on June 8. Invoice dated today for $18,600.

12   Received a purchase order from Stereo Depot for 400 Easy Rider systems at a per-unit cost of $80. Immediately shipped all 150 units on hand and recorded the sale of these units. Our sales invoice no. 753. Placed a "rush" order with Carnegie for 500 Easy Rider systems at a unit cost of $68.

Delivery of rush orders is guaranteed in two business days. (June 13 and 14 are the weekend; the order will arrive on Tuesday, June 16.) NEXT must pay the special freight charges for rush shipments.

12   Biweekly salaries were as follows: office salaries, $2,700; warehouse wages, $2,000. Issued cheque no. 932 in the amount of the total payroll, $4,700, to National Bank, which handles the payroll distribution to NEXT's employees. (Ignore amounts withheld from employees' pay and also payroll taxes on NEXT.)

15   Received $24,696 from the Buzzer in full settlement of its purchase on June 5, less the allowable 2% discount for prompt payment.

June 16 Received the rush shipment of 500 Easy Rider systems ordered on June 12; invoice dated today for $34,000. Immediately shipped the remaining 250 units ordered by Stereo Depot on that date, issuing sales invoice no. 754.

16 Issued cheque no. 933 to Overnight Air Transport for $206 in special-handling freight charges relating to the rush order of Easy Rider speakers received on June 16.

17 Bailey Renner removed from inventory one of the SuperScreen televisions for personal use in her home.

18 Sold 250 MegaMite systems on account to Electric City. Our sales invoice no. 755, $30,000.

18 Purchased supplies for cash. Issued cheque no. 934 to C & D Supply Co. for $2,206.

19 Made the monthly interest payment on the 9%, $300,000 note payable to Harbour Mortgage Co. Terms of the note call for the accrued interest ($2,250 per month) to be paid on the 20th day of each month. The entire principal amount of the note due on November 15, 2001. Issued cheque no. 935 for $2,250. (***Note:*** $750 of this interest has been accrued as of May 31.)

19 Received $27,440 from Atlantic Auto Supply in full payment within the discount period for the sale on June 10.

19 Renner contacted POW Stereo about its account, much of which is overdue. The controller of POW promised to contact Renner tomorrow to settle this matter.

20 The controller of POW Stereo visited Renner at her home, giving her a cheque for $7,000, and a 90-day, 12% promissory note to NEXT, dated today, for the remaining $90,000 balance of POW's account. The note calls for interest to accrue at the rate of 12% per annum, all payable upon the maturity date (September 17, 2000). Renner notified POW that until this note is paid, POW must pay cash for future purchases of merchandise from NEXT.

22 Electric City returned 30 of the MegaMite systems purchased on June 18, stating that they were overstocked in such products. (It is NEXT's policy to accept such returns without question.) The account receivable from Electric City was credited for the full amount of this sales return ($3,600), and credit memo no. 29 was issued to Electric City.

   The returned speaker systems were in perfect condition and were placed back in NEXT's inventory.

22 Received from Stereo Depot a cheque for $47,760 in full settlement of its account. This amount includes full payment of Stereo Depot's account balance at the beginning of the month, upon which the discount period has lapsed; and also payment for its credit purchases on June 12 and June 16, upon which Stereo Depot is entitled to a 2% cash discount.

23 Sold 150 Easy Rider systems on account to Atlantic Auto Supply. Our sales invoice no. 756, $12,000.

June 25 Received the 300 MegaMite systems ordered from Carnegie on June 19. Invoice dated June 23 for $27,900.

26 Ten of the MegaMite systems received on June 25 were found to be defective and were returned to Carnegie Acoustics. Issued debit memo no. 86 for $930. (Carnegie accepts such returns and credits the customer's account in its accounts receivable subsidiary ledger.)

26 Received $25,872 from Electric City in full payment for its purchase on June 18, less the merchandise returned on June 22, and less a 2% cash discount on the remaining balance.

26 Biweekly salaries were as follows: office salaries, $2,700; warehouse wages, $2,000. Issued cheque no. 936 for the total payroll, $4,700, to National Bank. (Ignore amounts withheld from employees' pay and also payroll taxes on NEXT.)

29 A lawyer for POW Stereo notifies Renner that POW is filing a lawsuit against NEXT. POW alleges $500,000 in damages caused by NEXT's refusal to sell merchandise to POW on the same credit terms as it extends to other customers. The lawyer states that NEXT's refusal to sell merchandise on account to POW may force POW to declare bankruptcy. However, the lawyer suggests that if NEXT agrees to cancel the $90,000 note receivable from POW, POW will not continue this lawsuit.

Renner is furious about POW's lawsuit and vows to fight it in court. She believes that NEXT has acted properly and has no liability to POW.

29 Received the 500 Easy Rider systems ordered from Carnegie on June 23. The purchase invoice, dated today, is in the amount of $34,000.

29 Sold 200 MegaMite systems on account to Stereo Depot. Our sales invoice no. 757, $24,000.

30 Paid the monthly balance of the Visa card that Renner uses for a variety of personal expenditures. Issued cheque no. 937 to Visa for $1,240.

30 Paid the monthly balance of the American Express card that Renner uses for entertaining customers. Issued cheque no. 938 to American Express for $208.

30 Issued cheque no. 939 to Bailey Renner in the amount of $6,000. Renner withdraws this amount from the business every month, which she considers "a reasonable salary."

30 Sold the remaining 11 SuperScreen televisions on account to Electric City. Our sales invoice no. 758, $15,400.

Information for End-of-Period Adjustments

Some of the information listed below may not require an adjusting entry at month-end. In such cases, enter the letter designating the information on the "explanation of adjustments" page to accompany your work sheet, write "No adjusting entry required," and briefly explain your reasoning.

a. The May 31 balance of unexpired insurance has expired. Also, one-half month has passed since the new policy, dated June 16, went into effect.

b. The balance in the Prepaid Advertising account represents advance payment for magazine advertising. On April 28, NEXT paid $3,000 to *Retail News,* a monthly trade journal, to run a small ad for 12 months, beginning with the May issue.

c. Supplies on hand at June 30 are estimated to amount to $2,400.

d. Monthly depreciation expense on the building amounts to $1,250.

e. Monthly depreciation expense on the warehouse equipment amounts to $750.

f. Office equipment is being fully depreciated over a period of five years (60 months). (Note for students familiar with alternative depreciation methods: NEXT uses straight-line depreciation on all of its assets.)

g. As of June 30, no bills had been received either from Megacity Gas & Electric or from C & P Telephone for utility services during June. Past experience shows that NEXT owes each of these companies about $200 to $225.

h. The last interest payment on NEXT's 9%, $300,000 note payable was made on June 20. Since then, 10 days' interest (one-third of a month's interest) has accrued on this note.

i. As of June 30, employees are owed salaries for two working days since the last biweekly payroll (June 26). (Employees earn wages and salaries at the same rates as indicated in the last biweekly payroll; each biweekly payroll covers 10 working days.)

j. Ten days' interest revenue (one-third of one month) has accrued on the 12%, $90,000 note receivable from POW Stereo dated June 20. (The accrual of interest is unaffected by the lawsuit filed by POW on June 29.)

k. The amount owed to Express Transport Co. for shipments of merchandise to customers in June totals $5,045. This amount is payable within 15 days.

l. A physical inventory taken at June 30 shows the following quantities of merchandise on hand:

Easy Rider systems	*600*
MegaMite systems	*214*
SuperScreen televisions	*0*

Shortages under $500 are charged directly to Cost of Goods Sold (account no. 501). Larger losses are charged to Inventory Shrinkage Losses (account no. 632).

Analysis of Sales and Gross Profit by Month and by Product

	June	May	April
Net sales (by product):			
SuperScreen TVs			
April—100 units @ $1,400			$140,000
May—20 units @ $1,400		$ 28,000	
June—29 units @ $1,400	$ 40,600		
Easy Rider systems:			
April—0			
May—1,000 units @ $80		80,000	
June—1,200 units @ $80	96,000		
MegaMite systems:			
April—0			
May—700 units @ $120		84,000	
June—570 units @ $120	68,400		
Discounts for prompt payment	(2,852)	(2,500)	(2,000)
Total net sales	$202,148	$189,500	$138,000
Cost of goods sold (by product):			
SuperScreen TVs			
April—100 units @ $1,029			$102,900
May—20 units @ $1,029		$ 20,580	
June—29 units @ $1,029	$ 29,841		
Easy Rider systems:			
April—0			
May—1,000 units @ $68		68,000	
June—1,200 units @ $68	81,600		
MegaMite systems:			
April—0			
May—700 units @ $93		65,100	
June—570 units @ $93	53,010		
Freight on RUSH orders	206	—0—	—0—
Total cost of goods sold	$164,657	$153,680	$102,900
Gross profit (by product):			
SuperScreen TVs	$ 10,759	$ 7,420	$ 37,100
Easy Rider systems	14,400	12,000	—0—
MegaMite systems	15,390	18,900	—0—
Less: Items not sorted by			
product (sales discounts			
and cost of RUSH orders):	(3,058)	(2,500)	(2,000)
Total gross profit	$ 37,491	$ 35,820	$ 35,100
Operating expenses	24,033	24,080	24,020
Operating income	$ 13,458	$ 11,740	$ 11,080
Nonoperating items (net)	(4,050)	(2,350)	(2,330)
Net income	$ 9,408	$ 9,390	$ 8,750

PART 3

Accounting for Assets and Liabilities; Accounting Principles

What's the most valuable asset in this picture? It isn't the bottle of coke, it's the name in the fancy print. But the coke is listed as part of the inventories in Coca-Cola's balance sheet, and the famous trademark isn't. If you want to understand accounting information, you must understand the assumptions and measurement techniques involved in the accounting process.

CHAPTER 7

The Control of Cash Transactions

Every business needs cash for its activities. Thus, the
proper management and control of cash is essential
for successful operations.

1. Describe the balance sheet presentation of cash and state the basic objectives of "cash management."
2. Explain the major steps in achieving internal control over cash transactions.
3. Describe how a voucher system contributes to internal control over cash disbursements.
4. Prepare a bank reconciliation and explain its purpose.
5. Describe the operation of a petty cash fund.

What Do Accountants Mean by "Cash"?

Accountants define **cash** as money on deposit in banks and any items that a bank will accept for deposit. These items include not only coins and paper money but also cheques, money orders, travellers' cheques, and the charge slips signed by customers using bank credit cards, such as Visa and MasterCard.

Most companies maintain several bank accounts and also may keep small amounts of cash on hand. Therefore, the Cash account in the general ledger is a *controlling account.* A cash subsidiary ledger includes a separate account corresponding to each of the company's bank accounts and also to each petty cash fund or change fund within the organization.

Reporting Cash in the Balance Sheet

LO 1: Describe the balance sheet presentation of cash and state the basic objectives of "cash management."

Cash is listed first in the balance sheet because it represents a resource that can be used immediately to pay any type of obligation. The term *liquid assets* is used to describe assets that can be converted quickly into cash. In the current asset section of the balance sheet, assets are listed in the order of their liquidity. Thus cash—being the ultimate in liquidity—is listed first.

For purposes of balance sheet presentation, however, the balance in the Cash controlling account generally is combined with the controlling account for cash equivalents. The balance in each bank account or the amount of cash on hand is not shown because such information is not useful to external users of financial statements.

Cash Equivalents   Some short-term or temporary investments are so liquid that they are termed **cash equivalents.** (Cash equivalents will be discussed fully in Chapter 19.) Examples include money market funds, treasury bills (T-Bills), guaranteed investment certificates (GICs) or sometimes called certificates of deposit (CDs), and high-grade commercial paper. These items are considered so similar to cash that they often are combined with the amount of cash in the balance sheet. Therefore, many businesses call the first asset shown in the balance sheet *"Cash and short-term investments."*

CASE IN POINT

The amount of cash and short-term investments held by a corporation can be quite substantial; it may be one of the largest current assets. A few examples from recent corporate balance sheets:

	Amount in Millions	Percentage of Current Assets
Air Canada	$650	47%
BCE Inc.	2,249	15%
Dofasco Inc.	162	12%
Hudson's Bay Company*	32	14%
Molson Companies Limited	669	62%

*Cash and short-term deposits

Evaluating Solvency   Bankers, credit managers, and other creditors who study a balance sheet always are interested in the amount of cash and short-term investments as compared to other balance sheet items, such as accounts payable. These users of a company's financial statements are interested in evaluating the company's *solvency*—that is, its ability to pay its debts as they come due. Creditors need to know the amount of the most liquid resources available to the business.

Lines of Credit   Many businesses have arranged **lines of credit** with their banks. A line of credit means that the bank has agreed in advance to lend the company any amount of money up to a specified limit. The company can borrow this money at any time, by drawing cheques upon a special bank account. A liability to the bank arises as soon as any of the money is borrowed—that is, as soon as a portion of the line of credit is used.

The *unused* portion of a line of credit is neither an asset nor a liability; it represents only the *ability* to borrow money quickly and easily. Although an unused line of credit does not appear as an asset or a liability in the balance sheet, it does affect the company's solvency. For this reason, unused lines of credit are *disclosed* in notes accompanying the financial statements.

CASE IN POINT

A recent annual report of Canadian Pacific Limited, a giant conglomerate, included the following note to the financial statements:

Unused lines of credit for short-term and long-term financing, subject to periodic review, repayable on demand and at various maturities, amounted to $1,064.8 million on which interest rates vary with bank prime or money market rates.

"Restricted" Cash   Some bank accounts are restricted as to their use, so that they are not available to meet normal operating needs of the business. For example, a bank account may contain cash specifically earmarked for the acquisition of plant assets. Bank accounts in some foreign countries are restricted by laws that prohibit transferring the money to another country. Restricted bank accounts are not regarded as current assets if their balances are not available for use in paying current liabilities. Therefore, "restricted cash balances" may be listed just below the current asset section of the balance sheet in the section entitled ***long-term investments.***

The Cash Flow Statement

The balance sheet indicates the amount of cash owned by the business at a particular date. A separate financial statement, called the cash flow statement, summarizes all of the cash ***activity*** (receipts and disbursements) during the accounting period. Interpreting this statement requires an understanding of many types of business transactions, including the operating, investing, and financing activities of large corporations. Therefore, we will defer discussion of this financial statement to Chapter 19.

Cash Management

The term **cash management** refers to planning, controlling, and accounting for cash transactions and cash balances. Efficient cash management is essential to the success—even to the survival—of every business organization. The basic objectives of cash management are:

- ***Provide accurate accounting for cash receipts, cash disbursements, and cash balances.*** A large portion of the total transactions of a business involve the receipt or disbursement of cash. Also, cash transactions affect every classification within the financial statements—assets, liabilities, owner's equity, revenue, and expenses. If financial statements are to be reliable, it is ***absolutely essential*** that cash transactions be recorded correctly.
- ***Prevent or minimize losses from theft or fraud.*** Cash is more susceptible to theft than any other asset and, therefore, requires physical protection.
- ***Anticipate the need for borrowing and assure the availability of adequate amounts of cash for conducting business operations.*** Every business organization must have sufficient cash to meet its financial obligations as they come due. Otherwise, its creditors may force the business into bankruptcy.
- ***Prevent unnecessarily large amounts of cash from sitting idle in bank accounts that produce little or no revenue.*** Well-managed corporations should frequently review their bank balances for the purpose of transferring any excess cash into short-term investments that generate more revenue.

How Much Cash Is "Enough?" Every business needs sufficient cash, cash equivalents, or lines of credit to meet the company's obligations on a timely basis. However, maintaining larger amounts of cash than necessary is ***not*** an efficient use of resources.

A large cash balance is a relatively nonproductive asset. Corporate accounts do not usually earn interest. Because cash equivalents are such safe and highly liquid investments, they earn very modest rates of return. Such investments are an efficient way of investing ***temporary*** surpluses of cash that soon will be needed for other purposes. However, if a business has large amounts of cash that can be invested on a long-term basis, it should try to earn a substantially **_higher_** rate of return than is available from cash equivalents.

Efficient uses of cash balances that are available on a long-term basis often include financing the growth and expansion of the business, taking advantage of unusual investment opportunities, and repaying interest-bearing liabilities. Simply holding large amounts of cash and cash equivalents increases a company's solvency but adds little to its profitability.

The amount of cash needed to keep a company operating smoothly varies greatly from one business to the next. Cash that cannot be utilized efficiently within a particular business should be distributed to the company's owners, so that they may invest it elsewhere.

Cash Balances and Corporate Dividends

In the early chapters of this textbook, most of our illustrations have involved businesses organized as sole proprietorships. In these organizations, the owner may withdraw excess cash balances from the business at will. In a corporation, however, the decision of whether to distribute company-owned cash to the owners (shareholders) rests with the company's **board of directors.**[1]

A distribution of cash by a corporation to its shareholders is called a **_dividend._**[2] The timing and dollar amounts of dividend payments are determined by the corporation's directors and top management. (Limits upon dividend payments also may be imposed by corporate laws and by contractual agreements with creditors.) Among the factors that most influence the amount of dividends that a corporation pays are the:

- Company's profitability in recent periods.
- Amount of cash on hand that is not needed in business operations.
- Goals and philosophy of the company's top management.

By studying financial statements, investors easily can determine for recent periods a company's net income, the amount of cash on hand, and the amounts of dividends paid to the shareholders. The relationships among these factors can shed much light upon management's attitude toward the payment of dividends and can assist investors in evaluating the prospects of receiving future dividend distributions.

Internal Control over Cash

Internal control over cash is sometimes regarded merely as a means of preventing fraud and theft. A good system of internal control, however, will also aid in achieving the other objectives of efficient cash management, including accurate accounting for cash transactions, anticipating the need for borrowing, and the maintenance of adequate but not excessive cash balances.

LO 2: Explain the major steps in achieving internal control over cash transactions.

1. Separate the function of handling cash from the maintenance of accounting records. Employees who handle cash **_should not have_**

---

[1]The board of directors is the highest level of corporate management.
[2]Accounting for dividends is explained and illustrated in later chapters.

access to the accounting records, and accounting personnel should not have access to cash.

2. Prepare for each department within the organization a **cash budget** (or forecast) of planned cash receipts, cash payments, and cash balances, scheduled month-by-month for the coming year. (Departmental budgets assume the use of a *responsibility accounting system.*[3])

3. Prepare a **control listing** of cash receipts at the time and place the money is received. For cash sales, this listing may be a cash register tape, created by ringing up each sale on a cash register. For cheques received through the mail, a control listing of incoming cheques should be prepared by the employee assigned to open the mail.

4. Require that all cash receipts be **deposited daily** in the bank.

5. Make all payments **by cheque.** The only exception should be for small payments to be made in cash from a **petty cash fund.** (Petty cash funds are discussed later in this chapter.)

6. Require that the validity and amount of every expenditure be verified **before** a cheque is issued in payment. Separate the function of approving expenditures from the function of signing cheques.

7. Promptly reconcile bank statements with the accounting records.

The application of these principles in building adequate internal control over cash can best be illustrated by considering separately the topics of cash receipts and cash disbursements. A company may supplement its internal control by obtaining a fidelity bond from an insurance company. Under a fidelity bond, the insurance company agrees to reimburse an employer for **proven** losses resulting from fraud or embezzlement by bonded employees.

Cash Receipts

Cash receipts consist primarily of two types: cash received through the mail as collections of accounts receivable, and cash received over the counter from cash sales.

Cash Received Through the Mail   Cash received through the mail should be in the form of cheques made payable to the company. When the mail is first opened, an employee should stamp the back of each cheque with a restrictive endorsement stamp, indicating that the cheque is *"For Deposit Only"* into the company's bank account. This *restrictive endorsement* prevents anyone else from being able to cash the cheque or deposit it into another bank account.

Next, the employee should prepare a **control listing** of the cheques received each day. This list shows each customer's name (or account number) and the amount received. One copy of this list is sent with the customers' cheques to the cashier, who deposits the money in the bank. Another copy is sent to the accounting department, to be recorded in the accounting records. Daily comparisons of this control listing with the

---

[3]A *responsibility accounting system* includes a chart of accounts sufficiently detailed to measure separately the activities of each department (or area of managerial responsibility) within the organization. These systems were described in Chapter 6.

amounts deposited by the cashier and with the receipts recorded by the accounting department should bring to light any cash shortages or recording errors.

Cash Received over the Counter   Cash sales should be rung up on a cash register so located that the customer can see the amount recorded. The register has a locked-in tape, which serves as a control listing for cash sales. When the salesperson ends a workday, he or she will count the cash in the register and turn it over to the cashier. A representative of the accounting department will remove the tape from the cash register, compare the total shown on the tape with the amount turned in to the cashier, and record the cash sales in the accounting records.

As explained in earlier chapters, most larger stores now use on-line ***point-of-sale terminals.*** When these terminals are in use, sales transactions are recorded instantly in the accounting records as the salesclerk passes the merchandise over an optical scanner. At first glance, it may appear that the salesclerk both handles cash and has access to the accounting records. Actually, the salesclerks do ***not*** have direct access to the accounting records; all entries in the accounting records are made automatically by the point-of-sale terminal.

Use of Prenumbered Sales Tickets   Another means of establishing internal control over cash sales is by writing out a prenumbered sales ticket in duplicate at the time of each sale. The original is given to the customer and the carbon copy is retained. Prenumbered sales tickets are often used in businesses such as restaurants in which one central cashier rings up the sales made by all salespeople.

At the end of the day, an employee computes the total sales figure from these sales tickets and also makes sure that no tickets are missing from the series. This total sales figure is then compared with the cash register tape and the total cash receipts.

Cash Over and Short   In handling over-the-counter cash receipts, a few errors in making change inevitably will occur. These errors will cause a cash shortage or overage at the end of the day, when the cash is counted and compared with the reading on the cash register.

Any cash shortage or overage is debited or credited to the account entitled Cash Over and Short. If the cash shortages during an entire accounting period are in excess of the cash overages, this account will have a debit balance and will be shown as miscellaneous ***expense*** in the income statement. On the other hand, if the overages exceed the shortages, this account will show a credit balance at the end of the period and should be treated as an item of miscellaneous ***revenue.*** Management should review the daily entries to this account so as to be aware of any material cash shortages or consistent pattern of small shortages.

Subdivision of Duties   Employees who handle cash receipts should ***not have access to the accounting records.*** This combination of duties might enable the employee to alter the accounting records and thereby conceal a cash shortage.

Employees who handle cash receipts also should ***not have authority to issue credit memoranda for sales returns.*** This combination of duties might enable the employee to conceal cash shortages by issuing fictitious credit memoranda. Assume, for example, that an employee with these responsibilities collects $500 cash from a customer as payment of the customer's account. The employee might remove this cash and issue a $500 credit memorandum, indicating that the customer had returned the merchandise instead of paying the account. The credit memoranda would cause the account receivable from this customer to be credited. However, the offsetting debit would be to the Sales Returns & Allowances account, not to the Cash account. Thus, the books would remain in balance, the customer would receive credit for the abstracted payment, and there would be no record of cash having been received.

Using Departmental Cash Budgets   Departmental cash budgets provide estimates of the cash receipts ***expected*** within each department during the accounting period. Management should investigate to determine ***why*** a department falls significantly short of the budgeted amounts. Perhaps this investigation will show that the budgeted amounts were overly optimistic; in this case, management will change the budget estimates for future months. On the other hand, the investigation may reveal weak departmental performance or fraud on the part of certain personnel. In either of these situations, management will want to initiate corrective action.

Cash Disbursements

To achieve adequate internal control over cash payments, all disbursements of significant dollar amount should be ***made by cheque.*** Cheques should be prenumbered. Any spoiled cheques should be marked "Void" and filed in sequence so that all numbers in the series can be accounted for.

Every transaction requiring a cash disbursement should be verified and approved before payment is made. The official designated to ***sign*** cheques should not be given authority to ***approve*** invoices for payment or to make entries in the accounting records. When a cheque is presented to a company official for signature, it should be accompanied by the approved invoice and voucher showing that the transaction has been fully verified and that payment is justified. When the cheque is signed, the supporting invoices and vouchers should be perforated or stamped "Paid" to eliminate any possibility of their being presented later in support of another cheque. If these rules are followed, it is almost impossible for a fraudulent cash disbursement to be concealed without the collusion of two or more persons.

The Voucher System

LO 3: Describe how a voucher system contributes to internal control over cash disbursements.

One widely used method of establishing control over cash disbursements is the **voucher system.** The basic idea of this system is that every transaction that will result in a cash disbursement must be verified, approved in writing, and recorded before a cheque is issued. A written authorization called a **voucher** is prepared for every transaction that will require a cash payment, regardless of whether the transaction is for payment of an expense, purchase of inventory or a plant asset, or for payment of a liability.[4] Notice that ***every purchase is treated as an independent transaction*** even though many purchases may be made from the same supplier. Vouchers are serially numbered so that the loss or misplacement of a voucher would be immediately apparent.

To demonstrate the internal control inherent in a voucher system, consider the way a voucher is used in verifying an invoice received from a supplier. A serially numbered voucher is attached to each incoming invoice. The voucher has spaces for listing the data from the invoice and for showing the ledger accounts to be debited and credited in recording the transaction. Space is also provided for approval signatures for each step in the verification and approval process. A completed voucher provides a description of the transaction and also of the work performed in verifying the liability and approving the cash disbursement.

Preparing a Voucher   To illustrate the functioning of a voucher system, let us begin with the receipt of an invoice from a supplier. A voucher is prepared by filling in the appropriate blanks with information taken from the invoice, such as the invoice date, invoice number, amount, and the creditor's name and address. The voucher with the supplier's invoice attached is then sent to the employees responsible for verifying the extensions and footings on the invoice and for comparing prices, quantities, and terms with those specified in the purchase order and receiving report. When completion of the verification process has been evidenced by approval signatures of the persons performing these steps, the voucher and supporting documents are sent to an employee of the accounting department, who indicates on the voucher the accounts to be debited and credited. The voucher is then reviewed by an accounting official to provide assurance that the verification procedures have been satisfactorily completed and that the liability is a proper one. A completed voucher is illustrated on the following page.

Recording Approved Vouchers

After receiving the supervisory approval explained above, the voucher is entered in a special journal called a **voucher register.** Entries in the voucher register indicate the nature of the expenditure by debiting the appropriate asset, expense, or liability accounts. The credit portion of each entry is always to a short-term liability account entitled Vouchers Payable. Note that the entry in the voucher register is not made ***until the liability has been verified and approved.***

In a company using the voucher system, the ledger account, Vouchers Payable, replaces Accounts Payable. For purposes of balance sheet presentation, however, most companies continue to use the more widely understood term Accounts Payable.

---

[4]Other names for a ***"voucher"*** include ***"invoice approval form"*** and ***"cheque authorization."***

Use of voucher ensures verification of invoice

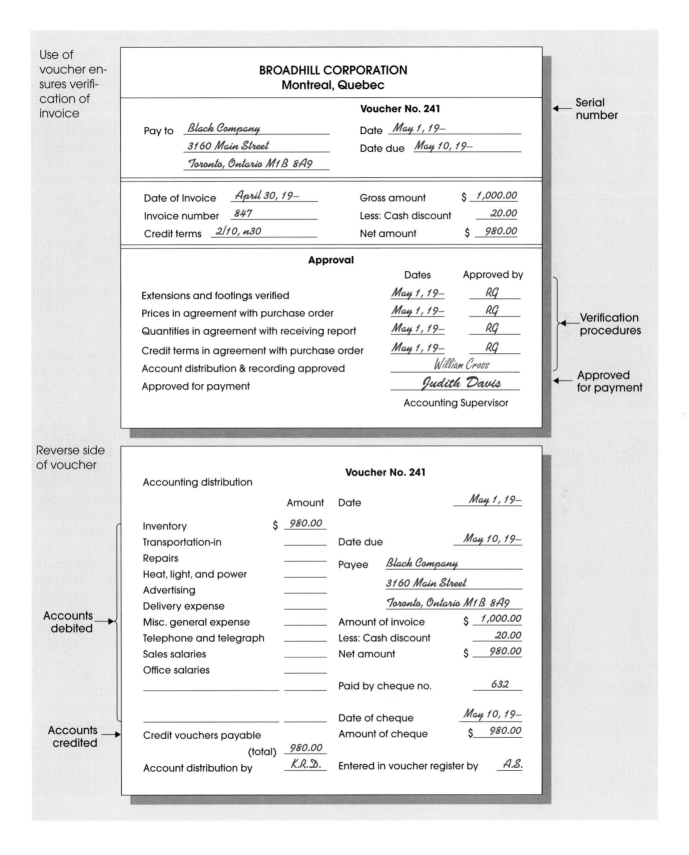

Serial number

Verification procedures

Approved for payment

Reverse side of voucher

Accounts debited

Accounts credited

BROADHILL CORPORATION
Montreal, Quebec

Voucher No. 241

Pay to *Black Company*   Date *May 1, 19–*
        3160 Main Street   Date due *May 10, 19–*
        Toronto, Ontario M1B 8A9

Date of Invoice *April 30, 19–*   Gross amount $ *1,000.00*
Invoice number *847*   Less: Cash discount *20.00*
Credit terms *2/10, n30*   Net amount $ *980.00*

Approval

	Dates	Approved by
Extensions and footings verified	*May 1, 19–*	*RG*
Prices in agreement with purchase order	*May 1, 19–*	*RG*
Quantities in agreement with receiving report	*May 1, 19–*	*RG*
Credit terms in agreement with purchase order	*May 1, 19–*	*RG*
Account distribution & recording approved		*William Cross*
Approved for payment		*Judith Davis*

Accounting Supervisor

Voucher No. 241

Accounting distribution

	Amount	Date	*May 1, 19–*
Inventory	$ *980.00*		
Transportation-in		Date due	*May 10, 19–*
Repairs		Payee	*Black Company*
Heat, light, and power			*3160 Main Street*
Advertising			*Toronto, Ontario M1B 8A9*
Delivery expense			
Misc. general expense		Amount of invoice	$ *1,000.00*
Telephone and telegraph		Less: Cash discount	*20.00*
Sales salaries		Net amount	$ *980.00*
Office salaries			
		Paid by cheque no.	*632*
		Date of cheque	*May 10, 19–*
Credit vouchers payable		Amount of cheque	$ *980.00*
(total)	*980.00*		
Account distribution by	*K.R.D.*	Entered in voucher register by	*A.S.*

Voucher systems are used principally by larger companies that process transactions by computer. Because our interest in voucher systems is in their internal control features and because manual voucher systems are rare, our discussion does not include illustration of a hand-operated voucher register.

Paying the Voucher within the Discount Period After the voucher has been entered in the voucher register, it is placed (with the supporting documents attached) in a tickler file according to the date of required payment. Cash discount periods generally run from the date of the invoice. Since a voucher is prepared for each invoice, the required date of payment is the last day on which a cheque can be prepared and mailed to the creditor in time to qualify for the discount.

When the payment date arrives, an employee in the accounting department removes the voucher from the unpaid file, draws a cheque for signature by the treasurer, and records payment of the voucher in a special journal called a ***cheque register.*** Since cheques are issued only in payment of approved vouchers, every entry in the cheque register represents a debit to Vouchers Payable and a credit to Cash.

An important factor in achieving internal control is that the employee in the accounting department who prepares the cheque ***is not authorized to sign it.*** The unsigned cheque and the supporting voucher are now sent to the treasurer or other designated official in the finance department. The treasurer reviews the voucher, especially the approval signatures, and signs the cheque. Thus, the invoice is ***approved for payment*** in the accounting department, but the actual cash disbursement is made by the finance department. ***No one person or department is in a position both to approve invoices for payment and to issue signed cheques.***

Once the cheque has been signed, the treasurer should mail it directly to the creditor. The voucher and all supporting documents are then perforated with a PAID stamp and are forwarded to the accounting department, which will note payment of the voucher in the voucher register and will file the paid voucher. The operation of a voucher system is illustrated in the flowchart on the following page. Notes have been made on the illustration identifying the most important internal control features in the system.

Establishing Control over the Issuance of Cheques In a small business, the officer authorized to sign cheques is held responsible for signing only those cheques that have been properly authorized. In a large company that issues hundreds or thousands of cheques daily, it is not practicable for a company official to sign each cheque manually. Instead, cheque-signing machines with various built-in control devices are used. This automation of the cheque-signing function does not weaken the system of internal control if attention is given to proper use of the machine and to control of the cheques both before and after they pass through the cheque-signing machine.

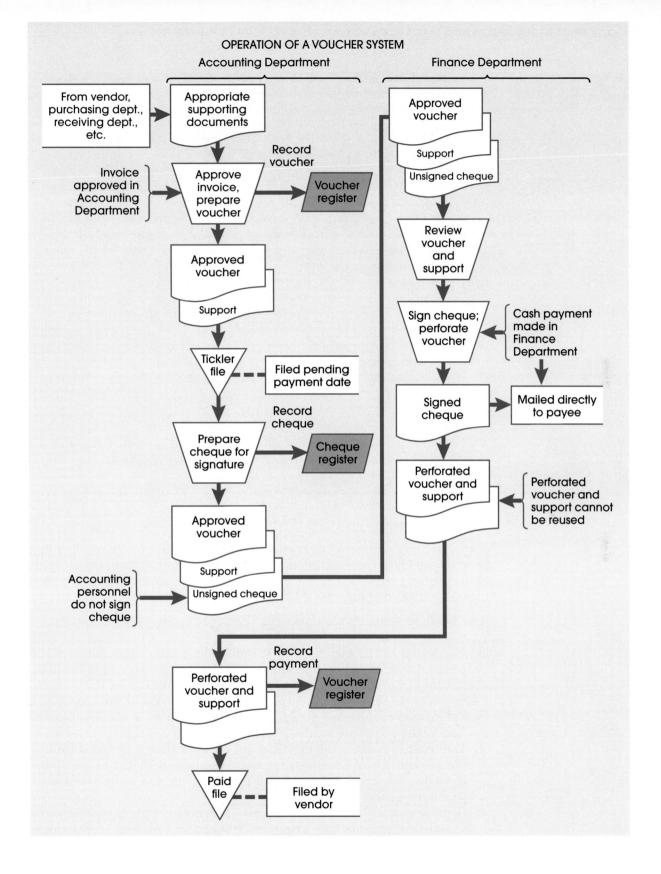

OPERATION OF A VOUCHER SYSTEM

Accounting Department

- From vendor, purchasing dept., receiving dept., etc.
- Appropriate supporting documents
- Invoice approved in Accounting Department
- Approve invoice, prepare voucher
- Record voucher → Voucher register
- Approved voucher / Support
- Tickler file — Filed pending payment date
- Prepare cheque for signature
- Record cheque → Cheque register
- Approved voucher / Support / Unsigned cheque
- Accounting personnel do not sign cheque
- Perforated voucher and support
- Record payment → Voucher register
- Paid file — Filed by vendor

Finance Department

- Approved voucher / Support / Unsigned cheque
- Review voucher and support
- Sign cheque; perforate voucher
- Cash payment made in Finance Department
- Signed cheque → Mailed directly to payee
- Perforated voucher and support
- Perforated voucher and support cannot be reused

387

CASE IN POINT

A large construction company issued a great many cheques every day but paid little attention to internal controls over its cash payments. Stacks of unissued cheques were kept in an unlocked supply closet along with Styrofoam coffee cups. Because the number of cheques issued was too great for the treasurer to sign them manually, a cheque-signing machine was used. This machine, after signing the cheques, ejected them into a box equipped with a lock. In spite of warnings from the company's auditors, company officials found that it was "too inconvenient" to keep the box locked. The company also failed to make any use of the cheque-counting device built into the cheque-signing machine. Although the company maintained very large amounts on deposit in its bank accounts, it did not bother to reconcile bank statements for weeks or months at a time.

These weaknesses in internal control led to a crisis when an employee was given a three-week-old bank statement and a bundle of paid cheques and told to prepare a bank reconciliation. The employee found that the bundle of paid cheques accompanying the bank statement was incomplete. No paid cheques were on hand to support over $700,000 of charges deducted on the bank statement. Further investigation revealed that over $1 million in unauthorized and unrecorded cheques had been paid from the corporation's bank accounts. These cheques had been issued out of serial number sequence and had been run through the company cheque-signing machine. It was never determined who had carried out the theft and the money was not recovered.

Chequing Accounts

Virtually every business organization maintains one or more chequing accounts, which are opened and maintained in much the same way as a personal chequing account. The use of chequing accounts contributes to strong internal control in many ways. For example:

1. Chequing accounts eliminate the need for keeping large amounts of currency on hand.
2. The owner of the business must notify the bank of the names of all persons authorized to sign cheques. Thus, access to cash is limited to those company officers and employees designated by the business owner (or, for a corporation, by the board of directors).
3. The person responsible for each cash disbursement is readily identified by the signature on the cheque.
4. The bank returns to the depositor all cheques that it has paid from the account. Thus, the depositor has documentary evidence showing the date and amount of each cash payment, and the identity of the person receiving the money.
5. Comparison of the monthly **bank statement** with the depositor's accounting records can bring to light many types of errors made either by the bank or by the depositor in accounting for cash transactions.

Bank Statements

Every month, banks provide each depositor with a bank statement summarizing the activity in the depositor's account.[5] The bank statement is accompanied by all of the cheques that the bank has paid from the account and also by documents indicating the nature and amount of any other changes in the account balance. As illustrated on the next page, a bank statement shows the balance on deposit at the beginning of the month, the deposits, the cheques paid, any other debits and credits during the month, and the new balance at the end of the month. (To keep the illustration short, we have shown only the beginning and ending portion of the statement.)

Reconciling the Bank Statement

LO 4: Prepare a bank reconciliation and explain its purpose.

A **bank reconciliation** is a schedule *explaining any differences* between the balance shown in the bank statement and the balance shown in the depositor's accounting records. Remember that both the bank and the depositor are maintaining independent records of the deposits, the cheques, and the current balance of the bank account. Each month, the depositor should prepare a bank reconciliation to verify that these independent sets of records are in agreement. This reconciliation may disclose internal control failures, such as unauthorized cash disbursements or failures to deposit cash receipts, as well as errors in either the bank statement or the depositor's accounting records. In addition, the reconciliation identifies certain transactions that must be recorded in the depositor's accounting records, and helps to determine the "actual" amount of cash on deposit.

For strong internal control, the employee who reconciles the bank statement should not have any other responsibilities for cash.

Normal Differences between Bank Statements and Accounting Records   The balance shown in a monthly bank statement seldom equals the balance appearing in the depositor's accounting records. Certain transactions recorded by the depositor may not have been recorded by the bank. The most common examples are:

1. **Outstanding cheques.** Cheques issued and recorded by the company but not yet presented to the bank for payment.
2. **Deposits in transit.** Cash receipts recorded by the depositor but that reached the bank too late to be included in the bank statement for the current month.

In addition, certain transactions appearing in the bank statement may not have been recorded by the depositor. For example:

1. **Service charges.** Banks often charge a fee for handling small accounts. The amount of this charge usually depends upon both the average balance of the account and the number of cheques paid during the month.
2. **Charges for depositing NSF cheques.** NSF stands for "Not Sufficient Funds." When cheques are deposited, the bank increases

---

[5]Large businesses usually receive bank statements on a weekly basis.

A bank statement provides an independent record of cash transactions.

NATIONAL BANK
260 Bland Street
Toronto, Ontario M4W 1G5

Under your agreement with the bank, this statement will be considered correct except as to errors or omissions of which you notify the bank within 30 days after it is delivered or mailed to you.
Please notify the bank of any change of address.

Account No. 238686

In account with

Parkview Company
109 Parkview Road
Toronto, Ontario M5K 1B9

	Date			Amount	
Balance Forward	30	6	99	5,029	30

Code	Description	Debits	Credits	Date D	M	Yr	Balance
CD			300.00	2	7	99	5,329.30
CD			1,250.00	3	7	99	6,579.30
Ch	Cheque No. 830	1,100.00		3	7	99	5,479.30
Ch	Cheque No. 836	415.20		4	7	99	5,064.10
DM	Cheque returned	50.25		28	7	99	2,798.82
CD			1,083.25	29	7	99	3,882.07
CM	Proceeds of note		500.00	30	7	99	4,382.07
DM	Collection fee	5.00		30	7	99	4,377.07
SC		12.00		31	7	99	4,365.07
CD			610.36	31	7	99	4,975.43
IN			24.74	31	7	99	5,000.17

NO. OF DEBITS	TOTAL AMOUNT– DEBITS	NO. OF CREDITS	TOTAL AMOUNT– CREDITS
60	28,367.54	36	28,338.41

EXPLANATION OF CHARACTERS

CC Certified Cheque	DD Direct Deposit	EX Foreign Exchange	OD Balance Overdrawn
CD Customer Deposit	DM Debit Memo	IN Interest	RI Returned Item
CH Cheque	EC Error Corrected	LT Total Several Cheques	SC Service Charge
CM Credit Memo			

(credits) the depositor's account. On occasion, one of these cheques may prove to be uncollectible, because the maker of the cheque does not have sufficient funds in his or her account. In such cases, the bank will reduce the depositor's account by a debit memorandum for the amount of this uncollectible item and return the cheque to the depositor marked "NSF."

The depositor should view an NSF cheque as an account receivable from the maker of the cheque, not as cash. The accounting entry required consists of a debit to the account receivable from the customer and credit to cash.

3. **Credits for interest earned.** Most banks offer some chequing accounts that earn interest. At month-end, this interest is credited to the depositor's account and reported on the bank statement.

4. **Miscellaneous bank charges and credits.** Banks charge for services—such as printing cheques, handling collections of notes receivable, and processing NSF cheques. The bank deducts these charges from the depositor's account and notifies the depositor by including a debit memorandum in the monthly bank statement.[6] If the bank collects a note receivable on behalf of the depositor, it adds the money to the depositor's account and issues a credit memorandum describing the collection.

In a bank reconciliation, the balances shown in the bank statement and in the accounting records both are adjusted for any unrecorded transactions. Additional adjustment may be required to correct any errors discovered in the bank statement or in the accounting records.

Steps in Preparing a Bank Reconciliation   To prepare a bank reconciliation, we determine those items that make up the difference between the ending *balance shown on the bank statement and the balance of cash according to the depositor's records.* By listing and studying these reconciling items we can determine the correct figure for cash owned. This is the amount that should appear in the balance sheet. The specific steps to be taken in preparing a bank reconciliation are:

1. Compare the deposits listed on the bank statement with the deposits shown in the company's records. Any deposits not yet recorded by the bank are deposits in transit and should be added to the balance shown in the bank statement. If there were any deposits in transit listed in the prior month's bank reconciliation, these amounts should appear as deposits in the current month's bank statement. If they do not appear, immediate investigation is necessary.

2. Arrange the paid cheques returned by the bank in sequence by serial numbers and compare each cheque with the corresponding entry in the cheque register. Any cheques issued but not yet paid by the bank should be listed as outstanding cheques to be deducted from the balance reported in the bank statement. Determine whether the cheques listed as *outstanding* (i.e., issued but not cashed) in the bank reconciliation for the *preceding month* have cleared the bank this month. If not, such cheques should still be listed as outstanding in the current reconciliation.

---

[6]Banks view each depositor's account as a liability. Debit memoranda are issued for transactions that *reduce* this liability, such as bank service charges. Credit memoranda are issued to recognize an *increase* in this liability, as results, for example, from interest earned by the depositor.

3. Add to the balance per the depositor's accounting records any credit memoranda issued by the bank that have not been recorded by the depositor. Examples in the illustrated bank statement on page 390 are the $500 credit from collection of a note receivable and the $24.74 credit for interest earned.

4. Deduct from the balance per the depositor's records any debit memoranda issued by the bank that have not been recorded by the depositor. Examples in the illustrated bank statement on page 390 are the $5 collection fee, the $50.25 NSF cheque, and the $12 service charge.

5. Make appropriate additions or deductions to correct any errors in the balance per bank statement or the balance per depositor's records. An example in the illustrated bank reconciliation on page 393 is the $27 error by the company in recording cheque no. 875.

6. Determine that the adjusted balance of the bank statement is equal to the adjusted balance in the depositor's records.

7. Prepare journal entries to record any items in the bank reconciliation listed as adjustments to the balance per the depositor's records.

Illustration of a Bank Reconciliation   The July bank statement sent by the bank to Parkview Company was illustrated earlier. This statement shows a balance of cash on deposit at July 31 of $5,000.17. Assume that on July 31, Parkview's ledger shows a bank balance of $4,262.83. The employee preparing the bank reconciliation has identified the following reconciling items:

1. A deposit of $410.90 made after banking hours on July 31 does not appear in the bank statement.

2. Four cheques, one issued in June and three issued in July, have not yet been paid by the bank. These cheques are:

Cheque No.	Date	Amount
801	June 15	$100.00
888	July 24	10.25
890	July 27	402.50
891	July 30	205.00

3. Two credit memoranda were included in the bank statement:

Date	Amount	Explanation
July 30	$500.00	Proceeds from collection of a non-interest-bearing note receivable from J. David. Parkview Company had left this note with the bank's collection department.
July 31	24.74	Interest earned on average account balance during July.

4. Three debit memoranda accompanied the bank statement:

Date	Amount	Explanation
July 28	$50.25	Cheque from customer J. B. Ball deposited by Parkview Company charged back as NSF.
July 30	5.00	Fee charged by bank for handling collection of note receivable.
July 31	12.00	Service charge by bank for the month of July.

5. Cheque no. 875 was issued July 20 in the amount of $85 but was erroneously recorded in the cash payments journal as $58. The cheque, in payment of telephone expense, was paid by the bank and correctly listed at $85 in the bank statement. In Parkview's ledger, the Cash account is **overstated** by $27 because of this error ($85 − $58 = $27).

The July 31 bank reconciliation for Parkview Company is shown below. (The numbered arrows coincide both with the steps in preparing a bank reconciliation listed on pages 391–392 and with the reconciling items listed above.)

PARKVIEW COMPANY
Bank Reconciliation
July 31, 1999

Balance per bank statement, July 31		$5,000.17
① → Add: Deposit of July 31 not recorded by bank		410.90
		$5,411.07
② → Deduct: Outstanding cheques:		
No. 801	$100.00	
No. 888	10.25	
No. 890	402.50	
No. 891	205.00	717.75
Adjusted cash balance		**$4,693.32**
Balance per depositor's records, July 31		$4,262.83
③ → Add: Note receivable collected for us by bank . . .	$500.00	
Interest earned during July	24.74	524.74
		$4,787.57 ⑥
④ → Deduct: NSF cheque of J. B. Ball	$ 50.25	
Collection fee	5.00	
Service charge	12.00	
⑤ → Error on cheque stub no. 875	27.00	94.25
Adjusted cash balance (as above)		**$4,693.32**

Updating the Accounting Records The last step in a bank reconciliation is to update the depositor's accounting records for any unrecorded cash transactions brought to light. In the bank reconciliation, every adjustment to the **balance per depositor's records** is a cash receipt or a cash payment that has not been recorded in the depositor's accounts. Therefore, **each of these items should be recorded.**

In this illustration and in our assignment material, we will follow a policy of making one journal entry to record the unrecorded cash receipts and another to record the unrecorded cash reductions. (Acceptable alternatives would be to make separate journal entries for each item or to make one compound entry for all items.) Based on our recording policy, the entries to update the accounting records of Parkview Company are:

Per bank credit
memoranda . . .

Cash	524.74	
Notes Receivable		500.00
Interest Revenue		24.74

To record collection of note receivable from J. David collected by bank and interest earned on bank account in July.

...per bank debit memoranda (and correction of an error)

Miscellaneous Expense (or Bank Service Charges)	17.00	
Accounts Receivable, J. B. Ball	50.25	
Telephone Expense	27.00	
Cash		94.25

To record bank charges (service charge, $12; collection fee, $5), to reclassify NSF cheque from customer J. B. Ball as an account receivable, and to correct understatement of cash payment for telephone expense.

Electronic Funds Transfer Systems

Banks today allow depositors to use a wide variety of **electronic funds transfer** systems. These systems enable depositors to transfer money in and out of their bank accounts without actually bringing deposits to the bank or writing cheques. Common examples of these systems include automatic teller machines, automatic bill payment plans, transfers authorized by telephone, and the use of "debit cards."

Many businesses now use electronic funds transfers in meeting their payrolls. Every "payday," the business provides the bank with data indicating the amounts owed to specific employees. The bank electronically transfers these amounts from the company's bank account to the employees' personal bank accounts. Thus, employees receive their money immediately, and the employer is spared the nuisance of issuing and distributing paycheques.

Banks take many precautions to ensure that all electronic funds transfers are properly authorized by the depositor. Also, these transactions are fully documented in the monthly bank statements.

Petty Cash Funds

LO 5: Describe the operation of a petty cash fund.

We have emphasized the importance of making all significant cash disbursements by cheque. However, every business finds it convenient to have a small amount of cash on hand with which to make some minor expenditures. Examples of these expenditures include such things as small purchases of office supplies, taxi fares, and doughnuts for an office meeting.

Establishing a Petty Cash Fund   To create a **petty cash fund,** a cheque is written payable to Petty Cash for a round amount such as $200 or $300, which will cover the small expenditures to be paid in cash for a period of two or three weeks. The issuance of the cheque creating a petty cash fund is recorded in the cheque register. This cheque is cashed and the money kept on hand in a locked petty cash box or drawer in the office. One employee is designated as the ***custodian*** of the fund.

Making Disbursements from a Petty Cash Fund   As cash payments are made from the petty cash box, the custodian of the fund is required to fill out a ***petty cash voucher*** for each expenditure. A petty cash voucher shows the date, the amount paid, the purpose of the expenditure, and the signature of the person receiving the money. A petty cash voucher should be prepared for every payment made from the fund. The petty cash box should, therefore, always contain cash and/or vouchers **totalling the exact amount of the fund.**

The petty cash custodian should be informed that occasional surprise counts of the fund will be made and that he or she is personally responsible for the fund being intact at all times.

Replenishing a Petty Cash Fund   Assume that a petty cash fund of $200 was established on June 1. On June 18, the custodian of the fund reports that the cash remaining in the fund is down to $20. Since the $200 originally placed in the fund is nearly exhausted, the fund should be replenished. To replenish a petty cash fund means to restore the fund to its original balance. Thus, a cheque is drawn for $180. This cheque is cashed and the money placed in the petty cash box.

The journal entry to record the issuance of the cheque includes debits to the expense accounts indicated by inspection of the vouchers and a credit to cash. As a practical matter, the entire debit portion of the entry often is charged to the Miscellaneous Expense account because the amount is not material. The petty cash vouchers are perforated to prevent their being resubmitted and are filed in support of the replenishment cheque.

Note that **expense accounts** are debited each time the fund is replenished. The Petty Cash account is debited only when the fund is first established. There ordinarily will be no further entries in the Petty Cash account after the fund is established, unless the fund is discontinued or a decision is made to change its size from the original $200 amount.

The Cash Budget as a Control over Departmental Expenditures

Many businesses prepare detailed cash budgets that include forecasts of the monthly cash receipts and expenditures of each department within the organization. Management (or the internal auditors) will investigate any cash receipts and expenditures that differ substantially from the budgeted amounts. Thus, each department manager is held accountable for the monthly cash transactions occurring within his or her department.

Frequent comparisons of actual results with budgeted levels of performance greatly reduce the risks of fraud and waste. Of course, such comparisons require the use of a **responsibility accounting system,** that is, a chart of accounts that is sufficiently detailed to measure separately the activities of each department.

End-of-Chapter Review

Key Terms Introduced or Emphasized in Chapter 7

Bank reconciliation *(p.389)* An analysis that explains the difference between the balance of cash shown on the bank statement and the balance of cash shown in the depositor's records.

Board of directors *(p.380)* The highest level of management within a business organized as a corporation.

Cash *(p.377)* Currency, coins, cheques, bank credit card charge slips, and any other media that a bank will accept for deposit.

Cash equivalent *(p.377)* Very short-term investments that are so liquid they are considered "equivalent" to cash. Examples include deposits in money market funds, treasury bills, certificates of deposit, and commercial paper.

Cash management *(p.379)* Planning, controlling, and accounting for cash transactions and cash balances.

Deposits in transit *(p.389)* Cash receipts that have been entered in the depositor's accounting records and mailed to the bank or left in the bank's night depository but reached the bank too late to be included in the current monthly bank statement.

Electronic funds transfer *(p.394)* The process of transferring money in or out of a bank account electronically, without the need for the depositor to physically bring in a deposit or write a cheque.

Line of credit *(p.378)* A prearranged loan agreement in which a bank stands ready to lend the borrower any amount up to the specified credit limit, without delay. The "unused" portion of a line of credit represents the ability to borrow cash immediately.

NSF cheque *(p.389)* A customer's cheque that was deposited but returned because of a lack of funds (Not Sufficient Funds) in the account on which the cheque was drawn.

Outstanding cheques *(p.389)* Cheques issued by a business to suppliers, employees, or other payees but not yet presented to the bank for payment.

Petty cash fund *(p.394)* A small amount of cash set aside for making minor cash payments for which writing of cheques is not practicable.

Voucher *(p.383)* A written authorization used in approving a transaction for recording and payment.

Voucher register *(p.384)* A special journal used in a voucher system for the purpose of recording liabilities to pay approved vouchers, and the nature of the expenditures.

Voucher system *(p.383)* An accounting system designed to provide strong internal control over cash disbursements. Requires that every transaction that will result in a cash payment be verified, approved, and recorded before a cheque is prepared.

DEMONSTRATION PROBLEM

The information listed below is available in reconciling the bank balance for the Red River Company on November 30, 19___ .

1. The bank statement at November 30 indicated a balance of $10,034.70. The ledger account for Cash showed a balance at November 30 of $12,761.94.

2. The November 30 cash receipts of $5,846.20 had been left in the bank's night depository on that date and did not appear among the deposits on the November bank statement.

3. Of the cheques issued in November, the following were not included among the paid cheques returned by the bank:

Cheque No.	Amount	Cheque No.	Amount
924	$136.25	944	$ 95.00
940	105.00	945	716.15
941	11.46	946	60.00
943	826.70		

4. A service charge for $40 by the bank had been made in error against the Red River Company account.

5. The paid cheques returned with the November bank statement disclosed two errors in the company's cash records. Cheque no. 936 for $504.00 had been erroneously recorded as $50.40, and cheque no. 942 for $245.50 had been recorded as $254.50. Cheque no. 936 was issued in payment of advertising expense and cheque no. 942 was for the acquisition of office equipment.

6. Included with the November bank statement was an NSF cheque for $220 signed by a customer, J. Wilson. This amount had been charged against the bank account on November 30.

7. A non-interest-bearing note receivable for $1,890 owned by the Red River Company had been left with the bank for collection. On November 30 the company received a memorandum from the bank indicating that the note had been collected and credited to the company's account after deduction of a $5 collection charge. No entry has been made by the company to record collection of the note.

8. A debit memorandum for $12 was enclosed with the paid cheques at November 30. This charge covered the printing of chequebooks bearing the Red River Company name and address.

INSTRUCTIONS

a. Prepare a bank reconciliation at November 30.

b. Prepare journal entries required at November 30 to bring the company's records up-to-date.

SOLUTION TO DEMONSTRATION PROBLEM

a.

RED RIVER COMPANY
Bank Reconciliation
November 30, 19__

Balance per bank statement, Nov. 30		$10,034.70
Add: Deposit of Nov. 30 not recorded by bank	$5,846.20	
Service charge made by bank in error	40.00	5,886.20
Subtotal		$15,920.90
Deduct: Outstanding cheques:		
No. 924	$ 136.25	
No. 940	105.00	
No. 941	11.46	
No. 943	826.70	
No. 944	95.00	
No. 945	716.15	
No. 946	60.00	1,950.56
Adjusted cash balance		$13,970.34
Balance per depositor's records, Nov. 30		$12,761.94
Add: Error in recording cheque no. 942 for office equipment:		
Recorded as	$254.50	
Correct amount	$245.50 $ 9.00	
Note receivable collected by bank	1,890.00	1,899.00
		$14,660.94
Deduct: Error in recording cheque no. 936 for advertising expense:		
Correct amount	$504.00	
Recorded as	50.40 $ 453.60	
NSF cheque (J. Wilson)	220.00	
Collection fee	$ 5.00	
Printing cheques	12.00 17.00	690.60
Adjusted cash balance (as above)		$13,970.34

b. Journal entries required at November 30 to bring the company's records up-to-date.

```
19__
Nov. 30  Cash ........................................  1,899.00
                Office Equipment .....................               9.00
                Notes Receivable  ....................           1,890.00
             To record increase in Cash account as indicated
             by bank reconciliation.

Nov. 30  Advertising Expense .........................   453.60
             Accounts Receivable (J. Wilson) ..........   220.00
             Miscellaneous Expense  ...................    17.00
                Cash .................................             690.60
             To record decreases in Cash account as indicated
             by bank reconciliation.
```

Self-Test Questions

Answers to these questions appear on page 420.

1. Which of the following practices contributes to efficient cash management?
   a. Never borrow money—maintain a cash balance sufficient to make all necessary payments.
   b. Record all cash receipts and cash payments at the end of the month when reconciling the bank statements.
   c. Prepare monthly forecasts of planned cash receipts, payments, and anticipated cash balances up to a year in advance.
   d. Pay each bill as soon as the invoice arrives.

2. Each of the following measures strengthens internal control over cash receipts *except:*
   a. The use of a voucher system.
   b. Preparation of a daily listing of all cheques received through the mail.
   c. The deposit of cash receipts intact in the bank on a daily basis.
   d. The use of cash registers.

3. When a voucher system is in use:
   a. The voucher and supporting documents are perforated when the cheque is prepared for signature.
   b. The finance department signs the cheque and perforates the voucher and supporting documents.
   c. The accounting department does not have access to the perforated vouchers and support.
   d. The finance department signs the cheque and returns the signed cheque to the accounting department to be mailed.

Use the following data for questions 4 and 5.
   Quinn Company's bank statement at January 31 shows a balance of $13,360, while the ledger account for Cash in Quinn's ledger shows a balance of $12,890 at the same date. The only reconciling items are the following:

   • Deposit in transit, $890.
   • Bank service charge, $24.
   • NSF cheque from customer Greg Denton in the amount of $426.
   • Error in recording cheque no. 389 for rent: it was written in the amount of $1,320, but was recorded in the bank statement as $1,230.
   • Outstanding cheques, $?????

4. What is the total amount of outstanding cheques at January 31?
   a. $1,048
   b. $868
   c. $1,900
   d. $1,720

5. Assuming a single journal entry is made to adjust Quinn Company's accounting records at January 31, the journal entry includes:
   a. A debit to Rent Expense for $90.
   b. A credit to Accounts Receivable, G. Denton, for $426.
   c. A credit to Cash for $450.
   d. A credit to Cash for $1,720.

ASSIGNMENT MATERIAL

Discussion Questions

1. If a company has accounts in three banks, should it maintain a separate ledger account for each? Should the company's balance sheet show as three separate items the amounts on deposit in the three banks? Explain.

2. What are **cash equivalents?** Provide two examples. Why are these items often combined with cash for the purpose of balance sheet presentation?

3. Does the expression "efficient cash management" mean anything more than procedures to prevent losses from fraud or theft? Explain.

4. Why are cash balances **in excess** of those needed to finance business operations sometimes viewed as relatively nonproductive assets?

5. Suggest several ways in which a corporation might efficiently utilize cash balances in excess of the amounts needed for current operations.

6. Among the various assets owned by a business, cash is probably the one for which strong internal control is most urgently needed. What specific attributes of cash cause this special need for internal control?

7. Mention some principles to be observed by a business in establishing strong internal control over cash receipts.

8. Explain how internal control over cash transactions is strengthened by compliance with the following rule: "Deposit each day's cash receipts intact in the bank, and make all disbursements by cheque."

9. Ringo Store sells only for cash and records all sales on cash registers before delivering merchandise to the customers. On a given day the cash count at the close of business indicated $10.25 less cash than was shown by the totals in the cash register. In what account would this cash shortage be recorded? Would the account be debited or credited?

10. With respect to a **voucher system,** what is meant by the terms **voucher, voucher register,** and **cheque register?**

11. Randall Company uses a voucher system to control its cash disbursements. With respect to a purchase of merchandise, what three documents would need to be examined to verify that the voucher should be approved?

12. Suggest an internal control procedure to prevent the documents supporting a paid voucher from being resubmitted later in support of another cash disbursement.

13. What information usually appears on a bank statement?

14. It is standard accounting practice to treat as cash all cheques received from customers. When a customer's cheque is received, recorded, and deposited, but later returned by the bank marked "NSF," what accounting entry or entries would be appropriate?

15. List two items often encountered in reconciling a bank account that may cause cash per the bank statement to be *larger* than the balance of cash shown in the accounts.

16. In the reconciliation of a bank account, what reconciling items necessitate a journal entry in the depositor's accounting records?

17. Briefly describe how an employer may use *electronic funds transfers* in meeting its payroll obligations. Describe the advantages of this system to (1) the employees and (2) the employer.

18. A basic concept of internal control is that all cash disbursements of substantial dollar amount should be made by cheque. What then is the purpose of a *petty cash fund?* Also, identify three types of expenditures that are likely to be made from such a fund.

19. Pico Stationery Shop has for years maintained a petty cash fund of $75, which is replenished twice a month.
    (a) How many debit entries would you expect to find in the Petty Cash account each year?
    (b) When would expenditures from the petty cash fund be entered in the ledger accounts?

20. Describe the nature and usefulness of a *cash budget.*

Exercises

EXERCISE 7-1
Accounting Terminology
(LO 1, 2, 3, 4, 5)

Listed below are nine technical accounting terms introduced in this chapter.

Cash equivalents	*Cash budget*	*Cheque register*
Cash management	*Voucher system*	*Bank reconciliation*
Petty cash fund	*NSF cheques*	*Cash Over and Short*

Each of the following statements may (or may not) describe one of these technical terms. For each statement, indicate the term described, or answer "None" if the statement does not correctly describe any of the terms.

a. Short-term and highly liquid investments that often are combined with cash for the purpose of balance sheet presentation.

b. A sequence of procedures for assuring that every potential expenditure has been reviewed and approved before a cheque is issued.

c. A control procedure that should bring to light any unrecorded cash disbursements.

d. The account in which errors in making change for cash customers are recorded.

e. Cheques issued by a business that have not yet been presented for payment.

f. A document used in determining whether a department's cash receipts and cash expenditures are consistent with management's prior expectations.

g. Includes measures to prevent the maintenance of excessively large balances in non-interest-bearing bank accounts.

h. A means of conveniently making small, incidental disbursements of cash.

EXERCISE 7-2
Effects of Errors and
Irregularities
(LO 1, 2, 3, 4, 5)

DodgeTown, Inc., is an automobile dealership. The company uses a voucher system and has several bank accounts. Shown below are a series of situations that may (or may not) represent errors or irregularities that affect the reliability of the company's accounting records.

a. Collection of an account receivable is recorded by debiting Sales Returns and Allowances and crediting Accounts Receivable.

b. A cheque was issued in payment of voucher no. 4600, but no entry was made in the cheque register. Voucher no. 4600 was for property taxes expense.

c. No entry was made to record the investment of cash in treasury bills, which are considered cash equivalents.

d. No entry was made to record the investment of cash in the stock of **Canadian Pacific Limited,** which is ***not*** considered a cash equivalent.

e. No entry was made to record the failure to earn any interest revenue on the large cash balances in the corporation's non-interest-bearing bank account.

f. No entry is made to adjust the company's accounting records for the amount of a deposit in transit listed in the year-end bank reconciliation.

g. No entry was made to adjust the company's accounting records for customers' cheques returned by the bank at year-end with the designation "NSF."

h. Last month, a particular supplier was paid in full for services classified as an expense. This month, the same supporting documents were recirculated through the voucher system, and a second voucher was recorded authorizing a duplicate payment. (No cheque has yet been issued for this second payment.)

i. The custodian "borrowed" $250 from the petty cash fund but replaced the money before the fund was counted or replenished.

INSTRUCTIONS

Indicate the effects (if any) of each of these situations upon the elements of the company's financial statements listed below. (Notice that Cash & Cash Equivalents is listed separately from other assets.) Use the code letters **O** to indicate overstatement, **U** to indicate understatement, and **NE** to indicate no effect. Organize your answer in tabular form, using the following column headings:

	Income Statement			Balance Sheet			
Trans-action	Net Sales −	Net Expenses =	Net Income	Cash & Cash Equivalents +	All Other Assets =	Liabilities +	Owners' Equity
a							

EXERCISE 7-3
Internal Control: Identifying
Strength and Weakness
(LO 1, 2, 3, 4, 5)

Some of the following practices are suggestive of strength in internal controls; others are suggestive of weakness. Identify each of the eight practices with the term **Strength** or **Weakness.** Give reasons for your answers.

a. Vouchers and all supporting documents are stamped "PAID" before being sent to the finance department for review and signing of cheques.

b. Personnel in the accounting department are not authorized to handle cash receipts. Therefore, accounts receivable records are maintained by the credit manager, who handles all collections from customers.

c. Accounting department personnel are not authorized to prepare bank reconciliations. This procedure is performed in the finance department and the accounting department is notified of any required adjustments to the accounts.

d. Cheques received through the mail are recorded daily by the person maintaining accounts receivable records.
e. All cash receipts are deposited daily.
f. Any difference between a day's over-the-counter cash receipts and the day's total shown by the cash register is added to or removed from petty cash.
g. After the monthly bank reconciliation has been prepared, any difference between the adjusted balance per the depositor's records and the adjusted balance per the bank statement is entered in the Cash Over and Short account.
h. Employees who handle cash receipts are not authorized to issue credit memoranda or to write off accounts receivable as uncollectible.

EXERCISE 7-4
Subdivision of Duties
(LO 2, 4)

Certain subdivisions of duties are highly desirable for the purpose of achieving a reasonable degree of internal control. For each of the following six responsibilities, explain whether or not assigning the duty to an employee who also handles cash receipts would represent a significant weakness in internal control. Briefly explain your reasoning.

a. Responsibility for executing both cash and credit sales transactions.
b. Responsibility for maintaining the general ledger.
c. Responsibility for maintaining the accounts receivable subsidiary ledger.
d. Responsibility for issuing credit memoranda for sales returns.
e. Responsibility for preparing a control listing of all cash collections.
f. Responsibility for preparing monthly bank reconciliations.

EXERCISE 7-5
Voucher System
(LO 3)

Laser Optic, Inc., uses a voucher system. The following transactions occurred early this month:

a. Voucher no. 100 prepared to purchase office equipment at cost of $4,000 from Coast Furniture Co. Ltd.
b. Cheque no. 114 issued in payment of voucher no. 100.
c. Voucher no. 101 prepared to establish a petty cash fund of $150.
d. Cheque no. 115 issued in payment of voucher no. 101.
e. Cheque no. 116 issued in payment of voucher no. 102 for $910.

INSTRUCTIONS

You are to record the transactions in general journal form (without explanations). Also indicate after each entry the journal (or book of original entry) in which in actual practice the transaction would be recorded. For example, your treatment of transaction **a** should be as follows:

```
(a)  Office Equipment .....................................    4,000
            Vouchers Payable ..............................              4,000
     (Voucher register)
```

EXERCISE 7-6
Short Bank Reconciliation
(LO 4)

The following information relating to the bank account is available for Music Hall at July 31:

Balance per bank statement at July 31	$19,893.25
Balance per depositor's records at July 31	18,681.35
Outstanding cheques	2,102.50
Deposits in transit	872.60
Service charge by bank	18.00

INSTRUCTIONS

Prepare a bank reconciliation for Music Hall at July 31.

EXERCISE 7-7
Another Short Bank
Reconciliation
(LO 4)

The following information relating to the bank account is available for Wild Bill's Barbeque at May 31.

Balance per bank statement at May 31	$9,740.15
Outstanding cheques	3,352.70
Deposit in transit	1,106.30
Service charge by bank	10.00
Interest credited by the bank	43.10
Balance per depositor's accounting records at May 31	7,460.65

INSTRUCTIONS

Prepare a bank reconciliation at May 31.

EXERCISE 7-8
Bank Reconciliation and
Entries to Update the
Accounting Records
(LO 4)

Shown below is the information needed to prepare a bank reconciliation for Data Flow, Inc., at December 31.

1. At December 31, cash per the bank statement was $15,981; cash per the company's records was $17,445.

2. Two debit memoranda accompanied the bank statement: service charges for December of $24, and a $600 cheque drawn by Jane Jones marked "NSF."

3. Cash receipts of $4,353 on December 31 were not deposited until January 2.

4. The following cheques had been issued in December but were not included among the paid cheques returned by the bank: no. 620 for $978, no. 630 for $2,052, and no. 641 for $483.

INSTRUCTIONS

a. Prepare a bank reconciliation at December 31.
b. Prepare the necessary journal entry or entries to update the accounting records of Data Flow, Inc.

EXERCISE 7-9
Analysis of Reconciling Items
(LO 4)

At September 30, the Cash account of Canvasback, a sole proprietorship, showed a balance of $72,900. The bank statement, however, showed a balance of $87,400 at the same date. The only reconciling items consisted of a $4,800 deposit in transit, a credit for interest earned of $200, and 30 outstanding cheques.

INSTRUCTIONS

a. Compute the amount of cash that should appear in the company's balance sheet at September 30.
b. Compute the total amount of the outstanding cheques.

EXERCISE 7-10
Adjustments to the Cash
Account
(LO 4)

In this exercise we focus on some of the basic computations required in almost all bank reconciliations. At the end of November, Glacier Lodge received a bank statement showing a balance of $105,000. The balance included interest earned during November of $450. All cheques issued by Glacier Lodge were returned with the November bank statement except for 10 cheques totalling $16,000 issued on November 30. Also, a late afternoon deposit of $8,000 by Glacier Lodge on November 30 did not appear on the November bank statement.

INSTRUCTIONS

a. Compute the amount of cash to appear on the November 30 balance sheet of Glacier Lodge. Show all computations.
b. Compute the amount of cash shown by Glacier Lodge's records *before* any month-end entries were made to update the company's records.

EXERCISE 7-11
Reconciling Items
(LO 4)

In reconciling the bank account of Lane Company, the accountant had to deal with the following six items.

1. Outstanding cheques.

2. Bank service charges.

3. Cheque no. 502 was issued in the correct amount of $350 and paid by the bank in that amount, but had been incorrectly recorded in Lane Company's accounting records as $530.

4. Collection by bank of note receivable left with bank by Lane Company for collection and credit to Lane Company's account.

5. Customers' cheques deposited by Lane Company but returned by bank marked "NSF."

6. Deposit in transit.

INSTRUCTIONS

You are to classify each of the above six items under one of the following headings: (a) an addition to the balance per the bank statement; (b) a deduction from the balance per the bank statement; (c) an addition to the balance per the depositor's records; (d) a deduction from the balance per the depositor's records.

Problems

PROBLEM 7-1
Internal Control Procedures
(LO 2, 3, 4)

Listed below are nine errors or problems that might occur in the processing of cash transactions. Also shown is a separate list of internal control procedures.

Possible Errors or Problems

a. In serving customers who do not appear to be attentive, a salesclerk often rings up a sale at less than the actual sales amount and then removes the additional cash collected from the customer.

b. John Davis, who has prepared bank reconciliations for Marlo Corporation for several years has noticed that some cheques issued by the company are never presented for payment. Davis, therefore, has formed the habit of dropping any cheques outstanding for more than six months from the outstanding cheques list and removing a corresponding amount of cash from the cash receipts. These actions taken together have left the ledger account for cash in agreement with the adjusted bank balance and have enriched Davis substantially.

c. A voucher was circulated through the system twice, causing the supplier to be paid twice for the same invoice.

d. Lisa Miller, an employee of Plaza Home Repairs, frequently has trouble in getting the bank reconciliation to balance. If the book balance is more than the bank balance, she writes a cheque payable to Cash and cashes it. If the book balance is less than the bank balance, she makes an accounting entry debiting Cash and crediting Cash Over and Short.

e. Without fear of detection, the cashier sometimes abstracts cash forwarded to him from the mailroom or the sales department instead of depositing these receipts in the company's bank account.

f. The monthly bank reconciliation continually shows a difference between the adjusted bank balance and the adjusted book balance because the cashier regularly deposits actual cash receipts, but the debits to the Cash account reflect cash register readings that differ by the amount of errors in making change in cash sales transactions.

g. All cash received from Monday through Thursday was lost in a burglary on Thursday night.

h. A salesclerk occasionally makes an error in the amount of change given to a customer.

i. The official designated to sign cheques is able to steal blank cheques and issue them for unauthorized purposes without fear of detection.

Internal Control Procedures

1. Periodic reconciliation of bank statements to accounting records.

2. Use of a Cash Over and Short account.

3. Adequate subdivision of duties.

4. Use of prenumbered sales tickets.

5. Depositing each day's cash receipts intact in the bank.

6. Use of electronic cash registers equipped with optical scanners to read magnetically coded labels on merchandise.

7. Immediate preparation of a control listing when cash is received, and the comparison of this listing to bank deposits.

8. Cancellation of paid vouchers at the time of signing the cheques.

9. Requirement that a voucher be prepared as advance authorization of every cash disbursement.

0. None of the above control procedures can effectively prevent this type of error or problem from occurring.

INSTRUCTIONS

List the letters (**a** through **i**) designating each possible error or problem. Beside this letter, place the number indicating the internal control procedure that should prevent this type of error or problem from occurring. If none of the specified internal control procedures would effectively prevent the error or problem, place a **0** opposite the letter.

PROBLEM 7-2
Internal Control Procedures
(LO 2, 3, 4)

Listed below are nine errors or problems that might occur in the processing of cash transactions. Also shown is a separate list of internal control procedures.

Possible Errors or Problems

a. The bookkeeper of Centre Hardware frequently has trouble in getting the bank reconciliation to balance. If the book balance is more than the bank balance, the bookkeeper writes a cheque payable to Cash and cashes it. If the book balance is less than the bank balance, the bookkeeper makes an accounting entry debiting Cash and crediting Cash Over and Short.

b. The cashier of Fun Toys Store abstracts cash forwarded to him from the mailroom or the sales department instead of depositing these receipts in the store's bank account.

c. The monthly bank reconciliation continually shows a difference between the adjusted bank balance and the adjusted book balance because the cashier regularly deposits actual cash receipts, but the debits to the Cash account reflect cash register readings that differ by the amount of errors in making change in cash sales transactions.

d. All cash receipts from Monday through Wednesday were stolen on Wednesday night.

e. A cashier occasionally makes an error in the amount of change given to a customer.

f. The official authorized to sign cheques is able to steal blank cheques and issue them for unauthorized purposes without fear of detection.

g. When serving customers who do not appear to be attentive, a cashier often rings up a sale at less than the actual sales amount and then removes the additional cash collected from the customer.

h. Teresa Hill, who has prepared bank reconciliations for Ross Stewart, Inc., for several years has noticed that some cheques issued by the company are never presented for payment. Hill, therefore, has formed the habit of dropping any cheques outstanding for more than six months from the outstanding cheques list and removing a corresponding amount of cash from the cash receipts. These actions taken together have left the ledger account for cash in agreement with the adjusted bank balance and have enriched Hill substantially.

i. A voucher was circulated through the system twice, causing the supplier to be paid for the same voucher the second time.

Internal Control Procedures

1. Periodic reconciliation of bank statements to accounting records.
2. Use of a Cash Over and Short account.
3. Adequate subdivision of duties.
4. Use of prenumbered sales tickets.
5. Depositing each day's cash receipts intact in the bank.
6. Use of electronic cash registers equipped with optical scanners to read magnetically coded labels on merchandise.
7. Immediate preparation of a control listing when cash is received, and the comparison of this listing to bank deposits.
8. Cancellation of paid vouchers at the time of signing the cheques.
9. Requirement that a voucher be prepared as advance authorization of every cash disbursement.
0. None of the above control procedures can effectively prevent this type of error or problem from occurring.

INSTRUCTIONS

List the letters (**a** through **i**) designating each possible error or problem. Beside this letter, place the number indicating the internal control procedure that should prevent this type of error or problem from occurring. If none of the specified internal control procedures would effectively prevent the error or problem, place a **0** opposite the letter.

PROBLEM 7-3
Preparing a Bank Reconciliation and Adjusting Entries
(LO 4)

Bluegrass Tonight is a nightclub in Halifax. The information necessary for preparing a bank reconciliation for the company at November 30 appears below:

1. As of November 30, cash per the bank statement is $41,631, per the accounting records, $48,609.
2. Cash receipts of $9,366 on November 30 were not deposited until December 1.
3. Among the paid cheques returned by the bank was a stolen cheque for $1,512 paid in error after Bluegrass Tonight had officially notified the bank not to make payment. Thus, payment of this cheque was a bank error and should not have been charged against Bluegrass Tonight's bank account.
4. The following memoranda accompanied the bank statement:
   a. A debit memo for service charges, $21
   b. A debit memo attached to an $1,167 cheque that Bluegrass had accepted from customer Lanlee Limited and deposited in its account, but that the bank had returned with the marking "NSF"
   c. A credit memo for interest earned on the account during November, $135
5. The following cheques had been issued by the nightclub but had not been paid by the bank as of November 30: no. 921 for $2,346; no. 924 for $1,446; and no. 925 for $1,161.

INSTRUCTIONS

Prepare the November 30 bank reconciliation and the adjusting entries (in general journal form) to update the accounts.

PROBLEM 7-4
Bank Reconciliation, Adjusting Entries, and Balance Sheet Presentation
(LO 1, 4)

During July the cash transactions and cash balances of Rapid Harvest were as follows:

1. The cash balance per the bank statement at July 31 was $28,945.27.
2. The ledger account for Cash had a balance at July 31 of $26,686.95.
3. Cash receipts on July 31 amounted to $4,000. These cash receipts were left at the bank in the night depository chute after banking hours on July 31 and therefore were not included by the bank in the July bank statement.

4. Included with the July bank statement was a credit memorandum showing interest earned by the depositor on this account in the amount of $80.

5. Another credit memorandum enclosed with the July bank statement showed that a non-interest-bearing note for $3,663 from Ralph Warde, left with the bank for collection, had been collected and the proceeds credited to the account of Rapid Harvest.

6. Also included with the July bank statement was a debit memorandum from the bank for $19.45 representing service charges for July.

7. Comparison of the paid cheques returned by the bank with the entries in the accounting records revealed that cheque no. 922 for $4,521.50 issued July 15 in payment for salaries expense had been erroneously entered in the accounting records as $5,421.50.

8. Examination of the paid cheques also revealed that three cheques, all issued in July, had not yet been paid by the bank: no. 921 for $944.32; no. 924 for $320.50; no. 935 for $538.15.

9. Included with the July bank statement was a $168.20 cheque drawn by Edward Jones, a customer of Rapid Harvest. This cheque was marked "NSF." It had been included in the deposit of July 28 but had been charged back against the company's account on July 31.

INSTRUCTIONS

a. Prepare a bank reconciliation for Rapid Harvest at July 31.
b. Prepare journal entries (in general journal form) to update the accounts at July 31. Assume that the accounts have not been closed.
c. State the amount of cash that should be included in the balance sheet at July 31.

PROBLEM 7-5
Bank Reconciliation, Adjusting Entries, and Balance Sheet Presentation
(LO 1, 4)

The information relating to Seaview Co-op's bank reconciliation for July was as follows:

1. The ledger account for Cash showed a balance at July 31 of $16,766.95.

2. The July bank statement showed a closing balance of $19,228.12.

3. The cash received on July 31 amounted to $4,017.15. It was left at the bank in the night depository chute after banking hours on July 31 and was therefore not recorded by the bank on the July statement.

4. Also included with the July bank statement was a debit memorandum from the bank for $7.65 representing service charges for July.

5. A credit memorandum enclosed with the July bank statement indicated that a non-interest-bearing note receivable for $4,545 from Rene Manes, left with the bank for collection, had been collected and the proceeds credited to the account of Seaview Co-op.

6. Comparison of the paid cheques returned by the bank with the entries in the accounting records revealed that cheque no. 821 for *$835.02,* issued July 15 in payment for office equipment, had been erroneously entered in Seaview's records as *$853.02.*

7. Examination of the paid cheques also revealed that three cheques, all issued in July, had not yet been paid by the bank: no. 811 for $861.12; no. 814 for $640.80; no. 823 for $301.05.

8. Included with the July bank statement was a $180 cheque drawn by Howard Williams, a customer of Seaview Co-op. This cheque was marked "NSF." It had been included in the deposit of July 27 but had been charged back against the company's account on July 31.

9. Examination of the June bank reconciliation showed that cheque no. 789 for $300 still had not been paid by the bank.

INSTRUCTIONS

a. Prepare a bank reconciliation for Seaview Co-op at July 31.
b. Prepare journal entries (in general journal form) to update the accounts at July 31. Assume that the accounts have not been closed.
c. State the amount of cash that should be included in the balance sheet at July 31.

PROBLEM 7-6
Bank Reconciliation and Adjusting Entries
(LO 4)

Daytona Recycling Centre reports the following information concerning its bank account for the month of September:

1. Cash balance per bank statement as of September 30 was $20,893.25.

2. Two debit memoranda accompanied the bank statement: one for $10 was for service charges for the month; the other for $64.60 was attached to an NSF cheque from A. Smith.

3. Included with the bank statement was $69 credit memorandum for interest earned on the bank account in September.

4. The paid cheques returned with the September bank statement disclosed an error in Daytona's cash records. Cheque no. 851 for $77.44 for telephone expense had erroneously been recorded as $44.77.

5. A collection charge for $26.00 (not applicable to Daytona) was erroneously deducted from the account by the bank.

6. Cash receipts of September 30 amounting to $585.25 were deposited in the bank too late to be included in the September bank statement.

7. Cheques outstanding as of September 30 were as follows: no. 860 for $151.93, no. 867 for $82.46, and no. 869 for $123.61.

8. The Cash account showed the following entries during September:

				Cash				
Sept	1	Balance		18,341.82	Sept	30	Month's payments	11,598.63
	30	Month's receipts		14,441.58				

INSTRUCTIONS

a. Prepare a bank reconciliation at September 30.
b. Prepare the necessary journal entries, in general journal form, to update the company's records.

PROBLEM 7-7
Bank Reconciliation, Adjusting Entries, and Balance Sheet Presentation
(LO 1, 4)

The information needed to prepare a bank reconciliation for Wicked Pony at March 31 is listed below.

1. Cash balance per the accounting records of Wicked Pony, $18,106.69.

2. The bank statement showed a balance of $22,734.27 at March 31.

3. Accompanying the bank statement was a debit memorandum relating to a cheque for $186 from a customer, D. Otay. The cheque was returned by the bank and stamped "NSF."

4. Cheques issued in March that were outstanding as of March 31 were: no. 84 for $1,841.02; no. 88 for $1,323.00; no. 89 for $16.26.

5. Also accompanying the bank statement was a debit memorandum for $44.80 for safety deposit box rent; the bank had erroneously charged this item to the account of Wicked Pony.

6. On March 29, the bank collected a non-interest-bearing note for Wicked Pony. The note was for $2,963.

7. A deposit of $2,008.50 on March 31 was made too late for the bank to record it on March 31.

8. In recording a $160 cheque received on account from a customer, Ross Company, the accountant for Wicked Pony erroneously recorded the amount collected as $16. The cheque appeared correctly among the deposits on the March bank statement.

9. The bank service charge for March amounted to $20.40; a debit memo in this amount was returned with the bank statement.

10. Cheque no. 68 for $600, listed among the outstanding cheques in the February bank reconciliation was still not cashed.

INSTRUCTIONS

a. Prepare a bank reconciliation at March 31.
b. Prepare the necessary journal entries to update the account at March 31.
c. What amount of cash should be included in the company's March 31 balance sheet?

PROBLEM 7-8
Bank Reconciliation and
Internal Control
(LO 2, 4)

Carriage Towne, a successful small business, had never given much consideration to the need for internal control, and the internal controls over cash transactions were inadequate. Thom Chan, the cashier-bookkeeper, handled cash receipts, made small disbursements from these cash receipts, maintained the accounting records, and prepared the monthly reconciliations of the bank account. Recognizing the weaknesses in internal control over cash transactions, Chan began pocketing some of the company's cash receipts.

At the end of April, the bank statement indicated a balance on deposit of $37,350.90. The following cheques were outstanding: no. 7552 for $612.30, no. 7573 for $1,219.00, no. 7574 for $468.30, no. 7611 for $1,321.10, no. 7613 for $402.20, and no. 7622 for $3,211.00. All cash receipts for April (except those stolen by Chan) had been deposited in the bank, and the deposits all were listed correctly in the April 30 bank statement. The cash balance shown in the company's accounting records at April 30 was $38,467.00, including $200.00 in cash on hand. This information was known to Chan; however, he concealed the amount of his theft by preparing the bank "reconciliation" improperly, as shown below:

Balance per bank statement, April 30		$37,350.90
Less: Outstanding cheques:		
No. 7611	$1,321.10	
No. 7613	402.20	
No. 7622	2,311.00	3,034.30
		$34,316.60
Add: Deposit not recorded by bank (April 30 receipts) ..	$3,650.40	
Cash on hand	500.00	4,150.40
Balance per accounting records, April 30		$38,467.00

INSTRUCTIONS

a. Determine the amount of the cash shortage concealed by Chan in his November bank reconciliation by preparing a correct bank reconciliation.
b. Carefully review Chan's bank reconciliation and explain in detail how he concealed the amount of the shortage. Include a listing of the dollar amounts that were concealed in various ways. This listing should total the amount of the shortage as determined in part **a.**
c. Suggest some specific internal control measures that appear to be necessary for Carriage Towne.

PROBLEM 7-9
"Charmed . . ."
(LO 2, 4)

Equipment Rental Company had poor internal control over its cash transactions. Facts about the company's cash position at November 30, 2000, were as described below.

The accounting records showed a cash balance of $29,959.00, which included a deposit of two days of cash receipts of $3,420.60 on November 30 not yet recorded by the bank. The balance indicated in the bank statement was $18,299.40. Included in the bank statement were the following debit and credit memoranda:

Debit Memoranda:
Cheque from customer G. Davis, deposited by Equipment	
Rental Co., but charged back as NSF	$1,500.00
Bank service charges for November	25.00

Credit Memorandum:
Proceeds from collection of a note receivable	
from Regal Farms that Equipment Rental Co.	
had left with the bank's collection department	3,000.00

Outstanding cheques as of November 30 were as follows:

Cheque No.	Amount
8231	$ 340.30
8263	800.50
8288	145.20
8294	2,100.00

Melanie Charm, the company's cashier, has been abstracting portions of the company's cash receipts for several months. Each month, Charm prepares the company's bank reconciliation in a manner that conceals her thefts. Her bank reconciliation for November is illustrated as follows:

Balance per bank statement, Nov. 30		$18,299.40
Add: Deposits of November 30 not recorded by bank . . .	$4,320.60	
Collection of note from Regal Farms	3,000.00	7,320.60
Subtotal		$26,620.00
Less: Outstanding cheques:		
No. 8231	$ 340.30	
8263	800.50	
8288	145.20	1,186.00
Adjusted cash balance per bank statement		$25,434.00
Balance per accounting records, Nov. 30		$29,959.00
Add: Credit memorandum from bank		3,000.00
Subtotal		$26,959.00
Less: Debit memoranda from bank:		
NSF cheque of G. Davis	$1,500.00	
Bank service charges	25.00	1,525.00
Adjusted cash balance per accounting records		$25,434.00

INSTRUCTIONS

a. Determine the amount of the cash shortage that has been concealed by Charm in her bank reconciliation by preparing a correct bank reconciliation.

b. Carefully review Charm's bank reconciliation and explain in detail how she concealed the amount of the shortage. Include a listing of the dollar amounts that were concealed in various ways. This listing should total the amount of the shortage determined in part **a.**

c. Suggest some specific internal control measures that appear to be necessary for Equipment Rental Company.

PROBLEM 7-10
Using Bank Statement and Records To Prepare Bank Reconciliation
(LO 4)

At September 30, 2000, Sheraton Company's bank reconciliation shows these items: a service charge by the bank of $12, interest income from the bank account of $28, and two outstanding cheques—No. 786 for $200, No. 860 for $300. The cash receipts and the cash payments from the data base showed the following transactions:

Cash Receipts			Cash Payments			
Date		Cash Dr	Date		Ch. No.	Cash Cr
Oct. 1		72.80	Oct. 1		865	130.00
3		361.00	1		866	90.00
6		280.00	1		867	35.48
8		510.00	2		868	31.15
10		205.60	4		869	60.00
13		180.14	4		870	70.00
15		345.00	5		871	515.00
18		427.50	8		872	62.50
20		90.00	9		873	13.30
22		360.00	10		874	28.00
27		625.00	13		875	650.00
28		130.25	19		876	125.06
29		280.50	19		877	40.00
31		690.50	19		878	85.00
		4,558.29	20		879	24.10
			21		880	38.60
			22		881	65.00
			22		882	162.40
			23		883	150.00
			26		884	15.00
			28		885	270.00
			28		886	105.20
			28		887	225.00
			28		888	355.00
			30		889	25.00
			31		890	35.00
			31		891	255.00
						3,660.79

On November 2, the company received from its bank the following bank statement covering the month of October. Enclosed with the bank statement were 24 cheques paid by the bank during October and a $24.75 debit memorandum for service charge and a $20.50 credit memorandum for interest.

CANADIAN ROYAL BANK
380 Campbell Street, Windsor, Ontario N9B 3P6

Account No. 126890

				Date	Amount
Sheraton Company			Balance		
169 Randolph Avenue			Forward	Sept. 30, 2000	$8,158.75
Windsor, Ontario N9C 6B9					

Cheques			Deposits	Date	Balance
31.15	35.48	130.00	72.80	Oct. 2	8,034.92
60.00	300.00		361.00	5	8,035.92
70.00	515.00		280.00	7	7,730.92
90.00				8	7,640.92
13.30	62.50		510.00	9	8,075.12
28.00			205.60	12	8,252.72
650.00			180.14	14	7,782.86
			345.00	16	8,127.86
85.00			427.50	19	8,470.36
24.10	125.06			20	8,321.20
40.00			90.00	21	8,371.20
162.40	65.00		360.00	23	8,503.80
15.00			625.00	27	9,113.80
355.00	270.00	225.00	130.25	29	8,394.05
255.00	25.00	24.75 SC	280.50		
			20.50 IN	31	8,390.30

INSTRUCTIONS

a. Compute the amount of cash balance at October 31 according to the depositor's records, assuming the necessary journal entry or entries to update the company's records at September 30 have been made.

b. Prepare a bank reconciliation at October 31.

c. Prepare general journal entries to update the company's records at October 31, based on information contained in the bank reconciliation in part **b.**

PROBLEM 7-11
Using Bank Statement and Records To Prepare Bank Reconciliation
(LO 4)

The May bank reconciliation of Carnavan Limited shows these items: an outstanding cheque (No. 569) for $100, an outstanding deposit of $590 and a bank service charge of $23.80. The cash receipts and cash payments from the database showed the following transactions during June.

Cash Receipts			Cash Payments			
Date		Cash Dr	Date		Ch. No.	Cash Cr
June 2		82.80	June 1		665	148.00
4		351.00	1		666	90.00
6		280.00	1		667	25.48
8		500.00	2		668	23.15
10		215.60	4		669	60.00
13		280.14	4		670	80.00
15		245.00	5		671	505.00
17		327.50	9		672	62.50
20		190.00	10		673	18.30
22		360.00	10		674	23.00
26		625.00	13		675	650.00
28		150.25	19		676	25.06
29		260.50	19		677	40.00
30		315.25	19		678	85.00
		4,183.04	20		679	124.10
			21		680	48.60
			22		681	65.00
			22		682	162.40
			23		683	100.00
			26		684	15.00
			28		685	290.00
			28		686	125.20
			28		687	225.00
			28		688	335.00
			29		689	45.00
			29		690	65.00
			30		691	135.00
						3,570.79

On July 3, Carnavan Limited received the following bank statement covering the month of June. Enclosed were 23 cheques paid by the bank during June, a $26.50 debit memorandum for service charges, a credit memorandum for $20 interest, and a debit memorandum for $50 for an NSF cheque from K. Jordan.

DOMINION BANK
176 Georgia Street, Vancouver B.C. V6E 4A2

Account No. 3691278

Statement of Account

Carnavan Limited
268 Front Street
Vancouver, B.C. V8L 1S2

		Date	Amount
Balance Forward		May 31, 2001	$7,168.75

Cheques			Deposits	Date	Balance
			590.00	June 1	7,758.75
23.15	25.48	148.00	82.80	3	7,644.92
60.00			351.00	5	7,935.92
80.00	505.00		280.00	7	7,630.92
90.00				8	7,540.92
62.50			500.00	9	7,978.42
23.00	18.30		215.60	12	8,152.72
650.00			280.14	14	7,782.86
			245.00	16	8,027.86
85.00			327.50	19	8,270.36
124.10	25.06			20	8,121.20
40.00			190.00	21	8,271.20
162.40	65.00		360.00	23	8,403.80
15.00			625.00	27	9,013.80
335.00	290.00	225.00	150.25	29	8,314.05
135.00	45.00	26.50 SC	260.50		
50.00 DM			20.00 IN	30	8,338.05

INSTRUCTIONS

a. Compute the amount of cash balance at June 30 according to the depositor's records, assuming the necessary journal entry to update the company's records at May 31 has been made.

b. Prepare a bank reconciliation at June 30.

c. Prepare general journal entries to update the company's records at June 30, based on information contained in the bank reconciliation in part **b.**

PROBLEM 7-12
Analysis of Bank
Reconciliation Items
(LO 4)

The following items are related to cash balances between Macao Company and its bank for the month of December.

1. Accompanying the bank statement was a debit memorandum for $62, representing bank service charges for Macor Limited for December. This amount was deducted from Macao's account.

2. The bank statement does not show the cash receipts of $1,500 deposited by Macao in the bank's night depository on December 31.

3. Enclosed with the bank statement was a credit memorandum stating that the bank had collected a $2,000 note receivable plus interest of $28 from G. Hogg. The bank charged a collection fee of $16.

4. Macao has two cheques (one issued in payment of office supplies in October for $100 and the other in November for $320 for advertising) that still have not been cashed by the payees.

5. Comparison of the paid cheques returned by the bank with the entries in the cash payments records revealed that a cheque for $160, in payment for advertising expense, had been erroneously recorded as $610.

6. A cheque issued in December for $260 to settle an accounts payable (Totten Limited) was outstanding.

7. Included with the paid cheques was a cheque for $180, marked NSF by the bank. The cheques were from Thai MacDonald in payment of his open account.

8. A debit memorandum for $92, representing the cost of printing new cheques and service charges for December, was included with the bank statement.

INSTRUCTIONS

a. Prepare the necessary entries, in general journal form but omit explanations, at December 31 to update the cash balance per company's (depositor's) records.
b. Identify the item (or items) and indicate whether it should be added or deducted from the balance per bank statement to arrive at the adjusted cash balance (a bank reconciliation is **not** required).

Analytical and Decision Problems and Cases

A&D 7-1
Cash Management
(LO 1)

Banks generally offer a variety of "cash management" options to individuals and small business.

INSTRUCTIONS

a. Arrange an interview with a representative of a local bank. Enquire as to the options that the bank provides for temporarily investing cash balances not needed in the near future. Gain an understanding of the various cash management options available to individuals and to small business, including the expected yields. (**Note:** All interviews are to be conducted in accordance with the guidelines in the *Preface* of this textbook.)
b. Briefly explain each of the options discussed in this interview, along with the expected yields (if determinable). Identify the option you consider best suited to:
1. An individual or a small business whose chequing account often has as much as $10,000 that will not be needed within the next 30 days.
2. A small business that has about $400,000 in liquid resources that will not be needed for the next nine months.

Explain the reasons for your choices and be prepared to explain these reasons in class.

A&D 7-2
Cash Management
(LO 1)

St. Jude Medical, Inc., is a large public corporation engaged in the manufacture of heart valves and other medical products. In recent years, the company has accumulated large amounts of cash and cash equivalents as a result of profitable operations. A recent annual report shows cash and cash equivalents amounting to more than 50% of the company's total assets. As these large holdings of cash and cash equivalents have been accumulated, the company has paid no dividends.

INSTRUCTIONS

Evaluate St. Jude's policies of accumulating liquid resources instead of paying dividends from the perspectives of:
a. The company's creditors.
b. The company's shareholders.

A&D 7-3
Embezzlement, She Wrote
(LO 2)

D. J. Fletcher, a trusted employee of Bluestem Products, found herself in personal financial difficulties and decided to "borrow" $3,000 from the company and to conceal her theft.

As a first step, Fletcher removed $3,000 in currency from the cash register. This amount represented the bulk of the cash received in over-the-counter sales during the three business days since the last bank deposit. Fletcher then removed a $3,000 cheque from the day's incoming mail; this cheque had been mailed in by a customer, Michael Adams, in full payment of his account. Fletcher made no journal entry to record the $3,000 collection from Adams but deposited the cheque in Bluestem Products' bank account in place of the $3,000 over-the-counter cash receipts she had stolen.

In order to keep Adams from protesting when his month-end statement reached him, Fletcher made a journal entry debiting Sales Returns and Allowances and crediting Accounts Receivable—Michael Adams. Fletcher posted this entry to the two general ledger accounts affected and also to Adams's account in the subsidiary ledger for accounts receivable.

INSTRUCTIONS

a. Did these actions by Fletcher cause the general ledger to be out of balance or the subsidiary ledger to disagree with the controlling account? Explain.
b. Assume that Bluestem Products prepares financial statements at the end of the month without discovering the theft. Would any items in the balance sheet or the income statement be in error? Explain.
c. Several weaknesses in internal control apparently exist in Bluestem Products. Indicate three specific changes needed to strengthen internal control over cash receipts.

A&D 7-4
Internal Control—A Challenging Case Study
(LO 2)

June Davis inherited a highly successful business, Solano, Inc., shortly after her twenty-second birthday and took over the active management of the business. A portion of the company's business consisted of over-the-counter sales for cash, but most sales were on credit and were shipped by truck. Davis had no knowledge of internal control practices and relied implicitly upon the bookkeeper-cashier, John Adams, in all matters relating to cash and accounting records. Adams, who had been with the company for many years, maintained the accounting records and prepared all financial statements with the help of two assistants, made bank deposits, signed cheques, and prepared bank reconciliations.

The monthly income statements submitted to Davis by Adams showed a very satisfactory rate of net income; however, the amount of cash in the bank declined steadily during the first 18 months after Davis took over the business. To meet the company's weakening cash position, a bank loan was obtained and a few months later when the cash position again grew critical, the loan was increased.

On April 1, two years after Davis assumed the management of the company, Adams suddenly left town, leaving no forwarding address. Davis was immediately deluged with claims of creditors who stated their accounts were several months past due and that Adams had promised all debts would be paid by April 1. The bank telephoned to notify Davis that the company's account was overdrawn and that a number of cheques had just been presented for payment.

In an effort to get together some cash to meet this emergency, Davis called on two of the largest customers of the company, to whom substantial sales on account had recently been made, and asked if they could pay their accounts at once. Both customers informed her that their accounts were paid in full. They produced paid cheques to substantiate their payments and explained that Adams had offered them reduced prices on merchandise if they would pay within 24 hours after delivery.

To keep the business from insolvency, Davis agreed to sell at a bargain price a half interest in the company. The sale was made to Helen Smith, who had had considerable experience in the industry. One condition for the sale was that Smith should become the general manager of the business. The cash investment by Smith for her half interest was sufficient for the company to meet the demands on it and continue operations.

Immediately after Smith entered the business, she launched an investigation of Adams's activities. During the course of this investigation the following fraudulent actions were disclosed:

1. During the last few months of Adams's employment with the company, bank deposits were much smaller than the cash receipts. Adams had abstracted most of the receipts and substituted for them a number of worthless cheques bearing fictitious signatures. These cheques had been accumulated in an envelope marked "Cash Receipts—For Deposit Only."

2. Numerous legitimate sales of merchandise on account had been charged to fictitious customers. When the actual customer later made payment for the goods, Adams abstracted the cheque or cash and made no entry. The account receivable with the fictitious customer remained in the records.

3. When cheques were received from customers in payment of their accounts, Adams had frequently recorded the transaction by debiting an expense account and crediting Accounts Receivable. In such cases Adams had removed from the cash receipts an equivalent amount of currency, thus substituting the cheque for the currency and causing the bank deposit to agree with the recorded cash receipts.

4. More than $3,000 a month had been stolen from petty cash. Fraudulent petty cash vouchers, mostly charged to the Inventory account, had been created to conceal these thefts and to support the cheques cashed to replenish the petty cash fund.

5. For many sales made over the counter, Adams had recorded lesser amounts on the cash register or had not rung up any amount. He had abstracted the funds received but not recorded.

6. To produce income statements that showed profitable operations, Adams had recorded many fictitious sales. The recorded accounts receivable included many from nonexistent customers.

7. In preparing bank reconciliations, Adams had omitted many outstanding cheques, thus concealing the fact that the cash in the bank was less than the amount shown by the ledger.

8. Inventory had been recorded at inflated amounts in order to increase reported profits from the business.

INSTRUCTIONS

a. For each of the numbered paragraphs, describe one or more internal control procedures you would recommend to prevent the occurrence of such fraud.

b. Apart from specific internal controls over cash and other accounts, what general precaution could June Davis have taken to assure herself that the accounting records were properly maintained and the company's financial statements complete and dependable? Explain fully.

A&D 7-5
Bank Reconciliation, Internal Control, and Cash Management
(LO 1, 2, 4)

The following is the bank reconciliation presented to the owner by the bookkeeper:

Balance per depositor's records, March 31			$32,550
Add: Outstanding cheques: no. 1985		$3,000	
no. 1988		6,200	
no. 1990		7,800	
no. 1994		2,466	
Notes receivable collected by bank, including interest of $275		7,025	
Interest earned during March		15	
Bank error		300	26,806
			$59,356
Deduct: Deposit of cash receipts for March 29, 30, and 31 not yet recorded by bank		$6,312	
NSF cheque of Wonders Ltd.		200	
Error on cheque no. 1989 for telephone expense		148	
Bank service charges		6	6,666
Balance per bank statement, March 31			$52,690

The excerpts of the conversation between the owner (O) and the bookkeeper (B) are as follows:

O: Thank you for the bank reconciliation. You have been doing so many things for the business—recording the transactions, making small payments from daily cash receipts, making the deposits, and reconciling the bank account, I really appreciate your hard work. You know, I sometimes wonder why the cheques for 50% of our monthly payments are usually outstanding. Maybe these companies don't need cash as badly as I do; I still owe the bank a $10,000 loan at 9% interest.

B: Maybe I should get a raise for doing all these important things, right? But seriously, it is a lot of work.

O: Well, I will think about your raise and let you know in a week's time. Okay?

B: That is wonderful!

INSTRUCTIONS

a. Indicate which items should be added or deducted from the balance per bank statement to arrive at the adjusted cash balance. A bank reconciliation is **not** required.

b. Prepare the necessary entries, in general journal format but omit explanations, at March 31 to update the cash balance per the depositor's records.

c. Identify three deficiencies in internal control and one deficiency in cash management and recommend a remedy for each deficiency.

A&D 7-6
Bank Reconciliation, Cash Management, and Internal Control
(LO 1, 2, 4)

Millien Prince, owner of a small business, just came back from a conference on cash management where she learned that one key ingredient to business success is the efficient management of cash. Before she could settle down in her office, Millien was handed the following bank reconciliation for her business by Joe, the bookkeeper:

Balance per depositor's records, June 30		$20,880
Add: Outstanding cheques: No. 918	$195	
925	360	
931	405	960
		$21,840
Deduct: Cash on hand (receipts for three days)		1,850
Balance per bank statement, June 30		$19,990
Deduct: Unrecorded bank credit		600
True cash, June 30		$19,390

Millien took one look at the reconciliation, shook her head and said: "Joe, I don't understand this reconciliation at all. You used to start the reconciliation from the balance per bank statement and the balance per our records to arrive at two equal adjusted balances. Are you trying to confuse me or what?"

Joe, somewhat uncomfortable and irritated, countered: "Millien, you are the boss and you have time to go to conferences. But I have a lot to do here. Just in case you have forgotten, I handle cash receipts and make small payments from these receipts, do the books, and prepare the monthly bank reconciliation. I also prepare a lot of cheques for you to sign—the $960 of the outstanding cheques listed in the reconciliation is roughly 10% of the total amount of cheques that I do every month. What I did in this new reconciliation saved me time. Just one example, I saved time by excluding the five old outstanding cheques totalling $730 from the reconciliation. Since these cheques are more than six months old and cannot be cashed, there is no sense in putting them in the reconciliation. By the way, the only item that you may not understand is the unrecorded bank credit. This item represents a note collected for us by the bank."

Shortly after, Joe had a heated argument with Millien and left the company. Now Millien comes to you to see whether Joe had done anything wrong with the handling of the bank reconciliation and the cash on hand. Also, she wonders whether she has efficiently managed her cash.

INSTRUCTIONS

a. Determine the adjusted cash balance per the depositor's records and the cash shortage, if any, for which Joe may be held responsible.

b. Comment on the efficiency of Millien's cash management and on the internal control on cash, and suggest any improvement you deem necessary.

A&D 7-7
Petty Cash?
(LO 2, 5)

Tom Pharro owns Pharro Concrete & Masonry, a small contracting business. On April 1, the company established a petty cash fund in the amount of $5,000, which was expected to last about three months. The cash was kept in a locked box in the desk of the company's receptionist. (The company has two part-time receptionists, who were designated the office custodians of the fund. The only other people with access to the petty cash box were Tom Pharro and his assistant, Chris Greer.) Vouchers were to be prepared for all disbursements from the fund, and these vouchers were to be placed in the petty cash box.

Unfortunately, the money in the petty cash fund did not last three months. On April 30, the receptionists reported that the vouchers in the fund totalled $4,390.90 but that the fund contained only $2.00 in cash. The vouchers were sent to the accounting department, reviewed, and cancelled. All of the vouchers included adequate documentation. Replenishment of the fund then was recorded by the following entry:

Office Supplies Expense	*160.20*	
Travel & Entertainment Expense	*1,501.00*	
Office Equipment	*804.70*	
Repairs Expense (Roof)	*925.00*	
Drawing, Tom Pharro	*1,000.00*	
Miscellaneous Expense	*607.10*	
Cash		*4,998.00*

To replenish the petty cash fund.

INSTRUCTIONS

Identify any control weaknesses relating to this fund. Explain your reasons for regarding any aspect of the fund's operations as a weakness, and make specific recommendations for improvement.

Answers to Self-Test Questions

1. c   **2.** a   **3.** b   **4.** d   **5.** c

CHAPTER 8

Accounts Receivable and Notes Receivable

The business world depends on selling goods and services on credit. Thus, proper accounting for and management of accounts and notes receivable are essential to efficient business operations.

1. Explain the nature, estimate, and statement presentation of uncollectible accounts receivable, write off any accounts known to be uncollectible, and record any later recoveries.
2. Compare the allowance method and the direct write-off method of accounting for uncollectible accounts.
3. Explain why accounts receivable may be viewed as "nonproductive" assets. Identify several ways of converting receivables quickly into cash.

4. Account for sales to customers using credit cards.
5. Explain promissory notes and the nature of interest.
6. Compute the accounts receivable turnover rate. Explain why this ratio is of interest to short-term creditors.
*7. Account for notes receivable with the interest charges included in the face amount.
*8. Discuss the concept of present value in accounting for long-term notes receivable.

ACCOUNTS RECEIVABLE

LO 1: Explain the nature, estimate, and statement presentation of uncollectible accounts receivable, write off any accounts known to be uncollectible, and record any later recoveries.

One of the key factors underlying the growth of our economy is the trend toward selling goods and services on credit. Accounts receivable are liquid assets, usually being converted into cash within a period of 30 to 60 days. Therefore, accounts receivable from customers are classified as current assets, appearing in the balance sheet immediately after cash and short-term investments.

CASE IN POINT

Examples from recent balance sheets of large companies:

Company	Current Assets	Dollars in Millions
BCE Inc.:	Cash and short-term investments	$2,249
	Accounts receivable	8,625
Domtar Inc.:	Cash	$ 9
	Short-term investments	274
	Receivables	242
Quebecor Inc.:	Cash	$ 38
	Accounts receivable	1,248

Sometimes companies sell merchandise on longer-term instalment plans, requiring 12, 24, or even 48 months to collect the entire amount receivable from the customer. By definition, the normal period of time required to collect accounts receivable is part of a company's *operating cycle.* Therefore, accounts receivable arising from normal sales transactions usually are classified as current assets, even if the credit terms extend beyond one year.[1]

---

*Supplemental Topic, "Notes Receivable with Interest Charges Included in the Face Amount"
[1]As explained in Chapter 5, the period used to define current assets and current liabilities is one year or the company's operating cycle, whichever is longer. The **operating cycle** is the period of time needed to convert cash into inventory, the inventory into accounts receivable, and the accounts receivable back into cash.

Uncollectible Accounts

No business wants to sell on credit to a customer who will prove unable or unwilling to pay his or her account. Therefore, most businesses have a credit department that investigates the creditworthiness of each prospective customer. This investigation usually includes obtaining a credit report from a national credit-rating agency such as **Dun & Bradstreet.** If the prospective customer is a business concern, its financial statements will be obtained and analyzed to determine its financial strength and the trend of its operating results.

A business that sells its goods or services on credit will inevitably find that some of its accounts receivable are uncollectible. Regardless of how thoroughly the credit department investigates prospective customers, some uncollectible accounts will arise as a result of errors in judgment or because of unexpected developments. In fact, a limited amount of uncollectible accounts or credit loss is evidence of a sound credit policy. If the credit department should become too cautious and conservative in rating customers, it may avoid most credit losses but, in so doing, lose many sales opportunities by rejecting customers who should have been considered acceptable credit risks.

Reflecting Uncollectible Accounts in the Financial Statements An account receivable that has been determined to be uncollectible is no longer an asset. The loss of this asset represents an **expense,** termed **uncollectible accounts expense** (also called bad debts expense).

In measuring business income, one of the most fundamental principles of accounting is that revenue should be **matched** with (offset by) the expenses incurred in generating that revenue. Uncollectible accounts expense is **caused by selling goods** on credit to customers who fail to pay their bills. Therefore, this expense is incurred in the accounting period in which the **related sales** are made, even though specific accounts receivable may not be determined to be uncollectible until a later accounting period. Thus, an account receivable that originates from a sale on credit in January and is determined to be uncollectible in August represents an expense in **January.** Unless each month's uncollectible accounts expense is **estimated** and reflected in the month-end income statement and balance sheet, these financial statements may show overstated earnings and overvalued assets, because they will show accounts that will never be collected. Thus, the estimating and recording of the uncollectible accounts expense is required by the **matching principle.**

To illustrate, assume that World Famous Toy Co. begins business on January 1, 2000, and makes most of its sales on account. At January 31, accounts receivable amount to $250,000. On this date, the credit manager reviews the accounts receivable and estimates that approximately $10,000 of these accounts will prove to be uncollectible. The following adjusting entry should be made at January 31:

Provision for uncollectible accounts	*Uncollectible Accounts Expense*	*10,000*	
	Allowance for Doubtful Accounts		*10,000*
	To record the portion of total accounts receivable estimated to be uncollectible.		

The ***Uncollectible Accounts Expense*** account created by the debit part of this entry is closed into the Income Summary account in the same manner as any other expense account. The ***Allowance for Doubtful Accounts*** that was credited in the above journal entry will appear in the balance sheet as a deduction from the face amount of the accounts receivable. It serves to reduce the accounts receivable to their ***net realizable value*** in the balance sheet, as shown by the following illustration:

WORLD FAMOUS TOY CO. Partial Balance Sheet January 31, 2000		
Current assets:		
Cash and short-term investments		*$75,000*
Accounts receivable	*$250,000*	
Less: Allowance for doubtful accounts	*10,000*	*240,000*

How much is the estimated net realizable value of the accounts receivable?

The Allowance for Doubtful Accounts

There is no way of telling in advance ***which*** accounts receivable will prove to be uncollectible. It is therefore not possible to credit the accounts of specific customers for our estimate of probable uncollectible accounts. Neither should we credit the Accounts Receivable controlling account in the general ledger. If the Accounts Receivable controlling account were to be credited with the estimated amount of doubtful accounts, this controlling account would no longer be in balance with the total of the numerous customers' accounts in the subsidiary ledger. The only practical alternative, therefore, is to credit a separate account called **Allowance for Doubtful Accounts** with the amount estimated to be uncollectible.

The Allowance for Doubtful Accounts often is described as a **contra-asset account** or a ***valuation*** account. Both of these terms indicate that the Allowance for Doubtful Accounts has a credit balance, which is offset against the asset Accounts Receivable to produce the proper balance sheet value for this asset.

Estimating the Amount of Uncollectible Accounts   Before financial statements are prepared at the end of the accounting period, an estimate of the expected amount of uncollectible accounts receivables should be made. This estimate is based upon past experience and modified in accordance with current business conditions. Losses from uncollectible receivables tend to be greater during periods of recession than in periods of growth and prosperity. Because the allowance for doubtful accounts is necessarily an estimate and not a precise calculation, professional judgment plays a considerable part in determining the size of this valuation account.

Conservatism as a Factor in Valuing Accounts Receivable   The larger the allowance established for doubtful accounts, the lower the net valuation of accounts receivable will be. Some accountants and some business executives tend to favour the most conservative valuation of assets that logically can be supported. **Conservatism** in the preparation of a balance sheet implies a tendency to resolve uncertainties in the valuation of assets by reporting assets at the lower end of the range of reasonable values rather than by establishing values in a purely objective manner.

The valuation of assets at conservative amounts is a long-standing tradition in accounting, stemming from the days when creditors were the major users of financial statements. From the viewpoint of bankers and others who use financial statements as a basis for granting loans, conservatism in valuing assets has long been regarded as a desirable policy.

In considering the argument for balance sheet conservatism, it is important to recognize that the income statement also is affected by the estimate made of uncollectible accounts. The act of providing a relatively large allowance for doubtful accounts involves a correspondingly heavy charge to expense. Setting asset values at a minimum in the balance sheet has the related effect of minimizing the amount of net income reported in the current period.

Monthly Adjustments of the Allowance Account   In the adjusting entry made by World Famous Toy Co. at January 31, the amount of the adjustment ($10,000) was equal to the estimated amount of uncollectible accounts. This is true because January was the first month of operations and this was the company's first estimate of its uncollectible accounts. In future months, the amount of the adjusting entry will depend upon two factors: (1) the *estimate* of uncollectible accounts and (2) the *current balance* in the Allowance for Doubtful Accounts. Before we illustrate the adjusting entry for a future month, let us first see why the balance in the allowance account may change during the accounting period.

Writing Off an Uncollectible Account Receivable

Whenever an account receivable from a specific customer is determined to be uncollectible, it no longer qualifies as an asset and should be written off. To **write off** an account receivable is to reduce the balance of the customer's account to zero. The journal entry to accomplish this consists of a credit to the Accounts Receivable controlling account in the general ledger (and to the customer's account in the subsidiary ledger) and an offsetting debit to the **Allowance for Doubtful Accounts.**

To illustrate, assume that on February 15, World Famous Toy Co. learns that a customer, Discount Stores, has gone out of business and that the $4,000 account receivable from this customer is now worthless. The entry to write off this uncollectible account receivable is:

Writing off a receivable "against the allowance"	*Allowance for Doubtful Accounts*	*4,000*
	Accounts Receivable (Discount Stores)	*4,000*
	To write off the receivable from Discount Stores as uncollectible.	

The important thing to note in this entry is that the debit is made to the **Allowance for Doubtful Accounts** and **not** to the Uncollectible Accounts Expense account. The estimated expense of credit losses is charged to the Uncollectible Accounts Expense account at the end of each accounting period. When a particular account receivable is later determined to be worthless and is written off, this action does not represent an additional expense but merely confirms our previous estimate of the expense. If the Uncollectible Accounts Expense account were first charged with **estimated** credit losses and then later charged with **proven** credit losses, we would be double counting the actual uncollectible accounts expense.

After the entry writing off the receivable from Discount Stores has been posted, the Accounts Receivable controlling account and the Allowance for Doubtful Accounts appear as follows:

Both accounts reduced by write-off of worthless receivable

Accounts Receivable			
2000		2000	
Jan. 31	250,000	Feb. 15 (write-off)	4,000

Allowance for Doubtful Accounts			
2000		2000	
Feb. 15 (write-off)	4,000	Jan. 31	10,000

Notice also that the entry to write off an uncollectible account receivable reduces both the asset account and the contra-asset account by the same amount. Thus, writing off an uncollectible account **does not change** the net realizable value of accounts receivable in the balance sheet. The following illustration shows the net realizable value of World Famous Toy Co.'s accounts receivable before and after the write-off of the account receivable from Discount Stores:

Net value of receivables unchanged by write-off

Before the Write-Off		**After the Write-Off**	
Accounts receivable $250,000		Accounts receivable $246,000	
Less: Allowance for		Less: Allowance for	
doubtful accounts 10,000		doubtful accounts 6,000	
Net value of receivables . . $240,000		Net value of receivables . . $240,000	

The fact that writing off a worthless receivable against the Allowance for Doubtful Accounts does not change the net carrying value of accounts receivable shows that no expense is entered in the accounting records when an account receivable is written off. This example bears out the point stressed earlier in the chapter. **Credit losses belong in the period in which the sale is made, not in a later period in which the account receivable is discovered to be uncollectible.** This is another example of the use of the **matching principle** in determining net income.

Write-Offs Seldom Agree with Previous Estimates   The total amount of accounts receivable actually written off will seldom, if ever, be exactly equal to the estimated amount previously credited to the Allowance for Doubtful Accounts.

If the amounts written off as uncollectible turn out to be less than the estimated amount, the Allowance for Doubtful Accounts will continue to show a credit balance. If the amounts written off as uncollectible are greater than the estimated amount, the Allowance for Doubtful Accounts will acquire a ***temporary debit balance,*** which will be eliminated by the adjustment at the end of the period.

Recovery of an Account Receivable Previously Written Off

Occasionally a receivable that has been written off as worthless will later be collected in full or in part. Such collections are often referred to as ***recoveries*** of uncollectible accounts or bad debts. Collection of an account receivable previously written off is evidence that the write-off was an error; the receivable should therefore be reinstated as an asset.

Let us assume, for example, that a past-due account receivable in the amount of $200 from J. B. Barker was written off on February 16 by the following entry:

Barker account considered uncollectible	*Allowance for Doubtful Accounts* *200*	
	Accounts Receivable (J. B. Barker)	*200*
	To write off the receivable from J. B. Barker as uncollectible.	

On February 27, the customer, J. B. Barker, pays the account in full. The entry to restore Barker's account will be:

Barker account reinstated	*Accounts Receivable (J. B. Barker)* *200*	
	Allowance for Doubtful Accounts	*200*
	To reinstate as an asset an account receivable previously written off.	

Notice that this entry is ***exactly the opposite*** of the entry made when the account was written off as uncollectible. A separate entry will be made to record the collection from Barker. This entry will debit Cash and credit Accounts Receivable (J. B. Barker).

Monthly Estimates of Credit Losses

At the end of each month, management should again estimate the probable amount of uncollectible accounts ***and adjust the Allowance for Doubtful Accounts to this new estimate.***

To illustrate, assume that at the end of February the credit manager of World Famous Toy Co. analyzes the accounts receivable and estimates that approximately ***$11,000*** of these accounts will prove uncollectible. Currently, the Allowance for Doubtful Accounts has a credit balance of only ***$6,000,*** determined as follows:

Current balance in the allowance account	*Balance at January 31 (credit)*		*$10,000*
	Less: Write-offs of accounts considered worthless:		
	Discount Stores	*$4,000*	
	J. B. Barker	*200*	*4,200*
	Subtotal		*$ 5,800*
	Add: Recoveries of accounts previously written off: J. B. Barker		*200*
	Balance at end of February (prior to adjusting entry)		*$ 6,000*

To increase the balance in the allowance account to $11,000 at February 28, the month-end adjusting entry must add $5,000 to the allowance because the $6,000 of accounts receivable that were considered uncollectible at the end of January are included again in the $11,000 at the end of February. The entry will be:

Increasing the allowance for doubtful accounts

Uncollectible Accounts Expense	*5,000*	
Allowance for Doubtful Accounts		*5,000*

To increase the Allowance for Doubtful Accounts to $11,000,
computed as follows:

Required allowance at Feb. 28	*$11,000*
Credit balance prior to adjustment	*6,000*
Required adjustment	*$ 5,000*

Estimating Credit Losses—The "Balance Sheet" Approach The most widely used method in reviewing and analyzing accounts receivable to estimate the probable amount of uncollectible accounts is the **aging of the accounts receivable.** This method is sometimes called the ***balance sheet*** approach, because the method emphasizes the proper balance sheet valuation of accounts receivable.

"Aging" accounts receivable means classifying each receivable according to its age. An aging schedule for the accounts receivable of Valley Ranch Supply is illustrated below:

Analysis of Accounts Receivable by Age
December 31, 2000

	Total	Not Yet Due	1–30 Days Past Due	31–60 Days Past Due	61–90 Days Past Due	Over 90 Days Past Due
Animal Care Centre	*$ 9,000*	*$ 9,000*				
Butterfield, John D.	*2,400*			*$ 2,400*		
Citrus Groves, Inc.	*4,000*	*3,000*	*$ 1,000*			
Dairy Fresh Farms	*1,600*				*$ 600*	*$1,000*
Eastlake Stables	*13,000*	*7,000*	*6,000*			
(Other customers)	*70,000*	*32,000*	*22,000*	*9,600*	*2,400*	*4,000*
Totals	*$100,000*	*$51,000*	*$29,000*	*$12,000*	*$3,000*	*$5,000*

An aging schedule is useful to management in reviewing the status of individual accounts receivable and in evaluating the overall effectiveness of credit and collection policies. In addition, the schedule is used as the basis for estimating the amount of uncollectible accounts.

The longer an account is past due, the greater the likelihood that it will not be collected in full. Based upon past experience, the credit manager estimates the percentage of credit losses likely to occur in each age group of accounts receivable. This percentage, when applied to the total dollar amount in the age group, gives the estimated uncollectible portion for that group. By adding together the estimated uncollectible portions for all age groups, the ***required balance*** in the Allowance for Doubtful Accounts is determined. The following schedule lists the group totals from the aging schedule and shows how the estimated total amount of uncollectible accounts is computed:

Estimated Uncollectible Accounts Receivable
December 31, 2000

	Age Group Total	Percentage Considered Uncollectible*	Estimated Uncollectible Accounts
Not yet due	$51,000	1	$510
1–30 days past due	29,000	3	870
31–60 days past due	12,000	10	1,200
61–90 days past due	3,000	20	600
Over 90 days past due	5,000	50	2,500
Totals	$100,000		$5,680

These percentages are estimated each month by the credit manager, based upon recent experience and current economic conditions.

At December 31, Valley Ranch Supply has total accounts receivable of $100,000, of which $5,680 are estimated to be uncollectible. Thus, an adjusting entry is needed to increase the Allowance for Doubtful Accounts from its present level to $5,680. If the allowance account currently has a credit balance of, say, $4,000, the month-end adjusting entry should be in the amount of **$1,680** as follows:[2]

The "balance sheet" approach

Uncollectible Accounts Expense	1,680	
Allowance for Doubtful Accounts		1,680
To increase the Allowance for Doubtful Accounts to $5,680 from $4,000.		

An Alternative Approach to Estimating Credit Losses The procedures above describe the ***balance sheet*** approach to estimating and recording credit losses. This approach is based upon an aging schedule, and the Allowance for Doubtful Accounts is ***adjusted to a required balance.*** An alternative method, called the ***income statement*** approach, focuses upon estimating the uncollectible accounts ***expense*** for the period. Based upon past experience, the uncollectible accounts expense is estimated at some percentage of net credit sales. The adjusting entry is made in the ***full amount of the estimated expense,*** without regard for the current balance in the Allowance for Doubtful Accounts.

---

[2]If accounts receivable written off during the period ***exceed*** the Allowance for Doubtful Accounts at the last adjustment date, the allowance account temporarily acquires a ***debit balance.*** This situation seldom occurs if the allowance is adjusted each month but often occurs if adjusting entries are made only at year-end.

If Valley Ranch Supply makes only an annual adjustment for uncollectible accounts, the allowance account might have a debit balance of, say, $10,000. In this case, the year-end adjusting entry should be for ***$15,680*** in order to bring the allowance to the required credit balance of $5,680.

Regardless of how often adjusting entries are made, the balance in the allowance account of Valley Ranch Supply should be ***$5,680 at year-end.*** Uncollectible accounts expense will be the same for the year regardless of whether adjusting entries are made annually or monthly. The only difference is in whether this expense is recognized in one annual adjusting entry or in 12 monthly adjusting entries, each for a smaller amount.

To illustrate, assume that a company's past experience indicates that about 2% of its net credit sales prove to be uncollectible. If net credit sales for September amount to $150,000, the month-end adjusting entry to record uncollectible accounts expense is:

<table>
<tr><td>The "income statement" approach</td><td>Uncollectible Accounts Expense . . . .</td><td>3,000</td><td></td></tr>
<tr><td></td><td>   Allowance for Doubtful Accounts . . . .</td><td></td><td>3,000</td></tr>
<tr><td></td><td colspan="3">To record uncollectible accounts expense, estimated at 2% of net credit sales ($150,000 × 2% = $3,000).</td></tr>
</table>

This approach is fast and simple—no aging schedule is required and no consideration is given to the existing balance in the Allowance for Doubtful Accounts. The aging of accounts receivable, however, provides a more reliable estimate of uncollectible accounts because of the consideration given to the age and collectibility of specific accounts receivable at the balance sheet date.

In past years, many small companies used the income statement approach as a shortcut in preparing monthly financial statements but used the balance sheet method in preparing annual financial statements. Today, however, most businesses have computer software that quickly and easily prepares monthly aging schedules of accounts receivable. Thus, most businesses today use the **balance sheet approach** in their monthly as well as annual financial statements.

Direct Write-Off Method

Some companies do not use the **allowance method** to value their accounts receivable. Instead of making end-of-period adjusting entries to record uncollectible accounts expense on the basis of estimates, these companies recognize no uncollectible accounts expense until specific receivables are determined to be worthless. This method makes no attempt to match revenue and related expenses. Uncollectible accounts expense is recorded in the period in which individual accounts receivable are determined to be worthless rather than in the period in which the sales were made.

LO 2: Compare the allowance method and the direct write-off method of accounting for uncollectible accounts.

When a particular customer's account is determined to be uncollectible, it is written off directly to Uncollectible Accounts Expense, as follows:

<table>
<tr><td>Uncollectible Accounts Expense . . . .</td><td>250</td><td></td></tr>
<tr><td>   Accounts Receivable (Bell Products) . . . .</td><td></td><td>250</td></tr>
<tr><td colspan="3">To write off the receivable from Bell Products as uncollectible.</td></tr>
</table>

When the **direct write-off method** is in use, the accounts receivable will be listed in the balance sheet at their gross amount, and **no valuation allowance** will be used. The receivables, therefore, are not stated at estimated net realizable value.

In some situations, use of the direct write-off method is acceptable. If a company makes most of its sales for cash, the amount of its accounts receivable will be small in relation to other assets. The expense from uncollectible accounts should also be small. Consequently, the direct write-off method is acceptable because its use does not have a **material** effect on the reported net income. Another situation in which the direct write-off method works satisfactorily is in a company that sells all or most of its output to a few large companies that are financially strong. In this setting there may be no basis for making advance estimates of any credit losses.

Internal Controls for Receivables

One of the most important principles of internal control is that employees who have custody of cash or other negotiable assets must not maintain accounting records. In a small business, unfortunately, it is not uncommon to find that one employee has responsibility for handling cash receipts from customers, maintaining the accounts receivable records, issuing credit memos for goods returned by or for allowance to customers, and writing off receivables judged to be uncollectible. Such a combination of duties is an invitation to errors and fraud. The errors made in performing these four functions can be covered up by the employee. Thus, the information so generated is misleading. Also, the employee in this situation is able to remove the cash collected from a customer without making any record of the collection. The next step is to dispose of the balance in the customer's account. This can be done by issuing a credit memo indicating that the customer has returned merchandise, or has been given an allowance on the sale, or by writing off the customer's account as uncollectible. Thus, the employee has the cash, the customer's account shows a zero balance due, and the books are in balance.

To avoid errors and fraud in the handling of receivables, some of the most important rules are that employees who maintain the accounts receivable subsidiary ledger must **not have access** to cash receipts, and employees who handle cash receipts must not have access to the records of receivables. Furthermore, **neither** the employees who maintain records of receivables **nor** those who handle cash receipts should have authority to issue credit memoranda or to authorize the write-off of receivables as uncollectible. These are classic examples of incompatible duties.

Management of Accounts Receivable

LO 3: Explain why accounts receivable may be viewed as "nonproductive" assets. Identify several ways of converting receivables quickly into cash.

Management has two conflicting objectives with respect to the accounts receivable. On the one hand, management wants to generate as much sales revenue as possible. Offering customers lengthy credit terms, with little or no interest, has proven to be an effective means of generating sales revenue.

Every business, however, would rather sell for cash than on account. Unless they earn interest, accounts receivable are a nonproductive asset that produce no revenue as they await collection. Therefore, another objective of management is to minimize the amount of money "tied up" in the form of accounts receivable.

Several tools are available to a management that must offer credit terms to its customers yet wants to minimize the company's investment in accounts receivable. We have already discussed offering credit customers cash discounts (such as 2/10, n/30) to encourage early payment. Other tools include factoring accounts receivable and selling to customers who use national credit cards.

Factoring Accounts Receivable

The term **factoring** describes transactions in which a business either sells its accounts receivable to a financial institution (often called a *factor*) or borrows money by pledging its accounts receivable as **collateral** (security) for the loan. In either case, the business obtains cash immediately instead of having to wait until the receivables can be collected.

The **factoring** of **accounts receivable** may create a potential liability to reimburse the factor for any losses sustained if some of the factored accounts are uncollectible. This "potential" liability is an example of ***off-balance-sheet risk*** that must be disclosed in notes to the financial statements. The disclosure of off-balance-sheet risk such as contingencies is discussed in Chapter 11.

Factoring accounts receivable is a practice limited primarily to small business organizations that do not have well-established credit. Large and solvent organizations usually are able to borrow money using unsecured lines of credit, so they need not factor their accounts receivable.

Credit Card Sales

LO 4: Account for sales to customers using credit cards.

Many retailing businesses maximize sales opportunities while minimizing their investment in accounts receivable by making credit sales to customers who use well-known credit cards such as American Express, Visa, and MasterCard. A customer who makes a purchase using one of these cards must sign a multiple-copy form, which includes a ***credit card draft.*** A credit card draft is similar to a cheque that is drawn upon the funds of the credit card company rather than upon the personal bank account of the customer. The credit card company promptly pays cash to the merchant to redeem these drafts. At the end of each month, the credit card company bills the credit card holder for all the drafts it has redeemed during the month. If the credit card holder fails to pay the amount owed, it is the credit card company that sustains the loss.

By making sales through credit card companies, merchants receive cash more quickly from credit sales and avoid uncollectible accounts expense. Also, the merchant avoids the expenses of investigating customers' credit, maintaining an accounts receivable subsidiary ledger, and making collections from customers.

Bank Credit Cards Some widely used credit cards (such as Visa and MasterCard) are issued by banks. When the credit card company is a bank, the retailing business may deposit the signed credit card drafts directly in its bank account, along with the currency and personal cheques received from customers. Since banks accept these credit card drafts for immediate deposit, sales to customers using bank credit cards are recorded as ***cash sales.***

In exchange for handling the credit card drafts, the bank makes a monthly service charge that usually runs between 1½ and 5% of the amount of the drafts deposited by the merchant during the month. This monthly service charge is deducted from the merchant's bank account and appears with other bank service charges in the merchant's monthly bank statement.

Other Credit Cards When customers use nonbank credit cards (such as EnRoute, Diners Club, and Discover), the retailing business cannot deposit the credit card drafts directly in its bank account. Instead of debiting Cash, the merchant records an account receivable from the credit card company. Periodically, the credit card drafts are mailed (or transmitted electronically) to the credit card company, which then sends a cheque to the merchant. Credit card companies, however, do not redeem the drafts at the full sales price. The agreement between the credit card company and the merchant usually allows the credit card company to take a discount of between 3½% and 5% when redeeming the drafts.

To illustrate the procedures in accounting for these credit card sales, assume that Bradshaw Camera Shop sells a camera for $200 to a customer who uses a Quick Charge credit card. The entry would be:

This receivable is from the credit card company

Accounts Receivable (Quick Charge Company)	*200*	
Sales		*200*
To record sale to customer using Quick Charge credit card.		

At the end of the week, Bradshaw Camera Shop mails credit card drafts totalling $1,200 to Quick Charge Company, which redeems the drafts after deducting a 5% discount. When payment is received by Bradshaw, the entry is

Cash	*1,140*	
Credit Card Discount Expense	*60*	
Accounts Receivable (Quick Charge Company)		*1,200*
To record collection of account receivable from Quick Charge, less 5% discount.		

The expense account, Credit Card Discount Expense, should be included among the selling expenses in the income statement of Bradshaw Camera Shop.

NOTES RECEIVABLE

LO 5: Explain promissory notes and the nature of interest.

A promissory note is an unconditional promise in writing to pay on demand or at a future date a definite sum of money.

The person who signs the note and thereby promises to pay is called the **maker** of the note. The person to whom payment is to be made is called the **payee** of the note. In the illustration below, G. L. Smith is the maker of the note and A. B. Davis is the payee.

From the viewpoint of the maker, G. L. Smith, the illustrated note is a liability and is recorded by crediting the Notes Payable account. However,

Simplified form of promissory note

$100,000	Vancouver, British Columbia	July 10, 19__

One year **after date** I **promise to pay**

to the order of A. B. Davis

—One hundred thousand and no/100— **dollars**

payable to Canadian National Bank

for value received, with interest at 12% per annum

G. L. Smith

from the viewpoint of the payee, A. B. Davis, this same note is an asset and is recorded by debiting the Notes Receivable account. The maker of a note expects to pay cash at the **maturity date** (or due date); the payee expects to receive cash at that date.

Nature of Interest

Interest is a charge made for the use of money. A borrower incurs interest expense. A lender earns interest revenue. When you encounter notes payable in a company's financial statements, you know that the company is borrowing and you should expect to find interest expense. When you encounter notes receivable, you should expect interest revenue.

Computing Interest   A formula used in computing interest is as follows:

Principal × Rate of Interest × Time = Interest

(Often expressed as $P \times R \times T = I$)

Of the three elements in the above formula, the rate and time elements need a brief explanation. The rate is usually stated on an annual basis, unless otherwise indicated. The time can be expressed in days, months, or on an annual basis. All notes, other than those payable on demand, are *legally due* and payable *three days* after the due date indicated on the notes. These extra three days are called the **three days of grace.** Thus, in counting the exact number of days for interest computation, the day on which a note is dated is not included; the date on which a note falls due is included, that is, the last day of the added three days of grace.

Suppose, for example, that a 60-day, 12% note for $100,000 is drawn on June 10. The interest charge, with the three days of grace added, is computed as follows:

$$100{,}000 \times 0.12 \times \tfrac{63}{365} = \$2{,}071.23$$

The principal of the note ($100,000) plus the interest ($2,071.23) equals $102,071.23 and this amount (the **maturity value**) will be payable on ***August 12.*** The computation of days to maturity is as follows:

<table>
<tr><td>Note the three days of grace added</td><td>*Days remaining in June (30–10; date of note is not included)* ....</td><td align="right">*20*</td></tr>
<tr><td></td><td>*Days in July* ....</td><td align="right">*31*</td></tr>
<tr><td></td><td>*Days in August to maturity date (date of payment is included, 9 days plus 3 days of grace)* ....</td><td align="right">*12*</td></tr>
<tr><td></td><td>*Total days called for by note* ....</td><td align="right">*63*</td></tr>
</table>

Accounting for Notes Receivable

In some fields of business, notes receivable are seldom encountered; in other fields they occur frequently and may constitute an important part of total assets. Business concerns that sell high-priced durable goods such as automobiles and farm machinery often accept notes receivable from their customers. Many companies obtain notes receivable in settlement of past-due accounts receivable.

All notes receivable are usually posted to a single account in the general ledger. A subsidiary ledger is not essential because the notes themselves, when filed by due dates, are the equivalent of a subsidiary ledger and provide any necessary information as to maturity, interest rates, collateral pledged, and other details. The amount debited to Notes Receivable is always the *face amount* of the note, regardless of whether or not the note bears interest. When an interest-bearing note is collected, the amount of cash received may be larger than the face amount of the note, depending on whether the interest charge is included in the face amount of the note. (Notes receivable with interest included in the face amount will be covered in the "Supplemental Topic" at the end of this chapter.) The interest collected is credited to an Interest Revenue account, and only the face amount of the note is credited to the Notes Receivable account.

Illustrative Entries   Assume that on December 1 a 90-day, 12% note receivable is acquired from a customer, Marvin White, in settlement of an existing account receivable of $30,000. The entry for acquisition of the note is as follows:

Note received to replace account receivable	*Notes Receivable*	*30,000*
	Accounts Receivable (Marvin White)	*30,000*
	Accepted 90-day, 12% note in settlement of account receivable.	

At December 31, the end of the company's fiscal year, the interest earned to date on notes receivable should be accrued by an adjusting entry as follows:

Adjusting entry for interest revenue earned in December	*Interest Receivable*	*295.89*
	Interest Revenue	*295.89*

To accrue interest for the month of December on Marvin White note ($30,000 × 12% × $\frac{30}{365}$ = $295.89).

On March 4, 93 days after the date of the note (90 days plus 3 days of grace), the note matures. The entry to record collection of the note will be:

Collection of principal and interest	*Cash* *30,917.26*	
	Notes Receivable	*30,000.00*
	Interest Receivable	*295.89*
	Interest Revenue	*621.37*

Collected 90-day, 12% note from Marvin White ($30,000 × 12% × $\frac{93}{365}$ = $917.26 interest of which $621.37 was earned in current year).

The preceding three entries show that interest is being earned throughout the life of the note and that the interest should be apportioned between years on a time basis. The revenue of each year will then include the interest actually earned in that year.

If the Maker of a Note Defaults   A note receivable that cannot be collected at maturity is said to have been **defaulted** by the maker. Immediately after the default of a note, an entry should be made by the holder to transfer the amount due from the Notes Receivable account to an account receivable from the debtor.

To illustrate, assume that on March 4, our customer, Marvin White, had defaulted on the note used in the preceding example. In this case, the entry on March 4 would have been:

Accounts Receivable (Marvin White)	*30,917.26*	
Notes Receivable		*30,000.00*
Interest Receivable		*295.89*
Interest Revenue		*621.37*

To record default by Marvin White on 90-day, 12% note, plus three days of grace.

Notice that the interest earned on the note is recorded through the maturity date and is included in the account receivable from the maker. The interest receivable on a defaulted note is just as valid a claim against the maker as is the principal amount of the note.

If the account receivable from White cannot be collected, it ultimately will be written off against the Allowance for Doubtful Accounts. Therefore, the balance in the Allowance for Doubtful Accounts should provide for estimated uncollectible ***notes*** receivable as well as uncollectible ***accounts*** receivable.

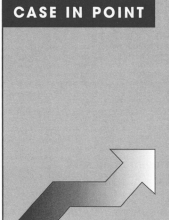

CASE IN POINT   For many companies, the provision for doubtful accounts is small and does not have a material effect upon net income for the period. Notes receivable, however, are the largest and most important asset for nearly every bank. Interest on these notes is a bank's largest and most important type of revenue. Thus, the collectibility of notes owned by a bank is a key factor in determining the success or failure of that bank.

A few years ago, six Canadian chartered banks (also the six largest) added a staggering $4 billion to their allowance for doubtful loans to less developed countries. The total allowance for these doubtful loans ranges from 61% to almost 100% of the loans to these countries. This wide margin in the estimate of the allowance for doubtful loans clearly manifests the role of personal judgment in determining the size of the allowance, as pointed out in the early part of this chapter.

Renewal of a Note Receivable   Sometimes the two parties to a note agree that the note shall be renewed rather than paid at the maturity date. In this situation a new note should be prepared and the old one cancelled. If the old note does not bear interest, the entry could be made as follows:

Renewal of note should be recorded

Notes Receivable	*10,000*	
Notes Receivable		*10,000*

A 60-day, non-interest-bearing note from Bell Company renewed today with new 60-day, 14% note.

Since the above entry causes no change in the balance of the Notes Receivable account, a question may arise as to whether the entry is necessary. The renewal of a note is an important transaction requiring managerial attention; a general journal entry is needed to record the action taken by management and to provide a permanent record of the transaction. If journal entries were not made to record the renewal of notes, confusion might arise as to whether some of the notes included in the balance of the Notes Receivable account were current or defaulted. Alternatively, a memorandum noting the renewal may be attached to the new note.

Discounting Notes Receivable   In past years, some companies sold their notes receivable to banks in order to obtain cash prior to the maturity dates of these notes. As the banks purchased these notes at a "discount" from their maturity values, this practice became known as **discounting notes receivable.**

Discounting notes receivable is not a widespread practice today, because most banks no longer purchase notes receivable from their customers. Interestingly, the discounting of notes receivable remains a common practice among banks themselves. Many banks sell large "packages" of notes receivable (loans) to other financial institutions.

If a business organization wants to convert its receivables into cash prior to their maturity dates, it usually enters into some type of factoring arrangement. Accounting for the factoring of receivables varies with the terms and conditions of the contract between the company and the factor. Various factoring arrangements will be discussed in more advanced accounting courses.

Evaluating the Quality of Notes and Accounts Receivable

In the annual audit of a company by a public accounting firm, the independent auditors will verify receivables by communicating directly with the customers of the company and with the makers of notes receivable. This **confirmation** process is designed to provide evidence that the customers and other debtors actually exist, and that they acknowledge the indebtedness. The auditors may also verify the credit rating of major debtors.

Any company with large amounts of receivables needs the assurance of an annual audit to guard against the possibility that sizable but worthless notes and accounts receivable from bankrupt firms or fictitious customers may have been disguised as genuine assets. The quality of receivables may also be appraised by an internal auditing staff that will study the adequacy of the internal controls over such activities as the granting of credit, accounting for receivables, and the prompt recognition of credit losses.

LO 6: Compute the accounts receivable turnover rate. Explain why this ratio is of interest to short-term creditors.

Accounts Receivable Turnover   Collecting accounts receivable **on time** is important; it spells the success or failure of a company's credit and collection policies. A past-due receivable is a candidate for write-off as a credit loss. To help us judge how good a job a company is doing in granting credit and collecting its receivables, we compute the ratio of net sales to average receivables. This **accounts receivable turnover rate** tells us how many times the receivables were converted into cash during the year. The ratio is computed by dividing annual net sales by average accounts receivable.[3]

CASE IN POINT

Recent financial statements of Shell Canada Limited show net sales of $5.3 billion. Receivables were $.77 billion at the beginning of the year and $.72 billion at the end of the year. Adding these two amounts and dividing the total by 2 gives us average receivables of $.75 billion. Now we divide the year's net sales by the average receivables ($5.3 ÷ $.75 = 7.1); the result indicates an accounts receivable turnover rate of 7.1 times per year for Shell Canada. The higher the turnover rate the more liquid the company's receivables.

Another step that will help us judge the liquidity of a company's accounts receivable is to convert the accounts receivable turnover rate to the number of days (on average) required for the company to collect its accounts receivable. This is a simple calculation: divide the number of days in the year by the turnover rate.

CASE IN POINT

Divide 365 days by turnover of 7.1 for Shell (365 ÷ 7.1 = 51), we have 51 days. This calculation tells us that on average, Shell Canada waited approximately 51 days to make collection of a sale on credit.

The data described above in the two Cases in Point for computing the accounts receivable turnover rate and the average number of days to collect accounts receivable can be concisely stated as shown in the following equations:

Accounts Receivable Turnover

$$\frac{\text{Net Sales}}{\text{Average Accounts Receivable}} = \frac{\$5.3}{(\$.77 + \$.72) \div 2} = \frac{\$5.3}{\$.75} = 7.1 \text{ times}$$

Average Number of Days to Collect Accounts Receivable

$$\frac{\text{Days in Year}}{\text{Accounts Receivable Turnover}} = \frac{365}{7.1} = 51 \text{ days}$$

Management closely monitors these ratios in evaluating the company's policies for extending credit to customers and the effectiveness of its collection procedures. Short-term creditors, such as factors, banks, and merchandise

---

[3]From a conceptual point of view, net **credit** sales should be used in computing the accounts receivable turnover rate. It is common practice, however, to use the net sales figure, as the portion of net sales made on account usually is not disclosed in financial statements.

suppliers, also use these ratios in evaluating a company's ability to generate the cash necessary to pay it short-term liabilities.

Concentrations of Credit Risk   Assume that a business operates a single retail store in a town in which the major employer is a steel mill. What would happen to the collectibility of the store's accounts receivable if the steel mill were to close, leaving most of the store's customers unemployed? This situation illustrates what accountants call a **concentration of credit risk,** because many of the store's credit customers *share a characteristic* that can be affected *in a similar manner* by certain changes in economic conditions. Concentrations of credit risk occur if a significant portion of a company's receivables are due from a few major customers or from customers operating in the same industry or geographic region. This is called *shared characteristic.*[4]

Section 3860.67 of the *CICA Handbook* requires companies to disclose all *significant* concentrations of credit risk in the notes accompanying their financial statements. The disclosure includes (1) a description of the shared characteristic that identifies each concentration and (2) the amount of the maximum credit risk exposure of the assets sharing that characteristic.[5] The basic purpose of these disclosures is to assist users of the financial statements in evaluating the extent of the company's vulnerability to credit losses stemming from changes in economic conditions.

---

[4]CICA, *CICA Handbook* (Toronto), section 3860.77.
[5]Ibid.

*Supplemental Topic

NOTES RECEIVABLE WITH INTEREST CHARGES INCLUDED IN THE FACE AMOUNT

LO 7: Account for notes receivable with the interest charges included in the face amount.

In our discussion to this point, we have used notes receivable with the interest rate **stated separately.** We now want to compare this form of note with an alternative form in which the interest charge is **included in the face amount** of the note. For example, assume that Genetic Services has a $10,000 account receivable from a customer, Biolab. The customer is short of cash and wants to postpone payment, so Genetic Services agrees to accept a 181-day promissory note from Biolab with interest at the rate of 12% a year to replace the $10,000 account receivable. The interest for the 181-day note plus 3 days of grace (a total of 184 days) will amount to $605 ($10,000 × 12% × $\frac{184}{365}$ = $605, rounded) and the total amount to be received at maturity will be $10,000 principal plus $605 interest, or $10,605 altogether.

If the note is drawn with interest stated separately, as in the illustration below, the wording will be ". . . Biolab promises to pay to Genetic Services the sum of $10,000 with interest at the rate of 12% per year."

This note is for the principal amount with interest stated separately

Montreal, Quebec	November 1, 19__
_____181 days_____ **after this date** _____	Biolab
promises to pay to Genetic Services the sum of $ _____	10,000
with interest at the rate of _____	12% per year
	Signed _____ George Harr
	Title _____ Treasurer, Biolab

If the alternative form of note is used, the $605 interest will be included in the face amount and the note will appear as shown below:

Interest is included in face amount of this note

Montreal, Quebec	November 1, 19__
_____181 days_____ **after this date** _____	Biolab
promises to pay to Genetic Services the sum of $ _____	10,605
	Signed _____ George Harr
	Title _____ Treasurer, Biolab

Notice that the face amount of the note ($10,605) is **greater** than the $10,000 account receivable that it replaces. However, the value of the note receivable at November 1 is only $10,000; the other $605 included in the face amount of the note represents **unearned interest revenue.** As this interest revenue is earned over the life of the note, the value of the note will rise to $10,605 at maturity.

The journal entry by Genetic Services at November 1 to record the acquisition of the note will be as follows:

Interest included in face of note		

Notes Receivable 10,605
  Discount on Notes Receivable 605
  Accounts Receivable 10,000
Obtained from Biolab a 181-day note with a $605 interest charge included in the face amount, plus 3 days of grace.

The asset account, Notes Receivable, was debited with the full face amount of the note ($10,605). It is, therefore, necessary to credit a contra-asset, Discount on Notes Receivable, for the $605 of future interest revenue included in the face amount of the note. The Discount on Notes Receivable will appear in the balance sheet as a deduction from Notes Receivable. In our illustration, the amounts in the balance sheet will be Notes Receivable, $10,605 **minus** Discount on Notes Receivable, $605, or a **net** asset value of $10,000 on November 1.

Discount on Notes Receivable   The $605 balance of the account **Discount on Notes Receivable** at November 1 represents **unearned interest revenue.** As this interest revenue is earned over the life of the note, the amount in the discount account will be gradually transferred into Interest Revenue. Thus, at the maturity date of the note, Discount on Notes Receivable will have a zero balance and the value of the note receivable will have increased to $10,605. The process of transferring the amount in the Discount on Notes Receivable account into the Interest Revenue account is called **amortization** of the discount.

Amortization of the Discount   The discount on **short-term** notes receivable usually is amortized by the straight-line method, which allocates the **same amount** of discount to interest revenue for each month of the note's life.[6] Thus, the $605 discount on the Biolab note will be transferred from Discount on Notes Receivable into Interest Revenue at a uniform rate over the 184-day period.

Adjusting entries should be made to amortize the discount at the end of each accounting period and at the date the note matures. At December 31, Genetic Services will make the following adjusting entry to recognize the 60-days' interest revenue earned since November 1:

Amortization of discount

Discount on Notes Receivable 197
  Interest Revenue 197
*To record interest revenue earned to end-of-year on the 181-day note (plus 3 days of grace) dated Nov. 1 ($605 discount ×
$\frac{60}{184}$ = $197, rounded)*

---

[6]When an interest charge is included in the face amount of a **long-term** note, the effective interest method of amortizing the discount is often used instead of the straight-line method. The effective interest method of amortization is covered in intermediate accounting courses.

At December 31, the net valuation of the note receivable will appear in the balance sheet of Genetic Services as shown below:

Asset shown net of discount

Current assets:
Notes receivable $10,605
Less: Discount on notes receivable 408 $10,197

The net asset valuation of $10,197 consists of the $10,000 principal amount receivable from Biolab plus the $197 interest that has been earned since November 1.

When the note matures on May 4 of the following year, Genetic Services will recognize the $408 interest revenue earned since December 31 and will collect $10,605 from Biolab. The entry is:

Interest applicable to second year

Cash 10,605
Discount on Notes Receivable 408
    Interest Revenue 408
    Notes Receivable 10,605
To record collection of 181-day note (plus 3 days of grace) due today and to recognize interest revenue earned since year-end ($605 discount × $\frac{124}{184}$ = $408, rounded).

Comparison of the Two Forms of Notes Receivable

We have illustrated two alternative methods that Genetic Services could use in accounting for its $10,000 receivable, depending upon the form of the note. Journal entries for both methods, along with the resulting balance sheet presentations of the asset at November 1 and December 31, are summarized on the next page. Notice that both methods result in Genetic Services recognizing the **same amount of interest revenue** and the **same overall asset valuation** in the balance sheet. The form of the note does **not change the economic substance** of the transaction.

THE CONCEPT OF PRESENT VALUE

LO 8: Discuss the concept of present value in accounting for long-term notes receivable.

Consider again the note receivable from Biolab in which interest is included in the face amount. The only dollar amount that appears in this note is **$10,605**—the maturity value. Yet this note appears in Genetic Services' November 1 balance sheet at a net valuation of only **$10,000.** Where did this $10,000 amount come from, and what does it represent?

At November 1, $10,000 is the **present value** to Genetic Services of the right to collect $10,605 184 days in the future. The term present value means the economic value **today** of a cash flow that will occur at some future date.

It is helpful to think of present value as the **amount that a knowledgeable investor would pay today for the right to receive the future cash amount.** Because an investor expects to earn a profit (or interest) on an investment, the present value is **always less** than the full amount of the future cash flow.

The **difference** between the present value and the actual future amount is viewed as an **interest charge** included in the future amount. Often the present value of a note receivable is apparent from the current market values of the assets or services that are **given in exchange** for the note. In our

Comparison of the Two Forms of Notes Receivable

Note Written for $10,000 Plus 12% Interest

Entry to record acquisition of note on Nov. 1

Notes Receivable	10,000	
Accounts Receivable		10,000

Partial balance sheet at Nov. 1

Current assets:
Notes receivable $10,000

Adjusting entry at Dec. 31

Interest Receivable	197	
Interest Revenue		197

Partial balance sheet at Dec. 31

Current assets:		
Notes receivable	$10,000	
Interest receivable	197	$10,197

Entry to record collection of note on May 4

Cash	10,605	
Notes Receivable		10,000
Interest Receivable		197
Interest Revenue		408

Note Written with Interest Included in Face Amount

Entry to record acquisition of note on Nov. 1

Notes Receivable	10,605	
Discount on Notes Receivable		605
Accounts Receivable		10,000

Partial balance sheet at Nov. 1

Current assets:		
Notes receivable	$10,605	
Less: Discount on notes receivable	605	$10,000

Adjusting entry at Dec. 31

Discount on Notes Receivable	197	
Interest Revenue		197

Partial balance sheet at Dec. 31

Current assets:		
Notes receivable	$10,605	
Less: Discount on notes receivable	408	$10,197

Entry to record collection of note on May 4

Cash	10,605	
Discount on Notes Receivable	408	
Interest Revenue		408
Notes Receivable		10,605

current illustration, for example, Genetic Services accepts the note from Bio-lab at November 1 in full settlement of a $10,000 account receivable. This provides evidence that the current economic value (present value) of the note receivable on this date is $10,000.

In the assignment material for this chapter, the present value of notes receivable will be apparent from the value of the assets given in exchange. In practice, however, this is not always the case. When the present value of future cash flows is not apparent from the other values in a transaction, it must be computed by mathematical techniques.[7]

An Illustration of Notes Recorded at Present Value

To illustrate the use of present value in transactions involving long-term notes receivable, let us assume that on September 1, Tru-Tool, Inc., sells equipment to Everts Company and accepts as payment a one-year note (with the 3 days of grace included) in the face amount of $218,000 with no mention of an interest rate. It is not logical to assume that Tru-Tool, Inc., would extend credit for one year without charging any interest. Therefore, some portion of the $218,000 face amount of the note **should be regarded as a charge for interest.**

Let us assume that the regular sales price of the equipment sold in this transaction is $200,000. In this case the **present value** of the note is apparently **$200,000,** and the remaining $18,000 of the face amount represents a charge for interest. (The rate of interest that will cause the $200,000 present value of the note to increase to the $218,000 maturity value in one year is 9%. Thus, the face amount of the note actually includes an interest charge computed at the **effective annual interest rate** of 9%.)

The selling company, Tru-Tool, Inc., should use the **present value** of the note in determining the amount of revenue to be recognized from the sale. The $18,000 interest charge included in the face amount of the note receivable from Everts Company represents **unearned interest revenue** to Tru-Tool, Inc., and is **not part of the sales price of the equipment.** If Tru-Tool, Inc., were to treat the entire face amount of the note receivable as the sales price of the equipment, the result would be to overstate sales revenue and notes receivable by $18,000, and also to understate interest revenue by this amount over the life of the note.

At September 1, the date of sale, Tru-Tool, Inc., should record as sales revenue only an amount equal to the **present value** of the note receivable. The portion of the note that is regarded as unearned interest revenue ($18,000) should be credited to the contra-asset account, Discount on Notes Receivable. Thus, the entry to record the sale of equipment to Everts Company at September 1 is as follows:

Present value of the note begins at $200,000—the sales price

Notes Receivable	*218,000*	
Discount on Notes Receivable		*18,000*
Sales		*200,000*

Sold equipment to Everts Company and received a one-year note (3 days of grace included) with an $18,000 interest charge included in the face amount.

---

[7]The mathematical computation of present values is discussed in Appendix C, which is presented at the end of Chapter 16.

As the $18,000 interest is earned over the life of the note, this amount gradually will be transferred into Interest Revenue. At December 31, Tru-Tool, Inc., will have earned 121 days interest revenue and will make the following entry:

Present value has increased $5,967 by Dec. 31

Discount on Notes Receivable	*5,967*	
Interest Revenue		*5,967*

To record interest earned from Sept. 1 through Dec. 31 on Everts Company note ($18,000 discount × $\frac{121}{365}$ = $5,967, rounded).

On September 1 of the following year, when the note receivable is collected from Everts Company, the required entry will be:

Present value has risen to $218,000 by maturity date

Cash	*218,000*	
Discount on Notes Receivable	*12,033*	
Interest Revenue		*12,033*
Notes Receivable		*218,000*

To record collection of Everts Company note and to recognize interest earned since year-end.

Instalment Receivables

Another application of present value is found in the recording of ***instalment sales.*** Many retailing businesses sell merchandise on instalment sales plans, which permit customers to pay for their credit purchases through a series of monthly payments. The importance of instalment sales is emphasized by the recent balance sheets of large companies that show receivables in millions of dollars, nearly all of which call for collection in monthly instalments.

When merchandise is sold on an instalment plan, substantial interest charges are usually added to the "cash selling price" of the product in determining the total dollar amount to be collected in the series of instalment payments. The amount of sales revenue recognized at the time of sale, however, is limited to the ***present value*** of these instalment payments. In most cases, the present value of these future payments is equal to the regular sales price of the merchandise. The portion of the instalment account receivable that represents unearned finance charges is credited to the contra-asset account, Discount on Instalment Receivables. Thus, the entry to recognize the revenue on an instalment sale consists of a debit to Instalment Contracts Receivable, offset by a credit to Discount on Instalment Receivables for the unearned finance charges and a credit to Sales for the regular sales price of the merchandise. The balance of the contra-asset account, Discount on Instalment Receivables, is then amortized into Interest Revenue over the length of the collection period.

Although the collection period for an instalment receivable often runs as long as 24 to 36 months, such receivables are regarded as current assets if they correspond to customary credit terms of the industry. In published balance sheets, the Discount on Instalment Receivables is often called ***Deferred Interest Income*** or ***Unearned Finance Charges.*** A typical balance sheet presentation of instalment accounts receivable is illustrated below:

Trade accounts receivable:

Accounts receivable	$ 75,040,000
Instalment contracts receivable, including $31,000,000 due after one year...	52,640,000
	$127,680,000
Less: Deferred interest income ($8,070,000) and allowance for doubtful accounts ($1,872,000)	9,942,000
Total trade accounts and notes receivable	$117,738,000

End-of-Chapter Review

Key Terms Introduced or Emphasized in Chapter 8

Accounts receivable turnover *(p.438)* A ratio used to measure the liquidity of accounts receivable and the reasonableness of the accounts receivable balance. Computed by dividing net sales by average receivables.

Aging the accounts receivable *(p.429)* The process of classifying accounts receivable by age groups such as current, past due 1–30 days, past due 31–60 days, etc. A step in estimating the uncollectible portion of the accounts receivable.

Allowance for Doubtful Accounts *(p.425)* A valuation account or contra account relating to accounts receivable and showing the portion of the receivables estimated to be uncollectible.

Collateral (for a loan) *(p.432)* Assets pledged to secure a borrower's promise to repay a loan. In the event that the borrower fails to repay the loan, the creditor may foreclose against (take title to) the collateral.

Concentration of credit risk *(p.440)* A significant portion of receivables due from one customer or from a group of customers with a shared characteristic that is likely to be affected in a similar manner by changes in economic conditions.

Conservatism *(p.425)* A traditional practice of resolving uncertainties by choosing an asset valuation at the lower point of the range of reasonableness. Also refers to the policy of postponing recognition of revenue to a later date when a range of reasonable choice exists. Designed to avoid overstatement of financial strength and earnings.

Contra-asset account *(p.425)* A ledger account that is deducted from or offset against a related account in the financial statements—for example, Allowance for Doubtful Accounts and Discount on Notes Receivable.

Default *(p.436)* Failure to pay interest or principal of a promissory note at the due date.

Direct write-off method *(p.431)* A method of accounting for uncollectible receivables in which no expense is recognized until individual accounts are determined to be worthless. At that point the account receivable is written off with an offsetting debit to uncollectible accounts expense. Fails to match revenue and related expenses.

*Discount on Notes Receivable *(p.442)* A contra-asset account representing any unearned interest included in the face amount of a note receivable. Over the life of the note, the balance of the Discount on Notes Receivable account is amortized into Interest Revenue.

Discounting notes receivable *(p.438)* Selling a note receivable prior to its maturity date.

*Effective interest rate *(p.445)* The rate of interest that will cause the present value of a note to increase to the maturity value by the maturity date.

Factoring accounts receivable *(p.433)* Transactions in which a business either sells its accounts receivable to a financial institution (often called a **factor**) or borrows money by pledging its accounts receivable as collateral.

Interest *(p.435)* A charge made for the use of money. The formula for computing interest is Principal $\times$ Rate of interest $\times$ Time = Interest $(P \times R \times T = I)$.

Maker (of a note) *(p.434)* A person or an entity who issues a promissory note.

Maturity date *(p.435)* The date on which a note becomes due and payable.

Maturity value *(p.435)* The value of a note at its maturity date, consisting of principal plus interest.

Payee *(p.434)* The person named in a promissory note to whom payment is to be made (the creditor).

*Present value (of a future cash receipt) *(p.443)* The amount of money that an informed investor would pay today for the right to receive that future cash receipt. The present value is always less than the future amount, because money available today can be invested to earn interest and thereby become equivalent to a larger amount in the future.

Three days of grace *(p.435)* The extra three days added to the due date on all notes, other than the demand notes, to determine the legal date on which the note is due and payable.

DEMONSTRATION PROBLEM

Mui Home Centre sells custom wood furniture to decorators and the general public. Selected transactions relating to the company's receivables for the month of March follow. The company uses the allowance method in accounting for uncollectible accounts.

---

*Supplemental Topic, "Notes Receivable with Interest Charges Included in the Face Amount"

March 8   A $380 account receivable from Tanya Firmas was determined to be worthless and was written off.

March 13   Sold merchandise to Designer Interiors and received a $15,000, 60-day, 8% note dated March 13.

March 21   Received full payment from J. Porter of a $4,500, 60-day, 12% note dated January 17. Accrued interest receivable of $62 had been recorded in prior months.

March 23   An account receivable of $325 from G. Davis had been written off in January; full payment was unexpectedly received from Davis.

March 24*   Received a 60-day note from StyleCraft Co. in settlement of $3,600 open account. Interest computed at 8% was included in the face amount of the note.

March 29   Sales to ExtraCash credit card customers during March amounted to $14,800. (Summarize all credit card sales in one entry. ExtraCash Inc. is a credit card company.)

March 30   Collected cash from ExtraCash Inc. for the March credit card sales, less a 5% discount charged by ExtraCash.

March 31   As a result of substantial write-offs, the Allowance for Doubtful Accounts has a debit balance of $320. Aging of the accounts receivable indicates that the estimated uncollectible accounts are $1,800 at the end of March.

INSTRUCTIONS

a. Prepare journal entries in general journal form for the March transactions.
b. Prepare the necessary adjusting entries at March 31.

Solution to Demonstration Problem

a.   **General Journal**

March 8	Allowance for Doubtful Accounts		380	
		Accounts Receivable, Tanya Firmas			380
	Wrote off uncollectible account from Tanya Firmas			
13	Note Receivable, Designer Interiors		15,000	
		Sales			15,000
	Sale of merchandise for a 60-day, 8% note.			
21	Cash		4,593	
		Notes Receivable			4,500
		Interest Receivable			62
		Interest Revenue			31
	Collected note from J. Porter, including $93 interest.			
	($4,500 × .12 × $\frac{21}{365}$ = $31, rounded)			
23	Account Receivable, G. Davis		325	
		Allowance for Doubtful Accounts			325
	To reinstate Davis receivable previously written off.			
23	Cash		325	
		Accounts Receivable, G. Davis			325
	To record collection of Davis account.			
24	Notes Receivable		3,650	
		Discount on Notes Receivable			50
		Accounts Receivable, StyleCraft Co.			3,600
	Received 60-day note with interest at 8% included			
	in face amount in settlement of open account			
	($3,600 × .08 × $\frac{63}{365}$ = $50, rounded)			

Supplemental Topic, "Notes Receivable with Interest Charges Included in the Face Amount"

29	Accounts Receivable, ExtraCash Inc.	14,800	
	Sales		14,800
	To record credit card sales for March.		

30	Cash	14,060	
	Credit Card Discount Expense	740	
	Accounts Receivable, ExtraCash Inc.		14,800
	Collected March credit card sales invoices, less 5%.		

b.   **Adjusting Entries**

| March 31 | Uncollectible Accounts Expense . . . . | 2,120 | |
| | Allowance for Doubtful Accounts . . . . | | 2,120 |

To provide for estimated uncollectibles as follows:

Required allowance at March 31	$1,800
Present balance (debit)	320
Required increase in allowance	$2,120

| 31 | Interest Receivable . . . . | 59 | |
| | Interest Revenue . . . . | | 59 |

To accrue interest on the Designer Interiors' note: $15,000 \times .08 \times \frac{18}{365} = 59 (rounded).

| 31 | Discount on Notes Receivable . . . . | 6 | |
| | Interest Revenue . . . . | | 6 |

To record interest earned through March 31 on StyleCraft note receivable ($50 discount $\times \frac{7}{63} = 6, rounded)

Self-Test Questions

The answers to these questions appear on page 467.

1. Which of the following best describes the application of generally accepted accounting principles to the valuation of accounts receivable?
   a. Realization principle—Accounts receivable are shown at their net realizable value in the balance sheet.
   b. Matching principle—The loss due to an uncollectible account is recognized in the period in which the sale is made, not in the period in which the account receivable is determined to be worthless.
   c. Cost principle—Accounts receivable are shown at the initial cost of the merchandise to customers, less the cost the seller must pay to cover uncollectible accounts.
   d. Principle of conservatism—Accountants favour using the lowest reasonable estimate for the amount of uncollectible accounts shown in the balance sheet.

2. On January 1, Dillon Company had a $3,100 credit balance in the Allowance for Doubtful Accounts. During the year, sales totalled $780,000 and $6,900 of accounts receivable were written off as uncollectible. A December 31 aging of accounts receivable indicated the amount probably uncollectible to be $5,300. (No recoveries of accounts previously written off were made during the year.) Dillon's financial statements for the current year should include:
   a. Uncollectible accounts expense of $9,100.
   b. Uncollectible accounts expense of $5,300.
   c. Allowance for Doubtful Accounts with a credit balance of $1,500.
   d. Allowance for Doubtful Accounts with a credit balance of $8,400.

3. Under the ***direct write-off*** method of accounting for uncollectible accounts:
   a. The current year uncollectible accounts expense is less than the expense would be under the income statement approach.

    b. The relationship between the current period net sales and current period uncollectible accounts expense illustrates the matching principle.

    c. The Allowance for Doubtful Accounts is debited when specific accounts receivable are determined to be worthless.

    d. Accounts receivable are not stated in the balance sheet at net realizable value, but at the balance of the Accounts Receivable ledger account.

4. On October 1, Blaine Company sold a parcel of land in exchange for a nine-month (3 days of grace included), 12% note receivable in the amount of $300,000. Interest is not included in the face amount of this note and the proper adjusting entry was made with respect to this note at December 31. Blaine's journal entry to record collection of this note at July 1 of the following year (maturity date) includes (compute interest on a monthly rather than daily basis):

    a. A debit to Cash for $318,000.

    b. A credit to Interest Revenue of $18,000.

    c. A debit to Interest Receivable of $9,000.

    d. A credit to Notes Receivable of $327,000.

*5. On September 1, 2000, Vickers Industries sold machinery in exchange for a six-month (3 days of grace included) note receivable. An interest charge, computed at an annual rate of 12%, was included in the face amount of the note. In its December 31, 2000, balance sheet, Vickers correctly presented the note receivable as follows:

Note Receivable, due March 1, 2001 .... $143,100
Less: Discount on note receivable .... (2,700) $140,400

What was the total amount of interest charge included in the face amount of the note on **September 1, 2000** (interest is computed on a monthly rather than daily basis):

    a. $2,700

    b. $5,400

    c. $8,100

    d. $8,586

ASSIGNMENT MATERIAL

Discussion Questions

1. Wolf Brothers, a retailer, makes most of its sales on credit. In the first 10 years of operation, the company incurred some uncollectible accounts (bad debts) expense each year. Does this record indicate that the company's credit policies are in need of change? Explain.

2. Company A and Company B are virtually identical in size and nature of operations, but Company A is more conservative in valuing accounts receivable. Will this greater emphasis on conservatism cause A to report higher or lower net income than Company B? Assume that you are a banker considering identical loan applications from A and B and you know of the more conservative

---

*Supplemental Topics, "Notes Receivable with Interest Charges Included in the Face Amount"

policy followed by A. In which set of financial statements would you have more confidence? Explain.

3. Explain the relationship between the **matching principle** and the need to estimate uncollectible accounts receivable.

4. Kitchen Company determines at year-end that its Allowance for Doubtful Accounts should be increased by $5,200. Give the adjusting entry to carry out this decision.

5. Familyroom Fungames Company, which has accounts receivable of $371,520 and an allowance for doubtful accounts of $4,320, decides to write off as worthless a past-due account receivable for $1,800 from Kassy Company. What effect will the write-off have upon total current assets? Upon net income for the period? Explain.

6. In making the annual adjusting entry for uncollectible accounts, a company may utilize a **balance sheet approach** to make the estimate or it may use an **income statement approach.** Explain these two alternative approaches.

7. At the end of its first year in business, Arthur Yokotake, Inc., had accounts receivable totalling $148,500. After careful analysis of the individual accounts, the credit manager estimated that $146,100 would ultimately be collected. Give the journal entry required to reflect this estimate in the accounts.

8. In February of its second year of operations, World Travel Network learned of the failure of a customer, Dale Corporation, which owed $800. Nothing could be collected. Give the journal entry to recognize the uncollectibility of the receivable from Dale Corporation, assuming World uses an allowance method.

9. Posner Company, which uses the allowance method of accounting for uncollectible accounts, wrote off as uncollectible a $1,500 receivable from Webb Company. Several months later, Webb Company obtained new long-term financing and promptly paid all its old debts in full. Give the journal entry or entries (in general journal form) that Posner Company should make to record this recovery of $1,500.

10. What is the direct write-off method of handling credit losses as opposed to the allowance method? What is its principal shortcoming?

11. Caballeros, Inc., had decided to write off its account receivable from Leisure Now because the latter has entered bankruptcy. What general ledger accounts should be debited and credited, assuming that the allowance method is in use? What general ledger accounts should be debited and credited if the direct write-off method is in use?

12. What are the advantages to a retailer of making credit sales only to customers who use nationally recognized credit cards?

13. Jade Palace, a restaurant that had always made cash sales only, adopted a new policy of honouring several nonbank credit cards. Sales did not increase, but many of its regular customers began charging dinner bills on the credit cards. Has the new policy been beneficial to Jade Palace? Explain.

14. Determine the maturity date of each of the following:
    a. A three-month note dated March 10.
    b. A 30-day note dated August 15.
    c. A 90-day note dated July 2.

15. On April 10, Hilltop Growers receives a 60-day, 9% note receivable from Jane Stream, a customer, in settlement of a $6,000 account receivable due today. Give the journal entries to record (1) the receipt of this note and (2) its collection at the maturity date.

16. How are the accounts receivable turnover rate and the average number of days to collect accounts receivable computed? Why is this information significant to short-term creditors?

17. How does an annual audit by a public accounting firm provide assurance that a company's accounts receivable and notes receivable are fairly presented in the company's financial statements?

*18. Define the **present value** of a future amount. Is the present value larger or smaller than the face amount of the future cash flow? Why?

*19. Williams Gear sold merchandise to Dayco in exchange for a one-year (3 days of grace included) note receivable. The note was drawn with a face amount of $13,310, **including** a 10% interest charge. Compute the amount of sales revenue to be recognized by Williams Gear.

*20. Maxline Stores sells merchandise with a sales price of $1,260 on an instalment plan requiring 12 monthly payments of $120 each. How much revenue will this sale ultimately generate for Maxline Stores? Explain the nature of this revenue and when it should be recognized in the accounting records.

*21. With reference to Question **20** above, make the journal entries required in the accounting records of Maxline Stores to record:
    a. Recognition of revenue from sale of merchandise on instalment contract.
    b. Collection of the first monthly instalment payment. (Assume that an equal portion of the discount is amortized at the time that each instalment payment is received.)

Exercises

EXERCISE 8-1
Accounting Terminology
(LO 1, 2, 3, 5, 6)

Listed below are nine technical accounting terms introduced in this chapter.

Uncollectible accounts expense	*Allowance for Doubtful Accounts*	*Accounts receivable turnover*
Aging schedule	*Conservatism*	*Direct write-off method*
Factoring	*Default*	*Maturity value*

Each of the following statements may (or may not) describe one of these technical terms. For each statement, indicate the term described, or answer "None" if the statement does not correctly describe any of the terms.
a. The principal amount of an interest-bearing note.
b. Resolving uncertainties in the valuation of assets by reporting assets at the lower end of the range of reasonable values rather than by estimating values in a purely objective manner.
c. The account indicating the portion of the year-end accounts receivable that are expected to prove uncollectible.
d. The account indicating the amount of accounts receivable originating during the year that are expected to prove uncollectible.

---

*Supplemental Topic, "Notes Receivable with Interest Charges Included in the Face Amount"

e. Failure to make payment of the principal or interest per the terms of a promissory note.

f. A computation useful in determining how quickly a company is able to collect its accounts receivable.

g. Recognition of credit losses when specific accounts receivable are determined to be uncollectible.

EXERCISE 8-2
Accounting for Uncollectible Accounts—The "Balance Sheet" Approach
(LO 1)

At May 31, the accounts receivable of Biway Central amounted in total to $705,600. The company uses the balance sheet approach to estimate uncollectible accounts and has prepared an aging schedule of accounts receivable at May 31 that indicates $17,568 to be uncollectible. You are to prepare as of May 31 the adjusting entry required under each of the following independent assumptions. The explanation portion of each entry should include appropriate supporting computations.

a. The Allowance for Doubtful Accounts has a credit balance of $12,672.

b. The Allowance for Doubtful Accounts has a debit balance of $4,262.

EXERCISE 8-3
Accounting for Uncollectible Accounts—The "Income Statement" Approach
(LO 1)

The income statement approach to estimating uncollectible accounts expense is used by Burgess Wholesale. On March 31 the firm had accounts receivable in the amount of $630,000. The Allowance for Doubtful Accounts had a credit balance of $3,950. The controller estimated that uncollectible accounts expense would amount to one-half of 1% of the $5,200,000 of net credit sales made during March. This estimate was entered in the accounts by an adjusting entry on March 31.

On April 12, an account receivable from Conrad Stern of $3,110 was determined to be worthless and was written off. However, on April 24, Stern won several thousand dollars in a lottery and immediately paid the $3,110 past-due account.

INSTRUCTIONS

Prepare four journal entries in general journal form to record the above events.

EXERCISE 8-4
Uncollectible Accounts Expense—Allowance Method and Direct Write-Off Method
(LO 1, 2)

The credit manager of Olympic Sporting Goods has gathered the following information about the company's accounts receivable and credit losses during the current year:

Net credit sales for the year		$3,000,000
Accounts receivable at year-end		360,000
Uncollectible accounts receivable:		
Actually written off during the year	$43,650	
Estimated portion of year-end receivables expected to		
prove uncollectible (per aging schedule)	18,000	61,650

INSTRUCTIONS

Prepare one journal entry summarizing the recognition of uncollectible accounts expense for the entire year under each of the following independent assumptions:

a. Uncollectible accounts expense is estimated at an amount equal to 1½% of net credit sales.

b. Uncollectible accounts expense is recognized by adjusting the balance in the Allowance for Doubtful Accounts to the amount indicated in the year-end aging schedule. The credit balance in the allowance account at the beginning of the current year was $15,000.

c. The company uses the direct write-off method of accounting for uncollectible accounts.

EXERCISE 8-5
Write-Offs and Recoveries
(LO 1)

The balance sheet of Omni, Inc., at the end of last year included the following items:

Notes receivable from customers	$ 540,000
Interest receivable	10,800
Accounts receivable	$2,268,000
Less: Allowance for doubtful accounts	54,000

INSTRUCTIONS

You are to record the following related events of the current year in general journal entries:

a. Accounts receivable of $51,840 are written off as uncollectible.

b. A customer's note for $14,850, on which interest of $810 has been accrued in the accounts, is deemed uncollectible, and both balances are written off against the Allowance for Doubtful Accounts.

c. An account receivable for $7,020 previously written off is collected.

d. Aging of accounts receivable at the end of the current year indicates a need for an $81,000 allowance to cover possible failure to collect accounts currently outstanding.

EXERCISE 8-6
How Fast Are Accounts Receivable Collected?
(LO 6)

In your analysis of the financial statements of Rayscan, Inc., you note that net sales for the year were $17,000,000; accounts receivable were $1,500,000 at the beginning of the year and $1,900,000 at the end of the year.

INSTRUCTIONS

a. Compute the accounts receivable turnover rate for the year.

b. Compute the number of days (on average) required to collect accounts receivable.

c. Assume that during the following year sales increase and the accounts receivable turnover rate also increases. Would you regard this as a favourable development? Explain.

EXERCISE 8-7
Notes and Interest
(LO 7)

On September 1, a six-month (3 days of grace included), 15% note receivable is acquired from Shaun Young, a customer, in settlement of his $12,000 account receivable. (Interest is computed on a monthly rather than daily basis.)

INSTRUCTIONS

Prepare journal entries to record:

a. The receipt of the note on September 1.

b. The adjustment to record accrued interest revenue on December 31.

c. Collection of the principal and interest on February 28.

*EXERCISE 8-8
Two Forms of Notes Receivable
(LO 5, 7)

On October 1, Blackwood Company made a loan of $300,000 to a supplier, Niagara Mills. The loan agreement provided for repayment of the $300,000 in 12 months plus interest at an annual rate of 10%. (Compute interest on a monthly basis and assume the 3 days of grace has been included.)

INSTRUCTIONS

You are to prepare two different presentations of the note receivable from Niagara Mills on Blackwood Company's balance sheet at December 31, assuming that the note was drawn as follows:

a. For $300,000 with interest stated separately and payable at maturity.

b. With the total interest charge included in the face amount of the note.

*EXERCISE 8-9
Interest Included in Face Amount of Note
(LO 7, 8)

West Motors, a truck dealer, sold three trucks to Day & Night Truck Lines on July 1, for a total price of $78,600. Under the terms of the sale, West Motors received $21,000 cash and a promissory note due in full in 24 months. The face amount of the note was $67,968, which included interest on the note for the 24 months.

West Motors uses a perpetual inventory system. The trucks sold to Day & Night Truck Lines were carried in West's inventory at an aggregate cost of $69,000.

INSTRUCTIONS

Prepare entries in general journal form for West Motors relating to this transaction and to the note for the year ended December 31. Include the adjusting entry needed to record interest earned to December 31. (Adjusting entries are made only at year-end. Assume the discount is amortized by the straight-line method—that is, an

---

Supplemental Topic, "Notes Receivable with Interest Charges Included in the Face Amount"

equal amount of interest revenue is considered earned in each month. Also, compute interest on a monthly basis and assume the 3 days of grace have been included in the 24-month note.)

Problems

PROBLEM 8-1
Aging Accounts Receivable;
Write-Offs
(LO 1)

Popular Image, a firm specializing in marketing and publicity services, uses the balance sheet approach to estimate uncollectible accounts expense. At year-end (December 31) an aging of the accounts receivable produced the following classification:

(1) Not yet due	*$222,000*
(2) 1–30 days past due	*90,000*
(3) 31–60 days past due	*39,000*
(4) 61–90 days past due	*9,000*
(5) Over 90 days past due	*15,000*
Total	*$375,000*

On the basis of past experience, the company estimated the percentages probably uncollectible for the above five age groups to be as follows: Group 1, 1%; Group 2, 3%; Group 3, 10%; Group 4, 20%; and Group 5, 50%.

The Allowance for Doubtful Accounts before adjustment at December 31 showed a credit balance of $5,400.

INSTRUCTIONS

a. Compute the estimated amount of uncollectible accounts based on the above classification by age groups.
b. Prepare the adjusting entry needed to bring the Allowance for Doubtful Accounts to the proper amount.
c. Assume that on January 16 of the following year, Popular Image learned that an account receivable that had originated on September 1 in the amount of $5,700 was definitely uncollectible because of the financial difficulties of the customer, Cranston Manufacturing. Prepare the journal entry required on January 16 to write off this account.

PROBLEM 8-2
Aging Accounts Receivable;
Write-Offs
(LO 1)

Nelson Associates Inc., uses the balance sheet approach to estimate uncollectible accounts and maintains an allowance account to reduce accounts receivable to realizable value. An analysis of the accounts receivable at December 31 (year-end date) produced the following age groups:

(1) Not yet due	*$116,000*
(2) 1–30 days past due	*60,000*
(3) 31–60 days past due	*26,000*
(4) 61–90 days past due	*6,000*
(5) Over 90 days past due	*10,000*
Total accounts receivable	*$218,000*

In reliance upon its past experience with collections, the company estimated the percentages probably uncollectible for the above five age groups to be as follows: Group 1, 1%; Group 2, 4%; Group 3, 10%; Group 4, 30%; and Group 5, 50%.

Prior to adjustment at year-end, the Allowance for Doubtful Accounts showed a credit balance of $4,200.

INSTRUCTIONS

a. Compute the estimated amount of uncollectible accounts based on the above classification by age groups.

b. Prepare the adjusting entry needed to bring the Allowance for Doubtful Accounts to the proper amount.

c. Assume that on February 8 of the following year, Nelson Associates learned that an account receivable that had originated on October 6 in the amount of $2,400 was worthless because of the bankruptcy of the customer, Weaver Company. Prepare the journal entry required on February 8 to write off this account receivable.

PROBLEM 8-3
Estimating Uncollectible
Accounts
(LO 1)

Kiln Kraft, Inc., owned by Abby Powers, had for the past five years been engaged in selling a line of ceramic merchandise to retail stores. Sales are made on credit and each month the company has estimated its uncollectible accounts expense as a percentage of net credit sales. The percentage used has been ½ of 1% of net credit sales. However, it appears that this provision has been inadequate because the Allowance for Doubtful Accounts has a debit balance of $12,400 at May 31 prior to making the monthly provision. Powers has therefore decided to use another approach of estimating uncollectible accounts expense and to rely upon an analysis of the accounts receivable at the end of each month.

At May 31, the accounts receivable totalled $760,000. This total amount included past-due accounts in the amount of $172,000. None of these past-due accounts was considered hopeless; all accounts regarded as worthless had been written off as rapidly as they were determined to be uncollectible. After careful investigation of the past-due accounts at May 31, Abby Powers decided that the probable loss contained therein was 10%, and that in addition she should anticipate a loss of 1% of the current amounts receivable.

INSTRUCTIONS

a. Compute the probable amount of uncollectible accounts included in the accounts receivable at May 31, based on the analysis by the owner.

b. Prepare the journal entry necessary to carry out the change in company policy with respect to providing for uncollectible accounts expense.

PROBLEM 8-4
Estimating Uncollectible
Accounts, Write-Offs, and
Recovery
(LO 1)

At December 31 last year, the balance sheet of Quality Wholesale included $504,000 in accounts receivable and an allowance for doubtful accounts of $26,400. During January of the current year selected transactions are summarized as follows:

(1) Sales on account *$360,640*
(2) Cash collections from customers (no cash discounts) *364,800*
(3) Account receivable from Acme Company written off as worthless . . *9,280*

After a careful aging and analysis of all customers' accounts at January 31, it was decided that the allowance for doubtful accounts should be adjusted to a balance of $29,280 in order to reflect accounts receivable at net realizable value in the January 31 balance sheet.

INSTRUCTIONS

a. Prepare entries in general journal form summarizing for the entire month of January the activity described in the three numbered items. Also show the adjusting entry at January 31 to provide for uncollectible accounts.

b. Show the amounts of accounts receivable and the allowance for doubtful accounts as they would appear in a partial balance sheet at January 31.

c. Assume that three months after the receivable from Acme Company had been written off as worthless, Acme Company won a large award in the settlement of patent litigation and immediately paid the $9,280 debt to Quality Wholesale. Give the journal entry or entries (in general journal form) to reflect this recovery of a receivable previously written off.

PROBLEM 8-5
Estimating Uncollectible Accounts
(LO 1)

Rivero Graphics, owned by Maria Rivero, sells paper novelty goods to retail stores. All sales are made on credit and the company has regularly estimated its uncollectible accounts expense as a percentage of net credit sales. The percentage used has been 1% of net credit sales. However, it appears that this provision has been inadequate because the Allowance for Doubtful Accounts has a debit balance of $3,900 at July 31 prior to making the monthly provision. Rivero has therefore decided to change the approach of estimating uncollectible accounts expense and to rely upon an analysis of the age and character of the accounts receivable at the end of each month.

At July 31, the accounts receivable totalled $260,000. This total amount included past-due accounts in the amount of $46,000. None of these past-due accounts was considered worthless; all accounts regarded as worthless had been written off immediately. After a careful review of the $46,000 of past-due accounts at July 31, Rivero decided that the estimated loss contained therein was 10%. In addition she decided to provide for a loss of 1% of the current accounts receivable.

INSTRUCTIONS

a. Compute the estimated amount of uncollectible accounts included in the $260,000 of accounts receivable at July 31, based on the analysis by the owner.
b. Prepare the journal entry necessary to carry out the change in company policy with respect to providing for uncollectible accounts expense.

PROBLEM 8-6
Accounts Receivable: A Comprehensive Problem
(LO 1)

Nagano International has 420 accounts receivable in its subsidiary ledger. All accounts are due in 30 days. On December 31, an aging schedule was prepared. The results are summarized below:

Customer	Total	Not Yet Due	1–30 Days Past Due	31–60 Days Past Due	61–90 Days Past Due	Over 90 Days Past Due
(418 names) Subtotals	$863,125	$458,975	$236,700	$108,350	$22,500	$36,600

Two accounts receivable were accidentally omitted from this schedule. The following data is available regarding these accounts:
1. J. Ardis owes $10,625 from two invoices; invoice no. 218, dated Sept. 14, in the amount of $7,450; and invoice no. 568, dated Nov. 9, in the amount of $3,175.
2. N. Selstad owes $9,400 from two invoices; invoice no. 628, dated Nov. 19, in the amount of $3,375; and invoice no. 718, dated Dec. 5, in the amount of $6,025.

INSTRUCTIONS

a. Complete the aging schedule as of Dec. 31 by adding to the column subtotals an aging of the accounts of Ardis and Selstad.
b. Prepare a schedule to compute the estimated portion of each age group that will prove uncollectible and the required balance in the Allowance for Doubtful Accounts. Arrange your schedule in the format illustrated in this chapter. The following percentages of each age group are estimated to be uncollectible: Not yet due, 1%; 1–30 days, 4%; 31–60 days, 10%; 61–90 days, 30%; over 90 days, 50%.
c. Prepare the journal entry to bring the Allowance for Doubtful Accounts up to its required balance at Dec. 31. Prior to making this adjustment, the account has a credit balance of $34,500.
d. Show how accounts receivable would appear in the company's balance sheet at Dec. 31.
e. On Jan. 7 of the following year, the credit manager of Nagano International learns that the $10,625 account receivable from J. Ardis is uncollectible because Ardis has declared bankruptcy. Prepare the journal entry to write off this account.

PROBLEM 8-7
Accounting for Uncollectible Accounts
(LO 1)

Maps & Globes, Inc., is a manufacturer that makes all sales on 30-day credit terms. Annual sales are approximately $25 million. At the end of 2000, accounts receivable were presented in the company's balance sheet as shown below:

Accounts receivable from customers $2,350,000
Less: Allowance for doubtful accounts   70,000

During 2001, $740,000 in accounts receivable were written off as uncollectible. Of these accounts written off, receivables totalling $24,000 were unexpectedly collected. At the end of 2001, an aging of accounts receivable indicated a need for an $80,000 allowance to cover possible failure to collect the accounts currently outstanding.

Maps & Globes makes adjusting entries in its accounting records ***only at year-end.*** Monthly and quarterly financial statements are prepared from work sheets, without any adjusting or closing entries actually being entered in the accounting records.

INSTRUCTIONS

a. Prepare the following in the form of general journal entries:
   1. One entry to summarize all accounts written off against the allowance for doubtful accounts during 2001.
   2. Entries to record the $24,000 in accounts receivable that were unexpectedly collected in 2001.
   3. The adjusting entry required at December 31, 2001 to increase the allowance for doubtful accounts to $80,000.
b. Notice that the allowance for doubtful accounts was only $70,000 at the end of 2000, but uncollectible accounts during 2001 totalled $716,000 ($740,000 less the $24,000 reinstated). Do these relationships appear reasonable, or was the allowance for doubtful accounts greatly understated at the end of 2000? Explain.

PROBLEM 8-8
Turnover of Accounts Receivable
(LO 6)

Shown below are the net sales and the average amounts of accounts receivable of two computer makers in a recent year:

	(Dollars in Millions)	
	Average Accounts Receivable	Net Credit Sales
Hewlett-Packard Company	$1,297	$7,102
Digital Equipment Corporation	2,108	9,390

INSTRUCTIONS

a. For each of these companies, compute:
   1. The number of times that the average balance of accounts receivable turned over during this fiscal year. (Round to the nearest tenth.)
   2. The number of days (on average) that each company must wait to collect its accounts receivable. (Round to the nearest day.)
b. Based upon your computations in part **a,** which company's accounts receivable appear to be the more "liquid" asset? Explain briefly.

PROBLEM 8-9
Hey, Pal . . . When You Gonna Pay for This Beer?
(LO 6)

Shown below are the sales and the average amounts of accounts receivable of three beverage companies in a recent year:

	(Dollars in Millions)	
	Average Accounts Receivable	Sales
Molson Companies Limited	$123	$ 1,465
Adolph Coors Company	147	1,764
Anheuser-Busch Companies, Inc.	652	11,394

INSTRUCTIONS

a. For each of these companies, compute:
   1. The number of times that the average balance of accounts receivable turned over during this fiscal year. (Round to the nearest tenth.)
   2. The number of days (on average) that each company must wait to collect its accounts receivable. (Round to the nearest day.)
b. Based upon your computations in part **a,** which company's accounts receivable appear to be the more "liquid" asset? Explain briefly.

PROBLEM 8-10
Note Receivable: Entries for Collection and for Default
(LO 5)

Hanover Mills sells merchandise to retail stores on 30-day credit, but insists that any customer who fails to pay an invoice when due must replace it with an interest-bearing note. The company adjusts and closes its accounts at December 31. Among the transactions relating to notes receivable were the following.

Nov. 1   Received from a customer (Jones Brothers) a 90-day, 9% note for $20,000 in settlement of an account receivable due today.

Feb. 2   Collected in full the 90-day, 9% note receivable from Jones Brothers, including interest.

INSTRUCTIONS

a. Prepare journal entries in general journal form to record: (1) the receipt of the note on November 1, (2) the adjustment for interest on December 31, and (3) collection of principal and interest on the following February 2. Assume that the company does not use reversing entries.
b. Assume that instead of paying the note on the following February 2, the customer (Jones Brothers) had defaulted. Give the journal entry by Hanover Mills to record the default. Assume that Jones Brothers has sufficient resources to pay the amount owed.

PROBLEM 8-11
Note Receivable: Entries for Collection and for Default
(LO 5)

Five Corners Imports sells a variety of merchandise to retail stores on open account. It has a policy that requires that any customer who fails to pay an invoice when due must replace it with an interest-bearing note. The company adjusts and closes its accounts at December 31. Among the transactions relating to notes receivable were the following:

Dec. 1   Received from a customer, Party Plus, a 60-day, 9% note for $42,000 in settlement of an account receivable due today.

Feb. 2   Collected in full the 60-day, 9% note receivable from Party Plus, including interest.

INSTRUCTIONS

a. Prepare journal entries (in general journal form) to record: (1) the receipt of the note on December 1; (2) the adjustment for interest on December 31; and (3) collection of principal and interest on February 2. Assume that the company does not use reversing entries.
b. Assume that instead of paying the note on February 2, the customer (Party Plus) had defaulted. Give the journal entry by Five Corners Imports to record the default. Assume that Party Plus has sufficient resources that the amount owed eventually will be collected.

***PROBLEM 8-12**
Notes Receivable: A Comprehensive Problem
(LO 5, 7, 8)

Following are selected receivables of Douglas Agricultural Supply Company at December 1, 2000. The company adjusts and closes its accounts only at year-end.

---

*Supplemental Topic, "Notes Receivable with Interest Charges Included in the Face Amount"

Notes receivable:

Flag-Is-Up; 90-day, 10% note dated Sept. 7	$10,000
Trust-House Co-op; 60-day, 9% note dated Oct. 29	20,000
Applegate Farm; 45-day, 10% note dated Nov. 1	28,800
W. B. McCoy; 90-day, 12% note dated Dec. 1	32,000

Accounts receivable:

Morgan-Hill Farms	$ 8,000
T. J. Peppercorn	12,700

Instalment contracts receivable:

M. Twain (19 monthly payments of $900)	$17,100

Unearned finance charges on instalment contracts:

Applicable to M. Twain contract	$ 2,280

During December, transactions affecting these receivables were as follows:

Dec. 7   T. J. Peppercorn paid $700 on account and gave a 30-day, 10% note to cover the $12,000 balance of his account.

Dec. 9   Collected in full the maturity value of the Flag-Is-Up 90-day note.

Dec. 11   Received a 60-day note receivable from Morgan-Hill Farms in full settlement of its account receivable. The face amount of this note was $8,120, which included an interest charge.

Dec. 19   Tom Applegate wrote that Applegate Farm would be unable to pay the note due today. However, he enclosed a cheque for the interest due, along with a new 30-day, 10% note replacing the old note. Douglas Agricultural decided to accept this renewal of the Applegate note.

Dec. 31   Received notice from Trust-House Co-op that it was unable to pay its note due today. The defaulted note was not renewed, but Douglas expects that the amount owed will eventually be collected.

Dec. 31   Received the $900 payment from M. Twain on her instalment contract. The payment included $120 interest for the month of December. The interest charges included in the face amount of the instalment contract originally had been credited to the contra-asset account, Unearned Finance Charges on Instalment Contracts.

INSTRUCTIONS

a. Prepare journal entries for the six December transactions listed above.
b. Prepare the adjusting entries necessary at December 31 to recognize interest accrued on notes receivable through year-end.

Use one adjusting entry to accrue interest receivable on the three notes in which interest is stated separately (the Applegate, Peppercorn, and McCoy notes). Use a separate adjusting entry to recognize interest revenue earned on the note with interest included in the face amount (the Morgan-Hill note).

c. Prepare the current asset section of Douglas Agricultural Supply Company's balance sheet at Dec. 31, 2000. In addition to the receivables described above, include the following items:

Cash	$ 42,500
Accounts receivable (other than described above)	120,000
Allowance for doubtful receivables (all types)	10,000
Inventory	105,000

In listing the company's receivables, include captions indicating any unamortized discount, unearned finance charges, and accrued interest. Do **not,** however, identify the individual debtors. (Combine all four notes under the caption "Notes receivable.")

*PROBLEM 8-13
Notes Receivable: A
Comprehensive Problem
(LO 5, 7, 8)

Selected receivables of Hartford Building Supply at December 1, 2001, are shown below. Hartford adjusts and closes its accounts only at December 31.

Notes receivable:

Weiss Construction Co.; 90-day, 12% note dated Sept. 29	$25,000
Mr. Remodel; 60-day, 10% note dated Oct. 12	18,000
Tillamook Homes; 45-day, 10% note dated Nov. 1	16,000
J. D. Walters; 60-day, 9% note dated Dec. 1	30,000

Accounts receivable:

Regal Construction	$12,000
Dexter Dalton	8,200

Instalment contracts receivable:

Jesse Cole (14 monthly payments of $600)	$ 8,400

Unearned finance charges on instalment contracts:

Applicable to Jesse Cole contract	$ 728

During the month of December, transactions affecting these receivables were as follows:

Dec. 1 Received an 87-day note receivable from Regal Construction in full settlement of its account receivable. The face amount of this note was $12,360, which included an interest charge.

Dec. 11 Dexter Dalton paid $2,200 on his account and gave a 30-day, 12% note to cover the $6,000 balance of his account.

Dec. 14 Collected in full the maturity value of the Mr. Remodel 60-day note.

Dec. 19 Tillamook Homes paid in cash the interest due on its $16,000 note but renewed the note for the $16,000 principal amount for another 30 days. The interest rate in the new note is 12%.

Dec. 31 Received the $600 payment from Jesse Cole on his instalment contract. The payment included $52 interest for the month of December. The interest charges included in the face amount of the instalment contract originally had been credited to the contra-asset account, Unearned Finance Charges on Instalment Contracts.

Dec. 31 Received notice from Weiss Construction Co. that it was unable to pay its note due today. The defaulted note was not renewed, but Hartford expects that the amount due will eventually be collectible.

INSTRUCTIONS

a. Prepare journal entries for the six December transactions listed above.
b. Prepare the adjusting entries necessary at December 31 to recognize interest accrued on notes receivable through year-end.
    Use one adjusting entry to accrue interest receivable on the three notes in which interest is stated separately. Use a separate adjusting entry to recognize interest revenue earned on the note with interest included in the face amount.
c. Prepare the current asset section of Hartford Building Supply's balance sheet at Dec. 31, 2001. In addition to the receivables described above, include the following items:

Cash	$ 67,900
Accounts receivable (other than described above)	250,000
Allowance for doubtful receivables (all types)	24,000
Inventory	350,000

---

*Supplemental Topic, "Notes Receivable with Interest Charges Included in the Face Amount"

In listing the company's receivables, include captions indicating any unamortized discount, unearned finance charges, and accrued interest. Do ***not,*** however, identify the individual debtors.

*PROBLEM 8-14
Long-Term Note Receivable
with Interest Included in Face
Amount
(LO 7, 8)

On April 1, 2000, Merrimac Corporation sold merchandise to Jefferson Davis Company in exchange for a note receivable due in ***one year*** (3 days of grace included). The note was drawn in the face amount of $189,200, which included the principal amount and an interest charge. In its December 31, 2000, balance sheet, Merrimac Corporation correctly presented the note receivable as follows:

Note receivable, due Mar. 31, 2001	*$189,200*	
Less: Discount on note receivable	*3,300*	*$185,900*

INSTRUCTIONS

a. Determine the monthly interest revenue earned by Merrimac Corporation from this note receivable.
b. Compute the amount of interest revenue recognized by Merrimac Corporation from the note during 2000.
c. Compute the amount of sales revenue recognized by Merrimac Corporation on April 1, 2000, when this note was received.
d. Compute the effective annual rate of interest (stated as a percentage) represented by the interest charge originally included in the face amount of the note.
e. Prepare all journal entries relating to this note in the accounting records of Merrimac Corporation for 2000 and 2001. Assume that adjusting entries are made only at December 31 and that reversing entries are not used. Assume also that the note was collected on the maturity date.

*PROBLEM 8-15
Long-Term Note Receivable
with Interest Included in Face
Amount
(LO 7, 8)

On June 1, 2000, Monitor Corporation sold merchandise to Potomac Shipping in exchange for a note receivable due in ***one year*** (3 days of grace included). The note was drawn in the face amount of $325,500, which included the principal amount and an interest charge. In its December 31, 2000, balance sheet, Monitor Corporation correctly presented the note receivable as follows:

Note receivable, due May 31, 2001	*$325,500*	
Less: Discount on note receivable	*10,625*	*$314,875*

INSTRUCTIONS

a. Determine the monthly interest revenue earned by Monitor Corporation from this note receivable.
b. Compute the amount of interest revenue recognized by Monitor Corporation from the note during 2000.
c. Compute the amount of sales revenue recognized by Monitor Corporation on June 1, 2000 when this note was received.
d. Compute the effective annual rate of interest (stated as a percentage) represented by the interest charge originally included in the face amount of the note.
e. Prepare all journal entries relating to this note in the accounting records of Monitor Corporation for 2000 and 2001. Assume that adjusting entries are made only at December 31, and that the note was collected on the maturity date.

---

*Supplemental Topic, "Notes Receivable with Interest Charges Included in the Face Amount"

Analytical and Decision Problems and Cases

A&D 8-1
All about Uncollectible Accounts
(LO 1)

The following information pertains to the accounts receivable of Sergio Company for the year ended December 31:

1. Net sales: $1,000,000
2. A recent study shows that the industry's uncollectible accounts expense over the past few years is approximately 1% of its total net sales. The company is considered as one of the most representative companies in the industry.
3. Accounts receivable aging schedule

Number of Days Outstanding	Amount	Percentage Considered Uncollectible
1–30	$ 70,000	0%
31–60	30,000	20%
61–90	20,000	40%
91 and over	6,000	50%
Total accounts receivable balance	$126,000	

4. Details of the Allowance for Doubtful Accounts (the entry to record the uncollectible accounts expense for the year is not shown but is included in the December 31 balance).

	Allowance for Doubtful Accounts		
		January 1, balance	8,210
June 10	810	September 30	260
		December 31, balance	17,000

INSTRUCTIONS

a. What approach of estimating uncollectible accounts expense is used by the company? Explain.
b. Based on the information in the Allowance for Doubtful Accounts, record the two transactions that occurred during the year (in general journal format).
c. Compute the amount of uncollectible accounts expense for the year.
d. Prepare an adjusting entry to record the uncollectible accounts expense for the year.
e. What would the amount be for the entry in **d** if an equally acceptable alternative approach for estimating uncollectible accounts expense were used?

A&D 8-2
Which Approach for Credit Losses Did We Use?
(LO 1)

The controller for Naturejoy Inc. is in the process of computing the uncollectible accounts expense for 2001. Unfortunately, a computer virus attacked Naturejoy's accounting system one night and destroyed the information regarding the approach that Naturejoy has consistently used for computing the uncollectible accounts expenses for the past three years. However, the following information is provided by the credit manager.

	1998	1999	2000
Accounts receivable, December 31	$136,000	$184,000	$166,000
Allowance for doubtful accounts			
(credit balance), December 31	37,600	24,000	36,800
Accounts receivable, written off during the year	1,600	40,000	11,200
Sales: cash	480,000	648,000	560,000
credit	720,000	880,000	800,000

The credit manager explains that the large write off in 1999 was due to an unexpected bankruptcy of a major customer even though the age distribution of accounts receivable has been very consistent over the past three years.

INSTRUCTIONS

The controller wants you to determine the approach that Naturejoy has used for computing the uncollectible accounts expense for the past three years so that he can use it for 2001 to comply with the accounting principle of consistency.

A&D 8-3
If Things Get Any Better, We'll Be Broke
(LO 1, 2, 3, 4, 6)

Loud Max, Inc., sells stereo equipment. Traditionally, the company's sales have fallen into the following categories: cash sales, 25%; customers using national credit cards, 35%; sales on account (due in 30 days), 40%. With these policies, the company earned a modest profit, and monthly cash receipts exceeded monthly cash payments by a comfortable margin. Uncollectible accounts expense was approximately 1% of net sales. (The company uses the direct write-off method in accounting for uncollectible accounts receivable.)

Two months ago, the company initiated a new credit policy that it calls "Double Zero." Customers may purchase merchandise on account, with no down payment and no interest charges. The accounts are collected in 12 monthly payments of equal amounts.

The plan has proven quite popular with customers, and monthly sales have increased dramatically. Despite the increase in sales, however, Loud Max is experiencing cash flow problems—it hasn't been generating enough cash to pay its suppliers, most of which require payment within 30 days.

The company's bookkeeper has prepared the following analysis of monthly operating results:

	Before Double Zero	Last Month
Sales:		
Cash	$12,500	$ 5,000
National credit card	17,500	10,000
30-day accounts	20,000	–0–
Double Zero accounts	–0–	75,000
Total monthly sales	$50,000	$ 90,000
Cost of goods sold and expenses	40,000	65,000
Net income	$10,000	$ 25,000
Cash receipts:		
Cash sales	$12,500	$5,000
National credit card companies	17,500	10,000
30-day accounts	19,500	–0–
Double Zero accounts	–0–	11,250
Total monthly cash receipts	$49,500	$ 26,250
Accounts written off as uncollectible	$ 500	$ –0–
Accounts receivable at month-end	$20,000	$122,000

The bookkeeper offers the following assessment: "Double Zero is killing us. Since we started that plan, our accounts receivable have increased more than six-fold, and they're still growing. We can't afford to carry such a large nonproductive asset on our books. Our cash receipts are down to nearly half of what they used to be. If we don't go back to more cash sales and receivables that can be collected more quickly, we'll become insolvent."

Maxwell "Loud Max" Swartz, founder and chief executive officer, shouts back: "Why do you say that our accounts receivable are nonproductive? They're the most productive asset we have! Since we started Double Zero, our sales have nearly doubled, our profits have more than doubled, and our uncollectible accounts expense has dropped to nothing!"

INSTRUCTIONS

a. Is it logical that the Double Zero plan is causing sales and profits to increase while also causing a decline in cash receipts? Explain.

b. Why has the uncollectible accounts expense dropped to zero? What would you expect to happen to the company's uncollectible accounts expense in the future—say, next year? Why?

c. Do you think that the reduction in monthly cash receipts is permanent or temporary? Explain.

d. In what sense are the company's accounts receivable a "nonproductive" asset?

e. Suggest several ways that Loud Max (the company) may be able to generate the cash it needs to pay its bills without terminating the Double Zero plan.

f. Would you recommend that the company continue offering Double Zero financing, or should it return to the use of 30-day accounts? Explain the reasons for your answer and identify any unresolved factors that might cause you to change this opinion in the future.

*A&D 8-4
How Much Is the "True" Net Income?
(LO 1, 2, 8)

Record House and Concert Sound are two similar companies engaged in selling stereo equipment to the public. Customers may pay cash, purchase on 30-day accounts, or make instalment payments over a 36-month period. The instalment receivables include a three-year interest charge in the face amount of the contract. Condensed income statements prepared by the companies for their first year of operations follow:

	Record House	Concert Sound
Sales	$387,000	$288,000
Cost of goods sold	210,000	192,000
Gross profit	$177,000	$ 96,000
Operating expenses	63,000	60,000
Operating income	$114,000	$ 36,000
Interest revenue	-0-	10,800
Net income	$114,000	$ 46,800

When Record House makes a sale of stereo equipment on the instalment plan it immediately credits the Sales account with the face amount of the instalment receivable, which includes interest charges. The interest charges included in Record House's instalment receivables originating in the first year amount to $72,000, of which $52,000 is unearned at the end of the first year. Record House uses the direct charge-off method to recognize uncollectible accounts expense. During the year, accounts receivable of $2,100 were written off as uncollectible, but no entry was made for $37,200 of accounts estimated to be uncollectible at year-end.

Concert Sound records sales revenue equal to the present value of its instalment receivables and recognizes the interest earned during the year as interest revenue. Concert Sound provides for uncollectible accounts by the allowance method. The company wrote off $6,180 of its uncollectible accounts during the year and estimated its uncollectible accounts to be $11,100 at year end and this amount appeared to be adequate.

INSTRUCTIONS

a. Identify the accounting principles that have been violated by one of the companies and determine the dollar effect of each violation on its reported net income. Also show the net income after the corrections.

---

*Supplemental Topic, "Notes Receivable with Interest Charges Included in the Face Amount"

b. Based on the information in **a,** what do you believe to be the key factor responsible for making one of these companies more profitable than the other? What corrective action would you recommend be taken by the less profitable company to improve future performance?

Answers to Self-Test Questions

1. b   **2.** a   **3.** d   **4.** b   **5.** c [($2,700 ÷ 2 months) × 6 months].

CHAPTER 9

Inventories and the Cost of Goods Sold

Inventory is the most costly asset that many companies own. And its cost can be measured in several different ways, with very different effects upon the amounts of current assets, gross profit, and net income. In evaluating the financial position or the profitability of a business, one of your first questions should be, "How do they value their inventory?"

1. In a perpetual inventory system, determine the cost of goods sold using (a) specific identification, (b) average cost, (c) FIFO, and (d) LIFO. Discuss the advantages and shortcomings of each method.
2. Explain the need for taking a physical inventory.
3. Record shrinkage losses and other year-end adjustments to inventory.
4. In a periodic inventory system, determine the ending inventory and cost of goods sold using (a) specific identification, (b) average cost, (c) FIFO, and (d) LIFO.
5. Explain the effects of errors in inventory valuation upon the income statement.
6. Estimate the cost of goods sold and ending inventory by the gross profit method and by the retail method.
7. Compute the inventory turnover rate and explain its uses.
8. Identify several factors that management should consider in determining the optimal size of the company's inventory.

Inventory Defined

One of the largest current assets of a retail store or of a wholesale business is the *inventory* of merchandise. The sale of this merchandise is the major source of revenue. In a merchandising company, the inventory consists of all goods owned and held for sale to customers. Inventory is converted into cash within the company's *operating cycle* and, therefore, is regarded as a current asset.[1] In the balance sheet, inventory is listed immediately after accounts receivable, because, with the exception of cash sales, it is just one step further removed from conversion into cash than are the accounts receivable.

CASE IN POINT Examples from recent balance sheets of large corporations:

Corporation	Current Assets	Dollars in Millions
Loblaw Companies Limited:	Cash and short-term investments	$ 776
	Accounts receivable	150
	Inventories	707
Quebecor Inc.:	Cash	$ 38
	Accounts Receivable	1,248
	Inventories*	754
*Disclosed in a note:	Raw materials and supplies	$ 447
	Work in process	134
	Finished goods	173
		$ 754

---

[1] As explained in Chapter 5, the *operating cycle* of a merchandising business is the period of time required to convert cash into inventory, inventory into accounts receivable, and these accounts receivable into cash. Assets expected to be converted into cash within one year or the operating cycle, whichever is longer, are regarded as current assets.

In a merchandising company, all of the inventory is purchased in a ready-to-sell condition. A manufacturing company, however, has three types of inventory: (1) *finished goods,* which are ready to sell; (2) *work in process,* which are goods in the process of being manufactured; and (3) *direct or raw materials,* which are the raw materials and component parts used in the manufacture of finished products. All three classes of inventory are included in the current asset section of the balance sheet.[2]

THE FLOW OF INVENTORY COSTS

Inventory is an asset and—like most other assets—usually is shown in the balance sheet at its cost.[3] As items are sold from this inventory, their costs are removed from the balance sheet and transferred into the cost of goods sold, which is offset against sales revenue in the income statement. This "flow of costs" is illustrated in the following diagram:

"Flow" of costs through financial statements

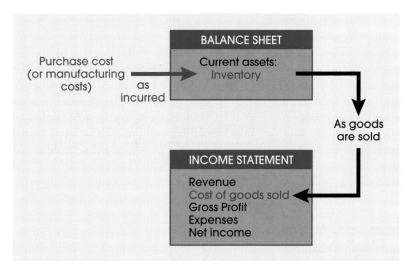

In a perpetual inventory system, entries in the accounting records parallel this flow of costs. When merchandise is purchased, its cost (net of allowable cash discounts) is debited to the asset account Inventory. As the merchandise is sold, its cost is removed from the Inventory account and debited to the Cost of Goods Sold account.

The valuation of inventory and of the cost of goods sold are of critical importance to managers and to users of financial statements. In most cases, inventory is a company's largest current asset, and the cost of goods sold is its largest expense. These two accounts have a significant effect upon the financial statement subtotals and ratios used in evaluating the solvency and profitability of the business.

---

[2]In a manufacturing company, the manufacturing process is part of the operating cycle. Therefore, direct materials and work in process are considered current assets even if completion of the manufacturing process requires more than one year.
[3]Some companies deal in inventories that can be sold in a worldwide market at quoted market prices. Examples include mutual funds, stock brokerages, and companies that deal in commodities such as agricultural crops or precious metals. Often these companies value their inventories at market price, rather than at cost. Our discussions in this chapter are directed to the far more common situation in which inventories are valued at cost.

Several different methods of "pricing" inventory and of measuring the cost of goods sold are acceptable under generally accepted accounting principles. These different methods may produce significantly different results in a company's financial statements. Therefore, managers and investors alike should understand the usual effects of the different inventory valuation methods.

Which Unit Did We Sell? Does It Really Matter?

Purchases of merchandise are recorded in the same manner under all of the inventory valuation methods. The differences in these methods lie in determining **which costs** should be removed from the Inventory account when merchandise is sold.

We illustrated the basic entries relating to purchases and sales of merchandise in Chapter 5. In that introductory discussion, however, we made a simplifying assumption: all of the units in inventory had been acquired at the same unit cost. In practice, a company often has in its inventory units of a given product that were acquired at **different costs.** Acquisition costs may vary because the units were purchased at different dates, or from different suppliers.

When identical units of inventory have different unit costs, a question naturally arises as to **which of these costs** should be used in recording sales transactions.

Data for an Illustration

To illustrate the alternative methods of measuring the cost of goods sold, assume that Mead Electric Company sells electrical equipment and supplies. Included in the company's inventory are five Elco AC-40 generators. These generators are identical; however, two were purchased on January 5 at a per-unit cost of **$1,000,** and the other three were purchased a month later, shortly after Elco had announced a price increase, at a per unit cost of **$1,200.** These purchases are reflected in Mead's inventory subsidiary ledger as shown below:

Inventory subsidiary ledger record

ITEM Elco AC-40 PRIMARY SUPPLIER Elco Manufacturing
DESCRIPTION Portable generator SECONDARY SUPPLIER Vegas Wholesale Ltd.
LOCATION Daily St. warehouse INVENTORY LEVEL: MIN: 2 MAX: 5

	Purchased			Sold			Balance		
Date	Units	Unit Cost	Total	Units	Unit Cost	Cost of Goods Sold	Units	Unit Cost	Total
Jan. 5	2	$1,000	$2,000				2	$1,000	$2,000
Feb. 5	3	1,200	3,600				2	1,000	
							3	1,200	5,600

Notice that on February 5, the balance columns contain two "layers" of unit cost information, representing the units purchased at the two different unit costs. A new **cost layer** is created whenever units are acquired at a different per-unit cost. (As the units comprising a cost layer are sold, the layer is eliminated from the inventory. Therefore, a business is unlikely to have more than three or four cost layers in its inventory at any given time.)

Now assume that on March 1, Mead sells one of these Elco generators to Boulder Construction Company for $1,800, cash. What cost should be removed from the Inventory account and recognized as the cost of goods sold—$1,000 or $1,200?

In answering such questions, accountants may use an approach called **specific identification**, or they may adopt a **cost flow assumption**. Either of these approaches is acceptable. Once an approach has been selected, however, it should be ***applied consistently*** in accounting for all sales of this particular type of merchandise.

Specific Identification

LO 1: In a perpetual inventory system, determine the cost of goods sold using (a) specific identification, (b) average cost, (c) FIFO, and (d) LIFO. Discuss the advantages and shortcomings of each method.

The specific identification method can be used only when the actual costs of individual units of merchandise can be determined from the accounting records. For example, each of the generators in Mead's inventory may have an identification number, and these numbers may appear on the purchase invoices. With this identification number, Mead's accounting department can determine whether the generator sold to Boulder Construction had cost $1,000 or $1,200. The ***actual cost*** of this particular unit then is used in recording the cost of goods sold.

Cost Flow Assumptions

If the items in inventory are ***homogeneous*** in nature (identical, except for insignificant differences), it is ***not appropriate*** for the seller to use the specific identification method. Rather, the seller should follow the more convenient practice of using a ***cost flow assumption.*** (In practice, the phrase "cost flow assumption" often is shortened to "flow assumption.")

When a flow assumption is in use, the seller simply makes an ***assumption*** as to the sequence in which units are withdrawn from inventory. For example, the seller might assume that the oldest merchandise always is sold first, or that the most recently purchased items are the first to be sold.

Three flow assumptions are in widespread use:

1. **Average cost**. This assumption values all merchandise—units sold and units remaining in inventory—at the ***average*** per-unit cost. (In effect, the average-cost method assumes that units are withdrawn from the inventory in random order.)
2. **First-in, first-out (FIFO)**. As the name implies, FIFO involves the assumption that goods sold are the ***first*** units that were

purchased—that is, the ***oldest*** goods on hand. Thus, the remaining inventory is comprised of the most recent purchases.

3. **Last-in, first-out (LIFO).** Under LIFO, the units sold are assumed to be those **most recently** acquired. The remaining inventory, therefore, is assumed to consist of the earliest purchases.

The cost flow assumption selected by a company ***need not*** correspond to the actual physical movement of the company's merchandise. When the units of merchandise are identical (or nearly identical), it ***does not matter*** which units are delivered to the customer in a particular sales transaction. Therefore, in measuring the income of a business that sells units of identical merchandise, accountants consider the flow of ***costs*** to be more important than the physical flow of the merchandise.

The use of a flow assumption ***eliminates the need for separately identifying each unit sold and looking up its actual cost.*** Experience has shown that these flow assumptions provide useful and reliable measurements of the cost of goods sold, as long as they are applied consistently to all sales of the particular type of merchandise.

Average-Cost Method

When the average-cost method is in use, the ***average cost*** of all units in the inventory is computed after every purchase. This average cost is computed by dividing the total cost of goods available for sale by the number of units in inventory. As the average cost may change following each purchase, this method also is called ***moving average.***

As of January 5, Mead has only two Elco generators in its inventory, each acquired at a purchase cost of $1,000. Therefore, the average cost is $1,000 per unit. After the purchase on February 5, Mead has five Elco generators in inventory, acquired at a total cost of $5,600 (2 units @ $1,000, plus 3 units @ $1,200 = $5,600). Therefore, the ***average*** per-unit cost now is ***$1,120*** ($5,600 ÷ 5 units = $1,120).

On March 1, two entries are made to record the sale of one of these generators to Boulder Construction for $1,800. The first recognizes the revenue from this sale, and the second recognizes the cost of the goods sold. These entries follow, with the cost of goods sold measured by the average-cost method:

Cash	*1,800*	
Sales		*1,800*
To record the sale of one Elco AC-40 generator sold for cash. ...		

Cost of Goods Sold	*1,120*	
Inventory		*1,120*
To record the cost of one Elco AC-40 generator sold to Boulder Construction. Cost determined by the average-cost method.		

(The entry to recognize the $1,800 in sales revenue remains the same, regardless of the inventory method in use. Therefore, we will not repeat this entry in our illustrations of the other cost flow assumptions.)

When the average-cost method is in use, the inventory subsidiary ledger is modified slightly from the format illustrated on page 471. Following the sale on March 1, Mead's subsidiary ledger card for Elco generators will appear as follows, modified to show the average unit cost.

Inventory subsidiary record—average cost basis

	Purchased			Sold			Balance		
Date	Units	Unit Cost	Total	Units	Average Unit Cost	Cost of Goods Sold	Units	Average Unit Cost	Total
Jan. 5	2	$1,000	$2,000				2	$1,000	$2,000
Feb. 5	3	1,200	3,600				5	1,120*	5,600
Mar. 1				1	$1,120	$1,120	4	1,120	4,480

*$5,600 total cost ÷ 5 units = $1,120.

Notice that the unit cost column for purchases still shows actual unit costs—$1,000 and $1,200. The unit cost columns relating to sales and to the remaining inventory, however, show the **average unit cost** ($5,600 total ÷ 5 units = $1,120). As all units are valued at this same average cost, the inventory has only one cost layer.

Under the average-cost assumption, all items in inventory are assigned the **same** per-unit cost (the average cost). Hence, it does not matter which units are sold; the cost of goods sold always is based upon the current average unit cost. When one generator is sold on March 1, the cost of goods sold is $1,120; if four generators were sold on this date, the cost of goods sold would be $4,480 (4 units × $1,120 per unit).

First-In, First-Out Method

The first-in, first-out method, often called **FIFO,** is based upon the assumption that the **first merchandise purchased is the first merchandise sold.** Thus, the accountant for Mead Electric would assume that the generator sold on March 1 was one of those purchased on **January 5.** The entry to record the cost of goods sold would be:

Cost of Goods Sold   1,000
     Inventory   1,000
To record the cost of one Elco AC-40 generator sold to Boulder
Construction. Cost determined by the FIFO flow assumption.

Following this sale, Mead's inventory ledger would appear as follows:

Inventory subsidiary
record—FIFO basis

	Purchased			Sold			Balance		
Date	Units	Unit Cost	Total	Units	Unit Cost	Cost of Goods Sold	Units	Unit Cost	Total
Jan. 5	2	$1,000	$2,000				2	$1,000	$2,000
Feb. 5	3	1,200	3,600				2	1,000	
							3	1,200	5,600
Mar. 1				1	$1,000	$1,000	1	1,000	
							3	1,200	4,600

Notice that FIFO uses actual purchase costs, rather than an average cost. Thus, if merchandise has been purchased at several different costs, the inventory will include several different cost layers. The cost of goods sold for a given sales transaction also may involve several different cost layers. To illustrate, assume that Mead had sold *four* generators to Boulder Construction, instead of only one. Under the FIFO flow assumption, Mead would assume that it first sold the two generators purchased on January 5, and then two of those purchased on February 5. Thus, the total cost of goods sold ($4,400) would include items at *two different unit costs,* as shown below:

2 generators from January 5 purchase @ $1,000 .... $2,000
2 generators from February 5 purchase @ $1,200 2,400
Total cost of goods sold (4 units) $4,400

As the cost of goods sold always is recorded at the oldest available purchase costs, the units remaining in inventory are valued at the more recent acquisition costs.

Last-In, First-Out Method

The last-in, first-out method, commonly known as *LIFO,* is one of the most interesting methods of determining the cost of goods sold and valuing inventory. As the name suggests, the *most recently* purchased merchandise (the "last-in") is assumed to be sold first. If Mead were using the LIFO method, it would assume that the generator sold on March 1 was one of those acquired on *February 5,* the most recent purchase date. Thus, the cost transferred from inventory to the cost of goods sold would be *$1,200.*

The journal entry to record the cost of goods sold is illustrated below, along with the inventory subsidiary ledger record after this entry has been posted:

Cost of Goods Sold 1,200
    Inventory 1,200
*To record the cost of one Elco AC-40 generator sold to Boulder
Construction. Cost determined by the LIFO flow assumption.*

Inventory subsidiary
record—LIFO basis

	Purchased			Sold			Balance		
Date	Units	Unit Cost	Total	Units	Unit Cost	Cost of Goods Sold	Units	Unit Cost	Total
Jan. 5	2	$1,000	$2,000				2	$1,000	$2,000
Feb. 5	3	1,200	3,600				2	1,000	
							3	1,200	5,600
Mar. 1				1	$1,200	$1,200	2	1,000	
							2	1,200	4,400

The LIFO method uses actual purchase costs, rather than an average cost. Thus, the inventory may have several different cost layers. If a sale includes more units than are included in the most recent cost layer, some of the goods sold are assumed to come from the next most recent layer. For example, if Mead had sold four generators (instead of one) on March 1, the cost of goods sold determined under the LIFO assumption would be $4,600, as shown below:

3 generators from February 5 purchase @ $1,200 . . . . $3,600
1 generator from January 5 purchase @ $1,000   1,000
Total cost of goods sold (4 units) $4,600

As LIFO transfers the most recent purchase costs to the cost of goods sold, the goods remaining in inventory are valued at the oldest acquisition costs.

Evaluation of the Methods

All three of the cost flow assumptions described above are acceptable for use in financial statements. As we have explained, it is not necessary that the physical flow of merchandise correspond to the cost flow assumption. Different flow assumptions may be used for different types of inventory.

CASE IN POINT   In a recent survey of 129 Canadian companies, the most common methods of valuing inventory at cost are first-in, first-out and average cost, with last-in, first-out as a distant third, and specific identification as a distant fourth.[4]

The only requirement for using a flow assumption is that the units to which the assumption is applied should be ***homogeneous*** in nature—that is, nearly identical to one another. If each unit is unique, the specific identification method is needed in order to achieve a proper matching of sales revenue with the cost of goods sold.

[4]Clarence Byrd and Ida Chen, *Financial Reporting in Canada,* Twenty-second Edition (CICA Toronto, 1997), p. 168.

As discussed below, each inventory valuation method has certain advantages and shortcomings. In the final analysis, the selection of inventory valuation methods is a managerial decision. However, the method (or methods) used in financial statements always should be disclosed in notes accompanying the statements.

Specific Identification   The specific identification method is best suited to inventories of high-priced, low-volume, non-homogeneous items. This is the only method that exactly parallels the physical flow of the merchandise. If each item in the inventory is unique, as in the case of valuable paintings, custom jewellery, and most real estate, specific identification is clearly the logical choice.

The specific identification method has an intuitive appeal, because it assigns actual purchase costs to the specific units of merchandise sold or in inventory. However, when the units in inventory are identical (or nearly identical), the specific identification method may produce ***misleading results*** by implying differences in value that—under current market conditions—do not exist.

As an example, assume that a coal dealer has purchased 100 tonnes of coal at a cost of $60 per tonne. A short time later, the company purchases another 100 tonnes of the ***same grade*** of coal—but this time, the cost is $80 per tonne. The two purchases are in separate piles; thus, it would be possible for the company to use the specific identification method in accounting for sales.

Assume now that the company has an opportunity to sell 10 tonnes of coal at a retail price of $120 per tonne. Does it really matter from which pile this coal is removed? The answer is ***no;*** the coal is a homogeneous product. Under current market conditions, the coal in each pile is equally valuable. To imply that it is more profitable to sell coal from one pile rather than the other is an argument of questionable logic.

Average Cost   Identical items will have the same accounting values only under the average-cost method. Assume for example that a hardware store sells a given size nail for 65 cents per kilogram. The hardware store buys the nails in 100-kilogram quantities at different times at prices ranging from 40 to 50 cents per kilogram. Several hundred kilograms of nails are always on hand, stored in a large bin. The average-cost method properly recognizes that when a customer buys a kilogram of nails it is not necessary to know exactly which nails the customer selected from the bin in order to measure the cost of goods sold. Therefore, the average-cost method avoids the shortcomings of the specific identification method. It is not necessary to keep track of the specific items sold and of those still in inventory. Also, it is not possible to manipulate income merely by selecting the specific items to be delivered to customers.

A shortcoming in the average-cost method is that changes in current replacement costs of inventory are concealed because these costs are averaged with older costs. Thus, neither the valuation of ending inventory nor the cost of goods sold will quickly reflect changes in the current replacement cost of merchandise.

First-In, First-Out The distinguishing characteristic of the FIFO method is that the oldest purchase costs are transferred to the cost of goods sold, while the most recent costs remain in inventory.

Over the last 50 years, we have lived in an inflationary economy, which means that most prices tend to rise over time. When purchase costs are rising, the FIFO method assigns **lower** (older) costs to the cost of goods sold and the higher (more recent) costs to the goods remaining in inventory.

By assigning lower costs to the cost of goods sold, FIFO usually causes a business to report somewhat **higher profits** than would be reported under the other inventory valuation methods. Some companies favour the FIFO method for financial reporting purposes, because their goal is to report the highest net income possible.

Some accountants and decision makers believe that FIFO tends to **overstate** a company's profitability. Revenue is based upon current market conditions. By offsetting this revenue with a cost of goods sold based upon older (and lower) prices, gross profits may be overstated consistently.

A conceptual advantage of the FIFO method is that inventory is valued at recent purchase costs. Therefore, this asset appears in the balance sheet at an amount closely approximating its current replacement cost.

Last-In, First-Out The LIFO method is the exact opposite of FIFO. Under LIFO, the most recent purchase costs are transferred to cost of goods sold, while the oldest purchase costs remain in inventory.

Supporters of the LIFO method contend that the measurement of income should be based upon **current market conditions.** Therefore, current sales revenue should be offset by the **current** cost of the merchandise sold. Under the LIFO method, the costs assigned to the cost of goods sold are relatively current, because they stem from the most recent purchases. Under the FIFO method, on the other hand, the cost of goods sold is based upon "older" costs.

Income tax considerations, however, provide the principal reason for the popularity of the LIFO methods in the United States. Remember that the LIFO method transfers the most recent purchase costs to the cost of goods sold. In the common situation of rising prices, these "most recent" costs are also the highest costs. By reporting a higher cost of goods sold than results from the other inventory valuation methods, the LIFO method usually results in a **lower income for tax purposes.** In short, if purchase costs are rising, **a company in the United States** can reduce the amount of its income tax obligation by using the LIFO method in its income tax returns. Consequently, many companies in the United States use LIFO in their income tax returns. However, income tax regulations allow a corporation to use LIFO in its income tax return only if the company also uses LIFO in its financial statements. Thus, income tax considerations often provide an important reason for selecting the LIFO method.

However, the Canadian situation for LIFO is quite different from that for the United States. **In Canada, LIFO is not acceptable for income tax purposes.** This explains why only a small number of Canadian companies use LIFO.[5]

---

[5]Op. cit., *Financial Reporting in Canada,* p. 168. However, Shell Canada Limited, one of the largest corporations in Canada, uses LIFO.

There is one significant shortcoming to the LIFO method. The valuation of the asset inventory is based upon the company's "oldest" purchase costs. After the company has been in business for many years, these "oldest" costs may greatly understate the current replacement cost of the inventory. Thus, when an inventory is valued by the LIFO method, the company also should disclose the current replacement cost of the inventory in a note to the financial statements.

During periods of rising inventory replacement costs, the LIFO method results in the lowest valuation of inventory and measurement of net income. Therefore, LIFO is regarded as the most *"conservative"* of the inventory pricing methods. FIFO, on the other hand, is the "least conservative" method.[6]

Do Inventory Methods Really Affect Performance?

The answer to this question is *no.*

During a period of rising prices, a company might *report* higher net income by using FIFO instead of LIFO. But the company would not really *be* any more profitable. An inventory valuation method affects only the *allocation of costs* between the Inventory account and the Cost of Goods Sold account. It has *no effect* upon the total costs actually *incurred* in purchasing or manufacturing inventory. Differences in the profitability reported under different inventory methods exist "only on paper."

In the United States, LIFO is allowed for tax purposes. Thus, the inventory method in use *does* affect the amount of income taxes owed. To the extent that an inventory method reduces these taxes, it *does* increase profitability.

The table on the following page summarizes characteristics of the basic inventory valuation methods.

The Principle of Consistency

The principle of **consistency** is one of the basic concepts underlying reliable financial statements. This principle means that once a company has adopted a particular accounting method, it should *follow that method consistently,* rather than switch methods from one year to the next. Thus, once a company has adopted a particular inventory flow assumption (or the specific identification method), it should continue to apply that assumption to all sales of that type of merchandise.

The principle of consistency does *not* prohibit a company from *ever* changing its accounting methods. A company may change its method when the circumstances warrant such a change.[7] If a change is made, however, the reasons for the change must be explained, and the effects of the change upon the company's net income must be fully disclosed.

---

[6]During a prolonged period of *declining* inventory replacement costs, this situation reverses: FIFO becomes the most conservative method, and LIFO the least conservative.
[7]CICA, *CICA Handbook* (Toronto), section 3030.01.

Inventory Valuation Methods: A Summary

Valuation Method	Costs Allocated to:		Comments
	Cost of Goods Sold	Inventory	
Specific identification	Actual costs of the units sold	Actual cost of units remaining	• Parallels physical flow • Logical method when units are unique • May be misleading when the units are identical
Flow assumptions (acceptable only for an inventory of homogeneous units): Average cost	Number of units sold, times the average unit cost	Number of units on hand, times the average unit cost	• Assigns all units the same average unit cost • Current costs are averaged in with older costs • Inventory not at current costs
First-in, first-out (FIFO)	Costs of earliest purchases on hand immediately prior to the sale (first-in, first-out)	Costs of most recently purchased units	• Cost of goods sold is based on older costs • Inventory valued at current costs • May overstate income during periods of rising prices
Last-in, first-out (LIFO)	Cost of most recently purchased units (last-in, first-out)	Costs of earliest purchases (assumed still to be in inventory)	• Cost of goods sold shown at recent prices • Inventory shown at old (and perhaps out-of-date) costs • Most conservative method during periods of rising prices

Just-in-Time (JIT) Inventory Systems

In recent years, much attention has been paid to the **just-in-time** inventory concept in manufacturing operations. The phrase "just-in-time" usually means that purchases of direct materials arrive just in time for use in the manufacturing process—often within a few hours of the time they are scheduled for use. A second application of the just-in-time concept is completing the manufacturing process just in time to ship the finished goods to customers.

One advantage of a just-in-time system lies in reducing the amount of money "tied-up" in inventories of direct materials and finished goods. Also, the manufacturing company does not need to maintain large inventory storage facilities. A disadvantage of a just-in-time system is that a delay in the arrival of direct materials may bring manufacturing operations to a halt. Therefore, just-in-time scheduling of incoming direct materials is feasible only when the suppliers—and the transportation systems—are highly reliable.

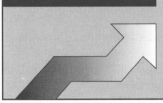

CASE IN POINT One of the pioneers of just-in-time manufacturing is Toyota, a Japanese automaker. Toyota's main plant is located in an area of Japan called "Toyota City." Many of the company's suppliers of direct materials also are located in Toyota City and produce materials primarily for Toyota. Thus, the suppliers' economic survival depends upon meeting their delivery schedules at the Toyota plant.

Although a just-in-time system reduces the size of a company's inventories, it does not eliminate them entirely. A recent annual report of Toyota, for example, shows inventories in excess of *$3 billion.* (Toyota values some of these inventories by the specific identification method, and others by LIFO.)

The concept of minimizing inventories applies more to manufacturing operations than to retailers. Ideally, manufacturers have buyers "lined up" for their merchandise even before the goods are produced. Many retailers, in contrast, want to offer their customers a large selection of in-stock merchandise—which means a big inventory.

The just-in-time concept actually involves much more than minimizing the size of inventories. It has been described as the "philosophy" of constantly working to increase efficiency throughout the organization. One basic goal of an accounting system is to provide management with useful information about the efficiency—or inefficiency—of operations.

TAKING A PHYSICAL INVENTORY

LO 2: Explain the need for taking a physical inventory.

In Chapter 5, we explained the need for businesses to make a complete physical count of the merchandise on hand at least once a year. The primary reason for this procedure of "taking inventory" is to adjust the perpetual inventory records for unrecorded **shrinkage losses**, such as theft, spoilage, or breakage.

The **physical inventory** usually is taken at (or near) the end of the company's fiscal year.[8] Often a business selects a fiscal year ending in a season of low activity. For example, most large retailers use a fiscal year ending in January.

Recording Shrinkage Losses

LO 3: Record shrinkage losses and other year-end adjustments to inventory.

In most cases, the year-end physical count of the inventory reveals some shortages or damaged merchandise. The costs of missing or damaged units are removed from the inventory records using the same flow assumption as is used in recording the costs of goods sold.

To illustrate, assume that a company's inventory subsidiary ledger shows the following 158 units of a particular product in inventory at year-end:

Purchase on November 2: 8 units @ $100	$ 800
Purchase on December 10: 150 units @ $115	17,250
Total (158 units)	$18,050

A year-end physical count, however, discloses that only **148** of these units actually are on hand. Based upon this physical count, the company should adjust its inventory records to reflect the loss of 10 units.

The inventory flow assumption in use affects the measurement of shrinkage losses in the same way it affects the cost of goods sold. If the company uses **FIFO,** for example, the missing units will be valued at the oldest purchase costs shown in the inventory records. Thus, 8 of the missing units will be assumed to have cost $100 per-unit and the other 2, $115 per-unit. Under FIFO, the shrinkage loss amounts to **$1,030** (8 units @ $100 + 2 units @ $115). But if this company uses **LIFO,** the missing units all will be assumed to have come from the most recent purchase (on December 10). Therefore, the shrinkage loss amounts to **$1,150** (10 units @ $115).

If shrinkage losses are small, the costs removed from inventory may be charged (debited) directly to the Cost of Goods Sold account. If these losses are **material** in amount, the offsetting debit should be entered in a special loss account, such as Inventory Shrinkage Losses. In the income statement, a loss account is deducted from revenue in the same manner as an expense account.

Other Write-Downs of Inventory and LCM

In addition to shrinkage losses, the value of inventory may decline because the merchandise has become obsolete or is unsalable for other reasons.

---

[8]The reason for taking a physical inventory near year-end is to ensure that any shrinkage losses are reflected in the annual financial statements. The stronger the company's internal control over inventories, the further this procedure may be moved away from the balance sheet date.

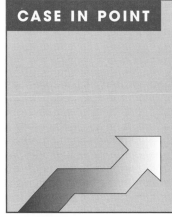

CASE IN POINT

Several years ago, a deranged individual in the United States inserted a deadly poison into a few packages of Tylenol, a widely used medication. This criminal act of "product tampering" resulted in several tragic deaths. In response, Johnson & Johnson, the maker of Tylenol, promptly recalled all packages of this product and destroyed the entire inventory. The company later reintroduced Tylenol—this time in tablet form (rather than capsules) and in a tamperproof container. Other drug manufacturers quickly followed Johnson & Johnson's lead and changed the form and the packaging of their over-the-counter products.

 The Tylenol tragedy often is studied by business managers and business students alike. The company's response is considered a classic example of fast, responsible, and effective action in a time of crisis.

If inventory has become obsolete or is otherwise unsalable, its carrying value in the accounting records should be *written down* to zero (or to its "scrap value," if any). A **write-down** of inventory reduces both the carrying value of the inventory and also the net income of the current period. The reduction in income is handled in the same manner as a shrinkage loss. If the write-down is relatively small, the loss is debited directly to the Cost of Goods Sold account. If the write-down is *material in amount,* however, it is charged to a special loss account, perhaps entitled Loss from Write-down of Inventory.

The Lower-of-Cost-and-Market (LCM) Rule An asset is an economic resource. It may be argued that no economic resource is worth more than it would cost to **replace** that resource in the open market. For this reason, accountants traditionally have valued inventory in the balance sheet at the lower of its (1) cost and (2) market value. In this context, "market value" means *current replacement cost* or *net realizable value.* Thus the inventory is valued at the lower of its purchase cost or its current replacement cost or net realizable value.

For a merchandising company, current replacement cost is the amount the concern would have to pay at the present time for the goods in question, purchased in the customary quantities through the usual sources of supply and including transportation-in. Net realizable value is the estimated selling price in the ordinary course of business less estimated costs of completion and sale such as selling expenses in a merchandising company. To avoid misunderstanding, many companies are disclosing both the cost method and the market method, such as "the lower of first-in, first-out and replacement cost," or "the lower of the average cost and net realizable value." The **lower-of-cost-and-market rule** is another example of the accounting concept of conservatism. A conservative valuation of inventory requires prompt recognition of losses, even though the exact amount of the loss cannot be conclusively determined.

The lower-of-cost-and-market rule may be applied in conjunction with any flow assumption and also with the specific identification method. If the current replacement cost or net realizable value of the ending inventory is substantially *below* the cost shown in the accounting records, the inventory is written down to the lower amount. The offsetting debit is charged to either the Cost of Goods Sold account or the Loss from Write-down of Inventory account, depending upon the materiality of the dollar amount.

In our inflationary economy, however, the lower-of-cost-and-market usually is cost, especially for companies using LIFO.[9] In their financial statements, most companies state that inventory is valued at the lower-of-cost-and-market.

CASE IN POINT

In a recent survey of 163 Canadian companies, 136 used the lower-of-cost-and-market rule for inventory valuation. The most common "market method" for valuation is net realizable value, with replacement cost as a very distant second.[10]

The Year-End Cutoff of Transactions

Making a proper **cutoff** of transactions is an essential step in the preparation of reliable financial statements. A "proper cutoff" simply means that the transactions occurring near year-end are **recorded in the correct accounting period.**

One aspect of a proper cutoff is determining that all purchases of merchandise through the end of the period are recorded in the inventory records and included in the physical count of merchandise on hand at year-end. Of equal importance is determining that the cost of all merchandise sold through the end of the period has been removed from the inventory accounts and charged to the Cost of Goods Sold. This merchandise should **not** be included in the year-end physical count.

If some sales transactions have not been recorded as of year-end, the quantities of merchandise shown in the inventory records will exceed the quantities actually on hand. When the results of the physical count are compared with the inventory records, these unrecorded sales easily could be mistaken for inventory shortages.

Making a proper cutoff may be difficult if sales transactions are occurring while the merchandise is being counted. For this reason, most businesses count their physical inventory during nonbusiness hours, even if they must shut down their sales operations for a day.

Matching Revenue and the Cost of Goods Sold   Accountants must determine that both the sales revenue and the cost of goods sold relating to sales transactions occurring near year-end are recorded in the **same** accounting period. Otherwise, the revenue and expense from these transactions will not be properly "matched" in the company's income statements.

---

[9]A notable exception is the petroleum industry, in which the replacement cost of inventory can fluctuate very quickly and in either direction. Large oil companies occasionally report LCM adjustments of several hundred million dollars in a single year.
[10]Clarence Byrd and Ida Chen, *Financial Reporting in Canada,* Twenty-second Edition (CICA Toronto, 1997), pp. 168–169.

Goods in Transit   A sale should be recorded ***when title to the merchandise passes to the buyer.*** In making a year-end cutoff of transactions, questions may arise when goods are in transit between the seller and the buyer as to which company owns the merchandise. The answer to such questions lies in the terms of shipment. If these terms are **F.O.B.** (free on board) **shipping point**, title passes at the point of shipment and the goods are the property of the buyer while in transit. If the terms of the shipment are **F.O.B. destination**, title does not pass until the shipment reaches its destination and the goods belong to the seller while in transit.

Many companies ignore these distinctions, because goods in transit always arrive within a day or two. In such cases, the amount of merchandise in transit usually is ***not material*** in dollar amount, and the company may follow the ***most convenient*** accounting procedures. It usually is most convenient to record all purchases when the inbound shipments arrive and all sales when the merchandise is shipped to the customer.

In some industries, however, goods in transit may be very material. Oil companies, for example, often have millions of dollars of inventory in transit in pipelines and supertankers. In these situations, the company must consider the terms of each shipment in recording its purchases and sales.

Periodic Inventory Systems

LO 4: In a periodic inventory system, determine the ending inventory and the cost of goods sold using (a) specific identification, (b) average cost, (c) FIFO, and (d) LIFO.

In our preceding discussions, we have emphasized the perpetual inventory system—that is, inventory records that are kept continuously up-to-date. Virtually all large business organizations use perpetual inventory systems.

Some small businesses, however, use ***periodic*** inventory systems. In a periodic inventory system, the cost of merchandise purchased during the year is debited to a ***Purchases*** account, rather than to the Inventory account. When merchandise is sold to a customer, an entry is made recognizing the sales revenue, but no entry is made to reduce the inventory account or to recognize the cost of goods sold.

The inventory on hand and the cost of goods sold for the year are not determined until year-end. At the end of the year, all goods on hand are counted and priced at cost. The cost assigned to this ending inventory is then used in computing the cost of goods sold, as shown below. (The dollar amounts are assumed for the purpose of completing the illustration.)

Inventory at the beginning of the year	$10,000
Add: Purchases during the year	80,000
Cost of goods available for sale during the year	$90,000
Less: Inventory at the end of the year	7,000
Cost of goods sold	$83,000

The only item in this computation that is kept continuously up-to-date in the accounting records is the Purchases account. The amounts of inventory at the beginning and end of the year are determined by annual physical counts.

Determining the cost of the year-end inventory involves two distinct steps: counting the merchandise and pricing the inventory, that is, determining the cost of the units on hand. Together, these procedures determine the proper valuation of inventory at cost and also the cost of goods sold.

Applying Flow Assumptions in a Periodic System   In our discussion of perpetual inventory systems, we have emphasized the costs that are transferred from inventory *to the cost of goods sold.* In a periodic system, the emphasis shifts to determining the costs that should be assigned *to inventory* at the end of the period.

To illustrate, assume that The Kitchen Counter, a retail store, uses a periodic inventory system. The year-end physical inventory indicates that 12 units of a particular model food processor are on hand. Purchases of these food processors during the year are as follows:

	Number of Units	Cost Per Unit	Total Cost
Beginning inventory	10	$ 80	$ 800
First purchase (Mar. 1)	5	90	450
Second purchase (July 2)	5	100	500
Third purchase (Oct. 1)	5	120	600
Fourth purchase (Dec. 31)	5	130	650
Available for sale	30		$3,000
Units in ending inventory	12		
Units sold	18		

This schedule shows that 30 food processors were available for sale in the course of the year, of which 12 are still on hand. Thus, 18 of these food processors apparently were sold.[11] We will now use this data to determine the cost of the year-end inventory and the cost of goods sold using the specific identification method, and the average-cost, FIFO, and LIFO flow assumptions.

Specific Identification   If specific identification is used, the company must identify the 12 food processors on hand at year-end and determine their actual costs from purchase invoices. Assume that these 12 units have an actual total cost of $1,240. The cost of goods sold then is determined by subtracting this ending inventory from the cost of goods available for sale:

Cost of goods available for sale	$3,000
Less: Ending inventory (specific identification)	1,240
Cost of goods sold	$1,760

Average Cost   The average cost is determined by dividing the total cost of goods available for sale during the year by the total number of units available for sale. Thus, the average per-unit cost is *$100* ($3,000 ÷ 30 units). Under the average-cost method, the ending inventory would be priced at $1,200 (12 units × $100 per unit), and the cost of goods sold would be *$1,800* ($3,000 cost of goods available for sale, less $1,200 in costs assigned to the ending inventory).

FIFO   Under the FIFO flow assumption, the oldest units are assumed to be the first sold. The ending inventory therefore is assumed to consist of

---

[11]The periodic inventory method does not distinguish between merchandise sold and shrinkage losses. Shrinkage losses are included automatically within the cost of goods sold.

the *most recently* acquired goods. (Remember, we are now talking about the goods *remaining in inventory,* not the goods sold.) Thus, the inventory of 12 food processors would be valued at the following costs:

5 units from the December 31 purchase @ $130	$ 650
5 units from the October 1 purchase @ $120	600
2 units from the July 2 purchase @ $100	200
Ending inventory, 12 units at FIFO cost	$1,450

The cost of goods sold would be *$1,550* ($3,000 − $1,450).

Notice that the FIFO method results in an inventory valued at relatively recent purchase costs. The cost of goods sold, however, is based upon the older acquisition costs.

LIFO   Under LIFO, the last units purchased are considered to be the first goods sold. Therefore, the ending inventory is assumed to contain the *earliest* purchases. The 12 food processors in inventory would be priced as follows:

10 units from the beginning inventory @ $80	$800
2 units from the March 1 purchase @ $90	180
Ending inventory, 12 units at LIFO cost	$980

The cost of goods sold under the LIFO method is *$2,020* ($3,000 − $980).

Notice that the cost of goods sold under LIFO is *higher* than that determined by the FIFO method ($2,020 under LIFO, as compared with $1,550 under FIFO). LIFO always results in a higher cost of goods sold when purchase costs are rising. Thus, LIFO tends to minimize reported net income during periods of rising purchase prices.

Notice also that the LIFO method may result in an ending inventory that is priced *well below* its current replacement cost.

Pricing the Year-End Inventory by Computer   If purchase records are maintained by computer, the computer can compute the value of the ending inventory automatically using any of the flow assumptions discussed above. The computer operator must only enter the number of units on hand at year-end. A computer also can apply the specific identification method, but the computer operator then must enter an identification number for each unit in the ending inventory. This is one reason why the specific identification method usually is not used for inventories consisting of a large number of low-cost items.

Comparison between Perpetual and Periodic Inventory Systems   For the FIFO and the specific identification methods, the perpetual and periodic inventory systems would both produce the same amount for cost of goods sold and for ending inventory. However, the average-cost and LIFO methods produce different amounts for cost of goods sold and for ending inventory under the perpetual and periodic inventory systems. If purchase costs are rising, the cost of goods sold for the average cost method under the perpetual inventory system will be smaller than that under the periodic inventory system. The reason is that the perpetual system computes the cost of goods sold on a moving average basis throughout the year while the periodic system computes cost of goods sold on the average cost for the whole year. Similarly, the LIFO method under the perpetual system produces a smaller amount of cost of goods sold than that under the periodic system when purchase costs are rising. Under the perpetual system, the amount transferred from inventory to cost of goods sold is done periodically throughout the year. Under the periodic system, the amount transferred from inventory to cost of goods sold is computed on a yearly basis. Consequently, certain "older" but lower purchase costs that would have been transferred to cost of goods sold under the perpetual system would remain in the ending inventory under the periodic system.

Importance of an Accurate Valuation of Inventory

The most important current assets in the balance sheets of most companies are cash, accounts receivable, and inventory. Of these assets, inventory often is the largest. It also is the only current asset for which alternative valuation methods are considered acceptable.

Because of the relatively large size of inventory, and the fact that products may be stored in many different locations, an error in inventory valuation may not be readily apparent. But in many cases, even a small error in the valuation of inventory may have a material effect upon net income. Therefore, care should be taken in counting and pricing the inventory at year-end.

An error in the valuation of inventory will affect several balance sheet measurements, including current assets, the current ratio, and total owners' equity. It also will affect key figures in the ***income statement,*** including the cost of goods sold, gross profit, and net income. And remember that the ending inventory of one year is the beginning inventory of the next. Thus, an error in inventory valuation will ***"carry over"*** into the income statement of the following year.

Effects of an Error in Valuing Ending Inventory   To illustrate, assume that some items of merchandise in a company's inventory are overlooked during the year-end physical count. As a result of this error, the ending inventory will be ***understated.*** The costs of the uncounted merchandise erroneously will be transferred out of the Inventory account and included in the cost of goods sold. This overstatement of the cost of goods sold, in turn, results in an understatement of gross profit and net income.

Inventory Errors Affect Two Years   An error in the valuation of ending inventory affects not only the financial statements of the current year, but also the income statement for the ***following*** year.

LO 5: Explain the effects of errors in inventory valuation upon the income statement.

Assume that the ending inventory in ***1999*** is ***understated*** by $10,000. As we have described above, the cost of goods sold in 1999 will be overstated by this amount, and both gross profit and net income will be ***understated.***

The ending inventory in 1999, however, becomes the ***beginning inventory*** in ***2000.*** An understatement of the beginning inventory results in an understatement of the cost of goods sold and, therefore, an ***overstatement*** of gross profit and net income in 2000.

Notice that the original error has exactly the ***opposite effects*** upon the net incomes of the two successive years. Net income was ***understated*** by the amount of the error of 1999, and ***overstated*** by the same amount in 2000. For this reason inventory errors are said to be "counterbalancing" or "self-correcting" over a two-year period.

The fact that offsetting errors occur in the financial statements of two successive years does not lessen the consequences of errors in inventory valuation. Rather, this ***exaggerates*** the misleading effects of the error upon ***trends*** in the company's performance from one year to the next.

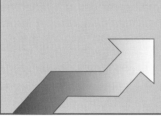

CASE IN POINT Some small businesses purposely have understated ending inventory in their income tax returns as an easy—though fraudulent—means of understating taxable income. In the following year, however, the effects of this error will reverse, and taxable income will be overstated. To avoid paying income taxes on this overstated income, the business may again understate its ending inventory, this time by an even greater amount. If this type of tax fraud continues for very long, the inventory becomes so understated that the situation becomes obvious.

Effects of Errors in Inventory Valuation: A Summary   The following table summarizes the effects of an error in the valuation of ending inventory over two successive years. In this table we indicate the effects of the error on various financial statement measurements using the code letters ***U*** (Understated), ***O*** (Overstated), and ***NE*** (No Effect). The effects of errors in the valuation of inventory are the same regardless of whether the company uses a perpetual or a periodic inventory system.

Original Error: Ending Inventory Understated

	Year of the Error	Following Year
Beginning inventory	NE	U
Cost of goods available for sale	NE	U
Ending inventory	U	NE
Cost of goods sold	O	U
Gross profit	U	O
Net income	U	O
Owner's equity at year-end	U	NE

Original Error: Ending Inventory Overstated

	Year of the Error	Following Year
Beginning inventory	NE	O
Cost of goods available for sale	NE	O
Ending inventory	O	NE
Cost of goods sold	U	O
Gross profit	O	U
Net income	O	U
Owner's equity at year-end	O	NE

Techniques for Estimating the Cost of Goods Sold and the Ending Inventory

Taking a physical inventory every month would be very expensive and time-consuming. Therefore, if a business using a periodic inventory system is to prepare monthly or quarterly financial statements, it usually *esti-mates* the amounts of its inventory and cost of goods sold. One approach to making these estimates is called the **gross profit method**; another—used primarily by retail stores—is the **retail method**.

The Gross Profit Method

LO 6: Estimate the cost of goods sold and ending inventory by the gross profit method and by the retail method.

The gross profit method is a quick, simple technique for estimating the cost of goods sold and the amount of inventory on hand. In using this method, it is assumed that the rate of gross profit earned in the preceding year will remain the same for the current year. When we know the rate of gross profit, we can divide the dollar amount of net sales into two elements: (1) the gross profit and (2) the cost of goods sold. We view net sales as 100%. If the gross profit rate, for example, is 40% of net sales, the cost of goods sold must be 60%. In other words, the cost of goods sold percentage (or **cost ratio**) is determined by deducting the gross profit rate from 100%.

When the gross profit rate is known, the ending inventory can be estimated by the following procedures:

1. Determine the *cost of goods available for sale* from the general ledger records of beginning inventory and net purchases.
2. Estimate the *cost of goods sold* by multiplying the net sales by the cost ratio.
3. Deduct the *cost of goods sold* from the *cost of goods available for sale* to find the estimated ending inventory.

To illustrate, assume that Metro Hardware has a beginning inventory of $50,000 on January 1. During the month of January, net purchases amount to $20,000 and net sales total $30,000. Assume that the company's normal gross profit rate is 40% of net sales; it follows that the cost ratio is **60%**. Using these facts, the inventory on January 31 may be estimated as follows:

Cost of goods available for sale:			
Beginning inventory, Jan. 1			*$50,000*
Purchases			*20,000*
Step 1 ...	Cost of goods available for sale		*$70,000*
	Deduct: Estimated cost of goods sold:		
	Net sales	*$30,000*	
	Cost ratio (100% − 40%)	*60%*	
Step 2 ...	Estimated cost of goods sold ($30,000 × **60%**)		*18,000*
Step 3 ...	*Estimated ending inventory, Jan. 31*		*$52,000*

The gross profit method of estimating inventory has several uses apart from the preparation of monthly financial statements. For example, if an inventory is destroyed by fire, the company must determine the amount of the inventory on hand at the date of the fire in order to file an insurance claim. The most convenient way to determine this inventory amount is often the gross profit method.

The gross profit method is also used at year-end after the taking of a physical inventory to confirm the overall reasonableness of the amount determined by the counting and pricing process.

The Retail Method

The retail method of estimating inventory and the cost of goods sold is quite similar to the gross profit method. The basic difference is that the retail method is based upon the cost ratio of the *current period,* rather than that of the prior year.

To determine the cost ratio of the current period, the business must keep track of both the cost of all goods available for sale during the period and also the *retail sales prices* assigned to these goods. To illustrate, assume that during June the cost of goods available for sale in Tennis Gallery totalled $45,000. The store had offered this merchandise for sale to its customers at retail prices totalling $100,000. The cost ratio in June was *45%* ($45,000 ÷ $100,000). This cost ratio is used to estimate the monthly cost of goods sold and the month-end inventory by the same procedures as are applied under the gross profit method.

Many retail stores also use their current cost ratio as a quick method of pricing the inventory counted at year-end. In a retail store, the retail sales price is clearly marked on the merchandise. Therefore, employees quickly can determine the retail price of the ending inventory. This retail price may be reduced to a close approximation of cost simply by multiplying by the cost ratio.

Assume, for example, that the annual physical inventory at Tennis Gallery indicates the merchandise on hand at year-end has a retail sales price of $120,000. If the cost ratio for the year has been 44%, the cost of this inventory is approximately $52,800 ($120,000 × 44%). This version of the retail method approximates valuation of the inventory at average cost.

"Textbook" Inventory Systems Can Be Modified . . . and They Often Are

In this chapter we have described the basic characteristics of the most common inventory systems. In practice, businesses often modify these systems to suit their particular needs. Some businesses also use *different inventory systems for different purposes.*

We described one modification in Chapter 5—a company that maintains very little inventory may simply charge (debit) all purchases directly to the cost of goods sold. Another common modification is to maintain perpetual inventory records showing only the *quantities* of merchandise bought and sold, with no dollar amounts. Such systems require less record keeping than a "full-blown" perpetual system, and they still provide management with useful information about sales and inventories. To generate the dollar amounts needed in financial statements, these companies might use the gross profit method, the retail method, or a periodic inventory system.

Businesses such as restaurants often update their inventory records by physically counting products on a daily or weekly basis. In effect, they use frequent periodic counts as the basis for maintaining a perpetual inventory system.

In summary, "real-world" inventory systems often differ from the illustrations in a textbook. But the underlying principles remain much the same.

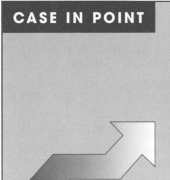

CASE IN POINT

Apple Computer maintains a perpetual inventory system. The daily entries reflect only the *quantities* of units produced and sold—not the dollar costs. Dollar amounts are computed and recorded in the inventory records at the end of the month. In transferring costs from inventory accounts to the cost of goods sold, Apple uses a FIFO flow assumption. But the inventory "cost layers" don't represent units purchased at different prices—they represent units manufactured in different months.

Sears and Wal-Mart maintain perpetual inventory records showing both quantities and dollar amounts. But the dollar amounts are recorded at *retail prices.* When cost data are needed, these companies apply cost ratios to the retail amounts.

EVALUATING THE LIQUIDITY OF INVENTORY

Inventory often is the largest of a company's current assets. But how liquid is this asset? How quickly will it be converted into cash? As a step toward answering these questions, short-term creditors often compute the **inventory turnover rate.**

Inventory Turnover Rate

LO 7: Compute the inventory turnover rate and explain its uses.

The inventory turnover rate is equal to the cost of goods sold divided by the average amount of inventory (beginning inventory plus ending inventory, divided by 2). This ratio indicates how many *times* in the course of a year the company is able to sell the amount of its average inventory. The higher this rate, the more quickly the company sells its inventory. We can also compute the *number of days* required for the company to sell its inventory by dividing 365 days by the turnover rate.

CASE IN POINT

A recent annual report of Domtar Inc. shows a cost of goods sold of $1,615 million and average inventory of $325 million. The inventory turnover rate for Domtar, therefore, is *5 to 1* ($1,615 million ÷ $325 million). To compute the number of *days* required for the company to sell its inventory, divide 365 days by the turnover rate. Thus, Domtar requires *73 days* to turn over (sell) the amount of its average inventory (365 days ÷ 5).

Users of financial statements find the inventory turnover rate useful in evaluating the liquidity of the company's inventory. In addition, managers and independent auditors use this computation to help identify inventory that is not selling well and that may have become obsolete. A declining turnover rate indicates that merchandise is not selling as quickly as it used to.

Converting the Inventory into Cash   Most businesses sell merchandise on account. Therefore, inventory often is not converted into cash as soon as it is sold. To determine how quickly inventory is converted into cash, we must combine the number of days required to *sell the inventory* with the number of days required to *collect the accounts receivable.*

Computation of the number of days required to collect accounts receivable was illustrated and explained in the preceding chapter. To review, the *accounts receivable turnover rate* is computed by dividing net sales by the average accounts receivable. The number of days required to collect these receivables then is determined by dividing 365 days by this turnover rate. Data for the Domtar annual report indicate that the company needed *46 days* (on average) to collect its accounts receivable.

Length of the Operating Cycle   The *operating cycle* of a merchandising company is the average time period between the purchase of merchandise and the conversion of this merchandise back into cash. In other words, the merchandise acquired as inventory gradually is converted into accounts receivable by selling the goods on account, and these receivables are converted into cash through the process of collection.

The operating cycle of Domtar was approximately *119 days,* computed by adding the average 73 days required to sell its inventory and the 46 days required to collect its accounts receivable from customers. From the viewpoint of short-term creditors, the shorter the operating cycle, the higher the quality of the company's current assets.

Accounting Methods Can Affect Analytical Ratios

The accounting methods selected by a company may affect the ratios and financial statement subtotals used in evaluating the company's financial position and the results of its operations. To illustrate, let us consider the effects of inventory valuation methods upon inventory turnover rates.

Assume that during a period of rising prices Alpha Company uses LIFO, whereas Beta Company uses FIFO. In all other respects, the two companies *are identical;* they have the same size inventories, and they purchase and sell the same quantities of merchandise at the same prices and on the same dates. Thus, each company *physically* "turns over" its inventory at *exactly the same rate.*

Because Alpha uses the LIFO method, however, its inventory is valued at older (and lower) costs than is the inventory of Beta Company. Also, Alpha's cost of goods sold includes more recent (and higher) costs than does Beta's. When these amounts are used in computing the inventory turnover rate (cost of goods sold divided by average inventory), Alpha *appears* to have the higher turnover rate.

We already have stated that the inventories of these two companies are turning over at exactly the same rate. Therefore, the differences in the turnover rates computed from the companies' financial statements are caused *solely by the different accounting methods used in the valuation of the companies' inventories.*

Inventory turnover is not the only ratio that will be affected. Alpha will report lower current assets than Beta and, therefore, a lower current ratio and less working capital. In addition, using LIFO will cause Alpha to report less gross profit and lower net income than Beta.

Users of financial statements must understand the typical effects of different accounting methods. Also, a financial analyst should be able to restate on a **comparable basis** the financial statements of companies that use different accounting methods. Notes accompanying the financial statements usually provide the information necessary for comparing the operating results of companies using LIFO with those of companies using the FIFO method.

Inventory Management

LO 8: Identify several factors that management should consider in determining the optimal size of the company's inventory.

How much inventory should a business keep on hand? The answer to this question is based upon many factors, including the nature of a company's business operations, the reliability and proximity of its suppliers, the physical characteristics of the inventory, marketing strategies, and management's willingness to risk the consequences of running out of merchandise or direct materials.

Inventory stored in a warehouse is an idle asset. Not only does this asset produce no revenue, it may require substantial storage and other costs.

Today, many manufacturing companies are implementing just-in-time inventory systems, designed to minimize their inventories of direct materials and finished goods. Although these systems can reduce the costs associated with carrying substantial inventories, they also involve considerable risk. As stated earlier, even a temporary delay in the arrival of key materials may bring the company's manufacturing operations to a halt.

Many retailing companies maintain large inventories to attract customers by offering them a wide selection of merchandise. Such advertising slogans as "Largest selection in town," and "Available for immediate delivery" reflect marketing strategies that involve a large inventory.

In contrast, retailers that sell merchandise tailored to customers' specifications often maintain little or no inventory. These companies do not purchase their merchandise until **after** they have an order (and usually a deposit) from their customer. In essence, these businesses have just-in-time inventory systems.

Among the advantages of maintaining a **minimum**-size inventory are:

- Less money is tied up in an asset that generates little or no revenue while it is stored in a warehouse or on a shelf. (Many companies, such as automobile dealerships, finance their purchases of inventory. Thus, a smaller inventory reduces the company's interest expense.)
- Storage and insurance costs are minimized (including the need for maintaining storage facilities).
- The risk of loss from merchandise becoming obsolete, out-of-fashion, or otherwise unsalable is held to a minimum.

On the other hand, the following considerations favour maintaining a **larger** inventory:

- A large selection of merchandise may attract more customers. For retailers, fewer sales opportunities are lost because items are temporarily "out of stock." In most cases, a large inventory is required to generate a high volume of sales in a retail business.

- Suppliers may offer substantial discounts if merchandise is purchased in large quantities. (Automobile manufacturers, for example, offer larger discounts to dealerships that purchase more cars.)
- For manufacturers, larger inventories of direct materials reduce the risk that manufacturing operations will be interrupted by shortages of key materials.

In summary, the decision as to the appropriate size of an inventory involves not only financial considerations, but also management's marketing strategy and its willingness to take risks. These issues, and the related topic of determining the optimal reorder quantity, are discussed further in later accounting courses.

End-of-Chapter Review

Key Terms Introduced or Emphasized in Chapter 9

Average-cost method (*p.472*) A method of valuing all units in the inventory at the same average per-unit cost, which is recomputed after every purchase (for perpetual inventory system) or at the end of the year (for periodic inventory system).

Consistency (in inventory valuation) (*p.479*) An accounting standard that calls for the use of the same method of inventory pricing from year to year, with full disclosure of the effects of any change in method. Intended to make financial statements comparable.

Cost flow assumptions (*p.472*) Assumptions as to the sequence in which units are removed from inventory for the purpose of sale. Need not parallel the physical movement of merchandise if the units are homogeneous.

Cost layer (*p.472*) Units of merchandise acquired at the same unit cost. An inventory comprised of several cost layers is characteristic of all inventory valuation methods except ***average cost.***

Cost ratio (*p.490*) The cost of merchandise expressed as a percentage of its retail selling price. Used in inventory estimating techniques, such as the ***gross profit method*** and the ***retail method.***

First-in, first-out (FIFO) method (*p.472*) A method of computing the cost of inventory and the cost of goods sold based on the assumption that the first merchandise acquired is the first merchandise sold, and that the ending inventory consists of the most recently acquired goods.

F.O.B. destination (*p.485*) A term meaning the seller bears the cost of shipping goods to the buyer's location. Title to the goods remains with the seller while the goods are in transit.

F.O.B. shipping point (*p.485*) The buyer of goods bears the cost of transportation from the seller's location to the buyer's location. Title to the goods passes at the point of shipment and the goods are the property of the buyer while in transit.

Gross profit method (*p.490*) A method of estimating the cost of the ending inventory based upon the assumption that the rate of gross profit remains approximately the same from year to year.

Inventory turnover rate (*p.492*) The cost of goods sold divided by the average amount of inventory. Indicates how many times the average inventory is sold during the course of the year.

Just-in-time (JIT) inventory system (*p.481*) A technique designed to minimize a company's investment in inventory. In a manufacturing company, this means receiving purchases of direct materials just in time for use in the manufacturing process, and completing the manufacture of finished goods just in time to fill existing sales orders. Just-in-time also may be described as the philosophy of constantly becoming more efficient.

Last-in, first-out (LIFO) method (*p.473*) A method of computing the cost of goods sold by use of the prices paid for the most recently acquired units. Ending inventory is valued on the basis of prices paid for the units first acquired.

Lower-of-cost-and-market (LCM) rule (*p.483*) A method of inventory pricing in which goods are valued at original cost and net realizable value or replacement cost, whichever is lower.

Physical inventory (*p.482*) A systematic count of all goods on hand, followed by the application of unit prices to the quantities counted and development of a dollar valuation of the ending inventory.

Retail method (*p.490*) A method of estimating the cost of goods sold and ending inventory. Similar to the gross profit method, except that the cost ratio is based upon current cost-to-retail price relationships rather than upon those of the prior year.

Shrinkage losses (*p.481*) Losses of inventory resulting from theft, spoilage, or breakage.

Specific identification (*p.472*) Recording as the cost of goods sold the actual costs of the specific units sold. Required when each unit in inventory is unique, but not appropriate when the inventory consists of homogeneous products.

Write-down (of an asset) (*p.483*) A reduction in the carrying value of an asset because it has become obsolete or its usefulness has otherwise been impaired. Involves a credit to the asset account, with an offsetting debit to a loss account.

DEMONSTRATION PROBLEM

The Audiophile sells high-performance stereo equipment. Ottawa Acoustic recently introduced the Carnegie-440, a state-of-the-art speaker system. During the current year, The Audiophile purchased 9 of these speaker systems at the following dates and acquisition costs:

Date	Units Purchased	Unit Cost	Total Cost
Oct. 1	2	$3,000	$ 6,000
Nov. 17	3	3,200	9,600
Dec. 1	4	3,250	13,000
Available for sale during the year	9		$28,600

On **November 21,** The Audiophile sold 4 of these speaker systems to the Metro Symphony. The other 5 Carnegie-440s remained in inventory at December 31.

INSTRUCTIONS

Assume that The Audiophile uses a **perpetual inventory system.** Compute (1) the cost of goods sold relating to the sale of Carnegie-440 speakers to the Metro Symphony, and (2) the ending inventory of these speakers at December 31, using each of the following flow assumptions:

   a. Average cost
   b. First-in, first-out (FIFO)
   c. Last-in, first-out (LIFO)

Show the number of units and the unit costs of the cost layers comprising the cost of goods sold and the ending inventory.

SOLUTION TO DEMONSTRATION PROBLEM

a. (1) Cost of goods sold (at average cost):
    Average unit cost at Nov. 21
      (($6,000 + $9,600) ÷ 5 units) . . . . $ 3,120
      Cost of goods sold (4 units × $3,120 per unit) $12,480

   (2) Inventory at Dec. 31 (at average cost):
    Average unit cost at Dec. 31:
      Units remaining after sale of November 21
        (1 unit @ $3,120) . . . . $ 3,120
        Units purchased on Dec. 1 (4 units @ $3,250)   13,000
      Total cost of 5 units in inventory $16,120
      Average unit cost at Dec. 31 . . . . $ 3,224
      Inventory at Dec. 31 (5 units × $3,224 per unit) $16,120

b. (1) Cost of goods sold (FIFO basis): (2 units @ $3,000 +
      2 units @ $3,200) $12,400
   (2) Inventory at Dec. 31 (4 units @ $3,250 +
      1 unit @ $3,200) $16,200
c. (1) Cost of goods sold (LIFO basis): (3 units @ $3,200 +
      1 unit @ $3,000) $12,600
   (2) Inventory at Dec. 31 (4 units @ $3,250 +
      1 unit @ $3,000) $16,000

Self-Test Questions

The answers to these questions appear on page 514.

   1. The primary purpose for using an inventory flow **assumption** is to:
     a. Parallel the physical flow of units of merchandise.
     b. Offset against revenue an appropriate cost of goods sold.

    c. Minimize income taxes.

    d. Maximize the reported amount of net income.

2. Ace Auto Supply uses a perpetual inventory system. On March 10, the company sells 2 Shelby four-barrel carburetors. Immediately prior to this sale, the perpetual inventory records indicate 3 of these carburetors on hand, as shown below:

Date	Quantity Purchased	Unit Cost	Units on Hand	Total Cost
Feb 4	1	$220	1	$220
Mar. 2	2	235	3	690

With respect to this sale on March 10: (More than one of the following answers may be correct.)

    a. If the average-cost method is used, the cost of goods sold is $460.

    b. If these carburetors have identification numbers, Ace must use the specific identification method in determining the cost of goods sold.

    c. If the company uses LIFO, the cost of goods sold will be $15 higher than if it were using FIFO.

    d. If the company uses LIFO, the carburetor *remaining* in inventory after the sales will be assumed to have cost $220.

3. T-Shirt City uses a *periodic* inventory system. During the first year of operations, the company made four purchases of a particular product. Each purchase was for 500 units and the prices paid were: $9 per unit in the first purchase, $10 per unit in the second purchase, $12 per unit in the third purchase, and $13 per unit in the fourth purchase. At year-end, 650 of these units remained unsold. Compute the cost of goods sold under the FIFO method and LIFO method, respectively.

    a. $13,700 (FIFO) and $16,000 (LIFO)

    b. $8,300 (FIFO) and $6,000 (LIFO)

    c. $16,000 (FIFO) and $13,700 (LIFO)

    d. $6,000 (FIFO) and $8,300 (LIFO)

4. Trent Department Store uses a perpetual inventory system but adjusts its inventory records at year-end to reflect the results of a complete physical inventory. In the physical inventory taken at the ends of 2000 and 2001, Trent's employees failed to count the merchandise in the store's window displays. The cost of this merchandise amounted to $13,000 at the end of 2000 and $19,000 at the end of 2001. As a result of these errors, the cost of goods sold for 2001 will be:

    a. Understated by $19,000.

    b. Overstated by $6,000.

    c. Understated by $6,000.

    d. None of the above.

5. In July, 2001, the accountant for LBJ Imports is in the process of preparing financial statements for the quarter ended June 30, 2001. The physical inventory, however, was last taken on June 5 and the accountant must establish the approximate cost at June 30 from the following data:

Physical inventory, June 5, 2001	$900,000
Transactions for the period June 5—June 30:	
Sales	700,000
Purchases	400,000

The gross profit on sales has consistently averaged 40% of sales. Using the gross profit method, compute the approximate inventory cost at June 30, 2001.
    a. $420,000   **b.** $880,000   **c.** $480,000   **d.** $1,360,000

6. Allied Products maintains a large inventory. The company has used the LIFO inventory method for many years, during which the purchase costs of its products have risen substantially. (More than one of the following answers may be correct.)
   a. Allied would have reported a *higher* net income in past years if it had been using the average-cost method.
   b. Allied's financial statements imply a *higher* inventory turnover rate than they would if the company were using FIFO.
   c. If Allied were to let its inventory fall far below normal levels, the company's gross profit rate would *rise.*
   d. Allied's current ratio is *lower* than it would be if the company were using FIFO.

ASSIGNMENT MATERIAL

Discussion Questions

1. Is the cost of merchandise acquired during the period classified as an asset or an expense? Explain.

2. Briefly describe the advantages of using a cost flow assumption, rather than the specific identification method.

3. Under what circumstances do generally accepted accounting principles permit the use of an inventory cost flow assumption? Must a flow assumption closely parallel the physical movement of the company's merchandise?

4. Assume that a company has in its inventory units of a particular product that were purchased at several different per-unit costs. When some of these units are sold, explain how the cost of goods sold is measured under each of the following flow assumptions:
   a. Average cost
   b. FIFO
   c. LIFO

5. A large art gallery has in inventory more than one hundred paintings. No two are alike. The least expensive is priced at more than $1,000 and the higher-priced items carry prices of $100,000 or more. Which of the four methods of inventory valuation discussed in this chapter would you consider to be most appropriate for this business? Give reasons for your answer.

6. During a period of steadily increasing purchase costs, which inventory flow assumption results in the highest reported profits? The valuation of inventory that is closest to current replacement cost? Briefly explain your answers.

7. Assume that during the first year of Hatton Corporation's operation, there were numerous purchases of identical items of merchandise. However, there was no change during the year in the prices paid for this merchandise. Under these special circumstances how would the financial statements be

affected by the choice between the FIFO and LIFO methods of inventory valuation?

8. Apex Corporation sells two different types of products. The FIFO method is used in accounting for inventories for one type and the specific identification method is used for the other. Does this concurrent use of two inventory methods indicate that Apex is violating the accounting principle of consistency? Explain.

9. What are the characteristics of a *just-in-time* inventory system? Briefly explain some advantages and risks of this type of system.

10. Why do most companies that use perpetual inventory systems also take an annual *physical inventory?* When is this physical inventory usually taken? Why?

11. Under what circumstances might a company write down its inventory to carrying value below cost?

12. What is meant by the year-end *cutoff* of transactions? If merchandise in transit at year-end is material in dollar amount, what determines whether these goods should be included in the inventory of the buyer or the seller? Explain.

13. Briefly explain the operation of a *periodic* inventory system. Include an explanation of how the cost of goods sold is determined.

14. Assume that a *periodic* inventory system is in use. Explain which per-unit acquisition costs are assigned to the year-end inventory under each of the following inventory costing procedures:
    a. The average-cost method
    b. FIFO
    c. LIFO

15. When purchase costs are rising, do the perpetual and periodic inventory systems under LIFO produce the same amount for cost of goods sold? Explain.

16. Explain why errors in the valuation of inventory at the end of the year are sometimes called "counterbalancing" or "self-correcting."

17. Briefly explain the *gross profit method* of estimating inventories. In what types of situations is this technique likely to be useful?

18. Estimate the ending inventory by the gross profit method, given the following data: beginning inventory $40,000, net purchases $100,000, net sales $112,000, average gross profit rate of 25% of net sales.

19. A store using the *retail inventory method* takes its physical inventory by applying current retail prices as marked on the merchandise to the quantities counted. Does this procedure indicate that the inventory will appear in the financial statements at retail selling price? Explain.

20. How is the *inventory turnover rate* computed? Why is this measurement of interest to short-term creditors?

21. Baxter Corporation has been using FIFO during a period of rising costs. Explain whether you would expect each of the following measurements to be higher or lower if the company had been using LIFO.
    a. Net income
    b. Inventory turnover rate
    c. Current ratio

Exercises

EXERCISE 9-1
Accounting Terminology
(LO 1, 3, 6)

Listed below are nine technical accounting terms introduced in this chapter.

Retail method	*FIFO method*	*Average-cost method*
Gross profit method	*LIFO method*	*Lower-of-cost-and-market*
Flow assumption	*Shrinkage loss*	*Specific identification*

Each of the following statements may (or may not) describe one of these technical terms. For each statement, indicate the term described, or answer "None" if the statement does not correctly describe any of the terms.

a. A pattern of transferring unit costs from the Inventory account to the cost of goods sold, which may (or may not) parallel the physical flow of merchandise.

b. The excess of the cost of the inventory determined by the perpetual records over the cost of the physical inventory of merchandise.

c. The only flow assumption in which all units of merchandise are assigned the same per-unit cost.

d. The method used in recording the cost of goods sold when each unit in the inventory is unique.

e. The most conservative of the flow assumptions during a period of sustained inflation.

f. The flow assumption that provides the most current valuation of inventory in the balance sheet.

g. A technique for estimating the cost of goods sold and the ending inventory that is based upon the relationships between cost and sales price during the ***current*** accounting period.

EXERCISE 9-2
Flow Assumptions
(LO 1)

On May 10, Merlin Computers sold 80 Portex lap-top computers to College Text Publishers. At the date of this sale, Merlin's perpetual inventory records included the following cost layers for the Portex lap-tops:

Purchase Date	Quantity	Unit Cost	Total Cost
April 9	60	$800	$48,000
May 1	40	850	34,000
Total on Hand	100		$82,000

Prepare journal entries to record the cost of the 80 Portex lap-tops sold on May 10, assuming that Merlin Computers uses the:

a. Specific identification method (50 of the units sold were purchased on April 9, and the remaining units were purchased on May 1).

b. Average-cost method.

c. FIFO method.

d. LIFO method.

EXERCISE 9-3
Evaluating Alternative
Inventory Methods
(LO 1)

Notes to the financial statements of two clothing manufacturers are shown below:

Stevens Limited
    Inventories: The inventories are stated at the lower of cost, determined principally by the LIFO method, or market.

Brooks Incorporated
    Inventories: Inventories are stated at the lower of cost (first-in, first-out method) or market value.

Assuming a period of rising prices, which company is using the more "conservative" method of pricing its inventories? Explain.

EXERCISE 9-4
Effects of Different Flow
Assumptions
(LO 1)

Forbidden Beach, a chain of retail stores, uses FIFO. Shown below are selected data from the corporation's most recent financial statements (dollar amounts are in thousands):

Cost of goods sold $48,000
Net income   6,500

A footnote to the statements disclosed that had Forbidden Beach been using **LIFO,** the cost of goods sold would have been $51,200.

a. Explain how LIFO can result in a higher cost of goods sold. Would you expect the LIFO method to result in the company's inventory being shown at a greater amount?

b. Assuming that Forbidden Beach had been using **LIFO,** compute the net income for the current year. Show supporting computations, with dollar amounts in thousands.

EXERCISE 9-5
F.O.B. Shipping Point and F.O.B.
Destination
(LO 2, 3)

Fraser Company had two large shipments in transit at December 31. One was a $90,000 inbound shipment of merchandise (shipped December 28, F.O.B. shipping point) that arrived at the Fraser receiving dock on January 2. The other shipment was a $55,000 outbound shipment of merchandise to a customer that was shipped and billed by Fraser on December 30 (terms F.O.B. shipping point) and reached the customer on January 3.

In taking a physical inventory on December 31, Fraser counted all goods on hand and priced the inventory on the basis of average cost. The total amount was $480,000. No goods in transit were included in this figure.

What amount should appear as inventory on the company's balance sheet at December 31? Explain. If you indicate an amount other than $480,000, state which asset or liability other than inventory also would be changed in amount.

Exercises 9-6 and 9-7 are based on the following data: Late in 2000, Software City began carrying WordCrafter, a new word processing software program. At December 31, Software City's perpetual inventory records included the following cost layers in its inventory of WordCrafter programs:

Purchase Date	Quantity	Unit Cost	Total Cost
Nov. 14	6	$400	$2,400
Dec. 12	20	310	6,200
Total available for sale at Dec. 31	26		$8,600

EXERCISE 9-6
Recording Shrinkage Losses
(LO 1, 3)

(This exercise is based upon the data presented above.) At December 31, Software City takes a complete physical inventory and finds only 23 WordCrafter programs on hand. Prepare the journal entry to record the shrinkage loss assuming that Software City uses (a) FIFO and (b) LIFO. Any write-down in excess of $1,000 is considered "material" in dollar amount.

EXERCISE 9-7
Lower-of-Cost-and-Market
(LO 3)

(This exercise is based upon the data presented above Exercise **9-6.**) Assume that at December 31, all 26 units of WordCrafter are on hand, but that the net realizable value of this product is $250 per unit.

Prepare journal entries to record:

a. The write-down of the inventory of WordCrafter programs to the lower-of-cost-and-market at December 31. (Company policy is to charge LCM adjustments of less than $2,000 to Cost of Goods Sold and larger amounts to a separate loss account.)

b. The cash sale of 10 WordCrafter programs on January 9 at a retail price of $350 each. Assume that Software City uses the FIFO flow assumption.

EXERCISE 9-8
Costing Inventory in a Periodic System
(LO 4)

Herbor Company uses a ***periodic*** inventory system. The company's records show the beginning inventory of product no. T12 on January 1 and the purchases of this item during the current year to be as follows:

Jan.	1	Beginning inventory	900 units @ $10.00	$ 9,000
Feb.	23	Purchase	1,200 units @ $11.00	13,200
Apr.	20	Purchase	3,000 units @ $11.20	33,600
May	4	Purchase	4,000 units @ $11.60	46,400
Nov.	30	Purchase	900 units @ $13.00	11,700
		Totals	10,000 units	$113,900

A physical count indicates 1,600 units in inventory at year-end.

Determine the cost of the ending inventory, based upon each of the following methods of inventory valuation. (Remember to use ***periodic*** inventory costing procedures.)

a. Average cost
b. FIFO
c. LIFO

EXERCISE 9-9
Periodic Inventory Costing Methods
(LO 4)

Pacific Plumbing uses a ***periodic*** inventory system. One of the company's products is a 2 cm brass gate valve. The company purchases these valves several times a year and makes sales of the item daily. Shown below are the inventory quantities, purchases, and sales for the year.

	Number of Units	Cost Per Unit	Total Cost
Beginning inventory (Jan. 1)	9,100	$4.00	$ 36,400
First purchase (Feb. 20)	20,000	4.10	82,000
Second purchase (May 10)	30,000	4.25	127,500
Third purchase (Aug. 24)	50,000	4.60	230,000
Fourth purchase (Nov. 30)	10,900	5.00	54,500
Goods available for sale	120,000		$530,400
Units sold during the year	106,000		
Ending inventory (Dec. 31)	14,000		

Compute the cost of the ending inventory of gate valves, using the following ***periodic*** inventory valuation methods:

a. FIFO
b. LIFO
c. Average cost

EXERCISE 9-10
Periodic LIFO, Comparison with Perpetual LIFO, and Inventory Shrinkage
(LO 1, 4)

Marston Products uses a perpetual inventory system and a LIFO flow assumption. At year-end, the perpetual inventory records indicate the following units of Product RB-21 are in inventory:

Purchase Date	Quantity	Unit Cost	Total Cost
Beginning inventory	50	$40	$ 2,000
June 18	300	45	13,500
Nov. 7	150	50	7,500
Total available for sale at Dec. 31	500		$23,000

A physical count of the merchandise indicates that only 490 units of Product RB-21 are on hand. Applying *periodic LIFO* costing procedures, these 490 units would be assigned the following unit costs:

Purchase Date	Quantity	Unit Cost	Total Cost
Beginning inventory	220	$40	$ 8,800
June 18	270	45	12,150
Total available for sale at Dec. 31	490		$20,950

a. Prepare a journal entry to record the shrinkage loss of 10 units in the LIFO-based perpetual inventory records. (Charge any loss of less than $1,000 directly to Cost of Goods Sold.)

b. Prepare a journal entry to record the shrinkage loss of 10 units under the periodic LIFO costing procedures.

c. Explain *why* the perpetual LIFO inventory system produces a higher year-end inventory than the periodic LIFO costing procedures.

EXERCISE 9-11
Effects of Errors in Inventory Valuation
(LO 5)

Norfleet Company prepared the following condensed income statements for two successive years:

	2000	1999
Sales	$1,500,000	$1,440,000
Cost of goods sold	879,600	914,400
Gross profit	$ 620,400	$ 525,600
Operating expenses	460,500	447,000
Net income	$ 159,900	$ 78,600

At the end of 1999 (right-hand column above) the inventory was understated by $50,400, but the error was not discovered until after the accounts had been closed and financial statements prepared at the end of *2000*. The balance sheets for the two years showed owner's equity of $414,200 at the end of 1999 and $460,400 at the end of 2000. (Norfleet is organized as a sole proprietorship and does not incur income taxes expense.)

a. Compute the corrected net income figures for 1999 and 2000.

b. Compute the gross profit amounts and the gross profit percentages for each year based upon corrected data.

c. What correction, if any, should be made in the amounts of the company's owner's equity at the end of 1999 and at the end of 2000?

EXERCISE 9-12
Estimating Inventory by the Gross Profit Method
(LO 6)

When Anne Blair arrived at her store on the morning of January 29, she found empty shelves and display racks; thieves had broken in during the night and stolen the entire inventory. Blair's accounting records showed that she had had $55,800 inventory on January 1 (cost value). From January 1 to January 29, she had made net sales of $200,000 and net purchases of $142,800. The gross profit during the last several years had consistently averaged 30% of net sales. Blair wishes to file an insurance claim for the theft loss. You are to use the *gross profit method* to estimate the cost of her inventory at the time of the theft. Show computations.

EXERCISE 9-13
Estimating Inventory by the Retail Method
(LO 6)

Westlake Accessories uses a periodic inventory system, but needs to determine the approximate amount of inventory at the end of each month without taking a physical inventory. From the following information, you are to estimate the cost of goods sold and the cost of the July 31 inventory by the *retail method* of inventory valuation.

	Cost Price	Retail Selling Price
Inventory of merchandise, June 30	$264,800	$400,000
Purchases during July	170,400	240,000
Goods available for sale during July	$435,200	$640,000
Net sales during July		$275,200

EXERCISE 9-14
Inventory Turnover Rate
(LO 7)

A recent annual report of **Algoma Steel Inc.** shows: cost of goods sold, $1,015; inventory at the beginning of the year, $371; and inventory at the end of the year, $380. (These dollar amounts are in millions.)

a. Compute the inventory turnover rate for the year (round to the nearest tenth).
b. Using the assumption of 365 days in a year, compute the number of days required for the company to sell the amount of its average inventory (round to the nearest day).
c. Assume that an average of 46 days are required for Algoma to collect its accounts receivable. What is the length of Algoma's *operating cycle?*

Problems

PROBLEM 9-1
Evaluating Different Inventory Methods
(LO 1)

A note to the financial statements of *The Quaker Oats Company* includes the following information:

Inventories: Inventories are valued at the lower-of-cost-and-market, using various cost methods. The percentage of year-end inventories valued using each of the methods is as follows:

June 30 (fiscal year-end)
Average cost	*54%*
Last-in, first-out (LIFO)	*29%*
First-in, first-out (FIFO)	*17%*

INSTRUCTIONS

a. Does the company's use of three different inventory methods violate the accounting principle of consistency?
b. Assuming that the purchase costs of inventories have been steadily rising, would the company's reported net income be higher or lower if all inventories were valued by the FIFO method?
c. Assume that management's primary objective is to minimize income taxes and that the three inventory valuation methods are acceptable for income tax purposes. Which inventory valuation method would you recommend? Explain.

PROBLEM 9-2
Perpetual Inventory Records
(LO 1)

Black Hawk Inc. uses a perpetual inventory system and maintains an inventory record of each type of product in stock. The following transactions show beginning inventory, purchases, and sales of CT-300, a cellular telephone, for the month of May:

May 1	Balance on hand, 20 units, cost $40 each	$800
May 5	Sale, 8 units, sales price $60 each	480
May 6	Purchase, 20 units, cost $45 each	900
May 21	Sale, 10 units, sales price $60 each	600
May 31	Sale, 15 units, sales price $65 each	975

INSTRUCTIONS

a. Record the beginning inventory, the purchases, the cost of goods sold, and the running balance on an inventory record card like the one illustrated in this chapter. Use the *first-in, first-out* (FIFO) method.
b. Prepare general journal entries to record the purchases and sales in May. Assume that all transactions were on account.

PROBLEM 9-3
Perpetual Inventory Records in a Small Business
(LO 1)

Executive Suites Inc. uses a perpetual inventory system. This system includes a perpetual inventory record card for each of the 60 types of products the company keeps in stock. The following transactions show the purchases and sales of a particular desk chair (product code DC-7) during September.

Sept. 1	Balance on hand, 50 units, cost $60 each	$3,000
Sept. 4	Purchase, 20 units, cost $65 each	1,300
Sept. 8	Sale, 35 units, sales price $100 each	3,500
Sept. 9	Purchase, 40 units, cost $65 each	2,600
Sept. 20	Sale, 60 units, sales price $100 each	6,000
Sept. 25	Purchase, 40 units, cost $70 each	2,800
Sept. 30	Sale, 5 units, sales price $110 each	550

INSTRUCTIONS

a. Record the beginning inventory, the purchases, the cost of goods sold, and the running balance on an inventory record card like the one illustrated in this chapter. Use the ***last-in, first out*** (LIFO) method.
b. Prepare general journal entries to record the purchases and sales in September. Assume that all transactions were on account.

PROBLEM 9-4
Four Methods of Inventory Valuation
(LO 1)

On January 15, 2000, California Irrigation sold 1,000 RainMaster-30 oscillating sprinkler heads to Rancho Landscaping. Immediately prior to this sale, California's perpetual inventory records for this sprinkler head included the following cost layers:

Purchase Date	Quantity	Unit Cost	Total Cost
December 12, 1999	600	$9.25	$ 5,550
January 9, 2000	900	9.50	8,550
Total on hand	1,500		$14,100

INSTRUCTIONS

(***Note:*** We present this problem in the sequence of the accounting cycle—that is, journal entries before ledger entries. However, you may find it helpful to work part **b** first.)
a. Prepare a separate journal entry to record the cost of goods sold relating to the January 15 sale of 1,000 RainMaster-30 sprinkler heads, assuming that California Irrigation uses:
  1. Specific identification (500 of the units sold were purchased on December 12, and the remaining 500 were purchased on January 9).
  2. Average cost.
  3. FIFO.
  4. LIFO.
b. Complete a subsidiary ledger record for RainMaster-30 sprinkler heads using each of the four inventory valuation methods listed above. Your inventory records should show both purchases of this product, the sale on January 15, and the balance on hand at December 12, January 9, and January 15. Use the formats for inventory subsidiary records illustrated in this chapter.

Problems 9-5 and 9-6 are based upon the following data: SK Marine sells high-performance marine equipment to power boat owners. Apollo Outboard recently introduced the world's first 400 horsepower outboard motor—the Apollo 400. During the current year, SK purchased 8 of these motors—all intended for resale to customers—at the following dates and acquisition costs:

Purchase Date	Units Purchased	Unit Cost	Total Cost
July 1	2	$4,450	$ 8,900
July 22	3	4,600	13,800
Aug. 3	3	4,700	14,100
Available for sale during the year	8		$36,800

On *July 28,* SK sold 4 of these motors to Mr. G Racing Associates. The other 4 motors remained in inventory at September 30, the end of SK's fiscal year.

PROBLEM 9-5
Alternative Flow Assumptions
(LO 1)

Assume that SK Marine uses a *perpetual inventory system.*
a. Compute (a) the cost of goods sold relating to the sale on July 28 and (b) the ending inventory of Apollo outboard motors at September 30, using each of the following flow assumptions:
 1. Average cost
 2. FIFO
 3. LIFO
 Show the number of units and the unit costs of each cost layer comprising the cost of goods sold and the ending inventory.
b. In part **a,** you have determined SK's cost of Apollo motors sold using three different inventory flow assumptions.
 1. Which of these methods will result in SK Marine reporting the *highest net income* for the current year? Would this always be the case? Explain.
 2. Assume that these methods are acceptable for income tax purposes, which method will *minimize the income taxes owed* by SK for the year? Would you expect this usually to be the case? Explain.

PROBLEM 9-6
Periodic Costing Procedures
(LO 4)

Assume that SK Marine uses a *periodic inventory system.*
a. Compute the ending inventory of Apollo motors at September 30 and the cost of goods sold through this date under each of the following periodic costing procedures:
 1. Average cost
 2. FIFO
 3. LIFO
 Show the number of units and the unit costs in each cost layer of the *ending inventory.* (You may determine the cost of goods sold by deducting ending inventory from the cost of goods available for sale.)
b. Would the amount of ending inventory for each of the methods in **a** be different if the perpetual inventory system were used? Explain.

PROBLEM 9-7
Year-End Adjustments;
Shrinkage Losses and LCM
(LO 2, 3)

Bunyon's Trees & Shrubs uses a perpetual inventory system. At December 31, 2000 the perpetual inventory records indicate the following quantities of a particular 5-gallon tree:

	Quantity	Unit Cost	Total Cost
First purchase (oldest)	230	$18	$ 4,140
Second purchase	200	19	3,800
Third purchase	170	20	3,400
Total	600		$11,340

A year-end physical inventory, however, shows only 570 of these trees on hand and alive.

In its financial statements, Bunyon's values its inventories at the lower-of-cost-and-market. At year-end, the per-unit net realizable value of this tree is $21. (Use $2,000 as the "level of materiality" in deciding whether to debit losses to Cost of Goods Sold or to a separate loss account.)

INSTRUCTIONS

Prepare the journal entries required to adjust the inventory records at year-end, assuming that:
a. Bunyon's uses:
 1. Average cost.
 2. Last-in, first-out.

b. Bunyon's uses the first-in, first-out method. However, the net realizable value of the trees at year-end is **$15** apiece, rather than the $21 stated originally. [Make separate journal entries to record (1) the shrinkage losses, and (2) the restatement of the inventory at a "market" value lower than cost. Record the shrinkage losses first.]

PROBLEM 9-8
Periodic Inventory Costing
Procedures
(LO 4)

Audio Shop uses a periodic inventory system. One of the most popular items carried in stock by Audio Shop is a 16-cm speaker unit. The inventory quantities, purchases, and sales of this unit for the most recent year are shown below.

	Number of Units	Cost Per Unit	Total Cost
Inventory, Jan. 1	2,700	$30.00	$ 81,000
First purchase (May 12)	3,540	30.60	108,324
Second purchase (July 9)	2,400	31.05	74,520
Third purchase (Oct. 4)	1,860	32.10	59,706
Fourth purchase (Dec. 18)	3,000	32.55	97,650
Goods available for sale	13,500		$421,200
Units sold during the year	10,400		
Inventory, Dec. 31	3,100		

INSTRUCTIONS

a. Using *periodic* costing procedures, compute the cost of the December 31 inventory and the cost of goods sold for the 16-cm speaker units during the year under each of the following cost flow assumptions:
  1. First-in, first-out
  2. Last-in, first-out
  3. Average-cost
b. Which of the three inventory pricing methods provides the most realistic balance sheet valuation of inventory in light of the current purchase cost of the speaker units? Does this same method also produce the most realistic measure of income in light of the costs being incurred by Audio Shop to replace the speakers when they are sold? Explain.

PROBLEM 9-9
Comparisons of Perpetual and
Periodic Inventory Systems
(LO 1, 4)

During 2001, Playground Specialists purchased 6 BigGym redwood playground sets at the following dates and acquisition costs:

Date	Units Purchased	Unit Cost	Total Cost
Aug. 4	2	$2,100	$ 4,200
Sep. 23	2	2,300	4,600
Oct. 2	2	2,560	5,120
Available for sale during the year	6		$13,920

On **September 25,** the company sold 3 of these BigGym sets to the Department of Parks and Recreation. The other 3 sets remained in inventory at December 31.

INSTRUCTIONS

a. Assume that Playground Specialists uses a *perpetual inventory system.* Using each of the flow assumptions listed below, compute (a) the cost of goods sold relating to the sale of BigGym playground sets on September 25 and (b) the cost of the BigGym sets in inventory at December 31.
  1. Average cost
  2. FIFO
  3. LIFO
Show the number of units and the unit costs of each cost layer comprising the cost of goods sold and the ending inventory.

b. Assume that Playground Specialists uses a ***periodic inventory system.*** Compute the ending inventory of BigGym playground sets at December 31 and the related cost of goods sold under each of the following year-end costing procedures:
   1. Average cost
   2. FIFO
   3. LIFO

Show the number of units and the unit costs in each cost layer of the ending inventory. (You may determine the cost of goods sold by deducting ending inventory from the cost of goods available for sale.)

c. Would the amount for ending inventory for each of the three methods be different between the perpetual and periodic inventory systems? Explain.

PROBLEM 9-10
Inventory Errors: Effects on Earnings
(LO 5)

The owners of Night & Day Window Coverings are offering the business for sale as a going concern. The income statements of the business for the three years of its existence are summarized below:

	2001	2000	1999
Net Sales	$860,000	$850,000	$800,000
Cost of goods sold	481,600	486,000	480,000
Gross profit	$378,400	$364,000	$320,000
Gross profit percentage	44%	43%*	40%

Rounded to nearest full percentage point.

In negotiations with prospective buyers of the business, the owners of Night & Day are calling attention to the rising trends of the gross profit and of the gross profit percentage as very favourable elements.

Assume that you are retained by a prospective purchaser of the business to make an investigation of the fairness and reliability of Night & Day's accounting records and financial statements. You find everything in order except for the following: (1) An arithmetical error in the computation of inventory at the end of 1999 had caused a $24,000 understatement in that inventory, (2) a counting error in the physical inventory at the end of 2000 had caused an overstatement of $10,000 in that inventory, and (3) a duplication of figures in the computation of inventory at the end of 2001 had caused an overstatement of $70,000 in that inventory. The company uses the periodic inventory system and these errors had not been brought to light prior to your investigation.

INSTRUCTIONS

a. Prepare a revised three-year schedule similar to the one illustrated above.
b. Comment on the trend of gross profit and gross profit percentage before and after the revision.

PROBLEM 9-11
Retail Method and Shrinkage
(LO 3, 6)

Cherry Vanilla is called a "record" store, but its sales consist almost entirely of tapes and CDs. The company uses a periodic inventory system but also uses the retail method to estimate its monthly, quarterly, and annual cost of goods sold and ending inventory.

During the current year, Cherry Vanilla offered for sale merchandise that had cost a total of ***$385,000.*** As required by the retail method, the company also kept track of the retail sales values of this merchandise, which amounted to ***$700,000.*** The store's net sales for the year were ***$620,000.***

INSTRUCTIONS

a. Using the retail method, estimate (1) the cost of goods sold during the year and (2) the inventory at the end of the year.
b. At year-end, Cherry Vanilla takes a physical inventory. The manager walks through the store counting each type of product and reading its retail price into a tape recorder. From this tape recording, an employee prepares a

schedule listing the entire ending inventory at retail sales prices. The inventory on hand at year-end had a retail sales value of **$70,400.**

1. Use the cost ratio determined in part **a** to reduce the inventory counted by the manager from its retail value to an estimate of its cost.
2. Determine the estimated shrinkage losses (measured at cost) incurred by Cherry Vanilla during the year.
3. Compute the store's gross profit for the year. (Include shrinkage losses in the cost of goods sold.)

PROBLEM 9-12
What If They'd Used FIFO?
(LO 1, 7)

OB Corporation uses LIFO. Recent financial statements included the following data (dollars in thousands):

Average inventory (throughout the year)	$ 81,554
Ending inventory	89,334
Current assets (at year-end)	115,852
Current liabilities (at year-end)	27,175
Net sales	315,076
Cost of goods sold	209,006
Gross profit	106,070

A note accompanying these statements indicated that had the company used the **FIFO** inventory method (dollars in thousands):

1. Average inventory would have been $88,474 ($6,920 **higher** than the LIFO amount).
2. Ending inventory would have been valued at a cost of $96,115 ($6,781 **higher** than the LIFO cost).
3. The cost of goods sold would have been $209,284 ($278 **higher** than that reported in the company's income statement).

Note to student: Notice that the cost of goods sold is **higher** under FIFO than LIFO. This is a somewhat unusual situation, indicating that the company has encountered **declining** purchase costs for its merchandise during the year.

INSTRUCTIONS

a. Using the data contained in the company's financial statements (based upon the LIFO method), compute the following analytical measurements. (Round to the nearest tenth.)
   1. Inventory turnover rate
   2. Current ratio
   3. Gross profit rate
b. **Recompute** the three ratios required in part **a** in a manner that will be **directly comparable** to those of a company using the FIFO method in its financial statements. (Round to the nearest tenth.)

Analytical and Decision Problems and Cases

A&D 9-1
Wanted: Better Results!
(LO 1, 4, 7, 8)

Designers Galore is a chain of retail stores that sell designer imitation jeans and shirts. The business has been steadily expanding and profitable, in spite of fierce competition and rising purchase costs of merchandise. The key to success is the policy of competitive pricing and wide selection of merchandise. Now, inventory is the largest asset on the balance sheet. To increase its profitability, the company plans to continue its expansion and to lower its purchase costs by getting a better volume discount from suppliers because of the increasing size of the purchases. To finance the expansion and the increasing size of inventory, the company needs a bank loan in the near future.

Anna Hall, the owner of Designers Galore, wants to show the most favourable operating results and financial position so that she can get a loan at a reasonable interest rate. She would like to achieve this through actual performance and generally accepted accounting principles. She understands that, for financial reporting, the company can use any one of the three cost flow assumptions for its inventory, under either the periodic or perpetual system.

INSTRUCTIONS   What would be your advice to Anna Hall?

A&D 9-2
Have I Got a Deal for You!
(LO 1)

You are the sales manager of Continental Motors, an automobile dealership specializing in European imports. Among the automobiles in Continental Motors' showroom are two Italian sports cars, which are identical in every respect except for colour: one is red and the other white. The red car had been ordered last February, at a cost of $48,300. The white car had been ordered early last March, but because of a revaluation of the Italian lira relative to the dollar, the white car had cost only $47,000. Both cars arrived on the same boat and had just been delivered to your showroom. Since the cars were identical except for colour and both colours were equally popular, you had listed both cars at the same suggested retail price, $58,000. This price is about $2,000 less than competing dealerships are asking for this particular model.

Smiley Miles, one of your best sales agents, comes into your office with a proposal. He has a customer in the showroom who wants to buy the red car for $58,000. However, when Miles pulled the inventory card on the red car to see what options were included, he happened to notice the inventory card of the white car. Continental Motors, like most automobile dealerships, uses the specific identification method to value inventory. Consequently, Miles noticed that the red car had cost $48,300, while the white one had cost Continental Motors only $47,000. This gave Miles the idea for the following proposal.

"Have I got a deal for you! If I sell the red car for $58,000, Continental Motors makes a gross profit of $9,700. But if you'll let me discount that white car $500, I think I can get my customer to buy that one instead. If I sell the white car for $57,500, the gross profit will be $10,500, so Continental Motors is $800 better off than if I sell the red car for $58,000. Since I came up with this plan, I feel I should get part of the benefit, so Continental Motors should split the extra $800 with me. That way, I'll get an extra $400 commission, and the company still makes $400 more than if I sell the red car."

INSTRUCTIONS   Would you accept Miles's proposal? Explain your reasoning.

A&D 9-3
Just-in-Time or NQIT (Not-Quite-in-Time)
(LO 1)

Fargo Manufacturing is located in Windsor, Ontario. In the past, the company has rented several warehouses to store its inventories of materials and finished goods. Recently, management has been working to implement the principles of a just-in-time inventory system. At present, almost 70% of the company's materials arrive on a just-in-time basis, and all finished goods are shipped to customers immediately upon completion of the production process.

INSTRUCTIONS   a. Explain what is meant by "just-in-time," with respect to both materials and finished goods.
   b. What are the advantages to Fargo of just-in-time manufacturing? What is the biggest risk?

A&D 9-4
Are these Inventory Transactions Okay?
(LO 3)

The bookkeeper of FunBuy Souvenir Shop is not sure whether the following transactions have been handled properly. FunBuy uses a perpetual inventory system.
1. Merchandise costing $1,000 was shipped to FunBuy by a supplier on December 30, 1999. Since the merchandise was not received until January 3, 2000, it was not included in the physical ending inventory of 1999. The supplier's invoice, with terms n/30, F.O.B. shipping point, was received on December 31, 1999 and was recorded immediately.

2. Merchandise costing $2,900 was shipped to a regular customer in the late afternoon of December 31, 1999, after it was counted and included in the physical inventory. Since this customer had done a lot of business with the company, FunBuy did not want to bill the customer until January 8, 2000. On that day, the invoice for $3,600, with terms 2/10, n/30, F.O.B. shipping point, was prepared and the transaction was recorded.

INSTRUCTIONS

Indicate, in a tabulation format, the items in the 1999 and 2000 income statements and in the 1999 balance sheet that are affected by the manner in which the two transactions were handled and how these items are affected (that is, whether they are understated or overstated and by what amount). FunBuy charges inventory shrinkage loss to cost of goods sold.

A&D 9-5
Inventory Management
(LO 8)

In this chapter, we discussed several factors that management should consider in deciding upon the size of inventory to be kept on hand. In each of the following cases, you are to indicate what you consider to be the most important factor (or factors) favouring (1) increasing the size of the company's inventory and (2) **not** increasing the size of the inventory.

a. Morgan Chevrolet is an automobile dealership in a large metropolitan area. It currently has an opportunity to buy several hectares of land adjacent to the dealership that it could use to store additional inventory. The cost of this land would be approximately $200,000. General Motors—Morgan Chevrolet's supplier—allows substantial discounts to dealers that purchase a large volume of cars. Like most auto dealers, Morgan Chevrolet finances purchases of inventory through a bank and repays the bank as individual automobiles are sold.

b. Marc's Furniture sells name-brand furniture to homeowners at discount prices. The company is located in a small rented office. At present, the company's inventory consists of five or six different pieces of furniture that are kept on hand primarily for purposes of display. Customers place their orders from catalogues and wait six to eight weeks for delivery. The manager has noticed that customers most frequently order those items that the company has on display.

c. Captain's Choice is a fish market located near the waterfront. All of the fish is purchased fresh each day from the local fishing fleet. Captain's Choice sells the fish at a retail price of approximately five times its cost.

A&D 9-6
Comparison of LIFO and FIFO
(LO 1, 7)

You are making a detailed analysis of the financial statements of two companies in the same industry: APM and BFC. Both businesses are organized as corporations and, therefore, must pay income taxes on their earnings. Both companies maintain large inventories, and the replacement costs of their products have been rising steadily for several years. A note to APM's financial statements discloses that the company's inventory is shown at a cost that is **far below** current replacement cost. BFC's inventory, in contrast, is presented at a cost that is **very close** to its current replacement cost.

INSTRUCTIONS

Answer the following questions. Explain the reasoning behind your answers.
a. What method of inventory valuation is probably used by APM? By BFC?
b. If we assume that the two companies are identical except for the method used in valuing inventory:
   1. Which company probably has been reporting the higher net income in recent years?
   2. Which company's financial statements probably imply the higher inventory turnover rate?

3. Which company's financial statements probably imply the higher current ratio?

4. Comment upon your answers to parts **2** and **3** above. If the only difference between these companies is their method of inventory valuation, is one company actually more solvent than the other? Assume that the inventory valuation methods are all acceptable for income tax purposes.

c. If both companies sold their entire inventory at the same sales prices, which company would you expect to report the larger amount of gross profit?

A&D 9-7
Inventory: Attracting Attention?
(LO 5, 7)

Carla Fontana is an auditor with Revenue Canada. She has been assigned to audit the income tax return of Square Deal Lumber Company (a corporation). Selected figures from the company's income tax return are shown below.

Sales	*$12,000,000*
Beginning inventory	*360,000*
Purchases of merchandise	*9,600,000*
Ending inventory	*260,000*
Cost of goods sold	*9,700,000*
Gross profit	*2,300,000*

As Fontana examined these figures, she became suspicious that Square Deal had understated its taxable income by a significant amount and may have been engaging in this practice for several years.

Fontana looked up several ratios for the retail lumber industry in a recent publication of industry averages. She found that retail lumberyards, on average, had annual sales of $10 million, an inventory turnover rate of 10, and a gross profit rate of 20%. Fontana also noticed a newspaper advertisement by Square Deal, which read, "Many unique products in our huge yard. We carry what the other yards don't. This week's special: roofing materials—15% discount on shake, shingle, and composition. Large selection in stock." Fontana then sent a letter to Square Deal to arrange a date for visiting the company and performing an audit of its latest income tax return.

When Fontana arrived at Square Deal Lumber, she was met in the parking lot by Sam "Square Deal" Delano, president and owner of the business. Fontana noticed that Square Deal looked like most other retail lumberyards. There was one main building, containing offices and displays of such merchandise as power tools and electrical supplies. Behind this building was a large fenced yard, with many stacks of lumber, and several storage sheds. These sheds contained plywood, fibreglass insulation, and other products that required protection from the weather.

Fontana asked to see the company's perpetual inventory records. Delano told her that Square Deal uses a periodic inventory system, as it is not a publicly owned company and does not have to issue quarterly financial statements to shareholders or other outsiders. He pointed out that he and the general manager were on hand every day, and they both knew exactly what was in stock—down to the very last board.

By examining various accounting records, Fontana concluded that the amounts of sales revenues and merchandise purchases were correctly stated in Square Deal's income tax return. She noticed, however, that most types of merchandise were reordered at intervals of about five weeks.

INSTRUCTIONS

a. What was it about the figures in Square Deal Lumber Company's income tax return that originally made Fontana suspect that the company might be understating its taxable income?

b. What happened to confirm Fontana's suspicions? Identify all of the factors that have come to her attention and yours.

c. Does it appear that Square Deal is engaging in a deliberate scheme to evade income taxes, or that the company has simply made an "honest mistake"? Explain.

d. Assume that the industry averages correctly approximate the financial position and operating results of the Square Deal. Estimate for the current year the correct amounts of the company's (1) cost of goods sold, (2) gross profit, (3) average amount of inventory. (Show supporting computations.)

e. Estimate the amount by which Square Deal appears to have understated its taxable income over a period of years. Explain the basis for your conclusion.

Answers to Self-Test Questions

1. b   2. a, c, d   3. a   4. b   5. b   6. a, b, c, d

CHAPTER 10

Capital Assets: Plant and Equipment, Intangible Assets, and Natural Resources

Just as different flow assumptions may be used in accounting for inventories, different depreciation methods may be used in accounting for plant assets. Also, estimates such as useful life and residual value of plant assets are involved. These methods and estimates affect the measurement of net income. If this is beginning to sound familiar, you're developing a "feel" for accounting information.

1. Determine the cost of plant assets.
2. Distinguish between capital expenditures and revenue expenditures.
3. Compute depreciation by the straight-line, the declining-balance, and the units-of-production (output) methods.
4. Account for disposals of plant assets.
5. Explain the nature of intangible assets, including goodwill.
6. Account for the depletion of natural resources.

The *CICA Handbook* uses the general term **capital assets**[1] to encompass three groups of long-term assets: property, plant, and equipment; intangible assets; and natural resources. Each of these three groups of assets is usually presented separately in the financial statements, and they will be discussed individually in this chapter.

The term **plant and equipment (plant assets)** describes long-lived capital assets acquired for use in business operations rather than for resale to customers. The term *fixed assets* has long been used in accounting literature to describe all types of plant and equipment and is still used in the published financial statements of large corporations. *Plant and equipment,* however, appears to be a more descriptive term. Another alternative title used on many corporation balance sheets is *property, plant, and equipment.* Regardless of the term used, these assets comprise the largest category of assets for many corporations.

CASE IN POINT Some examples from recent corporate balance sheets:

| | | Dollars in Millions | | |
Corporation	Term	Cost	Accumulated Depreciation	Percentage of Total Assets
Shell Canada Limited	*Properties, plant and equipment*	*$7,360*	*$3,647*	*62%*
Maple Leaf Foods Inc.	*Property and equipment*	*912*	*336*	*38%*
Abitibi-Consolidated Inc.	*Fixed assets*	*6,355*	*2,251*	*65%*

Plant and Equipment as a "Stream of Future Services"

Plant and equipment are similar to long-term prepaid expenses. Ownership of a delivery truck, for example, may provide about 100,000 kilometres of transportation. The cost of the truck is entered in an asset account, which

---

[1]Section 3060. Also, the terms "property, plant and equipment," and "intangible assets" are most widely used in published financial statements. In the four examples (four companies from four industries) cited by the most recent CICA's *Financial Reporting in Canada* (Twenty-second Edition, 1997), two use the term "property, plant, and equipment," and the other two use "property and equipment," and "fixed assets" respectively.

in essence represents the ***advance purchase*** of these transportation services. Similarly, a building represents the advance purchase of many years of housing services. As the years go by, these services are utilized by the business, and the cost of the plant or equipment gradually is transferred to depreciation expense.

Major Categories of Plant and Equipment

Plant and equipment items are often classified into the following groups:

1. **Tangible plant assets.** The term "tangible" denotes physical substance, as exemplified by land, a building, or a machine. This category may be subdivided into two distinct classifications:
   a. Plant property subject to depreciation; included are plant assets of limited useful life such as buildings and office equipment.
   b. Land. The only plant asset not subject to depreciation is land, which has an unlimited term of existence.
2. **Intangible assets.** The term "intangible assets" is used to describe capital assets that are used in the operation of the business but have no physical substance and are noncurrent. Examples include patents, copyrights, trademarks, franchises, and goodwill. Current assets such as accounts receivable or prepaid rent are not included in the intangible classification, even though they are lacking in physical substance.
3. **Natural resources.** A site acquired for the purpose of extracting or removing some valuable resource such as oil, minerals, or timber is classified as a ***natural resource,*** not as land. This type of plant asset is gradually converted into inventory as the natural resource is extracted from the site.

Accountable Events in the Lives of Plant Assets

For all categories of plant assets, there are three basic "accountable events": (1) acquisition, (2) allocation of the acquisition cost to expense over the asset's useful life (depreciation), and (3) sale or disposal.

ACQUISITIONS OF PLANT ASSETS

The cost of a plant asset includes all expenditures that are ***reasonable*** and ***necessary*** for getting the asset to the desired location and ***ready for use.***

LO 1: Determine the cost of plant assets. Thus, many incidental costs may be included in the cost assigned to a plant asset. These include, for example, sales taxes on the purchase price, delivery costs, and installation costs.

But only reasonable and necessary costs should be included. Assume, for example, that a machine is dropped and damaged while it is being unloaded. The cost of repairing this damage should be recognized as expense of the current period, ***not*** added to the cost of the machine. Although it was necessary to repair the machine, it was not necessary to drop it—and that's what brought about the need for the repairs.

Companies often purchase plant assets on an instalment plan, or by issuing a note payable. Interest charges after the asset is ready for use are recorded as interest expense, not as part of the cost of the asset. But if a company constructs a plant asset for its own use, the interest charges ***dur-***

ing the construction period are viewed as part of the asset's cost when it is the company's accounting policy to capitalize such costs.[2]

Determining Cost: An Example

The concept of including in the cost of a plant asset all of the incidental charges necessary to put the asset in use is illustrated by the following example. A company in Windsor orders a machine from a tool manufacturer at a list price of $10,000. Payment will be made in 48 monthly instalments of $250, which include $2,000 in interest charges. Sales taxes of $800 must be paid, as well as freight charges of $1,050. Installation and other "start-up" costs amount to $400. The cost of this machine to be debited to the Machinery account is ***$12,250,*** computed as follows below:

All reasonable and necessary costs are capitalized

*List price**	*$10,000*
*Sales taxes***	*800*
Transportation charges	*1,050*
Cost of installation and set-up	*400*
Total	*$12,250*

*The $2,000 in interest charges on the instalment purchase will be recognized as interest expense over the next 48 months. (Accounting for instalment notes payable is discussed in the next chapter.)

**Since the company is entitled to an input tax credit on the goods and services tax, it is not part of the cost of the machine.

Some Special Considerations

Land   When land is purchased, various incidental costs are generally incurred, in addition to the purchase price. These additional costs may include commissions to real estate brokers, land transfer tax, legal fees for examining the title, delinquent taxes paid by the purchaser, and fees for surveying, draining, clearing, and grading the property. All these expenditures become part of the cost of the land.

Sometimes land purchased as a building site has on it an old building that is not suitable for the buyer's use. In this case, the only useful "asset" being acquired is the land. Therefore, the entire purchase price is charged to the Land account, along with the costs of tearing down and removing the unusable building.

Land Improvements   Improvements to real estate such as driveways, fences, parking lots, landscaping, and sprinkler systems have a limited life and are therefore subject to depreciation. For this reason they should be recorded in a separate account entitled Land Improvements.

Buildings   Old buildings are sometimes purchased with the intention of repairing them prior to placing them in use. Repairs made under these circumstances are charged to the Buildings account. After the building has been placed in use, ordinary repairs are considered to be maintenance expense when incurred.

---

[2]CICA, *CICA Handbook* (Toronto), section 3060.26.

Equipment When equipment is purchased, all of the sales taxes, delivery costs, and costs of getting the equipment "in good running order" are treated as part of the cost of the asset. Once the equipment has been placed in operation, maintenance costs—including interest, insurance, and property taxes—are treated as expenses of the current period.

Allocation of a Lump-Sum Purchase Several different types of plant assets often are purchased at one time. Separate controlling accounts are maintained for each type of plant asset, such as land, buildings, and equipment.[3]

When land and buildings (and perhaps other assets) are purchased for a lump sum, the purchase price must be *allocated* among the types of assets acquired. An appraisal may be needed for this purpose. Assume, for example, that Holiday Workout purchases a complete fitness centre from Golden Health Spas. Holiday purchases the entire facility at a bargain price of $800,000. The allocation of this cost on the basis of an appraisal is illustrated below:

Total cost is allocated in proportion to appraised values

	Value per Appraisal	Percentage of Appraised Value	Allocation of $800,000 Cost
Land	$ 250,000	25%	$200,000
Land improvements	50,000	5%	40,000
Building	300,000	30%	240,000
Equipment	400,000	40%	320,000
Total	$1,000,000	100%	$800,000

Assuming that Holiday purchased this facility for cash, the journal entry to record this acquisition would be:

The journal entry allocating the total cost

Land	200,000	
Land Improvements	40,000	
Building	240,000	
Equipment	320,000	
Cash		800,000
To record purchase of fitness centre from Golden Health Spas.		

Capital Expenditures and Revenue Expenditures

LO 2: Distinguish between capital expenditures and revenue expenditures.

Expenditures for the purchase or expansion of plant assets are called **capital expenditures** and are recorded in asset accounts. Accountants often use the verb **capitalize** to mean charging an expenditure to an asset account rather than to an expense account. Expenditures for ordinary repairs, maintenance, fuel, and other items necessary to the ownership and use of plant and equipment are called **revenue expenditures** and are recorded by debiting expense accounts. The charge to an expense account is based on the assumption that the benefits from the expenditure will be used up in the current period, and the cost should therefore be deducted from the revenue of the period in determining the net income. Charging an expenditure directly to an expense account is often called "expensing" the item.

---

[3]Each controlling account is supported by a subsidiary ledger providing information about the cost, annual depreciation, and book value of each asset (or group of similar assets).

A business may purchase many small items that will benefit several accounting periods but that have a relatively low cost. Examples of such items include auto batteries, wastebaskets, and pencil sharpeners. Such items are theoretically capital expenditures, but if they are recorded as assets in the accounting records it will be necessary to compute and record the related depreciation expense in future periods. We have previously mentioned the idea that the extra work involved in developing more precise accounting information should be weighed against the benefits that result. Thus, for reasons of convenience and economy, expenditures that are **not material** in dollar amount are treated in the accounting records as expenses of the current period.

In brief, any material expenditure that will benefit several accounting periods is considered a **capital expenditure.** Any expenditure that will benefit only the current period or that is not material in amount is treated as a **revenue expenditure.**

Many companies develop formal policy statements defining capital and revenue expenditures as a guide toward consistent accounting practice from year to year. These policy statements often set a minimum dollar amount (such as $500) for expenditures that are to be capitalized.

DEPRECIATION

We first introduced the concept of depreciation in Chapter 3. We will now expand that discussion to address such topics as residual values and alternative depreciation methods.

Allocating the Cost of Plant and Equipment over the Years of Use

Tangible plant assets, with the exception of land, are of use to a company for only a limited number of years. **Depreciation,** as the term is used in accounting, is the **allocation of the cost of a tangible plant asset to expense in the periods in which services are received from the asset.**[4] In short, the basic purpose of depreciation is to achieve the **matching principle**—that is, to offset the revenue of an accounting period with the costs of the goods and services being consumed in the effort to generate that revenue.

Earlier in this chapter, we described a delivery truck as a stream of "transportation services" to be received over the years that the truck is owned and used. The cost of the truck initially is debited to an asset account, because this purchase of these "transportation services" will benefit many future accounting periods. As these services are received, however, the cost of the truck gradually is removed from the balance sheet and allocated to expense in the income statement, through the process called "depreciation."

The journal entry to record depreciation expense consists of a debit to Depreciation Expense and a credit to Accumulated Depreciation. The credit

---

[4]While section 3060 of the *CICA Handbook* uses the term "amortization" to encompass the commonly used terms "depreciation" and "depletion," it indicates that the latter two terms may also be used. In practice, the terms "depreciation" and "depletion" are still most widely used. These two terms are used in all four examples (four companies from four industries) cited in the most recent CICA's *Financial Reporting In Canada* (Twenty-second Edition, 1997). Accordingly, the terms "depreciation" and "depletion" are used in this text.

Depreciation: a process of
allocating the cost of an
asset to expense

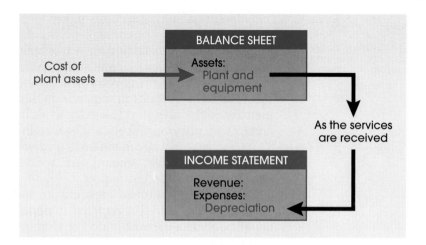

portion of the entry removes from the balance sheet that portion of the asset's cost estimated to have been used up during the current period. The debit portion of the entry allocates this expired cost to expense.

Separate Depreciation Expense and Accumulated Depreciation accounts are maintained for different types of depreciable assets, such as factory buildings, delivery equipment, and office equipment. These separate accounts help accountants to measure separately the costs of different business activities, such as manufacturing, sales, and administration.

Depreciation Is Not a Process of Valuation   Depreciation is a process of *cost allocation,* not a process of valuation. Accounting records do not attempt to show the current market values of plant assets. The market value of a building, for example, may increase during some accounting periods within the building's useful life. The recognition of depreciation expense continues, however, without regard to such temporary increases in market value. Accountants recognize that the building will render useful services only for a limited number of years, and that the full cost of the building should be *systematically allocated to expense* during these years.

Depreciation differs from most other expenses in that it does not depend upon cash payments at or near the time the expense is recorded. For this reason, depreciation often is called a "noncash" expense. Bear in mind, however, that cash payments may be required at the time depreciable assets are purchased or over a period of time.

Book Value   Plant assets are shown in the balance sheet at their book values (or *carrying values*). The **book value** of a plant asset is its *cost minus the related accumulated depreciation.* Accumulated depreciation is a contra-asset account, representing that portion of the asset's cost that has *already* been allocated to expense. Thus, book value represents the portion of the asset's cost that remains to be allocated to expense in future periods.

Causes of Depreciation

The two major causes of depreciation are physical deterioration and obsolescence.

Physical Deterioration   Physical deterioration of a plant asset results from use, as well as from exposure to sun, wind, and other climatic factors. When a plant asset has been carefully maintained, it is not uncommon for the owner to claim that the asset is as "good as new." Such statements are not literally true. Although a good repair policy may greatly lengthen the useful life of a machine, every machine eventually reaches the point at which it must be discarded. In brief, the making of repairs does not lessen the need for recognition of depreciation.

Obsolescence   The term ***obsolescence*** means the process of becoming out of date or obsolete. A computer, for example, may become obsolete even though it is in excellent physical condition; it becomes obsolete because better computers of superior design and performance have become available.

Methods of Computing Depreciation

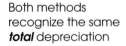
LO 3: Compute depreciation by the straight-line, the declining-balance, and the units-of-production (output) methods.

In preceding chapters, we have computed depreciation only by the **straight-line depreciation** method. Companies actually may use any of several different depreciation methods. Generally accepted accounting principles require only that a depreciation method result in a ***rational and systematic*** allocation of cost over the asset's useful life.

The straight-line method allocates an ***equal portion*** of depreciation expense to each period of the asset's useful life. Most of the other depreciation methods are various forms of accelerated depreciation. The term **accelerated depreciation** means that larger amounts of depreciation are recognized in the early years of the asset's life, and smaller amounts are recognized in the later years. Another depreciation method is the **units-of-production (output)** that allocates the cost based on the actual production or output of the period. Over the entire life of the asset, however, all these three methods recognize the same ***total*** amount of depreciation.

The differences between the straight-line methods and accelerated methods are illustrated in the following graphs:

Both methods recognize the same ***total*** depreciation

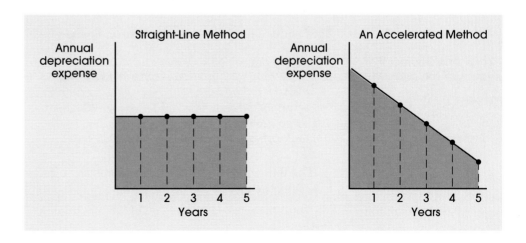

There is only one straight-line method and only one units-of-production method. But there are several different accelerated methods, each producing slightly different results. Different depreciation methods may be used for different assets. Of course, the depreciation methods in use should be disclosed in notes accompanying the financial statements.

In this chapter, we illustrate and explain straight-line depreciation, the most widely used accelerated method, which is called **fixed-percentage-of-declining-balance,** and the units-of-production (output) method.

Data for Our Illustrations   Our illustrations of depreciation methods are based upon the following data: On January 2, S&G Wholesale Grocery acquires a new delivery truck. The data and estimates needed for the computation of the annual depreciation expense are:

Cost $17,000
Estimated residual value . . . . $ 2,000
Estimated useful life . . . .   5 years (or 100,000 kilometres)*

The estimated life stated in kilometres will be used only in the units-of-production depreciation method.

The Straight-Line Method

The straight-line method was introduced in Chapter 3. Under this method an **equal portion** of the asset's cost is recognized as depreciation expense in each period of the asset's useful life.

Annual depreciation expense is computed by deducting the estimated **residual value** (or salvage value) from the cost of the asset and dividing the remaining **depreciable cost** by the years of estimated useful life. Using the data in our example, the annual straight-line depreciation is computed as follows:

$$\frac{\text{Cost} - \text{Residual Value}}{\text{Years of Useful Life}} = \frac{\$17,000 - \$2,000}{5 \text{ years}} = \$3,000 \text{ per year}$$

This same depreciation computation is shown below in tabular form.

Computing depreciation by straight-line method

Cost of the depreciable asset	$17,000
Less: Estimated residual value (amount to be realized by sale of asset when it is retired from use)	2,000
Total amount to be depreciated (depreciable cost)	$15,000
Estimated useful life	5 years
Depreciation expense each year ($15,000 ÷ 5)	$ 3,000

The following schedule summarizes the effects of straight-line depreciation over the entire life of the asset:

Depreciation Schedule: Straight-Line Method

Year	Computation	Depreciation Expense	Accumulated Depreciation	Book Value
				$17,000
First	$15,000 × ⅕	$ 3,000	$ 3,000	14,000
Second	$15,000 × ⅕	3,000	6,000	11,000
Third	$15,000 × ⅕	3,000	9,000	8,000
Fourth	$15,000 × ⅕	3,000	12,000	5,000
Fifth	$15,000 × ⅕	3,000	15,000	2,000
Total		$15,000		

Constant annual depreciation expense

Notice that the depreciation expense over the life of the truck totals **$15,000**—the cost of the truck **_minus the estimated residual value._** The residual value is **_not_** part of the cost "used up" in business operations. Instead, the residual value is expected to be recovered in cash upon disposal of the asset.

In practice, residual values are ignored if they are not expected to be **_material_** in amount. Traditionally, buildings, office equipment, furniture, fixtures, and special-purpose equipment seldom are considered to have significant residual values. Assets such as vehicles, aircraft, and computer systems, in contrast, often do have residual values that are material in amount.

It often is convenient to state the portion of an asset's depreciable cost that will be written off during the year as a percentage, called the **_depreciation rate._** When straight-line depreciation is in use, the depreciation rate is simply **_1_** divided by the **_life_** (in years) of the asset. The delivery truck in our example has an estimated life of 5 years, so the depreciation expense each year is ⅕, or **20%,** of the depreciable amount. Similarly, an asset with a 10-year life has a depreciation rate of 1/10, or **10%;** and an asset with an 8-year life, a depreciation rate of ⅛, or **12½%.**

Depreciation for Fractional Periods When an asset is acquired in the middle of an accounting period, it is not necessary to compute depreciation expense to the nearest day or week. In fact, such a computation would give a misleading impression of great precision. Since depreciation is based upon an estimated useful life of many years, the depreciation applicable to any one year is **_only an approximation._**

One widely used method of computing depreciation for part of a year is to round the calculation to the nearest whole month. In our example, S&G acquired the delivery truck on January 2. Therefore, we computed a "full year's" depreciation for the year of acquisition. Assume, however, that the truck had been acquired later in the year, say, on **_October 1._** Thus, the truck would have been in use for only 3 months (or 3/12) of the first year. In this case, depreciation expense for the first year would be limited to only **$750,** or 3/12 of a "full year's" depreciation ($3,000 × 3/12 = $750).

An even more widely used approach, called the **half-year convention,** is to record six months' depreciation on all assets acquired during the year. This approach is based upon the assumption that the actual purchase dates will "average out" to approximately midyear. The half-year convention is widely used for assets such as office equipment, automobiles, and machinery.

Assume that S&G Wholesale Grocery uses straight-line depreciation with the half-year convention. Depreciation on the $17,000 delivery truck with the 5-year life is summarized below:

Depreciation Schedule
Straight-Line Method with Half-Year Convention

	Year	Computation	Depreciation Expense	Accumulated Depreciation	Book Value
					$17,000
Straight-line with the half-year convention	First	$15,000 × ⅕ × ½	$ 1,500	$ 1,500	15,500
	Second	$15,000 × ⅕	3,000	4,500	12,500
	Third	$15,000 × ⅕	3,000	7,500	9,500
	Fourth	$15,000 × ⅕	3,000	10,500	6,500
	Fifth	$15,000 × ⅕	3,000	13,500	3,500
	Sixth	$15,000 × ⅕ × ½	1,500	15,000	2,000
	Total		$15,000		

When the half-year convention is in use, we ignore the date upon which the asset was actually purchased. We simply recognize ***one-half year's depreciation*** in both the first year and last year of the depreciation schedule. Notice that our depreciation schedule now includes depreciation expense in **6** years, instead of 5. Taking only a partial year's depreciation in the first year always extends the depreciation program into one additional year.

The half-year convention enables us to treat similar assets acquired at different dates during the year as a single group. For example, assume that an insurance company purchases hundreds of desk-top computers throughout the current year at a total cost of $600,000. The company depreciates these computers by the straight-line method, assuming a 5-year life and no residual value. Using the half-year convention, the depreciation expense on all of the computers purchased during the year may be computed as follows: $600,000 ÷ 5 years × 6/12 = $60,000. If we did not use the half-year convention, depreciation would have to be computed separately for computers purchased in different months.

The Declining-Balance Method

By far the most widely used accelerated depreciation method is called **fixed-percentage-of-declining-balance (diminishing-balance).** However the method is used primarily for income tax purposes.

Under the declining-balance method, an accelerated ***depreciation rate*** is computed as a specified percentage of the straight-line depreciation rate. Annual depreciation expense then is computed by applying this accelerated depreciation rate to the undepreciated cost (current book value) of the asset. This computation may be summarized as follows:

$$\text{Depreciation Expense} = \text{Remaining Book Value} \times \text{Accelerated Depreciation Rate}$$

The accelerated depreciation rate *remains constant* throughout the life of the asset. Hence, this rate represents the "fixed-percentage" described in the name of this depreciation method. The book value (cost minus accumulated depreciation) *decreases every year,* and represents the "declining or diminishing balance."

Thus far, we have described the accelerated depreciation rate as a "specified percentage" of the straight-line rate. Quite often this specified percentage is *200%,* meaning that the accelerated rate is exactly twice the straight-line rate. As a result, the declining-balance method of depreciation often is called *double-declining-balance* (or 200%-declining-balance).

Double-Declining-Balance   To illustrate the double-declining-balance method, consider our example of the $17,000 delivery truck. The estimated useful life is 5 years; therefore, the straight-line depreciation rate is *20%* (1 ÷ 5 years). Doubling this straight-line rate indicates an accelerated depreciation rate of *40%.* Each year, we will recognize as depreciation expense 40% of the truck's current book value, as shown below:

Depreciation Schedule: Double-Declining-Balance Method

Year	Computation	Depreciation Expense	Accumulated Depreciation	Book Value
				$17,000
First	$17,000 × 40%	$ 6,800	$ 6,800	10,200
Second	$10,200 × 40%	4,080	10,880	6,120
Third	$ 6,120 × 40%	2,448	13,328	3,672
Fourth	$ 3,672 × 40%	1,469	14,797	2,203
Fifth	$ 2,203 × 40% = 8̶8̶1̶	203	15,000	2,000
Total		$15,000		

Declining-balance at twice the straight-line rate

Notice that the estimated residual value of the delivery truck *does not* enter into the computation of depreciation expense until the very end. This is because the declining-balance method provides an *"automatic"* residual value. As long as each year's depreciation expense is equal to only a portion of the undepreciated cost of the asset, the asset *will never be entirely written off.* However, if the asset has a significant residual value, depreciation should *stop at this point.* Since our delivery truck has an estimated residual value of *$2,000,* the depreciation expense for the fifth year should be *limited to $203,* rather than the $881 indicated by taking 40% of the remaining book value. By limiting the last year's depreciation expense in this manner, the book value of the truck at the end of the fifth year will be equal to its $2,000 estimated residual value.

In the schedule illustrated above, we computed a "full year's" depreciation in the first year, because the asset was acquired on January 2. But if the half-year convention were in use, depreciation in the first year would be *reduced by half,* to $3,400. The depreciation in the second year would be ($17,000 − $3,400) × 40%, or *$5,440.*

Units-of-Production (Output) Method   For certain kinds of assets, more equitable allocation of the cost can be obtained by dividing the cost (minus residual or salvage value, if significant) by the estimated units of production or output, rather than by the estimated years of useful life. A car rental company, for example, might compute depreciation on its vehicles on the kilometres used.

If we assume that the delivery truck in our example has an estimated useful life of 100,000 kilometres, the depreciation rate *per kilometre of operation is 15 cents* ($15,000 ÷ 100,000 kilometres). This calculation of the depreciation rate may be stated as follows:

$$\frac{\text{Cost} - \text{Residual Value}}{\text{Estimated Units of Production (Kilometres)}} = \frac{\text{Depreciation per}}{\text{Unit of Production (Kilometre)}}$$

$$\frac{\$17,000 - \$2,000}{100,000 \text{ kilometres}} = \frac{\$.15 \text{ depreciation per}}{\text{kilometre}}$$

At the end of each year, the amount of depreciation to be recorded would be determined by multiplying the 15-cent rate by the number of kilometres the truck had been driven during the year. After the truck has gone 100,000 kilometres, it is fully depreciated, and the depreciation program is stopped. This method is suitable only when the total units of production (output) of the asset over its entire useful life can be estimated with reasonable accuracy.

Which Depreciation Methods Do Most Businesses Use?

Most businesses use the straight-line method of depreciation in their financial statements and accelerated methods in their income tax returns. The reasons for these choices are easy to understand.

Accelerated depreciation methods result in higher charges to depreciation expense in the early years of the asset's life and, therefore, lower reported net income than straight-line depreciation in those early years. Most publicly owned companies want to appear as profitable and as early as possible—certainly as profitable as their competitors. Therefore, the overwhelming majority of publicly owned companies use straight-line depreciation in their financial statements.

CASE IN POINT In a recent survey of 198 companies, 170 used the straight-line method and 77 of these 170 companies also used either the diminishing (declining) balance or units-of-production method. Moreover, 7 of the 198 surveyed companies used only the diminishing balance, and 2 used only the units-of-production method.[5]

For income tax purposes, it's a different story. Management usually wants to report the *lowest* possible taxable income in the company's income tax returns. Accelerated depreciation methods can substantially reduce both taxable income and tax payments for a period of years.[6]

---

[5]Clarence Byrd and Ida Chen, *Financial Reporting in Canada,* Twenty-second Edition (CICA, Toronto, 1997), p. 201.
[6]For a *growing* business, the use of accelerated depreciation in income tax returns may reduce taxable income *every* year. This is because a growing business may always have more assets in the early years of the recovery period than in the later years.

Accounting principles and income tax laws both permit companies to use *different depreciation methods* in the financial statements and their income tax returns. Therefore, most companies use straight-line depreciation in their financial statements and accelerated methods in their income tax returns.

The Differences in Depreciation Methods: Are They "Real"?   Using the straight-line depreciation method will cause a company to *report* higher profits than would be reported if an accelerated method were in use. But *is* the company more profitable than if it had used an accelerated method? The answer is *no!* Depreciation—no matter how it is computed—*is only an estimate.* The amount of this estimate has *no effect* upon the actual financial position of the business.

Thus, a business that uses an accelerated depreciation method in its financial statements is simply measuring its net income *more conservatively* than a business that uses straight-line.

However, the benefits of using an accelerated method for income tax purposes *are* "real," because amount of depreciation (called capital cost allowance for tax purposes) claimed affects the amount of taxes owed.

Financial Statement Disclosures

A company should *disclose* in notes to its financial statements the methods used to depreciate plant assets. Readers of these statements should recognize that accelerated depreciation methods transfer the costs of plant assets to expense more quickly than does the straight-line method. Thus, accelerated methods result in more *conservative* (lower) balance sheet valuations of plant assets and measurements of net income in the early years in the life of the plant assets. Moreover, when a change is made, both the reason for the change and the effect of the change on net income should be disclosed in a note to the financial statements.

Estimates of Useful Life and Residual Value   Estimating the useful lives and residual values of plant assets is a *responsibility of management.* These estimates usually are based upon the company's past experience with similar assets, but they also reflect the company's current circumstances and management's future plans. Thus, the estimated lives and residual values of similar assets may vary from one company to another.

The estimated lives and residual values of plant assets affect the amount of net income reported each period. The longer the estimated useful life and the larger the residual value, the smaller the amount of cost transferred each period to depreciation expense, and the larger the amount of reported net income. Bear in mind, however, that all large corporations are *audited* annually by a firm of independent public accountants. One of the responsibilities of these auditors is to determine that management's estimates of the useful lives of plant assets and residual values are reasonable under the circumstances.

Automobiles typically are depreciated over relatively short estimated lives—say, from 3 to 5 years. Most other types of equipment are depreciated over a period of from 5 to 15 years. Buildings are depreciated over much longer lives—perhaps 25 to 40 years for a new building, and 15 years or more for a building acquired used.

CASE IN POINT

Some excerpts of financial statement disclosures from recent balance sheets:

Toromont Industries Ltd.

Property, plant, and equipment are recorded at cost. Depreciation is provided principally using the straight-line method over the estimated useful lives of the various classes of assets as follows:

Buildings	20–30 years
Machinery	3–10 years
EDP Equipment	3 years
Furniture and Fixtures	3–5 years
Vehicles	3–5 years

Maple Leaf Foods Inc.

Property and equipment are recorded at cost. . . . Depreciation is calculated on a straight-line basis at the following rates, which are based on the expected useful life of the assets.

	Rate
Buildings	2% to 6%
Machinery and equipment	6% to 33%

Quebecor Inc.

Fixed assets are recorded at cost,. . . . Depreciation is provided on the straight-line basis over the following estimated useful lives:

Assets	Life
Buildings and hydroelectric power plant	20 years to 40 years
Machinery and equipment	3 years to 20 years

The Principle of Consistency   The *consistent* application of accounting methods is a generally accepted accounting principle. With respect to depreciation methods, this principle means that a company should *not change* from year to year the method used in computing the depreciation expense for a given plant asset. However, management *may* use different methods in computing depreciation for different assets. Also, as we have stressed earlier, a company may use different depreciation methods in its financial statements and income tax returns.

Revision of Estimated Useful Lives   What should be done if, after a few years of using a plant asset, management decides that the asset actually is going to last for a considerably longer or shorter period than was originally estimated? When this situation arises, a *revised estimate* of useful life should be made and the periodic depreciation expense decreased or increased accordingly.

The acceptable procedure for correcting the depreciation program is to spread the remaining undepreciated cost of the asset *over the years of remaining useful life.*[7] This correction affects only the amount of depreciation expense that will be recorded in the current and future periods. The financial statements of past periods are *not* revised to reflect changes in the estimated useful lives of depreciable assets. It is desirable to disclose the nature and effect of such a change.[8]

To illustrate, assume that a company acquires a $10,000 asset that is estimated to have a 5-year useful life and no residual value. Under the straight-line method, the annual depreciation expense is $2,000. At the end of the third year, accumulated depreciation amounts to $6,000, and the asset has an undepreciated cost (or book value) of $4,000.

At the beginning of the fourth year, it is decided that the asset will last for 5 *more* years. The revised estimate of useful life is, therefore, a total of 9 years. The depreciation expense to be recognized for the fourth year and for each of the remaining years is $800, computed as follows:

Revision of depreciation program

Undepreciated cost at end of third year ($10,000 − $6,000)	*$4,000*
Revised estimate of remaining years of useful life	*5 years*
Revised amount of annual depreciation expense ($4,000 ÷ 5)	*$ 800*

DISPOSAL OF PLANT AND EQUIPMENT

LO 4: Account for disposals of plant assets.

When depreciable assets are disposed of at any date other than the end of the year, an entry should be made to record depreciation for the *fraction of the year* ending with the date of disposal. If the half-year convention is in use, six months' depreciation should be recorded on all assets disposed of during the year. In the following illustrations of the disposal of items of plant and equipment, it is assumed that any necessary entries for fractional-period depreciation already have been recorded.

As units of plant and equipment wear out or become obsolete, they must be scrapped, sold, or traded in on new equipment. Upon the disposal or retirement of a depreciable asset, the cost of the property is removed from the asset account, and the accumulated depreciation is removed from the related contra-asset account. Assume, for example, that office equipment purchased 10 years ago at a cost of $20,000 has been fully depreciated and is no longer useful. The entry to record the scrapping of the worthless equipment is as follows:

Scrapping fully depreciated asset

Accumulated Depreciation: Office Equipment	*20,000*	
Office Equipment		*20,000*
To remove from the accounts the cost and the accumulated depreciation on fully depreciated office equipment now being scrapped. No salvage value.		

Once an asset has been fully depreciated, no more depreciation should be recorded on it, even though the property is in good condition and is still in use. The objective of depreciation is to spread the *cost* of an asset over the estimated period of its usefulness; in no case can depreciation expense be greater than the amount paid for the asset. When a fully depreciated

---

[7]CICA, *CICA Handbook* (Toronto), section 1506.25.
[8]Ibid.

asset remains in use beyond the original estimate of useful life, the asset account and the Accumulated Depreciation account should remain in the accounting records without further entries until the asset is retired.

Gains and Losses on Disposals of Plant and Equipment

Since the residual values and useful lives of plant assets are only estimates, it is not uncommon for plant assets to be sold at prices that differ from their book value at the date of disposal. When plant assets are sold, any gain or loss on the disposal is computed by comparing the ***book value with the amount received from the sale.*** A sales price in excess of the book value produces a ***gain;*** a sales price below the book value produces a ***loss.*** These gains or losses, if material in amount, should be shown separately in the income statement by computing the income from operations.

Disposal at a Price above Book Value   Assume that a machine that cost $10,000 and has a book value of $2,000 is sold for $3,000 cash. The journal entry to record this disposal is as follows:

Gain on disposal of plant asset

Cash	*3,000*	
Accumulated Depreciation: Machinery	*8,000*	
Machinery		*10,000*
Gain on Disposal of Plant Assets		*1,000*
To record sale of machinery at a price above book value.		

Disposal at a Price below Book Value   Now assume that the same machine is sold for $500 cash. The journal entry in this case would be as follows:

Loss on disposal of plant asset

Cash	*500*	
Accumulated Depreciation: Machinery	*8,000*	
Loss on Disposal of Plant Assets	*1,500*	
Machinery		*10,000*
To record sale of machinery at a price below book value.		

The disposal of a depreciable asset at a price equal to book value would result in neither a gain nor a loss. The entry for such a transaction would consist of a debit to Cash for the amount received, a debit to Accumulated Depreciation for the balance accumulated, and a credit to the asset account for the original cost.

Trading in Used Assets on New

Certain types of depreciable assets, such as automobiles and trucks, sometimes are traded in on new assets of the same kind. In most instances, a trade-in is viewed as both a ***sale*** of the old asset and a purchase of a new one as the cash payment involved is significant.[9]

---

[9]The CICA's Accounting Standards Board takes the position that, in general, when 10% or more of the transaction value is comprised of monetary consideration (cash or monetary obligations), the transaction should be viewed as ***monetary,*** rather than nonmonetary. Thus, gains and losses on most routine trade-ins should be ***recognized in full.*** See *CICA Handbook,* section 3830.04.

To illustrate, assume that Rancho Landscape has an old pickup truck that originally cost $15,000 but that now has a book value of $2,000. Rancho trades in this old truck on a new one with a fair market value of $23,000. The truck dealership grants Rancho a "trade-in allowance" of $3,500 for the old truck, and Rancho pays the remaining $19,500 cost of the new truck in cash. Rancho Landscape should record this transaction as follows:

Entry to record a typical trade-in

Vehicles (new truck)	*23,000*	
Accumulated Depreciation: Trucks (old truck)	*13,000*	
Vehicles (old truck)		*15,000*
Gain on Disposal of Plant Assets		*1,500*
Cash		*19,500*

Traded-in old truck on a new one costing $23,000. Received $3,500 trade-in allowance on the old truck, which had a book value of $2,000.

Notice that Rancho views the $3,500 trade-in allowance granted by the truck dealership as the ***sales price*** of the old truck. Thus, Rancho recognizes a ***$1,500 gain*** on the disposal (trade-in) of this asset ($3,500 trade-in allowance − $2,000 book value = $1,500 gain).

However, if the trade-in allowance is $1,200 rather than $3,500 a ***loss of $800*** ($2,000 book value − $1,200 trade-in allowance) is incurred by Rancho in this transaction. Also, the amount of cash to be paid is $21,800 rather than $19,500.

Accordingly, gains and losses on routine trade-ins are recorded in the accounting records whenever the transaction involves the payment of a significant amount of cash (or the creation of debt).

INTANGIBLE ASSETS

Characteristics

LO 5: Explain the nature of intangible assets, including goodwill.

As the word ***intangible*** suggests, assets in this classification have no physical substance. Leading examples are goodwill, patents, and trademarks. Intangible assets are classified in the balance sheet as a separate section called intangible assets (or other assets), following plant assets. However, not all assets that lack physical substance are regarded as intangible assets. An account receivable, for example, or a short-term prepayment is of nonphysical nature but is classified as a current asset and is not regarded as an intangible. In brief, ***intangible assets are assets that are used in the operation of the business but that have no physical substance and are noncurrent.***

The basis of valuation for intangible assets is cost. In some companies, certain intangible assets such as trademarks may be of great importance but may have been acquired without incurring any significant cost. Intangible assets appear in the balance sheet at their ***cost.*** Therefore, the assets are listed only if significant costs are incurred in their acquisition or development. If these costs are ***insignificant,*** they are treated as revenue expenditures.

Operating Expenses Versus Intangible Assets

For an expenditure to qualify as an intangible asset, there must be ***reasonable evidence*** of future benefits. Many expenditures offer some prospects of yielding benefits in subsequent years, but the existence and life-span of these benefits is so uncertain that most companies treat these expenditures as operating expenses. Examples are the expenditures for intensive advertising campaigns to introduce new products and the expense of training employees to work with new types of machinery or office equipment. There is little doubt that some benefits from these outlays continue beyond the current period, but because of the uncertain duration of the benefits, it is almost universal practice to treat expenditures of this nature as expense of the current period.

Amortization

The term **amortization** is used to describe the systematic write-off to expense of the cost of an intangible asset over its useful life. The usual accounting entry for amortization consists of a debit to Amortization Expense and a credit to the intangible asset account. There is no theoretical objection to crediting an accumulated amortization account rather than the intangible asset account, but this method is seldom encountered in practice.

   Although it is difficult to estimate the useful life of an intangible such as a trademark, it is highly probable that such an asset will not contribute to future earnings on a permanent basis. The cost of the intangible asset should, therefore, be deducted from revenue during the years in which it may be expected to aid in producing revenue. Under current accounting practices, the maximum period for amortization of an intangible asset cannot exceed ***40 years*** unless a longer life can be estimated and clearly demonstrated.[10] The straight-line method normally is used for amortizing intangible assets.

Goodwill

Business executives used the term **goodwill** in a variety of ways before it became part of accounting terminology. One of the most common meanings of goodwill in a nonaccounting sense concerns the benefits derived from a favourable reputation among customers. To accountants, however, goodwill has a very specific meaning not necessarily limited to customer relations. It means the ***present value of future earnings in excess of the normal return on net identifiable assets.*** Above-average earnings may arise not only from favourable customer relations, but also from such factors as superior management and manufacturing efficiency.

   The **present value** of future cash flows is the amount that a knowledgeable investor would ***pay today*** for the right to receive those future cash flows. (The present value concept is discussed further in later chapters and in Appendix C.)

---

[10]CICA, *CICA Handbook* (Toronto), section 3060.32.

The phrase ***normal return on net identifiable assets*** also requires explanation. ***Net assets*** means the owners' equity in a business, or assets minus liabilities. Goodwill, however, is not an ***identifiable*** asset. The existence of goodwill is implied by the ability of a business to earn an above-average return; however, the cause and precise dollar value of goodwill are largely matters of personal opinion. Therefore, **net identifiable assets** mean all assets ***except goodwill,*** minus liabilities.

A ***normal return*** on net identifiable assets is the rate of return that investors demand in a particular industry to justify their buying a business at the fair market value of its net identifiable assets. A business has goodwill when investors will pay a ***higher*** price because the business earns ***more*** than the normal rate of return.

Assume that two similar restaurants are offered for sale, and that the normal return on the fair market value of the net identifiable assets of restaurants of this type is 15% a year. The relative earning power of the two restaurants during the past five years is shown below:

	Mandarin Coast	Golden Dragon
Fair market value of net identifiable assets	$1,000,000	$1,000,000
Normal rate of return on net assets	15%	15%
Normal earnings, computed as 15% of net identifiable assets	150,000	150,000
Average actual net income for past five years	150,000	200,000
Earnings in excess of normal	$ -0-	$ 50,000

Which business is "worth more"?

An investor presumably would be willing to pay $1,000,000 to buy Mandarin Coast, because this restaurant earns the normal 15% return that justifies the fair market value of its net identifiable assets. Although Golden Dragon has the same amount of net identifiable assets, an investor probably would be willing to pay ***more*** for Golden Dragon than for Mandarin Coast, because Golden Dragon has a long record of superior earnings. The ***extra amount*** that a buyer would pay to purchase Golden Dragon represents the value of this business's ***goodwill.***

Estimating Goodwill   How much will an investor pay for goodwill? Above-average earnings in past years are of significance to prospective purchasers only if they believe that these earnings ***will continue*** after they acquire the business. Investors' appraisals of goodwill, therefore, will vary with their estimates of the ***future earning power*** of the business. Very few businesses, however, are able to maintain above-average earnings for more than a few years. Consequently, the purchaser of a business will usually limit any amount paid for goodwill to not more than four or five times the amount by which annual earnings exceed normal earnings.

Arriving at a fair value for the goodwill of an ongoing business is a difficult and subjective process. Any estimate of goodwill is in large part a matter of personal opinion. The following are two methods that a prospective purchaser might use in estimating a value for goodwill:

1. Value the business as a whole, and then subtract the current market value of the net identifiable assets.

The value of a business often is expressed through the ***price-earnings ratio*** (p/e ratio). Assume that highly successful restaurants in this area currently sell at about 6½ times annual earnings. This p/e ratio suggests that Golden Dragon is worth about $1,300,000 ($200,000 average net income × 6½). As the net identifiable assets have a market value of $1,000,000, this implies the existence of ***$300,000*** in goodwill.

2. Capitalize the amount by which earnings exceed normal amounts.

"Capitalizing" an earnings stream means dividing those earnings by the investor's required rate of return. The result is the maximum amount that the investor could pay for the excess earnings in order to achieve the required rate of return on the investment. To illustrate, assume that the prospective buyer decides to capitalize the $50,000 annual excess earnings of Golden Dragon at a rate of 25%. This approach results in a ***$200,000*** estimate ($50,000 ÷ .25 = $200,000) for the value of goodwill. (Note that $50,000 per year represents a 25% return on a $200,000 investment.)

A weakness in the capitalization method is that ***no provision is made for the recovery*** of the investment. If the prospective buyer is to earn a 25% return on the $200,000 investment in goodwill, either the excess earnings must continue ***forever*** (an unlikely assumption) or the buyer must be able to recover the $200,000 investment at a later date by selling the business at a price above the fair market value of net identifiable assets.

Notice that our two approaches resulted in very different estimates of Golden Dragon's goodwill—$300,000 and $200,000. Such differences are likely to occur in practice. The value of goodwill depends upon ***future performance.*** Therefore, there is ***no*** "surefire way" of determining its real value. At best, the value of a company's goodwill is only an educated guess.

Recording Goodwill in the Accounts Because of the difficulties in objectively estimating the value of goodwill, this asset is recorded only when it is ***purchased.*** Goodwill is "purchased" when one company buys another. The purchaser records the identifiable assets it has purchased at their fair market values, and then debits any additional amount paid to an asset account entitled Goodwill.

Generally accepted accounting principles require that recorded goodwill be amortized to expense over a period that does not ***exceed*** 40 years (unless a longer life can be estimated and clearly demonstrated).[11] However, the accounting concept of ***conservatism*** suggests that goodwill usually should be amortized over a much shorter period. For this reason, many companies amortize purchased goodwill over periods of 10 or 20 years.

But Most Goodwill Never Gets Recorded! Many businesses have never purchased goodwill but have ***generated it internally*** by developing good customer relations, superior management, or other factors that result in

---

[11]Ibid.

above-average earnings. Because there is no objective way of determining the value of goodwill unless the business is sold, internally generated goodwill is **not recorded** in the accounting records. Thus, goodwill may be an important asset of a successful business, but **may not even appear** in the company's balance sheet.

The absence of internally generated goodwill is, perhaps, the principal reason why a balance sheet does not indicate a company's current market value.

Goodwill or Bad Judgment?   Some companies have paid huge amounts for "goodwill," only to discover that the businesses they have purchased do **not** continue to earn above-normal rates of return. In these cases, the "goodwill" is not an asset with future economic value. Rather, it indicates that the company paid too high a price in acquiring the other business. If it becomes apparent that purchased goodwill does **not** have real economic value, it should be written off immediately.

In summary, the best evidence of a company's goodwill is not the amount listed in the balance sheet. Rather, it is a long and on-going track record of **above-average earnings.**

Patents

A patent is an exclusive right granted by the federal government for manufacture, use, and sale of a particular product. The purpose of this exclusive grant is to encourage the invention of new products and processes. When a company acquires a patent by purchase from the inventor or other holder, the purchase price should be recorded by debiting the intangible asset account, Patents.

For patents filed before October 1, 1989, their duration is 17 years from the date of issue. For patents filed on or after October 1, 1989, their duration is 20 years from the date of application. Thus, the period of amortization for patents must not exceed their legal life of either 17 or 20 years. However, if the patent is likely to lose its usefulness in less than the legal life, amortization should be based on the shorter period of estimated useful life. Assume that a patent is purchased from the inventor at a cost of $100,000, after five years of its 17-year legal life have expired. The remaining **legal** life is, therefore, 12 years, but if the estimated **useful** life is only four years, amortization should be based on this shorter period. The entry to be made to record the annual amortization expense would be:

Entry for amortization of patent

Amortization Expense: Patents *25,000*
    Patents *25,000*
To amortize cost of patent on a straight-line basis over an estimated life of 4 years.

Trademarks and Trade Names

Coca-Cola's famous name, usually written in a distinctive typeface, is a classic example of a trademark known around the world. A trademark is a word, symbol, or design that identifies a product or group of products and affords a measure of protection to the owner whether or not registration has occurred. However, registration of a trademark in Canada serves as evidence of ownership and facilitates a higher degree of protection. Registration has a term of 15 years but may be renewed indefinitely for further terms of 15 years.

A trade name is the name under which a business is carried on whether or not it is the legally incorporated name of the business. If a trade name is used as a trademark it may be registered as a trademark.

The costs of developing a trademark or trade name often consist of advertising campaigns, which should be treated as expense when incurred. If a trademark or trade name is purchased, however, the cost may be substantial. Such cost should be capitalized and amortized to expense over a reasonable period of time, which generally would not be more than 40 years. If the use of the trademark is discontinued or its contribution to earnings becomes doubtful, any unamortized cost should be written off immediately.

Franchises

A franchise is a right granted by a company or a governmental unit to conduct a certain type of business in a specific geographical area. An example of a franchise is the right to operate a McDonald's restaurant in a specific neighbourhood. The cost of franchises varies greatly and often may be quite substantial. When the cost of a franchise is small, it may be charged immediately to expense or amortized over a short period such as 5 years. When the cost is material, amortization should be based upon the life of the franchise (if limited); the amortization period, however, may not exceed 40 years.

Copyrights

A copyright is an exclusive right granted by the federal government to protect the production and sale of literary or artistic materials for the life of the creator plus 50 years. The cost of obtaining a copyright in some cases is minor and therefore is chargeable to expense when paid. Only when a copyright is ***purchased*** will the expenditure be ***material enough*** to warrant its being capitalized and spread over the useful life. The revenue from copyrights is usually limited to only a few years, and the purchase cost should, of course, be amortized over the years in which the revenue is expected.

Other Intangibles and Deferred Charges

Among the other intangibles found in the published balance sheets of large corporations are moving costs, plant rearrangement costs, organization costs, formulas, processes, name lists, and film rights. Some companies group items of this type under the title of **Deferred Charges,** meaning expenditures that will provide benefits beyond the current year and will be written off to expense over their useful economic lives. It is also common practice to combine these items under the heading of Other Assets, which is listed at the bottom of the balance sheet.

Research and Development (R&D) Costs

The spending of millions of dollars a year on research and development leading to all kinds of new products is a striking characteristic of modern industry. In the past, some companies treated all research and development costs as expense in the year incurred; other companies in the same industry recorded these costs as intangible assets to be amortized over future years. This diversity of practice prevented the financial statements of different companies from being comparable.

The lack of uniformity in accounting for R&D was ended when the *CICA Handbook* recommended that all research and development costs be charged to expense when incurred except when the ***development costs*** have met the following specific criteria; (1) the product is clearly defined and the attributable costs can be identified, (2) the product is technically and commercially feasible and adequate resources are available to complete the project, and (3) the future benefits of the product could be considered as reasonably certain and the enterprise intends to sell or use the product.[12] Those development costs that have met ***all*** these criteria should be ***deferred*** to future periods. The amortization of these deferred development costs should be on a systematic and rational basis so as to result in a fair matching of such costs with related benefits.[13] In the United States, however, the FASB requires that all research and development costs be charged to expense when incurred.[14]

NATURAL RESOURCES

Accounting for Natural Resources

Mining properties, oil and gas reserves, and tracts of standing timber are leading examples of natural resources. The distinguishing characteristics of these assets are that they are physically removed from their natural environment and are converted into inventory. Theoretically, a coal mine might be regarded as an underground "inventory" of coal; however, such an "inventory" is certainly not a current asset. In the balance sheet, mining property and other natural resources are classified as property, plant, and equipment. Once the coal is removed from the ground, however, this coal ***does*** represent inventory.

We have explained that plant assets such as buildings and equipment depreciate because of physical deterioration or obsolescence. A mine or an oil reserve does not "depreciate" for these reasons, but it is gradually ***depleted*** as the natural resource is removed from the ground. Once all of the coal has been removed from a coal mine, for example, the mine is "fully depleted" and will be abandoned or sold for its residual value.

To illustrate the **depletion** of a natural resource, assume that Rainbow Minerals pays $45 million to acquire the Red Valley Mine, which is believed to contain 10 million tonnes of coal. The residual value of the mine after all of the coal is removed is estimated to be $5 million. The depletion that will occur over the life of the mine is the original cost minus the residual value, or $40 million. This depletion will occur at the rate of ***$4 per tonne*** ($40 million ÷ 10 million tonnes) as the coal is removed from the mine. If we

LO 6: Account for the depletion of natural resources.

[12]CICA, *CICA Handbook,* (Toronto), section 3450.20 and 3450.21.
[13]Ibid., section 3450.26, 3450.27, and 3450.28.
[14]FASB, *Statement No. 2,* "Accounting for Research and Development Costs" (Norwalk, Conn.: 1974), par. 12.

assume that 2 million tonnes are mined during the first year of operations, the entry to record the depletion of the mine would be as follows:

Recording depletion

Inventory	*8,000,000*	
Accumulated Depletion: Red Valley Mine		*8,000,000*

To record depletion of the Red Valley Mine for the year;
2,000,000 tonnes mined @ $4 per tonne.

Once removed from the mine, coal becomes merchandise available for sale. Therefore, the estimated cost of this coal is debited to the Inventory account. As the coal is sold, this cost is transferred from the Inventory account to the Cost of Goods Sold account.

Accumulated Depletion is a **contra-asset account** similar to the Accumulated Depreciation account; it represents the portion of the mine that has been used up (depleted) to date. In Rainbow Mineral's balance sheet, the Red Valley Mine now appears as follows:

The mine gradually is turned into inventory

Property, Plant & Equipment:
Mining properties: Red Valley Mine	*$45,000,000*	
Less: Accumulated depletion	*8,000,000*	*$37,000,000*

Depreciation of Buildings and Equipment Closely Related to Natural Resources   Buildings and equipment installed at a mine or drilling site may be useful only at that particular location. Consequently, such assets should be depreciated over their normal useful lives, or over the life of the natural resource, **whichever is shorter.** Often depreciation on such assets is computed using the units-of-product (output) method, thus relating the depreciation expense to the rate at which units of natural resources are removed.

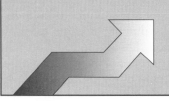

CASE IN POINT   Imperial Metals Corporation's recent balance sheet and related notes show:

MINERAL PROPERTIES

Producing mining property, plant and equipment	*$78,490,146*
Accumulated depletion and depreciation	*6,343,359*
	72,146,787
Exploration Properties	
Acquisition and deferred exploration costs	*10,553,505*
	$82,700,292

Producing mining property, plant and equipment is carried at cost less accumulated depletion and depreciation. Depletion and depreciation are computed by property on the unit-of-production method based upon estimated recoverable reserves.

Depreciation, Amortization, and Depletion—A Common Goal

The processes of depreciation, amortization, and depletion discussed in this chapter all have a common goal. That goal is to **allocate the acquisition** *cost of a long-lived asset to expense over the years in which the asset contributes to revenue.* By allocating the acquisition cost of long-lived assets over the years that benefit from the use of these assets, we stress again the importance of the *matching principle.* The determination of income requires the matching of revenue with the expenses incurred to produce that revenue.

The Impairment of Plant Assets

On occasion, it may become apparent that a company cannot reasonably expect to recover the cost of certain plant assets, either through use or through sale. For example, an oil company may pay a high price for land that it hopes contains large deposits of oil. If the company finds no oil, however, it may become apparent that the land is worth far less than its cost.

If the cost of an asset cannot be recovered through future use or sale, the asset should be *written down* to its net recoverable amount or net realizable value. The offsetting debit is to a loss account. These write-downs generally do *not* enter into the determination of taxable income.

End-of-Chapter Review

Key Terms Introduced or Emphasized in Chapter 10

Accelerated depreciation *(p.523)* Methods of depreciation that call for recognition of relatively large amounts of depreciation in the early years of an asset's useful life and relatively small amounts in the later years.

Amortization *(p.534)* The systematic write-off to expense of the cost of an intangible asset over the periods of its economic usefulness.

Book value *(p.522)* The cost of a plant asset minus the total recorded depreciation, as shown by the Accumulated Depreciation account. The remaining undepreciated cost is also known as *carrying value.*

Capital assets *(p.517)* Capital assets consist of property, plant, and equipment, intangible properties, and natural resources that are held for use in the operation of the business and not intended for sale to customers.

Capital expenditure *(p.520)* A cost incurred to acquire a long-lived asset. An expenditure that will benefit several accounting periods.

Capitalize *(p.520)* A verb with two different meanings in accounting. The first is to debit an expenditure to an asset account, rather than directly to expense. The second is to determine the value of an investment by dividing the annual return by the investor's required rate of return.

Deferred charge *(p.538)* An expenditure expected to yield benefits for several accounting periods and therefore capitalized and written off during the periods benefited.

Depletion *(p.539)* Allocating the cost of a natural resource to the units removed as the resource is mined, pumped, cut, or otherwise consumed.

Depreciation *(p.521)* The systematic allocation of the cost of an asset to expense over the years of its estimated useful life.

Fixed-percentage-of-declining-balance (diminishing-balance) depreciation *(p.526)* An accelerated method of depreciation in which the rate may be a multiple of the straight-line rate, which is applied each year to the *undepreciated cost* of the asset.

Goodwill *(p.534)* The present value of expected future earnings of a business in excess of the earnings normally realized in the industry. Recorded when a business entity is purchased at a price in excess of the fair value of its net identifiable assets (excluding goodwill) less liabilities.

Half-year convention *(p.525)* The practice of taking six months' depreciation in the year of acquisition and the year of disposition, rather than computing depreciation for partial periods to the nearest month.

Impairment (of an asset) *(p.541)* A change in economic conditions that reduces the economic usefulness of an asset. May necessitate writing down the carrying value of the asset.

Intangible assets *(p.518)* Those assets that are used in the operation of a business but that have no physical substance and are noncurrent.

Natural resources *(p.518)* Mines, oil fields, standing timber, and similar assets that are physically consumed and converted into inventory.

Net identifiable assets *(p.535)* Total of all assets *except goodwill,* minus liabilities.

Plant and equipment (plant assets) *(p.517)* Long-lived assets that are acquired for use in business operations rather than for resale to customers.

Present value *(p.534)* The amount that a knowledgeable investor would pay today for the right to receive future cash flows. The present value is always less than the sum of the future cash flows, because the investor requires a return on the investment.

Residual (salvage) value *(p.524)* The portion of an asset's cost expected to be recovered through sale or trade-in of the asset at the end of its useful life.

Revenue expenditure *(p.520)* Any expenditure assumed to benefit only the current accounting period.

Straight-line depreciation *(p.523)* A method of depreciation that allocates the cost of an asset (minus any residual value) equally to each year of its useful life.

Tangible plant assets *(p.518)* Plant assets that have physical substance, but that are not natural resources. Include land, buildings, and all types of equipment.

Units-of-production (output) *(p.523)* A depreciation method in which cost (minus residual value) is divided by the estimated units of lifetime output. The unit depreciation cost is multiplied by the actual units of output each year to compute the annual depreciation expense.

DEMONSTRATION PROBLEM

On April 1, 1997, Argo Industries purchased new equipment at a cost of $325,000. Useful life of this equipment was estimated at 5 years, with a residual value of $25,000. The estimated total units produced by this equipment amount to 150,000 units.

INSTRUCTIONS

Compute the annual depreciation expense for each year until this equipment becomes fully depreciated under each depreciation method listed below. Show supporting computations.

a. Straight-line, with depreciation for fractional years rounded to the nearest whole month.

b. Double-declining-balance, with the half-year convention. Limit depreciation in 2002 to an amount that reduces the undepreciated cost to the estimated residual value.

c. Units-of-production, assuming the units produced are: 1997: 20,000; 1998: 50,000; 1999: 30,000; 2000: 25,000; 2001: 15,000; 2002: 10,000.

SOLUTION TO DEMONSTRATION PROBLEM

	Method of Depreciation		
	a	b	c
Year	Straight-Line	Double-Declining-Balance	Units-of-Production
1997	$ 45,000	$ 65,000	$ 40,000
1998	60,000	104,000	100,000
1999	60,000	62,400	60,000
2000	60,000	37,440	50,000
2001	60,000	22,464	30,000
2002	15,000	8,696	20,000
Totals	$300,000	$300,000	$300,000

Supporting computations:

a.

1997: ($325,000 − $25,000) × ⅕ × ⁹⁄₁₂ = $45,000
1998–2001: $300,000 × ⅕ = $60,000
2002: $300,000 × ⅕ × ³⁄₁₂ = $15,000

b.

	Undepreciated Cost	Rate	Depreciation Expense
1997:	$325,000 ×	40% × ½ =	$ 65,000
1998:	260,000 ×	40% =	104,000
1999:	156,000 ×	40% =	62,400
2000:	93,600 ×	40% =	37,440
2001:	56,160 ×	40% =	22,464
2002:	33,696 −	$25,000 =	8,696

c.

$$1997: \quad (\$325{,}000 - \$25{,}000) \times \frac{20{,}000}{150{,}000} = \$40{,}000$$

$$1998: \quad \$300{,}000 \times \frac{50{,}000}{150{,}000} = \$100{,}000$$

$$1999: \quad \$300{,}000 \times \frac{30{,}000}{150{,}000} = \$60{,}000$$

$$2000: \quad \$300{,}000 \times \frac{25{,}000}{150{,}000} = \$50{,}000$$

$$2001: \quad \$300{,}000 \times \frac{15{,}000}{150{,}000} = \$30{,}000$$

$$2002: \quad \$300{,}000 \times \frac{10{,}000}{150{,}000} = \$20{,}000$$

Self-Test Questions

The answers to these questions appear on page 558.

1. In which of the following situations should the named company **not** record any depreciation expense on the asset described?
   a. Commuter Airline is required by law to maintain its aircraft in "as good as new" condition.
   b. Metro Advertising owns an office building that has been increasing in value each year since it was purchased.
   c. Computer Sales Company has in inventory a new type of computer designed "never to become obsolete."
   d. None of the above answers is correct—in each case, the named company should record depreciation on the asset described.

2. Which of the following statements is (are) correct?
   a. Accumulated depreciation represents a fund being accumulated for the replacement of plant assets.
   b. The cost of a machine includes the cost of repairing damage to the machine during the installation process.
   c. A company may use different depreciation methods in its financial statements.
   d. The use of an accelerated depreciation method causes an asset to wear out more quickly than does use of the straight-line method.

3. On April 1, 2000, Sanders Construction paid $10,000 for equipment with an estimated useful life of 10 years and a residual value of $2,000. The company uses the double-declining-balance method of depreciation and applies the half-year convention to fractional periods. In **2001,** the amount of depreciation expense to be recognized on this equipment is:
   a. $1,600
   b. $1,440
   c. $1,280
   d. Some other amount

4. Delta Company sold a plant asset that originally had cost $50,000 for $22,000 cash. If Delta correctly reports a $5,000 gain on this sale, the **accumulated depreciation** on the asset at the date of sale must have been:
   a. $33,000
   b. $28,000

      c. $23,000
      d. Some other amount

  5. In which of the following situations would Burton Industries include goodwill in its balance sheet?
      a. The fair market value of Burton's net identifiable assets amounts to $2,000,000. Normal earnings for this industry is 15% of net identifiable assets. Burton's net income for the past five years has averaged $390,000.
      b. Burton spent $800,000 during the current year for research and development for a new product that promises to generate substantial revenue for at least 10 years.
      c. Burton acquired Baxter Electronics at a price in excess of the fair market value of Baxter's net identifiable assets.
      d. A buyer wishing to purchase Burton's entire operation has offered a price in excess of the fair market value of Burton's net identifiable assets.

ASSIGNMENT MATERIAL

Discussion Questions

  1. Coca-Cola's distinctive trademark is more valuable than a bottling plant. But the company's bottling plants are listed in the balance sheet, and the famous trademark isn't. Explain.

  2. Identify the basic "accountable events" in the life of a depreciable plant asset. Which of these events directly affect the net income of the current period?

  3. Which of the following characteristics would prevent an item from being included in the classification of plant and equipment? (a) Intangible, (b) limited life, (c) unlimited life, (d) held for sale in the regular course of business, (e) not capable of rendering benefits to the business in the future.

  4. The following expenditures were incurred in connection with a large new machine acquired by a metals manufacturing company. Identify those which should be included in the cost of the asset. (a) Freight charges, (b) sales tax on the machine, (c) payment to a passing motorist whose car was damaged by the equipment used in unloading the machine, (d) wages of employees for time spent in installing and testing the machine before it was placed in service, (e) wages of employees assigned to lubrication and minor adjustments of machine one year after it was placed in service.

  5. What is the distinction between a ***capital expenditure*** and a ***revenue expenditure?***

  6. If a capital expenditure is erroneously treated as a revenue expenditure, will the net income of the current year be overstated or understated? Will this error have any effect upon the net income reported in future years? Explain.

  7. Shoppers' Market purchased for $220,000 a site upon which it planned to build a new store. The site consisted of three hectares of land, and included an old house and two barns. County property tax records showed the following appraised values for this property: land, $160,000, buildings, $40,000.

Indicate what Shoppers' should do with this $220,000 cost in its financial statements, and explain your reasoning.

8. Which of the following statements best describes the nature of depreciation?
   a. Regular reduction of asset value to correspond to the decline in market value as the asset ages.
   b. A process of correlating the book value of an asset with its gradual decline in physical efficiency.
   c. Allocation of cost in a manner that will ensure that plant and equipment items are not carried on the balance sheet at amounts in excess of net recoverable value.
   d. Allocation of the cost of a plant asset to the periods in which services are received from the asset.

9. Should depreciation continue to be recorded on a building when ample evidence exists that the current market value is greater than original cost and that the rising trend of market values is continuing? Explain.

10. Explain what is meant by an ***accelerated*** depreciation method. Are accelerated methods widely used in financial statements?

11. One accelerated depreciation method is called ***fixed-percentage-of-declining-balance.*** Explain what is meant by the terms "fixed-percentage" and "declining-balance."

12. Criticize the following quotation:
   "We shall have no difficulty in paying for new plant assets needed during the coming year because our estimated outlays for new equipment amount to only $80,000, and we have more than twice that amount in our accumulated depreciation account at present."

13. Explain two approaches to computing depreciation for a fractional period in the year in which an asset is purchased. (Neither of your approaches should require the computation of depreciation to the nearest day or week.)

14. a. Does the accounting principle of consistency require a company to use the same method of depreciation for all of its plant assets?
   b. Is it acceptable for a corporation to use different depreciation methods in its financial statements and its income tax returns?

15. After 4 years of using a machine acquired at a cost of $15,000, London Construction Company determined that the original estimated life of 10 years had been too short and that a total useful life of 12 years was a more reasonable estimate. Explain briefly the method that should be used to revise the depreciation program, assuming that straight-line depreciation has been used. Assume that the revision is made after recording depreciation and closing the accounts at the end of four years of use of the machine.

16. Define ***intangible assets.*** Would an account receivable arising from a sale of merchandise qualify as an intangible asset under your definition?

17. Over what period of time should the cost of various types of intangible assets be amortized by regular charges against revenue? (Your answer should be in the form of a principle or guideline rather than a specific number of years.) What method of amortization is generally used?

18. Under what circumstances should ***goodwill*** be recorded in the accounts?

19. In reviewing the financial statements of Digital Products Company Limited with a view to investing in the company's stock, you notice that net tangible assets total $1 million, that goodwill is listed at $400,000, and that average

earnings for the past five years have been $50,000 a year. How would these relationships influence your thinking about the company?

20. Mineral King recognizes $20 depletion for each tonne of ore mined. During the current year the company mined 600,000 tonnes but sold only 500,000 tonnes, as it was attempting to build up inventories in anticipation of a possible strike by employees. How much depletion should be deducted from revenue of the current year?

21. Explain the meaning of an *impairment* of an asset. Provide several examples. What accounting event should occur when an asset has become substantially impaired?

22. Several years ago March Metals purchased for $120,000 a well-known trademark for padlocks and other security products. After using the trademark for three years, March Metals discontinued it altogether when the company withdrew from the lock business and concentrated on the manufacture of aircraft parts. Amortization of the trademark at the rate of $3,000 a year is being continued on the basis of a 40-year life, which the owner of March Metals says is required by accounting standards. Do you agree? Explain.

Exercises

EXERCISE 10-1
Costs to be Capitalized
(LO 1, 2)

New machinery was purchased by HydroTech at a list price of $40,000, with a cash discount of $800. Payment of the invoice was made within the discount period. Sales taxes were $3,000. HydroTech also paid transportation charges of $610 on the new machinery as well as $760 for installing the machinery in the appropriate locations. During the unloading and installation work, some of the machines fell from a forklift and were damaged. Repair of the damaged parts cost $2,170. After the machinery had been in use for 3 months, it was thoroughly cleaned and lubricated at a cost of $260. Prepare a list of the items that should be capitalized by a debit to the Machinery account and state the total cost of the new machinery.

EXERCISE 10-2
Distinguishing Capital Expenditures from Revenue Expenditures
(LO 1, 2)

Identify the following expenditures as capital expenditures or revenue expenditures:
a. Immediately after acquiring a new delivery truck, paid $225 to have the name of the store and other advertising material painted on the vehicle.
b. Painted delivery truck at a cost of $250 after 2 years of use.
c. Purchased new battery at a cost of $98 for 2-year-old delivery truck.
d. Installed an escalator at a cost of $12,500 in a three-storey building that had previously been used for some years without elevators or escalators.
e. Purchased an electric pencil sharpener at a cost of $28.50.
f. Original life of the delivery truck had been estimated at 4 years and straight-line depreciation of 25% yearly had been recognized. After 3 years' use, however, it was decided to recondition the truck thoroughly, including a new engine.

EXERCISE 10-3
Depreciation for Fractional Years
(LO 3)

On November 2, Glass Recycling Company purchased special-purpose equipment at a cost of $600,000. Useful life of the equipment was estimated to be 5 years and the residual value $90,000. Compute the depreciation expense to be recognized in each calendar year during the life of the equipment under each of the following:
a. Straight-line (round computations for a partial year to the nearest full month).
b. Straight-line (use the half-year convention).

EXERCISE 10-4
Declining-Balance Method
(LO 3)

Machinery with an estimated useful life of 5 years was acquired by VPI Industries at the beginning of the current year. The machinery cost $100,000, and had an estimated residual value of $12,000. Compute the annual depreciation on this machinery in each of the next 5 years using the double-declining-balance method. Compute one "full year's" depreciation in each year.

EXERCISE 10-5
Units-of-Production Method
(LO 3)

During the current year, Airport Auto Rentals purchased 60 new automobiles at a cost of $13,000 per car. The cars will be sold to a wholesaler at an estimated $4,000 each as soon as they have been driven 50,000 kilometres. Airport Auto Rentals computes depreciation expense on its automobiles by the units-of-production (output) method, based upon kilometres used.

INSTRUCTIONS

a. Compute the amount of depreciation to be recognized for each kilometre that a rental automobile is driven.

b. Assuming that the 60 rental cars are driven a total of 1,650,000 kilometres during the current year, compute the total amount of depreciation expense that Airport Auto Rentals should recognize on this fleet of cars for the year.

c. Is this method matching expenses with revenue better than the straight-line method? Explain.

EXERCISE 10-6
Depreciation Methods
(LO 3)

On April 15, Year 1, Delta Company acquired a new machine with an estimated useful life of 5 years. Cost of the equipment was $55,000, with a residual value of $5,000.

a. Compute the amounts of depreciation recognized each of the first 3 years under each of the two depreciation methods listed below. In each case, assume the half-year convention is applied.

　1. Straight-line.

　2. Double-declining-balance.

b. Comment upon significant differences or similarities that you observe among the patterns of depreciation expense recognized under the two methods.

EXERCISE 10-7
Evaluation of Disclosures in
Annual Reports
(LO 3)

A recent annual report of **H. J. Heinz Company** includes the following note: ***Depreciation:*** For financial reporting purposes, depreciation is provided on the straight-line method over the estimated useful lives of the assets. Accelerated depreciation methods generally are used for income tax purposes.

a. Is the company violating the accounting principle of consistency by using different depreciation methods in its financial statements and in its income tax returns? Explain.

b. **Why** do you think that the company uses accelerated depreciation methods in its income tax returns?

c. Would the use of accelerated depreciation in the financial statements be more "conservative," or less "conservative," than the practice of using the straight-line method? Explain.

EXERCISE 10-8
Revision of Depreciation Rates
(LO 3)

Hull Products uses straight-line depreciation on all its depreciable assets. The accounts are adjusted and closed at the end of each calendar year. On January 4, 1999, the corporation purchased machinery for cash at a cost of $80,000. Useful life was estimated to be 10 years and residual value $12,000. Depreciation for partial years is recorded to the nearest full month.

　In 2001, after almost 3 years of experience with the equipment, management decided that the estimated life of the equipment should be revised from 10 years to 6 years. No change was made in the estimate of residual value. The revised estimate of useful life was decided upon ***prior*** to recording depreciation for the period ended December 31, 2001.

　Prepare journal entries in chronological order for the above events, beginning with the purchase of the machinery on January 4, 1999. Show separately the depreciation for 1999, 2000, and 2001.

EXERCISE 10-9
Disposal of Equipment by Sale, Trade-in, or as Scrap
(LO 4)

A tractor that cost $30,000 had an estimated useful life of 5 years and an estimated residual value of $10,000. Straight-line depreciation was used. Give the entry (in general journal form) required by each of the following alternative assumptions:
a. The tractor was sold for cash of $19,500 after 2 years' use.
b. The tractor was traded in after 3 years on another tractor with a fair market value of $37,000. Trade-in allowance was $21,000.
c. The tractor was scrapped after 5 years' use. Since scrap dealers were unwilling to pay anything for the tractor, it was given to a scrap dealer for his services in removing it.

EXERCISE 10-10
Accounting for Trade-ins
(LO 4)

Ogilvie Construction traded in a used crane on a similar new one. The original cost of the old crane was $60,000 and the accumulated depreciation was $48,000. The new crane cost $75,000, but Ogilvie was given a trade-in allowance of $15,000.
a. What amount of cash must Ogilvie pay?
b. Compute the gain or loss that would be reported on disposal of the old crane under generally accepted accounting principles.

EXERCISE 10-11
Nature and Recognition of Goodwill
(LO 5)

Food Lion, Inc., and **Safeway, Inc.,** are two profitable grocery chains. At the end of 1992, Food Lion's balance sheet showed total assets of $2,521 million, and no goodwill. Safeway's balance sheet showed total assets of $5,226 million, including $361 million in goodwill. The two companies' returns on assets for the three preceding years were:

	1992	1991	1990
Food Lion	13.5%	18.6%	20.0%
Safeway	8.4%	8.4%	11.2%

Assume that the industry average return on assets during these three years was **10%.**
a. Explain why Safeway includes goodwill on its balance sheet and why Food Lion, which is a successful, profitable business does not.
b. In writing about Food Lion, one analyst said that the company possessed unrecorded goodwill. What do you think the analyst meant by the phrase, "unrecorded goodwill"? Is there any evidence in this exercise that supports the analyst's statement? Explain.

EXERCISE 10-12
Estimating Goodwill
(LO 5)

During the past several years the annual net income of Goldtone Appliance Company has averaged $540,000. At the present time the company is being offered for sale. Its accounting records show the book value of net assets (total assets minus all liabilities) to be $2,800,000. The fair market value of Goldtone's net identifiable assets, however, is $3,000,000.

An investor negotiating to buy the company offers to pay an amount equal to the fair market value for the net identifiable assets and to assume all liabilities. In addition, the investor is willing to pay for goodwill an amount equal to net earnings in excess of 15% on the fair market value of net identifiable assets, capitalized at a rate of 25%.

On the basis of this agreement, what is the maximum price this investor should pay for Goldtone Appliance?

EXERCISE 10-13
Depletion: Recording and Reporting
(LO 6)

Westin Mining Limited purchased the Lost Creek Mine for $15,000,000 cash. The mine was estimated to contain 2 million tonnes of ore and to have a residual value of $3,000,000.

During the first year of mining operations at the Lost Creek Mine, 400,000 tonnes of ore were mined, of which 300,000 tonnes were sold.

a. Prepare a journal entry to record depletion of the Lost Creek Mine during the year.

b. Show how the mine and the accumulated depletion would appear in Westin Mining company's balance sheet after the first year of operations.

c. Will the entire amount of depletion computed in part **a** be deducted from revenue in determining the income for the year? Explain.

d. Indicate how the journal entry in part **a** affects the company's current ratio. Do you believe that the activities summarized in this entry do, in fact, make the company any more or less liquid?

Problems

PROBLEM 10-1
Determining the Cost of Plant Assets and Depreciation
(LO 1, 2, 3)

Early this summer, Crystal Car Wash purchased new "brushless" car washing equipment for all 10 of its car washes. The following information refers to the purchase and installation of this equipment.

1. The list price of the brushless equipment was $7,200 for the equipment needed at each car wash. Because Crystal Car Wash purchased 10 sets of equipment at one time, it was given a special "package price" of $68,000 for all of the equipment. Crystal paid $28,000 of this amount in cash (no cash discount was allowed) and issued a 90-day, 8% note payable for the remaining $40,000. Crystal paid this note promptly at its maturity date, along with $800 in accrued interest charges.

2. In addition to the amounts described above, Crystal paid sales taxes of $4,450 at the date of purchase.

3. Freight charges for delivery of the equipment totalled $3,320.

4. Crystal paid a contractor $2,250 per location to install the equipment at six of Crystal's car washes. Management was able to find a less expensive contractor who installed the equipment in the remaining four car washes at a cost of $1,900 per location.

5. During installation, one piece of new equipment was accidentally damaged by an employee of Crystal Car Wash. The cost to repair this damage, $914, was paid by Crystal.

6. As soon as the machines were installed, Crystal Car Wash paid $5,700 for a series of radio commercials advertising the fact that it now uses brushless equipment in all of its car washes.

INSTRUCTIONS

a. In one sentence, make a general statement summarizing the nature of the expenditures properly included in the cost of plant and equipment.

b. For each of the six numbered paragraphs, indicate which items should be included by Crystal Car Wash in the cost debited to the Equipment account. Also briefly indicate the accounting treatment that should be accorded to any items that you **do not** regard as part of the cost of the equipment.

c. Prepare a list of the expenditures that should be included in the cost of the equipment. (Determine the total cost of the equipment at all 10 locations; do not attempt to separate costs by location.)

d. Prepare a journal entry at the end of the current year to record depreciation on this equipment. Crystal depreciates this equipment by the straight-line method over an estimated useful life of 10 years, assumes zero salvage value, and applies the half-year convention.

PROBLEM 10-2
Determining Cost of Plant Assets and Depreciation
(LO 1, 2, 3)

Brenner Graphics, a newly organized corporation, purchased typesetting equipment having a list price of $219,200 from a manufacturer, plus sales taxes of $15,400. Brenner Graphics paid the invoice within the discount period and received a $4,080 discount. Other payments relating to the acquisition of the equipment were a freight bill of $2,596 and a labour cost for installing the equipment of $4,210.

During the installation process, an accident caused damage to the equipment, which was repaired at a cost of $5,900. As soon as the equipment was in place, the company obtained insurance on it for a premium of $1,800. All the items described above were charged to the Typesetting Equipment account. No entry for depreciation has yet been made and the accounts have not yet been closed.

INSTRUCTIONS

a. Prepare a list of the expenditures that should have been capitalized by debiting the Typesetting Equipment. Show the correct total cost for this asset.
b. Prepare one compound journal entry to **correct** the error or errors by the company in recording these transactions.
c. Prepare a journal entry at the end of the current year to record depreciation on this equipment. Brenner Graphics depreciates typesetting equipment by the straight-line method over an estimated useful life of 8 years, assumes no residual value, and applies the half-year convention.

PROBLEM 10–3
Basic Depreciation Methods—
No Fractional Years
(LO 3)

On January 2, 2000, Atlantic Iron Works acquired new machinery at a cost of $270,000. The useful life of the machinery was estimated at 5 years, with a residual value of $24,000. Total production of this machinery was estimated as 123,000 units, 25% of which in years 2000–2002, 15% in 2003, and 10% in 2004.

INSTRUCTIONS

Compute the annual depreciation expense throughout the 5-year life of this equipment under each of the following depreciation methods. As the equipment was acquired early in January, one full year's depreciation will be taken in each year.
a. Straight-line.
b. Units-of-production method.
c. Double-declining-balance.

PROBLEM 10–4
Basic Depreciation Methods—
Including Fractional Periods
(LO 3)

Micro Circuit Company purchased new equipment on September 4, 2000, at a cost of $80,000. Useful life of this equipment was estimated at 4 years, with an estimated residual value of $5,000. The units produced by the equipment would be: 2000, 10,000 units; 2001, 30,000 units; 2002, 20,000 units; 2003, 11,000 units; 2004, 4,000 units.

INSTRUCTIONS

Compute the annual depreciation expense for each year until this equipment becomes fully depreciated under each of the depreciation methods listed below. Show supporting computations.
a. Straight-line, with depreciation for fractional years rounded to the nearest whole month.
b. Units-of-production method.
c. Double-declining-balance, with the half-year convention.

PROBLEM 10–5
Basic Depreciation Methods—
Including Fractional Periods
(LO 3)

On March 29, 2001, Global Manufacturing purchased new equipment with a cost of $100,000, an estimated useful life of 5 years, and an estimated residual value of $10,000. The estimated production of the equipment was: 9,000 units in 2001; 13,000 units in 2002; 13,000 units in 2003; 10,000 units in 2004; 9,000 units in 2005; 6,000 units in 2006.

INSTRUCTIONS

a. Compute the annual depreciation expense for each year until this equipment becomes fully depreciated under each of the depreciation methods listed below. Show supporting computations.
1. Straight-line, with depreciation for fractional years rounded to the nearest whole month.
2. Double-declining-balance, with the half-year convention.
3. Units-of-production method.

b. Global has two conflicting objectives. Management wants to report the highest possible earnings to shareholders in the near future, yet also wants to minimize the taxable income. Indicate the depreciation method that the company will probably use in (1) its financial statements and (2) its income tax return. Explain the reasons for your answers.

PROBLEM 10-6
Disposal of Plant Assets
(LO 4)

During 19__, Crown Developers disposed of plant assets in the following transactions:

Feb. 10 Office equipment costing $14,000 was given to a scrap dealer. No proceeds were received from the scrap dealer. At the date of disposal, accumulated depreciation on the office equipment amounted to $11,900.

Apr. 1 Crown sold land and a building to Villa Associates for $630,000, receiving $200,000 in cash and a 5-year, 10% note receivable for $430,000. Crown's accounting records showed the following amounts: Land, $120,000; Building, $350,000; Accumulated Depreciation: Building (as of April 1), $115,000.

Aug. 15 Crown traded in an old truck for a new one. The old truck had cost $11,000, and accumulated depreciation amounted to $7,000. The price of the new truck was $17,000; Crown received a $5,000 trade-in allowance for the old truck and paid the $12,000 balance in cash. (Trucks are included in the Vehicles account.)

Oct. 1 Crown traded in its old computer system as part of the purchase of a new system. The old computer had cost $150,000 and, as of October 1, accumulated depreciation amounted to $110,000. The new computer had a price of $90,000. Crown was granted a $10,000 trade-in allowance for the old computer system, paid $30,000 in cash, and issued a $50,000, 2-year, 9% note payable to Action Computers for the balance. (Computers are included in the Office Equipment account.)

INSTRUCTIONS

Prepare journal entries to record each of these transactions. Assume that depreciation expense on each asset already has been recorded up to the date of disposal. Thus, you need not update the accumulated depreciation figures stated in the problem.

PROBLEM 10-7
Depreciation and Disposal
(LO 3, 4)

On March 2, 1999, Gourmet Market purchased a delivery truck for $20,000. This asset was depreciated by the straight-line method, using an estimated useful life of 5 years, a residual value of $4,000, and the half-year convention. On September 4, 2001, Gourmet Market sells the truck for $10,400 cash.

INSTRUCTIONS

a. Prepare a schedule showing the annual amounts of depreciation expense until the truck is fully depreciated.
b. Compute (1) the book value of the truck at the date of disposal and (2) the amount of gain or loss on the sale.
c. Prepare journal entries (in general journal form) to record in Gourmet Market's accounting records (1) depreciation on the truck for the year of disposal and (2) the sale of the truck.

PROBLEM 10-8
Depreciation and Disposal
(LO 3, 4)

On October 12, 1999, Speedy Print purchased colour photocopy equipment at a cost of $30,000. Management estimated that the equipment would have a useful life of 8 years and a residual value of $6,000. Speedy Print uses straight-line depreciation, and rounds depreciation for partial periods to the nearest full month.

   Speedy Print found that not many of its customers used the colour copier. Therefore, on March 19, 2001, Speedy Print sold this equipment to Commercial Graphics Company for $15,000 cash.

INSTRUCTIONS

a. Prepare a schedule showing the annual amounts of depreciation expense that management originally expects to recognize over the 8-year life of this copier.

b. Compute (1) the book value of the copier at the date of disposal and (2) the gain or loss on the sale.

c. Prepare journal entries to record in Speedy Print's accounting records (1) depreciation on the copier for 2001 and (2) the sale of the colour copier. (Prepare both entries in general journal form.)

PROBLEM 10–9
Acquisition and Disposal of Plant Asset; Depreciation and Revision of Depreciation
(LO 3, 4)

Granville Company makes "Wonder Toys" for young adults. It has a December 31 year-end. On January 3, 1999, it purchased high-tech toy making equipment for cash at a cost of $120,000. It was estimated that the equipment would produce 100,000 units during its 5-year useful life, after which it would be sold for $20,000.

In order to get operating information on a more timely basis, an advanced data processing system was purchased on March 8, 2000 for $38,000 cash. This system was estimated to have a useful life of 6 years and a residual value of $2,000.

Granville decided that the equipment should be depreciated by the units-of-production method and the data processing system by the straight-line method.

On December 31, 2001, Granville was disappointed that, based on the production of the equipment (20,000 units for 1999, 18,000 units for 2000, and 15,000 units for 2001), the total production for the toy making equipment during its five-year useful life would be 12,000 units less than the original estimate. The residual value also would be reduced by $10,000.

The early part of 2002 was also disappointing for Granville. Since the production for the equipment up to March 30 was only 2,000 units, the equipment was sold for $30,000 cash on that day. In addition, Granville finally decided to get a more sophisticated system even though the existing data processing system was working well and still was very popular. So, on April 18, the system was sold for $26,900 on account, payable in 30 days.

INSTRUCTIONS

Based on the above information, prepare the necessary journal entries for the period of January 3, 1999 to April 18, 2002. Depreciation in the year of acquisition and in the year of disposal should be rounded to the nearest full month.

PROBLEM 10–10
Acquisition, Disposal, and Trade-in of Plant Asset; Depreciation and Revision of Depreciation
(LO 1, 3, 4)

Malden Tool & Die purchased a precision machine on March 16, 1999 for $225,000 cash. The machine was installed in the factory for $5,000 cash. At this date, management considered it appropriate to depreciate this machine at an annual rate of 20%, based on the declining-balance method. This machine was to be used to make automobile parts and estimated to have a residual value of $30,000.

To accommodate added office staff, Malden purchased office equipment for $15,000 cash on June 7, 2000. The office equipment was estimated to have a useful life of 7 years and a residual value of $1,000. The straight-line method of depreciation was to be used for the equipment.

Late in 2001, Malden's management decided that the machine's annual depreciation rate should be changed from 20% to 40% because of its expected heavy usage. Also, the estimated residual value should be revised from $30,000 to $10,000.

On June 15, 2002, the office equipment was traded-in for the more sophisticated office equipment. Malden received a trade-in allowance of $9,500 for the old office equipment and paid $10,000.

On December 8, 2002, the pipes in the factory froze and broke, flooding the area where the precision machine was located. Because of the heavy damage, the machine was beyond repair. As a result, a cash payment of $70,000 was received from the insurance company that took possession of the machine.

Malden adjusts and closes its books at the end of each calendar year and uses the half-year convention for depreciation in the year of acquisition and disposal of its machines and equipment.

INSTRUCTIONS

Based on the above information, prepare the necessary journal entries from March 16, 1999 to December 8, 2002.

PROBLEM 10-11
Intangible Assets or Operating Expenses: GAAP
(LO 5)

During the current year, Homes Sales Corporation incurred the following expenditures that should be recorded either as operating expenses of the current year or as intangible assets:

a. Expenditures for the training of new employees. The average employee remains with the company for 7 years, but is retrained for a new position every 3 years.

b. Purchased from another company the trademark to a household product. The trademark has an unlimited legal life, and the product is expected to contribute to revenue indefinitely.

c. Incurred significant research and development costs to develop a dirt-resistant fibre. The company expects that the fibre will be patented and that sales of the resulting products will contribute to revenue for at least 50 years. The legal life of the patent, however, will be 20 years.

d. An expenditure to acquire the patent on a popular video game. The patent has a remaining life of 14 years, but Home Sales expects to produce and sell the game for only 3 years.

e. Spent a large amount to sponsor a television mini-series about the French Revolution. The purpose in sponsoring the program was to make television viewers more aware of the company's name and its product lines.

INSTRUCTIONS

Explain whether each of the above expenditures should be recorded as an operating expense or an intangible asset. If you view the expenditure as an intangible asset, indicate the number of years over which the asset should be amortized. Explain your reasoning.

PROBLEM 10-12
Depletion of an Oilfield; Units of Production Depreciation
(LO 6)

On March 17, 2000, Alberta Oil Company began operations at its Southfork Oil Field. The oil field had been acquired several years earlier at a cost of $14.4 million. The field is estimated to contain 4 million barrels of oil and to have a residual value of $2 million after all of the oil has been pumped out. Equipment costing $560,000 was purchased for use at the Southfork Field. This equipment will have no economic usefulness once Southfork is depleted; therefore, it is depreciated on a units-of-production basis.

Alberta Oil also built a pipeline at a cost of $3,400,000 to serve the Southfork Field. Although this pipeline is physically capable of being used for many years, its economic usefulness is limited to the productive life of the Southfork Field and there is no residual value. Therefore, depreciation of the pipeline also is based upon the estimated number of barrels of oil to be produced.

Production at the Southfork Field amounted to 460,000 barrels in 2000 and 530,000 barrels in 2001.

INSTRUCTIONS

a. Compute the per-barrel depletion rate of the oil field and the per-barrel depreciation rates of the equipment and the pipeline.

b. Make the year-end adjusting entries required at December 31, 2000, and December 31, 2001, to record depletion of the oil field and the related depreciation. (Make separate entries to record depletion of the oil field, depreciation of the equipment, and depreciation of the pipeline.)

c. Show how the Southfork Field should appear in Alberta Oil's balance sheet at the end of 2001. (Use "Oil Reserves: Southfork Field" as the title of the asset account; show accumulated depletion, but do not include the equipment or pipeline.)

Analytical and Decision Problems and Cases

A&D 10–1
Are Useful Lives "Flexible"?
(LO 3)

Robert Lynch is the controller of Print Technologies, a publicly owned company. The company is experiencing financial difficulties and is aggressively looking for ways to cut costs.

Suzanne Bedell, the CEO, instructs Lynch to lengthen from 5 to 10 years the useful life used in computing depreciation on certain special purpose machinery. Bedell believes that this change represents a substantial cost savings, as it will reduce the depreciation expense on these assets by nearly one-half.

(*Note:* The proposed change affects only the depreciation expense recognized in financial statements. Depreciation deductions in income tax returns will not be affected.)

INSTRUCTIONS

a. Discuss the extent to which Bedell's idea will, in fact, achieve a "cost savings." Also consider the effects upon net income.
b. Who is responsible for estimating the useful lives of plant assets?
c. Discuss any ethical issues that Lynch should consider with respect to Bedell's instructions.

A&D 10–2
Departures from GAAP—Are They Ethical?
(LO 1)

Martin Cole owns Delta Construction Co. The company maintains accounting records for the purposes of exercising control over its construction activities, and meeting its reporting obligations regarding payrolls and income tax returns. As it has no other financial reporting obligations, Delta does not prepare formal financial statements.

The company owns land and several other assets with current market values well in excess of their historical costs. Cole directs the company's accountant, Maureen O'Shaughnessey, to prepare a balance sheet in which assets are shown at estimated market values. Cole says this type of balance sheet will give him a better understanding of "where the business stands." He also thinks it will be useful in obtaining bank loans, as loan applications always ask for the estimated market values of real estate owned.

INSTRUCTIONS

a. Would the financial statements requested by Cole be in conformity with generally accepted accounting principles?
b. Is Delta Construction under any legal or ethical obligation to prepare financial statements that *do* conform to generally accepted accounting principles?
c. Discuss any ethical issues that O'Shaughnessey should consider with respect to Cole's request.

A&D 10–3
Depreciation Policies in Annual Reports
(LO 3)

Shown below is a note accompanying the financial statement of **International Paper Company:**

Plant, Properties, and Equipment

Plant, properties, and equipment are stated at cost less accumulated depreciation.

For financial reporting purposes, the company uses the units-of-production method of depreciating its major pulp and paper mills and certain wood products facilities, and the straight-line method for other plants and equipment.

Annual straight-line depreciation rates for financial reporting purposes are as follows: buildings 2½% to 8%; machinery and equipment 5% to 33%; woods equipment 10% to 16%. For tax purposes, depreciation is computed utilizing accelerated methods.

a. Are the depreciation methods used in the company's financial statements determined by current income tax laws? If not, who is responsible for selecting these methods? Explain.

b. Does the company violate the consistency principle by using different depreciation methods for its paper mills and wood products facilities than it uses for its other plant and equipment? If not, what does the principle of consistency mean? Explain.

c. What is the estimated useful life of the machinery and equipment being depreciated with a straight-line depreciation rate of:

1. 5%.

2. 33% (round to the nearest year).

Who determines the useful lives over which specific assets are to be depreciated?

d. Why do you think the company uses accelerated depreciation methods for income tax purposes, rather than using the straight-line method (assuming both are acceptable for income tax purposes)? Explain.

A&D 10–4
Effects of Depreciation Policies
upon Earnings
(LO 3)

Two independent cases are described below. You are to comment separately on each case.

Case A Assume that Adams Limited and Barnes Corporation are in the same line of business, have similar plant assets that were acquired a few years ago, and report the same amount of net income. In their financial statements, Adams uses straight-line depreciation and Barnes uses an accelerated method.

INSTRUCTIONS

Do you have any reason for considering one of these companies to be more profitable than the other? Explain.

Case B The income statement of Morris Foods includes depreciation expense of $200,000 and net income of $100,000. A note accompanying the financial statements discloses the following information about the company's depreciation policies:

Depreciation. For financial statement purposes, depreciation is computed by the straight-line method using the following estimated useful lives:

Automobiles	*10 years*
Furniture and equipment	*20 to 30 years*
Buildings	*50 to 80 years*

For tax purposes, depreciation is computed using accelerated methods.

INSTRUCTIONS

In general terms, evaluate the effects of these depreciation policies upon the net income reported by the company in its income statement.

A&D 10–5
Depreciation Method and
Journal Entries on Disposal
(LO 3, 4)

Holeless Donuts began operations on January 1, 1997. On that date, it purchased donut making equipment that was estimated to have a five-year useful life and a residual value of $15,000. The first year's business was a huge success. So, on January 1, 1998, a muffin making machine with a four-year useful life and a $6,000 residual value was purchased.

The equipment and machine were depreciated over their respective useful lives as follows:

		Donut Equipment	Muffin Machine
Depreciation expense for:	1997	*$72,000*	
	1998	*43,200*	*$12,000*
	1999	*25,920*	*10,000*
	2000	*15,552*	*6,000*
	2001	*8,328*	*4,000*

On January 1, 2002, the donut equipment was sold for $16,200 cash and the muffin machine was traded-in for a new one with a list price of $28,000. Since the trade-in allowance was $5,200, Holeless Donuts only paid $22,800 for the new muffin machine.

INSTRUCTIONS

a. Determine the depreciation method used for the donut equipment and for the muffin machine.

b. Prepare the entries, in general journal form, to record the sale of the donut equipment and the trade-in of the muffin machine.

A&D 10–6
Depreciation Method and Disposals
(LO 3, 4)

Evergreen Company, a clothing manufacturer, purchased a delivery truck on January 1, 1998. This truck was estimated to have a useful life of 5 years and a residual value of $3,000. Its depreciation expenses for 1998, 1999, 2000, and 2001 were: $12,000, $7,200, $4,320, and $2,592.

On July 1, 2000, the company purchased sewing equipment with a useful life of four years and a residual value of $3,000.

As Evergreen's business was booming, it needed a bigger truck. Accordingly, on January 1, 2002 the old delivery truck was traded in for a new truck with a retail price of $46,000. Since the trade-in allowance was $5,000, a cash payment of $41,000 was made. The gain on the trade-in was $1,112. On the same day, the sewing equipment was sold for $15,150 cash, resulting in a loss of $1,600. The depreciation expenses of the sewing equipment for 2000 and 2001 were: $2,750 and $5,500.

INSTRUCTIONS

a. Prepare the entries, in general journal form, to record the trade-in of the delivery truck and the sale of the sewing equipment.

b. Determine the depreciation method used for the delivery truck and for the sewing equipment.

A&D 10–7
Did I Do This Right?
(LO 3, 4, 5)

Protein Plus is a processor and distributor of frozen foods. The company's management is anxious to report the maximum amount of net income allowable under generally accepted accounting principles and, therefore, uses the longest acceptable lives in depreciating or amortizing the company's plant assets. Depreciation and amortization computations are rounded to the nearest full month.

Near year-end the company's regular accountant was in an automobile accident, so a clerk with limited accounting experience prepared the company's financial statements. The income statement prepared by the clerk indicated a net loss of $45,000. However, the clerk was unsure that he had properly accounted for the following items:

1. On April 4, the company purchased a small food processing business at a cost $80,000 above the value of that business's net identifiable assets. The clerk classified this $80,000 as goodwill on Protein Plus's balance sheet and recorded no amortization expense because the food processor's superior earnings are expected to continue indefinitely.
2. During the year the company spent $32,000 on a research project to develop a method of freezing avocados. The clerk classified these expenditures as an intangible asset on the company's balance sheet and recorded no amortization expense because it was not yet known whether the project would be successful.
3. Two gains from the disposal of plant assets were included in the income statement. One gain, in the amount of $4,300, resulted from the sale of a plant asset at a price above its book value. The other gain, in the amount of $2,700 on December 31, was based on receiving an offer for equipment that has not yet been sold.

4. A public accounting firm had determined that the company's depreciation expense for income tax purposes was $51,400. The clerk used this figure as depreciation expense in the income statement, although in prior years the company had used the straight-line method of depreciation in its financial statements. Depreciation for the current year amounts to $35,600 when computed by the straight-line method over realistic estimates of useful lives.

5. On January 4, the company paid $90,000 to purchase a 10-year franchise to become the exclusive distributor in three eastern provinces for a brand of Mexican frozen dinners. The clerk charged this $90,000 to expense in the current year because the entire amount had been paid in cash.

6. During the year, the company incurred advertising costs of $22,000 to promote the newly acquired line of frozen dinners. The clerk did not know how many periods would be benefited from these expenditures, so he included the entire amount in the selling expenses of the current year.

INSTRUCTIONS

a. For each of the numbered paragraphs, explain whether the clerk's treatment of the item is in conformity with generally accepted accounting principles.

b. Prepare a schedule determining the correct net income (or net loss) for the year. Begin with "Net loss originally reported . . . $45,000," and indicate any adjustments that you consider appropriate. If you indicate adjustments for the amortization of intangible assets acquired during the year, round the amortization to the nearest month.

Answers to Self-Test Questions

1. c (Depreciation is not recorded on inventory.)   2. c   3. d $1,800, computed 20% [$10,000 − ($10,000 × 20% × ½)]   4. a [Cost, $50,000, less book value, $17,000 (sales price, less gain)]   5. c

ALPINE VILLAGE AND NORDIC SPORTS

Concepts of Asset Valuation and Effects Upon Net Income

Chris Scott, a former Olympic skier, wants to purchase an established ski equipment and clothing shop in Banff, Alberta. Two such businesses currently are available for sale: Alpine Village and Nordic Sports. Both businesses are organized as sole proprietorships and have been in operation for three years. Summaries of the current balance sheet data of both shops are shown below:

Assets	Alpine Village	Nordic Sports
Cash	$ 38,700	$ 32,100
Accounts receivable	187,300	174,800
Inventory	151,400	143,700
Plant and equipment:		
Land	40,000	35,000
Building (net of accumulated depreciation)	99,900	72,900
Equipment (net of accumulated depreciation)	7,600	8,200
Goodwill	18,500	
Total assets	$543,400	$466,700
Liabilities & Owner's Equity		
Total liabilities	$199,900	$206,300
Owner's equity	343,500	260,400
Total liabilities & owner's equity	$543,400	$466,700

Income statements for the last three years show that Alpine Village has reported total net income of **$238,500** since the business was started. The income statements of Nordic Sports show total net income of **$199,400** for the same three-year period.

With the permission of the owners of the two businesses, Scott arranges for a public accountant to review the accounting records of both companies. This investigation discloses the following information:

Accounts Receivable   Alpine Village uses the direct write-off method of recording uncollectible accounts expense. The accountant believes that the $187,300 of accounts receivable appearing in the company's balance sheet includes about $15,000 in uncollectible accounts. Nordic Sports makes monthly estimates of its uncollectible accounts and shows accounts receivable in its balance sheet at estimated net realizable value.

Inventories   Alpine Village uses the first-in, first-out *(FIFO)*) method of pricing its inventory. Had the company used the last-in, first-out method *(LIFO),* the balance sheet valuation of inventory would be about $10,000 lower. Nordic Sports uses the LIFO method to value inventory; if it had used FIFO, the balance sheet valuation of inventory would be about $9,000 greater.

Buildings   Alpine Village depreciates its building over an estimated life of 40 years using the straight-line method. Nordic Sports depreciates its building over 20 years using the double-declining-balance method. Nordic has owned its building for three years, and the accumulated depreciation on the building now amounts to $27,100.

Goodwill   Three years ago, each business provided $20,000 in prize money for ski races held in the area. Alpine Village charged this expenditure to goodwill, which it is amortizing over a period of 40 years. Nordic Sports charged its $20,000 prize money expenditure directly to advertising expense.

INSTRUCTIONS

a. Prepare a revised summary of the balance sheet data in a manner that makes the information about the two companies more comparable. Use the format illustrated at the beginning of this problem. However, you are to adjust the asset values for one company or the other so that the balance sheet data for each company meets the following standards:
1. Accounts receivable are valued at estimated net realizable value.
2. Inventories are valued by the method that will minimize income during a period of rising prices.
3. Depreciation on the buildings is based upon the straight-line method and an estimated useful life of 40 years.
4. The cost of the $20,000 payment of prize money is treated in the manner required by generally accepted accounting principles.

After making the indicated adjustments to the valuation of certain assets, show "owner's equity" at the amount needed to bring total liabilities and owner's equity into agreement with total assets.

When you revalue an asset of either company, ***show supporting computations.***

b. Revise the ***cumulative amount*** of net income reported by each company during the last three years, taking into consideration the changes in accounting methods and policies called for in part **a.**

c. Assume that after revision of asset values as described in part **a,** the revised book value of net identifiable assets is not materially different from aggregate fair market value of net identifiable assets. Therefore, Scott is willing to buy either company at a price equal to the revised amount of owner's equity as determined in part **a,** plus an amount for goodwill. For goodwill, Scott is willing to pay four times the amount by which average annual net income exceeds a 20% return on this revised owner's equity.

Determine the price that Scott is willing to pay for each of the two companies. Base your computations on the revised data about owner's equity and net income that you developed in parts **a** and **b.**

CHAPTER 11

Liabilities Common to Most Business Organizations

Credit is essential to every business organization—but it should be kept under control.

1. Define *liabilities;* distinguish between debt and equity.
2. Distinguish between current and long-term liabilities.
3. Account for notes payable and interest expense, and other current liabilities.
4. Prepare an amortization table allocating instalment payments between interest and the repayment of principal.

5. Define *contingent losses and commitments* and explain their presentation in financial statements.
6. Evaluate the safety of creditors' claims.
*7. Describe the basic separation of duties in a payroll system, and explain how this plan contributes to strong internal control.
*8. Account for a payroll, including computation of amounts withheld and payroll taxes on the employer.

Now that you have an understanding of the major types of business assets, we will shift our attention to the *right* side of the balance sheet, which shows how the company's assets have been financed.

There are two basic ways of financing assets: with liabilities or with owners' equity. The "mix" of liabilities and owners' equity in a particular business is termed the company's **capital structure**. In this chapter we will begin our discussion of liabilities.

Our coverage of liabilities is split between this chapter and Chapter 16. In this chapter, we address the types of liabilities that are likely to arise in almost any type or size of business organization, and also the accounting and disclosure requirements relating to contingent losses and commitments. Accounting for payrolls is discussed in a **Supplemental Topic* section at the end of the chapter.

In Chapter 16, we will address the special types of liabilities that appear primarily in the balance sheets of large, publicly owned corporations.

The Nature of Liabilities

LO 1: Define liabilities; *distinguish between debt and equity.*

Liabilities may be defined as ***debts or obligations arising from past transactions or events,*** and requiring settlement at a future date. Put simply, liabilities are what a company owes to banks, suppliers, employees, and others. All liabilities have certain characteristics in common; however, the specific terms of different liabilities, and the rights of the creditors, vary greatly.

Distinction Between Debt and Equity   Businesses have two basic sources of financing: liabilities and owners' equity. Liabilities differ from owners' equity in several respects. The feature that most clearly distinguishes the claims of creditors from owners' equity is that all liabilities eventually ***mature***—that is, they come due. Owners' equity does not mature. The date upon which a liability comes due is called the maturity date.[1]

---

*Supplemental Topic, "Accounting for Payrolls."
[1]Some liabilities are ***due on demand,*** which means that the liability is payable upon the creditor's request. From a bank's point of view, customers' chequing accounts are "demand liabilities." Liabilities due on demand may come due at any time, and are classified as current liabilities.

Although all liabilities mature, their maturity dates vary. Some liabilities are so short in term that they are paid within a few days or a few weeks. Long-term liabilities, in contrast, may not mature for many years. The maturity dates of key liabilities may be a critical factor in the solvency of a business.

The providers of borrowed capital are ***creditors*** of the business, not owners. As creditors, they have financial claims against the business, but usually do ***not*** have the right to control business operations. The traditional roles of owners, managers, and creditors may be modified, however, in an ***indenture contract.*** Creditors sometimes insist upon being granted some control over business operations as a condition of making a loan, particularly if the business is in poor financial condition. Indenture contracts may impose such restrictions as limits upon management salaries and upon dividends, and may require the creditor's approval for additional borrowing or for large capital expenditures.

The claims of creditors have ***legal priority*** over the claims of owners. If a business ceases operations and liquidates, creditors must be ***paid in full*** before any distributions are made to the owners. The relative security of creditors' claims, however, can vary among the creditors. Sometimes the borrower pledges title to specific assets as collateral for a loan. If the borrower defaults on a secured loan, the creditor may foreclose upon the pledged assets. Assets that have been pledged as security for loans should be identified in notes accompanying the borrower's financial statements.

Liabilities that are not secured by specific assets are termed ***general credit obligations.*** The priorities of general credit obligations vary with the nature of the liability, and the terms of indenture contracts.

Most long-term liabilities, and some short-term ones, require the borrower to pay interest. Only interest payable ***as of the balance sheet date*** appears as a liability in the borrower's balance sheet. The borrower's obligation to pay interest in ***future*** periods sometimes is disclosed in the notes to the financial statements, but it is not shown as an existing liability.

The total amount of interest expense for a period appears in the company's income statement, and is also ***deductible*** for income tax purposes. The deductibility of interest is a major advantage of using liabilities to finance business assets. After considering the reduction in income taxes, the effective cost of borrowing is often only 60% to 70% of the stated rate of interest.

Estimated Liabilities Most liabilities are for a definite dollar amount, clearly stated by contract. Examples include notes payable, accounts payable, and accrued expenses, such as interest payable and salaries payable. In some cases, however, the dollar amount of a liability must be ***estimated*** at the balance sheet date.

Estimated liabilities have two basic characteristics: The liability is ***known to exist,*** but the precise dollar amount cannot be determined until a later date. For instance, the automobiles sold by most automakers are accompanied by a warranty obligating the automaker to replace defective parts for a period of several years. As each car is sold, the automaker ***incurs a liability*** to perform any work that may be required under the warranty. The dollar amount of this liability, however, can only be estimated.

CURRENT LIABILITIES

LO 2: Distinguish between current and long-term liabilities.

Current liabilities are obligations that must be paid within one year or within the operating cycle, whichever is longer. Another requirement for classification as a current liability is the expectation that the debt will be paid from current assets (or through the rendering of services). Liabilities that do not meet these conditions are classified as long-term liabilities.

The time period used in defining current liabilities parallels that used in defining current assets. As explained in Chapter 5, the amount of **working capital** (current assets less current liabilities) and the **current ratio** (current assets divided by current liabilities) are valuable indicators of a company's ability to pay its debts in the near future.

Among the most common examples of current liabilities are accounts payable, short-term notes payable, the current portion of long-term debt, accrued liabilities (such as interest payable, income taxes payable, and payroll liabilities), and unearned revenue.

CASE IN POINT

The recent balance sheets of Loblaw Companies Limited and Canadian Airlines Corporation show the following current liabilities:

In Millions of Dollars

Loblaw
Bank advances and notes payable	$ 362
Accounts payable and accrued liabilities	1,084
Taxes payable	21
Long-term debt and debt equivalents due within one year	12
	$1,479

Canadian Airlines
Accounts payable and accrued liabilities	$ 515
Advanced ticket sales	234
Current portion of long-term debt	129
	$ 878

Accounts Payable

Accounts payable often are subdivided into the categories of trade accounts payable and other accounts payable. **Trade accounts payable** are short-term obligations to suppliers for purchases of merchandise. Other accounts payable include liabilities for any goods and services other than merchandise.

Technically, the date at which a trade account payable comes into existence depends upon whether goods are purchased F.O.B. shipping point or F.O.B. destination. However, unless **material** amounts of merchandise are purchased on terms of F.O.B. shipping point, most companies follow the convenient practice of recording the transaction when the merchandise is received.

Accounts payable usually do not require the payment of interest. This makes this form of liability very desirable; it represents an "interest-free" loan from the supplier.

Notes Payable

Notes payable are issued whenever bank loans are obtained. Other transactions that may give rise to notes payable include the purchase of real estate or costly equipment, the purchase of merchandise, and the substitution of a note for a past-due account payable.

LO 3: Account for notes payable and interest expense, and other current liabilities.

Notes Payable with Interest Stated Separately   Notes payable usually require the borrower to pay an interest charge. Normally, the interest rate is stated separately from the **principal amount** of the note.

To illustrate, assume that on November 1 Porter Company borrows $10,000 from its bank for a period of six months (with the three days of grace included) at an annual interest rate of 12%. Six months later on May 1, Porter Company will have to pay the bank the principal amount of $10,000 plus $600 interest ($10,000 × .12 × $\frac{6}{12}$).[2]

The journal entry in Porter Company's accounting records for this November 1 borrowing is:

Face amount of note

Cash	*10,000*	
Notes Payable		*10,000*
Borrowed $10,000 for six months at 12% interest per year.		

Notice that no liability is recorded for the interest charges when the note is issued. At the date that money is borrowed, the borrower has a liability ***only for the principal amount of the loan;*** the liability for interest accrues day by day over the life of the loan. At December 31, two months' interest expense has been incurred, and the following year-end adjusting entry is made:

A liability for interest accrues day by day

Interest Expense	*200*	
Interest Payable		*200*
To record interest expense incurred through year-end on 12%, six-month note dated Nov. 1 ($10,000 × 12% × $\frac{2}{12}$ = $200).		

The entry on May 1 to record payment of the note will be:

Payment of principal and interest

Notes Payable	*10,000*	
Interest Payable	*200*	
Interest Expense	*400*	
Cash		*10,600*
To record payment of 12%, six-month note on maturity date and to recognize interest expense incurred since year-end ($10,000 × .12 × $\frac{4}{12}$ = $400).		

If Porter Company paid this note ***prior*** to May 1, interest charges usually would be computed only through the date of early payment.[3]

---

[2]For notes stated in months, interest will be computed on a basis of months rather than days so as to stress concept rather than unnecessary precision.
[3]Computing interest charges only through the date of payment is the normal business practice. However, some notes are written in a manner requiring the borrower to pay interest for the full term of the note even if payment is made early. Borrowers should look carefully at these terms.

Notes Payable with Interest Charges Included in the Face Amount Instead of stating the interest rate separately as in the preceding illustration, the note payable issued by Porter Company could have been drawn to *include the interest charge in the face amount of the note.* Thus, the face amount of this note is $10,600 ($10,000 + $600), $600 greater than the $10,000 amount borrowed. Porter Company's liability at November 1 is only $10,000—the *present value* of the note.[4] The other $600 included in the face amount of the note represents *future interest charges.* As interest expense is incurred over the life of the note, Porter Company's liability will grow to $10,600, just as in the preceding illustration.

The entry to record Porter Company's $10,000 borrowing from the bank at November 1 will be as follows for this type of note payable:

Interest included in face of note

Cash	10,000	
Discount on Notes Payable	600	
Notes Payable		10,600
Issued to bank a six-month, 12% note payable with interest charge included in the face amount of note.		

The liability account, Notes Payable, was credited with the full face amount of the note ($10,600). It is therefore necessary to debit a **contra-liability account, Discount on Notes Payable**, for the future interest charges included in the face amount of the note. Discount on Notes Payable is shown in the balance sheet as a deduction from Notes Payable. In our illustration, the amounts in the balance sheet would be Notes Payable, $10,600, minus Discount on Notes Payable, $600, or a net liability of $10,000 at November 1.

Discount on Notes Payable The balance of the account Discount on Notes Payable represents *interest charges applicable to future periods.* As this interest expense is incurred, the balance of the discount account gradually is transferred into the Interest Expense account. Thus, at the maturity date of the note, Discount on Notes Payable will have a zero balance, and the net liability will have increased to $10,600. The process of transferring the amount in the Discount on Notes Payable account into the Interest Expense account is called **amortization of the discount**

Amortization of the Discount The discount on *short-term* notes payable usually is amortized by the straight-line method, which allocates the same amount of discount to interest expense for each month the note is outstanding. Thus, the $600 discount on the Porter Company note payable will be transferred from Discount on Notes Payable into Interest Expense at the rate of $100 per month ($600 ÷ 6 months).

---

[4]The concept of present value was introduced in Chapter 8. The mechanics of computing present values is explained in Appendix C at the end of Chapter 16.

Adjusting entries should be made to amortize the discount at the end of each accounting period and at the date the note matures. At December 31, Porter Company will make the following adjusting entry to recognize the two months' interest expense incurred since November 1:

Amortization of discount

Interest Expense	*200*	
Discount on Notes Payable		*200*
To record interest expense incurred to end of year on a		
six-month, 12% note dated Nov. 1 ($600 discount $\times \frac{2}{6}$).		

Notice that the liability for accrued interest is recorded by crediting Discount on Notes Payable rather than Interest Payable. The credit to Discount on Notes Payable reduces the debit balance in this contra-liability account from $600 to $400, thereby increasing the **net liability** for notes payable by $200.

At December 31, Porter Company's net liability for the bank loan will appear in the balance sheet as shown below:

Liability shown net of discount

Current liabilities:		
Notes payable	*$10,600*	
Less: Discount on notes payable	*400*	*$10,200*

The net liability of $10,200 consists of the $10,000 principal amount of the debt plus the $200 interest that has accrued since November 1.

When the note matures on May 1, Porter Company will recognize the four months' interest expense incurred since year-end and will pay the bank $10,600. The entry is:

Two-thirds of interest applicable to second year

Notes Payable	*10,600*	
Interest Expense	*400*	
Discount on Notes Payable		*400*
Cash		*10,600*
To record payment of a six-month, 12% note due today		
and recognize interest expense incurred since year-end		
($10,000 $\times \frac{4}{12} \times$ 12% = $400).		

Comparison of the Two Forms of Notes Payable

We have illustrated two alternative methods that Porter Company could use in accounting for its $10,000 bank loan, depending upon the form of the note payable. The journal entries for both methods, along with the resulting balance sheet presentations of the liability at November 1 and December 31, are summarized on the next page. Notice that both methods result in Porter Company recognizing the **same amount of interest expense** in the income statement and the **same total liability** in its balance sheet. The form of the note does not change the economic substance of the transaction.

The Current Portion of Long-Term Debt

Some long-term debts, such as mortgage loans, are payable in a series of monthly or quarterly instalments. In these cases, the **principal** amount

Comparison of the Two Forms of Notes Payable

	Note Written for $10,000 Plus 12% Interest	Note Written with Interest Included in Face Amount

Entry to record borrowing on Nov. 1	Cash 10,000
	  Notes Payable 10,000
		Cash 10,000
		Discount on Notes Payable 600
		  Notes Payable 10,600

Partial balance sheet at Nov. 1	*Current liabilities:*
	  Notes payable $10,000
		Current liabilities:
		  Notes payable $10,600
		  Less: Discount on notes payable .. 600 ... $10,000

Adjusting entry at Dec. 31	Interest Expense 200
	  Interest Payable 200
		Interest Expense 200
		  Discount on Notes Payable 200

Partial balance sheet at Dec. 31	*Current liabilities:*
	  Notes payable $10,000
	  Interest payable .... 200 ... $10,200
		Current liabilities:
		  Notes payable $10,600
		  Less: Discount on notes payable .. 400 ... $10,200

Entry to record payment of note on May 1	Notes Payable 10,000
	Interest Payable 200
	Interest Expense 400
	  Cash 10,600
		Notes Payable 10,600
		Interest Expense 400
		  Discount on Notes Payable 400
		  Cash 10,600

due within one year (or the operating cycle) is regarded as a current liability, and the remainder of the obligation is classified as a long-term liability.

As the maturity date of a long-term liability approaches, the obligation eventually becomes due within the current period. Long-term liabilities that become payable within the coming year are *reclassified* in the balance sheet as current liabilities.[5] Changing the classification of a liability does not require a journal entry; the obligation merely is shown in a different section of the balance sheet.

Accrued Liabilities

Accrued liabilities arise from the recognition of expenses for which payment will be made in a future period. Thus, accrued liabilities also are called *accrued expenses.* The need to record accrued liabilities arises from the fact that certain expenses are incurred by the business before they are actually paid. Examples of accrued liabilities include interest payable, income taxes payable, and amounts related to payrolls. As accrued liabilities stem from the recording of expenses, the *matching* principle governs the timing of their recognition.

All companies incur accrued liabilities. In most cases, however, these liabilities are paid at frequent intervals. Therefore, they usually do not accumulate to large amounts. In a balance sheet, accrued liabilities frequently are included in the amount shown as "accounts payable."

Interest Payable   Interest—the cost of borrowing—accrues with the passage of time. When companies enter into long-term financing agreements, they may become committed to paying large amounts of interest for many years to come. At any balance sheet date, however, only a *small portion* of this total interest obligation represents a "liability."

Remember, liabilities stem from *past transactions.* Therefore, the only interest obligation that represents a "liability" is the unpaid interest that has *already* accrued. (At the end of each period, any accrued interest payable is recorded by debiting Interest Expense and crediting Interest Payable.)

To illustrate this point, assume that HighTech Stores borrows $500,000 from its bank for a period of five years at an interest rate of 12%. Although the principal amount of this loan will not be due for five years, interest is to be paid monthly—on the first day of each month.

The interest expense on this loan amounts to *$60,000* per year ($500,000 × 12%). Over the life of the loan, HighTech will pay *$300,000* in interest charges. At the end of each month, however, HighTech will have a liability for only *one month's interest*—the interest that has accrued since the last interest payment date. Thus, HighTech's balance

---

[5]Exceptions are made to this rule if the liability will be *refinanced* (that is, extended or renewed) on a long-term basis, or if a special *sinking fund* has been accumulated for the purpose of repaying this obligation. In these cases, the debt remains classified as a long-term liability, even though it will mature within the current period.

sheets normally will show accrued interest payable of only **$5,000** ($500,000 × 12% × ¹⁄₁₂).

If this loan had called for the accrued interest to be paid on the **last** day of each month, HighTech's balance sheets would include **no** liability for accrued interest payable.

A borrower's contractual obligation to pay interest in future periods is **not yet a liability** and **does not appear** in the borrower's balance sheet. However, this information may be of vital importance to investors and creditors evaluating the company's solvency and its ability to finance future growth. For this reason, accounting principles require businesses to **disclose** the terms of major financing arrangements in the notes that accompany their financial statements.

To determine the amount of a company's interest **expense** for the year, the reader of financial statements should look in the **income statement,** not the balance sheet. For information about the company's interest obligations in **future** years, this reader must study the **notes** that accompany the financial statements.

Income Taxes Payable   As discussed in Chapter 1, profitable corporations pay income taxes on their income. Therefore, income taxes expense accrues **as profits are earned.** At the end of each accounting period, the amount of accrued income taxes is estimated and recorded in an adjusting entry, as shown below:

```
Income Taxes Expense ....................................    72,750
        Income Taxes Payable  ............................              72,750
To accrue estimated income taxes expense for the first quarter
of the year (Jan. 1 through Mar. 31).
```

The account debited in the entry, Income Taxes Expense, is an expense account that usually appears as the very last deduction in the income statement. The liability account, Income Taxes Payable, ordinarily will be paid within a few months and, therefore, appears as a current liability section of the balance sheet.

Payroll Liabilities   Every business incurs a number of accrued liabilities relating to its payroll. The largest of these liabilities is the obligation to pay employees for services rendered during the period. Another is the liability for withholding the taxes from the employees' paycheques. This liability is settled by remitting the amount to the government. Payroll **expense** often is among the largest expenses of a business organization. Accrued payroll liabilities, however, seldom accumulate to large amounts because they are paid in full at frequent intervals.

Accounting for payrolls involves much more than merely recording the liability for accrued wages and salaries payable. Employers must compute numerous taxes that the government levies either upon employees or upon the employer. In fact, one might say that the total wages and salaries expense (or gross pay) represents only the "starting point" of payroll computations.

To illustrate, assume that a manufacturing company's monthly wages expense amounts to $100,000. The costs incurred by this employer in a "typical" monthly payroll might be as follows:

<table>
<tr><td>Notice the costs in addition
to employees' wages</td><td>*Gross pay (wages expense)* ....</td><td>*$100,000*</td></tr>
<tr><td></td><td>*Canada Pension Plan Contributions* ....</td><td>*2,916*</td></tr>
<tr><td></td><td>*Employment Insurance Taxes* ....</td><td>*3,884*</td></tr>
<tr><td></td><td>*Group dental and extended healthcare insurance premiums* ....</td><td>*9,500*</td></tr>
<tr><td></td><td>*Contributions to employee pension plan and other postretirement costs* ..</td><td>*5,200*</td></tr>
<tr><td></td><td>*Total payroll costs for January** ....</td><td>*$121,500*</td></tr>
</table>

*The cost is much higher when provincial payroll taxes on employers are added, as indicated in footnotes 16 and 17 later.

In our example total payroll-related costs exceed wages expense **by more than 20%.** This relationship will vary from one employer to the next, but our illustration is typical of many payrolls.

Every business student should have some familiarity with payrolls, including the purpose and relative size of the various payroll taxes, and whether these taxes are paid by the employees or by the employer. An introduction to accounting for payrolls is presented in the **Supplemental Topic* section at the end of this chapter.

Unearned Revenue

A liability for unearned revenue arises when a customer pays in advance. Upon receipt of an advance payment from a customer, the company debits Cash and credits a liability account such as Unearned Revenue, or Customers' Deposits. As the services are rendered to the customer, an entry is made debiting the liability account and crediting a revenue account. Notice that the liability for unearned revenue normally is "paid" by rendering services to the creditor, rather than by making cash payments.

Unearned revenue ordinarily is classified as a current liability, as the activities involved in earning revenue are part of the business's normal operating cycle.

LONG-TERM LIABILITIES

Long-term obligations usually arise from major expenditures, such as acquisitions of plant assets, the purchase of another company, or refinancing an existing long-term obligation that is about to mature. Thus, transactions involving long-term liabilities are relatively few in number, but often involve large dollar amounts. In contrast, current liabilities usually arise from routine operating transactions.

Many businesses regard long-term liabilities as an alternative to owners' equity as a source of "permanent" financing. Although long-term liabilities eventually mature, they often are **refinanced**—that is, the maturing obligation simply is replaced with a new long-term liability.

Maturing Obligations Intended to Be Refinanced

One special type of long-term liability is an obligation that will mature in the current period, but that is expected to be refinanced on a long-term basis. For example, a company may have a bank loan that "comes due" each year, but is routinely extended for the following year. Both the company and the bank may intend for this arrangement to continue on a long-term basis.

If management has made contractual arrangements to refinance soon-to-mature obligations on a long-term basis, these obligations are classified as long-term liabilities.[6] In this situation, the accountant also looks to the ***economic substance*** of the situation, rather than just to its legal form.

When the economic substance of a transaction differs from its legal form or its outward appearance, financial statements should reflect the ***economic substance.*** Accountants summarize this concept with the phrase, ***"Substance takes precedence over form."*** Today's business world is characterized by transactions of ever-increasing complexity. Recognizing those situations in which the substance of a transaction differs from its form is one of the greatest challenges confronting the professional accountant.

Instalment Notes Payable

Purchases of real estate and certain types of equipment often are financed by the issuance of long-term notes that call for a series of instalment payments. These payments (often called debt service) may be due monthly, quarterly, semiannually, or at any other interval. If these instalments continue until the debt is completely repaid, the loan is said to be ***fully amortizing.*** Often, however, instalment notes contain a "due date" at which the remaining unpaid balance is to be repaid in a single "balloon payment."

Some instalment notes call for instalment payments equal to the periodic interest charges (an "interest only" note). Under these terms, the principal amount of the loan is payable at a specified maturity date. More often, however, the instalment payments are ***greater*** than the amount of interest accruing during the period. Thus, only a portion of each instalment payment represents interest expense, and the remainder of the payment reduces the principal amount of the liability. As the amount owed is reduced by each payment, the portion of each successive payment representing interest expense will ***decrease,*** and the portion going toward repayment of principal will ***increase.***

Allocating Instalment Payments Between Interest and Principal In accounting for an instalment note, the accountant must determine the portion of

---

[6]CICA, *CICA Handbook* (Toronto), section 1510.06.

LO 4: Prepare an amortization table allocating instalment payments between interest and repayment of principal.

each payment that represents interest expense, and the portion that reduces the principal amount of the liability. This distinction is made in advance by preparing an **amortization table.**

To illustrate, assume that on October 15, 1999, King's Inn purchases furnishings at a total cost of $16,398. In payment, the company issues an instalment note payable for this amount, plus interest at 12% per annum (or 1% per month). This note will be paid in 18 monthly instalments of $1,000 each, beginning on November 15. An amortization table for this instalment note payable follows (amounts of interest expense are *rounded to the nearest dollar*):

		(A)	(B) Interest Expense (1% of the Last Unpaid Balance)	(C) Reduction in Unpaid Balance (A) − (B)	(D) Unpaid Balance
Interest Period	**Payment Date**	**Monthly Payment**			
Issue date	Oct. 15 1999	—	—	—	$16,398
1	Nov. 15	$1,000	$164	$836	15,562
2	Dec. 15	1,000	156	844	14,718
3	Jan. 15, 2000	1,000	147	853	13,865
4	Feb. 15	1,000	139	861	13,004
5	Mar. 15	1,000	130	870	12,134
6	Apr. 15	1,000	121	879	11,255
7	May 15	1,000	113	887	10,368
8	June 15	1,000	104	896	9,472
9	July 15	1,000	95	905	8,567
10	Aug. 15	1,000	86	914	7,653
11	Sept. 15	1,000	77	923	6,730
12	Oct. 15	1,000	67	933	5,797
13	Nov. 15	1,000	58	942	4,855
14	Dec. 15	1,000	49	951	3,904
15	Jan. 15, 2001	1,000	39	961	2,943
16	Feb. 15	1,000	29	971	1,972
17	Mar. 15	1,000	20	980	992
18	Apr. 15	1,000	8*	992	-0-

Amortization Table (12% Note Payable for $16,398; Payable in 18 Monthly Instalments of $1,000)

In the last period, interest expense is equal to the amount of the final payment minus the remaining unpaid balance. This compensates for the cumulative effect of rounding interest amounts to the nearest dollar.

Preparing an Amortization Table   Let us explore the content of this table. First, notice that the payments are made on a *monthly* basis. Therefore, the amounts of the payments (column A), interest expense (column B), and reduction in the unpaid balance (column C) are all *monthly amounts.*

The interest rate used in the table is of special importance; this rate must coincide with the period of time *between payment dates*—in this case, one month. Thus, if payments are made monthly, column B must be based upon the ***monthly*** rate of interest. If payments were made quarterly, this column would use the quarterly rate of interest.

An amortization table begins with the original amount of the liability ($16,398) listed at the top of the unpaid balance column. The amounts of the monthly payments, shown in column A, are specified by the instalment contract. The monthly interest expense, shown in column B, is computed for each month by applying the monthly interest rate to the unpaid balance at the ***beginning of that month.*** The portion of each payment that reduces the amount of the liability (column C) is simply the remainder of the payment (column A minus column B). Finally, the unpaid balance of the liability (column D) is reduced each month by the amount indicated in column C.

Rather than continuing to make monthly payments, King's Inn could settle this liability at any time by paying the amount currently shown as the unpaid balance.

Notice that the amount of interest expense listed in column B ***changes every month.*** In our illustration, the interest expense is ***decreasing*** each month, because the unpaid balance is continually decreasing.[7]

Preparing each horizontal line in an amortization table involves making the same computations, based upon a new unpaid balance. Thus, an amortization table of any length can be easily and quickly prepared by computer. (Most "money management" software includes a program for preparing amortization tables.) The data that must be entered into the computer consist of only three items: (1) the original amount of the liability, (2) the amount of periodic payments, and (3) the interest rate (per payment period).

Using an Amortization Table   Once an amortization table has been prepared, the entries to record each payment are taken directly from the amounts shown in the table. For example, the entry to record the first monthly payment (November 15, 1999) is:

Payment is allocated between interest and principal

Interest Expense	*164*	
Instalment Note Payable	*836*	
Cash		*1,000*

Made November payment on instalment note payable.

Similarly, the entry to record the ***second*** payment, made on ***December 15, 1999,*** is:

Notice that interest expense is less in December

Interest Expense	*156*	
Instalment Note Payable	*844*	
Cash		*1,000*

Made December payment on instalment note payable.

At December 31, 1999, King's Inn should make an adjusting entry to record one-half month's accrued interest on this liability. The amount of this

---

[7]If the monthly payments were ***less*** than the amount of the monthly interest expense, the unpaid balance of the note would ***increase*** each month. This, in turn, would cause the interest expense to increase each month. This pattern, termed ***negative amortization,*** occurs temporarily in some "adjustable-rate" home mortgages.

adjusting entry is based upon the unpaid balance shown in the amortization table as of the last payment (December 15). This entry is:

Year-end adjusting entry

Interest Expense 74
    Interest Payable   74
Adjusting entry to record interest expense on instalment note
for the last half of December: $14,718 × 1% × ½ = $74.

The Current Portion of Long-Term Debt   Notice that as of December 31, **1999,** the unpaid balance of this note is $14,718. As of December 31, **2000,** however, the unpaid balance will be only $3,904. Thus, the principal amount of this note will be reduced by **$10,814** during 2000 ($14,718 − $3,904 = $10,814). In the balance sheet prepared at December 31, 1999, the $10,814 portion of this debt that is scheduled for repayment within the **next 12 months** should be classified as a **current liability.** The remaining $3,904 should be classified as a long-term liability.

Disclosure Requirements for Long-Term Debt

A company should disclose in notes to its financial statements the interest rates, the assets pledged as security, and maturity dates of all long-term notes payable.[8] In addition, the company should disclose the total amounts of long-term debt maturing in each of the next five years. These disclosures are intended to assist users of the financial statements in evaluating the company's solvency—not just today, but over a period of several years.

ESTIMATED LIABILITIES, CONTINGENT LOSSES, AND COMMITMENTS

Estimated Liabilities

The term **estimated liabilities** refers to **liabilities that appear in financial statements at estimated dollar amounts.** Let us again consider the example of the automaker's liability to honour its "new car warranties." A manufacturer's liability for warranty work is recorded by an entry debiting Warranty Expense and crediting Liability for Warranty Claims. The **matching principle** requires that the expense of performing warranty work be recognized in the period in which the products are **sold,** in order to offset this expense against the related sales revenue. As the warranty may extend several years into the future, the dollar amount of this liability (and expense) must be estimated. Rather than estimate when warranty work will be performed, accountants traditionally have classified the liability for warranty claims as a current liability.

By definition, estimated liabilities involve some degree of uncertainty. However, the liabilities are (1) known to exist, and (2) the uncertainty is **not so great** as to prevent the company from making a reasonable estimate and recording the liability.

---

[8]If a company has many different notes payable, it is not practicable to disclose separately the terms of each note. In such cases, the notes are grouped into categories of similar liabilities, and the **range** of interest rates and maturity dates of each category is disclosed. Drafting disclosures that are informative, yet not excessively detailed, requires professional judgment.

Contingent Losses

LO 5: Define contingent losses and commitments and explain their presentation in financial statements.

Contingent losses are similar to estimated liabilities, but may involve much more uncertainty. A ***contingent loss*** is a ***possible loss*** (or expense), stemming from ***past events,*** that will be resolved as to existence and amount by some future event confirming or rejecting the loss.

Central to the definition of a contingent loss is the element of ***uncertainty***—uncertainty to the amount of loss and, in some cases, uncertainty as to ***whether or not any loss actually has been incurred.*** A common example of a contingent loss is a lawsuit pending against a company. The lawsuit is based upon past events, but until the suit is resolved, uncertainty exists as to the amount (if any) of the company's liability.

Contingent losses differ from estimated liabilities in two ways. First, a contingent loss involves a ***greater degree of uncertainty.*** Often the uncertainty extends to whether or not any loss or expense actually has been incurred. In contrast, the loss or expense relating to an estimated liability is ***known to exist.***

Second, the concept of a contingent loss extends not only to possible liabilities but also to possible ***impairments of assets.*** Assume, for example, that a bank has made large loans to a foreign country that is now experiencing political instability. Uncertainty exists as to the amount of loss, if any, associated with this loan. From the bank's point of view, this loan is an ***asset that may be impaired,*** not a liability.

Contingent Losses in Financial Statements   The manner in which contingent losses are presented in financial statements depends upon the ***degree of uncertainty involved.***

Contingent losses are ***recorded*** in the accounting records only when both of the following criteria are met: (1) it is ***likely*** that a loss has been incurred, and (2) the amount of loss can be ***reasonably estimated.***[9] When these criteria are ***not*** met, contingent losses still are ***disclosed*** in financial statements if the occurrence of the confirming future event (1) is likely but the amount of loss cannot reasonably be estimated, or (2) is likely and there exists an exposure to loss in excess of the amount accrued in the records, or (3) is not determinable.[10] Pending lawsuits, for example, usually are disclosed in notes accompanying the financial statements, but the loss, if any, is not recorded in the accounting records until the lawsuit is settled.

Companies generally need not disclose contingent losses if the risk of a material loss is considered ***remote.***

Notice the ***judgmental nature*** of the criteria used in accounting for contingent losses. These criteria involved assessments as to whether the risk of material loss is "likely," "not determinable," or "remote." Thus, the ***professional judgment*** of the company's management, accountants, legal counsel, and auditors is the deciding factor in accounting for contingent losses.

When contingent losses are disclosed in a note to the financial statements, the note should describe the nature of the contingency and, if possible, provide an estimate of the amount of possible loss. If a reasonable estimate of the amount of possible loss cannot be made, the note should include the range of

---

[9]CICA, *CICA Handbook* (Toronto), section 3290.12
[10]Ibid. section 3290.15

possible loss or a statement that an estimate cannot be made. The following note is an example of the disclosure of the contingent loss arising from pending litigation:

Note disclosure of a contingent loss

Note 8: Contingencies
In October of the current year, the Company was named as defendant in a lawsuit alleging patent infringement and claiming damages of $408 million. The Company denies all charges in this case and is preparing its defenses against them. The Company is advised by legal counsel that it is not possible at this time to determine the ultimate legal or financial responsibility with respect to this litigation.

CASE IN POINT

The extent of disclosure on contingencies varies among companies. Many describe contingencies only in very general terms. The following are more extensive and informative:

Bombardier Inc.

The Corporation is the defendant in certain legal cases presently pending before various courts in relation to product liability. The Corporation is also party to several actions associated with waste disposal sites. These actions include possible obligations to remove or mitigate the negative effects on the environment of wastes deposited at various sites. There are also some asbestos-related claims to compensate railway workers for various diseases which allegedly result from their workplace exposure to asbestos materials relating to past businesses involving locomotives.

The Corporation intends to vigorously defend its position in these matters. Management believes the Corporation has set up adequate provisions to cover potential losses and amounts recoverable under insurance coverage, if any, in relation with these legal actions.

IPL Energy Inc. (which owns 100% of Consumers Gas)

In 1994, a class action was commenced against Consumers Gas by a customer alleging that the OEB approved late payment penalties charged to customers were contrary to federal law and seeking certification of the action as a class action. The claim sought $112 million in restitutionary payments and other relief on behalf of all people who were customers of Consumers Gas who had paid or been charged such penalties since April 1, 1981. The class action was not certified by the Court although the Class Proceedings Committee, established under the Ontario Class Proceedings Act, 1992, decided that is would fund the action. On February 13, 1995, Mr. Justice Winkler, of the Ontario Court of Justice, General Division, issued a judgment in favour of Consumers Gas dismissing the class action lawsuit. He concluded that the late payment charge is not interest payable on a credit transaction, but is an incentive to customers to pay their bills by a certain date. He held that Section 347 of the Criminal Code of Canada, which deals with interest on credit transactions, did not apply. On March 10, 1995, the plaintiff's solicitors filed a notice of an appeal of the decision of the trial judge. The appeal was heard on September 12, 1996, and on September 19, 1996, the Court of Appeal dismissed the appeal. The plaintiff has sought leave to appeal to the Supreme Court of Canada from the decision of the Court of Appeal. The submissions of the parties have been filed with the Supreme Court, but the Court has not yet issued its decision as to whether leave to appeal will be granted. Consumers Gas is continuing to collect the penalties and will defend the action which it believes has no validity.

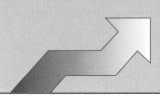

As mentioned earlier, in certain cases, a ***portion*** of a contingent loss qualifies for immediate recognition, whereas the remainder only meets the criteria for disclosure. Assume, for example, that a company has been sued for $10 million. Legal counsel cannot predict the outcome of this litigation, but considers it "likely" that the company will lose at least $1 million. The company should recognize this $1 million expected loss and record it as a liability. In addition, the company should disclose the nature and amount of the litigation, stating that the loss ultimately may exceed the recorded amount.

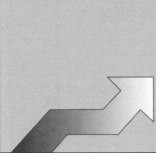

CASE IN POINT   Several years ago, the U.S. Federal Food and Drug Administration (FDA) imposed an indefinite moratorium on the use of silicone breast implants, saying there wasn't enough evidence of the products' safety.

Dow Corning Corp., the nation's largest manufacturer of silicone implants, promptly closed its production lines and accrued a $25 million liability for pending and future lawsuits and claims concerning these implants. Although the company could not estimate with precision the outcome of current and future lawsuits, it believed that losses of at least $25 million were "probable." Subsequently, Dow Corning filed for bankruptcy-court protection, claiming that it couldn't fight an estimated 19,000 lawsuits and stay in business.

Potential Significance of Contingent Losses   Users of financial statements should pay close attention to the notes disclosing contingent losses. Even if no loss has yet been recorded in the accounting records, contingent losses may be so material as to threaten the continued existence of the company.

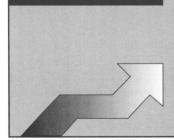

CASE IN POINT   Recently, Dow Corning Corp. and negotiators for women with silicone breast implants agreed to a $3.2 billion (U.S.) court settlement for approximately 400,000 women. While the average compensation payment for disease and disability would be about $31,000 per woman, payments would range from $12,000 to $60,000. Additional payments for rupture and explant surgery would also be made. The agreement must be ratified in a vote by women in the U.S. with Dow Corning implants. This agreement may mean the $50 million settlement approved by the Quebec Superior Court for Canadian women with such implants is one step closer to reality.

The risk that losses may result from ***future*** events is ***not*** a contingent loss. The risk of future losses generally is ***not*** disclosed in financial statements for several reasons. For one, any disclosure of future losses would be sheer speculation. For another, no one can foresee all of the events that might give rise to future losses.

Commitments

Contracts for future transactions are called **commitments**. They are not liabilities. However, commitments (contractual obligations) that are significant or material should be disclosed in the notes to the financial statements. For example, a professional baseball club may issue a three-year contract to a player at an annual salary of, say, $3 million. This is a commitment to pay for services to be rendered in the future. There is no obligation to make payment until the services are received. As liabilities stem only from *past transactions,* this commitment has not yet created a liability.

Other examples of commitments include long-term employment contracts, a contract for construction of a new plant, and a contract to buy or sell inventory at future dates. The common quality of all these commitments is an intent to enter into transactions *in the future.*

CASE IN POINT

Commitments can vary and can be quite substantial. Two companies disclosed the following in the notes to their recent financial statements:

Canadian Airlines Corporation The Corporation is committed to expenditures, estimated at U.S. $464,000,000 for ten A320-200 aircraft and related support equipment with delivery dates between 2000 and 2001. Deposits of U.S. $17,200,000 have been made and recorded as property and equipment at December 31, 1997.

Quebecor Inc. As of December 31, 1997, Quebecor Printing Inc., a subsidiary of Quebecor Inc. had commitments to purchase fixed assets valued at approximately $188,650,000. Quebecor Printing Inc. announced cash offers for the acquisition of Watmoughs (Holdings) Plc, a publicly traded company in the United Kingdom. The offers at 257 pence per common share and 120 pence per preferred share establishes Watmoughs (Holdings) Plc's total value at £188,300,000. If this acquisition materializes, Quebecor Printing Inc. will use its available revolving bank credits to finance the transaction.

EVALUATING THE SAFETY OF CREDITORS' CLAIMS

LO 6: Evaluate the safety of creditors' claims.

Creditors, of course, want to be sure that their claims are safe—that is, that they will be paid on time. Actually, ***everyone*** associated with a business—management, owners, employees—should be concerned with the company's ability to pay its debts. If a business becomes ***insolvent*** (unable to pay its obligations), it may be forced into bankruptcy.

Not only does management want the business to remain solvent, it wants the company to maintain a high ***credit rating*** with agencies such as Dun & Bradstreet and Standard & Poor's. A high credit rating helps a company borrow money more easily and at lower interest rates.

Analysis by Short-Term Creditors

In evaluating debt-paying ability, short-term creditors and long-term creditors look at different financial relationships. Short-term creditors are interested in the company's immediate solvency and look toward such measures of liquidity as working capital, the current ratio, and the lines of credit. They also compute the turnover rates for receivables and for inventory and the operating cycle to evaluate the liquidity of these assets. These short-term solvency measures were introduced in earlier chapters. A more stringent measure, called the quick ratio, is discussed below.

Quick Ratio   Although inventories and prepaid expenses are classified as current assets, they are further removed from conversion into cash than are other current assets. Therefore, short-term creditors often use a statistic called the **quick ratio** or **acid test ratio,** rather than the current ratio, to provide a quick evaluation of a company's short-term solvency.

The quick ratio is computed by dividing **quick assets** by current liabilities. Quick assets include only cash, investments in marketable securities,[11] and short-term receivables. Thus, the quick ratio provides a more rigid test of short-term solvency than does the current ratio.

A quick ratio of 1.0 to 1 or better usually is considered satisfactory, and a quick ratio of over 1.5 to 1 indicates a high degree of liquidity. Of course, all ratios vary substantially among companies of different sizes or in different industries. However, an analyst familiar with the nature of a company's operations generally can determine from the quick ratio whether the company represents a good credit risk in the short run.

Analysis by Long-Term Creditors

Long-term creditors are less concerned than short-term creditors with the amount of liquid assets a business has on hand today. Rather, they are interested in the borrower's ability to meet its interest obligations **over a period of years,** and also its ability to repay or refinance large obligations years in the future.

Debt Ratio   One measurement often used in evaluating the overall safety of long-term creditors' investments is the **debt ratio**. This ratio is computed by dividing total liabilities by total assets. Basically, the debt ratio indicates the **percentage** of total assets that are financed with borrowed money (liabilities), in comparison with the percentage financed with equity capital.

Creditors prefer a **low** debt ratio, as this means that their claims amount to only a small percentage of total assets. This relationship increases the prospects that the creditors will be paid in full, even if the company ceases operations and liquidates its assets.

Of course, individual creditors should look beyond the overall debt ratio to determine the safety of their claims. Holders of subordinated debt, for example, should consider the priority of their claims relative to those of other creditors. The holders of secured debt should consider the value and salability of the specific assets that secure their claims.

Interest Coverage Ratio   Creditors, investors, and managers all feel more comfortable when a company has enough operating income to cover its

---

[11]Investments in marketable securities are investments that can be sold readily at quoted market prices. They include, for example, investments in government bonds and in the stocks and bonds issued by major corporations. Marketable securities are discussed in Chapter 17.

interest payment obligations by a wide margin. One widely used measure of the relationship between earnings and interest expense is the **interest coverage ratio**.

The interest coverage ratio is computed by dividing annual **operating income** by the annual interest expense. From the creditor's point of view, the higher this ratio, the better.

Trend in Net Income   Long-term creditors are keenly interested in the financial viability of the company over a period of time. One measure of this is the trend of net income. A financially viable company generally shows a growing trend of net income.

Summary

The measures used to evaluate the solvency of the company by the short-term and long-term creditors are summarized below.

Measures of Debt-Paying Ability	
Short-Term	**Long-Term**
Quick ratio—Quick assets divided by current liabilities; a more stringent measure of solvency.	*Debt ratio*—Total liabilities divided by total assets. Measures percentage of capital structure financed by creditors.
Current ratio—Current assets divided by current liabilities; the most common measure of solvency, but less stringent than the quick ratio.	*Interest coverage ratio*—Operating income divided by interest expense. Shows how many times the company "earns" its annual interest obligations.
Working capital—Current assets less current liabilities; the "uncommitted" liquid resources.	*Trend in net income*—Not directly related to debt-paying ability, but still an excellent measure of long-term financial health.
Turnover rates—Measures of how quickly receivables are collected or inventory is sold. (Computed separately for receivables and inventory.)	
Operating cycle—The period of time required to convert inventory into cash.	
Lines of credit—Indicates ready access to additional cash should the need arise.	

Less Formal Means of Determining Creditworthiness

Not all decisions to extend credit involve formal analysis of the borrower's financial statements. Most suppliers of goods or services, for example, will sell "on account" to almost any long-established business—unless they know the customer to be in severe financial difficulty. If the customer is not a well-established business, these suppliers may investigate the customer's "credit history" by contacting a credit-rating agency.

In lending to small businesses organized as corporations, lenders usually require key shareholders to ***personally guarantee*** repayment of the loan.

Topics Deferred to Chapter 16

In this chapter, we have discussed the types of liabilities that are common to almost every business organization. Our discussion, however, does not address some of the largest liabilities of many large, publicly owned corporations.

In a large corporation, such liabilities as bonds payable, pensions and other postretirement benefits, and future (deferred) income taxes often dwarf such obligations as accounts payable and instalment debt.[12] Liabilities that relate primarily to large corporations will be discussed in Chapter 16, after we have explored more fully the nature and characteristics of the corporate form of business entity.

---

[12]The term "deferred income taxes" will be replaced by "future income tax liabilities" when section 3465 of the *CICA Handbook* on income taxes becomes effective on January 1, 2000.

*Supplemental Topic

ACCOUNTING FOR PAYROLLS

In most business organizations, the largest expense accruing on a daily basis is payroll. In the airlines industry, for example, labour costs usually represent about 30% of total operating expenses.

The task of accounting for payroll costs would be an important one simply because of the large amounts involved; however, it is further complicated by the many federal and provincial laws that require employers to maintain certain specific information in their payroll records not only for the business as a whole but also for each individual employee. Frequent reports of wages paid and amounts withheld must be filed with government authorities. These reports are prepared by every employer and must be accompanied by *payment* to the government of the amounts withheld from employees and of the payroll taxes levied on the employer.

A basic rule in most business organizations is that every employee must be paid on time, and the payment must be accompanied by a detailed explanation of the computations used in determining the net amount received by the employee. The payroll system must therefore be capable of processing the input data (such as employee names, social insurance numbers, hours worked, pay rates, overtime, and taxes) and producing a prompt and accurate output of paycheques, payroll records, withholding statements, and reports to governmental authorities. In addition, the payroll system must have built-in safeguards against overpayments to employees, the issuance of duplicate paycheques, payments to fictitious employees, and the continuance on the payroll of persons who have been terminated as employees.

INTERNAL CONTROL OVER PAYROLLS

Every business needs to establish adequate internal control over payrolls. With such controls, a business has assurance that employees will be paid the correct amounts and that payroll-related taxes will be computed correctly and paid on time. Failure to pay employees promptly and in the proper amounts is certain to damage employee morale. Failures to remit payroll taxes to tax authorities on schedule may result in fines and penalties. Finally, payroll historically has been an area in which poor internal control has sometimes led to employee fraud.

Payroll fraud can take many forms. Small-scale payroll fraud may consist of employees overstating the number of hours (or days) that they have actually worked. "Padding" the payroll—adding fictitious employees to the payroll in order to generate extra paycheques—is a larger-scale payroll fraud.

LO 7: Describe the basic separation of duties in a payroll system, and explain how this plan contributes to strong internal control.

A basic means of achieving adequate internal control over payrolls is an appropriate separation of duties. In most organizations, payroll activities include (1) employing workers, (2) timekeeping, (3) payroll preparation and record keeping, and (4) the distribution of pay to employees. Internal control is strengthened if each of these functions is handled by a separate department.

Human Resources Department The work of the human resources department begins with interviewing and hiring job applicants. When a new employee is hired, the department prepares records showing the date of employment, the authorized rate of pay, and payroll deductions. It then sends a written notice to the payroll department to place the new employee on the payroll. The human resources department also is responsible for notifying the payroll department of changes in employees' rates of pay and of persons whose employment has been terminated.

Timekeeping For employees paid by the hour, the time of arrival and departure should be punched on time cards. A new time card should be placed in the rack by the time clock at the beginning of each week or other pay period. Control procedures should exist to ensure that each employee punches his or her own time card and no other. The timekeeping function should be lodged in a separate department that will control the time cards and transmit these source documents to the payroll department.

In a computer-based payroll system, record keeping is simplified if the time clocks are on-line devices—that is, if they are connected directly with the computer system. In this way, the hours worked by each employee are entered automatically into the payroll accounting system.

The Payroll Department The input of information to the payroll department consists of hours reported by the timekeeping department and authorized names, pay rates, and payroll deductions received from the human resources department. The output of the payroll department includes (1) payroll cheques, (2) individual employee records of earnings and deductions, and (3) regular reports to the government showing employee earnings and taxes withheld.

Distribution of Paycheques The paycheques prepared in the payroll department are transmitted to the ***paymaster,*** who distributes them to the employees. The paymaster should ***not*** have responsibility for hiring or firing employees, timekeeping, or preparation of the payroll.

Paycheques for absent employees should never be turned over to other employees or to supervisors for delivery. Instead, the absent employee should later pick up the paycheque from the paymaster after presenting proper identification and signing a receipt. The distribution of paycheques by the paymaster provides assurance that paycheques will not continue to be issued to fictitious employees or employees who have been terminated.

The Operation of a Payroll System: A Summary

The operation of a typical payroll system is illustrated in the following flowchart. Notes have been made indicating the major internal control points within the system.

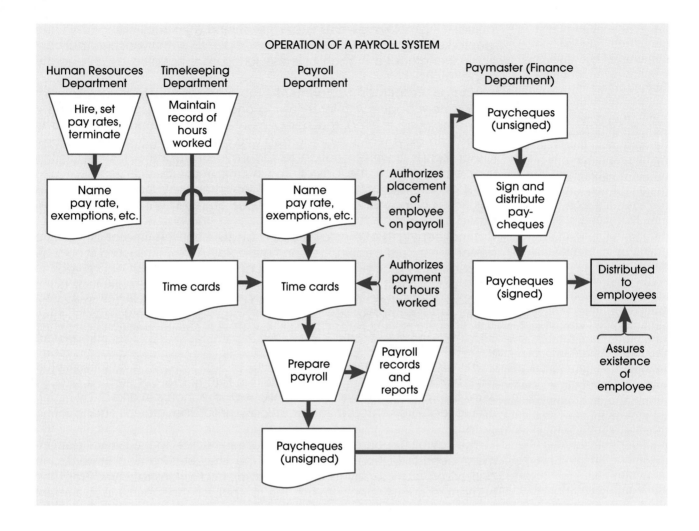

OPERATION OF A PAYROLL SYSTEM

THE COMPUTATION OF PAYROLL AMOUNTS

LO 8: Account for a payroll, including computation of amounts withheld and payroll taxes on the employer.

The actual preparation of a payroll, including the computation of dollar amounts, maintenance of payroll records, and printing of paycheques, is the responsibility of the payroll department. The dollar amounts associated with payrolls fall into three categories: (1) employees' gross pay, (2) amounts withheld from employees' gross pay, and (3) payroll taxes levied on the employer.

Gross Pay

Gross pay (earnings) is the amount earned by the employees during the pay period. Except to the extent that employers **withhold** amounts for taxes or other purposes, all gross pay is payable directly to the employees.

Gross pay also includes compensation during sick days, holidays, and vacations. However, it does not include **fringe benefits,** such as group life insurance paid by the employer or the use of a "company car." The distinction is that fringe benefits are not payable directly to the employees.

Gross pay must be computed separately for each employee. For employees paid an hourly wage, the payroll system must keep track of the **number of hours** that each employee works each day. In many cases, current laws require that employees be paid at an overtime rate for hours worked in excess of 8 per day or 40 per week. For employees who receive sales commissions, the system must record separately the sales revenue attributable to each salesperson. The amount of an employee's gross pay affects the amounts of taxes that must be withheld and also the payroll taxes levied upon the employer.

Amounts Withheld from Employees' Pay

The **net pay** (or "take-home pay") of most employees is substantially less than their gross pay. This is because government authorities require employers to **withhold** specified amounts of income taxes, employment insurance premiums, and Canada Pension Plan contributions from each employee's gross pay. (Employees often refer to amounts withheld as **deductions.**)

Taxes withheld from employees' pay are taxes levied **on the employees,** not taxes on the employer. The employer's role in withholding taxes is that of a tax **collector.** The amounts withheld must be forwarded to governmental tax authorities weekly, twice-monthly, monthly, or quarterly, depending on the size of the amount involved. Therefore, the employer records the amounts withheld as **current liabilities.**

Federal and Provincial Income Taxes   The amount of income taxes withheld depends upon the amount of the earnings and upon the "claim amount" (income tax exemptions) to which the employee is entitled. To ensure that the proper amount of income tax is withheld, each employee is required to file with the employer a **Personal Tax Credit Return, TD1** form, showing the total claim amount, the Claim Code, and the supporting details. However, this return may not need to be filed by employees claiming the "basic personal amount" only—i.e., claiming the minimum amount for tax credit.

Based on the earnings and the amount claimed, the employer can determine the income tax to be withheld from the employee by referring to the income tax deduction tables provided by Revenue Canada, Taxation. The amount withheld from employees is remitted to Revenue Canada, Taxation. This amount includes both the federal and provincial income taxes for all provinces except the province of Quebec, which collects its own income tax. Employers in Quebec must withhold separate deductions for federal and Quebec income taxes.

Employment Insurance   Since its inception in 1940, federal Unemployment Insurance legislation has undergone significant changes, including a recent change of its name from unemployment insurance to **employment insurance.** The current law requires, with a few exceptions, both employers and employees to contribute to employment insurance on remuneration from insurable employment. Insurable employment includes most employment in Canada under a contract of service, that is, employee–employer relationship. Also, there is no age limit for contribution to employment insurance. The purpose of the legislation is to provide relief from financial hardships for those who are unemployed even though they are willing and able to work. The eligibility for, and the amount of, unemployment benefits depend on a number of factors, including past insurable earnings, length of insurable employment, and regional unemployment rate.

The employers are responsible for withholding an appropriate amount of employment insurance premium from their employees. The amount of premium withheld together with the premium contributed by the employer is remitted to Revenue Canada, Taxation. For the year 1998, the employees' premium is 2.7% of their insurable earnings; the employers' premium is 1.4 times that of the employees'. For example, if an employee's monthly insurable earnings are $1,000, the premiums for the employee and the employer are $27 (1,000 × 2.7%) and $38 ($27 × 1.4) respectively. In 1998, the rate of premium of 2.7% is applicable to annual insurable earnings of up to a maximum of $39,000. In other words, employees with annual earnings of $39,000 or more are required to pay premium on the annual maximum amount of $39,000. Accordingly, the maximum annual premium for an employee is $1,053 ($39,000 × 2.7%). Since contributions are made periodically, employees with annual insurable earnings exceeding the maximum may pay up the $1,053 maximum annual premium in the early part of the year. The premium rate as well as the maximum amounts subject to employment insurance premium may change from year to year.

On occasion, employees may have contributed more than the maximum amount of premium. In such cases, the employees should claim a refund by reporting the overpayment in their income tax returns.

While the individual contribution is small, the total contribution for employment insurance is huge. For example, the total contribution of employment insurance in a recent year was more than $18 billion.

Canada Pension Plan   The Canada Pension Plan Act requires, with a few exceptions, both employers and employees (between the ages of 18 to 70), including those who are self-employed, to make contributions to the Canada Pension Plan. Its purpose is to provide retirement, disability, and similar benefits. The eligibility for, and the amount of, benefits depend on a number of factors, including the amount of pensionable earnings, the length of the contribution period, and the age of the individual.

The employers are responsible for withholding an appropriate amount of Canada Pension Plan contribution from the pensionable earnings of each of their employees and are required to contribute an amount equal to that of the employees'. The amount withheld together with the amount contributed by the employers is remitted to Revenue Canada, Taxation. For the year 1998, the employees' contribution is 3.2% of the maximum annual pensionable earnings of $36,900, with the first $3,500 exempted, and the employers' contribution is the same as that of the employees'. For example, if an employee's annual pensionable earnings are $18,500, both the employee and the employer are required to contribute $480 each (($18,500 less $3,500 basic annual exemption) times 3.2%). Thus, in 1998, the rate of contribution of 3.2% is applicable to annual pensionable earnings of over $3,500, up to a maximum of $33,400 (i.e., earnings of $36,900 less the $3,500 basic annual exemption). In other words, employees with annual pensionable earnings of $3,500 or less are not required to contribute, and employees with pensionable earnings of $36,900 or more are required to contribute on the maximum amount of $33,400. Accordingly, the maximum annual contribution for an employee is $1,068.80 ($33,400 × 3.2%).

Since contributions are made periodically, employees with annual earnings exceeding the maximum pensionable earnings may pay up the $1,068.80 maximum contribution in the early part of the year. If an employee, for example, earns $60,000 a year, the monthly contribution is $150.67 ($5,000 less the monthly exemption of $291.67 at 3.2%), and the employee will have contributed $1,054.69 in the first seven months and will only be required to contribute the balance of $14.11 in the eighth month.[13] The rate, and the amount subject to, Canada Pension Plan, may change from year to year. On occasion, an employee may have contributed more than the maximum amount. In such cases, the employee should claim a refund by reporting the overpayment in his or her income tax return.

The Canada Pension Plan applies to all provinces except the province of Quebec, which has its own similar pension plan. The two plans are closely coordinated so that contributing employees are protected wherever they may work in Canada.

The total contribution to Canada Pension Plan is very large; a recent year's contribution amounted to more than $14 billion.

Other Deductions from Employees' Earnings   In addition to the compulsory deductions for employment insurance, Canada (or Quebec) Pension Plan, and income taxes, many other deductions are voluntarily authorized by employees. Union dues, insurance premiums, savings bond purchases, charitable contributions, retirement programs, and pension plans are examples of voluntary payroll deductions.

Employer's Responsibility for Amounts Withheld   In withholding amounts from an employee's earnings for either voluntary or involuntary deductions, the employer acts merely as a collection agent. The amounts withheld are paid to the designated organization, such as governmental authorities or a labour union. The employer is also responsible for maintaining accounting records that will enable it to file required reports and make timely payments of the amounts withheld. From the employer's viewpoint, the amounts withheld from employee's earnings represent current liabilities.

Basic Payroll Records

The formats of payroll records vary greatly among different businesses, depending upon the number of employees and the extent of automation. However, there are two basic records common to the payroll system of every organization: the ***payroll register*** and the ***employees' individual earnings records.***

---

[13]The monthly exemption is arrived at by dividing the annual exemption of $3,500 by 12. The proper amounts of contributions can be obtained from the deduction tables provided by Revenue Canada, Taxation. Since the exemption has already been taken into account in these tables, there is no need to deduct the monthly or weekly exemption from the earnings. For example, if the monthly earnings plus taxable benefits, if any, are $5,000, look up the earnings' bracket between $4,995.26 and $5,005.25 to obtain the proper amount of contribution, which is $150.68.

Payroll Register   The **payroll register** is a special journal used for developing all of the information needed for processing and recording the payroll of a specific pay period. This journal includes a separate line of data about each employee. On this line, the employee's gross pay, various amounts withheld, and net pay are entered in separate columns. Thus, each line of the payroll register provides the data necessary for preparing one employee's paycheque, and also for updating the employee's individual earnings record. Totalling each column, on the other hand, provides information about the **entire** payroll, which is posted to the general ledger accounts.

To illustrate, assume that Data Management Limited has 35 salaried employees, who are paid monthly. A payroll register containing data relating to the March payroll is illustrated on the following page (along with the individual earnings record for one employee).

The illustrated payroll register includes separate columns for gross pay, four different types of withholding, and net pay.[14] The **totals** of these columns represent the expenses and liabilities associated with the issuance of paycheques to employees. (These totals do **not** reflect the payroll taxes on the employer for March.)

One common practice is to summarize the column totals of the payroll register in the form of a general journal entry, as follows:[15]

Journal entry summarizing the March payroll—except for taxes on the employer

Salaries Expense	*80,000*	
Liability for Income Tax Withheld		*14,210*
Liability for Employment Insurance Withheld		*2,160*
Liability for Canada Pension Plan Withheld		*2,251*
Liability for Group Insurance Withheld		*1,890*
Accrued Payroll		*59,489*

To record the monthly payroll for March.

All of the accounts credited in this entry are current liabilities of the employer. Accrued payroll represents the net pay owed to employees; this liability will be discharged almost immediately through the issuance of paycheques. The liabilities for amounts withheld will be discharged within a short period of time by remitting these amounts to the appropriate recipients.

Employees' Individual Earnings Records   An employer also must maintain an **individual earnings record** for each employee. These records contain basically the same information as does the payroll register: each employee's gross pay, amounts withheld, and net pay. The differences between a payroll register and the employees' individual earnings records are primarily in the manner in which the data are **organized.**

---

[14]The illustrated payroll register is highly simplified. An actual payroll register includes many more columns for such items as employees' social insurance numbers and several other types of withholding. For employees paid an hourly wage, additional columns would indicate pay rates and regular hours and overtime hours worked during the pay period. Actual payroll registers generally are a computer printout with, perhaps, 15 or more data columns.

[15]A general journal entry is not actually necessary; the column totals could be posted directly from the payroll register to the general ledger accounts.

PAYROLL REGISTER

Payroll period ended: March 31, 19___

| Employee | Gross Pay | Amounts Withheld | | | | Net Pay | Cheque No. |
		Income Taxes	Employment Insurance	Canada Pension Plan	Group Insurance		
Abrams, H	$ 1,600	$ 245	$ 43	$ 42	$ 35	$ 1,235	841
Boice, C	2,000	324	54	55	42	1,525	842
Cato, Y	3,000	594	81	87	66	2,172	843

| Zucco, R | 2,400 | 354 | 65 | 67 | 51 | 1,863 | 875 |
| Totals | $80,000 | $14,210 | $2,160 | $2,251 | $1,890 | $59,489 | – – |

EMPLOYEE EARNINGS RECORD

Name: Carol Boice
Address: 900 Lake View Lane, Apt. F
Windsor, Ontario, N9B 8P9
Position: Commercial artist-grade 1
Marital status: M
Claim Code: 2

Soc. Ins. # 483-724-690
Date of Birth: July 4, 1975
Date employed: July 24, 1997
Date of termination:
Reason for termination:
Monthly salary: $2,000

| Pay Period | Gross Pay | Year-to-Date | Amounts Withheld | | | | Net Pay | Cheque No. |
			Income Taxes	Employment Insurance	Canada Pension Plan	Group Insurance		
Jan.	$2,000	$2,000	$ 324	$ 54	$ 55	$ 42	$1,525	772
Feb.	2,000	4,000	324	54	55	42	1,525	807
Mar.	2,000	6,000	324	54	55	42	1,525	842
Total for quarter	$6,000	$6,000	$972	$162	$165	$126	$4,575	– –
Apr.								
May								

A payroll register shows in one place all of the payroll data for *one pay-roll period*, including data for all employees. An earnings record shows in one place all of the payroll data *for one employee*, including data for every payroll period. The individual earnings record for one of Data Management's salaried employees is illustrated on page 591.

An employee's earnings record always includes a column showing the employee's *cumulative* gross pay earned thus far during the year. This year-to-date earnings figure determines when (and if) the employee's earnings exceed the bases subject to employment insurance and Canada Pension Plan contribution. In addition, employers must report each employee's gross earnings for the year to the employee and to Revenue Canada.

By the end of February of each year, employers must furnish each employee and Revenue Canada with a copy of the **Statement of Remuneration Paid (T4),** showing the employee's gross earnings for the preceding calendar year and the amounts of all taxes withheld. When the employee files an income tax return, he or she must attach a copy of this statement.

Payroll Taxes Levied upon the Employer

As discussed earlier in this chapter, employers are required to contribute to employment insurance and Canada Pension Plan. These contributions are expenses to the business and are commonly called "payroll taxes expense."[16]

Entry Recording an Employer's Payroll Taxes The entry to record the employer's payroll taxes is made at the end of each pay period, along with the entry recording the payroll. To illustrate, let us again consider the $80,000 March payroll of Data Management Limited. The entry to record this payroll, including the taxes withheld from employees, appeared on page 590. Now, however, we are addressing the payroll taxes levied directly upon the **employer.**

The employer's liability for employment insurance premium is 1.4 times the amounts withheld from the employees—$3,024 (1.4 × $2,160). The employer's liability for Canada Pension Plan is equal to the amount withheld from the employees—$2,251. A general journal entry recording the payroll taxes levied upon Data Management in March appears below:

Journal entry to record payroll taxes on the employer

Payroll Taxes Expense	*5,275*	
Employment Insurance Taxes Payable		*3,024*
Canada Pension Plan Taxes Payable		*2,251*
To record employer's payroll taxes relating to the March payroll.		

All of the accounts credited represent current liabilities that must be paid within a short period of time.

Payroll by Computer

Because of the repetitive nature of payroll computations, payrolls are ide-ally suited to computer processing. In fact, accounting for payrolls was

---

[16]There are also payroll taxes at the provincial level. For example, employers in Ontario must pay employer health tax and insurance premium under the Workplace Safety and Insurance Act (formerly Workers' Compensation Act).

among the first applications of the computer in the business world. As an alternative to accounting for payrolls "in-house," small businesses often delegate this function to an outside agency.

Given the complexities of payroll accounting, computer-based payroll systems are amazingly efficient. Often, the only input required for processing the entire payroll is the **number of hours** worked by each employee receiving an hourly wage. If time clocks are on-line devices, payrolls sometimes can be prepared without any manual input of data or manual computations. (Of course, the computer-based files must be updated for changes in pay rates, tax rates, or the personnel comprising the work force.)

In conclusion, it simply is **not cost-efficient** to account for payrolls manually in a business that has more than just a few employees.

Fringe Benefits

Many companies provide employees with various fringe benefits, such as dental and extended health care insurance, group life insurance, and a pension plan. The cost of fringe benefits usually is determined for the work force as a whole, rather than computed separately for each employee. Separate expense accounts and liability accounts are used in recording each type of fringe benefit.

To illustrate, assume that Data Management pays dental and extended health care insurance and life insurance for its employees and also contributes an amount equal to 5% of their gross pay to an employees' registered pension plan. A general journal entry recording the cost of fringe benefits relating to the March 31 payroll is shown below:

Journal entry to record the cost of fringe benefits	*Dental and Extended Health Care Insurance Expense* *6,800*	
	Life Insurance Expense *4,600*	
	Pension Expense *4,000*	
	Insurance Premiums Payable	*11,400*
	Liability to Employees' Pension Plan	*4,000*
	To record the cost of fringe benefits provided to employees in March.	

The Total Cost of Employee Compensation

Our discussion of payrolls has been based upon the $80,000 March payroll of Data Management Limited. Notice, however, that the company's **total** payroll cost in March actually amounts to **$100,675**—a figure substantially higher than the employees' gross pay. The "total payroll cost" includes the following elements:[17]

Employees cost more than they're paid	*Gross pay earned by employees*	*$ 80,000*
	Payroll taxes levied upon employer	*5,275*
	Fringe benefits paid by employer	*15,400*
	Total employee compensation costs for the pay period	*$100,675*

---

[17]As noted earlier, the total cost will be much higher when the provincial payroll taxes are added.

These results are not at all unusual. An employer's total payroll cost generally exceeds employees' gross pay by 15% to 25%.

Distinction between Employees and Independent Contractors

Every business obtains personal services from **employees** and also from **independent contractors.** The employer–employee relationship exists when the company paying for the services has a right to direct and supervise the person rendering the services. Independent contractors, on the other hand, are retained to perform a specific task and exercise their own judgment as to the best methods for performing the work. Examples of independent contractors include public accountants engaged to perform an audit, lawyers retained to represent a company in a law suit, and a plumber called in to repair a broken pipe.

The **fees** paid to independent contractors are not included in payroll records and are **not subject to withholding or payroll taxes.** Also, independent contractors do not participate in the fringe benefits provided to employees.

End-of-Chapter Review

Key Terms Introduced or Emphasized in Chapter 11

Accrued liabilities *(p.570)* The liability to pay an expense that has accrued during the period. Also called ***accrued expenses.***

Amortization of discount *(p.567)* The process of systematically writing off to interest expense each period a portion of the discount on a note payable. Causes the carrying value of the liability to rise to the face value of the note by the maturity date.

Amortization table *(p.574)* A schedule that indicates how instalment payments are allocated between interest expense and repayments of principal.

***Canada Pension Plan** *(p.588)* A national plan established by a federal act that requires both the employer and the employee to make contributions to the plan. Its purpose is to provide retirement, disability, and similar benefits.

Capital structure *(p.563)* The combination of liabilities and owners' equity used in financing total assets. It is described by the "right-hand" side of the balance sheet.

Commitments *(p.579)* Agreements to carry out future transactions. Not a liability because the transaction has not yet been performed, but should be disclosed in notes to the financial statements if the commitment is significant.

Contingent loss *(p.577)* A possible loss that either will develop into a full-fledged loss or will be eliminated entirely by a future event.

Contra-liability account *(p.567)* A ledger account that is deducted from or offset against a related liability account in the balance sheet; for example, Discount on Notes Payable.

Debt ratio *(p.581)* Total liabilities divided by total assets. Indicates the percentage of total assets financed by borrowing.

Discount on Notes Payable *(p.567)* A contra-liability account representing any interest charges applicable to future periods included in the face amount of a note payable. Over the life of the note, the balance of the Discount on Notes Payable account is amortized into Interest Expense.

***Employment insurance** *(p.587)* An insurance plan established by federal legislation that imposes a premium contribution on both the employer and the employee. Its purpose is to provide relief from financial hardships for the unemployed.

Estimated liabilities *(p.564)* Liabilities known to exist but that must be recorded in the accounting records at estimated dollar amounts.

* **Fringe benefits** *(p.586)* Portions of the compensation package offered to employees that are not paid directly to the employees. Paid life insurance is an example.

* **Gross pay** *(p.586)* The total amount earned by an employee that is payable, at least in part, to that employee. Does not include fringe benefits.

* **Independent contractor** *(p.594)* A person or firm providing services to a company for a fee or commission. Not controlled or supervised by the client company. Not subject to payroll taxes.

Interest coverage ratio *(p.582)* Operating income divided by interest expense. Indicates the number of times that the company was able to earn the amount of its interest charges.

Operating income *(p.582)* A subtotal in the income statement representing the revenue earned from customers less only operating expenses. Widely used in evaluating the relationship between earnings and interest expense, as operating income represents the earnings ***before*** deductions for interest expense and other "nonoperating" items.

* **Payroll register** *(p.590)* A form of payroll record showing for each pay period all payroll information for employees individually and in total.

* **Personal Tax Credit Return (TD1)** *(p.587)* A form prepared and signed by the employee that shows the total amount of claims and the supporting details. It is used to determine the proper amount of income tax to be withheld from the employee's remuneration.

Principal amount *(p.566)* That portion of the maturity value of a note that is attributable to the amount borrowed or to the cost of the asset acquired when the note was issued, rather than being attributable to interest charges.

Quick ratio *(p.581)* Quick assets divided by current liabilities. A more stringent measure of immediate solvency than the current ratio.

* **Statement of Remuneration Paid (T4)** *(p.592)* A form furnished by the employer to every employee that shows the gross earnings for the calendar year and the amounts withheld for employment insurance, Canada Pension Plan, income tax, and other items such as registered pension plan.

---

*Supplemental Topic, "Accounting for Payrolls"

DEMONSTRATION PROBLEM

Listed below are selected items from the financial statements of S & H Pump Mfg. Corporation for the year ended December 31, 2000:

Note payable to TD Bank	$100,000
Discount on note payable (to TD Bank)	1,000
Income taxes payable	63,000
Contingent liability relating to lawsuit	200,000
Accounts payable	163,230
Mortgage note payable	240,864
Interest payable (mortgage note)	1,606
Accrued payroll	18,700
Amounts withheld from employees' pay	2,940
Payroll taxes payable	1,260
Unearned revenue	25,300

OTHER INFORMATION

1. The note payable owed to TD Bank is due in 30 days. S & H has arranged with this bank to renew the note for an additional 2 years.

2. S & H has been sued for $200,000 by someone claiming the company's pumps are excessively noisy. It is not determinable that a loss has been sustained.

3. The mortgage note is payable at $8,000 per month over the next 3 years. During the next 12 months, the principal amount of this note will be reduced to $169,994.

INSTRUCTIONS

a. Using this information, prepare the current liabilities and long-term liabilities sections of a classified balance sheet at December 31, 2000.

b. Explain briefly how the information in each of the three numbered paragraphs affected your presentation of the company's liabilities.

SOLUTION TO DEMONSTRATION PROBLEM

a.

S & H PUMP MFG. CORPORATION
Partial Balance Sheet
December 31, 2000

Liabilities:			
Current liabilities:			
Accounts payable			$163,230
Income taxes payable			63,000
Interest payable (mortgage note)			1,606
Accrued payroll			18,700
Amounts withheld from employees' pay			2,940
Payroll taxes payable			1,260
Unearned revenue			25,300
Current portion of long-term debt (mortgage note)			70,870
Total current liabilities			$346,906
Long-term liabilities:			
Note payable		100,000	
Less: Discount on note payable		1,000	$ 99,000
Mortgage note payable			169,994
Total long-term liabilities			$268,994
Total liabilities			$615,900

b. 1. Although the note payable to TD Bank is due in 30 days, it is classified as a long-term liability as it will be refinanced on a long-term basis.

   2. The pending lawsuit is a contingent liability requiring disclosure, but it is not listed in the liability section of the balance sheet.

   3. The $70,870 of the mortgage note that will be repaid within the next 12 months ($240,864 − $169,994) is a current liability; the remaining balance, due after December 31, 2000, is long-term debt.

Self-Test Questions

The answers to these questions appear on page 612.

1. Which of the following is characteristic of liabilities, rather than of equity? (More than one answer may be correct.)
   a. The obligation matures.
   b. Compensation paid to the provider of the capital is deductible for income tax purposes.
   c. The capital providers' claims are *residual* in the event of liquidation of the business.
   d. The capital providers normally have the right to exercise control over business operations.

2. Which of the following situations require recording a liability in 2000? (More than one answer may be correct.)
   a. In 2000, a company manufactures and sells stereo equipment that carries a three-year warranty.
   b. In 2000, a theatre group receives payments in advance from season ticket holders for productions to be performed in 2001.
   c. A company is a defendant in a legal action. At the end of 2000, the company's lawyer feels it is possible the company will lose, and that the amount of the loss might be material.
   d. During 2000, an agricultural co-operative is concerned about the risk of loss if inclement weather destroys the crops.

Use the following data for questions 3 and 4.
   On May 1, 2000, Thompkins Company borrowed $350,000 from the bank and agreed to repay that amount plus 12% interest at the end of one year (including the three days of grace).

3. Assume the note payable is drawn in the amount of $350,000 with interest stated separately. With respect to this note, Thompkins's financial statements for the year ended December 31, 2000 include:
   a. Interest expense of $42,000.
   b. An overall current liability for this loan of $392,000.
   c. An overall current liability for this loan of $378,000.
   d. Unamortized Discount on Notes Payable of $14,000.

4. Assume the note payable is drawn with interest included in the face of the note. Thompkins's adjusting entry on December 31, 2000 with regard to this note includes:
   a. A credit to Notes Payable of $14,000.
   b. A debit to Interest Expense of $14,000.
   c. A credit to Interest Payable of $28,000.
   d. A credit to Discount on Notes Payable of $28,000.

5. Identify those types of information that can readily be determined from an amortization table for an instalment loan. (More than one answer may be correct.)
   a. Interest expense on this liability for the current year.
   b. The present value of the future payments under current market conditions.
   c. The unpaid balance remaining after each payment.
   d. The portion of the unpaid balance that is a current liability.

6. A basic difference between **contingent losses** and "real" liabilities is:
   a. Liabilities stem from past transactions; contingent losses stem from future events.
   b. Liabilities always are recorded in the accounting records, whereas contingent losses never are.
   c. The extent of uncertainty involved.
   d. Liabilities can be large in amount, whereas contingent losses are immaterial.

*7. Each of the following indicates a significant weakness in internal control over payrolls **except:**
   a. The paymaster is responsible for timekeeping and for distributing paycheques to employees.
   b. The human resources department is responsible for hiring and firing employees and for the distribution of paycheques.
   c. The payroll department is responsible for preparing the payroll cheques for signature by the paymaster, maintaining individual employees' earnings records of earnings and deductions, and filing required payroll reports with the government.
   d. The payroll department prepares the payroll, the paymaster prepares and signs paycheques, and the paycheques are distributed by the timekeeping department.

*8. Hennesey receives a salary of $60,000 per year from Carling Limited. Income taxes withheld amounted to $17,112. Employment insurance premium and Canada Pension Plan contribution withheld were $1,053 and $1,068.80 respectively. Registered pension plan of $3,500 and union dues of $860 were also withheld. Hennesey's take-home pay and the total cost to Carling of having Hennesey on the payroll are, respectively:
   a. $36,406.20 and $62,543
   b. $42,888 and $62,121.80
   c. $36,406.20 and $62,121.80
   d. $38,528 and $64,243.60

ASSIGNMENT MATERIAL

Discussion Questions

1. Define liabilities. Identify several characteristics that distinguish liabilities from owners' equity.

2. Explain the relative priority of the claims of owners and of creditors to the assets of a business. Do all creditors have equal priority? Explain.

3. Define **current liabilities** and **long-term liabilities.** Under what circumstances might a 5-year note payable be classified as a current liability?

---

*Supplemental Topic, "Accounting for Payrolls."

Under what circumstances might a note payable maturing 30 days after the balance sheet date be classified as a long-term liability?

4. Jonas Company issues a 3-month (3 days of grace included), 12% note payable to replace an account payable to Smith Supply Company in the amount of $8,000. Draft the journal entries (in general journal form) to record the issuance of the note payable and the payment of the note at the maturity date.

5. What kind of account is Discount on Notes Payable? Where and how should it appear in the financial statements? What is the eventual disposition of amounts in Discount on Notes Payable?

6. Explain why an employer's "total cost" of a payroll may exceed by a substantial amount the total wages and salaries earned by employees.

7. Why is it often said that the "effective cost of borrowing" is less than the stated rate of interest?

8. Ace Garage has an unpaid mortgage loan of $63,210, payable at $1,200 per month. An amortization table indicates that $527 of the current monthly payment represents interest expense. What will be the amount of this mortgage obligation immediately ***after*** Ace makes this current payment?

9. A friend of yours has just purchased a house and has incurred a $50,000, 11% mortgage, payable at $476.17 per month. After making the first monthly payment, he received a receipt from the bank stating that only $17.84 of the $476.17 had been applied to reducing the principal amount of the loan. Your friend computes that at the rate of $17.84 per month, it will take over 233 years to pay off the $50,000 mortgage. Do you agree with your friend's analysis? Explain.

10. Is the failure to record an accrued liability likely to affect the income statement as well as the balance sheet? Explain.

11. Trong Corporation had a $300,000 note payable outstanding throughout the entire year. The note calls for interest to be computed at the annual rate of 9% and to be paid monthly on the last day of each month. How much accrued interest payable will appear in Trong's December 31 balance sheet? Explain.

12. Among the long-term liabilities listed on Reese Corporation's balance sheet is "Long-term instalment debt . . . $2,300,000." What ***disclosures*** should be made concerning this debt to assist users of the financial statements in evaluating the company's financial position?

13. Define ***estimated liabilities*** and provide two examples. Are estimated liabilities recorded in accounting records?

14. What is the meaning of the term ***contingent loss?*** Give two examples. How are contingent losses presented in financial statements? Explain.

15. What is the meaning of the term ***commitment?*** Give several examples. How are commitments usually presented in financial statements? Explain.

16. A company is considering hiring a new employee at a wage rate of $12.00 per hour. Would it be appropriate for the company to budget the cost of the new employee at this rate? Explain.

17. Ellison Corporation has been named as a defendant in a large lawsuit alleging negligence in development of one of its products. How would this lawsuit

affect the financial statements of Ellison, assuming the loss from the lawsuit can be reasonably estimated and the probability of loss is:
a. Remote
b. Not determinable
c. Likely

18. Why is the *quick ratio* often considered a more useful measure of short-term solvency than the current ratio?

19. Would long-term creditors prefer that a corporation's *debt ratio* be high or low? How about its *interest coverage ratio?* Explain your answers.

20. As a result of incurring a great deal of long-term debt, Low-Cal Foods now has an interest coverage ratio of .75 to 1. Should this ratio be of greater concern to short-term creditors or to shareholders? Explain.

*21. MetroScape has 210 employees, but no liability for accrued payroll appears in the company's balance sheet. Assuming no error has been made, how can this be? Explain.

22. The human resources department of Meadow Company failed to notify the payroll department that five hourly factory workers had been terminated at the end of the last pay period. Assuming a normal subdivision of duties regarding human resources, timekeeping, preparation of payroll, and distribution of paycheques, what control procedure will prevent the payroll department from preparing paycheques for these five employees in the current period?

*23. Explain which of the following taxes relating to an employee's wages are borne by the employee and which by the employer:
a. Employment insurance
b. Canada Pension Plan
c. Income taxes

*24. Is the Salaries Expense account equal to take-home pay or to gross pay? Why?

*25. Why is the cost to an employer of having an employee on the payroll greater than that person's gross pay?

*26. Distinguish between an employee and an independent contractor. Why is this distinction important with respect to payroll accounting?

Exercises

EXERCISE 11-1
Accounting Terminology
(LO 3, 4, 5, 6)

Listed below are nine technical terms introduced or emphasized in this chapter:

Contingent losses	*Principal amount*	*Quick ratio*
Amortization table	*Estimated liability*	*Debt ratio*
Maturity value of a	*Discount on notes*	*Interest coverage*
note payable	*payable*	*ratio*

Each of the following statements may (or may not) describe one of these technical terms. For each statement, indicate the term described, or answer "None" if the statement does not correctly describe any of the terms.
a. Warranty liability.
b. Future interest charges included in the face amount of a note payable.
c. A more stringent measure of short-term solvency than the current ratio.
d. A schedule allocating payments on an instalment note payable between the portion representing interest expense of the current period and the portion reducing the principal amount of the debt.

Supplemental Topic, "Accounting for Payrolls."

e. Total liabilities divided by annual interest expense.

f. The risk that a loss may occur in a future period as a result of risks inherent in the nature of a company's business operations.

g. The amount owed on a note payable *excluding* any interest charges.

EXERCISE 11-2
Effects of Transactions on the Accounting Equation
(LO 1, 2, 3, 5, 8)

Listed below are eight events or transactions of GemStar Corporation.

a. Made an adjusting entry to record interest on a short-term note payable.

b. Made a monthly instalment payment of a fully amortizing, six-month, interest-bearing instalment note payable.

c. Entered into a contractual commitment with a television network to purchase sixty 30-second commercials in each of the next 18 months. The cost is $75,000 per month, payable on the last day of the month in which the commercial aired.

d. Came within 12 months of the maturity date of a note payable originally issued for a period of 18 months.

e. Made an adjusting entry to accrue monthly interest payable on a long-term mortgage.

f. Estimated the income taxes expense relating to the month's business income.

*g. Recorded a regular bi-weekly payroll, including the amounts withheld from employees, the issuance of paycheques, and payroll taxes upon the employer.

*h. Remitted the amounts withheld from employees' paycheques to the designated recipients.

Indicate the effects of each of these transactions upon the following financial statement categories. Organize your answer in tabular form, using the illustrated column headings. Use the following code letters to indicate the effects of each transaction upon the accounting element listed in the column heading:

$$I = \text{Increase} \qquad D = \text{Decrease} \qquad NE = \text{No Effect}$$

	Income Statement			Balance Sheet			
Transaction	*Revenue* − *Expenses* =		*Net Income*	*Assets* =	*Current Liab.* +	*Long-Term Liab.* +	*Owners' Equity*
a.							

EXERCISE 11-3
Financial Statement Presentation of Liabilities
(LO 2, 3, 5)

Using the following information, prepare a listing and descriptions of the amounts that you would classify as (a) current liabilities and (b) long-term liabilities. If you do not list part or all of an item in either classification, briefly explain your reasoning.

Interest expense that will arise on interest bearing notes over the next 12 months	*$134,000*
Long-term mortgage note payable (of which $3,200 will be paid within the next 12 months)	*800,000*
Interest payable on the mortgage note payable	*2,600*
Lawsuit pending against the company, claiming $500,000 in damages. Legal counsel can make no reasonable estimate of company's potential liability at this time	*500,000*
Note payable due in 60 days, but which will be extended for an additional 18 months	*75,000*
Three-year commitment to Charlene Doyle as chief financial officer at a salary of $140,000 per year	*420,000*
Amounts withheld from employees' paycheques	*6,100*

---

*Supplemental Topic, "Accounting for Payrolls."

EXERCISE 11-4
Use of an Amortization Table
(LO 4)

Blue Cays Marina has a $200,000 mortgage liability. This mortgage is payable in monthly instalments of $2,057, which include interest computed at the rate of 12% per year (1% per month).

a. Prepare a partial amortization table showing the original balance of this loan and the allocation of the **first two** monthly payments between interest expense and reduction in the unpaid balance. (Round amounts to the nearest dollar.)

b. Prepare the journal entry to record the **second** monthly payment.

EXERCISE 11-5
The Nature of an Accrued Liability
(LO 3)

Late in 1999, Marco Construction borrowed $1 million, signing a 5-year (with three days of grace included), 7.2% note payable. The note calls for payment of interest charges monthly, on the sixteenth day of each month. Compute the following amounts relating to this note payable:

a. Total interest that will be paid over the life of the note.

b. Interest expense that will appear in Marco's income statement for **2001.**

c. Accrued interest payable that will appear in Marco's balance sheet at **December 31, 2001.** (Compute interest payable based on a 365-day year.)

EXERCISE 11-6
Two Forms for Notes Payable
(LO 3)

On November 1, Metals Exchange, Inc., borrowed $250,000 from a bank, and promised to repay that amount plus 12% interest (per year) at the end of 6 months (three days of grace included). You are to prepare two different presentations of the liability to the bank on Metals Exchange's December 31 balance sheet, assuming that the note payable to the bank was drawn as follows:

a. For $250,000, with interest stated separately and payable at maturity.

b. With the total interest charge included in the face amount of the note.

EXERCISE 11-7
Interest Included in Face Amount of Note Payable
(LO 3)

On April 1, Tiger Truck Lines bought four trucks from Freeway Motors for a total price of $272,000. The transactions required Tiger Truck Lines to pay $80,000 cash and to issue a promissory note due in full 18 months later (three days of grace included). The face amount of the note was $215,040, which included interest on the note for the 18 months.

Prepare all entries (in general journal form) for Tiger Truck Lines relating to the purchase of the trucks and the note for the current fiscal year ended December 31. Include the adjusting entries to record interest expense and depreciation expense to December 31. (The trucks are to be depreciated over an 8-year service life by the straight-line method. There is no estimated salvage value.)

EXERCISE 11-8
Safety of Creditors' Investments
(LO 6)

Shown below are data from the recent annual reports of two large toy makers. Amounts are stated in thousands.

	Mattel Inc.	Hasbro Inc.
Total assets	$830,273	$1,246,485
Total liabilities	554,103	444,161
Interest expense	50,029	24,288
Operating income	163,116	170,079

a. Compute for each company (1) the debt ratio and (2) the interest coverage ratio. (Round the debt ratio to one-tenth of 1%, and interest coverage to one decimal place.)

b. In your opinion, which of these companies would a long-term creditor probably view as the safer investment? Explain.

*EXERCISE 11-9
Internal Control over Payroll
(LO 7)

A supervisor in the factory of Barton Products, a large manufacturing company, discharged an employee but did not notify the human resources department of this action. The supervisor then began forging the employee's signature on time cards. When giving out paycheques, the supervisor diverted to his own use the paycheques drawn payable to the discharged worker. What internal control measure would be most effective in preventing this fraudulent activity?

*EXERCISE 11-10
Journal Entries for Payroll and Payroll Taxes
(LO 8)

The payroll record of ALG Company for the month of January showed the following amounts for total earnings: sales employees, $16,000; office employees, $10,000. Amounts withheld consisted of employment insurance premiums, $702, Canada Pension Plan, $757, and income tax, $5,830.

a. Prepare a general journal entry to record the payroll. Do not include taxes on the employer.
b. Prepare a general journal entry to record the payroll taxes expense to ALG Company relating to this payroll. Assume that the employer's rate for employment insurance is 1.4 times the employees' premium and that the employer's contribution to Canada Pension Plan is the same as the employees'.

*EXERCISE 11-11
Employer's Payroll Taxes
(LO 8)

The payroll of Fields Company may be summarized as follows:

Gross earnings of employees *$250,000*
Employee earnings subject to employment insurance *238,000*
Employee earnings subject to Canada Pension Plan *221,000*

Assuming that the employer is required to contribute employment insurance at 1.4 times the employee's rate of 2.7% and to contribute 3.2% to Canada Pension Plan, compute the amount of Fields Company's payroll taxes expense for the year, showing separately the amount of each of the two taxes and prepare a general journal entry to record the company's payroll taxes expense.

Problems

PROBLEM 11-1
Effects of Transactions on Financial Statements
(LO 2, 3, 5)

Twelve transactions or events affecting Laptop Computer, Inc., are listed below:
a. Made a year-end adjusting entry to accrue interest on a note payable.
b. A liability classified for several years as long-term becomes due within the next 12 months.
c. Earned an amount previously recorded as unearned revenue.
d. Made arrangements to extend for another 18 months a bank loan due in 60 days.
e. Made a monthly payment on a fully amortizing instalment note payable. (Assume this note is classified as a current liability.)
f. Recorded income taxes expense for the fourth quarter in the year (October 1 through December 31). Payment will be made within 3 months.
g. Recorded an estimated liability for future warranty claims on products sold during the current year.
h. Entered into a 2-year commitment to buy all hard drives from a particular supplier at a price 10% below market.
i. Paid the interest on a note payable.
j. Received notice that a lawsuit has been filed against the company for $7 million. The amount of the company's liability, if any, cannot be reasonably estimated at this time.

---

*Supplemental Topic, "Accounting for Payrolls."

k. Made a year-end adjusting entry to amortize the discount on a 4-month note payable with interest included in the face amount.

*__l.__ Recorded the regular bi-weekly payroll, including amounts withheld from employees, the issuance of paycheques, and payroll taxes levied upon the employer.

INSTRUCTIONS

Indicate the effects of each of these transactions upon the following elements of the company's financial statements. Organize your answer in tabular form, using the column headings shown below. Use the following code letters to indicate the effects of each transaction upon the accounting element listed in the column heading:

$$I = \text{Increase} \qquad D = \text{Decrease} \qquad NE = \text{No Effect}$$

	Income Statement			Balance Sheet			
Transaction	Revenue −	Expenses =	Net Income	Assets =	Current Liab. +	Long-Term Liab. +	Owners' Equity
a.							

PROBLEM 11-2
Balance Sheet Presentation of Liabilities
(LO 1–5)

Listed below are selected items from the accounting records of GOOD 'N' LITE Candy Co. for the year ended December 31, 2000:

Note payable to Scotia Bank	$200,000
Discount on note payable to Scotia Bank	2,000
Income taxes payable	43,000
Accrued expenses and payroll taxes	59,800
Mortgage note payable	301,080
Accrued interest on mortgage note payable	2,508
Trade accounts payable	129,345
Unearned revenue	52,100
Potential liability in pending lawsuit	750,000

OTHER INFORMATION

1. The note payable to Scotia Bank is due in 60 days. Arrangements have been made to renew this note for an additional 12 months.
2. The mortgage note payable requires payments of $10,000 per month for the next 36 months. An amortization table shows that as of December 31, **2001,** this note will be paid down to $212,430.
3. Accrued interest on the mortgage note payable is paid monthly.
4. GOOD 'N' LITE has been sued for $750,000 in a contract dispute. It is not possible at this time to make a reasonable estimate of the possible loss, if any, which the company may have sustained.

INSTRUCTIONS

a. Using this information, prepare the current liabilities section and long-term liabilities section of a classified balance sheet at December 31, 2000. (Within each classification, items may be listed in any order.)
b. Explain briefly how the information in each of the four numbered paragraphs affected your presentation of the company's liabilities.
c. Where might a creditor look to obtain additional information about the lawsuit described in **4,** above?

PROBLEM 11-3
Notes Payable; Adjusting Entries for Interest
(LO 3)

During the fiscal year ended December 31, Dunleer Corporation carried out the following transactions involving notes payable.

---

*Supplemental Topic, "Accounting for Payrolls."

Aug.	6	Borrowed $11,200 from Tom Hutchins, issuing to him a 2-month (3 days of grace included), 12% note payable.
Sept.	15	Purchased office equipment from Harper Company. The invoice amount was $16,800 and Harper Company agreed to accept as full payment a 3-month (3 days of grace included), 12% note for the invoice amount.
Oct.	6	Paid the Hutchins note plus accrued interest.
Oct.	31	Borrowed $235,200 from National Bank at an interest rate of 12% per annum; signed a 3-month (3 days of grace included) note payable for $242,256, which included a $7,056 interest charge in the face amount.
Dec.	1	Purchased merchandise in the amount of $3,000 from Kramer Company. Gave in settlement a 3-month note (3 days of grace included) bearing interest at 14%. (A perpetual inventory system is in use.)
Dec.	15	The $16,800 note payable to Harper Company matured today. Paid the interest accrued and issued a new 1-month (3 days of grace included), 12% note to replace the maturing note.

INSTRUCTIONS

a. Prepare journal entries (in general journal form) to record the above transactions.

b. Prepare the adjusting entries needed at December 31, prior to closing the accounts. Use one entry for the two notes on which interest is stated separately and a separate entry for the note in which interest is included in the face amount of the note.

c. In preparing your adjusting entries to accrue the interest on the notes, explain why you did **not** accrue the total amount of interest due at maturity on the note.

PROBLEM 11-4
Notes Payable; Adjusting
Entries for Interest—An
Alternate Problem
(LO 3)

In the fiscal year ended October 31, Harbour Corporation carried out several transactions involving notes payable. Listed below are the transactions relating to notes payable.

June	1	Borrowed $20,000 from Holden Investments Inc., by issuing a 2-month (3 days of grace included), 12% note payable to Holden as evidence of the indebtedness.
July	15	Bought office equipment from Western Office Supply. The invoice amount was $18,000 and Western Office Supply accepted as full payment a 3-month (3 days of grace included), 10% note for this amount.
Aug.	1	Paid the Holden note for $20,000 plus interest.
Sept.	1	Borrowed $240,000 from Royal Bank at an annual interest rate of 8%; signed a 3-month note (3 days of grace included) with interest included in the face amount of the note.
Oct.	1	Purchased merchandise for $16,200 from Earthware Imports. Gave in settlement a 3-month note (3 days of grace included) bearing interest at 10%. (Harbour Corporation uses a perpetual inventory system.)
Oct.	15	The $18,000 note payable to Western Office Supply matured today. Paid the interest accrued and issued a new 1-month (3 days of grace included), 12% note to replace the matured note.

INSTRUCTIONS

a. Prepare journal entries (in general journal form) to record the above transactions.

b. Prepare the adjusting entries needed at October 31, prior to closing the accounts. Use one adjusting entry to accrue interest on the two notes in which interest is stated separately. Use a separate adjusting entry to record interest expense accrued on the note with interest included in the face amount.

    c. Explain whether the total amount of interest due at maturity on the notes should be accrued at October 31, the year-end date.

PROBLEM 11-5
Note Payable with Interest
Included in Face Amount
(LO 3)

On August 1, 2000, Kennedy Limited purchased from Warden Corporation merchandise in exchange for a note payable due in **one year** (3 days of grace included). The note's face amount was $65,100, which included the principal amount and an interest charge. At December 31, 2000, Kennedy Limited's accounting records show, after the year-end adjustments, a note payable of $65,100 and a discount on note payable of $2,975.

INSTRUCTIONS

    a. Determine the monthly interest expense.

    b. Determine the amount of interest expense incurred during 2000.

    c. Determine the cost of the merchandise purchased on August 1, 2000. Kennedy uses a perpetual inventory system.

    d. Determine the effective annual rate of interest (in percentage) of the note payable.

    e. Prepare all journal entries relating to this note in the accounting records of Kennedy Limited for 2000 and 2001. Assume that adjusting entries are made only at December 31, and that the note was paid on the maturity date.

PROBLEM 11-6
Notes Payable: A
Comprehensive Problem
(LO 3)

The following transactions relating to notes payable were completed by Desktop Graphics during the three months ended June 30.

Apr.   **1**   Bought office equipment for use in the business from Stylecraft, Inc., for $39,000, making a $5,400 cash down payment and issuing a 1-year (3 days of grace included) note payable for the balance. The face amount of the note was $38,976, which included a 16% interest charge.

Apr. **15**   Paid $15,000 cash and issued a 3-month (3 days of grace included), 8%, $27,000 note to Hall Limited in settlement of open account payable in the amount of $42,000.

Apr. **25**   Purchased office equipment from ADM Company for $52,200, issuing a 2-month (3 days of grace included), 9% note payable in settlement.

May **15**   Borrowed $216,000 from Scotia Bank, issuing a 3-month (3 days of grace included) note payable as evidence of indebtedness. An interest charge computed at 17% per year was included in the face amount of the note.

June 10   Purchased merchandise on account from Courtway Limited, $54,000. (The company uses a perpetual inventory system.)

June 15   Issued a 2-month (3 days of grace included) note bearing interest at 9% in settlement of the account payable to Courtway Limited.

June 25   Paid the 2-month, 9% note due to ADM Company, which matured today.

INSTRUCTIONS

    a. Prepare journal entries (in general journal form) to record the listed transactions for the 3 months ended June 30.

    b. Prepare adjusting entries to record the interest expense on notes payable through June 30. Prepare one adjusting entry to record the accrued interest payable on the two notes for which interest is stated separately. The other adjusting entry should record the amortization of discount on the two notes in which interest is included in the face amount.

c. Prepare a partial balance sheet at June 30 reflecting the above transactions. Show "Notes Payable to Bank" as one item and "Notes Payable: Other" as a separate liability. Also include the interest payable in the current liability section of the balance sheet.

PROBLEM 11-7
Preparation and Use of an Amortization Table
(LO 4)

On September 1, 1999, AMC Steak House signed a 30-year, $540,000 mortgage note payable to Laurentian Bank in conjunction with the purchase of a restaurant. This mortgage note calls for interest at the rate of 12% per year (1% per month), and monthly payments of $5,555. The note is fully amortizing over a period of 360 months (30 years).

Laurentian Bank sent AMC Steak House an amortization table showing the allocation of the monthly payments between interest and principal over the life of the loan. A small part of this amortization table is illustrated below. (For convenience, amounts have been rounded to the nearest dollar.)

AMORTIZATION TABLE
(12%, 30-Year Mortgage Note Payable for $540,000;
Payable in 360 Monthly Instalments of $5,555)

Interest Period	Payment Date	Monthly Payment	Interest Expense	Reduction in Unpaid Balance	Unpaid Balance
Issue date	Sept. 1, 1999	—	—	—	$540,000
1	Oct. 1	$5,555	$5,400	$155	539,845
2	Nov. 1	$5,555	5,398	157	539,688

INSTRUCTIONS

a. Explain whether the amounts of interest expense and the reductions in the unpaid balance are likely to change in any predictable pattern from month to month.

b. Prepare journal entries to record the first two monthly payments on this mortgage.

c. Complete this amortization table for two more monthly instalments—those due on December 1, 1999, and January 1, 2000. (Round amounts to the nearest dollar.)

d. Will any amounts relating to this 30-year mortgage be classified as ***current*** liabilities in the December 31, 1999, balance sheet of AMC Steak House? Explain, but you need not compute any additional dollar amounts.

PROBLEM 11-8
Amortization Table and Instalment Debt
(LO 4)

On December 31, 2000, Kay Architectural Services purchased equipment at a cost of $20,215, paying $5,000 cash and issuing a 2-year instalment note payable for $15,215. This note calls for four semiannual instalments of $4,800, which include interest computed at the annual rate of 20% per year (10% per semiannual period). Payments are due on June 30 and December 31. The first payment is due June 30, 2001, and the note will be fully amortized at December 31, 2002.

Kay can retire this note at any interest payment date by paying the unpaid balance plus any accrued interest.

INSTRUCTIONS

a. Prepare an amortization table showing the allocation of each of the four semiannual payments between interest expense and reductions in the principal amount of the note.

b. Prepare journal entries to record the issuance of this note and each of the four semiannual payments in 2001 and 2002.

c. Assume that on December 31, **2001,** Kay decided to pay the entire unpaid balance of this note. Prepare a journal entry to record the early retirement of this note. (Assume that the semiannual payment due on this date already has been paid.)

d. Illustrate the presentation of this note in the company's balance sheet at December 31, **2000.** (Show separately the current and long-term portions of this debt.)

PROBLEM 11-9
Liabilities: Recognition and Measurement
(LO 1, 2, 3, 5)

The eight events listed below occurred at National Products on or near the end of the fiscal year, December 31, 1999:

a. On October 12, the company was named as a defendant in a lawsuit alleging $20 million in damages caused by lead paint used on products manufactured by the company in the early 1990s. National's legal counsel believes it is likely that National has liability of at least $2 million. The suit is not expected to be settled for several years.

b. On November 1, borrowed $900,000 from a bank, signing a 3-month (3 days grace included), 8% note payable.

c. On December 15, signed a contract for the purchase of 50,000 barrels of oil per month in 2000 at a price of $18 per barrel, a price slightly below current market price.

d. On December 31, purchased machinery at a price of $200,000 and signed a note payable due in 6 months with interest stated at the annual rate of 9%.

e. On December 31, signed a 2-year contract with a labour union providing for a 6% increase in wage rates each year. The increase in wages for the first year is estimated at $540,000.

*f. On December 31, processed the bi-weekly payroll. Paycheques totalling $289,000 were issued to employees. As these cheques were issued after banking hours on December 31, no cash will be disbursed from National's payroll bank account until early in January 2000. The amount withheld from employees' pay and payroll taxes on the employer of $67,600 was remitted to tax authorities on January 3, 2000.

g. On December 31, estimated that warranty work costing $200,000 probably will need to be performed in future months on products that were sold in 1999 with a 12-month warranty.

h. On January 5, 2000, a preliminary estimate was made of the company's income taxes expense for 1999. This expense was estimated at $2,800,000, of which $2,100,000 had already been paid in quarterly tax payments made during 1999. In March 2000 the company completed the preparation of its 1999 income tax return, and income taxes expense for 1999 was determined to be $2,779,806.

INSTRUCTIONS

For each of these eight events, indicate the dollar amounts (if any) that should appear in either the current or long-term liability sections of National's 1999 year-end balance sheet. Also indicate any information that should be disclosed in the notes accompanying the 1999 financial statements. Briefly explain the reasons underlying your answers. (**Note:** As a practical matter, much of the task of preparing the 1999 financial statements must be performed in January 2000. Assume the financial statements are completed and issued on January 31.)

*PROBLEM 11-10
Payroll—A Short Problem
(LO 8)

The payroll records of Oakland Ltd. for the first week in January showed total salaries earned by employees of $25,000.

---

*Supplemental Topic, "Accounting for Payrolls."

The amounts withheld from employees' pay consisted of employment insurance of $720, Canada Pension Plan of $756, income taxes of $4,272, and union dues of $380.

As a fringe benefit, Oakland Ltd. contributes an amount equal to 3% of employees' gross pay to an employee registered pension plan and 1% to an employee group life insurance plan.

The weekly payroll is recorded on Friday, January 6, and paycheques will be issued to employees on Monday, January 9.

INSTRUCTIONS

a. Prepare separate general journal entries to record the (1) salaries earned by employees, amounts withheld, and liability for net pay; (2) payroll taxes levied upon the employer; (3) cost of fringe benefits; and (4) issuance of paycheques.

b. Compute the ***total cost*** to Oakland Ltd. of employee compensation for the first week of January.

c. Assuming no change in pay rates, tax rates, or number of employees, would you expect the total cost of Oakland's weekly payroll to increase or decrease as the year progresses? Explain.

*PROBLEM 11-11
Payroll—A Comprehensive Problem
(LO 8)

The individual employees' earnings records of Surveillance Systems show the following cumulative gross pay (earnings) as of year-end.

Employee	Cumulative Gross Pay	Employee	Cumulative Gross Pay
Arthur, D. S.	$28,500	Hamilton, A. J.	$35,000
Barnett, S. T.	42,000	Maison, G. R.	49,600
Donahue, E. G.	60,000		

Assume that the rate of employment insurance for employees is 2.7% and the rate for the employer is 1.4 times that of the employees. The maximum annual insurable earnings for each employee is $39,000. The rate for Canada Pension Plan is assumed to be 3.2% for both the employees and the employer and the rate is applied to the employees' first $33,400 annual pensionable earnings (i.e., gross pay of $36,900 less $3,500 exemption).

During the year, the employer has withheld income taxes of $54,920 from employees' pay and has incurred costs of $23,120 relating to fringe benefits.

INSTRUCTIONS

a. Prepare a schedule with four data columns for each employee. In the first column, enter the employee's cumulative gross pay, as indicated above. In the remaining three columns, indicate the amounts of this gross pay that were subject to (1) employment insurance and (2) Canada Pension Plan. Show totals for each column.

b. Compute the following total amounts for the current year (round amounts to the nearest dollar):

1. Total amount withheld from employees' pay (combine all types of withholdings).
2. Employees' net pay.
3. Payroll taxes levied upon the employer.
4. The employer's total payroll costs.

c. Reconcile the total amount of employees' net pay [**b(2)**] with the total payroll costs incurred by the employer [**b(4)**].

---

*Supplemental Topic, "Accounting for Payrolls."

*PROBLEM 11-12
Payroll—A More
Comprehensive Problem
(LO 8)

The Daily Chronicle is a large business organization, with perhaps 1,500 employees. For illustrative purposes, however, we will demonstrate certain payroll procedures using the earnings of **only three** of these employees in the month of July.

The monthly salaries of these three employees, and their cumulative gross pay for the year as of June 30, appear below:

Employee	Monthly Salary	Year-to-Date, June 30
Adams	$5,600	$33,600
Colbert	2,000	6,500**
Henderson	6,800	40,800

Colbert started work in late March.

This information is obtained from the employees' individual earnings records.

Assume that the rate of employment insurance for employees is 2.7% and the rate for the employer is 1.4 times that of the employees. The maximum annual insurable earnings for each employee is $39,000. The rate for Canada Pension Plan is assumed to be 3.2% for both the employees and the employer and the rate is applied to the employees' first $33,400 pensionable earnings (i.e., gross earnings of $36,900 less $3,500 exemption).

The Daily Chronicle provides the following fringe benefits to all employees:

- Paid group life insurance (cost: $100 per month for the three employees)
- Contributions to an employees' registered retirement pension plan (at the rate of 5% of each employee's monthly salary)

Liabilities relating to fringe benefits are paid at the end of each calendar quarter.

INSTRUCTIONS

a. Prepare a three-column schedule showing payroll data for each employee. In the first column, enter each employee's gross pay for July. In the remaining columns, show the amount of this July's gross pay that is subject to (1) employment insurance and (2) Canada Pension Plan. (If none of an employee's July salary is subject to a particular tax, explain why not. If only part of the employee's July salary is subject to a particular type of tax, show a supporting computation. Round amounts to the nearest dollar.)

Show totals in each of the three columns.

b. Prepare three separate general journal entries, each dated **July 31,** summarizing for the month:

1. The gross pay, amounts withheld, and net pay of these employees. In addition, the amounts withheld for income taxes is $4,860. Paycheques will be issued on the next business day (August 3).
2. The payroll taxes **levied upon the employer.**
3. The cost of fringe benefits.

c. Compute the **total cost** to The Daily Chronicle of having these three employees on the payroll during the month of July.

d. List all of the current liabilities at July 31 resulting from this monthly payroll.

Analytical and Decision Problems and Cases

A&D 11-1
The Nature of Liabilities
(LO 1, 2, 3, 5)

Listed below are seven publicly owned corporations and a liability that regularly appears in each corporation's balance sheet:

a. Bank of Montreal: Deposits
b. Maclean Hunter Publishing Limited: Unearned revenue

Supplemental Topic, "Accounting for Payrolls."

c. **The Windsor Raceway Inc.** (horse racing): Outstanding mutuel tickets
d. **American Greetings** (greeting cards and gift wrap products manufacturer): Sales returns
e. **Dofasco Inc.**: Current requirements on long-term debt
f. **Club Med., Inc.** (resorts): Amounts received for future vacations
g. **Apple Computer, Inc.**: Accrued marketing and distribution

INSTRUCTIONS

Briefly explain what you believe to be the nature of each of these liabilities, including how the liability arose and the manner in which it is likely to be discharged.

A&D 11-2
Contingent Losses?
(LO 5)

Discuss each of the following situations, indicating whether the situation is a contingent loss that should be recorded or disclosed in the financial statements of Aztec Airlines. If the situation is not a contingent loss, explain how (if at all) it should be reported in the company's financial statements. (Assume that all dollar amounts are material.)

a. The company's president is in poor health and has previously suffered two heart attacks.
b. As with any airline, Aztec faces the risk that a future airplane crash could cause considerable loss.
c. Aztec is being sued for $2 million for failing to adequately provide for passengers whose reservations were cancelled as a result of the airline overbooking certain flights. This suit will not be resolved for a year or more.

A&D 11-3
Liabilities, Contingencies, or ???
(LO 1, 2, 3, 5)

Anna Held, a CA on the audit staff of a national public accounting firm, is in charge of the annual audit of Crystal Corporation, a successful medium-size client. On December 31, Held receives a telephone call from John Arnold, the controller of Crystal. Arnold explains that the company's board of directors has just signed two contractual arrangements with its former president, who has just retired. The first agreement provides that Crystal will pay its former president $10,000 a month for five years if during that time he does not compete with the company in a rival business. The second agreement states that Crystal will pay the former president $8,000 per month for five years, for which he is to provide such advisory services as the company may request.

The controller asks Held if the year-end balance sheet would include $216,000 as a current liability to the former president and $864,000 as a long-term liability, or whether the total amount of $1,080,000 should be disclosed as a contingency in a note to the financial statements. The controller emphasized that these amounts were material in terms of the company's earnings and resources.

INSTRUCTIONS

Explain fully how you think Anna Held should respond to the question raised by the controller.

*A&D 11-4
"Hey—Can't We Do This by Computer?"
(LO 7, 8)

A W Clausen's is a large department store with a highly automated accounting system. The computer program used in processing payrolls includes all tax rates and withholding tables, employees' individual earnings records, and every employee's rate of compensation. Employees' gross pay is determined as follows:

Warehouse workers . . . . *Hourly wages*
Office workers and management . . . . *Monthly salaries*
Salespeople . . . . *Monthly salaries plus commissions*

Sales commissions are based upon the sales generated by the individual salesperson during the pay period.

---

*Supplemental Topic, "Accounting for Payrolls."

Employees are paid twice each month. Every payroll period, the computer program compiles a payroll register, updates the employees' earnings records, prints paycheques, and records in the general ledger both the payroll and the payroll taxes upon the employer.

INSTRUCTIONS

a. Indicate the **_additional information_** that must be entered into this computerized system **_each pay period_** to enable the computer to perform the processing tasks described above. Suggest means by which each type of additional information might be entered into the computerized payroll system **_automatically,_** instead of manually.

b. Describe a plan for distributing paycheques to the company's employees that is both efficient and contributes to strong internal control.

*A&D 11-5
Payrolls
(LO 8)

Interview the owner of a small business, or an employee responsible for payrolls. (You may find this more interesting if you select a business in which the employees are exposed to some job-related risk of injury, such as construction.) Determine the items that cause differences between gross wages and salaries expense earned by employees during a pay period and both:

1. The employees' take-home pay.

2. The employer's total related payroll costs.

Also inquire as to whether any of these amounts tend to increase or decrease in later pay periods.

Be prepared to explain in class the relative size of each item as a percentage of gross wages and salaries expense. Also be prepared to explain the **_absence_** of any of the payroll costs discussed in this text.

(**_Note:_** All interviews are to be conducted in accordance with the guidelines discussed in the _Preface_ of this textbook.)

Answers to Self-Test Questions

1. a, b   **2.** a, b   **3.** c   **4.** d   **5.** a, c, d   **6.** c   *7. c   *8. a

---

*_Supplemental Topic, "Accounting for Payrolls."_

CHAPTER 12

Accounting Concepts, Professional Judgment, and Ethical Conduct

Congratulations! You have met the challenge. In completing this semester, you have achieved something worthwhile. You now know more about accounting and the business environment than most people ever will.

We will use this chapter to pause and look back at the territory you've covered—not the details and procedures, but at the broad understanding of accounting that we hope you will "take with you."

1. Explain the need for recognized accounting standards.
2. Discuss the nature and sources of generally accepted accounting principles.
3. Discuss the accounting principles presented on pages 617–628.
4. Apply the percentage-of-completion method of income recognition.
5. Describe the role of professional judgment in the financial reporting process.
6. Discuss international accounting standards.
7. Describe the nature of ethics and explain the basic purpose of a code of ethics within a profession.
8. Identify and explain the basic principles underlying a professional code of ethics.
9. Apply the basic principles of ethical conduct to situations likely to arise in an accountant's work.

The Need for Recognized Accounting Standards

LO 1: Explain the need for recognized accounting standards.

The basic purpose of financial statements is to provide information about a business entity—information that will be *useful in making economic decisions.* Investors, managers, creditors, financial analysts, economists, and government policy makers all rely upon financial statements and other accounting reports in making the decisions that shape our economy. Therefore, it is of vital importance that the information contained in financial statements possess certain characteristics. The information should be:[1]

1. *Relevant* to the information needs of the decision makers.
2. As *reliable* as possible.
3. *Comparable* to the financial statements of prior accounting periods and also to the statements of other companies.
4. *Understandable* to the users of the financial statements.

We need a well-defined body of accounting principles or standards to guide accountants in preparing financial statements that possess these characteristics. The users of financial statements also must be familiar with these principles in order to interpret properly the information contained in these statements.

GENERALLY ACCEPTED ACCOUNTING PRINCIPLES (GAAP)

The principles that constitute the ground rules for financial reporting are called **generally accepted accounting principles.** Accounting principles may also be termed *standards, assumptions, conventions,* or *concepts.* The various terms used to describe accounting principles stem from the many efforts that have been made to develop a satisfactory framework of accounting theory.[2] For example, the word *standards* was chosen rather than *principles* by the CICA for its Accounting Standards Board

---

[1]Adapted from *CICA Handbook* (Toronto) section 1000.18-.23.
[2]See, in Canada, *Corporate Reporting: Its Future Evolution,* CICA (Toronto: 1980). In the United States, see for example, *Accounting Research Study No. 3,* "A Tentative Set of Broad Accounting Principles for Business Enterprises," AICPA (New York: 1962), *APB Statement No. 4,* "Basic Concepts and Accounting Principles Underlying Financial Statements of Business Enterprises," AICPA (New York: 1970); and *Statements of Financial Accounting Concepts Nos. 1–6,* FASB (Norwalk, Conn.: 1978–1985).

as the top standard-making body. The effort to construct a satisfactory body of accounting theory is an ongoing process, because accounting theory must continually change with changes in the business environment and changes in the needs of financial statement users.

When a new accounting principle is promulgated, it must be adopted by the companies in their financial reporting. The application of the new principle can have a very significant impact on the financial statements.

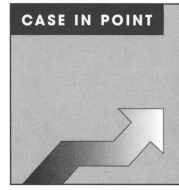

CASE IN POINT   When the **Financial Accounting Standards Board** in the United States issued a new accounting principle that required companies to recognize the costs of future retiree health care benefits in the year they were incurred rather than when they were actually paid, the impact was pervasive and staggering. The adoption of this new principle in financial reporting resulted in huge charges to income in one single year: American Telephone and Telegraph, $7 billion; Ford Motor, $7.5 billion; and General Motors, $21 billion. One estimate put the total charges created by this new principle on the Standard & Poor's 500 index at $148 billion.

Nature of Accounting Principles

LO 2: Discuss the nature and sources of generally accepted accounting principles.

Accounting principles do not exist in nature; rather, they are developed by humans in light of what we view as the most important objectives of financial reporting. In Chapter 1, we drew a parallel between generally accepted accounting principles and the rules established for an organized sport, such as hockey or football. For example, both accounting principles and sports rules originate from a combination of experience, tradition, and official decree. Also, both may change over time as gaps or shortcomings in the existing rules come to light.

An important aspect of accounting principles is the ***need for consensus*** within the economic community. If these principles are to provide a useful framework for financial reporting, they must be understood and observed by the participants in the financial reporting process. Thus, the words ***generally accepted*** are an important part of the phrase "generally accepted accounting principles."

As accounting principles are closely related to the needs, objectives, and traditions of a society, they vary somewhat from one country to another. Our discussion is limited to accounting principles "generally accepted" within Canada. An effort is underway to create greater uniformity in accounting principles among nations (as discussed in a later section of this chapter), but this effort will be a difficult and slow process.

Authoritative Support for Accounting Principles

To qualify as generally accepted, an accounting principle must have substantial authoritative support. This support may come from official sources, such as the CICA, or from unofficial sources, such as common sense, tradition, and widespread use.

Official Sources of GAAP   The most influential authoritative group in Canada is the **Accounting Standards Board (AcSB)** of the Canadian Institute of Chartered Accountants (CICA).[3] The AcSB is responsible for the development and promulgation of accounting principles, and its recommendations are contained in the "Accounting Recommendations" section of the *CICA Handbook*. These recommendations are considered as generally accepted accounting principles (GAAP) by the accounting profession, the administrators of provincial securities commissions, and a number of corporations acts, including the Canada Business Corporations Act.

In the United States, the official sources of accounting principles include (1) the American Institute of Certified Public Accountants, (2) the Financial Accounting Standards Board, and (3) the Securities and Exchange Commission.

Unofficial Sources of GAAP   Not all of what we call generally accepted accounting principles can be found in the "official pronouncements" of the standard-setting organizations. The business community is too complex and changes too quickly for every possible type of transaction to be covered by an official pronouncement. Thus, practicing accountants often must account for situations that have never been addressed by the official sources.

When the method of accounting for a particular situation is not explained in any official literature, generally accepted accounting principles are based upon such considerations as:

- Accounting practices that are in widespread use.
- Accounting guidelines and consensus issued by the CICA's Accounting Standards Board and the **Emerging Issues Committee** respectively.
- Broad theoretical concepts that underlie most accounting practices.

Thus, an understanding of generally accepted accounting principles requires a familiarity with (1) authoritative accounting literature, (2) accounting practices in widespread use, and (3) the broad theoretical concepts that underlie accounting practices. We will discuss these "broad theoretical concepts" in the following sections of this chapter.

The Accounting Entity Concept

LO 3: Discuss the accounting principles presented on pages 617–628.

One of the basic principles of accounting is that information is compiled for a clearly defined accounting entity. An ***accounting entity*** is any economic unit that controls resources and engages in economic activities. An individual is an accounting entity. So is a business enterprise, whether organized as a proprietorship, partnership, or corporation. Governmental agencies are accounting entities, as are nonprofit clubs and organizations.

---

[3]The CICA's Accounting Standards Board is composed of a cross section of individuals with various backgrounds and occupations: eight members are appointed by the CICA, and one member is appointed by each of these five organizations—the Canadian Academic Accounting Association, Canadian Council of Financial Analysts, Certified General Accountants' Association of Canada, Financial Executives Institute Canada, and Society of Management Accountants of Canada. However, the Certified General Accountants' Association of Canada has declined to appoint its representative to serve on the Board. At least two-thirds of the voting board members will be members of the CICA.

An accounting entity may also be defined as an identifiable economic unit *within a larger accounting entity.* For example, the Chevrolet Division of General Motors may be viewed as an accounting entity separate from GM's other activities.

The basic accounting equation, Assets = Liabilities + Owner's Equity, reflects the accounting entity concept because all elements of the equation must relate *to the particular entity whose financial position is being reported.* Although we have considerable flexibility in defining our accounting entity, we must be careful to use the *same definition* in the measurement of assets, liabilities, owners' equity, revenue, and expense. An income statement would not make sense, for example, if it included all the revenue of General Motors but listed the expenses of only the Chevrolet Division.

Although the entity concept appears straightforward, it can pose some judgmental allocation problems for accountants. Assume, for example, that we want to prepare an income statement for only the Chevrolet Division of General Motors. Also assume that a given plant facility is used in the production of Chevrolets, Pontiacs, and school buses. How much of the depreciation on this factory building should be regarded as an expense of the Chevrolet Division? Such situations illustrate the importance of the entity concept in developing meaningful financial information.

The Going-Concern Assumption

An underlying assumption in accounting is that an accounting entity will continue in operation for a period of time sufficient to carry out its existing commitments. The assumption of continuity, especially in the case of corporations, is in accord with experience in our economic system. This assumption leads to the concept of the **going concern.** In general, the going-concern assumption justifies ignoring immediate liquidation values in presenting assets and liabilities in the balance sheet.

For example, suppose that a company has just purchased a three-year insurance policy for $5,000. If we assume that the business will continue in operation for three years or more, we will consider the $5,000 cost of the insurance as an asset that provides services (freedom from certain risks) to the business over a three-year period. On the other hand, if we assume that the business is likely to terminate in the near future, the insurance policy should be reported at its cancellation value—that is, the amount refundable upon cancellation.

Although the assumption of a going concern is justified in most normal situations, it should be dropped when it is not in accord with the facts. Accountants are sometimes asked to prepare a statement of financial position for an enterprise that is about to liquidate. In this case the assumption of continuity is no longer valid, the accountant drops the going-concern assumption and reports assets at their current liquidation value and liabilities at the amount required to settle the debts immediately.

The Time Period Principle

The users of financial statements need information that is reasonably current. Therefore, for financial reporting purposes, the life of a business is divided into a series of relatively short accounting periods of equal length. This concept is called the **time period principle.**

The need for periodic reporting creates many of the accountant's most challenging problems. Dividing the life of an enterprise into relatively short time segments, such as a year or a quarter of a year, requires numerous estimates and assumptions. For example, estimates must be made of the useful lives of depreciable assets and judgment must be made as to appropriate depreciation methods. Thus periodic measurements of net income and financial position are at best only informed estimates. The tentative nature of periodic measurements should be understood by those who rely on periodic accounting information.

The Stable-Dollar Assumption

The **stable-dollar assumption** means that money is used as the basic measuring unit for financial reporting. The dollar, or any other monetary unit, is a measure of value—that is, it indicates the relative price (or value) of different goods and services.

When accountants add or subtract dollar amounts originating in different years, they imply that the dollar is a ***stable unit of measure,*** just as the litre, the hectare, and the kilometre are stable units of measure. Unfortunately, the dollar is ***not*** a stable measure of value.

To illustrate, assume that in 1980, you purchased land for $20,000. In 2000, you sell this land for $30,000. Under generally accepted accounting principles, which include the stable-dollar assumption, you have made a $10,000 "gain" on the sale. Economists would point out, however, that $30,000 in 2000 represents less "buying power" than did $20,000 in 1980. When the relative buying power of the dollar in 1980 and 2000 is taken into consideration, you came out behind on the purchase and the sale of this land.

Despite its shortcomings, the stable-dollar assumption remains a generally accepted accounting principle. In periods of low inflation, this assumption does not cause serious problems. During periods of severe inflation, however, the assumption of a stable dollar may cause serious distortions in accounting information.

The Objectivity Principle

The term **objectivity** refers to making measurements that are ***unbiased*** and subject to verification by independent experts. For example, the price established in an arm's-length transaction is an objective measure of exchange value at the time of that transaction. Exchange prices established in business transactions constitute much of the data from which accounting information is generated. Accountants rely on various kinds of evidence to support their financial measurements, but they usually seek the most objective evidence available. Invoices, contracts, paid cheques, and physical counts of inventory are examples of objective evidence.

If a measurement is objective, 10 competent investigators who make the same measurement will come up with substantially identical results. However, 10 competent accountants who set out independently to measure the net income of a given business would ***not*** arrive at an identical result.

Despite the goal of objectivity, *it is not possible to insulate accounting information from opinion and personal judgment.* For example, the cost of a depreciable asset can be determined objectively but not the periodic depreciation expense. Depreciation expense is merely an estimate, based upon estimates of the useful life and the residual value of the asset, and a judgment as to which depreciation method is most appropriate. Such estimates and judgments can produce significant variations in the measurement of net income.

Objectivity in accounting has its roots in the quest for reliability. Accountants want to make their economic measurements reliable and, at the same time, as relevant to decision makers as possible. However, the most relevant information may not be the most reliable. Thus, where to draw the line in the trade-off between *reliability* and *relevance* is one of the crucial issues in accounting theory. Accountants are constantly faced with the necessity of compromising between what users of financial information would like to know, and what it is possible to measure with a reasonable degree of reliability.

Asset Valuation: The Cost Principle

Both the balance sheet and the income statement are affected by the **cost principle.** Assets are initially recorded in the accounts at cost. In most cases no adjustment is made to this valuation in later periods, except to allocate a portion of the original cost to expense as the assets expire. At the time an asset is originally acquired, cost represents the "fair market value" of the goods or services exchanged, as evidenced by an arm's-length transaction. With the passage of time, however, the fair market value of such assets as land and buildings may change greatly from their historical cost. These later changes in fair market value generally have been ignored in the accounts, and the assets have continued to be shown in the balance sheet at historical (acquisition) cost (less the portion of that cost which has been allocated to expense.)

The cost principle is derived, in large part, from the principle of objectivity. Those who support the cost principle argue that it is important that users have confidence in financial statements, and that this confidence can best be maintained if accountants recognize changes in assets and liabilities only on a basis of completed transactions. Objective evidence generally exists to support cost; current fair market values, however, often may be largely a matter of personal opinion.

The question of whether to value assets at cost or estimated market value is a classic illustration of the "trade-off" between the relevance and the reliability of accounting information.

Revenue Recognition: The Realization (Recognition) Principle

When is revenue realized and when should it be recognized in the accounting records? Under the assumptions of accrual accounting, revenue should be recognized "when it is earned." However, the "earning" of revenue usually is an extended *economic process* and does not actually take place at a single point in time.

Some revenue, such as interest earned, is directly related to time periods. For this type of revenue, it is easy to compute the amount of revenue earned during the accounting period. However, the process of earning sales revenue is related to **economic activities** rather than to a specific period of time. In a manufacturing business, for example, the earning process involves (1) acquisition of direct (raw) materials, (2) production of finished goods, (3) sale of the finished goods, and (4) collection of cash from credit customers.

In the manufacturing example, there is little objective evidence to indicate how much revenue has been earned during the first two stages of the earning process. Accountants therefore usually do not recognize revenue until the revenue has been **realized.** Section 3400 of the *CICA Handbook* stipulates these criteria for revenue realization or recognition: (1) the significant risks and rewards of ownership of goods have been transferred from the seller to the buyer or the services have been performed, (2) reasonable assurance exists regarding the measurement of the consideration from the sale of goods or service rendered, and the extent to which goods may be returned, and (3) ultimate collection of the consideration from the sale of goods or services rendered is reasonably assured.[4] Accordingly, revenue is realized when both of the following conditions are met: (1) the earning process is **essentially complete** and (2) **objective evidence** exists as to the amount of revenue earned.

In most cases, the **realization (recognition) principle** indicates that revenue should be recognized **at the time goods are sold or services are rendered.**[5] At this point the business has essentially completed the earning process and the sales value of the goods or services can be measured objectively. At any time prior to sale, the ultimate sales value of the goods or services sold can only be estimated. After the sale, the only step that remains is to collect from the customer, and this is usually a relatively certain event.

In Chapter 3, we described a **cash basis** of income measurement whereby revenue is recognized only when cash is collected from customers and expenses are recorded only when cash is actually paid out. Cash basis accounting **does not conform** to generally accepted accounting principles, but it may be used by individuals in income tax returns. (Remember that the accounting methods used in income tax returns often differ from those used in financial statements.)

The Instalment Method   Under the **instalment method,** the seller recognizes the gross profit on instalment sales gradually as the cash is actually collected from customers. If the gross profit rate on instalment sales is 30%, then 30% of all cash received from the customer is viewed as gross profit.

To illustrate, assume that on December 15, 2000, a retailer sells for $400 a television set that costs $280, or 70% of the sales price. The terms of the sale call for a $100 cash down payment with the balance payable in 15

---

[4]CICA, *CICA Handbook* (Toronto), section 3400.06, .07 and .08.
[5]Ibid., section 3400.06, .07, .08 and .11.

monthly instalments of $20 each, beginning on January 1, 2001. (Interest charges are ignored in this illustration.) The collections of cash and recognition of profit under the instalment method are summarized as follows:

Instalment method: Profit recognized as cash is collected

Year	Cash Collected	− Cost Recovery (70%)	= Gross Profit (30%)
2000	$100	$ 70	$ 30
2001	240	168	72
2002	60	42	18
Totals	$400	$280	$120

Since the instalment method delays the recognition of profit beyond the point of sale, there is little theoretical justification for its use. Under generally accepted accounting principles, use of the instalment method is permissible only when the amounts likely to be collected on instalment sales are so uncertain that no reasonable basis exists for estimating an allowance for doubtful accounts. However, this is usually a rare occurrence. Consequently, the instalment method is seldom used for financial reporting.

Percentage-of-Completion   Under certain circumstances, accountants may recognize income ***during the production process.***[6] An example arises in the case of long-term construction contracts, such as the building of a dam over a period of several years. Clearly the income statements of a company engaged in such a project would be of little use to managers or investors if no profit or loss were reported until the dam was finally completed. The accountant therefore estimates the portion of the project completed during each accounting period, and recognizes the profit on the project ***in proportion*** to the work completed. This is known as the **percentage-of-completion** method of accounting for long-term contracts.

LO 4: Apply the percentage-of-completion method of income recognition.

The percentage-of-completion method works as follows:

1. An estimate is made of the total costs to be incurred and the total profit to be earned over the life of the project.
2. Each period, an estimate is made of the portion of the total project completed during the period. This estimate is usually made by expressing the costs incurred during the period as a percentage of the estimated total cost of the project.
3. The percentage figure determined in step **2** is applied to the estimated total profit on the contract to compute the amount of profit applicable to the current accounting period.
4. No estimate is made of the percentage of work done during the final period. In the period in which the project is completed, any remaining profit is recognized.

To illustrate, assume that Reed Construction Limited enters into a contract with the government to build an irrigation canal at a price of $50,000,000. The canal will be built over a three-year period at an estimated total cost of $40,000,000. Therefore, the estimated total profit on the project is $10,000,000. The following schedule shows the actual costs

---
[6]Op. cit., *CICA Handbook,* Section 3400.08 and .14.

incurred and the amount of profit recognized in each of the three years under the percentage-of-completion method:

Percentage-of-Completion: Profit recognized as work progresses

Year	(A) Actual Costs Incurred	(B) Percentage of Work Done in Year (Column A ÷ $40,000,000)	(C) Profit Considered Earned ($10,000,000 × Column B)
1	$ 6,000,000	15%	$1,500,000
2	20,000,000	50%	5,000,000
3	14,520,000	*	2,980,000 balance
Totals	$40,520,000		$9,480,000

Balance required to complete the contract.

The percentage of the work completed during Year 1 was estimated by dividing the actual cost incurred in the year by the estimated total cost of the project ($6,000,000 ÷ $40,000,000 = 15%). Because 15% of the work was done in Year 1, 15% of the estimated total profit of $10,000,000 was considered earned in that year ($10,000,000 × 15% = $1,500,000). Costs incurred in Year 2 amounted to 50% of the estimated total costs ($20,000,000 ÷ $40,000,000 = 50%); thus, 50% of the estimated total profit was recognized in Year 2 ($10,000,000 × 50% = $5,000,000). Note that no percentage-of-work-completed figure was computed for Year 3. In Year 3, the total actual cost is known ($40,520,000, including a cost overrun of $520,000), and the actual total profit on the contract is determined to be $9,480,000 ($50,000,000 − $40,520,000). Since profits of $6,500,000 were previously recognized in Years 1 and 2, the **remaining** profit ($9,480,000 − $6,500,000 = $2,980,000) is recognized in Year 3.

Although an expected **profit** on a long-term construction contract is recognized in proportion to the work completed, a different treatment is accorded to an expected **loss.** If at the end of any accounting period it appears that a loss will be incurred on a contract in progress, the **entire loss should be recognized at once.**

The percentage-of-completion method is used only when the total profit expected to be earned can be **reasonably estimated in advance** and the **ultimate collection** of the contract price is **reasonably assured.** If there are substantial uncertainties in the amount of profit that will be earned or in the amount of the contract price to be collected, no profit is recognized until the job is completed. This approach is called the **completed-contract method.** If the completed-contract method had been used in the preceding example, no profit would have been recognized in Years 1 and 2; the entire profit of $9,480,000 would have been recorded in Year 3.

Expense Recognition: The Matching Principle

The relationship between expenses and revenue is one of **cause and effect.** Expenses are **causal factors** in the earning of revenue. To measure the profitability of an economic activity, we must consider not only the revenue earned, but also all the expenses incurred in the effort to produce this revenue. Thus, accountants attempt to **match** (or **offset**) the revenue appearing in an income statement with all the expenses incurred in generating that revenue. This concept, called the **matching principle,** governs the timing of expense recognition in financial statements.

To illustrate, assume that in June a painting contractor purchases paint on account. The contractor uses the paint on jobs started and completed in July, but does not pay for the paint until August. In which month should the contractor recognize the cost of the paint as expense? The answer is *July,* because this is the month in which the paint was *used in the process of earning revenue.*

Because of the matching principle, costs that are expected to benefit future accounting periods are debited to asset accounts. These costs are then allocated to expense in the periods that the costs contribute to the production of revenue. The matching principle underlies such accounting practices as depreciating plant assets, measuring the cost of goods sold, and amortizing the cost of unexpired insurance policies. All end-of-the-period adjusting entries involving recognition of expense are applications of the matching principle.

Costs are matched with revenue in one of two ways:

1. *Direct association of costs with specific revenue transactions.* The ideal method of matching revenue with expenses is to determine the amount of expense associated with the specific revenue transactions occurring during the period. However, this approach works only for those costs and expenses that can be directly associated with specific revenue transactions. The cost of goods sold and commissions paid to salespeople are examples of costs and expenses that can be *directly associated* with the revenue of a specific accounting period.

2. *Systematic allocation of costs over the "useful life" of the expenditure.* Many expenditures contribute to the earnings of revenue for a number of accounting periods, but cannot be directly associated with specific revenue transactions. Examples include the costs of insurance policies, depreciable assets, and intangible assets such as goodwill. In these cases, accountants attempt to match revenue and expenses by *systematically allocating the cost to expense* over its useful life. Straight-line amortization and the various methods of depreciation are examples of the "systematic allocation" techniques used to match revenue with the related costs and expenses.

Unfortunately, it is not possible to apply the matching principle objectively to every type of expenditure. Many expenditures offer at least some hope of producing revenue in future periods; however, there may be little or no objective evidence to support these hopes. Accountants defer recognition of an expense to the future only when there is *reasonable evidence* that the expenditure will, in fact, benefit future operations. If this evidence is not available, or is not convincing, accountants do not attempt to apply the matching principle; rather, they charge the expenditure *immediately to expense.* Expenditures generally considered "too subjective" for accountants to apply the matching principle include advertising, research, and the cost of employee training programs.[7]

---

[7]Section 3450.16 of the *CICA Handbook* recommends that research costs be charged to expense immediately.

CASE IN POINT

Large pharmaceutical companies such as Merck, Upjohn, BioChem Pharma, and Marion Labs spend hundreds of millions of dollars each year in research. Ten or more years may be spent researching and testing a new product. During this time, no revenue is received from the product, but related research costs totalling hundreds of millions of dollars are charged to expense. Every now and then, these companies discover a "blockbuster" drug, which can bring in revenue of perhaps $1 billion per year for a decade or more. The costs of manufacturing pharmaceutical products are relatively small; the primary costs incurred in generating the companies' revenues are the research expenditures incurred in prior years.

As a result of accountants' inability to match research costs against the subsequent revenue, the income of pharmaceutical companies is understated during the years of product research and is overstated in the years that a successful product brings in revenue. Unfortunately, there is no simple solution to this problem. How are accountants to determine objectively whether or not today's research expenditures will result in a "blockbuster" product 10 years down the road?

The Consistency Principle

The principle of **consistency** implies that a particular accounting method, once adopted, will not be changed from period to period. This assumption is important because it assists users of financial statements in interpreting changes in financial position and changes in net income between periods.

Consider the confusion that would result if a company ignored the principle of consistency and changed its method of depreciation every year. The company could cause its net income for any given year to increase or decrease merely by changing its depreciation method.

The principle of consistency does not mean that a company should *never* make a change in its accounting methods. In fact, a company *should* make a change if a proposed new accounting method will provide more useful information than does the method presently in use. But when a significant change in accounting methods does occur, the fact that a change has been made, the reason for the change, and the dollar effects of the change should be *fully disclosed* in the financial statements.

Consistency applies to a single accounting entity and increases the comparability of financial statements from period to period. Different companies, even those in the same industry, may follow different accounting methods. For this reason, it is important to determine the accounting methods used by companies whose financial statements are being compared.

The Disclosure Principle

Adequate **disclosure** means that all *material* and *relevant facts* concerning financial position and the results of operations *are communicated to users.* This can be accomplished either in the financial statements or in the notes accompanying the statements. Such disclosure should make the financial statements more useful and less subject to misinterpretation.

Adequate disclosure does not require that information be presented in great detail; it does require, however, that no important facts be withheld. For example, if a company has been named as a defendant in a large lawsuit, this information must be disclosed. Other examples of information that should be disclosed in financial statements include:

1. A summary of the ***accounting policies*** (principles and methods) used in the preparation of the statements.
2. Dollar effects of any **changes** in these accounting policies during the current period.
3. Any ***contingent losses*** that may have a material effect upon the financial position of the business.
4. Contractual provisions that will affect future cash flows, including the terms and conditions of borrowing agreements, employee pension plans, and commitments to buy or sell material amounts of assets.

Even significant events that occur ***after*** the end of the accounting period but before the financial statements are issued may need to be disclosed. The reason for such a disclosure is to ensure that financial statements remain fairly presented when they are available to users.

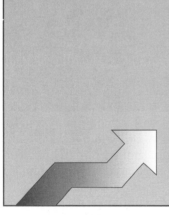

CASE IN POINT

The financial statements of Hudson's Bay Company for the year ended January 31, 1998 were available in April, 1998. The acquisition on February 27, 1998 of Kmart Canada Co. was disclosed as a subsequent event in a note to the financial statements: "On February 27, 1998 the Company acquired all of the outstanding shares of Kmart Canada Co., which operates discount department stores in Canada, for a consideration of approximately $260 million. This amount does not include costs of acquisition that might be incurred for employee terminations, store closures, professional fees, and other related costs."

Similarly, in its notes to the December 31, 1997 financial statements, Bell Canada disclosed the following: "Under an agreement dated January 13, 1998, Bell Canada will sell thirteen commercial properties to TrizecHahn Corporation. . . . The transaction is expected to close in the first quarter of 1998 and will be reflected in the financial statements of Bell Canada at such time. . . . Net proceeds from the sale of approximately $750 million will be used to meet outstanding debt maturities and for general corporate purposes."

Naturally, there are practical limits to the amount of disclosure that can be made in financial statements and the accompanying notes. The key point to bear in mind is that the supplementary information should be ***relevant to the interpretation*** of the financial statements.

Materiality

The term **materiality** refers to the ***relative importance*** of an item or an event. An item is "material" if knowledge of the item might reasonably ***influence the decisions*** of users of financial statements. Accountants must use their professional judgment to make sure that all material items are properly reported in the financial statements.

However, the financial reporting process should be ***cost-effective***—that is, the value of the information should exceed the cost of its preparation. By definition, the accounting treatment accorded to ***immaterial*** items is of little or no value to decision makers. Therefore, accountants should not waste time accounting for immaterial items; these items may be treated in the ***easiest and most convenient manner.*** In short, the concept of materiality allows accountants to ignore other accounting principles with respect to items that are not material.

An example of the materiality concept is found in the manner in which most companies account for low-cost plant assets, such as pencil sharpeners or wastebaskets. Although the matching principle calls for depreciating plant assets over their useful lives, these low-cost items usually are charged immediately to an expense account. The resulting "distortion" in the financial statement is too small to be of any importance.

If a large number of immaterial items occur in the same accounting period, accountants should consider the ***cumulative effect*** of these items. Numerous "immaterial" items may, in aggregate, have a material effect upon the financial statements. In these situations, the numerous immaterial events must be properly recorded to avoid a material distortion of the financial statements.

We must recognize that the materiality of an item is a relative matter; what is material in a small business organization may not be material in a larger one. The materiality of an item depends not only upon its dollar amount but also upon its nature. In a large corporation, for example, it may be immaterial whether a given $50,000 expenditure is classified as an asset or as an expense. However, if the $50,000 item is a misuse of corporate funds, such as an unauthorized payment of the personal living expense of the chief executive, the ***nature*** of the item may make it quite material to users of the financial statements.

Accordingly, in deciding materiality, accountants use professional judgment in assessing the financial statement impact of the dollar amount and the nature of the item involved.

CASE IN POINT   Hedy Lamarr, a glamorous movie star of the 1930s and 1940s, is suing Corel Corp. for damage in excess of $15,000 (U.S.) in a Florida circuit court. She alleges that Corel has profited from the use of her likeness in a stylized picture on the cover of CorelDraw 8 (Corel's flagship graphic software product) and on Corel's Web site. She also alleges that Corel's actions have disturbed her peace of mind and violated her privacy.

Corel is one of the 500 largest companies in Canada, with assets and revenue of $233 million and $359 million respectively. So, how material is this lawsuit? Should it or would it be disclosed in the financial statements? Reach your own conclusion and check it with Corel's annual financial statements.*

Source: The Globe and Mail, April 8, 1998

**Maclean's* reported on December 14, 1998 that the lawsuit was settled, allowing Corel to use Lamarr's image on its packaging, and that the original claim was for $23 million in royalties and damages. However, the financial terms of the settlement were not released. So it would be interesting to see what may be disclosed in Corel's financial statements.

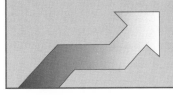

Conservatism as a Guide in Resolving Uncertainties[8]

We have previously referred to the use of **conservatism** in connection with the measurement of net income and the reporting of accounts receivable and inventories in the balance sheet. Although the concept of conservatism may not qualify as an accounting principle, it has long been a powerful influence upon asset valuation and income determination. Conservatism is most useful when matters of judgment or estimates are involved. Ideally, accountants should base their estimates on sound logic and select those accounting methods that neither overstate nor understate the facts. When some doubt exists about the valuation of an asset or the realization of a gain, however, accountants traditionally select the accounting option that produces a lower net income for the current period and a less favourable financial position.

An example of conservatism is the traditional practice of pricing inventory at the lower-of-cost-and-market. Decreases in the market value of the inventory are recognized as a part of the cost of goods sold in the current period, but increases in market value of inventory are ignored. Failure to apply conservatism when valuations are especially uncertain may produce misleading information and result in losses to creditors and shareholders.

PROFESSIONAL JUDGMENT: AN ESSENTIAL ELEMENT IN FINANCIAL REPORTING

LO 5: Describe the role of professional judgment in the financial reporting process.

Judgment plays a major role in financial reporting. For those situations not specifically covered by an official pronouncement, accountants must exercise **professional judgment** in determining the treatment that is most consistent with generally accepted accounting principles. Judgment also is exercised in selecting appropriate accounting methods (as for example, deciding whether to use the FIFO or LIFO method of inventory valuation), in estimating the useful lives of depreciable assets, and in deciding what events are "material" to a given business entity.

Judgment is a personal matter; different accountants often will make different judgments, even for similar situations. This explains why the financial statements of different companies are not likely to be directly comparable in all respects.

International Accounting Standards

LO 6: Discuss international accounting standards.

The increasing growth in international trade and capital financing as well as the rapid expansion of multinational enterprises have made international accounting standards (that is, international GAAP) an indispensable element in financial reporting. The fundamental rationale for internationalization of accounting standards is to enhance the comparability of external financial reporting by multinational and other large enterprises whose economic and financial influences and effects transcend national boundaries.

While the root for the development of international accounting standards can be traced back to the first conference of the International Congress of Accountants in 1904, the establishment of The Accountants International

---

[8]CICA, *CICA Handbook* (Toronto), section 1000.21.

Study Group (AISG) in 1966 by the accounting profession of Canada, the United Kingdom, and the United States provided an impetus to the creation of the International Accounting Standards Committee (IASC).

In 1973, the International Accounting Standards Committee was established by the professional accounting bodies in Australia, Canada, France, Germany, Japan, Mexico, the Netherlands, the United Kingdom and Ireland, and the United States as an independent, private sector standard setting organization. The primary objective of the IASC is to formulate and publish basic international accounting standards and to promote their worldwide acceptance and observance. Since its inception, the IASC has devoted its effort to expand its membership and to harmonize the divergence of accounting standards among nations. At present, it has about 100 accounting bodies from some 80 nations as members. (Canada has three members: The Canadian Institute of Chartered Accountants, the Certified General Accountants' Association of Canada, and the Society of Management Accountants of Canada.) It has issued more than thirty pronouncements on international accounting standards. These pronouncements provide sufficient flexibility by allowing the use of a fair number of accounting alternatives. However, the IASC has attempted to eliminate a number of free choices among alternative accounting treatments.

While the establishment of international accounting standards is a difficult and slow process, the IASC has accomplished a certain degree of harmonizing the standards by refining the boundaries for acceptable accounting standards. It has been able to narrow the choice of the number of accounting alternatives in some cases. Also, it has provided a source of accounting standards for some countries. For example, Malaysia, Singapore, and Yugoslavia, which do not have their own standards, have recognized the IASC's standards as the accepted standards. Recently, China has also recognized the IASC's standards as accepted standards. Moreover, in countries such as Nigeria and India where standard setting is emerging, the IASC's standards are the basis for the development of their accounting standards. Another significant manifestation of the IASC's accomplishment is that some stock exchanges, such as London and the Netherlands, consider the IASC's standards as generally accepted accounting principles in granting listing of foreign-based companies.

It is important to note two limitations of the IASC's accounting standards. First, compliance with these standards is voluntary; their acceptance is dependent on the persuasion of the IASC and the goodwill of its members. Second, these standards do not override those of the member countries.

ETHICAL CONDUCT IN THE ACCOUNTING PROFESSION

What Are "Ethics"?

LO 7: Describe the nature of ethics and . . .

Ethics are the moral principles that an individual uses in governing his or her behaviour. In short, ethics are the personal criteria by which an individual distinguishes "right" from "wrong."

Every society has a strong interest in the ethical standards of its citizens. If people had no ethics, for example, they would see nothing "wrong" in cheating, stealing, or even committing murder as a means of achieving their goals. Obviously a society without ethics would be a chaotic and dangerous place in which to live. For this reason, governments, organized religions, and educators have long attempted to create or promote certain ethical standards among all members of society. Governments pass laws requiring or prohibiting certain types of behaviour; organized religions attempt to define "right" and "wrong" through sermons and religious teachings. Throughout the educational process, educators attempt to teach students to distinguish between "right" and "wrong" using criteria (ethics) acceptable to the greater society.

Ethics Relating to Certain Types of Activities   Some ethical concepts, such as a belief that it is wrong to steal, apply to almost all situations. Other ethical concepts, however, apply specifically to some particular type of activity. For example, many of us have ethical principles relating directly to sports. Assume that you are playing a competitive sport and the umpire or referee makes a "bad call" *in your favour.* Do you challenge the call? Your answer to this question will depend upon your *personal* ethical principles concerning participation in competitive sports.

Some ethical concepts relate specifically to doing business. For example, if a member of the royal family or a government official in a foreign country demands a secret cash payment before allowing you to do business in that country, is it "ethical" for you to make this payment? If you manufacture a product that is useful, legal, and profitable, but evidence shows that its use is harmful to the environment, should you continue to produce this product? These are ethical decisions relating specifically to the field of business. There also are many ethical decisions that relate specifically to the practice of *professions,* such as medicine, law, and accounting.

To understand and appreciate the ethics applicable to a specialized type of activity, one must first understand the *nature of that activity.* Consider, for example, a painter who encounters a building badly in need of new paint. The painter has no "ethical obligation" to stop and paint this building. Now consider a physician encountering an accident victim who is unconscious and badly in need of immediate medical attention. The physician *does* have an ethical obligation to stop and render emergency medical care. The obligation to render immediate service simply because it is needed is an ethical concept applicable to the medical profession, because that profession is devoted to the public's health and safety.[9]

Ethics Relating to the Practice of Accounting   Accountants, too, have unique ethical responsibilities. For example, public accountants auditing financial statements have an ethical obligation to be *independent* of the company issuing the statements. An accountant preparing an income tax return has an ethical obligation to prepare the return *honestly,* even though the taxpayer paying the accountant's fee may want the return prepared in a manner that understates taxable income. An accountant employed by a private company has the conflicting ethical obligations of respecting the *confidentiality* of information gained on the job and also making *appropriate disclosures* to people outside the organization.

---

[9]Similar ethical responsibilities also exist for people working in a variety of "public safety" occupations.

The Concept of a "Profession"   Accountants are proud to consider themselves members of a recognized **_profession._** But just what is a "profession"? Actually, there is no single definition or criterion that distinguishes a profession from other fields of endeavour. Over time, however, some occupations have come to be regarded as professions, while others have not. Among the occupations most commonly regarded as professions are the practices of medicine, law, engineering, architecture, and theology. Accounting, too, is widely viewed as having achieved the status of a profession.

Although a profession is not easily defined, all professions do have certain characteristics in common. Perhaps the most important of these characteristics is the special responsibility of persons practicing a profession to **_serve the public interest,_** even at the sacrifice of personal gain.

Professional Codes of Ethics

All recognized professions have developed **_codes of professional ethics._** The basic purpose of these codes is to provide members of the profession with guidelines for conducting themselves **_in a manner consistent with the responsibilities of the profession._** Codes of ethics relating to the practice of accounting have been developed by several professional organizations of accountants. In addition to these codes, there are laws, income tax regulations, and professional pronouncements that govern the conduct of professional accountants.

LO 7: . . . explain the basic purpose of a code of ethics within a profession.

Codes of ethics developed by professional organizations generally hold their members to **_higher_** standards of conduct than do the laws regulating that profession. In part, this tendency evolves from the fact that professional organizations have a vested interest in enhancing the public image of the profession. Also, these organizations have a better understanding than do lawmakers of the special problems confronting the professional. For these reasons, all professions are, to some extent, **_self-regulating._** (The term self-regulating means that society expects the profession to establish its own rules of "professional conduct" for its members, and also to develop methods of enforcing these rules.)

LO 8: Identify and explain the basic principles underlying a professional code of ethics.

In this introductory discussion of ethical principles applicable to the accounting profession, we will explore briefly the following fundamental principles underlying the rules of professional conduct of the Institute of Chartered Accountants of Ontario[10]:

1. A member or student shall conduct himself or herself at all times in a manner that will maintain the good reputation of the profession and its ability to serve the public interest.
2. A member or student shall perform his or her professional services with integrity and care and accept an obligation to sustain his or her professional competence by keeping himself informed of, and complying with, developments in professional standards.

---

[10]Since these principles express the general spirit underlying the rules of professional conduct, they are essential in governing the conduct of professional accountants, regardless of the organization of affiliation. However, these principles are selected for purposes of illustration only.

3. A member who is engaged in an attest function such as an audit or review of financial statements shall hold himself or herself free of any influence, interest, or relationship, in respect of his or her client's affairs, that impairs his or her professional judgment or objectivity or that, in the view of a reasonable observer, would impair the member's professional judgment or objectivity.

4. A member or student has a duty of confidence in respect of the affairs of any client and shall not disclose, without proper cause, any information obtained in the course of his or her duties, nor shall he or she in any way exploit such information to his or her advantage.

5. The development of a member's practice shall be founded upon a reputation for professional excellence, and the use of methods of advertising that do not uphold professional good taste, that could be characterized as self-promotion, and that solicit, rather than inform, is not in keeping with this principle.

6. A member shall act in relation to any other member with the courtesy and consideration due between professional colleagues and that, in turn, he or she would wish to be accorded by the other member.

While these principles focus mainly on **public accountants** (those who practise public accounting), they also apply to **management accountants** (those who are employed by private companies, not-for-profit organizations, and governmental agencies). For example, the principles of integrity and confidentiality, to a large extent, are applicable to public accountants as well as management accountants. Also, the principle of independence applies primarily to attestation engagements such as an audit or a review (attesting to the plausibility of financial information or financial statements), not to income tax work or the rendering of other professional services.

These principles call for an unswerving commitment to honourable behaviour, even at the sacrifice of personal advantage. A member or student who is found guilty of violating any provisions of the rules of professional conduct derived from these principles will be admonished, reprimanded, suspended, or expelled. A member who is expelled will lose his or her professional accounting certificate.

A Closer Look at Some Key Principles

LO 9: Apply the basic principles of ethical conduct to situations likely to arise in an accountant's work.

Three ethical principles of special importance to public accountants and management accountants are independence (or objectivity), integrity, and confidentiality.

Independence or Objectivity   When public accountants *audit* a company's financial statements, they express their *professional opinion* as to whether the financial statements represent a fair representation of the company's financial position and the results of its operations. Shareholders, creditors, and potential investors all rely on these audited financial statements in deciding how to allocate their investment resources. The auditors' report will lend *credibility* to audited financial statements only if users of the statements view the auditors as impartial.

For auditors to be viewed as impartial, the profession feels that they must be *independent* of the company issuing the financial statements. By "*independent,*" we mean in fact and in appearance. Independence *in fact* refers to the ability of public accountants to maintain an objective mental attitude in all aspects of their work. Since it is not subject to objective measurement, mental attitude can usually be judged only by the public accountants themselves. On the other hand, independence *in appearance* means that the auditor must not be perceived as being under the company's influence or control, or as having any *vested interest* in the results reported in the financial statements. Assume, for example, that an auditor owned shares in the common stock of an audit client. Many users of the financial statements might assume that the auditor would be reluctant to insist upon the disclosure of facts that might lower the price of the company's shares. Thus, the auditor would not be regarded as impartial by these users of the statements.

Public accountants take extensive measures *to appear* independent of their audit clients. This aspect of independence places a number of constraints upon the auditors' relationship with the audit client. Auditors must not have any financial interest in a client firm, must not accept expensive gifts from the client, and must not be officers or employees of the client organization. Other restrictions require that close relatives of the auditors not have major investments or hold key management positions with a client company. In terms of inspiring public confidence, the *appearance* of independence is just as important as being independent in fact.

Public accountants need be independent only when they are expressing an opinion on the representations made by another party. Thus, the concept of independence applies *primarily* to the public accountant's role as an *auditor.* In rendering income tax services, consulting services, and many types of accounting services, public accountants are *not* required to be independent of their clients.

An important distinction between a management accountant and a public accountant is that the management accountant is an *employee* of the company for which he or she performs accounting services. The public accountant, on the other hand, is an independent contractor who provides services for a variety of different clients. Employees are not regarded as independent of their employers, so management accountants cannot perform independent audits of their employers' financial statements.

Although management accountants are not independent of their employers, they still are expected to develop accounting information that is fair, honest, and free from bias.

Integrity   One of the most important principles underlying professional conduct is that both public and management accountants shall *not knowingly misrepresent facts.* This concept of integrity goes to the very heart of the professional accountant's responsibility to the public interest.

Facts may be misrepresented even if the facts themselves are stated correctly. For example, facts are considered to be misrepresented if the financial statements or accounting documents do not contain *adequate disclosure* of relevant information that may reasonably influence the intended user's *interpretation* of the facts.

Accordingly, public and management accountants **must not be associated** with misleading financial statements, income tax returns, or other accounting reports. If a client or employer insists upon preparing financial statements or documents in a misleading manner, the public or management accountant must **resign from the engagement or employment.**

Confidentiality If individuals are to discuss sensitive and private matters openly with professionals, they must trust those professionals not to misuse the information provided. Thus, most professions have ethical requirements that information provided to the professionals must be held in strict confidence. Physicians, lawyers, and clergy, for example, are ethically and legally prohibited from disclosing to others personal information obtained from persons who have sought their professional services.

By the nature of their work, public and management accountants must have access to much financial information about their clients or their employers, information that is regarded as "confidential." If public and management accountants are to earn the trust and respect of their clients, their employers, and the public, they must respect the confidential nature of this information. They should not divulge sensitive information about a client or employer company to the company's competitors or to other outsiders, or use that information for their personal gain.

CASE IN POINT Both public and management accountants often have advance knowledge that a company's earnings for the year will be higher or lower than most investors are expecting. It would be unethical for the accountants to use this confidential information to profit from changes in the company's stock price, either personally or by passing such information to third parties.

The principle that information obtained by public and management accountants is to be held in confidence differs somewhat between the accounting profession and other professions. In all aspects of their work, these accountants have an ethical obligation **not to misrepresent facts.** They may face a conflict between their professional obligation to correctly and fully disclose facts, and a company's desire that certain information be held in confidence. In such a situation, they should insist that the company make the necessary disclosure. If such disclosure is not made, they should resign.

It should be noted that the confidentiality requirement is not valid when there is a legal obligation for the accountants to make such disclosure.

The Challenge of Adhering to a Code of Ethics

In principle, a professional code of ethics is a good thing. Society benefits when professionals conduct themselves in an honourable and ethical manner. (Surely, no one would argue against professionals striving toward such goals as increased competence and integrity.) A professional code of ethics provides professionals with some general guidelines in conducting themselves in an ethical manner.

However, even an "honest" person may find it difficult to act in an ethical manner in some situations. Let us briefly consider a few of the "barriers" to ethical conduct.

The "Price" of Ethical Behaviour   We would like to think that professionals will do the "right" (ethical) thing, regardless of the amount of personal sacrifice involved. This is an easier course of action to advocate than to follow. Management accountants, interestingly, may have to pay a far greater "price" for ethical conduct than public accountants. Let us first consider the case of a public accountant.

Assume that a public accountant has a client that intends to issue misleading financial statements or to understate taxable income in an income tax return. The public accountant should not be associated with such misrepresentation and should resign from the engagement. This, of course, may mean that the public accountant is unable to collect his or her fee from this engagement, but this is a relatively small price to pay.

First, this "unethical" client is but one of many clients for the typical public accountant. Thus, the fee from this engagement probably represents only a small percentage of the public accountant's total revenue. More importantly, public accountants simply ***cannot afford*** to be associated with misleading financial statements or fraudulent income tax returns. Such associations could leave the public accountant personally liable to persons deceived by the misleading accounting documents, create adverse publicity that could destroy the public accountant's practice, cause the public accountant to lose his or her licence to practise public accounting, and result in the public accountant going to prison for committing fraud. Thus, the public accountant's choice is relatively clear: it is far better to give up an unethical client than to continue the association.

Now consider the situation of the management accountant. If the management accountant's employer rejects the accountant's concerns over an ethical problem, the management accountant may have no further recourse other than to resign. This may mean giving up a high and steady income, losing future pension rights, and joining the ranks of the unemployed. Clearly, this management accountant is asked to pay a much higher price for choosing the "ethical path" than is the public accountant in the preceding example.

Incomplete Information   A professional accountant may "suspect" that activities in which he or she is asked to participate are unethical, but not be sure.

CASE IN POINT   Wilson, a management accountant for International Equipment Company, is asked to process the paper work to reimburse the Vice-President of International Operations for a $50,000 "advertising expenditure" claimed in the executive's expense account. Wilson considers it improbable that the Vice-President actually spent $50,000 in personal funds for company advertising. More likely, Wilson thinks, the funds were paid as a bribe to some foreign official. However, Wilson has no facts concerning the expenditure, other than that top management wants the vice-president reimbursed.

In most situations, accountants have neither the responsibility nor the right to investigate their employers or clients. If a further investigation of the facts is not directly related to the accountant's professional responsibilities, the accountant simply may never have enough information to reach an informed decision as to whether or not specific activities are "ethical."

Just What Is the "Ethical" Thing to Do?   Codes of ethics consist of broad, general guidelines, intended to be useful to practitioners in identifying and resolving ethical problems. However, no code of ethics can address every situation that might arise. Every "ethical dilemma" is somewhat unique, having its own facts and circumstances.

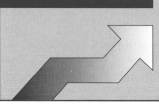

CASE IN POINT   Barnes, a public accountant, is performing income tax services for Regis Limited: Regis insists that Barnes prepare the company's income tax return in a manner that understates the amount of taxes owed. What should Barnes do?

Answer: Barnes cannot ethically comply with the client's instructions. Therefore, Barnes should resign from the engagement.

In many situations, however, the ethical course of action *is not readily apparent.*

CASE IN POINT   Riley, a public accountant, is auditing the 2000 financial statements of Quest Corporation. During this audit, Quest Corporation is acquired by Gordon Communications. Riley's step-brother is the Controller of Gordon Communications. Has Riley's independence been impaired with respect to the Quest audit? Must Riley resign from this engagement?

Answer: ???[11]

Codes of ethics, including the "official interpretations," typically do not address such specific questions. Therefore, it often is not possible to simply "look up" the solution to an ethical problem. In deciding when an ethical problem exists, and in determining what constitutes ethical behaviour, the practitioner must often rely primarily upon his or her own *professional judgment.*

In addition to studying a code of ethics, professionals attempting to resolve an ethical dilemma might ask themselves the following questions: "Would the action that I am considering be fair to everyone involved?" and "If my friends and family knew all the facts, would they be proud of my actions?" "Ethical conduct" means more than abiding by a list of rules; it means an *unswerving commitment to honourable behaviour;* even at the sacrifice of personal advantage.

---

[11]Our Case in Point involving Riley and his step-brother is intended to show that ethical dilemmas *do not always have clear-cut answers.* This case hinges upon personal judgments, including the closeness of the relationship between Riley and his step-brother, and what impairs the "appearance" of independence. Thus, even with all the facts in hand, experts are likely to disagree on the answer to this case.

End-of-Chapter Review

Key Terms Introduced or Emphasized in Chapter 12

Accounting Standards Board (AcSB) *(p.617)* The unit authorized by the CICA to issue recommendations with respect to matters of accounting practices. The board's recommendations are recognized as an authoritative source of generally accepted accounting principles.

Conservatism *(p.628)* A traditional practice of resolving uncertainties by choosing an asset valuation at the lower point of the range of reasonableness. This term refers to the policy of postponing recognition of revenue to a later date when a range of reasonable choice exists. Conservatism is designed to avoid overstatement of financial strength and earnings.

Consistency *(p.625)* An assumption that once a particular accounting method is adopted, it will not be changed from period to period. Consistency is intended to make financial statements of a given company comparable from year to year.

Cost principle *(p.620)* The traditional, widely used policy of accounting for assets at their historical (acquisition) cost determined through arm's-length bargaining. Justified by the need for objective evidence to support the valuation of assets.

Disclosure principle *(p.625)* Financial statements should include all material and relevant information about the financial position and operating results of the business. The notes accompanying financial statements are an important means of making the necessary disclosures.

Emerging Issues Committee *(p.617)* The committee established by CICA's Accounting Standards Board to review emerging accounting issues and to provide guidance so as to minimize divergent or unsatisfactory treatments in practice.

Entity concept *(p.617)* Any economic unit that controls economic resources and is accountable for these resources may be considered an accounting entity.

Ethical conduct *(p.629)* Doing "what is right," even at the sacrifice of personal advantage.

Financial Accounting Standards Board (FASB) *(p.616)* The organization in the United States with primary responsibility for formulating new accounting standards. The FASB is part of the private sector and is not a governmental agency.

Generally accepted accounting principles (GAAP) *(p.615)* The "ground rules" for financial reporting. This concept includes principles, concepts, and methods that have received authoritative support, such as the accounting recommendations in the *CICA Handbook,* or that have become "generally accepted" through widespread use.

Going-concern assumption *(p.618)* An assumption that a business entity will continue in operation indefinitely and thus will carry out its existing commitments.

Instalment method *(p.621)* An accounting method that provides for recognition of realized profit on instalment contracts in proportion to cash collected.

Management accountant *(p.632)* An accountant employed within a specific organization. Management accountants develop accounting information to meet the various needs of the organization and also assist management in the interpretation of this information.

Matching principle *(p.624)* The accounting principle that governs the timing of expense recognition. This principle indicates that expenses should be offset against revenue on a basis of cause and effect. That is, the revenue of an accounting period should be offset by those costs and expenses that were causal factors in producing that revenue.

Materiality *(p.626)* The relative importance of an amount or item. An item that is not significant enough to influence the decisions of users of financial statements is considered to be **not** material. The accounting treatment of immaterial items may be guided by convenience rather than by theoretical principles.

Objectivity (objective evidence) *(p.619)* The valuation of assets and the measurement of income are to be based as much as possible on objective evidence, such as exchange prices in arm's-length transactions.

Percentage-of-completion method *(p.622)* A method of accounting for long-term construction projects that recognizes revenue and profits in proportion to the work completed, based on an estimate of the portion of the project completed each accounting period.

Professional judgment *(p.628)* Using one's professional knowledge, experience, and ethics to make decisions that have no prescribed or obvious answer.

Public Accountant *(p.632)* A person who is licensed or otherwise permitted by provincial laws to engage in the practice of public accounting, the primary functions of which are to attest to the fairness of financial statements or financial information and to provide accounting services.

Realization (recognition) principle *(p.621)* The principle of recognizing revenue in the accounts only when the earning process is virtually complete, which is usually at the time of sale of goods or rendering service to customers.

Stable-dollar assumption *(p.619)* In using money as a measuring unit and preparing financial statements expressed in dollars, accountants make the assumption that the dollar is a stable unit of measurement.

This assumption is faulty in an environment of continued inflation.

Time period principle *(p.619)* The idea that to be useful, financial statements should be prepared for relatively short accounting periods of equal length. While this principle contributes to the timeliness of financial statements, it conflicts with the objectivity principle by forcing accountants to make many estimates, such as the useful lives of depreciable assets.

DEMONSTRATION PROBLEM

In each of the following situations, indicate the accounting principles or concepts, if any, that have been violated and explain briefly the nature of the violation. If you believe the treatment **is in accord with generally accepted accounting principles,** state this as your position and defend it.

a. Westin Manufacturing purchased an expensive special-purpose machine with an estimated useful life of 8 years. Proper installation of the machine required that it be set in the concrete of the factory floor. Once the machine was installed, Westin's controller felt that it had no resale value, so he charged the entire cost of the machine to expense in the current period.

b. Gold Mountain Exploration Limited reported on its balance sheet as an intangible asset the total of all wages, supplies, depreciation on equipment, and other costs related to the drilling of a producing oil well and then amortized this asset as oil was produced from the well.

c. A large lawsuit pending against Comfort Products Co. Ltd. was not mentioned in the notes to the company's financial statements because the lawsuit had not actually been filed with the court until seven days after the end of the current year.

d. Tanya Douglas is president of Double Joy Mines. During the current year, geologists and engineers revised upward the estimated amount of ore deposits on the company's property. Douglas instructed the company's accountant to record goodwill of $2 million, representing the estimated value of unmined ore in excess of previous estimates. The offsetting credit was made to a revenue account.

e. Opensky Airlines follows the practice of charging the purchase of hand tools with a unit cost of less than $50 to an expense account rather than to an asset account. The average life of these tools is about three years.

SOLUTION TO DEMONSTRATION PROBLEM

a. Charging the entire cost of an asset with an 8-year life to expense in a single period violates the principle of ***matching*** revenue with the costs of generating that revenue. The cost of the special-purpose machine is one of the costs of generating revenue over the next 8 years. Therefore, the cost of the machine would be charged to an asset account and depreciated over the machine's useful life. The market value of the machine after installation is not relevant, because Westin Manufacturing intends to benefit from use of the machine, not from selling it. The ***going-concern assumption*** also is being ignored by Westin's controller. This concept assumes continuity of operations and therefore calls for a balance sheet presentation based on cost rather than on current resale values.

b. This treatment is in accord with generally accepted accounting principles. An asset is an expected future economic benefit or right, and a producing oil well clearly falls within this definition. The cost of bringing such a well to the stage where it can produce oil is a part of the cost of the barrels of oil ultimately produced from the well, and may be reported as an asset to be amortized as oil is actually produced.

c. Failure to disclose the lawsuit violates the principle of **disclosure.** All information that is necessary for the reasonable interpretation of the financial statements should be disclosed, either in the face of the financial statements or in notes to the statements. The requirement for disclosure applies to events occurring after, as well as before, the balance sheet date.

d. The procedure followed by Double Joy Mines violates both the **objectivity principle** and the **realization (recognition) principle.** The revenue should not be recorded in the accounts until the ore is removed from the ground and the revenue is fully realized. Furthermore, assets should be carried at cost. The upward valuation is subject to a wide margin of error and violates the cost principle. To permit such appraisals would open the doors to possible abuses by business executives who often view their affairs optimistically. Finally, the write-up in the value of ore should not be recorded as goodwill; goodwill is the value of a going concern in excess of the value of net identifiable assets.

e. This procedure does not violate any accounting principles. Treating small dollar amounts in an expedient manner, rather than capitalizing them and depreciating them over a period of years, is justified by the principle of **materiality.**

Self-Test Questions

The answers to these questions appear on page 651.

1. Generally accepted accounting principles (GAAP):
   a. Include only the official pronouncements of the standard-setting organizations, such as the CICA and FASB.
   b. May include customary accounting practices in widespread use even if not mentioned specifically in official pronouncements.
   c. Eliminate the need for professional judgment in the area in which an official pronouncement exists.
   d. Are laws of the provincial and federal governments.

2. Which of the following situations best illustrates the application of the **realization** (recognition) principle?
   a. A company sells merchandise on the instalment method and recognizes gross profit as the cash is collected from customers.
   b. A construction company engaged in a three-year project determines the portion of profit to be recognized each year using the percentage-of-completion method.
   c. A construction company engaged in a three-month project during the year recognizes no profit until the project is completed.
   d. A manufacturer that sells washing machines with a three-year warranty recognizes warranty expense related to current year sales, based upon the estimated future liability.

3. Which of the following concepts has the **least** influence in determining the depreciation expense reported in the income statement under current GAAP?
   a. Reliability—The price of a depreciable asset established in an exchange transaction can be supported by verifiable, objective evidence.

    b. Cost principle—Assets are initially recorded in the account at cost and no adjustment is made to this valuation in subsequent periods, except to allocate a portion of the original cost to expense as assets expire.

    c. Relevance—Amounts shown in the financial statements should reflect current market values, as these are the most relevant to decision makers.

    d. Matching principle—Accountants attempt to match revenue with the expenses incurred in generating that revenue by systematically allocating an asset's cost to expense over its useful life.

4. The existence of generally accepted accounting principles has eliminated the need for professional judgment in:

    a. Estimating the useful lives and residual values of depreciable plant assets.

    b. Selecting an appropriate inventory valuation method, such as LIFO, FIFO, average cost, or specific identification.

    c. Determining which events are "material" to a given entity.

    d. None of the above is correct; each of the above situations requires the use of professional judgment.

5. The concept of ethical conduct would ***prohibit*** a professional accountant from which of the following?

    a. Resolving issues based upon professional judgment.

    b. After resigning because of an ethical dispute with an employer, accepting employment elsewhere in the same industry.

    c. Using for personal gain information that has not yet been released to the public about the financial position of a publicly owned employer or client.

    d. Investing in the common stocks of any publicly owned companies.

ASSIGNMENT MATERIAL

Discussion Questions

1. Briefly explain the meaning of the term ***generally accepted accounting principles.***

2. Why is it important that the accounting principles be "generally accepted"?

3. Name the organization in Canada that has been the most influential in developing generally accepted accounting principles.

4. To be "generally accepted," must an accounting method be set forth in the official pronouncements of an accounting standard-making organization? Explain.

5. Are generally accepted accounting principles in worldwide use? Explain.

6. What is the ***time period principle?*** Does this principle tend to increase or decrease the objectivity of accounting information? Explain.

7. What is meant by the term ***stable-dollar assumption?*** Is this assumption completely valid? Explain.

8. What is the meaning of the term ***objectivity*** as it is used by accountants? Is accounting information completely objective? Explain.

9. An argument has long existed as to whether assets should be valued in financial statements at cost or at estimated market value. Explain the implications of the **objectivity principle** in this controversy.

10. Explain what is meant by the expression "trade-off between **reliability** and **relevance**" in connection with the preparation of financial statements.

11. What two conditions should be met before accountants consider revenue to be **realized?**

12. Long-term construction projects often are accounted for by the percentage-of-completion method.
    a. Is this method consistent with the realization (recognition) principle? Explain.
    b. What is the justification for the use of this method?

13. Briefly explain the **matching principle.** Indicate two approaches that accountants follow in attempting to "match" revenue with expense.

14. Does the concept of **consistency** mean that all companies should use the same accounting methods? Explain.

15. Briefly define the principle of **disclosure.** List four examples of information that should be disclosed in financial statements or in notes accompanying the statements.

16. Briefly explain the concept of **materiality.** If an item is not material, how is the item treated for financial reporting purposes?

17. Does **conservatism** mean that assets should be deliberately understated in accounting records? Explain fully.

18. Indicate how the concept of **conservatism** would apply to:
    a. Estimating the allowance for doubtful accounts receivable.
    b. Estimating the useful lives of depreciable assets.

19. Professional judgment plays an important role in financial reporting. Identify at least three areas in which the accountant preparing financial statements must make professional judgments that will affect the content of the statements.

20. Briefly explain why society benefits from "ethical conduct" by all citizens. Next, explain why a society expects professionals to observe additional ethical standards, beyond those which pertain to all citizens.

21. Explain why all recognized professions have developed their own codes of professional ethics.

22. Identify an ethical concept that is unique to the auditing of financial statements. Explain why this ethical concept is important in the auditing function.

23. Briefly describe the ethical concept of **confidentiality.** Does this concept apply to public accountants, to management accountants, or to both? Does this concept prevent public accountants from insisting that their clients make "adequate disclosure" in financial statements intended for use by outsiders?

24. Why may a management accountant have to "pay a higher price" in resolving an ethical conflict than the "price paid" by a public accountant?

25. Briefly explain several reasons why even an honest person may have difficulty in always following the "ethical" course of action.

Exercises

EXERCISE 12-1
Accounting Terminology
(LO 2, 3, 5)

Listed below are nine technical accounting terms introduced or emphasized in this chapter.

GAAP   *Professional judgment*   *Realization*
CICA   *Materiality*   *Matching*
Objectivity   *Conservatism*   *Consistency*

Each of the following statements may (or may not) describe one of these technical terms. For each statement, indicate the accounting term described, or answer "None" if the statement does not correctly describe any of the terms.

a. The concept of associating expenses with revenue on a basis of cause and effect.

b. An essential element for an accountant making estimates, selecting appropriate accounting methods, and resolving trade-offs between the goals of conflicting accounting principles.

c. The organization that is primarily responsible for developing new accounting standards in Canada.

d. The goal of having all companies use the same accounting methods.

e. The accounting principles developed by the CICA.

f. The accounting principle used in determining when revenue should be recognized in financial statements.

g. An accounting concept that may justify departure from other accounting principles for purposes of convenience and economy.

EXERCISE 12-2
Asset Valuation
(LO 3)

Milestone Manufacturing Limited has just purchased expensive machinery that was custom-made to suit the company's manufacturing operations. Because of the custom nature of this machinery, it would be of little value to any other company. Therefore, the controller of Milestone is considering writing these machines down to their estimated resale value in order to provide a conservative valuation of assets in the company's balance sheet. In the income statement, the write-down would appear as a "loss on revaluation of machinery."

Separately discuss the idea of writing down the carrying value of the machinery in light of each of the four following accounting concepts:

a. The going-concern assumption

b. The matching principle

c. Objectivity

d. Conservatism

EXERCISE 12-3
Revenue Recognition
(LO 3)

In deciding when to recognize revenue in financial statements, accountants normally apply the realization (recognition) principle.

a. Revenue is considered realized when two conditions are met. What are these conditions?

b. Indicate when the conditions for recognition of revenue have been met in each of the following situations. (Assume that financial statements are prepared monthly.)

    1. An airline sells tickets several months in advance of its flights.

    2. An appliance dealer sells merchandise on 24-month payment plans.

    3. A professional sports team sells season tickets in July for eight home games to be played in the months of August through December.

    4. Interest revenue relating to a 2-year note receivable is all due at the maturity of the note.

EXERCISE 12-4
Expense Recognition
(LO 3)

Mystery Playhouse prepares monthly financial statements. At the beginning of its 3 month summer season, the company has programs printed for each of its 48 upcoming performances. Under certain circumstances, either of the following accounting treatments of the costs of printing these programs would be acceptable. Justify both of the accounting treatments using accounting principles discussed in this chapter.

a. The cost of printing the programs is recorded as an asset and is allocated to expense in the month in which the programs are distributed to patrons attending performances.

b. The entire cost of printing the programs is charged to expense when the invoice is received from the printer.

EXERCISE 12-5
Violations of Accounting Principles
(LO 3)

For each situation described below, indicate the principle of accounting that is being violated. You may choose from the following:

Accounting entity	*Materiality*
Consistency	*Objectivity*
Disclosure	*Realization (recognition)*
Matching	*Stable-dollar assumption*

a. The bookkeeper for a large metropolitan auto dealership depreciates metal wastebaskets over a period of 5 years.

b. Upon completion of the construction of a condominium project that will soon be offered for sale, Townhome Developers increased the balance sheet valuation of the condominiums to their sales value and recognized the expected profit on the project.

c. Plans to dispose of a major segment of the business are not communicated to readers of the financial statements.

d. The cost of expensive, custom-made machinery installed in an assembly line is charged to expense because it is doubtful that the machinery would have any resale value if the assembly line were shut down.

e. A small commuter airline recognizes no depreciation on its aircraft because the planes are maintained in "as good as new" condition.

EXERCISE 12-6
Profit Recognition: Instalment Method
(LO 3)

On September 15, 1999, Susan Moore sold a piece of property that cost her $56,000 for $80,000, net of commissions and other selling expenses. The terms of sale were as follows: down payment, $8,000; balance, $3,000 on the fifteenth day of each month for 24 months, starting October 15, 1999. Compute the gross profit to be recognized by Moore in 1999, 2000, and 2001 using (a) the ***accrual basis*** of accounting and (b) the ***instalment basis*** of accounting. Moore uses a fiscal year ending December 31.

EXERCISE 12-7
Profit Recognition: Percentage-of-Completion Method
(LO 4)

The Clinton Corporation recognizes the profit on a long-term construction project as work progresses. From the information given below, compute the profit that should be recognized each year, assuming that the original cost estimate on the contract was $6,000,000 and that the contract price is $7,500,000.

Year	Costs Incurred	Profit Considered Realized
1999	$1,800,000	$?
2000	3,000,000	?
2001	1,171,000	?
Total	$5,971,000	$1,529,000

EXERCISE 12-8
Developing New Accounting Standards
(LO 1, 2)

Answer the following questions relating to the creation of new accounting standards:

a. Why will a need for new standards always exist?

b. What organization has primary responsibility for setting new accounting standards?

c. Should all elements of the economic community be invited to comment and to express their views during the standard-setting process?

EXERCISE 12-9
Ethical Responsibilities of a Public Accountant
(LO 8, 9)

Teresa Ortiz, a public accountant, was engaged to audit the financial statements of Meglo Corporation and also to prepare the company's income tax return. During the course of her work, Ortiz discovered that in its income tax return, Meglo had claimed $75,000 of the amortization of goodwill even though this amount is not deductible for income tax purposes. Ortiz discussed this problem with her client, but the client insisted on deducting the amortization. A representative of management stated: "If 100% amortization of goodwill isn't deductible, it should be. After all, it's the same as any other expenses that the company incurred."

Also during this engagement, Ortiz learned that Meglo has owed $36,000 to Martin Advertising Agency for a period of 17 months. Apparently, Martin had underbilled Meglo for services rendered 2 years ago and has made no request for the $36,000 additional payments due.

In the financial statements, Meglo included appropriate amounts of income taxes expense and income taxes payable. The company also properly included the $36,000 among its liabilities. However, management has told Ortiz that it has no intention of making payment of this amount unless it receives a bill from Martin.

Discuss Ortiz's ethical responsibilities with respect to (a) completing her professional engagements for Meglo, and (b) personally disclosing the facts directly to the affected third parties (Revenue Canada and/or Martin).

EXERCISE 12-10
Responsibilities of a Management Accountant
(LO 8, 9)

Hong-Ching Chan, CMA, was hired this year as a management accountant for Drexel, Inc. While working for Drexel, Chan learns that in the preceding year the company understated its tax liability in its income tax return by more than $400,000.
a. Can Chan ethically report Drexel to Revenue Canada?
b. Would your answer be different if Chan had been fired by Drexel?
c. Would your answer be different if Chan were a public accountant engaged by Drexel to conduct an audit of the company's financial statements?

Problems

PROBLEM 12-1
Rationale Behind Acceptable Practices
(LO 3)

Paragraphs **a** through **e** describe accounting practices that ***are in accord*** with generally accepted accounting principles. From the following list of accounting principles, identify those principles that you believe justify or explain each described accounting practice. (Most of the described practices are explained by a single principle; however, more than one principle may relate to a given practice.) Briefly explain the relationship between the described accounting practice and the underlying accounting principle.

Accounting Principles

Consistency	*Accounting entity concept*
Materiality	*Matching revenue with expense*
Objectivity	*Going-concern assumption*
Realization	*Disclosure*
Conservatism	*Stable-dollar assumption*

Accounting Practices

a. If land costing $60,000 were sold for $65,000, a $5,000 gain would be reported regardless of inflation during the years that the land has been owned.
b. When equipment is purchased an estimate is made of its useful life and its residual value, and the equipment is then depreciated over this period.
c. The personal assets of the owner of a sole proprietorship are not disclosed in the financial statements of the business, even when these personal assets are sufficient to assure payment of all the business's liabilities.

d. In estimating the appropriate size of the allowance for doubtful accounts, most accountants would, under conditions of uncertainty, rather see this allowance be a little too large than a little too small.

e. The methods used in the valuation of inventory and for the depreciation of plant assets are described in a note to the financial statements.

PROBLEM 12-2
Accounting Principles
(LO 3)

Paragraphs **a** through **e,** below, describe accounting practices that *are in accord* with generally accepted accounting principles. From the following list of accounting principles, identify those principles that you believe justify or explain each described accounting practice. (Most of the practices are explained by a single principle; however, more than one principle may relate to a particular practice.) Briefly explain the relationship between the described accounting practice and the underlying accounting principle.

Accounting Principles

Consistency	Accounting entity concept
Materiality	Matching revenue with expense
Objectivity	Going-concern assumption
Realization	Disclosure
Conservatism	Stable-dollar assumption

Accounting Practices

a. The purchase of a 2-year fire insurance policy is recorded by debiting an asset account even though no refund will be received if the policy is cancelled.

b. Hand tools with a small unit cost are charged to expense when purchased even though the individual tools have a useful life of several years.

c. An airline records depreciation on its aircraft even though an excellent maintenance program keeps the planes in "as good as new" condition.

d. A lawsuit filed against a company is described in notes to the company's financial statements even though the lawsuit was filed with the court shortly after the company's balance sheet date.

e. A real estate developer carries an unsold inventory of condominiums in its accounting records at cost rather than at estimated sales value.

PROBLEM 12-3
Violations of GAAP
(LO 3)

Six independent situations are described below.

a. Morris Construction, Inc., does not have sufficient current assets to qualify for a much needed loan. Therefore, the corporation included among its current assets the personal savings accounts of several major shareholders, as these shareholders have promised to invest more money in the corporation if necessary.

b. First Bank incurred large losses on uncollectible agricultural loans. On average, these loans call for payments to be received over a period of 10 years. Therefore, First Bank is amortizing its losses from the uncollectible loans against the revenue that will be earned over this 10-year period.

c. The Ghost of Yonge Street, a popular play, has sold out in advance for the next 2 years. These ticket sales were recognized as revenue at the time cash was received from the customers.

d. Bay Street Advisory Service has been sued by clients for engaging in illegal securities transactions. No mention is made of this lawsuit in the company's financial statements, as the suit has not been settled and the company cannot objectively estimate the extent of its liability.

e. Carver Company sold for $200,000 land that had been purchased 10 years ago for $150,000. As the general price level had doubled during this period, Carver Company restated the cost of the land at $300,000 and recognized a $100,000 loss.

f. In a recent downturn in the economy, many small businesses have become bankrupt. Although Red River Stores was in no danger of bankruptcy, it reduced the carrying value of its assets to liquidation value to make its financial statements more in tune with the economy.

INSTRUCTIONS

For each situation, identify the accounting principle that has been violated and explain the nature of the violation.

PROBLEM 12-4
Applying Accounting
Principles
(LO 3)

Five independent situations are described below.

a. Pearl Cove Hotel recognizes room rental revenue on the date that a reservation is received. For the summer season, many guests make reservations as much as a year in advance of their intended visit.

b. In prior years Regal Corporation had used the declining-balance method of depreciation for both financial reporting purposes and for income tax purposes. In the current year, Regal began to use straight-line depreciation on all assets for financial reporting purposes but continued to depreciate assets by the declining-balance method for income tax purposes.

c. The liabilities of Ellis Construction are substantially in excess of the company's assets. In order to present a more impressive balance sheet for the business, Roy Ellis, the owner of the company, included in the company's balance sheet such personal assets as his saving account, automobile, and real estate investments.

d. On January 9, 2000, Gable Corporation's only plant was badly damaged by a tornado and will be closed for much of the coming year. No mention was made of this event in the financial statements for the year ended December 31, 1999, as the tornado occurred after year-end.

e. Friday Production Limited follows a policy of valuing its plant assets at liquidation values in the company's balance sheet. No depreciation is recorded on these assets. Instead, a loss is recognized if the liquidation values decline from one year to the next. If the liquidation values increase during the year, a gain is recognized.

INSTRUCTIONS

For each situation, indicate the accounting principle or concept, if any, that has been violated and explain briefly the nature of the violation. If you believe the treatment *is in accord with generally accepted principles,* state this as your position and briefly defend it.

PROBLEM 12-5
Evaluating Applications of
Accounting Principles
(LO 3)

Assume that you are an independent public accountant performing audits of financial statements. In the course of your work, you encounter the following situations:

a. Reliable Appliance Limited sells appliances on long-term payment plans. The company uses the instalment method of recognizing revenue in its financial statements. Uncollectible accounts consistently range between 1.5% and 2.0% of net sales.

b. Akron Labs has spent $700,000 during the year in a very imaginative advertising campaign. The controller is sure that the advertising will generate revenue in future periods, but he has no idea how much revenue will be produced or over what period of time it will be earned. Therefore, he has decided to follow the "conservative" policy of charging the advertising expenditures to expense in the current period.

c. Taylor Corporation has purchased special-purpose equipment, designed to work with other machinery already in place in Taylor's assembly line. Due to the special nature of this equipment, it has virtually no resale value to any other company. Therefore, Taylor's accountant has charged the entire cost of this special-purpose equipment to expense in the current period.

d. Architectural Associates charges all purchases of drafting supplies directly to expense. At year-end, the company makes no entry to record the fact that $200 to $300 of these supplies remain on hand.

e. Newton Company prepares financial statements four times each year. For convenience, these statements are prepared when business is slow and the accounting staff is not busy with other matters. Last year, financial statements were prepared for the two-month period ended February 28, the five-month period ended July 31, the three-month period ended October 31, and the one-month period ended November 30.

INSTRUCTIONS

Discuss each of the above situations. If you consider the treatment to be in conformity with generally accepted accounting principles, explain why. If you do not, explain which principle or principles have been violated, and also explain how the situation should have been reported.

PROBLEM 12-6
Alternative Methods of Income Recognition
(LO 3, 4)

Early in 1999, Roadbuilders, Inc., was notified that it was the successful bidder on the construction of a section of a highway. The bid price for the project was $24 million. Construction began in 1999 and will take about 27 months to complete; the deadline for completion is in April of 2001.

The contract calls for payments of $6 million per year to Roadbuilders, Inc., for 4 years, beginning in 1999. (After the project is complete, the government will also pay a reasonable interest charge on the unpaid balance of the contract.) The company estimates that construction costs will total $16 million, of which $6 million will be incurred in 1999, $8 million in 2000, and $2 million in 2001.

The controller of the company, Joe Morgan, recognizes that there are a number of ways he might account for this contract. He might recognize income at the time the contract is completed (completed-contract method), in April of 2001. Alternatively, he might recognize income during construction (percentage-of-completion method), in proportion to the percentage of the total cost incurred in each of the 3 years. Finally, he might recognize income in proportion to the percentage of the total contract price collected in instalment receipts during the 4-year period (instalment method).

INSTRUCTIONS

a. Prepare a schedule (in millions of dollars) showing the profit that would be recognized on this project in each of the 4 years (1999 through 2002) under each of the three accounting methods being considered by the controller. Assume that the timing and construction costs go according to plan. (Ignore the interest revenue relating to the unpaid balance of the contract.)

b. Explain which accounting method you consider to be ***most*** appropriate in this situation. Also explain why you consider the other two methods less appropriate.

PROBLEM 12-7
Alternative Methods of Revenue Recognition
(LO 3, 4)

Halifax Boat Works builds custom sailboats. During the first year of operations, the company built four boats for Island Charter, a well-established and profitable company. The four boats had a total cost of $216,000 and were sold for a total price of $360,000, due on an instalment basis. Island Charter paid $120,000 of this sales price during the first year, plus an additional amount for interest charges.

At year-end, work is in progress on two other boats that are 40% complete. The contract price for these two boats totals $250,000 and costs incurred on these boats during the year total $60,000 (40% of estimated total costs of $150,000).

INSTRUCTIONS

a. Compute the gross profit for Halifax Boat Works during its first year of operations under each of the following methods. (Interest earned from Island Charter Company does not enter into the computation of gross profit.)
   (1) Gross profit is recognized by a percentage-of-completion method.
   (2) Gross profit is recognized by the instalment method.

b. Which method is more appropriate from the revenue recognition viewpoint? Explain.

PROBLEM 12-8
Ethical Dilemmas
(LO 8, 9)

Below are five independent cases that may confront professional accountants. In each case, identify the specific fundamental principle(s) that should guide the accountant's conduct, and indicate the ethical course of action. If the situation does not create any ethical problem, briefly explain why not.

a. Brewster, a management accountant, works for the Department of National Defence. Part of her job is to evaluate bids of various defence contractors for the Department business. In the course of her work, she has come to know many people in the defence industry quite well. Today John Helms, a vice-president with General Systems Corporation, a defence contractor, offered Brewster the use of a condominium at a nearby ski resort any time she wanted to use it. He explained, "I know you like to ski. Our company owns this condominium, but no one ever seems to use it. Here's the key; just consider the place yours."

b. Bello, a public accountant, has been requested to audit the financial statements of Bello Corporation, a family business. The business is owned and operated entirely by Bello's parents, brothers, and sisters. Bello has no direct financial interest in the business and does not personally participate in its management.

c. Ross, a management accountant, works for One Million Auto Parts. The vice-president of marketing has asked Ross to prepare a summary of the market value of the company's inventory, arranged by geographic sales territories. Ross does not know the intended use of this summary. He does know, of course, that generally accepted accounting principles do not permit the valuation of inventories at market value in financial statements.

d. Jacobs is a member of a public accounting firm that audits two banks. Jacobs is the firm's specialist in the banking industry. Yesterday, she received a request that her firm audit the financial statements of First National, one of the largest banks in the country.

e. Two months ago, Arnold Chiou, a management accountant, worked as a cost accountant for Ewing Oil, but he is now employed by WestStar Oil. A manager at WestStar tells Chiou that WestStar is thinking of cutting its prices to win market share from Ewing. However, the manager needs to know Ewing Oil's per-litre production cost in order to know which company is likely to win a price war.

PROBLEM 12-9
More Ethical Dilemmas
(LO 8, 9)

Below are five independent cases that may confront professional accountants. In each case, identify the specific fundamental principles that should guide the accountant's conduct, and indicate the ethical course of action. If the situation does not create any ethical problem, briefly explain why not.

a. Brown, a public accountant, has been engaged by Marshal Corporation to help the company design a more efficient accounting system. In the course of this engagement, Brown learns that in the preceding year, Marshal prepared its income tax return in a manner that understated the amount of income taxes due. Brown was not involved in the preparation of this tax return. However, assume that she will receive a 10% "finder's fee" by providing information that assists the government in collecting additional taxes owed by another taxpayer.

Brown is considering alerting the government to the additional taxes owed by Marshal.

b. Huang, a management accountant, is asked by his employer to prepare financial statements in which depreciation expense is computed by the straight-line method. Huang knows that the company uses the declining-balance depreciation method in its income tax return.

c. Porter, a public accountant, considers Commuter Airlines to be a well-managed company with a good future. For years, Porter has been purchasing stock in Commuter Airlines as a means of saving for her children's university education. Recently, Porter has received a request from Commuter Airlines to assist them in the preparation of its income tax return.

d. DMX Corporation does custom manufacturing and bills each of its customers on a "cost plus" basis. In advertising, DMX uses the slogan, "We'll treat you like our only customer."

DMX has just purchased for $300,000 special machinery that will be used on seven separate contracts. Swartz, a management accountant at DMX, is told by his supervisor to charge each of these contracts with the entire $300,000 cost. The supervisor explains, "We would have had to buy this machinery if we were working on just one contract, and in that case, the customer would be charged the entire $300,000. So we'll just treat each customer as if it were our only customer."

e. Mandella, a public accountant, is engaged in the audit of Wells Medical Products. Wells is in financial difficulties and will be using the audited financial statements in its effort to raise much needed capital. The company hopes to issue 10-year bonds payable in the near future.

Mandella learns that Wells is a defendant in numerous lawsuits alleging that Microtain, a product produced by Wells in the early 1990s, caused birth defects. The lawsuits probably will not be resolved for perhaps 5, 10, or 15 years. If Wells should lose the suit, the damages awarded to the plaintiffs could bankrupt the company.

The chief financial officer for Wells tells Mandella, "Look, we aren't about to disclose this stuff in our financial statements. First, we're innocent; Microtain never hurt anyone. When it's all said and done, we won't owe a dime. Also, if we lose, we'll appeal. These suits won't even be settled until long after our 10-year bond issue has been repaid. If you insist on disclosing this mess in the financial statements, we'll never get our financing. We'll have to close up, and thousands of our employees will lose their jobs. In short, I can't allow disclosure of this information; you'll just have to regard it as 'confidential.' "

Analytical and Decision Problems and Cases

A&D 12-1
Gotta Match?
(LO 3)

In determining when to recognize an expenditure as expense, accountants attempt to apply the matching principle. Listed below are 10 types of costs frequently encountered by business organizations.

Types of Costs

1. The cost of merchandise purchased for resale.
2. The cost to an auto dealer of a training program for mechanics. On average, mechanics stay with the dealership for 4 years.
3. Sales commissions owed to employees for sales in the current period but payable in the next period.
4. The cost of a 2-year insurance policy.
5. The amount of accounts receivable estimated to be uncollectible.
6. The cost of expensive factory equipment with an estimated life of 10 years.
7. Research costs that may benefit the company for a decade or more if successful products are discovered and brought to market.
8. The cost of 10 wastebaskets with an estimated useful life of 10 years.
9. Interest on notes payable that has accrued during one period but is not payable until a future period.
10. The cost of an advertising campaign promoting the opening of a new store that is expected to remain in operation for 20 years.

INSTRUCTIONS

Indicate in which period or periods these costs should be recognized as expense.

A&D 12-2
"Trade-Offs" among
Accounting Principles
(LO 3)

It is not possible to be consistent with all accounting principles all the time. Sometimes trade-offs are necessary; accountants may need to compromise one accounting principle or goal in order to achieve another more fully.

INSTRUCTIONS

Describe a situation that requires a trade-off between the following sets of principles or goals:

a. The relevance of accounting information to decision makers and the need for this information to be reliable.

b. The comparability of information reported by different companies and the idea that a company should consistently apply the same accounting methods from year to year.

c. The realization (recognition) principle and the need for relatively timely information.

d. The desire to match revenue with expenses and the quest for objectivity.

A&D 12-3
GAAP from an Auditor's
Perspective
(LO 3)

Assume that you are an independent public accountant performing audits of financial statements. In the course of your work, you encounter the following situations:

a. Gala Magazine receives most of its revenue in the form of 12-month subscriptions. Even though this subscription revenue has already been received in cash, the company's controller defers recognition in the income statement; the revenue is recognized on a monthly basis as the monthly issues of the magazine are mailed to subscribers.

b. Due to the bankruptcy of a competitor, Regis Trucking was able to buy plant assets worth at least $400,000 for the "bargain price" of $300,000. In order to reflect the benefits of this bargain purchase in the financial statements, the company recorded the assets at a cost of $400,000 and reported a $100,000 "gain on purchase of plant assets."

c. Metro Development Company built a 400-unit furnished apartment complex. All materials and furnishings used in this project that had a unit cost of less than $200 were charged immediately to expense. The total cost of these items amounted to $6 million.

d. In January 2001, the main plant of Hillside Manufacturing Limited was destroyed in a fire. As this event happened in 2001, no loss was shown in the income statement for the year ended December 31, 2000. However, the event was thoroughly disclosed in notes to the 2000 financial statements.

e. In an effort to match revenue with all related expenses in an objective manner, Brentwood Company has established "useful life" standards for all types of expenditures. For example, expenditures for advertising are amortized over 3 years; the costs of employee training programs, 5 years; and research costs, 10 years.

INSTRUCTIONS

Discuss each of the above situations. If you consider the treatment to be in conformity with generally accepted accounting principles, explain why. If you do not, explain which principle or principles have been violated, and also explain how the situation should have been reported.

A&D 12-4
How Much Is the Restaurant?
(LO 3)

Rich & Famous, a luxury ski resort hotel located in Whistler, has been expanding its operation in the past few years to meet the increasing influx of affluent skiers from all over the globe. Last summer, Rich & Famous decided to add a gourmet restaurant for its wealthy guests. A contract was signed with a contractor to build the restaurant for $800,000. Since the skiing season usually begins in mid-December and the new restaurant was expected to attract more skiers to the hotel, Rich & Famous extracted a guarantee from the contractor to complete the construction of the restaurant by December 15; otherwise, a penalty of $8,000 a day will be deducted from the contract price until the restaurant is completed.

Unfortunately, the restaurant was not completed until December 31. Consequently, Rich & Famous deducted $128,000 (16 days × $8,000) from the contract price and paid only $672,000. In spite of the rather heavy penalty, Rich & Famous felt that it had lost not only some goodwill but also revenue as some of the guests left earlier than expected because the restaurant was not in place as promised.

At the end of the year, the president of Rich & Famous wanted to show the restaurant at its contract price of $800,000 and the penalty of $128,000 as revenue in the financial statements. However, the controller argued that the restaurant should be shown at its actual cost of $672,000. This upset the president and he shot back at the controller: "I don't know on what accounting principles you based your argument. But it simply doesn't make sense to me. Are you telling me that if the construction delay were 102 days rather than 16, you wouldn't even show the restaurant in the balance sheet because the contract price would be reduced to zero? Are you then saying that this new gourmet restaurant is not an asset? What do I do with the $16,000 penalty in excess of the contract price? I certainly think that it should be reported as revenue. Now, let me tell you one more thing: you and I know that the delay cost us more than $8,000 a day in revenue."

INSTRUCTIONS

Discuss the accounting principles and concepts underlying the position of the controller and of the president and defend their respective positions.

A&D 12-5
"What? Me? Fired?"
(LO 8, 9)

Christine Davis is a management accountant for CalTex Industries. Davis believes that she is being asked to accumulate inappropriate costs on a "cost plus" contract. All costs accumulated on the contract ultimately are billed to the customer (along with a markup representing CalTex's profit margin), an agency of the government.
a. Does this situation represent an ethical problem for Davis? Explain.
b. If you believe that an ethical problem exists, briefly explain how Davis should resolve it.
c. Assume that as a result of taking the steps that you suggested in part **b,** Davis is fired. Does Davis have an ethical obligation to inform the governmental agency of her suspicions that it is being overcharged? Explain.

A&D 12-6
Ethics in the "Real World"
(LO 8, 9)

Bring into class a copy of a newspaper or magazine article describing a situation in which professional accountants probably faced an ethical dilemma. (Your article need not specifically mention the accountants' roles in the situation. Also, your article need not be current; you may select any article from any business publication.)

Describe the ethical problems that you believe confronted the accountants in this situation and the courses of action that should have been considered. Also, express your ***personal opinion*** as to whether or not the accountants acted in an ethical manner, including the reasons behind your opinion. Finally, discuss what ***you*** would have done in the accountants' place, identifying any factors that may have made your decision difficult.

Answers to Self-Test Questions

1. b 2. c 3. c 4. d 5. c

ANNUAL REPORT OF LOBLAW COMPANIES LIMITED

On the following pages we present the 1997 annual report of Loblaw Companies Limited, a publicly held corporation. This report was selected to illustrate many of the financial reporting concepts discussed in this textbook. But not all of the terminology and accounting policies appearing in this report are consistent with our text discussions. This illustrates some of the diversity that exists in financial reporting.

Loblaw Companies Limited

Annual Report 1997

Loblaw Companies Limited is Canada's largest retail and wholesale food distributor with operations across the country.

Loblaw Companies strives to provide superior returns to its shareholders through a combination of share price appreciation and dividends. To this end, it follows certain fundamental operating principles. It concentrates on food retailing, with the objective of providing consumers with the best in one-stop shopping for everyday household needs. It maintains a significant program of reinvestment in and expansion of its existing markets. It is highly selective in acquisitions and continues to invest in products and technology. Loblaw seeks long term, stable growth, taking managed operating risks from a strong balance sheet position.

Loblaw Companies is one of the largest private employers in Canada with over 70,000 employees throughout the business and has a responsibility to provide fair wages and secure employment. Loblaw believes this responsibility can best be met in a stable, low cost operating environment where all associated with the Company accept the need to continuously improve its ability to serve our customers.

Contents

Geographic Divisions

		Total West	British Columbia	Alberta	Saskatchewan	Manitoba	Yukon	Ontario
Retail	Superstore	40	13	13	6	6	1	1
	WHOLESALE	19	7	5	4	1		2
	Extra Foods✦	68	3	25	24	16		
Wholesale	SHOP EASY	65	5	16	29	15		
	LUCKY·DOLLAR	206	22	19	109	56		
	SuperValu	37	35	2				
	Extra Foods✦	15	14	1				
West	Total	450	99	81	172	94	1	3
	Independents	3,446	43	1,400	1,871	132		

** The line of President's Choice™ products continues
to be actively marketed into select supermarket chains
in 18 States, Bermuda, Barbados, Israel and Colombia.*

1997 Review
West
- *Record sales and operating income.*
- *5 Superstores and 9 conventional stores opened.*
- *7 Wholesale Clubs opened, increasing the number of outlets by more than 50%.*
- *Retail sales increased 18%; same-store sales 8%.*
- *Increased market share.*
- *Average retail square footage increased 13%.*
- *Wholesale profits increased from higher retail volumes and warehouse and distribution network efficiencies.*

1998 Outlook
West
- *Continued focus on retail sales growth.*
- *Planned openings of 5 Real Canadian Superstores, 5 Real Canadian Wholesale Clubs and 12 conventional stores.*
- *Increased market share.*
- *Improved profitability.*

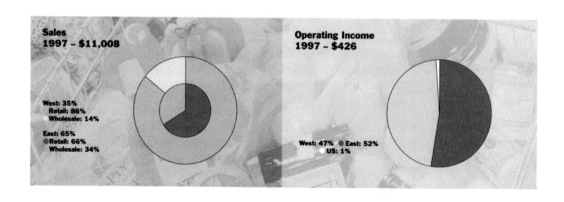

**Sales
1997 – $11,008**

West: 35%
Retail: 86%
Wholesale: 14%

East: 65%
Retail: 66%
Wholesale: 34%

**Operating Income
1997 – $426**

West: 47%　East: 52%
US: 1%

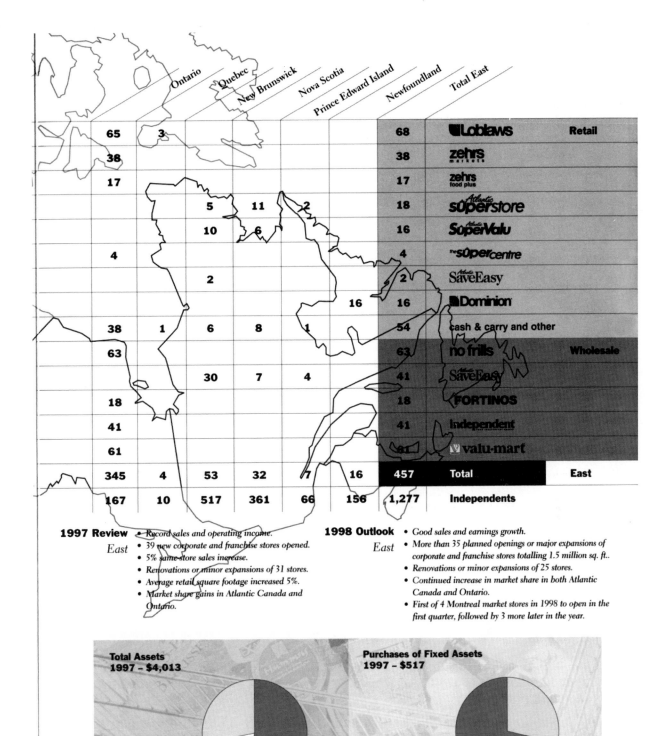

Ontario	Quebec	New Brunswick	Nova Scotia	Prince Edward Island	Newfoundland	Total East		
65	3					68	**Loblaws**	**Retail**
38						38	zehrs markets	
17						17	zehrs food plus	
		5	11		2	18	*Atlantic* superstore	
		10	6			16	*Atlantic* SuperValu	
4						4	the supercentre	
			2			2	*Atlantic* SaveEasy	
					16	16	Dominion	
38	1	6	8	1		54	cash & carry and other	
63						63	no frills	**Wholesale**
		30	7	4		41	*Atlantic* SaveEasy	
18						18	FORTINOS	
41						41	Independent	
61						61	valu-mart	
345	**4**	**53**	**32**	**7**	**16**	**457**	**Total**	**East**
167	10	517	361	66	156	1,277	**Independents**	

1997 Review
East
- Record sales and operating income.
- 39 new corporate and franchise stores opened.
- 5% same-store sales increase.
- Renovations or minor expansions of 31 stores.
- Average retail square footage increased 5%.
- Market share gains in Atlantic Canada and Ontario.

1998 Outlook
East
- Good sales and earnings growth.
- More than 35 planned openings or major expansions of corporate and franchise stores totalling 1.5 million sq. ft..
- Renovations or minor expansions of 25 stores.
- Continued increase in market share in both Atlantic Canada and Ontario.
- First of 4 Montreal market stores in 1998 to open in the first quarter, followed by 3 more later in the year.

Total Assets
1997 – $4,013

West: 28%   East: 53%
US: 19%

Purchases of Fixed Assets
1997 – $517

West: 29%   East: 71%

Financial Highlights

(in millions of dollars)		**1997**	1996	1995
Operating Results	Sales	**11,008**	9,848	9,854
	Trading profit (EBITDA) [1]	**573**	481	449
	Operating income (EBIT)	**426**	359	320
	Earnings before income taxes	**382**	313	271
	Net earnings	**213**	174	147
Financial Position	Total debt and debt equivalents	**1,289**	1,155	980
	Total shareholders' equity	**1,495**	1,311	1,160
	Total assets	**4,013**	3,531	3,197
Cash Flow	Cash flow from operations	**426**	262	270
	Purchases of fixed assets	**517**	389	302
Per Common Share (dollars)	Net earnings	**.88**	.72	.60
	Cash flow from operations	**1.76**	1.08	1.12
	Dividends declared	**.15**	.12	.11
	Year end dividend rate	**.16**	.12	.12
	Book value	**6.08**	5.35	4.74
	Market price – year end	**26.00**	14.25	10.29
	– high	**26.85**	14.50	10.50
	– low	**14.15**	10.33	7.75
Financial Ratios [2]	Return on common equity	**15.3 %**	14.2 %	13.4 %
	Return on total assets	**14.1 %**	13.5 %	12.2 %
	Return on sales			
	Trading profit (EBITDA) [1]	**5.2 %**	4.9 %	4.6 %
	Earnings before income taxes	**3.5 %**	3.2 %	2.8 %
	Net earnings	**1.9 %**	1.8 %	1.5 %
	Cash flow from operations	**3.9 %**	2.7 %	2.7 %
	Interest coverage on total debt and debt equivalents	**9.7:1**	7.9:1	6.0:1
	Total debt and debt equivalents to equity	**.34:1**	.33:1	.25:1

1. Trading profit is defined as operating income before depreciation and amortization (EBITDA).

2. For purposes of calculating financial ratios, debt is reduced by cash and short term investments net of bank advances and notes payable.

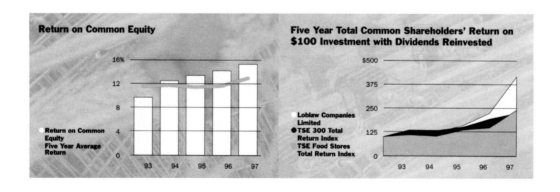

Report to Shareholders

W. Galen Weston
Chairman

Richard J. Currie
President

The year 1997 was an outstanding one for Loblaw Companies by any measure. Sales were up 12 percent from 1996, at $11.01 billion, with operating income of $426 million, net earnings of $213 million and earnings per share of $.88 all setting new highs.

Earnings per share have tripled ($.88 from $.29) in the last five years.

Sales throughout the Canadian business are now increasing rapidly, at the rate of about $1 billion in 1997, following a $.7 billion growth in 1996, as stores in existing markets are enlarged and modernized and as we enter new markets. This growth follows a six year period (1990 - 1995) of flat sales in the West of approximately $2.9 billion per year, during which time, store and customer rationalizations in wholesale operations were completed.

In fact, sales is the "big story" in Loblaw Companies today. In a total market (food sold through stores of any type) that is growing about 3 percent a year, our Canadian sales have grown by 20 percent in the last 2 years (26 percent in the West and 17 percent in the East). We expect sales to at least match these growth rates in 1998 and 1999.

The rapidly improving sales and operating performance has been driven over the last five years, by average corporate store size increasing 36 percent (from 32.0 thousand square feet in 1992 to 43.6 thousand square feet in 1997), while sales per average square foot also improved ($519 in 1992 vs. $534 in 1997). The larger store size has enabled us to provide consumers with a greater variety of everyday household needs, thereby increasing our gross margin dollars, without increasing our expenses at the same rate. One example of more fully meeting customer needs is that we now operate 167 full line pharmacies within corporate stores across Canada and an additional 29 pharmacies in franchised stores.

The financial implication of this change in store size and product mix is that Loblaw can increase sales and profitability rates at the same time. To illustrate, in 1995 operating income was 3.2% of sales, in 1996 it improved to 3.6% of sales and in 1997 a further improvement to 3.9% took place.

The present capital investment program and sales expectations are based on our belief that there is still much room for Loblaw Companies to grow across all of Canada. In March of 1998 we will open our first store in the Montreal area, the second-largest city in the country and one in which we currently have no presence. Plans are to open 3 to 5 stores per year in that market over the next several years. Growth opportunities in the West are also significant as current market shares in Alberta and British Columbia could triple before matching those already achieved in Ontario.

Growth is not only driven by asset investments but also by marketing initiatives emanating from our controlled label program, which continues to represent a unique and growing part of our product offering to consumers. In 1997, of the $11.01 billion total sales, $1.6 billion or 15 percent was controlled label, including the famous President's Choice™ and no name™ products. An important part of this program has been the establishment of our Club Pack™, or large-size and multipack packages in response to

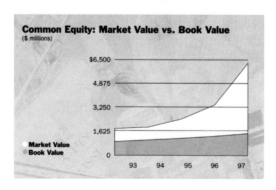

Common Equity: Market Value vs. Book Value
($ millions)

consumer demand. Their sales in 1997 approached $470 million, from a virtual standing start five years ago as we responded to the warehouse membership club incursion into Canada.

Again in 1997, Loblaw Companies increased its number of unionized employees, now at 55,700, compared with 50,200 at year end 1996 and 33,000 at the beginning of the decade. We continue to employ one of the largest number of unionized Canadians of any company in Canada and we are growing that number faster than any other business. Our union relations have been solid, based on straight talk and the ensuing respect on both sides. At present, we are working towards convincing union leadership that 100 percent unionization of stores or warehouses leads in many cases to less total union members than does a partial unionization. All our new food competitors, be they mass merchandisers (Wal-Mart, Zellers, etc.), warehouse clubs (Price-Costco) or promotional drug stores are not unionized. They are non-union for a reason and it is that non-union is a lower cost operation. Lower cost means lower prices. But no customer can be expected to pay higher prices to us because we pay higher wages to our workers. Just as we have adapted and reduced our costs in a creative fashion to grow despite these new, non-union non-traditional formats, so must unions now use their creative energies to increase and even maintain their membership in a changing retail world.

Loblaw Companies has no intention of pausing or resting on its laurels and it is operating from a clear strategic direction.

The massive capital investment program now well under way is increasing our total store square footage by about 10 percent a year. Large, modern stores will improve our market share and market share per store in every region.

Within that program, we are committed to making total perishables (from meat and produce to home meal solutions, i.e., in-store prepared meals) comparable in quality and value to the controlled label program that forms the base or core of our marketing activities. We intend that our perishables be superior to any other chain. To that end we have established and enhanced our own produce procurement operations in California, Florida and Texas to distinguish our quality from the products generally available to the Canadian market. We have also recently established a relationship with Mövenpick™, to expand into the best mix of in-store prepared home meal solutions.

With stores, controlled labels and perishables of the highest order, we are strongly building and positioning towards our objective of providing Canadian consumers with the best in "one-stop shopping for everyday household needs". Those

needs have increased dramatically over the years, from food to pharmacy, health and beauty care, to general merchandise, to photo finishing, dry cleaning, flowers and books. Those needs now even include banking, an industry to which we are bringing "fresh financial thinking" with President's Choice Financial™ in trials presently under way in Ottawa and St. Thomas, Ontario and Calgary, Alberta.

For some years we have noted in the Annual Report that "the success or failure of retailers depends on the attitude of the employees". The business is now investing over half a billion dollars a year in its future, over twice its net earnings and is also paying out well over $1 billion each year in wages and benefits to its employees. Such figures demonstrate more than words ever can the depth of our commitment to the business and its future. We believe that food retailing is about the seemingly conflicting elements of innovation and detail, growth and low cost, people and technology, and finally, fear and courage. Over the past 20+ years, this Company has faced and overcome risks of all types, both internally and in the marketplace. While the market value of Loblaw Companies has increased by over 150 times in that period, we think its best days are still ahead of it and we look forward to what is yet to come.

W. Galen Weston
Chairman

Richard J. Currie
President

Responsibility for Financial Reporting

Management is responsible for the preparation and presentation of the consolidated financial statements and all other information in the Annual Report. This responsibility includes the selection of appropriate accounting principles and methods in addition to making the judgements and estimates necessary to prepare financial statements in accordance with generally accepted accounting principles. It also includes ensuring that the other financial information presented elsewhere in the Annual Report is consistent with the financial statements.

To provide reasonable assurance that assets are safeguarded and that relevant and reliable financial information is being produced, management maintains a system of internal controls. Internal auditors who are employees of the Company, review and evaluate internal controls on management's behalf, coordinating this work with the independent shareholders' auditors. The financial statements have been audited by the independent shareholders' auditors, KPMG, whose report follows.

The Board of Directors, acting through an Audit Committee which is comprised solely of directors who are not employees of the Company, is responsible for determining that management fulfills its responsibilities in the preparation of financial statements and the financial control of operations. The Audit Committee recommends the independent auditors for appointment by the shareholders. It meets regularly with financial management, internal auditors and independent auditors to discuss internal controls, auditing matters and financial reporting issues. The independent shareholders' auditors have unrestricted access to the Audit Committee. The Committee reviews the Consolidated Financial Statements and the Management Discussion and Analysis prior to the Board approving them for inclusion in the Annual Report.

Richard J. Currie
President

Donald G. Reid
Executive Vice President

Stephen A. Smith
Senior Vice President, Controller

Toronto, Canada March 9, 1998

Auditors' Report

To the Shareholders of Loblaw Companies Limited:
We have audited the consolidated balance sheets of Loblaw Companies Limited as at January 3, 1998, December 28, 1996 and December 30, 1995 and the consolidated statements of earnings, retained earnings and cash flow for the 53, 52 and 52 week periods then ended. These consolidated financial statements are the responsibility of the Company's management. Our responsibility is to express an opinion on these consolidated financial statements based on our audits.

We conducted our audits in accordance with generally accepted auditing standards. Those standards require that we plan and perform an audit to obtain reasonable assurance whether the consolidated financial statements are free of material misstatement. An audit includes examining, on a test basis, evidence supporting the amounts and disclosures in the consolidated financial statements. An audit also includes assessing the accounting principles used and significant estimates made by management, as well as evaluating the overall consolidated financial statement presentation.

In our opinion, these consolidated financial statements present fairly, in all material respects, the financial position of the Company as at January 3, 1998, December 28, 1996 and December 30, 1995 and the results of its operations and the changes in its financial position for the periods then ended in accordance with generally accepted accounting principles.

KPMG

Chartered Accountants Toronto, Canada March 9, 1998

Consolidated Statement of Earnings

53 Weeks Ended January 3, 1998 (in millions of dollars)		**1997** **(53 Weeks)**	1996 (52 Weeks)	1995 (52 Weeks)
Sales		**$11,008**	$9,848	$9,854
Operating Expenses	Cost of sales, selling and			
	administrative expenses	**10,435**	9,367	9,405
	Depreciation and amortization	**147**	122	129
		10,582	9,489	9,534
Operating Income		**426**	359	320
Interest Expense (Income)	Long term	**78**	67	66
	Short term	**(34)**	(21)	(12)
		44	46	54
Net Gain on Sale of United States Retail Business (note 2)				5
Earnings Before Income Taxes		**382**	313	271
Income Taxes (note 3)		**169**	139	124
Net Earnings for the Period		**$ 213**	$ 174	$ 147
Net Earnings per Common Share (in dollars)		**$ .88**	$ .72	$ .60

Consolidated Statement of Retained Earnings

53 Weeks Ended January 3, 1998 (in millions of dollars)		**1997** **(53 Weeks)**	1996 (52 Weeks)	1995 (52 Weeks)
Retained Earnings, Beginning of Period		**$ 1,046**	$ 902	$ 783
	Net earnings for the period	**213**	174	147
		1,259	1,076	930
	Dividends declared			
	Preferred shares	**1**	1	2
	Common shares, per share – 15¢			
	(1996 – 12¢, 1995 – 11¢)	**37**	29	26
		38	30	28
Retained Earnings, End of Period		**$ 1,221**	$1,046	$ 902

Consolidated Balance Sheet

As at January 3, 1998
(in millions of dollars)

		1997	1996	1995
Assets				
Current Assets	Cash and short term			
	investments (note 4)	**$ 776**	$ 720	$ 692
	Accounts receivable	**150**	158	164
	Inventories	**707**	659	610
	Prepaid expenses and other assets	**48**	16	25
		1,681	1,553	1,491
Franchise Investments and Receivables		**113**	113	94
Fixed Assets (note 5)		**2,093**	1,738	1,491
Goodwill		**38**	40	42
Other Assets		**88**	87	79
		$4,013	$3,531	$3,197
Liabilities				
Current Liabilities	Bank advances and notes payable	**$ 362**	$ 413	$ 311
	Accounts payable and			
	accrued liabilities	**1,084**	938	937
	Taxes payable	**21**	40	42
	Long term debt and debt equivalents			
	due within one year (note 7)	**12**	8	22
		1,479	1,399	1,312
Long Term Debt and Debt Equivalents (note 7)		**915**	734	647
Other Liabilities		**47**	30	41
Deferred Income Taxes		**77**	57	37
		2,518	2,220	2,037
Shareholders' Equity				
Share Capital (note 8)		**274**	265	258
Retained Earnings		**1,221**	1,046	902
		1,495	1,311	1,160
		$4,013	$3,531	$3,197

Approved by the Board

W. Galen Weston

W. Galen Weston

Director

Richard J. Currie

Richard J. Currie

Director

Consolidated Cash Flow Statement

53 Weeks Ended January 3, 1998 (in millions of dollars)		**1997** **(53 Weeks)**	1996 (52 Weeks)	1995 (52 Weeks)
Operations	Net earnings	**$ 213**	$ 174	$ 147
	Depreciation and amortization	**147**	122	129
	Gain on sale of fixed assets	**(8)**	(5)	(6)
	Deferred income taxes	**15**	12	19
		367	303	289
Provided from (used for) Working Capital		**59**	(41)	(19)
Cash Flow from Operations		**426**	262	270
Investment	Purchases of fixed assets	**(517)**	(389)	(302)
	Sale of United States retail business (note 2)			368
	Proceeds from sale of fixed assets	**25**	25	19
	(Increase) in franchise investments and receivables		(19)	(8)
	Net decrease (increase) in other items	**24**	(11)	(25)
		(468)	(394)	52
Net Cash (Out) In Before Financing and Dividends		**(42)**	(132)	322
Financing	Long term debt and debt equivalents			
	– Issued	**200**	100	6
	– Retired	**(15)**	(27)	(78)
	Share Capital			
	– Issued	**9**	8	3
	– Retired		(1)	(60)
		194	80	(129)
Dividends		**(45)**	(22)	(28)
Increase (Decrease) in Cash		**107**	(74)	165
Cash at Beginning of Period		**307**	381	216
Cash at End of Period		**$ 414**	$ 307	$ 381

Cash is defined as cash and short term investments net of bank advances and notes payable.

Notes to Consolidated Financial Statements 53 Weeks Ended January 3, 1998
(In millions of dollars except Share Capital)

1. Summary of Significant Accounting Policies

Basis of Consolidation The consolidated financial statements include the accounts of the Company and all subsidiaries. The effective interest of Loblaw Companies Limited in the equity share capital of all principal subsidiaries is 100%.

Revenue Recognition Sales include retail sales revenues to consumers through corporate stores operated by the Company and wholesale sales to and service fees from franchised independent stores and independent accounts but exclude sales to corporate stores and other inter-company sales.

Cash Offsetting Cash balances, for which the Company has a right and intent of offset, are used to reduce reported short term borrowings.

Inventories Retail store inventories are stated at the lower of cost and net realizable value less normal profit margin. Wholesale inventories are stated at the lower of cost and net realizable value.

Fixed Assets Fixed assets are stated at cost, including capitalized interest. Depreciation is recorded principally on a straight line basis to amortize the cost of these assets over their estimated useful lives.

Estimated useful lives range from 25 to 40 years for buildings and 3 to 8 years for equipment and fixtures. Leasehold improvements are depreciated over the lesser of the applicable useful life and term of the lease.

Translation of Foreign Currencies Foreign currency balances are translated at the current exchange rate at each period end. Exchange gains or losses arising from the translation of foreign currency balances are included in the current period's earnings. Revenues and expenses are translated at the average exchange rate for the period.

Goodwill Goodwill arises on the acquisition of subsidiaries. It is the excess of the cost of the acquisition over the fair value of the underlying net tangible assets acquired. Goodwill is being amortized on a straight line basis determined for each acquisition over the estimated life of the benefit. The weighted average remaining amortization period is 23 years. Any permanent impairment in value, based on projected future earnings, is written off against earnings.

Derivative Financial Instruments The Company uses interest rate derivatives and cross-currency swaps to manage risks arising from fluctuations in exchange and interest rates. The income or expense arising from these instruments is included in interest expense. Unrealized gains or losses on cross-currency swaps are offset by unrealized gains or losses on the United States dollar net assets. The net exchange difference is recorded in the income statement.

Post Retirement Benefits The cost of post retirement health, insurance and other benefits, other than pensions, is expensed when paid. The cost of pension benefits is accrued as earned.

2. Sale of United States Retail Business
Substantially all of the assets of the United States retail business were sold at the end of the second quarter of 1995 for proceeds of $368. The net pre-tax gain of $5 included proceeds in excess of net book value, net of costs associated with the disposal. Operating income for the period to date of sale was not significant. Income taxes of $5 applicable to the disposal transaction were included in income taxes.

3. Income Taxes   The Company's effective income tax rate is made up as follows:

	1997	1996	1995
Combined basic Canadian federal and provincial income tax rate	**44.5 %**	44.2 %	43.5 %
Net impact of operating in foreign countries with lower effective tax rates	**(.6)**	(.3)	(1.5)
Other	**.3**	.6	3.9
	44.2 %	44.5 %	45.9 %

4. Cash and Short Term Investments   The Company has $773 (1996 – $717, 1995 – $685) in cash and short term investments held by its non-Canadian subsidiaries. The $41 (1996 – $37, 1995 – $31) income from these investments is included as a reduction of interest expense.

At year end, the Company has included in cash and short term investments an interest bearing demand note receivable of $214 ($150 U.S.) from George Weston Limited, the Company's majority shareholder. Interest has been set at market rates based on LIBOR plus .25%.

5. Fixed Assets

	1997					1996	1995
	Cost	**Accumulated Depreciation**	**Net Book Value**	Cost	Accumulated Depreciation	Net Book Value	Net Book Value
Properties held							
for development	**$ 93**		**$ 93**	$ 126		$ 126	$ 90
Land	**486**		**486**	380		380	332
Buildings	**1,148**	**$ 267**	**881**	996	$235	761	695
Equipment and fixtures	**1,057**	**637**	**420**	898	574	324	242
Leasehold improvements	**315**	**117**	**198**	225	98	127	108
	3,099	**1,021**	**2,078**	2,625	907	1,718	1,467
Capital leases –							
buildings and equipment	**56**	**41**	**15**	56	36	20	24
	$3,155	**$1,062**	**$2,093**	$2,681	$943	$1,738	$1,491

Interest capitalized as part of fixed assets during the period is $11 (1996 – $6, 1995 – $6).

6. Pensions   The Company maintains defined benefit pension plans. Current actuarial estimates indicate that the Company's registered pension plans have a present value of accrued pension benefits of $472 (1996 – $449, 1995 – $446) and a market related value of pension fund assets of $547 (1996 – $498, 1995 – $460). As at January 3, 1998, prepaid pension costs of $79 (1996 – $78, 1995 – $67) relating to these plans are included in other assets.

7. Long Term Debt and Debt Equivalents

	1997	1996	1995
Debentures			
Series 5, 10%, due 2006, retractable annually commencing 1996, redeemable in 2001	**$ 50**	$ 50	$ 50
Series 6, 9.75%, due 2001, retractable annually commencing 1993, redeemable in 1998	**75**	75	75
Series 7, 9%, redeemed 1996			14
Series 8, 10%, due 2007, redeemable in 2002	**61**	61	61
Notes			
11.4%, due 2031	**169**	172	175
8.75%, due 2033	**200**	200	200
Medium Term Notes			
7.34%, due 2001	**100**	100	
5.39% to 2000 and 7.91% thereafter, due 2007, redeemable in 2000	**100**		
6.65%, due 2027, redeemable on demand	**100**		
Other at a weighted average interest rate of 12.1%, due 1998 to 2009	**56**	67	77
Total long term debt	**911**	725	652
Total debt equivalents	**16**	17	17
	927	742	669
Less due within one year	**12**	8	22
Total long term debt and debt equivalents	**$915**	$734	$647

The five year schedule of repayments of long term debt and debt equivalents, at the earlier of maturity or first retraction date, excluding the Series 5 and Series 6 debentures which may be renewed dependent on market conditions at the time of renewal, is as follows: 1998 – $12; 1999 – $11; 2000 – $12; 2001 – $178; 2002 – $1.

Debentures The interest rates on the Series 5 and Series 6 debentures were reset in 1997 at 10% and 9.75% respectively. Current intentions are to reset the interest rate on the Series 5 debentures in 1998 to encourage renewal. The renewal of the Series 6 debentures in 1998 will depend on market conditions. Both Series 5 and Series 6 debentures are excluded from the amount due within one year.

Debt Equivalents First preferred shares, second series (authorized – 1,000,000) – $3.70 cumulative dividend redeemable at $70 each. In 1997, 253,782 shares were issued and outstanding (1996 – 260,006, 1995 – 266,429) in the amount of $16 (1996 – $17, 1995 – $17). Subject to certain exceptions, in each fiscal year, the Company is obligated to apply $.4 to the retirement of these shares.

Subsequent to year end, the Company filed a shelf prospectus to issue up to $500 of Medium Term Notes. During the first quarter of 1998, the Company issued $100 of these notes at 6.45%, due 2028, redeemable on demand.

8. Share Capital

	Number of shares issued			Capital stock (in millions of dollars)		
	1997	1996	1995	**1997**	1996	1995
First preferred shares, first series	**410,852**	410,852	432,752	**$ 20**	$ 20	$ 21
Common shares	**242,780,858**	241,341,158	240,119,838	**254**	245	237
Total capital stock				**$274**	$265	$258
Weighted average common shares	**242,033,135**	240,630,561	239,840,013			

Share Description (in dollars)

First preferred shares, first series (authorized – 1,000,000) – $2.40 cumulative dividend redeemable at $50 each.
Second preferred shares, fourth series - redeemed according to their terms at $500,000 each on March 1, 1995.
Common shares (authorized – unlimited) In 1997, the Company issued 1,439,700 (1996 – 1,221,320, 1995 – 655,800) common shares for cash consideration of $8,822,871 (1996 – $8,332,508, 1995 – $3,782,084) on exercise of employee stock options.

At year end, there were outstanding stock options, which were granted at the market price on the day preceding the grant, to purchase 6,656,965 (1996 – 7,216,450, 1995 – 8,522,920) common shares at prices ranging from $6.125 to $14.25 with a weighted average price of $8.491 (1996 – $7.029, 1995 – $7.01). All options expire on dates ranging from January 6, 1999 to January 3, 2004. The exercise of the stock options would not materially dilute net earnings per common share.

On March 9, 1998, the Company announced its intention to purchase on the Toronto Stock Exchange up to 12,218,040 of its common shares, representing 5% of the common shares outstanding pursuant to a Normal Course Issuer Bid effective March 18, 1998 to March 17, 1999. Purchases will be made by the Company in accordance with the rules and by-laws of the Toronto Stock Exchange and the price which the Company will pay for any such common shares will be the market price of such shares at the time of acquisition.

9. Financial Instruments

Derivatives The Company has entered into cross-currency swaps to exchange $704 Canadian dollar debt for United States dollar debt. The swaps provide a hedge against exchange rate fluctuations on United States dollar net assets, principally cash. The swaps mature as follows: 1999 – $7; 2000 – $119; 2001 – $85; 2002 – $77 and thereafter to 2007 – $416. Currency adjustments receivable or payable arising from the swaps may be settled in cash on maturity or the swap term can be extended. As at January 3, 1998, a currency adjustment of $38 (1996 – $8, 1995 – $8) has been included in other liabilities.

In addition, the Company has entered into interest rate derivatives, converting a net notional $314 of 7.8% fixed rate debt into floating rate debt. The net maturities are as follows: 1998 – $82; 1999 – $46; 2000 – $152; 2001 – $6 and thereafter to 2004 – $28.

An event of default by the counterparties to these derivatives does not create a significant risk because the principal amounts on cross-currency swaps are netted by agreement and there is no exposure to loss of the notional principal amounts on interest rate derivatives.

Fair Value of Financial Instruments The fair value of financial instruments is determined by reference to various market data and other valuation techniques as appropriate. With the exception of the following, the fair value of financial instruments including cash, short term investments, accounts receivable, bank advances, notes payable, accounts payable, accrued liabilities and taxes payable approximates their recorded values.

	1997		1996		1995	
	Carrying Amount	**Estimated Fair Value**	Carrying Amount	Estimated Fair Value	Carrying Amount	Estimated Fair Value
Long term debt and debt equivalents	**$927**	**$1,098**	$742	$898	$669	$760
Interest rate derivatives net asset		**$ 7**		$ 18		$ 2

The following methods and assumptions were used to estimate the fair value of each class of financial instrument for which it is practical to estimate that value.

Long Term Debt and Debt Equivalents The fair value of the Company's long term debt is estimated based on discounted cash flows of the debt using the estimated incremental borrowing rate of the Company for debt of the same remaining maturities. The fair value of the Company's debt equivalents is estimated based on market quotes or the last trade closest to the valuation date.

Interest Rate Derivatives The fair value of the net notional principal of the interest rate derivatives is estimated by discounting cash flows of the derivatives based on the market derivative rates for derivatives of the same remaining maturities.

10. Other Information

Segmented Information The Company's only significant industry segment is food distribution. Geographically segmented information is as follows:

		1997	1996	1995
Sales	Eastern Canada	**$7,182**	$6,514	$6,155
	Western Canada	**3,826**	3,334	3,034
	United States			665
Operating income	Eastern Canada	**$ 220**	$ 173	$ 165
	Western Canada	**200**	168	139
	United States	**6**	18	16
Total assets	Eastern Canada	**$2,122**	$1,875	$1,604
	Western Canada	**1,111**	936	870
	United States	**780**	720	723

United States Operating Income Operating income earned in 1997 is primarily net service fee revenue. The 1996 operating income earned includes $16 received for certain rights related to the cessation of an agreement with Wal-Mart, net service fee revenue and costs related to the disposition of some of the remaining net assets of the former United States businesses. In 1995, operating income is primarily net service fee revenue.

Contingent Liabilities and Commitments Commitments for net operating lease payments total $767 ($901 gross, net of $134 of expected sub-lease income). Net payments for each of the next five years and thereafter are as follows: 1998 – $121; 1999 – $103; 2000 – $79; 2001 – $62; 2002 – $56 and thereafter to 2056 – $346. Gross rentals under leases assigned at the time of sale of United States divisions for which the Company is contingently liable amount to $117.

Related Party Transactions The Company's majority shareholder, George Weston Limited and its subsidiaries are related parties. It is the Company's policy to conduct all transactions and settle balances with related parties on normal trade terms. Total purchases from related companies represent about 4% of cost of sales, selling and administrative expenses.

Pursuant to an investment management agreement, the Company, through a wholly owned subsidiary, manages certain United States cash and short term investments on behalf of a wholly owned subsidiary of George Weston Limited. Management fees are based on market rates and have been included in interest income.

Subsequent to year end, the Company sold its investment in an inactive subsidiary to George Weston Limited resulting in inter-company investment holdings. A legal right of offset exists to ensure no financial statement impact to either company.

Management Discussion and Analysis

Earnings per share improved to $.88 in 1997, a 22% increase from the $.72 earned in 1996. Sales for the year, which included an extra week in 1997, increased by 12% and exceeded $11 billion for the first time.

Operating income improved to $426 million, a 19% increase over the $359 million earned in 1996. After adjusting for the inclusion in 1996 operating income of a $20 million special provision for labour restructuring and a $16 million one time cessation payment received from Wal-Mart, operating income increased by 17% over 1996. The operating margin, defined as operating income (EBIT) divided by sales, improved to 3.9% from 3.6% in 1996 while trading margin, defined as operating income before depreciation and amortization (EBITDA) divided by sales, strengthened to 5.2% from 4.9% in 1996.

Interest expense declined by 4% to $44 million from $46 million in 1996. The effect of the increase in average borrowing levels was offset by lower effective borrowing rates and higher capitalized interest as a result of the increased capital expenditures.

The effective income tax rate declined marginally to 44.2% in 1997 from 44.5% in 1996.

Results of Operations

Sales Loblaw Companies, under an accounting convention common in the food distribution industry, follows a 52 week reporting cycle which periodically necessitates a fiscal year of 53 weeks. The current fiscal year is a 53 week year. The additional week in 1997 added approximately 2% to the year-over-year sales increase. The remaining 10% increase in sales is attributable to an increase in same-store sales and to additional square footage. Excluding the impact of the extra week, same-store sales increased by 4% in 1997 and 1996. Price inflation was not significant in either year. Volume increases were also driven by the addition during the last two years of approximately 3 million net square feet to the network of corporate and franchise stores, representing an increase of 15% in total square footage. As was the case in 1996, retail sales represent approximately 73% of total sales and the remaining 27% are wholesale sales.

Sales (in millions of dollars)	**1997**	**Change**	1996	Change	1995
Eastern Canada	**$ 7,182**	**10 %**	$6,514	6 %	$6,155
Western Canada	**3,826**	**15 %**	3,334	10 %	3,034
United States					665
	$11,008	**12 %**	$9,848		$9,854

Note: For an understanding of the geographic areas covered by these operating segments, please refer to the map at the beginning of the book.

Eastern Canadian sales represent 65% (1996 - 66%) of total Company sales and include sales from retail operations which generate 43% of total Company sales (1996 - 44%) and wholesale sales which account for 22% of total Company sales (1996 - 22%).

Retail sales increased by 9% in 1997. Substantial capital investment continued to expand the retail store network and strengthen the existing store base by renovating, expanding or replacing existing stores. Within the retail business, 24 new stores (1996 - 24) were opened and 24 stores (1996 - 10) underwent major renovation or minor expansion. New stores include major expansions to existing locations. When weighted for openings throughout the year and considering the impact of the closure of older, smaller stores, the net effect on average square footage in 1997 was an increase of approximately 5% as compared to an increase of 8% in 1996. Excluding the impact of the extra week, 1997 same-store sales grew 4% (1996 - 2%).

The 13% (1996 - 3%) increase in wholesale sales in Eastern Canada came from increased sales through franchised stores. Franchise retail sales growth of 15% surpassed the 1996 increase of 6%. During 1997, 15 new stores (1996 - 14) were opened and 7 underwent minor expansion (1996 - 12). Partially offsetting this franchised business growth was the decline in wholesale sales to independents.

In 1998, the Company plans to open, expand or remodel approximately 60 corporate and franchised independent stores in Eastern Canada with an expected net increase of 1.5 million square feet or a 10% average net increase which is expected to result in additional sales growth.

Western Canadian sales represent 35% (1996 - 34%) of total Company sales and include sales from retail operations which generate 30% of total Company sales (1996 - 29%) and wholesale sales which account for 5% of total Company sales (1996 - 5%).

Retail sales increased by 18% (1996 - 14%) driven once again by strong superstore sales growth. A total of 5 new superstores were opened in 1997 in addition to the 2 opened in 1996. These 5 new stores represented an increase in average net superstore square footage of 11%. An additional 7 Real Canadian Wholesale Clubs were added during 1997, increasing by more than 50% the number of wholesale club locations. Growth in retail sales during 1997 was further increased by the opening of 9 conventional stores (1996 - 10). All of this activity, when weighted for openings throughout the year, had the effect of increasing the average net square footage in Western Canada by 13% (1996 - 10%). Both in 1996 and 1997, sales increases were aided by competitors' work stoppages. The 1996 competitors' strike in British Columbia had a positive impact on 1996 sales in that region and a corresponding negative impact on 1997 comparative sales in that market. The 1997 competitor's strike in Alberta had less of a positive impact on total 1997 sales. Excluding the impact of the extra week, 1997 same-store sales grew 6% (1996 - 8%).

Wholesale sales decreased 3% following a decline of 6% in 1996. This decrease was due to a rationalization in the number of independent accounts and in the number of affiliated franchise stores. A partial offset to this decline was the sales growth in food services achieved through aggressive sales efforts and pricing.

In 1998, Western Canada's capital program includes the opening of 5 superstores, 5 Real Canadian Wholesale Clubs and 12 conventional stores resulting in an expected net increase of 1.1 million square feet or 19% average net increase which is expected to result in additional sales growth.

Operating Income Operating income has increased by 19% over 1996 to $426 million. In 1997, approximately 52% of operating income was generated in Eastern Canada, 47% in Western Canada and 1% in the United States. The operating margin improved to 3.9% in 1997 from 3.6% in 1996. This improvement was predominantly from continued focus on cost control, including the rationalization of administrative and buying functions, and from higher volumes leveraging off of fixed costs.

Operating Income (in millions of dollars)		**1997**	**Change**	1996	Change	1995
Eastern Canada	Operations	**$220**	**14 %**	$193	17 %	$165
	Store labour restructuring			$ (20)		
	Operating margin [1]	**3.1 %**		3.0 %		2.7 %
Western Canada	Operations	**$200**	**19 %**	$168	21 %	$139
	Operating margin	**5.2 %**		5.0 %		4.6 %
United States	Operations	**$ 6**	**(67)%**	$ 18	13 %	$ 16
Combined		**$426**	**19 %**	$359	12 %	$320
	Operating margin	**3.9 %**		3.6 %		3.2 %

1. 1996 operating margin is before store labour restructuring charge.

Eastern Canadian operating income improved to $220 million from $193 million excluding the one time charge of $20 million for store labour restructuring in 1996. This resulted in an increase in operating margin to 3.1% from 3.0% (excluding the one time labour charge) in 1996. Operations in both Ontario and in the Atlantic provinces have contributed to strengthening the margin.

Retail operating income increased by approximately 14% (1996 - 17% excluding the one time labour charge). Gross margins improved in 1997 but were still hampered by competitive pressures. Cost control contributed to the increased operating income which included reduced labour costs as the benefits from the store labour restructuring began to be realized.

Wholesale operating income increased by approximately 14% (1996 - 16%). Similar to retail, increased sales and containment of costs and a slight increase in gross margin provided the increase in operating income.

The results for 1998 are expected to maintain the trend of increasing sales and operating income.

Western Canadian operating income improved to $200 million from $168 million in 1996. These operations continue to generate a strong operating margin of 5.2% (1996 - 5.0%). In 1997, Western Canadian operations provided 47% of total Company operating income.

Retail operating income increased by approximately 15% (1996 - 27%), principally from the Real Canadian Superstores which continued to generate good sales increases while maintaining steady gross margins and containing costs.

Wholesale operating income increased by approximately 32% (1996 - 3%), buoyed by the increase of Western Canadian retail sales and the associated product flow through the distribution centres. In addition, 1996 results included costs associated with the closing of the Foremost Dairy milk processing operation.

Earnings growth in 1998 is expected to be consistent with 1997 as stores opened during the past couple of years continue to mature.

United States operating income is composed primarily of the net service fee revenue generated through the sale of selected President's Choice™ and no name™ products to non-affiliated retailers in the United States. The decrease in 1997 was attributable to the 1996 inclusion of the one time $16 million cessation payment from Wal-Mart, net of costs related to the disposition of some of the remaining net assets of the former United States businesses. As expected, service fee revenue declined in 1997 upon the expiration of the Wal-Mart agreement. Service fee revenue for 1998 is expected to increase marginally.

Interest Expense decreased $2 million in 1997 and $8 million in 1996. The 1997 decrease was due to a combination of declining Canadian interest rates and an increase in capitalized interest offset by an increase in the average net borrowing levels of approximately $170 million. Borrowing levels increased in 1997 due to the significant capital investment program offset by higher net earnings. In 1996, average net borrowing levels were $50 million lower than 1995, reflecting the impact of investing the proceeds from the sale of the United States business for a full year in 1996 versus a partial year in 1995. The positive impact of

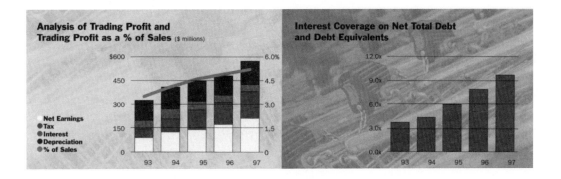

interest rate derivatives, as discussed in Note 9 to the financial statements, was partially offset in 1997 by the negative impact of cross-currency swaps. Total interest expense in 1998 is expected to be higher than the 1997 expense due to an anticipated increase in average net borrowing levels required to finance additional planned capital expenditures.

The **effective income tax rate** decreased in 1997 to 44.2% which was slightly lower than the 1996 level of 44.5%, and is expected to increase marginally in 1998.

Capital Resources and Liquidity   The sound financial position of the Company did not change significantly in 1997 nor is it expected to in 1998. The Company maintains treasury centres which operate under Company approved policies and guidelines covering funding, investing, foreign exchange and interest rate management. The 1997 **total debt and debt equivalents to equity** ratio, net of cash, increased slightly to .34:1 from .33:1 in 1996. The ratio continued to be relatively low, as the proceeds from the sale of the United States assets continue to be invested short term. The 1998 ratio is expected to remain consistent with 1997 and therefore, will be well within the Company's internal guideline of a ratio of less than 1:1. **Interest coverage** improved to 9.7 times in 1997 from 7.9 times in 1996 mainly from higher earnings. The 1998 interest coverage is expected to remain at the 1997 level.

The 1997 **capital expenditure** program reached a record high of $517 million and may be analyzed as follows:

Capital Expenditures (in millions of dollars)	**1998 Estimate**	1997	1996
Eastern Canada	**$355**	$367	$294
% of Total	**69 %**	71 %	75 %
Western Canada	**$160**	$150	$ 95
% of Total	**31 %**	29 %	25 %
	$515	$517	$389
% for Retail Stores	**86 %**	85 %	87 %

Note: Projects-in-progress which the Company has effectively committed to complete total approximately $130 million of the $515 million in 1998.

Capital expenditures increased significantly over 1996 reflecting the Company's commitment to invest for growth across Canada, including new stores and significant remodeling and refurbishing and an initial capital investment supporting the planned entry into the Montreal market.

Cash flow from operations increased to $426 million from $262 million in 1996 mainly reflecting improved net earnings and improved working capital management.

Short term liquidity is provided by a combination of internally generated cash flow, net cash and short term investments and access to the commercial paper market. The Company maintains a $500 million commercial paper program which is rated A-1 and R-1 (low) by the Canadian Bond Rating Service (CBRS) and the Dominion Bond Rating Service (DBRS) respectively. The Company's commercial paper program is supported by lines of credit, extended by several banks, totaling $600 million. This program serves to finance fluctuations in working capital. Financial instruments are used to manage the effective interest rate on total debt including underlying commercial paper and short term investments.

During the second quarter of 1996, the Company filed a shelf prospectus to issue up to $300 million of Medium Term Notes (MTN) with maturities of not less than one year. The Company issued $100 million during the third quarter of 1996 and two subsequent $100 million issues during each of the first quarter and fourth quarter of 1997.

In the first quarter of 1998, the Company filed another shelf prospectus to issue up to $500 million of MTN. This program enables the Company to issue, until January 7, 2000, unsecured debt obligations with maturities of not less than one year. This debt will be rated the same as other unsecured long term debt obligations of the Company. The Company expects to meet its 1998 cash requirements through internally generated funds and, when necessary, drawing on the $500 million MTN facility. During the first quarter of 1998, the Company issued $100 million of the new MTN at 6.45%, due 2028, redeemable on demand.

Longer term capital resources are provided by direct access to capital markets. The Company has a debt rating of A+ (low) from CBRS and A (high) from DBRS. In the fourth quarter of 1996, $14 million Series 7, 9% Debentures were redeemed. The 1997 year end weighted average interest rate on fixed rate long term debt (excluding capital lease obligations included in other long term debt, and debt equivalents) was 8.8%, down from 9.6% last year. The weighted average term to maturity, measured both on the basis of maturity date and on the earlier of maturity or first retraction date, was 21 and 20 years respectively at year end 1997 compared to 23 and 21 years at the end of 1996. The MTN issues in both 1996 and 1997, reduced the weighted average interest rate and marginally decreased the term to maturity.

Common shareholders' equity reached $1.5 billion in 1997, an increase of $184 million primarily from current earnings retained in the business. The Company's dividend policy is to declare dividends equal to approximately 20 to 25% of the prior year's earnings per common share giving consideration to year end cash flow position and future cash flow requirements and investment opportunities.

On March 9, 1998, the Company announced its intention to purchase on the Toronto Stock Exchange up to 5% or 12,218,040 of its common shares outstanding pursuant to a Normal Course Issuer Bid effective March 18, 1998 to March 17, 1999. Purchases will be made by the Company in accordance with the rules and by-laws of the Toronto Stock Exchange and the price which the Company will pay for any such common shares will be the market price of such shares at the time of acquisition.

Risk and Risk Management The Company successfully competes in the Canadian food distribution industry. Its operating philosophy is indicative of its long term objectives of security and growth. The Company employs various strategies, which may carry some short term risk, in order to achieve these objectives and to minimize the impact of perceived threats related to competitive erosion and loss of cost advantage.

Strategies employed by the Company include utilization and refinement of a variety of store formats, store banners and store sizes in order to appeal to the changing demographics of various markets. Developing and operating new departments and services which complement the traditional supermarket, allows the Company to compete effectively and efficiently in an evolving market. The

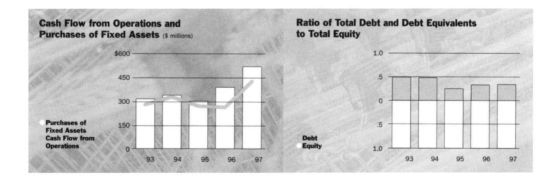

AR-26

Company follows a policy of enhancing profitability on a 'market-by-market' basis by selecting a store format, store size and store banner that is the best fit for each market. By successfully competing across Canada in both retail and wholesale operations, the Company has strategically minimized and balanced its exposure to regional and industry economic risk.

The Company maintains a significant portfolio of owned sites and, whenever practical, follows the strategy of purchasing sites. This enhances the Company's operating flexibility and also allows the Company to benefit from any long term property appreciation. A significant competitive advantage the Company has developed is its powerful controlled label products such as President's Choice™, no name™, Club Pack™, G•R•E•E•N™, "TOO GOOD TO BE TRUE!"™ and EXACT™ which enhance customer loyalty by providing superior overall value and some protection against national brand price cutting.

During the first quarter of 1998, the Company will enter the Montreal market and will also enter other new smaller markets and will review acquisitions when the opportunities arise. The Company will also exit a particular market and reallocate assets elsewhere when there is a strategic advantage to do so.

The success of these strategies depends to a large extent on the financial strength of the Company and the strategic deployment of the Company's financial resources. The Company maintains a strong balance sheet in order to minimize its vulnerability to short term earnings pressure and to provide a stable base for long term growth.

Low cost, non-union competitors are a threat to the Company's cost structure. The Company is willing to accept the short term costs of labour disruption in order to achieve competitive labour costs for the longer term which helps to ensure long term sustainable sales and earnings growth. In 1998, 27 labour agreements affecting approximately 5,200 employees will be negotiated with the single largest agreement covering 3,500 employees. Management's objective is to continue to negotiate longer term contracts to provide a more stable labour environment. The Company has good relations with its employees and unions and, although possible, no labour disruption is anticipated.

The Company self-insures its own risks to an appropriate level and limits its exposure through the purchase of excess insurance from financially stable insurance companies. The Company has comprehensive loss prevention programs in place and actively manages its claims handling and litigation processes to reduce the risk it retains.

Loblaw Companies Limited is aware of the year 2000 date change issues and is actively working to resolve the potential impact on the technology assets and processing of date-sensitive information by the Company's computerized information systems. A coordinated program is in place to ensure all vital business and technical issues are managed and appropriately dealt with, including consideration of electronic data interchange (EDI) with suppliers. During 1997, a number of critical systems within the various operations were successfully converted or modified to ensure year 2000 compliance. Throughout 1998, all remaining critical business systems will be converted or modified and compliance testing will be completed during 1998 and 1999. Loblaw is expensing all systems modification costs and these costs are not currently expected to have a material adverse impact on the Company's financial position or results of operations.

Loblaw endeavours to be a socially and environmentally responsible company and recognizes that the competitive pressures for economic growth and cost efficiency must be integrated with environmental stewardship and ecological considerations. Environmental committees throughout the Company meet regularly to monitor and enforce the maintenance of responsible business operations. This includes conducting environmental audits of warehouses, stores, equipment and gas stations and implementing packaging, waste reduction and recycling programs.

The Company is confident that it is well positioned to provide continued 1998 earnings growth and continued superior food industry returns.

Results by Quarter

(in millions of dollars)		**1997**	1996	1995
Sales	1st Quarter	$ **2,287**	$2,096	$2,303
	2nd Quarter	**2,497**	2,298	2,460
	3rd Quarter	**3,386**	3,070	2,867
	4th Quarter	**2,838**	2,384	2,224
		$**11,008**	$9,848	$9,854
Operating Income	1st Quarter	$ **74**	$ 61	$ 58
	2nd Quarter	**92**	82	76
	3rd Quarter	**113**	99	84
	4th Quarter	**147**	117	102
		$ **426**	$ 359	$ 320
Interest Expense	1st Quarter	$ **10**	$ 11	$ 17
	2nd Quarter	**8**	8	13
	3rd Quarter	**13**	16	13
	4th Quarter	**13**	11	11
		$ **44**	$ 46	$ 54
Net Earnings	1st Quarter	$ **36**	$ 28	$ 24
	2nd Quarter	**46**	40	35
	3rd Quarter	**56**	45	38
	4th Quarter	**75**	61	50
		$ **213**	$ 174	$ 147
Net Earnings Per Common Share (in dollars)				
	1st Quarter	$ **.15**	$ .12	$ .10
	2nd Quarter	**.19**	.16	.14
	3rd Quarter	**.23**	.19	.16
	4th Quarter	**.31**	.25	.20
		$ **.88**	$ .72	$ .60

Eleven Year Summary

Earnings Statement

(in millions of dollars)	1997	1996	1995	1994	1993	1992	1991	1990	1989	1988	1987
Sales	11,008	9,848	9,854	10,000	9,356	9,262	8,533	8,417	7,934	8,308	8,631
Trading profit[1]	573	481	449	410	326	313	328	324	295	260	290
Depreciation and amortization	147	122	129	138	126	120	109	109	104	100	100
Operating income	426	359	320	272	200	193	219	215	191	160	190
Interest expense	44	46	54	63	54	62	63	71	91	84	74
Income taxes	169	139	124	83	56	45	57	55	39	19	48
Minority interest									2	4	4
Earnings before extraordinary items	213	174	147	126	90	76	99	89	59	31	64
Extraordinary items										(15)	
Net earnings	213	174	147	126	90	76	99	89	59	16	64

Return on Sales (%)

	1997	1996	1995	1994	1993	1992	1991	1990	1989	1988	1987
Operating income	3.9	3.6	3.2	2.7	2.1	2.1	2.6	2.5	2.4	1.9	2.2
Trading profit[1]	5.2	4.9	4.6	4.1	3.5	3.4	3.8	3.8	3.7	3.1	3.4
Earnings before income taxes	3.5	3.2	2.8	2.1	1.6	1.3	1.8	1.7	1.3	.7	1.3
Net earnings	1.9	1.8	1.5	1.3	1.0	.8	1.2	1.1	.7	.2	.7
Cash flow from operations	3.9	2.7	2.7	3.2	2.9	2.8	2.4	2.8	2.8	1.6	1.7

Cash Flow

(in millions of dollars)	1997	1996	1995	1994	1993	1992	1991	1990	1989	1988	1987
Cash flow from operations	426	262	270	328	279	269	215	242	220	135	145
Purchases of fixed assets	517	389	302	339	315	198	159	171	166	192	248
Net cash (out) in before financing and dividends	(42)	(132)	322	3	(61)	55	61	103	21	44	(161)
Increase (decrease) in cash	107	(74)	165	(56)	64	(45)	222	15	56	29	(94)

1. Trading profit is defined as operating income before depreciation and amortization (EBITDA).

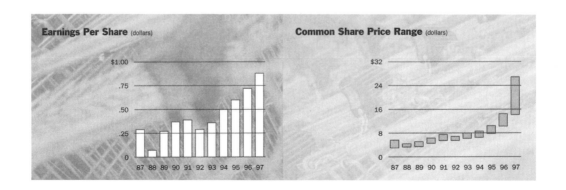

Earnings Per Share (dollars) — **Common Share Price Range** (dollars)

Financial Position

(in millions of dollars)	1997	1996	1995	1994	1993	1992	1991	1990	1989	1988	1987
Current assets	1,681	1,553	1,491	1,214	1,117	1,082	1,050	987	761	765	983
Current liabilities	1,479	1,399	1,312	1,185	969	937	788	937	727	685	843
Working capital	202	154	179	29	148	145	262	50	34	80	140
Fixed assets (net)	2,093	1,738	1,491	1,603	1,414	1,231	1,115	1,078	1,044	1,052	1,057
Total assets	4,013	3,531	3,197	3,042	2,743	2,504	2,362	2,282	2,040	2,004	2,214
Long term debt[1]	927	742	669	741	778	634	650	567	636	709	737
Total debt[1]	1,289	1,155	980	836	778	664	650	747	644	773	836
Retained earnings	1,221	1,046	902	783	684	618	568	499	434	390	396
Shareholders' equity	1,495	1,311	1,160	1,105	985	916	884	718	652	501	541
Average capital employed	2,730	2,385	2,114	1,911	1,726	1,624	1,479	1,360	1,379	1,433	1,393

Ratios[2]

	1997	1996	1995	1994	1993	1992	1991	1990	1989	1988	1987
Earnings Ratios[3] (percent)											
Return on common equity	15.3	14.2	13.4	12.5	9.7	8.8	13.4	14.6	11.7	5.9	12.5
Return on total assets	14.1	13.5	12.2	10.5	8.4	8.8	10.5	10.5	9.6	7.7	9.3
Financial Ratios (xx:1)											
Total debt to equity	.34	.33	.25	.48	.49	.46	.45	.75	.95	1.49	1.49
Cash flow from operations to long term debt	.83	.60	.94	.62	.58	.63	.54	.45	.35	.19	.20
Interest coverage on total debt[1]	9.68	7.88	5.97	4.32	3.68	3.11	3.50	3.03	2.11	1.90	2.56

Per Common Share

(dollars)	1997	1996	1995	1994	1993	1992	1991	1990	1989	1988	1987
Net earnings	.88	.72	.60	.50	.36	.29	.39	.37	.27	.07	.29
Dividends – declared	.15	.12	.11	.09	.08	.08	.08	.07	.07	.07	.07
– year end rate	.16	.12	.12	.09	.08	.08	.08	.07	.07	.07	.07
Book value	6.08	5.35	4.74	4.27	3.79	3.52	3.17	2.66	2.37	2.21	2.37
Price range – high	26.85	14.50	10.50	8.67	8.00	6.83	7.50	6.29	5.08	4.38	5.63
– low	14.15	10.33	7.75	6.50	6.17	5.46	5.46	4.54	3.42	3.29	3.00
Cash flow from operations[4]	1.76	1.08	1.12	1.35	1.15	1.11	.90	1.07	1.01	.62	.67

1. Debt includes debt equivalents.
2. For purposes of calculating financial ratios, debt is reduced by cash and short term investments net of bank advances and notes payable.
3. Earnings ratios have been computed as follows:
    Return on common equity – Earnings before extraordinary items less preferred dividends divided by average common share capital, retained earnings, foreign currency translation adjustment and the applicable portion of contributed surplus.
    Return on total assets – Operating income divided by average total assets (less cash and short term investments).
4. Cash flow from operations per common share is after preferred dividends.

Corporate Directory

Directors

W. Galen Weston, O.C., B.A., LL.D. [2]
Chairman, Loblaw Companies Limited
Chairman, George Weston Limited
Chairman, Wittington Investments, Limited
Chairman, Holt, Renfrew & Co., Limited
Chairman, Brown Thomas Group Limited
Chairman, The Windsor Club
President, The W. Garfield Weston Foundation
Director, Associated British Foods plc
Director, CIBC
Director, Fortnum & Mason plc
Director, United World Colleges

Richard J. Currie, C.M., MBA, LL.D., P.Eng. [2]
President, Loblaw Companies Limited
President, George Weston Limited
Director, Imperial Oil Limited
Director, BCE Inc.

Camilla H. Dalglish [4,5]
Corporate Director
Director, The W. Garfield Weston Foundation
Former Member of The Board of Directors, Royal Botanical Gardens

Robert J. Dart, FCA [1,3]
President, Wittington Investments, Limited
Former Senior Tax Partner, Price Waterhouse Canada
Director, Holt, Renfrew & Co., Limited
Director, Brown Thomas Group Limited

Sheldon V. Durtsche [1,4]
Corporate Director
Former Chairman, National Tea Co.

G. Joseph Reddington [2,3]
Chief Executive Officer, Breuners Home Furnishings Corp.
Former Chairman and CEO, The Signature Group
Former President and CEO, Sears Canada
Director, Trans World Airlines

T. Iain Ronald, FCA [1,5]
Corporate Director
Former Vice Chairman, CIBC Group of Companies
Director, Toronto Symphony Orchestra
Director, Northwest Company Inc.

Joseph H. Wright [3,5]
Corporate Director
Managing Partner, Crosbie & Co.
Former President and CEO, Swiss Bank Corporation (Canada)
Director, St. Laurent Paperboard Inc.
Director, Wolf Group Integrated Communications
Director, Brooke Capital Corporation
Director, Clarke Institute of Psychiatry Foundation

---

1 *member – Audit Committee*

2 *member – Executive Committee*

3 *member – Governance and Compensation Committee*

4 *member – Environmental, Health and Safety Committee*

5 *member – Pension Committee*

Corporate Officers Includes age and years of service:

W. Galen Weston, O.C., *57 and 26 years*
Chairman of the Board

Richard J. Currie, C.M., *60 and 26 years*
President

David K. Bragg, *49 and 14 years*
Executive Vice President

Serge K. Darkazanli, *55 and 23 years*
Executive Vice President

John A. Lederer, *42 and 16 years*
Executive Vice President

Donald G. Reid, *48 and 18 years*
Executive Vice President

Harold A. Seitz, *59 and 22 years*
Executive Vice President

John W. Thompson, *49 and 19 years*
Executive Vice President

David M. Williams, *55 and 21 years*
Executive Vice President

Robert G. Chenaux, *54 and 22 years*
Senior Vice President,
Corporate Brand Development

Roy R. Conliffe, *47 and 16 years*
Senior Vice President, Labour Relations

Stewart E. Green, *53 and 21 years*
Senior Vice President and Secretary

David R. Jeffs, *40 and 19 years*
Senior Vice President,
Sourcing and Procurement

Richard P. Mavrinac, *45 and 15 years*
Senior Vice President, Finance

David F. Poirier, *40 and 16 years*
Senior Vice President,
Logistics, Planning and Systems

Stephen A. Smith, *40 and 12 years*
Senior Vice President, Controller

Robert A. Balcom, *36 and 4 years*
Vice President, General Counsel

Manny Di Filippo, *38 and 5 years*
Vice President, Corporate Development

J. Bradley Holland, *34 and 4 years*
Vice President, Taxation

Michael Kimber, *42 and 13 years*
Vice President, Legal Counsel

Louise M. Lacchin, *40 and 14 years*
Vice President, Treasurer

Kevin P. Lengyell, *39 and 2 years*
Vice President, Internal Audit Services

Glenn D. Leroux, *43 and 11 years*
Vice President, Risk Management

Kenneth Mulhall, *35 and 14 years*
Vice President, Environmental Affairs

George D. Seslija, *42 and 18 years*
Vice President, Real Estate Development

Franca Smith, *34 and 9 years*
Vice President, Financial Control

Ann Marie Yamamoto, *37 and 11 years*
Vice President, Information Technology
and Systems Audit

Janice A. Hollett, *28 and 1 year*
Corporate Controller, Financial Reporting

Barbara T. Cook, *44 and 14 years*
Assistant Controller

Marian M. Burrows, *43 and 19 years*
Assistant Secretary

Shareholder Information

Executive Offices

22 St. Clair Avenue East
Toronto, Canada
M4T 2S8
Tel: (416) 922-8500
Fax: (416) 922-7791
Internet: www.loblaw.com

Stock Listings

Toronto, Montreal and Vancouver Stock Exchanges

Share Symbol — *"L"*

Common Shares Outstanding

71 percent of the common shares are owned beneficially by George Weston Limited.

Total outstanding	242,780,858
Shares available for public trading	71,577,288

Average Daily Trading Volume   26,422

Dividend Policy

It is the Company's policy to maintain a stable dividend payment of 20 to 25% of the prior year's earnings per common share.

Common Dividend Payment Dates

April 1
July 1
October 1
December 30

Normal Course Issuer Bid

The Company has a Normal Course Issuer Bid on the Toronto Stock Exchange effective from March 18, 1998 to March 17, 1999.

Value of Common Shares

December 22, 1971 (Valuation Day)	$ .958
February 22, 1994	$7.670

Investor Relations

Copies of the Company's Annual Information Form filed with regulatory authorities and additional copies of this Annual Report may be obtained from the Secretary upon specific request.

Other information requests should be directed to Mr. Donald G. Reid, Executive Vice President.

Transfer Agent and Registrar

Montreal Trust Company of Canada
151 Front Street West
Toronto, Canada
M5J 2N1

General Counsel

Borden & Elliot
Toronto, Canada

Auditors

KPMG
Toronto, Canada

Annual and General Meeting

April 28, 1998 at 11:00 a.m.
Toronto, Canada

Materials in this report are environmentally friendly. The cover and operating section papers are acid-free and recyclable. The financial section paper is acid-free and contains 20 percent post-consumer de-inked fibre.

INDEX

PHOTOGRAPH CREDITS

Volume 1
p. 1: James Balog/Tony Stone Images; p. 2: J.L. Pelaez/First Light; p. 56: Hulton Getty/Liaison Agency; p. 106: Carl Lavigne/Ottawa Senators; p. 166: Steven Weinberg/Tony Stone Images; p. 225: J. Feingersh/First Light; p. 226: J. Héguy/First Light; p. 375: "Coca-Cola" trademark appears courtesy of Coca-Cola Ltd. and the Coca-Cola Company; p. 376: J. Cochrane/First Light; p. 422: C. Gupton/First Light; p. 468: R. Watts/First Light; p. 516: T. Kitchin/First Light; p. 562: Steiner/First Light; p. 614: T. Bonderud/First Light.

Volume 2
p. 653: Hudson's Bay logo courtesy of Hudson's Bay Company, KPMG logo courtesy of KPMG Chartered Accountants, McGraw-Hill Ryerson logo courtesy of McGraw-Hill Ryerson Limited; p. 654: Logos courtesy of Arthur Andersen, Deloitte & Touche, Ernst & Young, KPMG Chartered Accountants, and PricewaterhouseCoopers; p. 696: David Madison/Tony Stone Images; p. 742: Steven Peters/Tony Stone Images; p. 786: D.C. Lowe/First Light; p. 862: Stock Certificate/PhotoDisc, Inc.; p. 936: Chris Windsor/Tony Stone Images; p. 992: Courtesy of the Toronto Stock Exchange; p. 1052: Jon Riley/Tony Stone Images.